*INTERMEDIATE
ECONOMIC
THEORY*

PRENTICE-HALL ECONOMICS SERIES

E. A. J. Johnson, Editor

INTERMEDIATE
ECONOMIC THEORY

by STEPHEN ENKE *Ph.D.* · *M.P.A.*

UNIVERSITY OF CALIFORNIA *&* THE *RAND* CORPORATION

NEW YORK: PRENTICE-HALL, INC.

to FAY

who sometimes helped
and often suffered

Preface

Intermediate Economic Theory has been planned as a textbook for upper-division students majoring in economics or business administration. It can be used as a text for a year course or, if certain chapters are omitted, for a single quarter or semester course. Certain of the more advanced chapters may aid graduate students by providing them with a handy reference.

Few books would ever be written if their authors did not believe that their publication would prove useful. *Intermediate Economic Theory* embraces three essential subjects of modern economic theory. Separate parts of the book are devoted to national income and to income and employment, as well as to the more conventional topics of prices, distribution, and money. Finally, the concluding part, on political economy, attempts to apply the theoretical apparatus of the book to the issue of socialism versus capitalism.

Naturally, *Intermediate Economic Theory* does not cover each of these topics exhaustively. To do so would be to sacrifice the purpose of the book. Instructors of undergraduate students should not expect them to understand the refinements of present-day doctrine on such varied topics as income and employment, prices, national income accounting, money, distribution, and the political organization of economic resources. Many Ph.D.'s are not so well equipped. The task of undergraduate work is surely to lay as complete a foundation as possible; the superstructure of economic theory can be erected later, during graduate work.

Some instructors and students may feel that *Intermediate Economic Theory* is lacking in description of actual markets, commodities, and regulations. Naturally, for pedagogical reasons, examples are cited whenever they seem illuminating enough to warrant extra reading by the student. However, the point is often overlooked that it is only in college, and as a student, that a person has a real opportunity to learn the skeleton of economics. Unless he learns in college how the bones are articulated, he will never be able to learn economic anatomy from the facts and figures that come his way in later life. The simple truth is that theory is always abstract and that so-called *principles texts* which are long on description are usually very short on analysis.

Intermediate Economic Theory contains more material than any normal upper-division student can master in a single semester. The instructor of a single-semester theory course must decide whether he wants to omit parts or chapters. It is likely that a great deal of the material in Part II (*Money*) and Part V (*Distribution*) will already have been covered in an elementary course; hence one recourse is to omit these two parts entirely.

If the instructor elects the other alternative, that of omitting certain chapters, he can either delete chapters that are not essential to continuity (in which case he can omit Chapters 2, 4, 5, 12, 14, 17, 22, 24, 28, 33, 34) or he can omit the chapters that are above the average in difficulty (in which case he should omit Chapters 4, 7, 12, 24, 25, 30, 32). By either standard he will probably omit Chapters 4, 12, and 24. However, in the event that this book is adopted for a year course or for use by graduate students, the entire book should be assigned.

No attempt has been made to credit each idea to its originator. Obviously Part III is neo-Keynesian; similarly, much of Part IV is neo-Chamberlinian. However, during the last decade, a great deal has been added to and subtracted from both income theory and value theory, until it is difficult to know which economist can lay undisputed claim to which parts of modern theory. The purpose of an undergraduate theory text is not to play intellectual detective but to spread out the generally accepted theories of the day for all who wish to see. The student who very properly declines to accept the author's dicta on faith can always turn to the references at the end of each chapter.

Nearly all the ideas contained in this book have been presented as lectures to students. The arrangement of the book has been developed from experience. Diagrams have been used rather lavishly because most students, in the end, seem to understand quantitative relations better when these relations are presented in diagram form.

The author wishes to acknowledge his indebtedness to Professor A. A. Alchian, and to those colleagues and former students who have played a part in the development of his ideas and the manner of their presentation here.

STEPHEN ENKE

Rancho Santa Ynez, Pacific Palisades, California

Contents

Part I: NATIONAL INCOME

1 THE ECONOMY'S TASK 3

Utility, Consumption, and Spending 3
Factors of Production 6
    Labor 6
    Land 7
    Concepts of Capital 7
    Enterprise 8
Opportunity Costs 9
The Inevitability of Scarcity 10

2 FOUR ECONOMIC GROUPS 15

Households 15
    Household Economics 15
    Households and Firms 16
    Households and Governments 18
    Households and Banks 20
Firms 20
    Gross Value Added 21
    Net Value Added 22
Governments and Banks 23

3 NATIONAL INCOME ACCOUNTING 28

Some Basic Ideas 28
Gross and Net National Product 31
National Income 33
Personal Income 36
National Income Estimates by the Department of Commerce 38
The Government Contribution 40
Market Price or Factor Cost? 42
Dual Aspects of National Income 43

4 GENERAL WELFARE AND NATIONAL INCOME . . 46

The Significance of Various Flows 46
Investment and Saving 50
Case 1—Firms and Households Only 50
Case 2—Governments, Firms, and Households 54
General Comments 57
Economic Welfare and Dynamic Change 57
Changes in Prices 58
Altered Composition of National Product 58
Quality Improvement 59
Altered Business Taxes 59
Variability of Investment 59
Population and Productivity Changes 60
Summary 60

Part II: MONETARY THEORY

5 THE NATURE AND QUANTITY OF MONEY . . . 65

What Is Money? 65
Legal Tender Money 65
Means of Payment 66
Near Money 67
Changes in the Stock of Money 67
The Federal Reserve System 68
Deposit Creation by Member Banks 69
The Federal Reserve Banks as a Central Bank 71
The Dilemma of Rival Goals 75
Ways of Looking at Money 76
The Commodity Theory 76
The Quantity Theory 76
The Circuit of Payments Approach 76
The Cash Balance Approach 76

6 PRICE LEVEL THEORIES 79

The Commodity Theory 79
The Original Theory 79

6 PRICE LEVEL THEORIES (*Cont.*):

The Qualified Version 80
Comments 81
The Quantity Theory 82
Crude and "Value of Trade" Versions 82
The Equation of Exchange 83
The Causal Problem 85
Current Thoughts on the Price Level 85
Importance of Motives 85
Price Relation Changes 86
Attempts at Measurement 86
Gross and Net Payments 87
Economic Significance of Changing Prices 88

7 THE CIRCUIT OF PAYMENTS 91

The Savings Bogey 91
Hoarding and Dishoarding 93
Expanding the Flow of Payments 96
Through Active Dishoarding 97
Through Bank Credits 98
Through Government Deficits 99
Why Increase Payments? 104

Part III: INCOME THEORY

8 INCOME THEORY ESSENTIALS 109

Introduction 109
Contrary Saving and Investing Plans 110
The Consumption Function 112
Investment Sets the Pace 114
The Investment Multiplier 115
The Marginal Efficiency of Capital 116
Liquidity Theory of Interest Rates 117
Summary Outline of Principal Relations 118

9 MULTIPLIERS OF INCOME 122

The Simple Investment Multiplier 122
The Compound Investment Multiplier 127
Investment Multipliers vs. Spending Multipliers 130
The Equilibrium Income 131
Supplementary Government Investment 133
A Reduction in Intended Savings 136
Summary 136

10 INDUCEMENTS TO INVEST 139

Finished Output Inventories 139
Working Capital Investment 140
Fixed Capital Investment 141
　　Marginal-Efficiency-of-Capital Mathematics 141
　　The Economics of Capital Efficiency 143
　　How Capitalistic Should a Firm Be? 145
The Principle of Acceleration 148
Which Inducement Dominates? 150

11 INTEREST AND LIQUIDITY 154

The Demand for Cash Balances 154
　　Transaction Motive 155
　　Precautionary Motive 155
　　Speculative Motive 156
Interest the Price of Money 157
Interest Expectations and Money Demand 158
Active and Passive Balances 160
The Liquidity Function 160
Other Aspects of Interest Theory 163

12 THE GENERAL THEORY 166

The Classical System 166
Income Introduced as an Extra Variable 168
Influence of the Demand for Money 169

12 THE GENERAL THEORY (*Cont.*):

Altered Human Attitudes 171
  Changed Saving Propensities 172
  Changed Investment Intentions 173
  Changed Liquidity Preferences 173
A Three-Dimensional Restatement 174
  Money Box Surfaces 174
  Savings and Investment Box Surfaces 175
  Equilibrium 176
Causes and Effects 177
  Increased Intention to Invest 178
  Increased Propensity to Save 178
  Increased Liquidity Preference 179
  Increased Money Supply 179
  Comparison with the Classicists 179

13 GOVERNMENT EMPLOYMENT POLICY 182

What the Analysis Has Shown 182
Soaking the Rich 184
Unbalancing the Budget 186
  Government Spending 186
  Reducing Taxes 191
  The Government Expenditure Multiplier 193
Financing Government Deficits 195

14 MONEY, INCOME, AND PRICES 200

Effective Demand 200
Money Stock and Effective Demand 201
The Influence of Supply on Prices 202
  Rising Labor Costs 203
  Diminishing Returns in the Short Run 204
  Temporary Bottlenecks 204
  Monopoly 204
  Full Employment 205
What's Wrong with Spiraling Prices? 205

CONTENTS

Part IV: PRICE THEORY

15 PRICE THEORY INTRODUCTION 211

Economic Significance of Price Theory 211
Role of the Firm 212
Three Product Types 213
Degrees of Competition 216
The Concept of Final and Temporary Equilibrium . . . 219
Analysis of Particular or General Equilibrium? 221
Statics and Dynamics 222

16 PURE COMPETITION 225

Price Determination in a Competitive Market 225
Price Ceiling Effects 228
Buyers' and Sellers' Surpluses 229
Commodity Tax Effects 231
Price Elasticity of Demand and Supply 233
The Cobweb Theorem 236

17 INTERDEPENDENT PRICES 239

Spatial Interdependence 239
Temporal Interdependence 242
Substitutes and Complements 244
Rival Supply 244
Rival Demand 246
Joint Supply 246
Joint Costs 247
Joint Demand 248
Cross-Elasticity and Product Interdependence 249

18 FORCES OF DEMAND 251

The Summing of Individuals' Demands 252
The Determination of a Consumer's Demand 253
Diminishing Marginal Utility 253
Budgeting Outlays 255

18 FORCES OF DEMAND (*Cont.*):

Marginal Utility of Money 257
Individual Demand for a Single Good 257
Income Changes and Individual Demand 258
Declining Marginal Importance of Money 259
Demand, Price, and Income 260
"Needs" and "Luxuries" 262

19 FORCES OF SUPPLY 266

Collective and Individual Supply Schedules 266
The Collective Supply 266
A Firm's Supply Schedule 266
Marginal Costs Vital 269
The Production Function 269
Four Cost Curves 272
The Planning Curve 276
Time and Supply 278
Concluding Comment 280

20 EQUILIBRIUM OF FIRM AND INDUSTRY 283

Competitive Firm Equilibrium 283
$MC = MR$ 283
Minimizing Losses in the Short Run 285
Concept of Quasi-Rent 286
The Industry's Adjustments 286
Short-Run Adjustments 286
Long-Run Adjustments 288
Industry-Wide Economies 290
Interaction of Demand and Supply 291

21 MONOPOLY AND MONOPSONY 295

The Concept of Monopoly and Monopsony 295
Price Policies of a Pure Monopolist 296
Demand as Seen by the Monopolist 296
Short-Run Pricing 300
Market Period Pricing 302

21 MONOPOLY AND MONOPSONY (*Cont.*):

Pricing by a Monopsonist 303
Monopoly with Monopsony 306
Long-Run Considerations 306

22 NON-PRICE COMPETITION 309

Price, Product, and Promotion 309
Promotion or Product as a Variable 310
   When Price and Quality Are Fixed 311
   When Sales and Quality Are Fixed 311
   Sales and Price Effects of Promotion 315
Controversies over Advertising 317
   Mass-Production Economies Argument 317
   Consumers-Pay-the-Cost Argument 318
   Economists' Approach to Evaluating Promotion . . . 318
Why Is Non-Price Competition so Prevalent? 319

23 MONOPOLISTIC COMPETITION 322

Interdependence Among Firms 322
   Measures of Interdependence 322
   Price with Oligopoly and Polypoly 323
   Attachments of Buyers 327
Long-Run Equilibrium 329
   Long-Run Profits 330
   Long-Run Output 331
   Firm Numbers and Price Policy 334
Composite Nature of Monopolistic Competition 334
   Substitutability of Rivals' Outputs 335
   Entry and Profits 335
   Firm Supply Schedules 335
   Output Formulae for Maximizing Profits 336
   Variables To Be Determined by the Management . . . 337

24 PRICE DISCRIMINATION 340

Examples of Discrimination 340
Discrimination Between Already Separated Markets . . . 342

24 PRICE DISCRIMINATION (*Cont.*):

Discrimination Between Markets Separable at Will . . . 345
Basing Points and "Freight Absorption" 348
Economic Desirability of Price Discrimination 350

25 PRIVATE PROFIT AND GENERAL WELFARE . . . 354

Real and Money Costs and Revenues 355
Interpersonal Utility Comparisons 357
The Monopoly Problem 358
   Resource Allocation Under Pure Competition 359
   Malallocation of Resources with Monopoly 361
   Reallocation by Government 363
Government Antimonopoly Policy 366

Part V: DISTRIBUTION OF INCOME

26 GENERAL PRINCIPLES OF INCOME DISTRIBUTION 373

Some Alternative Principles 373
Entrepreneurial Outlays for Productive Factors 376
   Entrepreneur's Demand for a Single Factor 376
   Supply Elasticity of an Employed Factor 380
   Pure Competition, Monopoly, and Monopsony 381
   Another Practical Example 382
   Optimum Outlays for Productive Factors 383
New Inventions and Marginal Productivity 385
Substitution of Factors 386
Exploitation 388
   Possible Exploitation of a Gifted Employee 389
   Ordinary Workers' Exploitation 389
General Summary 392

27 EARNINGS OF EMPLOYEES 395

Wages, Earnings, and Payrolls 395
   Some Important Relations 395
   Prosperity, Employment, and Labor Costs 396

27 EARNINGS OF EMPLOYEES (*Cont.*):

Economics of Overtime 399
Wage-Rate Differences 400
    Compensating Wage Differences 400
    Non-Competing Groups Within the Labor Force . . . 401
    Derived Demand 403
    Union Restrictions on Labor Supply 404
    Wage and Hours Laws 404
How Real Is Technological Unemployment? 407

28 UNION LEADERS AND WAGE RATES 412

Wages or Employment? 413
Some Union Wage Arguments 416
    Employee Purchasing Power 416
    Ability To Pay 417
    Productivity of Labor 418
    Comparable Wages for Comparable Jobs 420
Bargaining Power in Wage Negotiations 421
Summary 423

29 RENT ON LAND 427

Rent of Land in General 427
    Varying Factor Proportions 428
    Three Distinct Stages 430
    Comparisons of Efficiency 431
Specific Land Rent 432
Urban Site Rents 433
The Rent Concept 436
Should Rents Be Paid for Using Land? 437

30 INTEREST ON CAPITAL 441

Who Pays Interest? 441
Motives of Borrowers and Lenders 442
    Time Preference 442
    Productivity of Capital 443
    Liquidity Preference 444

30 INTEREST ON CAPITAL (*Cont.*):

The Demand and Supply of Loanable Funds 444
   Equations of an Individual 444
   The Loanable Funds Market 445
   Loanable Funds and Aggregate Investment 447
Full Equilibrium and the Interest Rate 449
Function and Justification of Interest 450

31 PROFITS OF ENTREPRENEURSHIP 454

The Functions of Entrepreneurship 454
Determining Economic Profits 456
Single Firm Profits 457
   Cheaply Acquired Assets 458
   Run of Luck 458
   Lack of Room 459
   Special Entrepreneurial Rents 459
   Originating 460
General Long-Run Profits 461
Are Profits Useful? 466

Part VI: POLITICAL ECONOMY

32 ECONOMIC AIMS AND POLITICAL ALTERNATIVES 471

Our Economic Aims 471
   Households 472
   Firms 475
   The Economy's Market 477
   Distribution of Income 478
   Fixed Capital Accumulation 478
   National Income and Aggregate Employment 479
The Political Alternatives 481

33 PROBLEMS OF SOCIALISM 485

Crude Socialist Planning 485
Individual Consumer Choice 488

33 PROBLEMS OF SOCIALISM (*Cont.*):

Incentive Incomes 490
Limited Worker Choice 492
Interacting Consumer and Worker Choice 493
The Rate of Investment 499
Decentralized Managerial Decisions 502
Leisure and Unemployment 503
Concluding Comment 505

34 WHY NOT CAPITALISM? 507

Three Necessary Reforms 507
Recurrent Mass Unemployment 507
Extreme Monopoly Distortion 511
Unproductive Income Inequalities 513
The Philosophy of Regulation 515
Perverted Regulation for Special Interests 517

APPENDICES

A Total Cost and Revenue Functions 523
B When Saving and Investment Plans Differ 527
C More on Savings and Investments 545
D Indifference Curves 548
E Glossary of Symbols 574

PART I

National Income

1

The Economy's Task

ECONOMICS is a social science that deals with the economic likes, dislikes, and abilities of people. This basic concern with human beings often is obscured by emphasis on markets, products, prices, and so on. However, such things, important as they are for economic theory, are properly only a means to an end.

Satisfaction of people's wants and of what the state considers are their needs is the goal of each national economy. In the main the satisfaction of these wants and needs depends ultimately upon production. Production, in turn, involves the use of the nation's natural resources, the inventing, making, and application of durable capital goods, and the employment of much of the adult population. Unfortunately, although production normally provides a means of satisfying wants and needs, it also occasions work, which most people dislike in anything but moderate amounts. Hence some sort of balance must be struck between the production of goods and services possessing utility and the disutility of the labor that production requires.

In a free enterprise economy, private firms and proprietors undertake most of the entrepreneurial functions of combining labor, capital, and natural resources, of innovating new products, methods, and equipment, and of risking their wealth in order to command the economy's factors of production. A major part of this book will consider the economics of a private and free enterprise economy. However, there are a number of economic problems that are common to all national economies, whether capitalistic or socialistic, and these universal problems will be discussed in this chapter.

Utility, Consumption, and Spending

Economic analysis is sometimes a confusing mixture of psychological, physical, and financial elements. For instance, we have said that the first objective of economic activity is usually to provide goods to satisfy human wants, but such a provision of utility (a psychological affair) is often linked in practice to consumption (a physical matter), and consumer spending (a financial act). Actually, although utility, consumption, and spending are frequently associated, this does not render them identical; in analysis they must be kept distinct.

Utility can be defined as the real or fancied ability of a good or service to satisfy a human want. Obviously, because utility is a psychological and sensory affair, it cannot be measured in any absolute manner. One cannot connect a meter to a man's body and read off the number of "utils" he experiences when drinking a cup of coffee. Also, because utility is subjective and individual, the utility of one person cannot be compared with that of another; one cannot, for example, know which of two men derived the most utility from a cup of coffee. Therefore, it is impossible to sum up directly the utilities of different consumers.

Consumption may be defined as "the using up and wearing out of goods and services from which utility is derived." Consumption and utility are often confused. In the case of goods, their wearing out is in part an incident of use, and when they are worn out they no longer provide utility; moreover, in the case of services, consumption and utility are nearly always simultaneous. However, if we consider almost any durable consumer good, such as an automobile or a suit of clothes, it is immediately evident that consumption and utility are distinct. If cars suddenly became twice as durable, so that, instead of 90,000 miles, an average family car had 180,000 miles of life in it, the consumption per mile would be halved, but the utility per mile would remain unchanged. Up to a point, automobiles also wear out when not in use or when parked outdoors, in which case consumption and utility have little to do with one another. In some ways consumption is a great enemy of utility. If consumer goods that never wore out could be invented, an economy might in time be able to attain a sufficient stock of each kind of these goods so that further production of them would be unnecessary. An invention that lessened consumption might occasion more utility at less cost than one that increased production.

Spending by consumers, after allowance is made for price changes, indicates the rate at which the public is acquiring consumer goods. In the case of services, spending and consumption are almost simultaneous—for example, telephone calls, movies, and bus trips. And where a durable good is purchased with the aid of an installment payment plan (for example, when a buyer has a year in which to pay for a suit of clothes), spending and consumption are not so very far apart in time. However, in periods of prosperity and depression, consumers' spending for houses, automobiles, furniture, clothing, and so forth is markedly different from their rate of consumption. Spending is higher than consumption during prosperity, and vice versa. The consuming public, no less than manufacturers and distributors, always has an inventory of durable consumer goods on hand, which it expands and contracts from time to time. These consumer inventories are often useful; for instance, during World War II, the economy's civilians, including war workers, were transported millions of miles in cars originally purchased before the war.

Spending, and sometimes consumption, unlike utility, is objective, measurable, and comparable among individuals. The spending of Jones can be compared with that of Smith, and the difference stated in dollar units. Then, too, Smith's consumption of eggs can be compared with that of Jones; but if they consume different goods at different rates their aggregate consumption cannot be compared so easily. Perhaps this is one reason why we often tend to forget about utility and come to speak and write as though consumption, and particularly consumer purchasing, were the goal of welfare economics.

Notwithstanding, utility is a key concept in economics, aiding in the definition of many other conceptual bricks in the theoretical structure. Any material thing that possesses utility, even indirectly, is said to be a "good"; and any human action that possesses utility, even indirectly, is called a "service." Goods and services are either free or they are economic. A "free good" (or a free service) is one that is so abundant, in relation to the demand for it, that it can be obtained without paying money, without exchanging another good, or without self-exertion. An "economic good" (or an economic service) is one that is scarce in relation to its supply, so that it can be obtained only by giving up money or other goods or by human effort. Real income consists of the utilities derived from both free and economic goods and services. However, economic science is not much concerned with free goods and services.

Economists usually assume that real income varies in the same direction as production. In other words they suppose, at least provisionally, that the flow of free utilities is constant and unaffected by the extent of economic activity. Production is defined as "any activity that, directly or indirectly, creates utilities and thereby augments real income." Such a concept of production is not limited to changing substances and shapes or to turning out something tangible and solid. An opera singer can provide as much utility as a blacksmith, and so prove herself equally, if not more, productive, provided people hear her sing and derive utility from listening.

It is evident that production is the source of most of a community's real income. Nature has not been generous in supplying free goods and services. Even air and water are as often economic as they are free. Warm air in winter, air in the bottom of a mine shaft, or clean water in a city are all examples of economic gods. Accordingly, economists look upon the national income as being more or less synonomous with the production of economic goods and services, which provide extra real income during some prescribed time period, such as a year.

Factors of Production

The factors of production—labor, land, capital, and enterprise—together provide the means of production and hence the means of satisfying the more urgent human wants and state needs. This four-way classification of productive agents is not especially significant for all purposes, but it is conventional and frequently helpful. The student should have a clear idea of the rather special meaning that economists have attributed to each of these terms.

Labor

Labor is defined as human effort undertaken for production. This definition excludes the work of mules and the like and rules out the exertion accompanying enjoyable sports. Labor includes mental effort as well as physical work. Actually, in a country such as the United States, work that requires merely brute strength is becoming relatively rare and unimportant; the higher labor incomes go to those paragons who can combine intelligence, skill, training, honesty, and industry with a pleasant manner. Both salaried executives and gravediggers paid by the hour supply labor, but naturally their incomes vary widely.

Land

Land is a synonym for natural resources, and in economics the term refers to all productive aids furnished by nature that are available without past or present labor cost. The unharnessed power of a Niagara Falls is "land," paradoxical as this may seem; so too are the cod fisheries of New England and the virgin timber stands of the Pacific Northwest. Land, in agriculture, refers to the indestructible powers of the soil. In some cases, it is important to distinguish between those "land" agents of production that are naturally renewed (for example, tidal energy) and those that are not naturally replaced and hence can be readily depleted (for example, mineral ores).

Labor and land are sometimes referred to as the two primary or original factors of production. It is certainly true that Robinson Crusoe, cast upon his desert island, had to start production with nothing except his own labor and the land he found. The most primitive type of economy would conceivably be one in which man relied solely on human effort applied to the natural environment without benefit of capital.

Fortunately, however, land and labor are usually allied with capital goods, in what are sometimes called "roundabout" methods of production. Even Robinson Crusoe did not long attempt to wrest a living with his bare hands from the tropic isle upon which he was shipwrecked. He directed some of his efforts toward making nets to catch fish, conduits to bring down water, and various implements to multiply the effectiveness of his labors. In other words he often worked in a roundabout way in order to provide himself with consumption goods, if in the long run such indirection seemed more productive. Capitalistic (that is, roundabout) methods of production are of course a feature of every advanced economy whether organized along free enterprise or socialistic lines.

Concepts of Capital

Capital goods are occasionally termed "produced means of production." Land and labor are also "means of production," of course, but they are not deliberately "produced" as are such capital goods as factories, machinery, pipelines, and semi-finished materials. In some parts of Scandinavia pulp wood trees are considered as capital because they are the result of deliberate silviculture. The value added to a hillside factory site when it is graded is also capital. Other names sometimes used to describe capital goods are "intermediate goods" and "producers' goods." Producers' goods only provide utility by indirectly aiding in the production of consumers' goods.

The term "capital," used alone, is often ambiguous; it may refer to capital goods (just described), capital funds (described below), or even sometimes to capital values (the present value of almost any future income stream).

Modern methods of production always require capital funds. Money must be spent before it can be recovered; the output to be sold must first be produced. Funds must be poured out for equipment, for materials, and for the labor and power needed to work up these materials to a point at which they are sufficiently processed for sale. The persons who provide the money needed to acquire fixed and working capital are advancing capital funds. These capitalists are "waiting" in the sense that there is a time interval between the date when the money is provided to purchase assets and the date when these funds are recouped.

Capital has several facets. On one side are the capital funds that are advanced, and on the other are the capital goods that the funds purchase. The identity of the capital goods is constantly changing as specific machines and goods in process are replaced; but the value of the capital funds in the business may remain approximately the same. Capital funds represent community saving, and capital goods represent community investment. For the economy as a whole, if certain special definitions are adopted, aggregate saving must equal aggregate investment in value.

Enterprise

Of course labor, land, and capital funds do not spontaneously combine themselves and impersonally decide what to produce and how to produce it. There is always a fourth factor involved in production, which is sometimes called "enterprise" or "enterpreneurship." The peculiar functions of entrepreneurship are combining the other factors of production, taking risks, and introducing new inventions and methods.

In all countries the state performs some of these functions. For example, in the United States the federal government owns and operates the post office; in Great Britain the government also operates the telephone, the telegraph, and the coal mines; and in the Soviet Union the government owns and operates all industrial, and most agricultural, undertakings. When the state assumes the role of entrepreneur, it may be able to transfer many risks to the shoulders of others, but it is still a risk-taker on behalf of the community. If it decides to use the economy's resources in unsound ways, the community will suffer a loss in well-being even though the government succeeds in balancing its books.

In the United States, and in other predominantly free enterprise economies, private interests assume most entrepreneurial responsibilities. There is usually some person who thinks he sees a profitable way to supply an anticipated demand, who is able to organize the necessary factors into an operating concern, and who is willing to gamble on the soundness of his judgment through an investment of money or effort. In the present century the entrepreneur of a corporation may consist of those management officials and stockholders who either originally promoted or now "spark" the concern.

The factors of land, labor, and capital are conglomerates. Land consists of such heterogeneous elements as farm land, mineral land, power-producing land, and so forth. Even farm land itself can be broken down into numerous kinds, such as grazing land, cereal land, and vegetable land. Similarly, there are all sorts of labor—for example, the services of accountants, elevator operators, newspaper columnists, and cow hands. Capital goods are extremely varied because there are numerous kinds of machinery and specialized structures employed to help labor use and process natural resources. However, despite the heterogeneous composition of land, labor, and capital, their unique sources of supply often permit us to treat them as distinct categories.

Opportunity Costs

In every economy, whether socialistic or capitalistic, it is naturally impossible for any given productive agent to be employed in two ways or in two places at once. Hence, at any given level of employment of land, labor, and capital, for the economy as a whole, it is presumably impossible, unless there is gross inefficiency somewhere in the system, to produce more of one good or service without producing less of some other good or service. This rather obvious fact lies beneath the idea of opportunity cost.

It is always theoretically possible, if the level and efficiency of resources employment is given, to assess the cost of producing "good A" in terms of the number of units of "good B" or "good C" that can no longer be produced if factors of production are diverted from making them and directed instead toward making A; for example (and this sort of dilemma is common in wartime), making 100 more airplanes may "cost" a production cut of 1,000 automobiles or 10,000 refrigerators. Opportunity costs stress alternatives and they are measured by what must be foregone.

A planned economy would need to know its various opportunity costs in order to determine the proper composition of the national output. If the price that the public will bid for a certain kind of car is 12 times as great as it will bid for a certain type of refrigerator, and the opportunity cost of each extra car is 10 refrigerators, some resources should be diverted from refrigerator to car production. The outputs of different goods are in proper proportion if the barter rates that the public would establish are equal to their opportunity-cost ratios. The above principle provides a valid standard of resource allocation for both socialistic and capitalistic economies.

The Inevitability of Scarcity

The concept of opportunity cost would be meaningless if it were possible to have more of A *without* having to accept less of B or C. The opportunity-cost idea has significance because there is always a general scarcity of goods and services. Why is it that most goods are economic goods and that all goods are not free goods? Why is not each and every one of us able to satisfy all his wants and needs? Do we exist in an "economy of scarcity" because of a conspiracy on the part of a rich and privileged few?

Occasionally people talk and write as though the only obstacles to their enjoying all they wanted were high prices and low incomes. However, second thought reveals that if the state doubled the money income of each of us, we would probably be able to buy no more goods and services than before because prices might easily double. Then too, the enactment of a law cutting all prices in half would also fail to make more goods and services available to us because sales receipts are the source of incomes.

The simple truth is that no economy will ever devise a way to enjoy goods and services not yet produced. The aggregate output of an economy, actual or potential, is limited. The principle limitations are (1) a preordained natural endowment, (2) the momentarily unchanging "state of the arts," (3) the disutility of labor, (4) unwillingness to postpone sumptuary pleasure, and (5) reluctance to incur undue financial risk.

(1) *Preordained Natural Resources.* The "land" factor of production is an unalterable fact that each economy must accept. Of course, it may be possible to reclaim land that previously was unusable, as the Dutch did in the Zuider Zee, but this is really an example of labor employed to create real capital. New mineral reserves may be discovered through exploration and prospecting, but this is also an example of a return to labor and possibly to capital. Permanent natural resources may acquire new value through an advance in the state of the arts (for example, the advent of the steam railroad made wheat-raising in the Canadian prairies commercially practical), but such additions to output do not depend upon the land factor. Each economy must be content to make the best use of the natural resources with which it has been endowed.

(2) *"State of the Arts."* Man's technology, that is his chemical, biological, and physical knowledge as applied to production, is constantly advancing. The rising living standards of the Occidental world during the past century and a half are probably due more to progress in the state of the arts than to any other influence. However, the acquisition of such knowledge, although apparently at an accelerating rate, is slow and gradual. Fortunately, each economy can, to some extent, hasten the discovery of new and more productive inventions.

(3) *Disutility of Labor.* The people of each economy could consume and produce more goods and services if they would work harder and longer. The tremendous combined military and civilian output of the United States during World War II, despite the fact that 11 million men were in the armed forces, was due to an expansion of the labor force and a lengthening of the work week.

Unfortunately, most people dislike their work. However, there are exceptions; some people work short hours and would be bored if they had nothing to do; some jobs are extremely interesting or carry fame or power. Nonetheless, work usually occasions disutility, and this is a real, albeit often a psychological, cost, which must be paid if economic goods and services are to be made available.

(4) *Unwillingness to Wait.* Often, known productive techniques, which in time would increase net output, are not put into practice because of the unwillingness of the community to invest the resources that these innovations would entail. In a free enterprise economy there are generally some productive inventions that, because of the rate of interest, are excluded from use; this is due partly to the unwillingness of people to postpone consumption and invest their savings. On the other hand, in a socialist economy, political pressures may make the leaders of the state refrain from public investment programs that cause a reduction in the current level of consumption, although in a thoroughgoing police state this consideration will have little weight. Technological discoveries are of limited use in themselves if the capital funds or directed resources needed to implement them are not forthcoming.

(5) *Reluctance to Take Risk.* In a free enterprise economy all private enterpreneurs must inevitably incur some risks. They are usually reluctant to subject themselves to financial uncertainty unless they believe the future holds odds that are slightly on their side. Such a belief may be mistaken and it may be unreasonable, but it must exist if the entrepreneur is to perform his role. This is because, in general, entrepreneurs probably place a lower subjective valuation on x dollars of profit than on x dollars of loss. Risk-taking in a socialist economy, although it must be incurred, is probably a weaker deterrent in most cases.

These five elements prevent, at any given moment, a sudden increase in output, except under special circumstances such as the outbreak of war, when the state may force more people into jobs or undertake investment itself. So far in the history of the world, except perhaps in some rather unusual places and cultures, these limitations on output have caused most goods and services to be economic rather than free. The needs and wants of most economies are too lavish in relation to the scarce means of satisfying them. The resulting condition of general scarcity is not due to unsound government, improper organization of the economy, or the selfish manipulations of a few. The sense of incomplete satisfaction that nettles most consumers could not be allayed for all of them as a group by lowering prices or increasing money incomes by edict.

Of course it is barely conceivable that there may be some paradise in the world where there is no economic problem and where human wants fall behind the means of satisfying them. In paradise everyone can have all he or she wants. Paradise might exist if (1) nature were extremely generous in growing fruit and vegetables and in providing fish and game, (2) infant mortality or sexual practices kept the population at a low level, and (3) the community culture emphasized play and sports rather than the possession of material goods. However, such places are certainly few and far between.

It is because generalized scarcity is the rule in all nations that economics exists as a social science. If everyone cannot have everything he wants, obviously it is desirable that the national means of production be used to best advantage. Land, labor, and capital must be economized; they must not be employed to produce goods and services of lesser importance than things that remain unproduced. It also becomes important that the available means of production, and especially labor, are not underemployed; underemployment in this sense means that extra goods and services, which possess more utility in use than the disutility of the labor necessary to produce them, could be made. In other words, it is desirable that the allocation among uses and the intensity of employment of all resources be optimum according to some standard. One of the principal tasks of economic theory is to evolve yardsticks of desirability. What is the best resource allocation? What is the best level of employment? Another task of theory is to consider methods of implementation. Will pure competition give us the results that have been defined as optimum? Will state socialism be more likely to employ resources in a better manner? Final and exact answers to these questions naturally do not exist. However, we shall, in the rest of this book, outline a number of principles and theorems that do throw light on these crucial matters.

Statements for Consideration

1. The real cost of production would be lessened in all respects if the population of each country were smaller.   *Evaluate*
2. Opportunity costs exist even when idle resources are available for employment.   *Discuss*
3. The factor "land" includes far more than rock and soil.   *Explain*
4. The notion of utility enters into many economic concepts.
                                                              Exemplify
5. There would be no economic problem if human nature would so improve that people would share their wealth.   *Evaluate*
6. The purpose of economics is to explain how prices are determined.
                                                              Evaluate
7. The real costs discussed in this chapter would also apply to a Socialist economy.   *Exemplify*
8. The consumption of different households can be compared but not their utility from consumption.   *Explain*
9. An invention that reduced physical consumption rates might increase real income.   *Evaluate*

References

Bowman, M. J., and Bach, G. L., *Economic Analysis and Public Policy,* Chapter 7.   New York: Prentice-Hall, 1949.

Due, J. F., *Intermediate Economic Analysis,* Chapter 1.   Chicago: Irwin, 1947.

Hicks, J. R., and Hart, A. G., *The Social Framework of the American Economy,* Chapters 1–3.   New York: Oxford University Press, 1945.

Marshall, A., *Principles of Economics,* Eighth Edition, Book II.   London: Macmillan, 1920.

Meyers, A. L., *Modern Economics,* Chapter 4.   New York: Prentice-Hall, 1946.

Morgan, T., *Income and Employment,* Chapter 1.   New York: Prentice-Hall, 1947.

Pigou, A. C., *Income,* Chapters 1–3.   London: Macmillan, 1946.

———, *The Economics of Welfare,* Fourth Edition, I, Chapters 1, 2.   London: Macmillan, 1942.

Robbins, L., *An Essay on the Nature and Significance of Economic Science,* Chapters 1, 2.   London: Macmillan, 1932.

Samuelson, P. A., *Economics,* Chapters 1, 2.   New York: McGraw-Hill, 1948.

Shoup, C. S., *Principles of National Income Analysis,* Chapter 1.   Boston: Houghton Mifflin, 1947.

Slichter, S. H., *The American Economy,* Chapter 1.   New York: Knopf, 1948.

2

Four Economic Groups

IN ORDER better to grasp the operations of an economy, it is helpful to imagine it populated by four different kinds of economic "persons." These four groups of "persons," each of which will be defined below, are households, firms, governments, and banks. Each of these groups carries on transactions within and without its group. In this chapter we shall consider the interrelations of households, firms, governments, and banks. The following description applies only to the United States, Great Britain, and other predominantly free enterprise economies.

Households

Half a century ago economic theory devoted considerable thought to the needs and behavior of consumers; but in many ways this emphasis on the consumer was not very useful. Babes-in-arms are consumers, but they certainly do not make economic decisions. Moreover, although a few individuals, such as bachelors, comprise single consuming units, the basic consuming unit is most often a household of people. A household comprises all those persons who live off and spend from the same pool of income or effort. At the present time there are probably forty-odd million households in the United States.

Household Economics

A fairly representative household might consist of a man, his wife, an adolescent boy, a girl in grade school, and an old mother-in-law. The man is the breadwinner, providing more than half the household income, but this income is supplemented by a small annuity of the mother-in-law and part-time work of the boy. The man is the net provider, actually enjoying only a fraction of the income he contributes to the household, whereas all the others are net detractors. In effect, the various members of the household

15

are pooling their income, and this is really a more significant criterion of a household than that these people exist under the same roof.

Another characteristic of households is that goods and services are usually distributed within the consuming unit according to the needs of its members rather than according to their incomes. In fact some breadwinners turn over their paychecks to their wives and receive in return a small allowance for personal spending. Junior's demands for an electric train may take precedence over Dad's need for a new hat. It is interesting to note that most households roughly practice the communist ideal, still unrealized even in the Soviet Union, of "from each according to ability, to each according to need." However, human nature usually prevents the operation of this principle beyond the immediate family.

A substantial part of the real income of most households is produced within them and enjoyed directly. The homemaker of a household cooks the food, cleans the house, and may even try her hand at dressmaking and interior decorating. (Perhaps someday housewives will present a weekly bill for all this work!) Rural households often raise part of their food supply, and some households short circuit the market place by exchanging goods and "taking in each other's washing." At the other extreme are single men in cities who buy all their sumptuary goods and services from the economy.

Households and Firms

In the United States, approximately three-quarters of the transactions of households, as measured in dollars, are with firms. A firm is any private combination of productive factors engaged in furnishing goods and services for profit; this definition includes all private industrial, distributive, and agricultural enterprises, whether legally organized as proprietorships, partnerships, or corporations. Naturally this three-quarters fraction varies, depending upon the household and upon its income. A bachelor, who spends relatively more on liquor, tobacco, and other things bearing heavy excise taxes, will find that fewer of his dollars go to firms and more go to the government than would those of a household with many children and with the same income.

Households obtain current income from firms in the form of wages and salaries, rents, royalties, interest, dividends, and profits.

This income is the return for the productive goods or services provided by members of the household. Naturally, the wages and salaries received for labor make up the bulk of all incomes except those of the wealthiest households.

The distinction between wages and profits and between firms and households is sometimes a little blurred in the case of proprietorships and especially in the case of farm families. Superficially, a farm may appear to have yielded a profit income of $5,400 to the farmer and his family in a year. But perhaps two of the farmer's grown sons and the farmer himself worked for nothing on the farm for most of the year, and the family slaughtered the farm hogs for food. Let us further assume that the farmer and

TABLE 1

U. S. HOUSEHOLDS RECEIPTS AND EXPENDITURES 1939, 1946, AND 1948 *
(Dollars in Billions)

	1939	1946	1948
Household Income	$73	$177	$212
Labor Income†	46	113	135
Proprietors' and Rental Income ..	15	42	49
Dividends	4	6	8
Personal Interest	5	8	8
Gifts (i.e., transfer payments)	3	11	11
Personal Taxes	2	19	21
Disposable Household Income	70	158	191
Household Consumption Expenditures ‡	67	144	179
Food and Tobacco	21	55	65
Clothing, Jewelry, etc.	8	22	24
Cosmetics	1	2	3
Housing	9	13	16
Household Operation (e.g., utilities)	9	18	24
Medical Care and Death Expenses	3	6	8
Personal Business (e.g., brokerage).	4	5	7
Transportation	6	11	18
Recreation	3	8	10
Private Education and Research ..	1	1	1
Religion and Welfare	1	2	2
Foreign Travel and Remittances §	—	—	1
Household Savings	3	15	12

* Source: U. S. Department of Commerce, National Income Supplement to the *Survey of Current Business.*
† Total employer disbursements, minus social insurance deductions, plus other labor income, such as board and lodging.
‡ Expenditure figures include excise taxes.
§ Less than half a billion dollars in 1939 and 1946.

his sons could have hired themselves out for $4,000 altogether and that the family ate up $200 worth of bacon, ham, and pork. The farm (as a firm) then provided the family (or household) with an income of $5,600, including a wages income of $4,000 and profits of $1,600.

Almost all the sumptuary goods and services that households specifically buy are purchased from firms. Table 1 shows the breakdown of household consumption expenditures by purpose and also the sources of household money receipts, personal taxes, and disposable income. The stable relation that each class of expenditure bears to total household consumption is noteworthy.

Households also have many money transactions with firms on capital account. They may buy or sell corporate securities; heads of families may invest funds in businesses that they own as proprietors; and rich men sometimes make direct loans to small enterprises. However, capital transactions of this kind are not always continuing in the same direction and are not part of the regular and inevitable flow of payments.

Households and Governments

Because there are so many government units, households pay more money to governments than is generally realized. In the United States, besides the federal government, there are states, counties, and municipalities, as well as various special assessment districts. If we were to consider every taxing unit as a separate government, there would be several thousand governments in the United States.

A relatively small sum is paid by households to governments in direct payment for specific purchases each year. For instance, the United States Post Office roughly covers its costs from the prices it charges for its services; on the state level, gasoline taxes and motor vehicle fees usually rather more than pay for construction, maintenance, and patrol of highways; and local special assessments are usually directly related to the cost of street lighting, paving, or other special improvements. In these cases a household, when it elects to make a current payment to a government, gets something in exchange. In a sense, the government is in business and playing the role of a private firm; however, its power to discriminate among its "customers" usually exceeds that of firms.

Most payments by households to governments (for example, personal income tax payments to the United States government, sales tax payments to certain states, and real property tax payments to municipalities) are not matched by any *quid pro quo*. These taxes go to finance the general purposes of government. Up to a point some of these taxes can be avoided, indirect taxes by living a very Spartan and ascetic life, and direct taxes by staying poor or moving to some other country; but for most people such escapes are a greater evil than taxes.   Hence many households pay for government services and gifts that they do not receive and even for the prosecution of government policies that they resent.

On the other hand there are many households that, for one reason or another, receive gifts of money that do not call for any *quid pro quo*.   Some so-called social insurance schemes are not genuinely self-supporting, but are in part financed by grants from unearmarked government receipts.   When this is so, the insurance beneficiaries, as a group, are to some extent receiving a gift. In the past, demobilized war veterans have been voted large bonuses, which were never contemplated during hostilities. Whether the gift element in these various payments and services is equitable or desirable need not concern us and probably cannot be determined.   These gifts are called "transfer payments."

Governments also provide a number of "free" goods and services, such as public education, libraries, and so on.   Of course these benefits are not free to the economy, for resources are used in providing them.   They are paid for indirectly through taxes instead of directly through prices.

It is obvious that governments can proceed a long way either in equalizing income equalities or at least in neutralizing their effect. Progressive tax rates on personal income and inheritance and proportionate taxes on real and personal property help to finance education, medical care, and some measure of security for the young, the sick, and the poor.   In Europe a number of national economies are slowly evolving into what have been described as "Welfare States," in which the central government stands ready to aid all those who may suffer undue hardship.

However, in value terms, most payments of governments to households are in exchange for goods and services.   Governments hire labor, rent land, borrow funds; in short, they require many of the same productive agents as do firms. In the United States the various government units employ several million persons and pay over a billion dollars a year in interest to households. In addition, on capital account, governments and households are of course constantly buying and selling assets, such as government bonds, land, and surplus government equipment; for instance, United States bonds were purchased in considerable amount by many households during World War II.

Households and Banks

In any rich and industrial economy, such as that of the United States, there are many corporations that serve as financial intermediaries between households, firms, and governments; for example, commercial and savings banks, life insurance companies, and investment trusts and syndicates. Throughout this book these financial intermediaries will often be referred to collectively and called "banks." Many households, perhaps a majority of them, at some time or another either entrust savings to banks or borrow from them. Household savings may either be placed in a savings account to be used to purchase stock of some investment trust with funds that are then reinvested by the trust or be paid as premiums to a life insurance company. Insurance premiums in part represent household savings if they are paid for policies that have an increasing cash surrender value. Life insurance companies are among the largest investors in real estate and securities. In the United States more households probably save and invest more money through life insurance than in any other way. Conversely, households are doing more and more borrowing from commercial banks and finance companies to pay for durable consumer goods, as well as to settle emergency bills. Occasionally these funds come from the purchase by the public of finance companies' securities. However, these funds are often the result of additional credit created by the commercial banks. During upswings of prosperity this extra credit, which is, in effect, new money, may push the upswing farther for a while.

Firms

Firms have been defined as "any private combination of productive factors engaged in furnishing goods and services for profit." Naturally this classification is too broad for some purposes, and it is often helpful to distinguish between manufacturing firms, farms, wholesaling and retailing firms, service establishments, and so on. However, all firms possess one common denominator, the *adding of value* incidental to seeking profits.

Gross Value Added

A typical firm is engaged in making the things it buys possess greater value. Thus a manufacturing firm may buy cereals to produce flour, or automobile parts to produce motor vehicles, or tobacco to produce cigarettes. A distributing firm, whether wholesaling or retailing, buys goods from suppliers, and then, after shipment and storage, resells them in smaller quantities at higher unit prices. An agricultural firm may buy range lambs and in time resell them, after special feeding, as fattened mutton. Usually, in each case, there will be an added value to the goods.

Obviously, the value added by a firm will be greater than its profits. There are many expense items to be charged against the value-added figure before one can tell what profit, if any, remains. An examination of these offsets reveals the relations that firms have with households, governments, and banks.

First, however, we must scrutinize a number of income categories. Gross value added may be viewed loosely as total receipts minus all purchase costs. But both "total receipts" and "purchase costs" are rather vague notions. "Total receipts" are really the value of the finished output during the time period in question; they are the receipts from the sale of the product plus the value of additions to finished inventories. This definition means that, if a firm produced nothing one year and sold entirely from inventory, it would have no value added for that period.

On the other hand "purchase costs" are really the cost of purchased goods and services that have been used, as distinct from expenditures for purchases; for example, a textile firm may purchase twice as much cotton in one year as it uses, in which case its purchase costs are payments for purchases minus the value of increases in purchased inventories. Purchased goods and services are usually obtained from other firms (for example, contracted advertising), occasionally from governments (for example, harbor and canal facilities), and from banks (for example, stock transfer services), but by definition exclude purchases from households.

Net Value Added

There are a number of offsets against gross value added. These offsets, with one exception, provide flows of income to households, or governments, or possibly banks. The one exception is depreciation, which is a drain on the economy; it is not income for any group.

It is the existence of depreciation that compels us to distinguish at this time between *gross value added* and *net value added*. The gross value added of a single firm, as we have seen, is the value of the produced output minus the value of the used purchases. In the case of a single firm again, gross value added minus depreciation is equal to what is called net value added. The significance of this distinction lies in the fact, as we shall see in the next chapter, that the sum of all firms' gross values added is equal to gross national product, whereas the sum of all firms' net values added is equal to net national product.

One of the other offsets against value added is indirect business taxes, such as excise taxes on output, real estate taxes on plants and their sites, and so on. If these so-called business taxes are deducted from net value added, we are left with a number of offsets that ultimately provide income for households. These remaining offsets are wages and salaries before deductions for social security payments, interest, rent, and profits. Of course, in the case of a single firm, some interest, rent, or profit may be paid to another firm. However, if all firms are aggregated, the remaining net payment-flows become household income.

Incidentally, in any year, profits are equal to the positive change in the value of a firm's assets minus liabilities, calculated prior to any profits' disbursement. From this basic definition it can be seen that profits need not be paid out and need not even take the form of money if retained; in fact they are usually already embodied in additions to equipment, inventories, or other real assets. These profits, which in reality are often increased real asset values, belong to the owners. When all firms are taken as a group, their net consolidated profits are considered the income of householders although no money is paid out.

Table 2 summarizes the relations described above.

TABLE 2

THE NATIONAL INCOME CONTRIBUTION AND VALUE ADDED OF A SINGLE FIRM

Sales Receipts,
  plus Value of Additions to Output Inventories,
  equals Value of Output.
Cost of Purchases,
  minus Value of Additions to Purchased Inventories
  equals Value of Used Purchases
Value of Output,
  minus Value of Used Purchases,
  equals Gross Value Added.
Gross Value Added,
  minus Depreciation,
  equals Net Value Added.
Net Value Added,
  equals Business Taxes
  plus Wages and Salaries (including Social Security),
  plus Interest,
  plus Rent,
  plus Profits.

Note: The percentage relations of "gross value added" to "value of output" differs consider-ably among industries, being about 15% in cereal milling, 20% in cigarette manufacturing, 25% in automobile making, 75% in ice manufacturing, and 80% in optical goods production.

The categories with which we have been concerned are needed to estimate the productive contribution of a firm toward national income. In a free enterprise economy, four-fifths or more of the paid-for national income is produced annually by firms. Hence a thorough understanding of the value-added concept and of the groups that share this addition to value will be developed in our subsequent analysis of national income.

Governments and Banks

We have already pointed out there are numerous government units in a country the size of the United States and that these vari-ous units have different functions and sources of revenue.

Governments must resort to banks for a number of reasons Just as firms borrow to buy buildings and equipment, so do gov-ernments borrow in advance to pay for highways, school build-ings, and other public works. This is especially true in areas where population is increasing rapidly. Another very human and potent reason for government borrowing is that in no country does the public relish taxes as avidly as it does "free" government benefits, and so there is always a tendency for government budgets to become unbalanced. And, in times of war, it is, of course, hardly conceivable that all the expenditures of the national government could be met from current taxes. In practice all governments must occasionally borrow, and although they often try to sell bonds and notes to households and firms, they must also borrow heavily from banks.

The banking system as a whole, that is the Federal Reserve Banks plus the commercial banks, alternately create and destroy money. The active money stock of the United States at any time is roughly the value of the legal tender and commercial bank accounts owned by governments, firms, and households. When the banking system extends credit, the value of commercial bank accounts rises, and in time some of this increase probably becomes circulating legal tender. The mechanics of these operations are described in Chapter 5.

As a general rule, in the United States, the Federal Reserve Banks and the commercial banks together expand their loans to firms and even households during periods of prosperity, thereby increasing the effective stock of money held by the non-bank public. The reverse normally occurs during periods of business depression. However, in the future, it is possible that a depression period contraction of credit and money may be somewhat mitigated by government efforts to borrow from the banks for public works and other forms of deficit spending.

The ever-increasing scope of federal fiscal operations has suggested the possibility to many economists that the United States government could seek indirectly to dampen future economic fluctuations. It is specifically argued that the Treasury should go into debt to the banking system during depressed times in order to lessen the normal contraction of money and *vice versa*. Just how effective this might be one naturally cannot predict.

However, there can be little debate over the ability of the federal government to increase the national money stock during wartime. Table 3 is offered in demonstration of this point. Line 7 shows that, between mid-1939 and mid-1945, the money stock owned by the non-bank public increased by 99.6 billion dollars to 267% of what it had been six years earlier.

What was the basis of this extra one-hundred-odd billion dollars, and from where did it come? The lower part of the table supplies the answer. The Federal Reserve Banks and the commercial banks together increased their holdings of federal secu-

rities by 87.6 billions.   Loans amounting to 7.3 billions were made
to war plants, farmers, and others.   These banks also purchased
4.1 billion dollars of imported and domestically mined gold.   It
is a rather startling realization that in six years the American banking system, excluding savings banks, created and advanced considerably more money to the U. S. Treasury, and indirectly to the
public, than the value of the entire national money stock owned
outside the banks in 1939.

TABLE 3

BANK FINANCING OF WORLD WAR II *

(Dollars in Billions)

	June 30, 1939	June 30, 1945	Change
Non-Bank Money Stock:			
1. Public's Demand Deposits	$27.4	$69.1	$41.7
2. Public's Time Deposits	15.1	27.2	12.1
3. Public's Legal Tender	6.0	25.1	19.1
4. Treasury Commercial Bank Balances	0.8	24.4	23.6
5. Treasury Legal Tender and FRB Balances	3.5	2.9	—0.6
6. Miscellaneous Bank Accounts	8.7	12.4	3.7
7. *Total Money Stock*	$61.4	$161.0	$99.6
Bank Assets:			
8. U. S. Securities	$18.3	$105.9	$87.6
9. Loans	16.4	23.7	7.3
10. Other Securities	7.2	6.8	0.4
11. Monetary Gold	16.1	20.2	4.1
12. Treasury Currency Outstanding	2.9	4.1	1.2
13. Miscellaneous Bank Assets	2.0	1.4	—0.6
14. *Total Bank Assets*	$62.9	$162.1	$99.2
Discrepancies	$1.5	$1.1	$.4

* Source: Federal Reserve Bulletins.
   Note: This table includes Federal Reserve Banks and Commercial Banks but excludes Savings Banks.

The banking system's holdings of federal obligations are now
so large that the future fiscal policy of the federal government will
inevitably affect the economy at large.   One cannot help but
wonder, although in terms of practical politics it is probably inconceivable, what would happen if Congress retired a substantial
fraction of the increased federal debt over a period of years.   On
the other hand, if these offsetting additions to the federal debt and

the national money stock are permanent, other commercial credit fluctuations will be less important in the future than hitherto.

An extreme and ludicrous supposition may make this clear. In 1939, if in some way all the loans shown on line 9 of Table 3 had been repaid to the banking system and all non-United States securities shown on line 10 had been sold by the banking system, the total money stock would have been reduced immediately by 39%; if this same unlikely event had occurred in 1945, the money stock would have been reduced only 18%. Alternatively, to consider a less far-fetched hypothesis, if one-half of all the balances and cash advanced by the banking system to the entire economy, other than the Treasury, were somehow retired, the national money stock would today be directly curtailed by about only ten per cent.

Hence, the debts owed to banks by firms, households, and lesser government units do not have the same monetary significance that they did as recently as one decade ago. Attention is centered nowadays on the interaction of Treasury and Federal Reserve policies and upon tax and appropriation votes of the Congress. An incidental result of World War II has been to place the federal government even more irrevocably in the center of the national economy.

Statements for Consideration

1. Communism is practiced in most American households.   *Discuss*
2. Households enjoy more real income than they buy.   *Explain*
3. A farmer's profit is the excess of his sales receipts over his money costs.   *Evaluate*
4. Many taxes could be legally avoided by living in a different manner.   *Discuss*
5. Social security deductions from wages and salaries should be considered a tax rather than the payment of an insurance premium.   *Evaluate*
6. No government service is free so far as the economy is concerned.   *Explain*
7. Depreciation is equal to "gross value added" minus "net value added."   *Explain*
8. If a firm sells goods one year, but entirely from finished goods inventories because it has undertaken no production, it will have nevertheless contributed a "net value added" to national income.   *Evaluate*
9. The debts owed to banks by firms and households do not have the same over-all economic importance that they did a decade ago.   *Explain*

References

Garver, F. B., and Hansen, A. H., *Principles of Economics,* Third Edition, Chapters 3, 4.   New York: Ginn, 1947.

Hicks, J. R., and Hart, A. G., *The Social Framework of the American Economy,* Parts II, III.   New York: Oxford University Press, 1945.

Morgan, T., *Income and Employment,* Chapters 2, 3.   New York: Prentice-Hall, 1947.

Samuelson, P. A., *Economics,* Chapters 4, 5.   New York: McGraw-Hill, 1948.

Shoup, C. S., *Principles of National Income Analysis,* Chapters 2–4. Boston: Houghton Mifflin, 1947.

Tarshis, L., *Elements of Economics,* Part II.   Boston: Houghton Mifflin, 1947.

3

National Income Accounting

IT IS logically possible to construct a system of accounts for a national economy, just as it is logically possible to set up an income statement for a single firm. Of course there are a number of practical differences; one of the most important of these differences is the lack or unreliability of some of the necessary national economic data. On the theoretical side, there is also an important difference; although one knows what a firm's income statement should try to show, there is not always complete agreement as to what national economic accounts should measure.

Some Basic Ideas

What constitutes annual income in the case of a national economy? Is national income the value of the money personally *received* for economic activity? Is it the *market value* or the *cost to firms* of all the goods and services produced but not reused in production? Is it the net value of the consumer goods and services *acquired* from the market or *used up* by households? Is the value of extra unused capital stocks a part of national income as well as that of consumer-goods output? These five questions demonstrate that national income can be an ambiguous concept despite the conventions that are becoming established.

Which definition of national income an economist finally selects will depend in part upon whom he believes an economy should serve and in part upon what are practical units of measurement. Should an economy function for the sake of governments, firms, or households? Naturally, political philosophies differ, but a majority of economists agree that ideally the performance of an economy should be judged by its ability to provide goods and services to households, whether through firms or governments or even home production.

On this basis, only consumer goods and services are, in the end, relevant to national income. If this is accepted, what then should the unit of measurement be? The real or psychic income of persons cannot be measured or compared, and so national income cannot practically be defined as collective *real* income. It is also impossible to adopt a physical measure of national income because there is no way of aggregating a ton of steel, a yard of cloth, a gallon of gasoline, and so on. Hence, in practice, national income has to be measured in money terms. Several reasons why this is an imperfect unit of measurement are set forth in the following chapter.

Various alternative definitions of national income, neglecting production by governments, remain, even after one decides to emphasize consumer goods and use money values. One might still view national income, as any one of the following:

(1) Production of consumer goods by firms;
(2) Household purchases of consumer goods;
(3) Household consumption of purchased consumer goods;
(4) Economy-wide production of consumer goods;
(5) Household consumption of all consumer goods.

Perhaps one can best distinguish these rival concepts by illustrating these categories in terms of women's dresses.

In a given year the following might all occur: (1) Firms produce $4 billions' worth of women's dresses (this is interesting but tells us little directly about the value of dresses used); (2) Women and their admirers purchase $6 billions' worth of dresses, $2 billion of which come from output inventories (however, we still do not know whether some of these are put away in closets and left unused); (3) Women use up $7 billions' worth of store dresses, $1 billion of which were bought in a previous, more prosperous year, and they are now "making them do"; (4) The economy as a whole produces $5 billions' worth of dresses, $1 billion of which are homemade; (5) Altogether, women wear out $8 billions' worth of dresses, $1 billion of which come from household stocks and another $2 billion from firms' stocks. Should the contribution of women's dresses to national income be listed at $4, $5, $6, $7, or $8 billions?

A strong theoretical case might be made for defining national income as aggregate household consumption (item 5) because this perhaps most closely approximates the concept of experienced real income.   Consumption, in turn, is equal to household spending on consumer goods, plus home production of consumer goods, plus decreases in household stocks of consumer goods.   Unfortunately, such a definition of national income is quite impractical because it requires unavailable data for measurement.   Specifically, the value of home production cannot be estimated, and the changing value of household stocks of consumer goods is largely unknown.

Hence, the realistic choice, although theoretically imperfect perhaps, is between household purchases of consumer goods or services (item 2) or the production of consumer goods or services for sale (item 1).

However, before going further, we must examine what is meant by consumer-goods production more closely.   Let us consider the case of women's dresses once again.   There are several stages in the making of dresses.   The fiber must be produced, it must be woven into fabric, and the fabric dyed, then cut, and so on.   At any moment there exist stocks of fiber, stocks of woven but undyed cloth, stocks of dyed but uncut cloth, and so forth, just as there also exist stocks of finished but unsold dresses.   Moreover, the size of each of these inventories may change between the beginning and end of a year.   If an increase in the stocks of finished but unsold dresses is considered to be production, it is only consistent to consider an increase in the stocks of dyed but uncut cloth as production.   In fact, an increase in any work in process inventory, between the beginning and end of a year, is part of production.

However, production includes even more than positive changes in materials and goods inventories.   In textile manufacturing, for example, machinery and fiber are both used up; the fact that the fiber is transformed immediately, whereas the machinery only depreciates gradually, does not alter the using-up process that is taking place.   Hence, if an increase in fiber stocks is part of production, an increase in machinery stocks should also be counted as production, after due allowance has been made for depreciation during the year.   After all, if the economy ends a year with capital equipment having greater use value than at the beginning, this is certainly a contribution to future welfare.

Production, in short, is equal to household spending for consumer goods plus investment, where investment is the algebraic sum of additions to the value of stocks of finished consumer goods, intermediate materials, and fixed capital. All these investment goods should naturally be valued at constant prices throughout the accounting period in any estimate of national production.

National income is very much like a long river with many tributaries flowing into it. The mouth of the river, where it discharges, can best be thought of as analogous to the using up of consumer goods by households, in which case the waters of the home-production tributaries are also recorded. However it is easier to record the river flow a little further up stream, below where the wholesale and retail tributaries come in but above the junction with the home production river. Then, as we proceed upstream, we pass the point where goods are in process and reach a stretch where goods are in raw material form. The water flowing in the tributaries we pass measures the value of the factors of production employed at each stage. The flow of water in the main river is the value of the goods passing the point of measurement. The measured rate of water flow halfway up the main stream will obviously be much smaller than at its mouth. Also, we clearly do not wish our estimate to depend upon the arbitrarily selected point of measurement. Either we must measure the water flow of each tributary where it joins the main river or take our recordings as close to the mouth of the river as possible. Actually, during certain flood stages, the former may exceed the latter. The water of the tributaries (production in the aggregate) then stores up in the river (investment) and only at a later day flows out into the sea (consumption).

Gross and Net National Product

During the past decade a great deal of experience in the measurement of national income has accumulated. Logical perfection has given way to practical possibility. For example, as already explained, the home work contributions of households to national income cannot be measured, and it is convenient to ignore them. In this case we must estimate such items as gross national product and net national product in terms of the activities of firms and governments. For the sake of simple exposition we shall first assume that only firms are truly productive and then amend this assumption by supposing that all government activities that produce goods and services are also productive.

In the previous chapter the value added of a single firm was defined as the value of output (i.e., output sold plus extra output inventory) minus the value of used purchases (i.e., cost of purchases minus extra purchased inventories). The difference remaining after this subtraction was called gross value added. It is obviously possible to sum together the gross value added of each and every firm in the economy. *If* all the production of an economy were carried on *only* by firms, the above total would be the value of what economists term the gross national product.

The gross national product (still assuming that only firms and not governments produce goods and services) can be computed by another means, algebraically identical with the one given in the preceding paragraph. The total sales receipts of all firms minus the total of all inter-firm purchases, plus all additions to all firms' working capital, fixed capital, and output inventories, will also equal gross national product.

Incidentally, gross national product is calculated in a manner that renders its magnitude immune to a greater or lesser degree of business integration. If the number of productive units were doubled, the gross value of firms' outputs would increase, but the value of used inter-firm purchases would increase by exactly the same amount. Gross national product can be loosely thought of as the "once counted output" of all the economy's producing units.

In reality governments as well as firms produce some goods and services that directly or indirectly benefit households. Whether these benefits are really commensurate with total government expenditures is a controversial subject and will be discussed toward the end of the chapter. For the moment, we shall prejudge this issue by assuming that all economic activities of governments are just as productive as those of firms, dollar for dollar.

The value of firms' outputs is estimated in terms of selling price. However, governments do not sell their goods and services, except in a few special instances, and so another rule for estimating the worth of government activities must be devised. A common method is to estimate the value of government activity according to its cost. The expenditures of government on providing goods and services, such as education and highways, are thus viewed as the gross value of government output.

However it is the value *added* by government that is significant for national income accounting. If a municipal government spends a million dollars on its police force each year, and $400,000 of this is for the purchase of automobiles and other equipment, the gross value *added* by government is only $600,000. Hence the contribution of governments to gross national product under our assumptions is their total outlay on providing goods and services minus the cost of all goods *purchased* from firms or other government units.

Gross national product overstates the value of goods and services that could be continuously sold to households for consumption or sold to others for net investment. One reason for this is that one of the offsets to gross value added by each firm is depreciation. Part of the use value of the structures and equipment of every firm and government is lost through depreciation each year. In some cases this depreciation may be a function of use and in others a function of time. In either event there has been a partial wearing out of fixed capital, just as some of the working capital inventories have disappeared through processing. Sooner or later this wearing out of fixed capital must be faced by the economy. Its eventual recognition is of course inevitable when buildings and machinery finally cease to work. However a sound system of national income accounting should make allowances for annual depreciation as it proceeds each year.

We may say therefore that the gross value added of a firm, minus allowance for depreciation within that firm, is equal to its net value added. If the net value added of each and every firm were summed up, and still assuming that only firms produce goods and services, we should have what many economists call net national income. Sometimes this is called national income at market price.

National Income

Firms make many current payments that are not purchases and for which there is no specific *quid pro quo*. Governments also make current payments to firms for reasons other than the purchase of goods and services. Most of these payments must be added to or subtracted from net national product to obtain what is sometimes called national factor income or just national income.

Let us first consider two kinds of non-purchase payments by firms. One of these is indirect business taxes. The other is business transfer payments.

Indirect business taxes are taxes paid by firms irrespective of their annual profit showing; examples are consumer sales taxes, excise taxes, and taxes on firms' real estate. Some firms, such as those that refine gasoline, make cigarettes, or produce whiskey, are substantial but unpaid tax collectors for the government. Indirect business taxes should be deducted from net national product as one step toward estimating national income.

The main reason for such a deduction is that the inclusion of business taxes involves double counting. They enter into the net value added of both firms and governments. The net value added of each government unit is equal to its expenditures, minus used purchases from other firms and governments, and minus current depreciation. Part of this net value added of government is financed by business taxes. However business taxes are also part of the net value added of firms. In order to prevent their inclusion twice they must be subtracted once.

An example may make this clearer. Let us suppose that the federal government plans extra activities costing and worth an additional $1,000 millions, of which $750 millions is to be spent on extra purchases from firms and $250 millions is to be paid directly to households as wages. It is decided to finance all this by raising business taxes $1,000 millions. The net value that is added directly by the federal government is $250 millions. However the net value added of all firms will probably increase about $1,750 millions. Has the national income really jumped $2,000 millions? No, it has not. Two dollars for one in this case is not modern magic but simply double counting.

The net value added of all firms will increase by about $1,750 millions, rather than merely $750 millions, because firms expect, and in the long run on an average they probably manage, at least to break even financially. If business taxes are increased, prices will sooner or later be increased too, although temporarily profits and other forms of personal income may be pinched, especially if the tax cannot be passed on to buyers immediately. The extra national income contribution of these firms is then really $750 millions, obtained by deducting the additional business taxes from the extra net value added of firms. The remaining $750 millions become personal income such as profits, rents, interest, or wages.

Of course it is conceivable that firms might only be able to shift $600 millions of these extra $1,000 millions of taxes on to consumers. In this case, the net value added of all firms will rise by only $1,350 millions, and national income, after deducting $1,000 millions in order to avoid double counting, will only rise by $600 millions. This $600 millions extra national income is made up of the $250 millions paid directly to government employees and the extra market value after business taxes of firms' outputs amounting to $350 millions. The $1,000 millions spent by the government has then increased national income by only $600 millions according to our accounting because there has been a reduction of $400 millions in profits and other factor incomes.

Business transfer payments are essentially gifts and are not made as part of an economic exchange. One example would be contributions to universities for endowing special laboratories; however, when the recipients spend this money for equipment, there will be a contribution to national income. Business transfer payments should also be deducted from gross national product in estimating national income because transfer payments are not matched by economic production.

On the other hand we have so far ignored government subsidies to business and agriculture. These payments are in fact not included in the sales receipts figures of firms and they are not a government purchase because possession of the subsidized output may remain in private hands. And yet these subsidies are conditional upon production and do occasion some increase in output. Extra output that is due to subsidization should be included in national income. Of course no one can ever know just how much of the production of beet sugar, or strategic minerals, or soybeans is due to a government subsidy or support price. Convention usually assumes that the extra output caused by the subsidy is equal in value to the total cost to the government of the subsidy. Incidentally, there are some government agencies that operate at a profit, and so obtain a reverse subsidy, as it were; one might as well cancel these government profits off against the government subsidies in a single adjustment.

We can now summarize by stating that national factor income is equal to net national product, minus indirect business taxes, minus business transfer payments, and plus subsidies to business less operating surpluses of government enterprises.

National factor income, obtained in this way, is an estimate of the value of the economy's production measured at factor cost. Factor cost refers to the income that is attributable to factors of production for their share in making the output. Stated in another way, national income at factor cost expresses the profit, wages, rent, and interest due to households because of their participation in production. Actually the spendable incomes received by households differ from national income at factor cost for a number of reasons to be set forth in the next section.

The distinction between net national product and national income is already evident. The former is valued at market prices and the latter at factor prices. In the United States there are in practice two major items that render the market price estimate different from the factor price estimate. The first is indirect business taxes, which firms collect from their customers but do not pay out to factors of production. The second is subsidies received by firms from governments, which are not included in market receipts but much of which are paid out to factors for additional output. In the United States, net national product is larger than national income, because indirect business taxes are greater than subsidies by governments. However this ranking of magnitude might conceivably be reversed in a country where enormous food and clothing subsidies were financed by other than business taxes.

Personal Income

National income, estimated at factor cost, is equal to the earnings of factors at source; but it is not equal to the money receipts of household members. There are a number of reasons why national factor income differs from personal income. The necessary adjustment items will now be considered.

First, some of the enterprises making profits are legally organized as corporations, and hence subject to corporate income taxes as well as excess profits taxes in certain years; these tax liabilities must be deducted from national factor income.

Second, many firms retain some of their profits, possibly as cash, but probably in the form of physical additions to working or fixed capital. These undistributed profits should also be deducted from national income in estimating personal incomes. Logically this subtraction should occur whether firms that retain profits are corporations, partnerships, or simply proprietorships; in practice, adequate data are readily available only for corporations.

Third, accounting statements of the profits and losses of business firms, as distinct from farm enterprises, include profits or losses occasioned by changes in the value of materials and inventories.

These profits and losses in money terms are quite real for those who receive or suffer them; for instance, in a period when prices are rising, a textile mill that sells cloth in one year, made out of cotton and wool bought during the previous year, will realize a special increment in dollar profits on this account. These inventory profits are properly included in personal income. However they are also quite properly excluded from gross national product, net national product, and national factor income, in estimating which average prices for the year are employed. Obviously an adjustment is necessary when the book value at which a firm has previously bought materials is different from their value as computed from average prices for the year in which they were liquidated. If the book value, based on purchase cost, is less than the mean price of the liquidating year, the difference must be added to obtain personal income from national factor income. Conversely, in a period of declining prices, personal incomes will fall even further below national factor income than usual because of inventory losses.

Fourth, a small percentage of many employees' wages or salaries are deducted by the employer and remitted to the federal government, and to some state governments, to finance social security benefits. Those employees who are "covered" have earned these deductions but they do not receive them, except perhaps later and indirectly as social security benefits. Social insurance deductions must be deducted from national income when estimating personal income.

Fifth, governments pay out far more as interest on their debts than they receive from those who are indebted to them; net interest paid by governments should be added, because it is excluded from national income for reasons explained in the next section.

Sixth, governments make very considerable transfer payments to individuals, and these must be included in personal income. A transfer payment is a payment for which no *quid pro quo* is exacted; payments to veterans and certain disability benefits are included in this category. Firms also make transfer payments to households. Some companies voluntarily decide to award pensions to old employees. Some consumers, by refusing to pay their debts to stores and other firms, in effect, through these bad debts, transform "sales" into "gifts." However only transfer payments by governments and firms to households should be added in estimating personal income. Transfer payments among individuals should be ignored, as for example when Dad gives his daughter $1,000 as a wedding present. Such a transfer does not increase the incomes of households in general but simply redistributes buying power among them.

Hence, in summary, personal income is equal to national income, minus corporate income and profits tax liability, minus undistributed profits, plus inventory adjustment when materials have been bought below average prices for the year, minus social security deductions, plus government net interest payments, plus government transfer payments, plus business transfer payments.

Personal income should logically include the value of income received in kind, as for example when a family's cook gets board and lodging in addition to her wage. However many of these supplements to income escape statistical detection. These real earnings and services of domestic employees should logically be included in national income also.

Personal income is not disposable income. For many people disposable income is much less than personal income because of income tax payments. Nor is aggregate disposable income necessarily the same thing as total consumer spending. Many households may save part of their incomes, not spending them all on consumer goods but investing through life insurance policies or savings deposits, or even hiding currency in strange places. Other households may of course dissave for a time.

National Income Estimates by the Department of Commerce

During recent years the Department of Commerce of the United States has evolved a systematic set of national income accounts. In various particulars the economists responsible for this remarkable development have been forced by reason of inadequate data to adopt procedures having welfare implications that are not universally accepted. Nevertheless, the Commerce Department estimates are, all in all, incomparable and outstanding. In time, although they are imperfect, the Commerce estimates, accounting systems, and terminology will probably become standard within the United States.

Table 4 furnishes estimates for certain income categories already defined and described. The item termed "statistical discrepancy," amounting to several billion dollars in some years, may arouse queries. The simple truth is that even an important government agency cannot possibly succeed in compiling sets of estimates that will exactly match. Gross national product estimates are based on one set of data. Personal income estimates are derived from another set of data. Moreover these different sets of data may have been originally collected by many different agencies for different reasons and employing different definitions. The statistical discrepancy item in Table 4 marries, as it were, the top and bottom parts of the table. How this discrepancy should be spread over the various other categories one naturally cannot know. Actually the arithmetic sum of all the errors and biases may be far greater than the algebraic difference cited in the table. This net discrepancy varies from about 1 to 3 per cent of national income. Under these circumstances, only an illusion of accuracy is created by estimating the values of accounts to the nearest million dollars, as is often done.

TABLE 4

PRINCIPAL COMPONENTS OF UNITED STATES NATIONAL INCOME
(Dollars to Nearest Billions)

	1939	1946	1948
Gross National Product	$91	$213	$262
Less Depreciation*	8	12	15
Net National Product	83	201	247
Less Indirect Business Taxes	9	17	20
Plus Subsidies†	–	1	–
Less Business Transfer Payments	–	1	1
Statistical Discrepancy	1	4	–
National (Factor) Income	73	180	226
Less Corporate Profits Taxes	1	10	14
Less Undistributed Profits‡	1	8	13
Plus Corporate Inventory Adjustment	1	5	2
Less Social Insurance Contributions	2	6	5
Plus Government Net Interest	1	4	4
Plus Government Transfer Payments	3	11	11
Plus Business Transfer Payments	–	1	1
Personal Income	73	177	212

* Includes other kinds of capital consumption, such as accidental losses from fire, and so forth.
† Subsidies here are net after deductions for government enterprise surpluses.
‡ Applies only to firms organized as corporations.
Source: U. S. Department of Commerce, *Survey of Current Business,* July 1939.

No intelligent person can long regard a set of estimates such as those contained in Table 4 without asking himself what they mean. The national income estimate for 1946 is $180 billions, whereas for 1939 it is $73 billions, for example.   Is this increase "good" or "bad" and in what sense and under what conditions? Some problems of inference are touched upon in the succeeding chapter.

The Government Contribution

One of the most vexing problems confronting economists concerned with estimating national income is how to value the contribution of governments.   Actually, and one might as well admit it at the outset, no definitive and entirely satisfactory conclusion has been reached in this regard.   However there are certain rather obvious comments that might be made.

Let us briefly review the orthodox Department of Commerce method of accounting for major types of government expenditure. Current government activities—for example, street lighting, public health regulation, and national defense—are all included in national income and valued at their current expense.   Government subsidies to business to encourage output are similarly valued and added to net national product to obtain national income at factor prices.   However government transfer payments to households, for which there is no economic *quid pro quo,* are not included in national income although these comprise part of personal income.   Net payments of interest by governments to households are handled in the same way as government transfer payments.

A number of objections can be raised against these accounting methods if one conceives of national income as a value estimate of production that contributes directly or indirectly to the satisfaction of household wants and needs.

For example, during some years of World War II, national defense was responsible for most of the federal budget and almost half the production of the economy.   Should these enormous disbursements for tanks, bombers, atomic weapons, and so on, none of which could be enjoyed by consumers, be considered part of national income?   It is true that expenditures for these things gave rise to personal incomes such as wages.   But war workers never produced anything they could buy with their earnings; tanks are not normally found on sale in department stores or elsewhere. The tendency of consumer goods prices to rise, often in violation of law, confirmed the fact that national defense outputs and expenditures are not national income. Against this it is sometimes asserted that national defense expenditures are the price the economy pays in certain years for freedom and liberty.

Regulation is an important function of government; for example, the federal government regulates the railroads through the Interstate Commerce Commission; also the states have factory safety laws, and the municipalities have building codes. The administration of these regulations costs money and such government expenditures enter into national income. Are these regulations worth more or less than what they cost? People often disagree violently on this subject, but no one really knows what these services are worth.

Government subsidies in many cases do not occasion an increase in net income proportionate to their cost despite the accounting convention that they do. For example, a typical mine may be producing ore having a metal equivalent of 1,000 tons, for which the pure metal price is $250 a ton. Perhaps the federal government wishes to stimulate production of this ore and metal for national defense reasons and so sets a support price of $300 for the equivalent of a ton of pure metal. The mine operator then pushes production to 1,200 tons under this stimulus. Before, his revenue was $250,000; now it is $360,000. Because of this incident, national income has supposedly risen $110,000, or 44 per cent; but output has only increased in fact by 200 tons or 20 per cent. On the other hand, perhaps the value of this ore to the economy has risen 20% per ton. On reflection, the orthodox method of estimating national income depends for its reasonableness in part on the assumption that subsidy prices reflect use values. However there is little reason to suppose that this is so.

In case of government transfer payments to households, it is evidently proper to exclude them from national income, even though they are included in personal income. There is no economic contribution on the part of a transfer payee by definition. If such transfer payments were included in national income it would be a simple matter to raise the national income. A law that required the federal government to give each U.S. citizen $1,000 a year would nominally increase the national income by about $150 billions, but where would be the extra goods for households to purchase with this extra personal income?

The conventional method of excluding net government interest from national income is probably sound in the main. Most of the interest paid on the federal debt is for past wars. In essence, the government is simply transferring money from taxpayers to bond-holders because of a debt incurred for the purchase of war goods that have long ago been destroyed, shot off, or abandoned. However, the situation may be somewhat different in the case of local governments, which often pay interest on money borrowed for durable public improvements, such as streets and sewers and utilities. The value of the services provided by these public works may be sufficient to cover interest payments as well as their other costs. If the interest paid by a private firm on money borrowed to obtain an increased private water supply is part of national income, why is not the interest on municipal borrowings undertaken to construct a sewer system? Perhaps it would be a better approximation if the interest paid by state and local governments were included in national income but if that paid by the federal government continued to be excluded.

A word should be added regarding capital transactions by governments. When governments borrow capital funds from households or firms in exchange for government securities, or when governments repay these loans, none of the various accounts appearing in Table 4 are directly affected. If governments purchase real capital goods, such as air route beacons, at exactly the rate at which they wear out, these replacements should enlarge gross national product but not net national product. When governments make net investments, as for example when the U.S. constructed Hoover Dam on the Colorado River, national income is increased as well as gross and net national products.

Market Price or Factor Cost?

The Department of Commerce, as we have seen, attempts in the main to value national income at what is often called "factor cost"; for instance, cigarettes are included in national income, not at the price paid for them by users, but according to the net price received by the seller after deducting excise and other business taxes. However, some economists have adopted the alternative approach of valuing each output, for national income purposes, according to its market price. What are some of the implications and problems of the market price approach?

One argument frequently advanced in favor of the market price method is that, inasmuch as it is the market price that buyers pay, market price valuations give a better idea of the relative use values of different kinds of goods.   A potential buyer of different goods makes up his mind in terms of their relative market prices; he does not stop to analyze how much of the cost of a carton of cigarettes or a case of whiskey is really tax.   On the other hand, if a good is suddenly taxed, and this tax is passed on to buyers through a higher price, it seems rather artificial to assert that this particular kind of good now contributes more satisfaction and national income just because it has been selected by government as a source of revenue.

One difficulty inherent in the market price approach is that it cannot be used to value the goods and services provided by government.   For example, we do not know the number of units of justice or health protection supplied by governments each year, and these benefits do not carry price tags.   Hence, in practice, the government output has almost entirely to be valued at cost; and, if the market price method is used for valuing firms' outputs, total business taxes must be deducted from total government outlay in order to avoid double-counting these taxes.   Incidentally, so-called business taxes constitute less than half of total government outlays and tend to be smaller in the aggregate than income taxes.

Actually the factor cost approach, as used by the Department of Commerce, should indicate changes in the relative contributions of different industries to national income.   These "factor costs" include profits.   Consequently, if the public demand for automobiles increases markedly one year, the net price of, and the profits on, each automobile will probably rise.   If the tax structure remains unchanged, market prices and revenues less taxes per unit will tend to move up and down together over time.   As long as entrepreneurial returns are included in factor costs, as they are, the factor cost and market price methods of valuing different outputs will probably indicate rather similar fluctuations in national income, both in the aggregate and by industries, from year to year.

Dual Aspects of National Income

It must now be evident that there are two different approaches that can be followed in estimating national income.   One is to start by summing the gross value added by the activities of firms and governments, and so obtaining gross national product; after this a deduction for depreciation, another for indirect business taxes, and an addition for subsidies are the principal adjustments in estimating national income.   However an alternative start can be made with personal income, after which a number of adjustments, the most important of which involve government interest and transfer payments, social security collections, and undistributed profits, are needed to reach national income.   If the statistical data were perfect in each case, these two divergent approaches should yield the same estimate of national income.

The existence of these two approaches stems from the nature of economic activity.   The economic activity of each firm gives rise to two kinds of flows; one is a flow of goods and services and the other is a flow of money to those who participated in their production.   The economic activities of governments also give rise to a flow of goods and services, although some of these may not be of much direct or indirect use to households—as well as a flow of money to government employees, men in the services, suppliers and contractors, and so on.

This dual aspect of economic activity is also evident when one considers investment and saving.   Investment is all that gross product which has not been sold for personal consumption, and which has not been used up in producing output; hence it is a physical affair, even though it has to be measured by a common denominator such as money.   Saving is all factor income at source minus personal expenditures for consumption.   These two definitions, when applied to our system of national income accounts, should give us similar estimates of the value of investment and of savings.   If they do not, it is because of the inadequate data available.   Logically investment and savings must be equal in value because conceptually they are identical.

Statements for Consideration

1. National income is measured in dollar values although logically this is invalid.   *Explain*
2. Household consumption, for two reasons, probably fluctuates less from periods of prosperity to depression than does household buying.   *Explain*
3. Production is like the inflow of a pipeline, and consumer purchases the outflow; although these may differ, either might just as logically be called national income.   *Discuss*
4. One effect of numerous small firms' being replaced by fewer large

ones is that gross national product exceeds net national product
by a smaller amount. *Evaluate*

5. The valuation of the national income contributions of governments and firms is logically different and this inconsistency is
rather unsatisfactory. *Discuss*

6. National income could conceivably exceed net national product
although the reverse is the case in the U. S. *Explain*

7. There are many steps between national income and personal income. *Exemplify*

8. The relationship of gross value added to net value added is almost
the same as that of gross national product to net national product.
Evaluate

9. Transfer payments may alter the magnitude of net national product, national income, and personal income. *Discuss*

10. The deduction of indirect business taxes from national product as
a step to national income only eliminates double counting if such
taxes do not affect business profits. *Evaluate*

11. Government services are just as much worth their cost as is the
output of firms. *Discuss*

12. Economic activity gives rise to two kinds of flows. *Explain*

References

Due, J. F., *Intermediate Economic Analysis*, Chapter 13. Chicago:
Irwin, 1947.

Hicks, J. R., and Hart, A. G., *The Social Framework of the American
Economy*, Chapters 12, 14, Appendices A, E. New York: Oxford University Press, 1945.

Kuznets, S., *National Income—A Summary of Findings*. New York:
National Bureau of Economic Research, 1946.

Meade, J. E., and Stone, R., *National Income and Expenditure*. New
York: Oxford University Press, 1944.

National Bureau of Economic Research, *Studies in Income and
Wealth*, vols. I–IX. New York: N.B.E.R.

Pigou, A. C., *The Economics of Welfare*, Fourth Edition, I, Chapters
3, 4, 6. London: Macmillan, 1946.

Samuelson, P. A., *Economics*, Chapter 11. New York: McGraw-Hill,
1948.

Shoup, C. S., *Principles of National Income Analysis*, Chapters 5–7.
Boston: Houghton Mifflin, 1947.

U. S. Department of Commerce, *Survey of Current Business*, July 1947
Supplement and subsequent issues.

4

General Welfare and National Income

WE MUST now consider the welfare significance of national income estimates. We have analyzed the system of accounts developed and publicized by the Department of Commerce. What welfare inferences can be drawn from these published estimates?

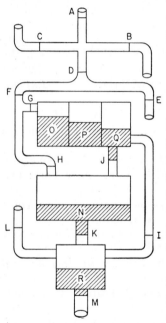

Fig. 1. The Hydraulics of National Income Flows and Stocks.

The Significance of Various Flows

Already a number of different flows have been mentioned. These include gross national product (GNP), net national product (NNP), national factor income (NFI), personal income (PI), and consumer spending (CS). The welfare significances of these flows differ and each concept is needed to answer different questions.

Figure 1 is designed to illustrate the relationships of certain major income flows. In some respects, national income accounting is not unlike a plumbing system, complete with connecting pipes, storage tanks, flow meters, valves, and taps. The locations of these flow meters are shown in Fig. 1 by capital letters. The national income flows that the meters record are as follows:

    A. Gross national product
    B. Indirect business taxes and business transfer payments
    C. Subsidies (minus current surpluses of government enterprises)
    D. National factor income before allowances for depreciation

E. Depreciation (includes all forms of capital consumption)
F. National factor income (NFI)
G. Private firm contributions to NFI
H. Government contributions to NFI
I. Consumer spending
J. Government purchases from firms
K. "Free" government aids to households
L. Home production
M. Experienced household income

There are also five tanks designated by letters, namely:

N. Government investment
O. Private fixed capital
P. Private working capital
Q. Unsold private output
R. Household stocks of consumer goods

If the flow at F (i.e., NFI) is greater than the combined flows
at K (i.e., free government aids to households) and I (i.e., consumer spending), it must be that the N, O, P, and Q tanks are on
balance filling up (i.e., there is net government and firm investment taken together).

In welfare economics we are presumably concerned with the
consumption of households (M); however, as already stated; we
have no reliable estimates of home production (L) or of changes in
households' stocks of consumer goods (R).   We are thus left with
consumer spending (I) and free government aids to households
(K).   Data on consumer spending (I) are adequate.   But estimates
of free government aids (K) are not satisfactory.

One might well ask how it is that, supposedly having definite
and reasonable estimates of National Factor Income (F) and consumer spending (I), we do not know free government aids (K).
The trouble is that the value of all the investment items that lie
between are uncertain.   Estimates are available for commodity
inventories; that is to say, for working capital (P) and unsold final
output (Q).   However, changes in fixed capital investment are
far less reliable.   There are estimates for gross private investment,
but the deductions for capital consumption allowances may be only
a rough approximation of yearly depreciation.   Net private fixed
investment (O) is in turn rendered rather problematical.   The
situation is even less satisfactory in the government investment
sector.   It is often difficult to know how much of the expenditures
by governments are for net investment (N) and how much for

current output of goods and services (K).   Naturally, the degree
of uncertainty varies.   In the case of streets and highways it is not
so impossible to estimate depreciation and the current expense of
providing current services.   But how much of the total outlay of
the military establishment is investment in any year?   If government net investment (N) were certain, one could make far more
definite estimates of "free" government aids (K).

Consequently, if one is primarily concerned with the experienced economic income of households (M), published national
income estimates do not tell the whole story.   Even if we ignore
home production (L), it is not unreasonable to believe that consumer spending (I) understates experienced economic income; and
consumer spending (I) and free government services (K) together
may then overstate it.   Obviously many government services, such
as "free" education, are an important contribution to household
incomes; however, national defense expenditures, part of which
are also included in free government services (K), hardly seem to
yield a utility return, dollar for dollar, comparable with consumer
spending (I).

National factor income (F) possesses all these imperfections as
an indirect measure of K and I together.   If there is considerable
net investment by governments and firms during any given year—
i.e., N, O, P, and Q are collectively increasing—the national factor
income will considerably overstate the economic income currently
being received by households from firms and governments.   Naturally, this net investment can contribute to real household income
in future years, but at the moment these potentialities remain unrealized.

Another flow of importance is national factor income before
allowances for depreciation (D).   Although this certainly overstates the economy's ability to produce continuously, it does suggest the maximum emergency production that might just be possible for short periods.   Although depreciation continues inexo-
rably year after year, it may often happen that in some years it is
possible to postpone equivalent replacements.   For instance, if a
lumber mill has 20 saws, with a service life of 5 years each, it does
not follow that it must replace 4 saws every year.   Belligerent
economies often postpone some capital replacements in wartime,
in order to produce a large volume of war and civilian goods,
through moderate disinvesting.   For example, in terms of Fig. 1

let us make the improbable assumption that no gross investment is undertaken at all, in which case the flows of K and I together would equal the flow at D; the inevitable flow of depreciation at E would be reflected in a falling of the investment levels in N, O, P, and Q.

Gross national product (A) probably overstates the value of almost any material welfare concept. In part this is because indirect taxes (B) in practice usually exceed government subsidies (C). In addition GNP ignores the very real and continual expense of depreciation (E).

A very simple but important equation in economic theory is that production equals investment plus consumption. It is now possible with the help of Fig. 1 to illustrate this maxim more specifically. However, a narrow or a broad illustration can be given.

If we limit ourselves to national income account estimates, as published by the Department of Commerce, the fundamental equation appearing above can be represented easily enough. Production is represented by F. Investment is interpreted to mean net firm investment as represented by any collective change in O, P, and Q. Consumption is production minus investment as so understood. In other words, it is assumed that "free" government aids (K) are equal to government expenditures in the form of purchases from firms (J) plus governments' net value added (obtained via H), there supposedly being no change in government net investment (N). And it is also assumed that consumer spending (I) is equal to firms' contributions to factor national income (G) minus all net increases in firms' investments (O, P, and Q).

However, if we were omniscient, we could give a broader and more logical content to the equality between production on the one hand and investment plus consumption on the other. Production would then comprise national factor income (F) plus home production (L). Consumption would be experienced economic income (M). Investment, equal to the difference, would consist of net increases in household stocks (R), firms' real capital (O, P, and Q), and in government investment (N). Consumption, expressed another way, would be home production (L) plus "free" government services (K) plus consumer spending (I) minus additions to household stocks (R).

Conceptually, it does not make so much difference whether we are omniscient or limited to available but inadequate statistics. The equation *production equals investment plus consumption* still stands. Normally, production will exceed consumption, except perhaps during years of depression or war. It is sometimes helpful to think of consumption as short-run national income, for it is the extent to which households make current use of the nation's economic activities. However, production is long-run national income, for in the end, the investment portion of this output can become consumption. It is for this reason that national income at factor cost is considered so important, for it is a rough measure of the economy's prolonged ability to produce for households.

Investment and Saving

The economic flows we have just been scrutinizing are real flows; that is to say, although measured and expressed in value terms, they relate to economic goods and services, such as locomotive building and shoe repairing. The provision of these goods almost always occasions some sort of monetary counter flow such as consumer spending or taxes. These twin but opposite flows—real and monetary—stem from almost all the economic activities of firms and governments. Investment and savings are two aspects of one particular economic activity that is of great significance for economic welfare. Investment is the real aspect of this activity and saving is the monetary aspect. The aggregate investment of an economy in a given year is obtained by summing various constituent real investment flows. The total saving of an economy is also made up of separate savings flows. It is important that we realize the identity of these flows and know how to aggregate them without double counting.

Case 1—Firms and Households Only

The relation between real investment and monetary saving can best be understood if we first consider an economy that comprises only firms and households. There are no governments and taxes. All consumer goods and services enjoyed by households are purchased from firms at the same rate as they are consumed, so that households do not *invest* in real goods, although it is expected that they will *save* money income. At first we shall also suppose that the nation's stock of cash, that is to say, the total of demand deposits and circulating legal tender, is constant from year to year.

One way of understanding national accounts that record investment and saving for the economy is to think of the manner in which the balance sheet of any ordinary firm is set up.   There are assets—real and monetary—on the left side.   The right side of the balance sheet shows the claims of different groups.   There are definite and contractual liabilities to creditors who have lent money or purchased bonds.   Also, the supposed equity or net worth of the owners or shareholders is shown on the right side, and this is equal to the value of all the assets minus the value of all liabilities.

A firm can invest in several ways.   One method is to borrow money and use it to buy materials, construct plants, and so on; in this case, the assets and liabilities increase by the same amount, so that the net worth of the firm to the owners is unchanged.   Another method is to "reinvest" profits; that is, instead of turning these profits into money and distributing these funds to owners, the firm allows its assets to increase in comparison with its liabilities so that the owners' equity is increased.   In the future the term "undistributed profits" will refer to an increase in the net worth of firms to their owners.

The assets of all the economy's firms taken together can only increase in value if either their liabilities to lenders increase or their net worth increases, or both.   An increase in their liabilities can only mean that the firms have done some borrowing from the households.   An increase in their net worth can only mean that owners have increased "undistributed profits."   Hence it might superficially seem that the value of investment by firms and the value of savings by households during a year is equal to the sum of the increases in the firms' liabilities and the increases in the firms' undistributed profits.

However this is not entirely correct because some of the extra assets of firms may take the form of extra bank balances rather than of extra plants and equipment.   For example, a firm might sell bonds to households and simply hold the proceeds as cash, in which case the combined sum of the firm's liabilities and net worths would increase but there would be no real investment.   Therefore, in assessing the value of the investment of all firms in the economy, it is necessary to sum algebraically the increases in their liabilities and net worths and to subtract algebraically the increases in their cash holdings.

All these changes have their counterpart in household transactions. If firms as a whole borrow, it must be that households as a whole have lent. If firms as a whole have had an increase in net worths, it must be that households as a whole have not taken all the current profits of the firms they own. And if firms as a whole hold less cash, it must be that, in view of our assumption of a constant money stock, households have increased their holdings of cash.

Thus the three flows that together make up the aggregate savings of the economy are—under our assumptions—increases in households' cash, increases in households' lending, and increases in households' share in undistributed profits. The sum of these flows is savings. And savings is equal to the total of all factor incomes at source minus what all households spend on consumer goods, in the absence of taxes.

There are also three classes of firm investment that can be distinguished. One is investment in fixed capital; another is additions to working capital; and the third is an increase in finished output inventories. The last may sometimes be rather involuntary.

TABLE 5

ILLUSTRATION OF SAVINGS AND INVESTMENT EQUALITY

(Hypothetical Economy Comprising Only Firms and Households)

Investment (Real)		Savings (Monetary)	
Firms' Fixed Capital	15x	−10x	.... Households' Cash Stock
Firms' Working Capital	10x	20x	.... Net Household Lending
Firms' Output Inventories.	−5x	10x	.... Undistributed Profits
Total Net Investment	20x	20x	.... Total Net Savings
Firms' Sales	80x	80x	.... Households' Purchases
National Factor Income	100x	100x	.... Households' Factor Earnings

Table 5 is hypothetical but it illustrates the relation of investment and savings to each other and to national income. The three kinds of investment by firms and the three modes of saving by households are distinguished. The total value of firms' sales and that of households' purchases—both of which exclude indirect taxes and excises—are necessarily equal, because selling and buy‹ ing are two aspects of the same transaction. The sum of firms' investment and firms' sales of finished output is equal to national income at factor cost. This last, in turn, must be equal to the sum of all household income at source, for the factor income of households is just another name for factor cost to firms.

It will be noted that aggregate saving equals aggregate invest- ment. In view of our definitions, this is inevitable and not an accident. After all, national product at factor cost and household income at source are identities, and firm sales and household pur- chases are also identities. Identities (sales and purchases) sub- tracted from identities (factor cost and factor income) must leave identities (investment and saving). And identities are always equal in magnitude.

If we admit the possibility of households' buying more than they currently consume, so that they are in effect accumulating furniture, appliances, and so on, this can be shown in the table by two insertions. On the investment side there will now have to be an item "Real Household Investment"; however, so that real national income will not be inflated artificially through double counting, this new item must be deducted from what previously was firms' sales. On the savings side there will now have to be a new item "Forward Consumer Buying"; and again, to avoid in- flating factor income at source, this must be deducted from what previously was household purchases. In the future the possibility of real household investment of this kind will be neglected.

It is also possible, reverting to Table 5, to trace through what might happen if we introduce banks into the model, and per- mit them to increase the combined cash holdings of firms and households through bank loans.

Let us suppose the banks loan 10x to firms. If the firms do nothing with this money—which is unlikely—there will be no increase in firm investments, firms' sales of output, or national income. In fact these loans would not be reflected by any change in any item in the table.

However, if this 10x were spent by firms in adding to their fixed capital, national income and household factor earnings might in- crease by 10x. Households would probably try to spend some of this extra income on consumer goods. If they now purchase

85x, firm sales will be 85x; but, if production should remain at only 80x, the firms' output inventories will experience a further change of –5x. The net investment of the economy will then be 25x. Net savings of households will also increase by 5x to 25x.

Naturally these bank loans might have other effects. If the economy were already fully extended, so that national income could not be increased above 100x, an addition of 10x to fixed capital would have to be offset by reductions somewhere on the left or "real" side of the table. In the future we shall ignore the activities of banks and the possibility that they can change the stock of money.

Case 2—Governments, Firms, and Households

In the real world the participation of governments in the investment and saving process cannot be disregarded. Governments cause real goods and services to be produced. Some or part of these constitute real investments that later provide benefits. However most of them are current goods and services, which we shall suppose are all provided without specific charges. Governments also spend money on gifts, but these do not contribute to national income and so can best be considered as a deduction from government receipts. Government receipts come from taxes, borrowing, and a few sales that henceforth will be disregarded.

It is useful to suppose that each government unit keeps a balance sheet and that all these are then consolidated into a governments' balance sheet. Perhaps, at the end of a year of generous hand-outs, we find that governments have increased their ownership of real assets by 5x, their cash holdings by 4x, and their obligations through bond sales to households by 17x. What has happened to what we shall term governments' net worth—i.e., the change in total government assets minus total government liabilities? It is –8x. That is to say, the equity that households have in their governments is now worth 8x less at the end of the year than at the start. Considered in isolation, this negative change is a form of dissaving for the economy; it may or may not be offset by other forms of positive saving.

It is now possible to construct an investment and savings table for an economy of governments, firms, and households. The first step is to consolidate all the balance sheets of all the firms with all the balance sheets of all the governments. If the data in Table 5 (which referred only to firms) is combined with that of the preceding paragraph (which relates only to governments) we have the investment and savings figures of Table 6. For instance, the net lending of households as a group is 37x, since they lent 20x to firms and 17x to governments. Whether or not firms lent to governments, or *vice versa,* does not matter; it will not be revealed in the table, since such loans would be offset by the consolidation of all firm and government balance sheets.

However, governments devote only part of their spending to real investment (for example, airfields) and spend rather more on current services (for example, teachers' salaries) and gifts (for example, veterans' pensions). The current services of governments are clearly not investments, but are part of national income, being in some ways analogous to the provision of current output by firms. Some of these services will be sold (for example, government printed documents) but most are provided free to the beneficiaries (for example, highways for motorists). In either event, they are part of real national income, and so appear on the left side of Table 6.

On the right or monetary side of Table 6 there are several new items, now that governments and firms are combined against households. The government net worth item is analogous to the undistributed profits of firms, for both refer to changes in assets minus liabilities. Another new item in Table 6 is "adjusted net levies."

The term "adjusted net levies" stands for the current payments by householders to governments for goods and services currently provided by governments. This concept can here be defined as taxes on households (for example, corporate profits taxes, social security deductions, and personal income taxes) plus fees paid by households (for example, postage stamps) minus transfer payments to households (such as veterans' benefits in cash rather than kind) and minus additions to government net worth. The transfer payments are deducted because there is no economic *quid pro quo.* The extra governments' net worths are deducted because that portion of taxes that buys government net worth does not provide a real current *quid pro quo* for householders. The involuntary purchase of government net worth by tax-paying households is a sort of prepayment.

TABLE 6

SAVINGS AND INVESTMENT AND NATIONAL INCOME

(Hypothetical Economy Comprising Governments, Firms, and Households)

Investment (Real)			Savings (Monetary)
Firms' Fixed Capital	15x	−14x	.... Households' Cash Stock
Firms' Working Capital	10x	37x	.... Net Household Lending
Firms' Output Inventories	−5x	10x	.... Undistributed Profits
Government Investment	5x	−8x	.... Government Net Worth
Total Net Investment	25x	25x	.... Total Net Saving
Government Current Services ...	20x	20x	.... Adjusted Net Levies *
Firms' Sales to Households †	80x	80x	..... Households' Purchases from Firms
National Factor Income	125x	125x	..... Households' Factor Income

* Equals direct taxes and fees paid by households, minus government transfer payments to households, and minus increases in government net worth.
† Excluding excise taxes.

Table 6 is based on Table 5 except that governments have now been introduced into the model and combined with firms on both sides. The numerical differences between these two tables are all due to the following assumed transactions of the governments: government investment of 5x, current government services of 20x, taxes of 18x, gifts of 6x, government borrowing from households of 17x, an increase in government cash holdings of 4x, and so a positive change in government net worth of −8x. These items, when added to the figures for firms and households represented in Table 5, produce Table 6.

Let us improve our understanding of Table 6 by tracing through one event. Let us suppose that governments increase taxes by 5x and use these funds for net investment: the first and temporary effect, after the government has collected the 5x but not yet spent it, is that households' cash declines 5x; government net worth increases 5x (because of the governments' extra cash assets), but levies remain unchanged (because the 5x of extra taxes is offset by the 5x improvement in the governments' cash). The next effect, after governments have spent 5x in wages for investment goods, is that households' cash rises 5x to its previous level, government net worth remains 5x above its original level, and levies remain unchanged because the taxes are offset by the increased net worth of governments.

General Comments

The real difficulty in keeping accounts of this kind is not a logical but a practical one.   It is often difficult to know how much of government expenditure is for investment and how much is for current service.   However, until this estimate has been made, it is impossible to assign values to many items of the table, such as government net worth, adjusted net levies, and, of course, government investment.

It will have been noted that total net investment is always equal to total net saving at the *end* of the year.   This does not mean that the total investment and savings that were expected or planned at the *start* of the year must have been equal.   And it certainly does not mean that each firm, each government, or each household has equal investments and savings at the end of the year.   The equality between aggregate savings and aggregate investment applies only to the economy as a whole and after the event.   The significance of this equality for full employment will be explained in Part III.

It is important to understand the place of savings and investment in the national income, not only because of the part they may play in determining the over-all level of income and employment, but because the rate at which an economy progresses over the years is bound up with the rate of investment.   Naturally each economy saves and invests more in certain years than in others.   However there are some economies that save and invest a higher percentage of their national income on an average than do other economies.   These economies are likely to be more technologically progressive and to be destined for a greater future.

Economic Welfare and Dynamic Change

The welfare significance of national income statistics, when they are considered over time, is ambiguous.   These special uncertainties are caused by the many dynamic changes affecting every economy, such as: inventions that may alter the relative importance of productive agents; special interest legislation that may alter the relative money incomes of farmers, workers, or landlords; international developments that may alter the relative importance of imports, exports, or the armed forces' takings; and so on.   In the face of such inevitable changes, the most complete and accurate national income data would still be ambiguous as regards changing economic welfare, for reasons soon to be stated.

Changes in Prices

One difficulty inherent in time comparisons is that price levels are changing from year to year, so that a dollar's worth of production means more at some times than at others. For example, the factor national income of the U.S. was about $180 billions in 1946, and about $40 billions in 1933, but possibly half of this apparent fourfold increase was due to higher prices. If each price changed by exactly the same proportion as every other price, it would be simple to apply a single adjusting coefficient; but the real difficulty is that individual prices rise and fall by different relative amounts, so that the price level is simply an average, and often not a very typical one. When price relations alter (for example, food prices rise relative to rents), large sectors of the population usually experience relative income changes (farmers gain more income and landlords gain less income). It is impossible to know whether the dollars gained by one group (which on the whole may be poor but may be better able to produce directly for itself) mean subjectively more or less than the dollars lost by another group (which may for the most part be rich but dependent upon purchases for consumption).

Altered Composition of National Product

Some of the other problems inherent in all time comparisons of national income change can perhaps best be understood if we think in physical terms. How can we know whether the national product in Year N is bigger than that of Year O if—as is almost inevitable—it is different in composition? Let us suppose that in Year N the economy produced more shoes, stoves, and radio quiz programs but fewer fur coats, station wagons, and concert broadcasts than in Year O, all other production being the same. A southern sharecropper might consider this an improvement, especially since the prices of shoes and stoves might fall. However, a gentleman farmer in Connecticut might disagree, especially as his wife prepares for Christmas! Should the economy be directed more toward the interests of one group and away from the needs of some other group?

Quality Improvement

Still another problem lies in the fact that the quality of goods normally improves as technology advances, even though the prices of these goods may not rise. For example, the automobile tires of 1940 had a longer service life than the tires of 1929, but their unit costs of production and their prices to users were no higher. Under such circumstances the changing outlays of households may indicate the changing quantity purchased but not the real change in services received. The effect of technological product advances, taken alone, would be to make national income statistics understate increases and overstate decreases in economic welfare. Over a period as long as a decade, this bias may become quite important in an economy that stresses durable manufactures.

Altered Business Taxes

It is difficult to know whether, in estimating changes in the magnitude of national production over time, one should value each output at its changing factor cost or at its changing market price. In other words, are changes in national factor income or changes in net national product the better guide to "real" changes in consumer goods output? It will be recalled that the market price of a good is equal to its factor cost plus indirect taxes minus government subsidies per unit. For example, the market price of a gallon of gasoline may be 27¢ and the tax on it 6¢; the factor price that includes profits will then be 21¢. If, in Year N, the economy produces and sells billions more gallons of gasoline, should these extra gallons be valued at 27¢ or 21¢? The market price clearly gives some indication of the extra gasoline's use value, as buyers do pay the 27¢. However, the factor cost of 21¢ may give a better idea of what it costs the economy to produce this extra gasoline, and especially the value of *other* goods that might have been produced instead.

Variability of Investment

So far in this discussion we have been implicitly assuming that net investment remains constant. Actually the composition of the national product in Year N may comprise more capital goods and fewer household use goods. Is this "good" or "bad"? An old man, alone in the world and about to die, might consider a diversion of production toward investment quite undesirable. A young officer, who believes it is necessary to expand the long-run economic war potential of the nation, might consider extra investment in steel-producing capacity absolutely vital. Whether or not an economy should produce less for immediate consumption, so that it will later have the capacity to produce more and better goods, cannot be decided except from some arbitrarily adopted point of view.

Population and Productivity Changes

There is yet another obstacle in the way of making economic welfare interpretations from annual changes in national income statistics. The national product in Year N might be exactly the same as that in Year O and yet economic welfare might be different. If the population has increased, the *per capita* availability of household goods may now be less than before. On the other hand, as increasingly productive methods of production are put into operation, it tends to be true that the real labor cost of output, for the whole economy, becomes less. The work week may now be shorter. However a reduction in total work time for the economy's population may be viewed with mixed feelings, depending upon whether it is experienced as involuntary unemployment or as enjoyably spent leisure.

Summary

Let us attempt to summarize part of this chapter by asking the question: In view of a fourfold increase of national factor income between 1933 and 1949, how much better off were the people of the United States in 1949? Any answering estimate would have to take account of the following: (1) the average change in prices; (2) the change in population; (3) changes in the quality of output per dollar of production cost; (4) changes in business taxes; (5) the relative utility of unemployed leisure as against more goods and services; (6) how much better it is to consume less now and invest, in order to be able to consume more later; and (7) how to evolve a common denominator for offsetting the gains and losses that dynamic changes occasion in different households. Unfortunately Solomon has been dead a long time.

Statements for Consideration

1. National income does not indicate the experienced economic or real income of households.   *Explain*
2. During a war emergency the economy might make more goods and services available, through its governments and firms, than would be indicated by national factor income statistics.   *Explain*
3. Production equals investment plus consumption whether or not we know the value of household stocks and home production.
                                                                 Discuss
4. In an economy comprising only firms and households, the saving of the economy is equal to the reduction in the cash holdings of households.   *Evaluate*
5. It is often alleged that certain government activities and expenditures represent real investment; in certain cases this seems reasonable, but in others the allegation is very questionable.   *Exemplify*
6. The savings of an economy, neglecting bank activities, are equal to the net increase in the combined net worths of firms, governments, and households.   *Evaluate*
7. That economic welfare doubled in the United States between 1939 and 1945 is evidenced by a doubling in the value of national income.
                                                                 Evaluate
8. The more unequal the distribution of income among households, the harder it is to know whether an increase in the value of national income is proportional to changes in the economy's physical output.
                                                                 Discuss
9. One cannot logically conclude whether an economy has become better or worse off if it produces more of some goods and less of others from one year to the next.   *Explain*

References

Ellis, H. S., (Ed.), *A Survey of Contemporary Economics.* Chapter 8. Philadelphia: Blakiston, 1948.

Hicks, J. R., and Hart, A. G., *The Social Framework of the American Economy,* Chapters 15, 16. New York: Oxford University Press, 1945.

National Bureau of Economic Research, *Studies in Income and Wealth,* vols. I-IX.

Pigou, A. C., *Income,* Chapters 4, 5. New York: Macmillan, 1946.

Pigou, A. C., *The Economics of Welfare,* I, Chapters 7, 8. London: Macmillan, 1942.

Shoup, C. S., *Principles of National Income Analysis,* Chapter 8. Boston: Houghton Mifflin, 1947.

Tarshis, L., *Elements of Economics,* Chapter 21. Boston: Houghton Mifflin, 1947.

PART II

Monetary Theory

5

The Nature and Quantity of Money

THERE ARE numerous reasons for studying money and there are several ways of looking at it. Certain theories of money are important, not only because they help to explain the occasional occurrence of mass unemployment, but because they suggest government policies that might be able to prevent or at least mitigate such calamities. Certain other theories of money help to explain why its purchasing power rises and falls, as prices in general dip and lift, so that the relative wealth of debtors and creditors is altered. A knowledge of what money is, and what it does, also enables one to "debunk" many of the crackpot panaceas, designed to make us all rich at once, that usually crop up during depression periods. Monetary theory is not only of interest to the economist. It concerns every voter, every person who is, on balance, either a creditor or a debtor, every businessman who plans the timing and extent of his investments, and every worker whose job may be wiped out by a depression.

What Is Money?

It is very difficult to study money until we have decided what it is and defined it for greater certainty. Money can be defined in various ways and each definition is useful for certain purposes. What are some of the more important classes of money?

Legal Tender Money

One well-known class of money is "legal tender." Legal tender money is money that the law requires creditors to accept when it is offered by debtors in discharge of their obligations. If *A* is owed $1,000 by *B*, and *B* is inspired to transfer his car to *A* in discharge of the debt, *A* can refuse the offer, as perhaps he will when he has seen the car! However, if *B* offers *A* $1,000 in Federal Reserve Notes, for example, which are legal tender, *A* must accept. If he does not, *B* can post the money with the appropriate court, which will rule that the debt has been discharged and that interest and other liabilities have ceased. At the moment, along with metallic money, seven different issues of paper money are legal tender. All paper money and coins bearing the stamp of the Treasury are legal tender, and of these the Silver Certificates (mostly small denominations such as $1 and $5 bills) are issued in the greatest aggregate value. However Federal Reserve Notes, which are individual obligations of the twelve Federal Reserve Banks, comprise at least 85 per cent of the nation's circulating legal tender. Naturally, the composition of legal tender money varies, becoming different every time Congress amends the law.

Means of Payment

For purposes of economic analysis, the legal tender definition of money is far too narrow. During 1948 the total stock of circulating legal tender was only about $25 billions. The national income for the same year was approximately $226 billions. It is extremely doubtful whether the economy could have produced a national income of this amount if only serviced with a money stock of $25 billions. Actually, businessmen, farmers, storekeepers, and everyone else made a great many of their payments in non-legal tender.

Most goods and services move from seller to buyer in exchange for what we shall call check money. Check money consists of deposits that can be withdrawn on demand and paid over to another person by writing a check. In other words, if *B* wishes to pay *A* $1,000, *B* makes out a check to *A* for this amount, drawn on *B*'s demand deposit in a bank located within the United States. The total value of demand deposits in January 1950—excluding those owed to one bank by another—was about $80 billions.

In the following chapters it will generally be assumed that "money" refers to circulating legal tender and non-bank-owned demand deposits. Of course the demand deposits do not possess quite the "moneyness" of legal tender. Sellers and employees do not have to accept checks in payment and it is often difficult to induce strangers to accept checks. However, in everyday commercial transactions, buyers and sellers and also employers and employees are known to each other, so that demand deposits can be and are used, rather than legal tender, as money.

Near Money

One way of deciding what is money is to realize what the functions of money are. It is generally agreed that money serves as a means of payment, a store of wealth, and a unit of account. Under normal circumstances legal tender and demand deposits perform these tasks. However there are obviously other assets that are almost money (in that they fill one or two of these three roles). Time deposits (of which there were about $55 billions in 1950) are an example of "near money" in this sense; they are a store of wealth, but they are not always a very good means of payment, since they cannot be readily drawn upon by check and since the bank can insist on a 30-day notice of withdrawal. United States Treasury bills, having a maturity of 90 days, are another example of near money. Both these varieties of near money must be converted into legal tender or demand deposits before they can be used as money.

Changes in the Stock of Money

One of the most remarkable characteristics of money is that its quantity is constantly changing. In 1933 the stock of money in the United States—as we have defined money—was about $19 billions; it rose to approximately $33 billions in 1939, and to $107 billions in 1949. Changes of this magnitude cause other changes on every hand.

It has already been explained (in Chapter 2) that the increase in the national money stock during World War II was largely due to the purchases of Treasury bonds by the Federal Reserve Banks and the commercial banks. The fundamental reason for this was, of course, the tremendous cost of the war, coupled with unwillingness or inability on the part of the United States Government to cover a larger percentage of the war's financial cost by taxes or forced loans. These new funds entered the circuit of payments and ultimately most of them became part of the receipts of households. At this point, if not before, these extra funds became a cause as well as a result of price changes, for the recipient households sought to spend most of their extra income on consumer goods, with the result that the prices of these goods tended to rise.

During normal times—by which we mean periods of peaceful prosperity—changes in the economy's money stock are brought about by firms and banks acting together and not as a result of government action.   When business is brisk, firms will need more working capital and may borrow capital funds to invest.   If this behavior becomes general, banks' loans to customers will increase considerably; in effect this means that new money has been created and that the national stock of money has increased.   Such a change may influence interest rates, prices, and the rate of economic activity.   In view of the far-reaching causes and effects of changes in the money stock, it is important to realize how these changes come about.

The Federal Reserve System

In the United States, the expansion and contraction of the money supply, for the most part, occurs within the legally prescribed framework of the Federal Reserve System, and so its structure must be briefly described.   The Federal Reserve System has several organs, of which the following are most important.   At the top is the Board of Governors, below the Board are the twelve Federal Reserve Banks, and below them are the commercial member banks.

The Board of Governors has authority to regulate the Federal Reserve Banks and the member banks in several respects.   Within limits it can vary their legal reserve rates.   The Board, through the powerful Federal Open Market Committee, upon which it has a majority, can direct the Federal Reserve Banks to buy or sell securities.   The Board can also pass on the rediscount rates set by the Federal Reserve Banks.

There is one Federal Reserve Bank for each of the twelve districts into which the country is divided.   The Reserve Banks are privately owned by the member banks of their districts, but one-third of their directors are appointed by the Board, and they are subject to the Board's control in many respects.   The member banks in each district keep their legal reserves in the local Federal Reserve Bank.   It is sometimes said that the Federal Reserve Banks are "bankers' banks" because their depositors are banks, the United States Treasury, and certain other government agencies.

Membership in the Federal Reserve System is not mandatory for state-licensed banks although it is for national banks.   Actually almost exactly 50 per cent of the banks in the United States are members of the System and collectively they hold about 85 per cent of the aggregate value of all demand deposits. Member banks are naturally subject to the regulations of the Board and the provisions of the Federal Reserve Act.

Most countries possess a single central bank, which is owned by the national government. In a few countries this national bank also acts as a treasury for the government, minting coins, issuing paper money, and holding all the government's funds from taxing and borrowing. In the United States the Board of Governors and the twelve Federal Reserve Banks together fulfill most of the usual duties of a central bank. To be at all effective, however, in its simultaneous regulation of money quantity and interest rates, the Federal Reserve must act in concert with the United States Treasury.

Deposit Creation by Member Banks

A bank makes a loan whenever it buys a piece of paper that establishes someone's indebtedness. The loan is direct if the "paper" is sold to the bank by its "maker." The "paper" may be the bond of a government or corporation; it may be a mortgage secured by real estate, equipment, or other asset; or it may be the promissory note of some businessman or other borrower. The purchased evidence of indebtedness becomes an asset of the bank.

Corporation XYZ may sell its I.O.U. to its bank if it wishes to increase its working capital. If the note matures in 90 days and is for $10,000, and the discount rate is 4.0 per cent a year, the bank simply *credits* XYZ's account with $9,900. The bank does not physically deposit legal tender in XYZ's account. Nothing is put into the account. It is merely written up by a bank official. The newly granted demand deposit becomes a liability of the bank. It would seem that the bank is about to earn $100 interest in three months on $9,900 that it has created out of nothing.

Obviously there must be some limit to this process or bankers would quickly own the earth. Three important limitations we shall discuss immediately are the drains imposed by (1) deficit balances at clearing house, (2) legal reserve requirements, and (3) the public's demand for hand currency to keep in its pockets and cash registers.

Clearing House Drain. Corporation XYZ, which borrowed the $9,900, will soon begin writing checks against this new credit. Only a minority will be made out to people who are also depositors

in the *same* bank.   Checks for most of this amount will be made
out to persons who will deposit them in *other* banks.   These other
banks will present these checks to the drawee bank for collection
when representatives of the various banks meet periodically at the
clearing house.   Settlement of net balances must be either in legal
tender or by transferring the ownership of commercial bank deposits held in the central bank.

A typical bank may lose about 80 per cent of any newly created
demand deposits at the clearing house.   The rate of retention may
be greater than 20 per cent if the bank in question dominates the
local banking scene and if most payments are made to people who
live in the region.   On the other hand, if new loans are going to
be spent for materials and equipment made far away, and not for
local labor and produce, the clearing house drain may well rise
above 80 per cent.

However a bank will not suffer a net drain upon clearing if it
can present "due *from* other banks" items equal in value to the
"due *to* other banks" items that it must honor.   If Bank *A* is receiving from its depositors checks drawn on other banks at the
same rate as other banks are receiving checks drawn on Bank *A,*
there will be no net balance between Bank *A* and the rest of the
banking system.   In general, a bank will have to pay at clearing
time if it is expanding loans more rapidly, or contracting loans
more slowly, than are other banks.   On the other hand, a cautious
policy of expanding slowly and contracting rapidly, relative to
the system, will result in net credits from other banks.   A single
bank that loans too much will not be able to settle at the clearing
house.   A bank that loans too little will accumulate excess reserves from the clearing house but will be sacrificing interest earnings.   Usually the most profitable policy for a single bank is to
keep pace with the system as a whole.

Legal Reserve Requirements.   In the United States, member
banks of the Federal Reserve System are required to keep a certain so-called legal reserve.   The amount to be reserved is a stipulated percentage of the member bank's demand deposit and the
reserve has to take the form of a deposit in the Federal Reserve
Bank of the District.   For example, if the legal reserve rate were
20 per cent, and a member bank had demand liabilities of 100
million dollars, it would have to maintain a deposit with the district's Federal Reserve Bank of 20 million dollars.   The cash a

member bank holds in its own vault is not part of its legal reserve, is of minor value in practice, and will be assumed constant. A *single* member bank can increase its account with the Federal Reserve Bank by depositing checks that it has taken in and that are drawn on other banks. However, the member banks as a group cannot increase their deposits with the Federal Reserve in this way, because the same check that causes the account of one member bank to be credited by the Federal Reserve will be debited by it from the account of another. The member banks, taken together, can only expand loans if they possess excess reserves. And the member banks can together increase their Federal Reserve deposits only if the latter increases its own investments or the public reduces its legal tender holdings.

The Currency Drain. The public always needs some pocket money for shopping and incidental spending, especially around Christmas and holidays, which it obtains through bank withdrawals. Depositors' withdrawals must be paid in legal tender. Experience suggests the fraction of deposits that will have to be released to the public to meet this drain. Obviously an increase in bank deposits will increase the sum drained away in this manner if the public demand for pocket and till money is a constant fraction of their bank balances. Member banks obtain the extra legal tender they need to meet their currency drain by sending for coin and notes from the Federal Reserve—just as you or I order carrots from the grocery—and having their excess reserves in the central bank correspondingly debited.

The Federal Reserve Bank Is a Central Bank

A central bank has no domestic clearing house drain, the currency drain does not inconvenience it, and there is no economic necessity for its being subjected to a legal reserve drain. Accordingly, the total value of the central bank's combined deposit and note liability is largely at the immediate discretion of its management, and indirectly of the national government. Hence, inasmuch as the value of a central bank's deposits is the basis of credit creation by commercial banks, the policies of the central bank can in part determine the nation's money supply.

In the United States, checks drawn on accounts in the Federal Reserve Banks, neglecting the case of an international withdrawal of funds, are almost inevitably redeposited with them. The reason for this is that the Federal Reserve's deposits are the source from which member banks meet all the three drains outlined above. A member bank holds its legal reserve in the form of Federal Reserve Bank deposits, meets its clearing house drain by writing a check on its Federal Reserve Bank account, and satisfies its currency drain by having this account debited as an incident to purchasing legal tender. In other words, a member bank cannot normally expand its loans, and thereby earn more interest and profits, unless it can first increase its deposit with the Federal Reserve and so acquire excess reserves. Hence a member bank usually redeposits any checks drawn on a Federal Reserve Bank account which it acquires in the course of its daily operations. Experience has taught the Federal Reserve that all checks drawn upon it will usually be redeposited. As a result, the Federal Reserve is not normally concerned with any clearing drain.

The Federal Reserve, like any other bank, must stand ready to pay off its depositors in legal tender. If Bank *A* suddenly asks for one million dollars in cash, perhaps to meet withdrawals that it is experiencing, the Federal Reserve can simply print off one million dollars worth of Federal Reserve Notes, deliver them by armored van to Bank *A,* and debit *A*'s account. The Federal Reserve has increased its note liability by one million and decreased its deposit liabilities by one million and its position is essentially unchanged. The Federal Reserve Banks cannot collectively be embarrassed by a currency drain.

A central bank may or may not have a legal reserve drain, depending upon the law of the land. In the United States, the twelve Federal Reserve Banks are required to hold gold or gold certificates amounting in value to 25 per cent of their deposit and note liabilities. In view of the gold certificate holdings of the Federal Reserve, this requirement is not an effective restraint; hence, in the following discussion, we shall ignore this requirement.

There are several ways in which the Federal Reserve can influence the supply of money. Some of the most important methods used by it are: (1) amending legal reserve requirements for commercial banks, (2) investing, and (3) changing its discount rate. These possibilities will now be taken up in turn.

Amended Reserve Ratios. Let us suppose that Bank *A* has a Federal Reserve Bank deposit of $10 million and deposit liabilities of its own amounting to $50 million, and that the legal reserve requirement is 20 per cent. Bank *A* is then "loaned up." It has no excess reserves, since all its Federal Reserve Bank account is legally required as a reserve against its deposit liabilities.

However, we shall suppose that the Federal Reserve reduces the legal reserve ratio to 15 per cent, although in fact these ratios differ depending upon the location of the bank. Deposit liabilities of $50 million will then only require the maintenance of $7.5 million as a legal reserve, and the balance of the account in the Federal Reserve, $2.5 million, is now excess reserves. The existence of excess reserves is always an invitation to a member bank to expand its loans and earn larger profits. In this case every member bank will have new excess reserves. Each private bank will probably begin to discount more notes and acceptances. If all commercial banks follow this course, no single member bank will experience a clearing house drain because its "due to banks" debits will be offset by "due from banks" credits. Bank *A* will, if we also neglect the currency drain, be able to expand its loans and deposits by $16.7 million ($2.5 million divided by .15), by which time all previous excess reserves will be needed as legal reserves.

It would be more realistic, of course, to take the currency drain into our calculations. If experience shows that a bank will have to pay out 10¢ cash on every extra dollar of deposits on demand with it, we should divide the excess reserves of $2.5 million by .25 (the .15 of legal reserve drain plus .10 for currency drain), in which case Bank *A* would only be able permanently to expand its loan-created deposits by $10 million. The final total increase in the money stock, as we have defined money, will be this $10 million of new demand deposits *plus* the $1 million of newly circulating legal tender, or $11 million.

Federal Reserve Investment. The Federal Reserve may invest by purchasing securities on the open market, subscribing to new bond issues, or discounting commercial paper. In every case the Federal Reserve Bank involved buys an evidence of indebtedness and pays for it with a draft on itself. The individual seller of the security or I.O.U. will deposit this draft in his own bank, which will soon present the draft to the Federal Reserve for collection, and will normally deposit the proceeds in its own account with the Federal Reserve. The deposits of the Federal Reserve Banks thus come to be increased, and the member bank, which now owns ad-

ditional deposits, finds itself with excess reserves that can be used
as a basis for expanding its loans and creating new commercial
bank deposits.   If the Federal Reserve invests $1 billion, its own
deposits will increase temporarily by $1 billion, the excess reserves
of member banks will temporarily increase by $1 billion, and,
assuming legal reserve and currency drains of .15 and .10 respectively, private bank deposits owned by the public will increase $4.0
billion.   Legal tender in circulation will increase by $.4 billion
(.1 of $4.0 billion).   The effective money supply—which combines
demand deposits of the commercial banks with legal tender circulating outside the banking system—has increased $4.4 billions.
Figure 2 illustrates this case.

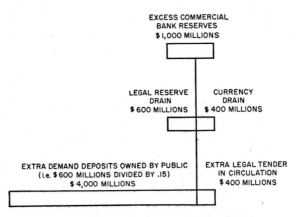

Fig. 2.   Federal Reserve Open Market Purchases.

Altered Rediscount Rates.   A member bank can usually borrow from its Federal Reserve Bank, either on its own note or on
certain kinds of commercial paper it has itself already discounted.
A member bank only borrows from the Federal Reserve in an
emergency, however.   For example, it may suddenly need legal
tender to meet a currency drain and have no excess reserves with
which to pay its Federal Reserve Bank, or the clearing drain may
have become unexpectedly heavy for some one bank.   The Federal Reserve Banks charge interest on the sums they advance to
member banks and consequently these commercial banks borrow
from the Federal Reserve Banks only as a last resort.   If the Federal Reserve Banks raise their interest charges and rediscount rates,
the commercial banks will be more loathe than usual to borrow

from them, and will take greater care not to be caught with insufficient Federal Reserve deposits or vault legal tender.   In other
words, the member banks will adopt more conservative loan policies and keep their own deposits at more moderate levels when the
rediscount rates of the Federal Reserve Banks are raised.

The Dilemma of Rival Goals

It was hinted at the beginning of this section that, in the United
States, the Board of Governors and the Treasury may at times
adopt policies that are in conflict.   The Board, with an eye to the
rate of economic activity and the price level, often seeks to encourage or discourage the creation of new demand deposits.   In
furtherance of its objectives, the Board, through the Federal Open
Market Committee, often requires the twelve Federal Reserve
Banks to buy Treasury obligations (if it wishes to ease credit) or to
sell them (to tighten credit).   Naturally this brings the Treasury
into the picture.

The Treasury has sold an enormous value of bills, certificates,
notes, and bonds to the banks and to the public.   A considerable
value of bills and certificates fall due every month or even every
week.   Unless Congress taxes far more heavily than it spends—
which is not in the nature of things—the Treasury can only pay
back what it has been lent by borrowing again.   Hence the Treasury has to borrow large sums, not net but gross, every few weeks.

It takes two to consummate a loan transaction, however, and
private banks may not choose to lend even though the Treasury
wishes to borrow.   For example, if the Board instructs the Federal
Reserve Banks to sell Treasury notes, in order to reduce member
banks' excess reserves, the latter can soon replace these excess
reserves by not relending to the Treasury the proceeds of currently redeemed government obligations.   In this case the Treasury must make its new issues more attractive by offering them at
a higher rate of interest.

As long as the commercial banks can elect whether or not to
relend to the Treasury, the Board of Governors cannot tighten
credit in the suggested manner without the risk of raising interest
rates against the Treasury.   On the other hand, if the Treasury
wishes to reborrow at low interest rates, the Board may have to
support the market for Treasury obligations by instructing the
Federal Reserve Banks to buy them.   During the period immedi

ately following World War II, the Board wished to limit credit (a plan that would have meant higher interest rates but probably lower price levels) whereas the Treasury wished to keep interest rates down (a practice that tended to ease credit and possibly to raise price levels further).

Ways of Looking at Money

Economists have analyzed money from a number of points of view, depending rather upon whether it was high prices or unemployment that bothered them.

For over a century, but especially immediately following the two World Wars, economists have sought to explain the causes of price level changes. An early approach to this problem, over a hundred years old in fact, was the commodity theory. Another price level theory of money, which has overlapped the commodity approach, is the quantity theory. For a while these two theories were in rivalry with one another, but the fires of controversy have since died down.

Of more immediate concern today are what might be termed the underemployment theories of money. Two views of money that are especially relevant to problems of underemployment are what we shall call the circuit of payments approach and the cash balances approach. Both these last two approaches are actively employed today.

These four viewpoints will soon be described in detail; meantime, however, so that they will be more than a mere set of names, the following rough statement on each is inserted.

The Commodity Theory

The commodity theory supposes that the purchasing power of money depends upon the exchange value of gold. It further supposes that the exchange value of gold, relative to other goods, is determined by the same demand and supply forces that determine the value of any other commodity. Hence, if the exchange value of gold falls, the price level rises. These two assumptions may have been reasonable a hundred years ago, but they are invalid today.

The Quantity Theory

The quantity theory stresses the aggregate value of the national stock of money. This money stock is supposed to have a velocity;

that is to say, it is conceived as turning over a certain number of times a year as goods and services are bought. These purchases are called transactions. The price level will rise if the quantity of money rises disproportionately to the volume of transactions and velocity is unaffected. In any more generalized and less indefensible form than this, the quantity theory becomes essentially a truism.

The Circuit of Payments Approach

The circuit of payments approach is a very useful way of thinking about money, but in itself it is hardly a theory in the rather definite and sometimes dogmatic way in which the commodity and quantity approaches are. It concentrates attention upon the relation between spending and receiving money and the identity and motives of those who receive and spend. Each receiving and spending unit—whether household or firm or government—is a link in a continuous chain of payments.

The Cash Balances Approach

The cash balances approach seeks to answer the question of why it is that persons—corporate and otherwise—prefer to hold some of their wealth as money rather than in some other way that will yield interest. The cash balances approach is indirectly concerned with the quantity of money but it is more interested in the ownership of money. The cash balances approach is also concerned with the flow of spending but relates it not so much to receipts as to money ownership. The liquidity theory of interest (discussed in Part III) stems from the cash balances approach. The other three ways of looking at money will be discussed in the next two chapters.

Statements for Consideration

1. Any money that people will accept in payment is legal tender.
   Evaluate
2. Money that has no intrinsic value is worthless.   *Discuss*
3. There are some assets that yield a return but are not quite money.
   Exemplify
4. A single bank will acquire excess reserves if it contracts more rapidly or expands more slowly than the system.   *Explain*
5. The effect of government sales of new Treasury bonds on the national money stock depends on who finally buys them.   *Exemplify*
6. Commerical banks create money out of nothing, upon which they earn interest, and they only limit their operations in this respect in

order to maintain the scarcity value of bank credit.   *Evaluate*
7. The Federal Reserve Banks are sometimes called "bankers' banks".
Explain
8. Vault cash on hand and excess reserves held with the Federal Reserve Bank cannot be used at the same monent to meet both legal reserve and currency drains, although indirectly and given time they can.   *Evaluate*
9. If the Treasury wishes to keep the interest cost of the national debt as low as possible, the Board of Governors cannot drastically limit bank credit, and vice versa.   *Explain*

References

Boulding, K. E., *Economic Analysis,* Chapters 13, 16. New York: Harper, 1948.

Bowman, M. J. and Bach, G. L., *Economic Analysis and Public Policy,* Chapters 9–11. New York: Prentice-Hall, 1949.

Currie, L. B., *The Supply and Control of Money in the U. S.* Cambridge, Mass.: Harvard University Press, 1934.

Ellis, H. S. (Ed.), *A Survey of Contemporary Economics,* Chapter 9. Philadelphia: Blakiston, 1948.

Garver, F. B., and Hansen, A. H., *Principles of Economics,* Chapters 18, 19. New York: Ginn, 1947.

Hart, A. G., *Money, Debt and Economic Activity,* Chapters 1, 2, 4. New York: Prentice-Hall, 1948.

Meyers, A. L., *Modern Economics,* Chapter 29. New York: Prentice-Hall, 1941.

Morgan, T., *Income and Employment,* Chapter 10. New York: Prentice-Hall, 1947.

Samuelson, P. A. *Economics,* Chapters 14, 15. New York: McGraw-Hill, 1948.

Tarshis, L., *Elements of Economics,* Part III. Boston: Houghton Mifflin, 1947.

6

Price Level Theories

SOME of the earliest theories of money help to explain why
prices alternately rise and fall, and especially why, following the
Napoleonic War, the Civil War, and World Wars I and II, they
have for a time risen so very markedly.   The interest of the professional economist in such phenomena has been matched by that
of the general public.   When price levels rise, all debts defined
in money lose real value, and this involves social injustices.
Households that placed their savings in bonds, bank accounts, or
life insurance policies tend to lose some of their real wealth.   On
the other hand, people who have borrowed money are now in a
position to repay in less valuable dollars.   A hyperinflation—
which multiplies prices millions of times and eventually destroys
the currency—has decimated the holdings of the middle classes of
more than one Central European country.   It is therefore not
surprising that both the commodity theory and the quantity theory
of money, more than most economic theories, have in one way or
another received a great deal of legislative and public attention.
Whether they have been generally understood is another matter.

The Commodity Theory

As is so often true of theories, there is more than one version of
the commodity theory of money; we shall distinguish between the
original theory and the qualified version of later years.

The Original Theory

The earliest version of the commodity theory viewed money as
though it were a commodity just like any other product.   Nor
was this so unreasonable a view a hundred years or so ago.   Most
of the effective money stock then consisted of gold or silver or
copper, which had intrinsic worth.   It is a reasonable statement
that in those times most money was gold.

The value of money was therefore thought to be determined by the value of gold. The value of gold was in turn held to be determined in the same manner as the value of copper, lead, or any other mineral is determined. In other words, the value of gold, just as that of any other commodity, was considered dependent upon demand and supply forces, and more especially upon the value of its uses and the costs of its production. Therefore, because it was both in demand and difficult to supply, gold was an economic good and possessed value.

Moreover, and this is more to the point, if gold is like any other commodity, its value should rise if demand increases or supply decreases. For example, in times of political unrest when people wish to hold their wealth in the form of gold, so that the demand for it is great, the value of gold and of money would be expected to increase and the prices of goods to fall. With new discoveries of gold, as in California and Australia in 1849, the cost of supplying gold should decrease, and the commodity theory suggests that the value of gold should fall as the prices of other goods rise.

The Qualified Version

Paper money came into general circulation during the nineteenth century. The bearer of paper money always had a right to demand legal tender from the bank issuing the note, and, if this legal tender was not gold, to demand gold from the bank or government that issued the legal tender. Originally, most of the paper money in circulation was fairly completely, although often indirectly, backed by gold; but in time the total issue of paper money became a larger and larger multiple of the gold stock that backed it. Realistically, although perhaps not legally, the connection between gold and money came to be more and more tenuous.

However, so long as a government maintained its money on a gold standard, some people held to the view that the value of money was at least not unaffected by the value of gold. They might perhaps be willing to admit that money could no longer be identified with gold, as it had been in pre-paper-money times, but they put their credence in the assertion that money was still a "shadow" of gold. This "shadow" could be lengthened, as it were, by lowering what used to be called the "gold content" of the national standard money.

The last serious attempt to formulate policy upon the basis of this qualified version of the old commodity theory may have occurred when the United States "devalued" the dollar in 1933–34. The New Deal Administration was anxious to raise commodity prices, and several agricultural economists advised the President to increase the Treasury's gold buying price to further this end. Their argument was that gold is a commodity, just as grains and minerals are commodities, and that the exchange values of commodities are based on their relative use value and supply cost. Hence, if the price of gold were increased by the Treasury, the prices of other commodities *versus* gold would remain approximately unchanged in the absence of new uses or supplies of gold. Actually, when the Treasury slowly raised its ounce price from $20.67 to $35.00, the exchange value of gold also rose by about 75 per cent, but the price level did not rise until later, and then probably for other reasons.

Comments

Several centuries ago the commodity theory made sense. It is not tenable today, however, when the possession of legal tender does not entitle one to demand a prescribed quantity of gold. With no gold standard remaining, there is no longer any light to cast gold's "shadow" upon the nation's money.

It is of course true that, if national governments ceased to deal in gold, the price of gold might fall back to its "commodity" value; that is to say, its value would again depend upon its costs of production and the importance of its uses. At the outset, in view of the enormous monetary gold stocks that would then become available for commercial use, the price of gold would probably fall to a level permitting its use as an electrical conductor, a liner for steel beer cans, and even perhaps a plating material for automobiles in place of chromium. However, at present official prices, gold is not an ordinary commodity, and its real or exchange value with other goods depends upon its relative price, rather than its price upon its exchange value.

One commodity aspect of gold will however continue to be important. Gold, being a commodity, can be produced, and so it is at today's high prices. The purchase of newly recovered gold by the Treasury creates new check money besides providing a base for further expansion of the nation's money stock.

The Quantity Theory

During the Napoleonic Wars in Europe and the Civil War in the United States, the warring governments issued large quantities of paper money, and almost immediately the prices of provisions began to rise.   Inevitably a great many people considered this almost simultaneous increase in prices and in the quantity of money to be more than a coincidence.   A theoretical explanation of price levels in terms of the money quantity was developed.

Crude and "Value of Trade" Versions

The most dogmatic form of the quantity theory of money is that price levels vary directly, that is to say proportionately, with the quantity of money.   If the quantity of money doubles, the price level presumably doubles.   Some people have thought it to be as simple as that.

Sometimes, of course, there is some doubt about what is meant by the quantity of money.   Is "money" mentioned in this connection limited to gold, to legal tender, to money issued by the Treasury and Federal Reserve Banks, to demand deposits, or to all bank deposits including interbank deposits and savings accounts? Probably the most useful concept of money in this connection is the one we adopted in the preceding chapter; namely, that "money" is whatever the customs and institutions of the time and place consider to be "means of payment."   Specifically, for the United States, we defined the total national money stock as circulating legal tender and demand deposits owned by the non-bank public.

As it happens, there is a rough correspondence, at least in the United States since 1895, between the quantity of money as just defined and the wholesale price level index.   It is true that the upward trend in the quantity of money is more pronounced than that of the price index, but then the population and per capita production and consumption of goods has increased tremendously during the last 50 odd years.   If this "growth of the economy" factor is eliminated from the money series, then the association between wholesale prices and money stock is far too great to be ascribed to chance.

Explanations of the quantity theory of money by economists, as distinct from the more popular but less reasoned versions, have usually stressed the fact that, especially over long periods of time, there are changes in the volume of trade. It would be ridiculous to suppose that the same quantity of money could support the same level of prices in 1950 (when the population of the United States was about 150 millions) as in 1900 (when the population was about 76 millions). More people normally cause more trade. Moreover, as a result of technological advances, individuals have come to enjoy a greater volume of goods and services. Finally, as production becomes more specialized, more goods and services go through the marketplace, at all stages of production, and this further increases the need for money.

Hence a more seriously held view of the quantity theory of money, one we might term the "volume of trade" version, is that the price level tends to vary, more or less directly, with the quantity of money that exists *relative* to the volume of trade. For example, if the quantity of money increased to 150 per cent of its former amount, but the physical volume of goods and services being traded for money rose to 125 per cent of its former rate, the price level might be expected to rise 150/125 per cent, which would entail an absolute increase of 20 per cent in prices. This modified version of the quantity theory is compatible with the wider price swings, but it does not "explain" smaller price fluctuations of short duration.

The Equation of Exchange

It is simpler to understand and evaluate these two versions of the quantity theory if one resorts to the symbolic logic of the equation of exchange.

It is an obvious truism that the total amount of money spent by purchasers of a good ($M \cdot V$) must be equal to the price of that good (P) times the number of units included in the transaction (T). For example, if 100 units of a good are sold at $7 each, the purchasers' outlays total $700. If $M \cdot V$ equals $P \cdot T$ for one good, $M \cdot V$ will equal $P \cdot T$ for every other good or service. Hence, aggregating all these equations, one for each and every good or service that is bought and sold for money, we can say that

$$M \cdot V = P \cdot T$$

for the economy as a whole.

Each side of the above equation requires further explanation.

The financial outlay ($M \cdot V$) is the product of the number of different units of money spent (M) and the average number of times each monetary unit was spent during the same period (V). For instance, the same ten dollar bill might be used four times during the period in question, in which case its contribution to aggregate $M \cdot V$ would be $40. Annual statistics, for any modern economy, will show that monetary outlays ($M \cdot V$) exceed the total stock of money (M), and so we can only surmise that money has an appreciable velocity of circulation (V). On the other side of the equation, we have $P \cdot T$, where T represents the physical quantity that is sold. If 50 pounds of butter were sold by the producer to several retailers, and by them resold again to housewives, it has been sold twice, and T would stand at 100 pounds, so far as these transactions are alone concerned. Resales always raise T whereas direct distribution from producer to consumer would tend to lower it.

The two versions of the quantity theory of money can best be understood and evaluated if the equation of exchange ($P \cdot T = M \cdot V$) is divided through by T so that it becomes a price level equation ($P = M \cdot V / T$). Certain features of this price level equation can be seen more readily if we re-express it in the form of three identities, as follows:

$$P = M \cdot \left(\frac{V}{T}\right) \equiv \frac{M}{T} \cdot (V) \equiv \frac{M \cdot V}{T}$$

The first identity highlights the basic and unreasonable assumption that underlies the more dogmatic version of the quantity theory. In the statement that the price level (P) varies directly with money stock (M), it is implicitly assumed that V/T remains a constant. In other words, if population and technological changes cause the volume of trade to double, it is in effect held that the velocity of money will also double. Under certain circumstances, V and T might rise together, but this is not necessary, and there is no reason to suppose that these changes would be proportionate.

The second identity serves to emphasize one of the basic defects of the "volume of trade" version of the quantity theory. Whereas the dogmatic version tended to forget the influence of V and T, the more sophisticated version tends to overlook V. The "trade" version of the theory is only valid if V is constant over time. If the money stock turns over on an average 3.0 times during one year, but has a velocity of only 2.5 during the next year, even the more refined version of the quantity theory will fail to explain the facts. However, fortunately for this more reasoned version, the velocity of money seems to be more stable over long periods of time than either M or T. Hence, for long-run analysis, the "volume of trade" version of the quantity theory, although still incomplete, probably stresses the three most important variables in the equation.

The Causal Problem

Another weakness of both versions of the quantity theory is that they seem to suggest that changes in prices are *caused* by changes in the money stock. For instance, one infers that M increases *originally* and that, after allowances for changes in either V or T, there is a *subsequent* change in P. It is by no means clear that there is either a causal or a chronological sequence of this kind. The path of events might be reversed. Rising prices, especially of raw materials, may stimulate firms to buy ahead of their needs and so drive them to the banks for loans; these new demand deposits are in effect an addition to the money stock. When prices are falling, buyers defer purchasing, so that T is influenced by P. During a period of hyperinflation, when everybody is competing to convert money into goods, P and V interact. Any theory of money, such as the quantity theory, that always casts prices in the role of a dependent variable should be scrutinized very carefully.

Current Thoughts on the Price Level

Today economists do not hold any definite theory explaining the magnitude and direction of price level changes. The equation of exchange is accepted as a truism and only valued as such. It is recognized that prices, the stock of money, its velocity, and the volume of trade are all variables and are all interacting. It is now generally understood that, while the equation of exchange can be used to describe what has happened, it does not explain why these changes occurred.

Importance of Motives

A more fundamental explanation of price level changes must be sought in the motives and expectations of households, firms, and

governments.   Prices tend to rise, other things being equal, whenever a substantial part of the economy's population commence to
spend, for some reason, at a more rapid rate.   One reason they
spend more rapidly (i.e., $M \cdot V$ increases) *may* be that each of them
holds more money (i.e., M has increased).   On the other hand, it
has happened in the past that, although M increased, the public
only slightly altered its spending habits, so that $M \cdot V$ rose only
slightly as V fell.   The expected course of future prices may influence public spending more than the size of the national money
stock.   Businessmen tend to spend more rapidly, especially for
plant and inventory additions, if business prospects appear favorable.   During World War II, $M \cdot V$ did not rise proportionately
with M, possibly because the fact that many durable consumer
goods were unobtainable led the public to bank its savings.   When
considering the possible effects of an increase in M, one must
discover who holds the extra money, whether prices are generally
expected to rise or fall, whether business prospects are bright or
dim, and many other facts and fancies. M may have a dominant
influence on P in the long run, but from quarter to quarter it can
be overshadowed by a host of factors that affect T and V.

Price Relation Changes

Today the tendency is less to discuss *the* price level than to
analyze the relative movements of groups of prices, such as commodity prices, cost-of-living goods' prices, security prices, and so
on.   More people are nowadays familiar with the construction of
price indexes and with the fact that while the average of all prices
may be rising the prices of many goods may actually be falling.
These price changes within the price level are often more enlightening than changes in the price level itself.

Attempts at Measurement

Another modern tendency is to cease arguing theories *pro* and
con and instead to attempt the measurement of some of these controversial relationships.

For instance, the average value of all circulating legal tender
(M') is reported by the Treasury and the average value of all demand deposits not owned by banks (M'') is also reported by the
Federal Reserve Board.   The ratio of bank debits to demand deposits gives an approximate estimate of the velocity of check
money.   If the turnover of legal tender is the same as that of

demand deposits, it is possible to estimate $M \cdot V$. Then $M \cdot V$ is the value of all money disbursements and it is naturally equal to $P \cdot T$, which is the value of all money receipts. The magnitude of these items in certain selected years is set forth in Table 7. The simultaneous rise in M' and fall in M'' between 1929 and 1934 is in part explained by panic bank withdrawals during the bottom of the 1933 depression.

TABLE 7

EQUATIONS OF EXCHANGE AND INCOME

(Dollars in Billions)

Year	M'	M''	M	V	$M \cdot V = P \cdot T$	$p \cdot O$	v
1929	$ 3.6	$22.9	$26.5	37.8	$ 1,002	87	3.29
1934	4.7	18.4	23.1	16.4	379	49	2.12
1940	6.7	32.7	39.4	13.2	512	81	2.06
1946	26.5	92.9	119.4	19.5	2,330	178	1.49

Sources: The Federal Reserve *Bulletin;* also U. S. Department of Commerce, *Survey of Current Business,* June 1947 Supplement.

The value of $2,330,000,000,000 for $M \cdot V$ or $P \cdot T$ in 1946 may appear startlingly large in view of the fact that the national (factor) income was only $178 billions and not $2,330 billions that year. This disparity is due to at least three reasons. First, part of $P \cdot T$ is occasioned by the sale of titles to wealth (for example, the trading of bonds). Second, part of $P \cdot T$ is the result of speculative transactions in commodities, in which the same trader may buy and sell but never use his purchases. Third, there is double counting when a firm buys materials and then sells them after some act of production (for example, when steel is purchased and then resold as a refrigerator). The value of all commercial transactions far exceeds the value of economic production.

Gross and Net Payments

The economist is not particularly interested in the turnover of money or in the gross volume of commercial transactions. He is more concerned with the net output of the national economy and the net income of its residents. If he has an interest in price changes, it is probably in the prices of finished goods, rather than the prices of everything bought and sold in the economy. Consequently, instead of an equation of transactions, the economist may on occasion wish to set up an equation embracing the national stock of money and the national income. Such an equation—which we shall call the equation of income—would be:

$$p \cdot O = M \cdot v$$

where O is net national output and v refers to the number of times each dollar of the money stock is earned as net income during a year.

The last two columns of Table 7 give estimated values of $p \cdot O$ and of v for certain selected years. In this case the value of v was obtained by dividing M into $p \cdot O$. On the whole, v tends to be about one-ninth of V and in more years than not they change in the same direction. An income velocity of 3.0, for example, means that we can think of each dollar of the national money stock entering into some household's income stream every four months or one-third of a year. The mean length of calendar time that intervenes between the moment a given dollar becomes part of the income of two successive households will be called the income period. On the other hand, a dollar becomes somebody's gross receipts about 30 times a year, or approximately once every twelve days, which lapse of time might be called the spending period. The income period is as many times longer than the spending period as V is larger than v because they are linked by the same sized stock of money.

The contrast between the exchange approach (which uses V and T) and the income approach (employing v and O) is enlightening. $P \cdot T$ is the total value of a year's commercial transactions whereas $p \cdot O$ is the value of the nation's annual income. T is the sum of the number of times each kind of good is sold, whereas O is the extra goods and services that are made available for use. V is the number of times a dollar changes hands, whereas v is the number of times a dollar becomes income, to be invested, spent, or taxed. Consequently the price symbol does not have the same meaning in each equation. The P of the equation of exchange is the average price paid for everything sold. The p of the income equation is the average price of a finished good that is added to capital or consumed.

Economic Significance of Changing Prices

The p of the income equation is of course equal to $M \cdot v$ divided by O. Naturally, national output does not consist of a "typical" product, and so p, which logically is the average price of an average final output, has no absolute significance. However changes in p are more meaningful.

Such changes in p indicate changes in the ratio of $M \cdot v$ to O, without explaining why they occur. It is as though your automobile had a fluid coupling between its engine (money income) and its wheels (real output) and a gauge (price) to indicate the degree of clutch slip. Going uphill (a business upswing) the engine drives the wheels and the clutch slips; going downhill (a business downswing) the wheels drive the motor and the clutch slips in the opposite direction.

If the flow of money income increases, because of an increase either in the quantity of money or in its income velocity, will there be a sympathetic increase in the flow of final goods and services? If there are idle factors of production waiting to be used, an increase in money income is likely to increase real income. However, during times of full employment, and when in addition lack of fabricating capacity may impose specific bottlenecks, a larger money income will begin to raise prices rather than output.

Statements for Consideration

1. It is an open question today whether the value of the dollar, or the value of gold, depends upon the dollar price paid for gold.
   Discuss
2. According to the original commodity theory of money, a new invention, which halved the cost of recovering gold, would tend to double the price level, even though the quantity of gold remained almost unaffected.
   Discuss
3. The commodity theory of money explains price movements within countries on a full gold standard.
   Evaluate
4. It cannot be a coincidence that price levels tend to reach new peaks soon after wars during which governments have expanded the means of payment.
   Discuss
5. The equation of exchange is essentially a truism possessing little significance.
   Evaluate
6. Both quantity theories of money completely overlook V. *Evaluate*
7. The equation of exchange in effect states that the price level is dependent upon changes in M, V, and T, rather than the other way around.
   Discuss
8. The expected course of future prices may influence public spending more than the size of the national money stock. *Exemplify*
9. A rising prise level means that all prices are rising. *Evaluate*
10. The P of the equation of exchange and the p of the equation of

income are the same in magnitude at any given moment. *Evaluate*
11. Rising price levels work an injustice upon those who own life insurance or endowment insurance policies.   *Explain*

References

Boulding, K. E., *Economic Analysis,* Chapter 14.   New York: Harper, 1948.

Bowman, M. J., and Bach, G. L., *Economic Analysis and Public Policy,* Chapter 8.   New York: Prentice-Hall, 1949.

Due, J. F., *Intermediate Economic Analysis,* Chapter 15.   Chicago: Irwin, 1947.

Fisher, I., *Purchasing Power of Money.*   New York: Macmillan, 1926.

Garver, F. B., and Hansen, A. H., *Principles of Economics,* Chapters 20, 21.   New York: Ginn, 1947.

Hart, A. G., *Money, Debt and Economic Activity,* Chapters 5, 6.   New York: Prentice-Hall, 1948.

Keynes, J. M., *A Treatise on Money,* Chapters 4, 9, 10.   London: Macmillan, 1930.

Meyers, A. L., *Modern Economics,* Chapter 30.   New York: Prentice-Hall, 1946.

Samuelson, P. A., *Economics,* Chapter 13.   New York: McGraw-Hill, 1948.

Wicksell, K., *Lectures on Political Economy,* Chapter 4.   London: Routledge, 1935.

7

The Circuit of Payments

EVER SINCE the Great Depression of the early 'thirties, and even before to some extent, money has been studied in relation to employment rather than to prices. Coupled with this shift in interest, there has occurred a change of viewpoint. Spending has come to be analyzed in terms of receipts rather than of money stocks. After all, the reason a rich man spends ten times more a year than I do is not that he keeps so much more money in the bank, but that his income is ten times greater than mine. Firms and governments also gear their spending to their receipts rather than to their bank balances. This rather simple and obvious fact has interesting theoretical consequences for employment theory.

The spending of money does not destroy it. In normal times, money circulates through a succession of recipients, each of whom eventually becomes a spender in turn. Opposed to this circulation of money—if we neglect debt transactions—there is a circulation of goods and services. It is an obvious idea, and a simple hope, that an increase in the circulation of money will increase the production and availability of goods and services, rather than simply bring about an increase in prices.

Unfortunately, people do not always spend their receipts; they hoard money instead. When this occurs, and there are no offsetting additions to the money stream, the entire flow of payments may slow down. Leakages of this kind will bring about a reduction in effective aggregate demand which in turn may cause unemployment.

The Savings Bogey

An alternative title for this section might be *Is Unemployment Caused by Underconsumption?*

Most households, and especially households enjoying relatively high incomes, spend only a fraction of their incomes on consump-

tion. Whereas a household possessing an income of $2,500 a year
may spend all of it and go into debt besides, a family having
$25,000 a year may spend only half this amount on consumer goods
and services. As one goes up the income scale, one finds that the
disposable income of households (i.e., their income after income
taxes) becomes a decreasing percentage of their gross income.
Moreover, the higher a household's disposable income, the greater
its proportionate savings will probably be. Some people have
thought that these income taxes and savings, which explain the
difference between gross income and consumer spending, are leakages that slow the flow of payments and so contribute to unemployment. It has sometimes been suggested that, if the distribution of household incomes were rendered less unequal by government action, business depressions would be avoided.

Is it true that direct household taxes and household savings are
"leakages" in the flow of payments?   It all depends upon whether
the agencies that receive these taxes and savings proceed to spend
them.   In the case of taxes, do the collecting governments spend
their tax receipts (in which case there is no leakage) or build up
budget surpluses (in which case there will probably be a leakage)?
Very few governments maintain substantial surpluses; it is particularly rare for them to do so during a depression, when public
works and unemployment relief usually occasion deficit government budgets instead.   Hence tax leakages are usually more than
offset by government spending.

The situation is more complex in the case of savings from disposable income. Savings may be invested directly in some family business or indirectly in the securities of some firm or government, which presumably will spend the money it is raising in this
way. Savings that are so employed are spent. By no means is all
the spending in an economy for consumer goods. Producer goods
are usually bought with money, too!

Not all savings are put to work in these ways, however. The
saved funds may simply be held, in a mattress, in a safety deposit
box, or in a bank account. The accumulating of money in this
way is sometimes described as hoarding. If households hoard
their savings rather than investing them, and there is no counter
dishoarding elsewhere in the economy by firms or governments,
the flow of payments will be slowed. It is not saving but hoarding that is the bogey of an economy.

At each rate of payments, firms and households will tend to save a certain sum and to invest a certain sum. At each rate of payments, governments will tend to tax a certain sum and to spend a certain sum. Hence, at each rate of payments, there will be a certain associated and combined private saving and government taxing. Also, at each rate of payments, there will be a certain associated and combined private investing and government spending. The circuit of payments, assuming the stock of money to be constant, cannot be forced below or above that rate at which private savings plus government taxes equal private investment plus government spending.

If, for some reason, the non-bank public decides that, at each rate of payment, it now wishes to save more or invest less than before, the circuit of payments will slow and contract unless the government undertakes offsetting policies. It might offset increased private saving with reduced government tax rates and reduced private investing with increased government spending. When the circuit of payments is in equilibrium, i.e., neither expanding nor contracting, any excess of private savings over private investment must, if the rate of payments is to remain unchanged, be offset by an excess of government spending over government taxes (see Appendix C).

Hoarding and Dishoarding

At any given moment the ownership of the national money stock is distributed among households, firms, and governments. Existing money—unless it is lost or destroyed—is always owned by someone. The desire to own wealth in the form of money has important repercussions on the flow of payments.

The main disadvantage of owning wealth in the form of money, rather than as securities or other earning assets, is that legal tender and demand deposits do not earn interest or profits. On the other hand, there are several reasons for wishing to hold some of one's wealth as money, and these are described in Chapter 11. One reason is convenience in carrying on day-to-day transactions.

Most people hold money income for a little while before they spend it. One explanation of this is that, while people spend from day to day, they receive income periodically. Dividends are frequently paid once every three months, salaries sometimes once a month, and even laborers are often paid by the week. However food, transportation, and entertainment expenditures may be made every day. Some money must be held to bridge the time gap between receipts and disbursements.

If a household spends its entire income on consumption, and its breadwinner receives a monthly salary of $500, it will have a spending time lag of at least half a month approximately. If it is "broke" just before each payday, its money holdings fluctuate between $500 and zero dollars, and its average cash balance will be $250. If it is receiving and spending $500 monthly, and on an average holds $250, then the average time interval between receiving a dollar and spending it is about 15 days, or half a month. Of course, if this household usually holds an additional "rainy day fund" of $750, which is not invested, its average money holding is $1,000; then its spending time lag, in view of the $500 "throughput" a month, is two months.

When a household or firm elects to hold more money, but its rate of receipts is unchanged, it lengthens its spending time lag. For example, if the above household saved and hoarded *another* $1,000 out of income, after which it began spending at its income rate of $500 a month again, its average spending time lag would now be four months, since its average money stock would now be $2,000. On the other hand, if a household decided to spend some of its money holdings for government bonds, its subsequent spending time lag would be shorter than before.

Obviously, with a given national money stock, all the households, firms, and governments in an economy cannot hoard more money at the same time. They may all simultaneously *attempt* to hoard. However they cannot all simultaneously *succeed* in their attempts to hold more money unless more money is created by the banking system.

Nevertheless, most units in the economy may try at times to hoard, and so increase their money stock, by spending at a slower rate. Given sufficient will power, most households can slow their rate of spending. However, this slows the receipts of the next units along the circuit of payments, so that the final consequence will be a reduction in income rather than larger money hoards.

A hypothetical example may clarify this. Let us suppose that the aggregate payments of a national economy total $2,000 billions a year, that the money stock in the hands of the non-bank public is $100 billions, and the average spending time lag is $\frac{1}{20}$

of a year, or about 18 days. Households, firms, and governments now attempt on balance to hold more money, and so slow their spending in relation to their consequently declining receipts. They cannot hold more money in actual fact, because the banks are "neutral," neither expanding nor contracting the means of payment. However, in attempting to hoard, they may succeed in lengthening the average payments time lag from $\frac{1}{20}$ to $\frac{1}{15}$ of a year. In this case, the aggregate of annual payments can only be 15 times the national money stock and will thus fall to $1,500 billions.

Another way to look at this shrinkage in the aggregate national payments would be to view it as a decrease in the transaction velocity of money. Before the hoarding attempt, the national money stock of $100 billions turned over as receipts 20 times a year, and our V of the previous chapter was 20.0. After the hoarding attempt V is 15.0 and the aggregate of national receipts has fallen from $2,000 billions to $1,500 billions.

We have just stated that all the units in an economy cannot succeed in simultaneously hoarding or dishoarding unless the national money stock changes. However, it is perfectly possible, and indeed usual, for some units to hoard while others dishoard. In this connection it is important to distinguish between active and passive hoarding and dishoarding.

If firms collectively decide to invest their cash holdings, and so dishoard, the income of households will tend to rise. These households, even though they do not lengthen their spending time lag, will find themselves with a larger holding of money. For example, our household that used to receive and spend $500 a month may now be paid an income of $600 once each month. If it continues to spend all its income every month, the average amount of money it holds to carry on daily transactions will be $300 instead of $250. Its spending time lag is still half a month but it holds $50 more. Such a household is a passive hoarder, and this behavior is due, in the assumed circumstances, to the active dishoarding of firms.

When a unit in the economy, such as a household or firm, maintains the same ratio of money to receipts, it cannot be described as an active hoarder. Hence one cannot detect active hoarders by noting which households or firms now hold more money than before. Active hoarding units are those that are lengthening their payments time lags or are holding a larger fraction of income as cash.

Hoarding must be distinguished from saving. A family that sells $1,000 worth of securities, but spends only $500 of the proceeds on consumer goods, is hoarding and dissaving at the same time. On the other hand, a firm that uses $100,000 of accumulated profits to pay off its outstanding notes is simultaneously dishoarding and saving.

Expanding the Flow of Payments

As already stated, unless prices rise, an acceleration of the flow of payments might very likely increase economic activity, employment, and welfare.

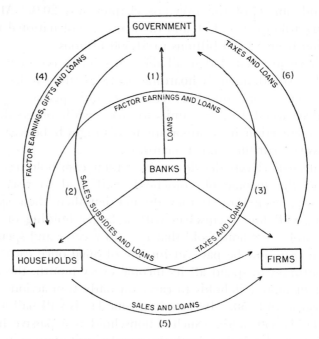

Fig. 3. A Circuit of Payments.

Some of the ways in which this might come about can best be understood by referring to Fig. 3, which is a schematic illustration of the pattern of payments. It breaks down the economy into households, firms, governments, and banks, as in Chapter 2. The arrows show the direction of payment and they are tagged in the way their recipients would describe them. Incidentally, "loans" include the money received upon the discharge of a loan, or the liquidation of real capital assets, as well as ordinary borrowing.

One development that would obviously speed the flow of payments would be if one of the non-bank groups would spend its receipts more rapidly. Another obvious possibility would be for the banks to advance new credits. The practical difficulty here is that in depression periods, when the flow of payments needs expanding, banks are usually unwilling to lend money to firms that want to borrow. It is for this reason that many people have recommended that governments, and especially the federal government, should expand the means of payment and the flow of payments through deficit financing during business depressions. The central government in effect has the power to force the central bank to loan it money to cover budget deficits.

Through Active Dishoarding

If there is active dishoarding in part of the economy, with no active and offsetting hoarding elsewhere, the flow of payments will be accelerated.

Let us suppose that governments hold no money, firms hold $80 billions, and households $20 billions. The spending time lag of firms is $\frac{1}{5}$ of a year, and that of households is $\frac{1}{20}$ of a year. Firms receive $400 billions from households each month and households also receive $400 billions from firms each month. Banks and governments are excluded from this model. Now let us suppose that firms reduce their spending time lag from $\frac{1}{5}$ to $\frac{1}{10}$ of a year. Flows 1 and 6 immediately increase. This causes flows 5, 3, 2, and 4 also to increase. And this in turn causes all six flows to increase. The whole circuit of payments has accelerated and expanded.

However, the zero and $\frac{1}{20}$ of a year time lags of governments and households, respectively, remain unchanged. Hence households will find themselves passive hoarders, holding more money because their receipts have increased. Moreover, the firms, which instigated all these developments by suddenly reducing their money holdings from $80 to $40 billions, i.e., by actively dishoarding, will begin to find that they too are passively hoarding as their receipts also rise.

This will continue until the $40 billions of actively dishoarded money stocks are passively hoarded. In the present case, if the new spending time lags are $\frac{1}{10}$ of a year for firms and $\frac{1}{20}$ of a year for households, on an average, the final distribution of the national money stock will be $67 billions among firms and $33 billions among households. The payments of households to firms, and of firms to households, will now be $667 billions a month in each direction, instead of $400 billions a month as hitherto. The autonomous spending of $40 billions by firms has increased their total flow of payments by $535 billions, or 13.3 times, because the spending time lag is now a little less than $\frac{1}{13}$ of a year, on an average, for the entire economy.

Through Bank Credits

The circuit of payments will be accelerated if new money is created through loans made by the banking system. It does not make much difference whether these loans are originally injected by way of governments, firms, or households. For instance, installment buying loans to households will increase flows 3 and 5, then increase flows 1, 2, 4, and 6, and then all six flows. After a few rounds of the circuit an injection anywhere along it will have become diffused throughout the whole pattern of payments.

What might happen if the bank, through new credits, maintains an injection of $10 billions via the rather improbable channel of installment credit loans to households, and so permanently increases the national money stock from $100 billions to $110 billions? This will increase flows 3 and 5, and then flows 1, 2, 4, and 6, and then all six flows together. When will equilibrium be established?

It rather depends upon whether the *average* rate of hoarding is equal to the *marginal* rate of hoarding. The average rate of hoarding for the entire economy is found by dividing the national money stock by the aggregate annual payments—it is, in other words, the reciprocal of V. We shall suppose that, before the new installment credits, this was $100 billions over $2,000 billions, or 0.05. However, does this mean that the various units of the economy would, if they received an *extra* $1.00 billions a year in receipts, wish to hold only an *extra* $0.05 billions in bank balances and legal tender? The ratio of *extra* money holdings to *extra* receipts is the marginal rate of hoarding. In the real world, the marginal rate of hoarding may well be different from the average rate, in which cases additions to the money stock have a disproportionate effect on the flow of patterns.

In order to answer the above question, we shall suppose that the average rate of hoarding was 0.05 and that the marginal rate of hoarding is 0.10. These rates apply to households and firms together. If governments spend their receipts immediately, they are, in effect, neutral in the present problem. The final result will be an increase in the aggregate national payments of $100 billions, because this is equal to the increment in the national money stock divided by the marginal rate of hoarding. The average rate of hoarding is now higher, the spending time lag is a little longer, and the transaction velocity of money has fallen.

Through Government Deficits

There is at least a theoretical possibility that full employment might be reached and held through large-scale expenditures of new money by the national government. Such new money would be provided to the government by the banking system and would then be injected into the circuit of payments. In this way the government might be able, not only to compensate for the tendency of the banking system not to renew maturing private loans during depressions, but actually to expand the flow of payments. Some economists hope and believe that an expansion of the flow of payments would be associated with a rise in real national income and a reduction in unemployment.

The consequence of a deficit in the budget of the United States Government is usually an injection of new bank credit into the circuit of payments because most of the deficit will probably be covered by the sale of United States Securities to the Federal Reserve. A deficit budget may come about through additional expenditures or a reduction in tax receipts. Actually, during depressions, budget deficits tend to arise from both causes; public relief designed to help the unemployed will increase disbursements, while simultaneously tax receipts will decline, not because tax rates are lower, but because the flow of income and goods upon which taxes are levied is contracted.

What will happen if the government suddenly makes a single injection of one hundred million dollars new credits obtained by borrowing from the central bank? As we have already seen, the consequences depend rather upon the marginal rate of hoarding, which we shall again suppose is $\frac{1}{10}$; in other words, recipients of extra money usually wait about one-tenth of a year before they spend it. Moreover, and this we have not yet taken into account, the government is not really "neutral." It does not always spend immediately what it receives and sometimes it spends before it receives. Governments have their hands in everybody's pockets, gathering excise taxes, excess profits taxes, and income taxes. Almost every time money changes hands in exchange for goods or services the government usually manages to be included. In the forthcoming analysis we shall suppose that 5 per cent of each money transfer on an average reverts to the federal government.

Induced Tax Leakages. Under these circumstances, if the government injects $100 millions, perhaps by giving bonuses to veterans or hiring more employees, the first group of recipients will wait $\frac{1}{10}$ of a year on an average before spending these incremental receipts. At the end of this period, these recipients will spend what is left after taxes on either consumer or producer goods. There will be $95 millions left to pass on to the second group. After another $\frac{1}{10}$ of a year, on an average, the second group will respend their increment in receipts. The government's share this time, obtained through cigarette and liquor taxes, income taxes, entertainment and travel taxes, and so on, will be 5 per cent of $95 millions, or $4.7 millions. The third group of recipients will be able to pass on only $(.95)^3$ of the original $100 millions. And so it goes, with another respending every tenth of a year, and with 5 per cent of the remaining amount reverting to the government as taxes on each respending. Eventually, after an infinite time, all the original injection would revert to the government, which could then completely discharge its debt to the central bank. The first three columns of Table 8 show the manner in which the original injection is gradually recovered through extra tax receipts.

What would happen if the government injected $100 millions of new money *every* tenth of a year? The circuit of payments would increase gradually, at a declining pace, until eventually a new and higher maximum flow of payments was attained. As the increment in the flow of payments becomes greater and greater, the government's 5 per cent share becomes larger and larger in terms of dollars, until eventually the extra tax receipts each tenth of a year are equal to the periodic injection of $100 millions. Eventually, but only after an infinitely long time, equilibrium would be established in this way.

TABLE 8

INJECTIONS, TAXES, AND PAYMENTS

(Dollars in Millions)

Spending Periods	Single Injection		Successive Injections	
	Extra Payts.	Extra Taxes	Extra Payts.	Extra Taxes
1	$100.0	$5.0	$ 100.0	$ 5.0
2	95.0	4.7	195.0	9.7
3	90.2	4.5	285.2	15.2
4	85.7	4.3	370.9	19.3
5	81.4	4.1	452.3	23.4
10	63.0	3.2	802.3	41.0
15	48.8	2.4	1,073.2	54.5
20	37.7	1.9	1,282.7	65.0
25	29.2	1.5	1,444.9	73.1
30	22.6	1.1	1,570.3	78.4
∞	0	0	2,000.0	100.0

Now, if the ratio of extra government tax receipts to extra public spending (t) is always .05 of the extra spending in each period, and eventually these extra tax receipts equal the periodic injection of $100 millions, we know that these extra tax receipts will eventually be $100 millions each period also. Hence we know that the eventual increase in the flow of payments each period must be 1.00/.05 of $100 millions, which is $20,000 millions.

The last two columns of Table 8 show the consequences, step by step, of periodic injections of $100 millions. In the first period the extra payments consist of a $100 millions injection. In the second period the second group receives $95.0 millions of the first injection while the first group is receiving the $100 millions second injection. In the third period, the third group is receiving the $90.2 millions remaining from the first injection spent by the second group, the second group is receiving the $95.0 remaining of the second injection spent by the first group, and the first group is receiving the third $100 millions injection. Hence the total increment in payments in the third period is $90.2 plus $95.0 plus $100 millions, which is $285.2 millions.

The extent to which the eventual increase in payments is a multiple of the government's periodic injection (m) depends upon the government's tax share of extra public spending (t). In the present case t is .05 and so the multiplier is 1.00/.05 or 20.0. If t had been one-fifth, the eventual multiplication of periodic payments would have been fivefold. The larger is t—whether as a decimal or as a fraction—the smaller is m.

However, these final m values will not be attained until an infinitely long time has elapsed. People do not live for an infinitely long time and so what is the value of these conclusions? Their value lies in the fact that, although the final increment in payments may never be actually reached, it may be approached in a fairly short time.

The Meaning of Periods. In the preceding paragraph, and in the table, reference has been made to "periods." These periods are marginal spending periods. They are the average length of time elapsing between the receipt of extra money and its spending. These marginal spending periods are actually $\frac{1}{10}$ of a year because the marginal rate of hoarding has been assumed to be .10. Marginal spending periods should not be confused with spending time lags, which are based on the average rate of hoarding and are equal to $1/V$ of a year.

Accordingly an economy might not have to wait so very long before it experienced a substantial multiplier effect from periodic injections. Column 4 of Table 8 shows that at the end of 10 periods (which is one year if the marginal hoarding rate is $\frac{1}{10}$) the increment in payments will be $802.3 millions or 40 per cent of the final increase of $2,000 millions. At the end of three years —or 30 periods—79 per cent of the final increment has been attained. In theory, at least, significant results might be obtained in a single Presidential administration.

The national money stock will be increased by periodic government injections of new money. The amount of this increase will—in the absence of other expansions or contractions of credit by the banking system—be equal to the increase in the government's debt. Hence an accumulation of all past injections minus an accumulation of the fifth column will give the extra national money stock at any time. This amount is actually shown in the fourth column and is eventually $2,000 millions also. It will always be equal to the final increase in payments per marginal spending period.

Annual Consequences. It is now time to consider the present case in terms of years rather than periods. If the marginal rate of hoarding is constantly .10, the marginal spending period will always be $\frac{1}{10}$ of a year. Hence a government injection of $100 millions a period is equal to $1.0 billions a year. Also, if the final increment in payments is $2.0 billions a period, the annual increment will be $20.0 billions. The latter amount is 10 times the increase in the national money stock, as it must be, because the marginal hoarding rate is .10.

If the marginal hoarding rate had been greater, say .2 instead of .1, then the extra national money stock, and the government's extra debt, would have been twice as great, given the same goals. Moreover, if there is a lag of $\frac{1}{5}$ of a year in spending extra receipts, it will take twice as long to achieve a given increment of payments; for example, it would take two years, instead of one year, to raise payments to $802.3 millions through successive periodic injections of $100 millions. However, a change in the marginal hoarding rate will leave m and t unaffected and the eventual increment in annual payments will still be $20.0 billions.

The injection of $1.0 billion a year, the effects of which we have been analyzing, might be the result of a reduction in tax rates rather than of an increase in disbursements. Let us suppose that, in a former state of equilibrium, the national payments flow was $2,000 billions and that .05 of this passed through the government's hands. The national government's budget was in balance with $100 billions income and outgo. Let us further suppose that it now reduced its tax rates on income, alcohol, entertainment, and so forth, so that now it collects .04 of the aggregate national payments. In the first year its receipts will be about $80 billions, but its disbursements, assuming it maintains the same establishment as before, will continue to be $100 billions. The resultant deficit of about $20 billions is in effect an injection. If t is now .04, m will be 25.0. Hence the increment in aggregate national payments will in time be $500 billions. Eventually, when this level of payments is attained, the government's receipts will have risen to .04 of $2,500 billions, or to $100 billions, and its budget will again be balanced. How many months or years will elapse before various intermediate levels of extra payments are attained depends upon the marginal rate of hoarding.

Points of Interest. The preceding discussion of payments multipliers resulting from deficit spending of new money should be concluded with the following comments. First, there are many multipliers in economics; the *m* ratio, which has been discussed here, relates the eventual increment in national *payments* to the rate of periodic injections of money. Second, the periodic injections in the table are gross injections; actually net injections decline with time, as offsetting periodic tax receipts rise. Third, multipliers work backwards as well as forwards; in the present case, if the government increased its tax rates and acquired a budget surplus, which it devoted to repurchasing its bonds from the central bank, aggregate national payments would decline.

Why Increase Payments?

Is the economy likely to be "better off" when the flow of payments expands? Will the national income increase by the same percentage as does the aggregate of payments? The answer is "Not necessarily, but possibly."

It is true, of course, that an increase in aggregate national payments might simply reflect a feverish buying back and forth of goods at inflated prices. In fact, during an upswing, there is usually more speculative buying and selling, and prices do tend to rise. However it is hard to believe that commercial activity will increase without there being some increase in economic activity.

Another danger is that the marginal rate of hoarding will rise rapidly as the level of payments increases. If this were to occur, it would enormously increase the net cost to the government of any experimenting along the lines laid down above. Also, if the marginal spending period were to lengthen, the calendar time it would require to achieve any given percentage of the final outcome would increase.

Government spending will have the most satisfactory results for economic welfare if events flatly contradict what we have described as the quantity theory of money. It is fervently to be hoped that, in terms of the equation of exchange (see Chapter 6), an increase in M has no tendency to raise P or lower V; i.e., that it will only affect T. The early and dogmatic version of the quantity theory would have held, however, that T would be unaffected

and that P would change proportionately. The practical usefulness of government spending as a panacea depends in part on
which elements in the monetary equation will vary.

Fundamentally the question is whether resources that were
formerly unemployed can become employed at no increase, or at
worst only a slight increase, in real costs. Specifically, can unemployed men be induced to work at a money wage no higher than
the wage that previously prevailed? Moreover, when a man is put
to work, will his output per man-hour be as high as that of those
workers who were always employed? If the answer to either of
these questions is "No," then money costs per unit of output will
increase. To avoid rising product prices, it is essential that formerly idle resources be as efficient as those already employed, and
that they take employment at former factor prices; or, if less efficient, that they take work at factor prices that are enough lower
than the former prices to match their relative inefficiency.

The above analysis ignores interest rates and the inducements
that lead private entrepreneurs to expand their operations by new
investments and spending. We also have not explained why an
economy might be in equilibrium below the level of full employment. These matters are taken up in Part III.

Statements for Consideration

1. A household's spending rate depends more upon its receipts rate
than upon the amount of money it holds. *Discuss*
2. The non-bank public can alter its hoarding rate but not its money
hoards without bank intervention. *Evaluate*
3. Rich people are responsible for depressions because they occasion
disproportionately large savings and tax leakages in the circuit of
payments. *Evaluate*
4. If firms decide to dishoard, other units, such as households, may
become passive hoarders, finally holding more money than before
but maintaining the same hoarding rate. *Explain*
5. Hoarding and saving are sometimes equal, but they are not necessarily so. *Explain*
6. A decrease in the community's spending time lag inevitably increases its velocity of money. *Discuss*
7. A decision to save more cannot slow the circuit of payments unless
it results in the holding of more money than before. *Discuss*
8. The circuit of payments approach to money is not concerned with
just the M or V alone of the equation of exchange but with MV.
Evaluate
9. People who believe that economic welfare will be advanced by

expanding *MV* are, consciously or unconsciously, making rather definite assumptions regarding the dependency or independency of *P* and *T* in the equation of exchange.   *Explain*

10. The effect on total spending of an increase in the national stock of money depends not upon the average hoarding rate but upon the marginal hoarding rate.   *Explain*

11. So far as the circuit of payments is concerned, additions to *M* and reductions in the average hoarding rate are approximately equivalent.   *Discuss*

References

Boulding, K. E., *Economic Analysis,* Chapter 15.   New York: Harper, 1948.

Bowman, M. J., and Bach, G. L., *Economic Analysis and Public Policy,* Chapters 12, 13.   New York: Prentice-Hall, 1949.

Garver, F. B., and Hansen, A. H., *Principles of Economics,* Chapter 22.   New York: Ginn, 1947.

Hart, A. G., *Money, Debt and Economic Activity,* Chapters 7, 10. New York: Prentice-Hall, 1948.

Meyers, A. L., *Modern Economics,* Chapter 31.   New York: Prentice-Hall, 1946.

Morgan, T., *Income and Employment,* Chapter 11.   New York: Prentice-Hall, 1947.

PART III

Income Theory

8

Income Theory Essentials

EVERYONE knows that an economy may operate at a slow rate, sometimes for years at a time, so that the level of real and money incomes is depressed while workers and other productive resources remain unemployed. Occasionally this slowdown of activity in a national economy continues for so long that almost permanent stagnation seems to have set in. At other times depressions may alternate with prosperity phases so that there appears to be a fairly regular cycle of bad and good years.

Introduction

Mere knowledge that depressions exist does not mean that economists and other students of the subject have always understood the circumstances that give rise to periods of stagnation and phases of depression. In fact formal economic theory a century ago did not accept the possibility of prolonged underemployment. It is only in the last few decades that economists have introduced additional variables into their theories in order to explain the familiar problem of depression.

Modern theories of employment, interest, and money demonstrate that an economy may be in equilibrium even when income and employment are below a desirable level. Psychological factors that lead individuals to save a fraction of any increase in income, expectations regarding the future course of interest rates, the desire to hold a portion of one's wealth in the form of money, and other factors too numerous to mention here can together depress the rate of economic activity. A national economy can be in equilibrium even in the midst of mass unemployment. There are no economic principles guaranteeing that a nation will realize the highest level of real income permitted by its available productive resources. A given level of income and employment may be consistent with a number of stability requirements, and hence be one of equilibrium, even though that level is incompatible with economic welfare.

Suboptimum equilibria are in large measure due to the beliefs, attitudes, and behavior of each entrepreneur, investor, and consumer in the economy. Economic stagnation is not caused by the folly or selfishness of a few key persons. Everyone is in general responsible, but no one in particular is to blame, for the collective misfortune of underemployment.

The following introductory sections present the highlights of modern income theory. Although they will be followed by a more intensive analysis in subsequent chapters, it is important that the manner in which the main pieces in the unemployment puzzle fit together be understood from the outset. In this way it is simpler to gain a realization of the places in the economy where the government might be able to intervene most beneficially. Modern income theory is an invitation to discard *laissez-faire* attitudes because it suggests that collective action rather than individual decisions can ensure full employment and high income.

Contrary Saving and Investing Plans

The necessary equality of aggregate savings and aggregate investment was stressed in Chapter 4. Such equality referred to past savings and investment. Indeed, in view of our adopted definitions of these terms, it would be impossible for savings and investment to differ in magnitude during some historical period.

However, this does not mean that the savings that savers plan must be equal in value to the investments investors plan. In fact one of the key ideas of income theory is that these savings plans and investment plans made by different households and firms will ordinarily differ. These *ex ante* savings and investments, as they are sometimes called, will be equal only by chance.

Here then is superficial paradox. Intended (or *ex ante*) savings and investments are ordinarily unequal. But actual (or *ex post*) savings and investments are necessarily equal. In some way during each year, the processes of the economy must compromise these dissimilar plans, so that in retrospect the actualities are reconciled. In the course of this "marriage," the employment and income of the economy are determined.

Incidentally, the term "investing" in income theory refers to the accumulating of real capital, such as factories, machines, and materials in process. Investing does not refer to the financial act of purchasing ten shares of some company's stocks. The lexicon of economies really needs a word, like "accumulating," to denote additions to real capital, because "investing" to most people means putting out savings to earn a return.

Most of the investing of the economy is planned and undertaken by firms. Most of the savings of an economy are planned and undertaken by households, although some firms also save and reinvest. The reconciliation of investment plans and savings plans is in large measure a reconciliation of the plans of firms and households.

The following sort of complication may easily arise. The firms in the economy may intend, during the coming year, to produce about $90 billions of consumer goods, plus $10 billions more producer goods than are needed for replacement. Hence, on an average, firms intend to invest about 10 per cent of their total output. However, when the national income is $100 billions, as is supposed here, households may intend to save 20 per cent of their factor income, in which case they will plan to save $20 billions. In this event, firms will not sell their entire output of consumer goods, but will find themselves with $10 billions more consumer goods inventories than they planned or desired. Firms have then invested $20 billions, $10 billions involuntarily in consumer goods inventories, and $10 billions according to plan. Next year, firms will probably reduce their output, and hence the factor income of households will fall. In fact, income will probably continue to fall until it reaches a level at which intended household saving is roughly equal to intended firm investments.

Several definitional matters regarding income (Y), consumption (C), and savings (S) and investment (I) merit attention. It is often stated that:

$$Y = C + I$$
$$S = Y - C$$
$$I = Y - C$$

In other words Y is defined in terms of I and C, while S and I are defined in terms of C and Y. Superficially the above system of definitions appears circular. However, Y can also be defined as the value of the real national income and C as household spending on consumption goods. If we use these more basic definitions,

Y and C are described independently of each other and independently of S or I. It is also interesting to note that $Y - C$ has two names. Sometimes the excess of income over consumption is called savings, and at other times it is called investment. Hence S and I are identities and must always be equal at the close of any given year. Because they are always identical and equal we shall sometimes use the symbol X to designate the savings-investment that actually takes place (see Appendix C).

The Consumption Function

Individuals have a tendency, especially marked as their incomes increase, of consuming only a part of their income and saving the balance. It seems that extra consumption, even though reconstituted and increasingly varied as income rises, begins to pall. Perhaps the accumulation of wealth as a means to power becomes a substitute motive with rising income. Fortunately we need not know the sensations and motives that cause people to consume ever smaller fractions of additions to their income. It is the economic consequences of this phenomenon that concern us.

Let us suppose that the consumption function, that is the relationship in some country between national income and aggregate consumer spending, is as set forth in Table 9.

TABLE 9

MARGINAL PROPENSITIES TO CONSUME AND SAVE
(Dollars in Billions)

Real Income	Actual Consumption	Extra Consumption	M.P.C.	M.P.S.
$ 80.0	$ 78.5			
90.0	86.5	$8.0	.80	.20
100.0	94.0	7.5	.75	.25
110.0	101.5	7.5	.75	.25
120.0	108.5	7.0	.70	.30

An increasing national income is associated with increased aggregate consumption. However the absolute increase in consumption is less than the absolute increase in national income. For example, when national income increases from $100 to $110 billions, consumption only increases from $94 to $101.5 billions. In this case the *marginal* propensity to consume, which is defined as the change in consumption divided by the change in income, is $7.5 billions divided by $10 billions, or .75. The extra amount saved must be $2.5 billions, since this is the difference between the extra national income and the extra consumption. The marginal propensity to save, which is defined as the change in saving divided by the change in national income, is then $2.5 billions divided by $10 billions, or .25. The sum of the marginal propensity to consume and the marginal propensity to save is always unity, because an extra dollar of real income must be either consumed or saved.

The *average* propensity to consume is simply the total consumption divided by the total national income. In the above example it is .94 when the national income is $100 billions. The average propensity to consume tends to fall as national income rises; the average propensity to save, therefore, tends correspondingly to increase in this example. Consequently the marginal propensity to save must normally be higher than the average propensity to save. The two average propensities must always add up to unity also. However, in economic analysis, it is these marginal propensities that are most important for public policy.

The extent to which one person's extra income will successively become extra income for other people depends in large measure on the marginal saving propensities of the community. Each person will naturally have his own individual marginal propensities to save. The rich will usually have higher marginal propensities to save than will the poor.

The character of the consumption function in the real world is statistically uncertain. In the United States, it is generally supposed that the average propensity to save increases with income —although, of course, the manner in which extra income is distributed among households is a material consideration. It is even possible that a given national income, distributed more unequally, might increase the amount of saving. The exact way, however, in which the marginal propensity to save varies with income size and distribution is a subject of controversy.

Modern income theory implicitly assumes that the consumption function, for any given national economy, is fairly stable, resting as it does on habits of thrift, savings institutions, and the extent of state social security schemes. More specifically, it is supposed that the consumption function does not shift markedly from one phase to another of the business cycle. It is also assumed that the consumption function is not affected by the rate of investment.

Investment Sets the Pace

Investment, given the consumption function of an economy, tends to determine the national income.   Such is the case for two reasons.   One is that the consumption function is held to be relatively stable, so that the value of savings depends upon aggregate money receipts.   The other is that money savings must equal real investment in the aggregate.

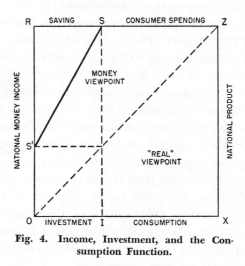

Fig. 4.   Income, Investment, and the Consumption Function.

A rather special kind of diagram (Fig. 4) helps to show why this is so.   The part above and to the left of the Z line, which is at 45° from the horizontal, depicts things from the money viewpoint. The part of the figure below and to the right of this line illustrates the "real" aspect of affairs.   The vertical axis represents national income (i.e., either money income or production) while the horizonal axis indicates its composition (i.e., either saving plus consumer spending *or* investment plus consumption).   The fact that the savings schedule SS' has an intercept on the vertical axis means that people do not save until a certain minimum money income has been attained.

Let us start by supposing that firms, and possibly others, continually undertake investments amounting to OI in value.   Now aggregate real investment of OI is impossible—for reasons given in Chapter 4—unless aggregate money savings are RS and hence equal in value.   At this point the consumption function, and especially its supplement the savings function, becomes crucial. There is a specific average propensity to save for each level of money income. Consequently, given investment, the level of money income must be such that, when it is multiplied by the average propensity to save, the resultant dollar savings will equal the value of the real investment. In the present case, if investment is *OI,* money income must be *OR,* so that the saving of *RS* will equal *OI.* That part of money income which is not saved goes for consumer spending, represented by *SZ.* If consumer spending is at a rate of *SZ* it follows that, neglecting household stockpiling, consumption is *TX.* Investment plus consumption is, of course, equal to production or, to use another term, to national income.

National income would be altered if either the consumption function or investment changed. If investment increases, savings and consumer spending, and hence money income, have to increase. If the consumption function shifts, so that savings increase at each income level (i.e., the savings schedule in the diagram shifts to the right), then national income, other things equal, falls.

In case the preceding analysis seems somewhat mechanical, it might be well to supplement it with a few realistic observations. In practice the flow of income to households depends primarily upon the spending of firms. Firms spend to produce consumer goods for immediate use and, from time to time, to obtain producer goods, most of which are highly durable. The production of consumer goods is relatively stable, and relatively well synchronized with the demand for them, at least in contrast with producer goods. Capital production, on the other hand, does not take place evenly, but in stops and starts, according to the principle of acceleration (see Appendix B). It is the extreme fluctuations in the production of capital goods, and in the flow of payments so generated, which gives investment an importance in the cyclical scheme of things out of all proportion to its monetary value.

The Investment Multiplier

Another reason why the rate of investment affects the level of income is that an increment or decrement of investment has a multiple effect. This multiple effect is due to circumstances already touched upon in the preceding chapter. The spending of firms for investment is respent, and then respent again, and so, apart from hoarding and tax leakages, enters into the income stream several times a year.

The extent to which investment is multiplied into extra income depends upon the consumption function and especially upon the marginal propensity to save. Under rather simple conditions, as for example when firms are not induced to invest more as income rises, the ratio of final extra income to the sustained investment increment is equal to the reciprocal of the marginal propensity to save. This ratio is ordinarily termed the investment multiplier and symbolized by k. If the marginal propensity to save is constantly $\frac{1}{5}$, the value of k will be 5. Alternatively, and quite often, k is defined as the reciprocal of one minus the marginal propensity to consume. In Fig. 4, the slope, from vertical, of a tangent to the savings curve indicates the marginal propensity to save at each and every point along it; hence, by imagining a little extra investment on the horizontal axis, one can visualize along the vertical scale the extra income that might eventually result.

Of course the situation is rather more complicated if an increment in income induces firms to invest more. The multiplier effect is then compounded. Some deficit financing theories assume that, once some deficit spending of new money is undertaken by government, business will provide additional injections by investing.

The Marginal Efficiency of Capital

The willingness of firms to invest depends in large measure upon their estimates of the future earning power of capital funds that might be invested in additional producer goods.

The anticipated earning power of a capital asset is based upon its cost of acquisition and the estimated net income it will produce during future years. There will always be some rate of discount that will render the present value of the asset's estimated income stream equal to the asset's supply price. The "efficiency" of a particular capital asset can be expressed in terms of this rate of discount. Take a very simple example: if an extra unit of capital costs $10,000 to acquire, and its net income stream, after deducting maintenance and depreciation and so on, is estimated to be $500 a year almost indefinitely, the marginal efficiency of this class of capital to this firm is .05. It is .05 because the present value of this income stream is almost exactly $10,000 when discounted, year by year, at 5 per cent.

The management of a firm will presumably purchase an asset if its estimated efficiency exceeds the rate of interest that is applicable to the situation at hand. In the above example, in which the marginal efficiency of capital was 5 per cent, management would probably buy the asset in question if the rate of interest were 4 per cent or lower. Another way of expressing the same idea is to say that a firm will probably buy an asset if its cost of acquisition is less than the present value of its net income stream discounted at current interest rates.

However, when we assert that investment will normally take place when it is believed that the marginal efficiency of capital exceeds the interest rate, we are still begging a lot of questions. The marginal efficiency of capital depends upon the cost of acquiring investment goods and their estimated net income streams. Their net income streams, in turn, depend upon the cost of other goods and services used with these capital goods, and upon the strength of demand for their outputs. Government regulations, changing fiscal policies, labor union demands, inventions, and acts of God will all affect the marginal efficiency of capital. In view of these numerous and relevant uncertainties, it is obvious that firms which acquire investments are doing so because they *believe* that their "efficiencies" exceed the rate of interest. Now beliefs, unlike knowledge, are mercurial, and hence the rate at which firms invest depends indirectly upon all sorts of psychological factors, including emotional outbursts of pessimism and optimism regarding business prospects.

Liquidity Theory of Interest Rates

It must be clear from the preceding discussion that the rate of interest plays a considerable role in determining the rate of investment. Investment proceeds at a more rapid pace if the marginal efficiency of capital is believed to have risen or if the interest rate falls. What determines the rate of interest?

The rate of interest depends upon a number of factors, described in Chapters 12 and 30. Two of these influences—to be discussed in Chapter 30—are the general reluctance of people to postpone consumption and the real productivity of invested capital. Two other factors that have been constantly stressed in the development of income theory, and almost to the exclusion of any others, are the national stock of money and the liquidity demand for money. In this respect we shall follow income theory traditions in Part III.

The liquidity explanation of interest—which is only a partial theory, as noted above—starts by asking a question: "Why do people want to hold some of their wealth as money when they could earn a return on this wealth by investing it?" There are several answers. One is that every household and firm must have some money to carry on day-to-day transactions. Another is that money is often held in case of an emergency. And still another answer is that people who believe that the prices of non-money assets will fall, and particularly that the prices of debts will fall, wish to wait and hold their wealth in money form until that eventuality occurs and bargains can be snapped up.

However, if people hold money rather than non-money assets, they forego a return on their wealth. The higher the rate of interest, the greater is the return that they forego by holding money wealth. Hence, the amount of money that firms and households decide to hold tends to be less at higher interest rates.

It is just as well that the amount of money people hold is influenced by the rate of interest. At any given moment, the total value of circulating legal tender and demand deposits is fixed, and somehow this money stock must be apportioned among the separate holdings of households, firms, and governments. The rate of interest—according to the liquidity theory—equates the aggregate demand for money to the national money stock. If the demand for money falls, or the stock of money is increased, interest rates will tend to fall.

Summary Outline of Principal Relations

The principal relations of modern income theory can briefly be summarized in terms of Fig. 5. There are three systems of overlapping relationships, involving at least seven variables. We shall call these systems the Income System, the Investment System, and the Interest System.

The Income System embraces income (Y) as the dependent variable, with the marginal propensity to save (β) and investment (I) as independent variables. Income increases if β falls or I rises.

Superficially, this relationship is quite mechanical, and can be expressed as $\Delta Y = \Delta I \cdot k$. The real question, however, is what determines the value and variation of the marginal propensity to save.

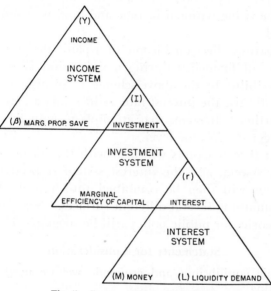

Fig. 5. Income Theory Relations.

The Investment System contains investment (I) as the dependent variable, with the marginal efficiency of capital and the interest rate (r) as independent variables. Investment increases if the marginal efficiency of capital rises or r falls. Entrepreneurs adjust their rate of investment so that the marginal efficiency of capital to them is equal to the going interest rate.

The Interest System includes the interest rate (r) as the dependent variable, with the liquidity demand for money (L) and the stock of money in the economy (M) as independent variables. The supposition is that r falls if L falls or M rises. The demand for money is a rather complicated affair, which depends in part upon the level of income and expectations regarding the rate of interest.

The possibility of government intervention to increase income is suggested by Fig. 5. The stock of money can be influenced by the central bank, as we have seen in preceding chapters. An increase in the stock of money will reduce the interest rate and induce entrepreneurs to invest more funds; this will have a multiple effect on income. However, such a tendency for income to rise will not continue, for a higher income is likely to lead to an increase in the marginal propensity to save and an increase in the demand for money. Both of these developments will act as a brake on the rising national income and hold it at some new and higher level.

The disastrous effect on income of a panic desire for liquidity on the part of financiers during a depression is revealed as a definite possibility by the above scheme. An urgent demand for liquidity will raise the interest rate, reduce investment, and lower incomes further. It seems that attempts to gain financial safety may endanger the income level.

The next three chapters will deal with the income system, the investment system, and the interest system respectively. These three systems will then be combined into a multi-dimensional diagram containing several different surfaces. Some implications of these theories for public policy will be suggested in conclusion.

Statements for Consideration

1. Economic equilibrium and economic welfare need not be the same thing.   *Discuss*
2. Income (Y) and the demand to hold wealth as money (L) are indirectly related.   *Explain*
3. Unemployment may be due to the frugality of the public and the timidity of investors.   *Evaluate*
4. Savings and investment for the economy may differ *ex ante* but not *ex post*.   *Explain*
5. Economic fluctuations might be less frequent and drastic if firms and households could only do their planning together.   *Explain*
6. The average propensity to savē can never be equal to the average hoarding rate, for M is a stock and Savings are a flow, so that they are really incomparable.   *Evaluate*
7. The fact that rich people save a larger fraction of their income than poor people do suggests, but does not prove, that for the economy over time, the marginal propensity to save exceeds the average propensity to save.   *Discuss*
8. The production of producer goods probably has a greater influence on economic fluctuations than does the production of consumer goods, despite the fact that the latter are greater in aggregate value.   *Explain*
9. A decrease in the marginal propensity to consume will reduce the value of the investment multiplier.   *Explain*
10. The marginal efficiency of capital is a useless concept because

investors do not know the future for certain but only have expectations concerning it.   *Discuss*

11. According to the liquidity theory of interest, if most people would be content to hold very little of their wealth in money form, interest rates might be zero.   *Evaluate*

References

Dillard, D., *The Economics of John Maynard Keynes*, Chapters 3, 4. New York: Prentice-Hall, 1948.

Due, J. F., *Intermediate Economic Analysis*, Chapter 14. Chicago: Irwin, 1947.

Hicks, J. R., *Value and Capital*, Note A to Chapter 14. New York: Oxford University Press, 1939.

Keynes, J. M., *The General Theory of Employment, Interest and Money*, Books I, II. New York: Harcourt, Brace, 1936.

Lerner, A. P., "Mr. Keynes' General Theory of Employment, Interest and Money," *International Labor Review*, October 1936.

Meade, J. E., "A Simplified Model of Mr. Keynes' System," *Review of Economic Studies*, February 1937. Also in *The New Economics*

Morgan, T., *Income and Employment*, Chapters 6, 7. New York: Prentice-Hall, 1947.

Pigou, A. C., *Income*, Chapter 6. London: Macmillan, 1946.

Robinson, J., *Introduction to the Theory of Employment*, Chapters 2–5, 8–10. London: Macmillan, 1937.

Samuelson, P. A., *Economics*, Chapter 12. New York: McGraw-Hill, 1948.

Schumpeter, J. A., "Keynes' General Theory of Employment," *Quarterly Journal of Economics*, November 1936.

Tarshis, L., *Elements of Economics*, Chapter 26. Boston: Houghton Mifflin, 1947.

Viner, J., "Mr. Keynes on the Causes of Unemployment," *Quarterly Journal of Economics*, November 1936.

9

Multipliers of Income

THE INCOME SYSTEM is concerned with the determination of the national income level by the consumption function and the rate of investment. Investment in this analysis refers to private real investment (for example, extra plants and equipment) plus government deficits (for example, the creation of new money to relieve the unemployed). An autonomous act of investment will occasion a large increase in income if the marginal propensity to save is small. Government attempts to raise income through "investment" will also prove more successful if they are supplemented by induced private investment. As the income level rises, private firms may feel prompted to expand capacity and to enlarge their inventories, thereby releasing more money for goods and services. On the other hand, certain government public works may discourage private investment, as, for example, when the government enters the business of producing hydroelectric power in competition with existing utility companies. The interactions of these possibilities must now be examined in detail.

The Simple Investment Multiplier

If an entrepreneur suddenly decides to release some of his money hoards, in order to invest in producer goods of some kind, there will be a multiple increase in the economy's real income, providing there is some stable relationship between extra real investment, consumption, and income.

Let us suppose a one-product economy, in which we distinguish between consumers, distributors, and manufacturers of the single good. We shall also distinguish between additional money transfers among these three groups, changes in the physical stocks of the distributors and manufacturers, and the additions to real investment, consumption, and income. The consumers use up their stocks as rapidly as they make purchases.

TABLE 10

SIMPLE MULTIPLICATION OF AUTONOMOUS INVESTMENTS

(Dollars in Millions)

	MONEY			INVENTORIES		NET		
	Distrs.	Manufs.	Households	Distrs.	Manufs.	Investment	Consumption	Income
Start	−1000	+1000	0	+1000	−1000	0	0	0
Round 1 a	0	−1000	+1000	0	+1000	+1000	0	+1000
b	+750	0	−750	−750	0	−750	+750	0
c	−750	+750	0	+750	−750	0	0	0
Total Round 1	0	−250	+250	0	+250	+250	+750	1000
Round 2 a	0	−750	+750	0	+750	+750	0	750
b	+562	0	−562	−562	0	−562	+562	0
c	−562	+562	0	+562	−562	0	0	0
Total Round 2	0	−188	+188	0	+188	+188	+562	+750
Round 3	0	−141	+141	0	+141	+141	+421	+562
Round 4	0	−105	+105	0	+105	+105	+316	+421
Round 5	0	−79	+79	0	+79	+79	+237	+316
Round 6	0	−59	+59	0	+59	+59	+178	+237
Round 7	0	−45	+45	0	+45	+45	+133	+178
Round 8	0	−33	+33	0	+33	+33	+100	+133
Round 9	0	−25	+25	0	+25	+25	+75	+100
and so on.								
Total All Rounds	(0)	(−1000)	(+1000)	(0)	(+1000)	(+1000)	(+3000)	(+4000)
All Rounds Plus Start	−1000	0	+1000	+1000	0	+1000	+3000	+4000

Table 10 shows what will happen if the distributors start by suddenly spending, from their idle money hoards, an extra $1,000 millions worth of goods for inventory.   (We shall eliminate 000,-000 in this discussion as in the table.)   The above transaction is indicated by a —$1,000 in the first column of dollar values (because the distributor has spent money), a $1,000 in the next column (because the manufacturer has received this sum), and the two physical stock columns show that the distributor now has larger inventories obtained from the manufacturers' finished stocks.   As yet there has been no over-all change in real investment, consumption, or income.

The next step (line 1a) is that manufacturers spend $1,000 in replacing the stocks they have just sold the distributors.   The resultant production occasions payments for labor, land, capital, and entrepreneurship, and provides incomes for households and families.   Real investment and income are equal for the economy because the production has gone into stock and there is still no consumption.

The next step (line 1b) is that households spend some of their new income (—$750 in the third dollar value column) and hoard the balance.   In other words, we are supposing a marginal propensity to consume (α) of .75.   The extra consumption comes out of consumer stocks and so there is no real income for the economy.

The final step in the first round (line 1c) is that distributors replace the stocks they have just sold consumers by ordering $750 worth of extra goods from the manufacturers.   There is simply a transfer of stocks between these two groups.   There is no production, and hence no income, nor is there investment or consumption.

The algebraic sum of lines 1a, 1b, and 1c, which together give the first round, show that, omitting the autonomous transactions that started this series of events, the manufacturers have $250 less in money and $250 more in inventories, the households have had $1,000 more income and $750 more consumption, and the distributors have been unaffected.   For the economy, there has been $250 extra investment, $750 extra consumption, and $1,000 extra income.   The same total stock of money exists in the system as before.

The second round is a repetition of the first, but on a smaller scale. The manufacturers try to replace the goods they sold the distributors. However, in the course of this attempt, the manufacturers create an additional $750 of income, which households receive, and .75 of which they spend, hoarding the remaining balance of $188. In turn the distributors replace their inventories by ordering $562 worth of extra goods from the manufacturers. Altogether, the second round causes $188 extra investment (by manufacturers), $562 extra consumption (by households), and $750 extra income for the whole economy.

If an infinite number of rounds are traced through (see the penultimate line) and added to the opening events (see the first line) we have the final outcome (see the last line). The distributors never recover any of the $1,000 they initially spent and so in the end their idle balances are still reduced by this amount. The manufacturers originally received $1,000 from the distributors, but the former have gradually spent this in rebuilding their finished stocks up to the initial level, so that ultimately their money hoards remain unchanged. It is the households that eventually receive the $1,000 in money initially spent by the distributors, even though at the outset they received none of it. In terms of physical stocks, the distributors maintain the $1,000 additional inventories they purchased in the beginning, and the manufacturers replace the goods they originally sold from finished stock. Ultimately, the economy's investment is increased by $1,000, its consumption by $3,000, and its real income by $4,000.

In this case the economy's marginal propensity to save (β), was .25. It has probably been noted that the final addition to real income (ΔY) is the reciprocal of the marginal propensity to save ($1/\beta$) times the original and autonomous increase in intended investment (ΔI) by distributors. Symbolically, we can define the investment multiplier (k) and estimate its value by remarking that

$$k = \frac{1}{\beta} = \frac{\Delta Y}{\Delta I}$$

and that

$$\Delta Y = k \cdot \Delta I \,*$$

---

* The final increase in the economy's income, if one extra dollar is invested by entrepreneurs, is then given by the following progression:
$$1 + (\alpha) + (\alpha)^2 + (\alpha)^3 + \cdots + (\alpha)^\infty$$

(over)

The investment multiplier will be high if the marginal propensity to consume is high and the marginal propensity to save is low. In the extreme and unlikely case that β was unity, any sums spent on investment would be completely absorbed by the first recipient, and the final increase in income would be equal to the original investment. Theoretically, if β were zero, an increment of real investment by some group (ΔI) would finally occasion an infinitely large addition to income (ΔY).

Extra money, which is released by intended investment into circulation, must finally be passively hoarded. It will be reabsorbed after a few transfers if the marginal propensity to save is high. Conversely, if the marginal propensity to consume is high, the initial injection will circulate many times before it becomes completely reabsorbed. In the end, the money hoards of some people (perhaps investors) are lower, and the money hoards of others (probably consumers) are higher. However there need be no change in the total stock of money at any time during the process of income multiplication.

It should be stressed, in the above example, that the entire process of adjustment, which eventually causes a fourfold increase in income, was set off by the *intention* of distributors to acquire and maintain higher investments in inventories. At the outset the investment of the economy did not increase because the intended investment of distributors occasioned an unintended disinvestment by manufacturers. It is not until the end of the process that the novel intentions of distributors result in an equivalent increase in the aggregate real investment of the economy.

Another noteworthy point is that the autonomous and intended investment of distributors is really a periodic injection because it is a sustained decision. At the end of each "round" distributors are found to be still clinging to their larger inventories. A sustained decision of this kind is analogous in many of its effects to the periodic injections discussed in Chapter 7.

This series will have a total value when summed of

$$\frac{1}{1-\alpha}$$

In the case described above, where the marginal propensity to consume (α) was supposed to be .75, the final value of the series will be $4.

The Compound Investment Multiplier

In the preceding analysis of the simple investment multiplier, it was supposed that one class of entrepreneurs (for example, distributors) suddenly decided to make and maintain extra investments, irrespective of the level of national income. Such an act will be termed *autonomous* investment. However, there may also be *induced* investment, if, at each successive level of national income, entrepreneurs are persuaded to invest more. Where there are autonomous *and* induced investments, there will be a compound investment multiplier (k_c).

Let us suppose, in terms of our previous example, that, whenever manufacturers make an extra $1,000 worth of output for distributors, they subsequently also produce an extra $200 worth of output, which they add to their finished stock. In practice, producers often do try to maintain their finished stocks at some level that is a fraction of their sales, and so this is a reasonable assumption. Such production represents an induced investment.

Table 11 shows what will happen if distributors make an autonomous decision to increase their stocks by $1,000 millions and manufacturers always produce 1.2 times their extra orders. The induced investment rate (δ), expressed as a fraction of ΔY, will then be .2/1.2, which is $\frac{1}{6}$. The marginal propensity to consume is still .75.

The "starting" line in Table 11 is the same as in Table 10. However, in the first step of the first round, it is seen that the manufacturers, when selling $1,000 (again eliminating 000,000) to distributors, produce $1,200 of output and income. The households (see line 1b) spend .75 of this, or $900, and hoard the balance of $300. Next (see line 1c) the distributors try to maintain their inventories at the new and higher level, and consequently order $900 of extra goods from the manufacturers for replacement. In the second round the consumers receive $1,080, consume $810 of this, and hoard $270, which is also the value of the manufacturers' extra investment. Total income is, of course, again equal to consumption plus investment.

Ultimately, after an infinite number of rounds, it is found that the distributors have released $1,000 of money, the manufacturers have released $2,000 of money, and the sum of $3,000 has been hoarded and saved by the consuming households. Distribu-

TABLE 11

COMPOUND MULTIPLICATION OF AUTONOMOUS INVESTMENT
(Dollars in Millions)

	MONEY TRANSFER			STOCK		REAL		
	Distrs.	Manufs.	Households	Distrs.	Manufs.	Investment	Consumption	Income
Start	−1000	+1000	0	+1000	−1000	0	0	0
Round 1 a	0	−1200	+1200	0	+1200	+1200	0	+1200
b	+900	0	−900	−900	0	−900	+900	0
c	−900	+900	0	+900	−900	0	0	0
Total Round 1	0	−300	+300	0	+300	+300	+900	+1200
Round 2 a	0	−1080	+1080	0	+1080	+1080	0	+1080
b	+810	0	−810	−810	0	−810	+810	0
c	−810	+810	0	+810	−810	0	0	0
Total Round 2	0	−270	+270	0	+270	+270	+810	+1080
Round 3	0	−243	+243	0	+243	+243	+729	+972
Round 4	0	−219	+219	0	+219	+219	+656	+875
Round 5	0	−197	+197	0	+197	+197	+590	+788
Round 6	0	−177	+177	0	+177	+177	+531	+709
Round 7	0	−159	+159	0	+159	+159	+488	+638
Round 8	0	−143	+143	0	+143	+143	+429	+574
Round 9	0	−129	+129	0	+129	+129	+386	+517
Round 10	0	−116	+116	0	+116	+116	+347	+465
and so on.								
Total All Rounds	(0)	(−3000)	(+3000)	(0)	(+3000)	(+3000)	(+9000)	(+12000)
All Rounds Plus Start	−1000	−2000	+3000	+1000	+2000	+3000	+9000	+12000

128

tors and manufacturers' stocks are increased by an amount equal
to the reduction in their money hoards. The total extra investment is hence $3,000 also. The final aggregate increase in con-
sumption is $9,000 and the aggregate increase in income is $12,000.
The compound investment multiplier (k_c) is 12.0.

It may be useful at this point to compare the simple investment
multiplier (k) and the compound investment multiplier (k_c). We
know that the value of k is 4.0 because the final increment in
income is four times the final total investment increment. However, the value of k_c is 12.0 because the final increment in income
is twelve times the value of the increase in *autonomous* investment. The difference in value between k and k_c is obviously due
to the induced investment. Actually, as we already know, k is
always equal to the reciprocal of the marginal propensity to save.
But k_c in the present example is equal to $1.0/(\frac{1}{4} - \frac{1}{6})$, which
is 12.0. The compound multiplier always has a higher value
than the simple multiplier, when there is induced investment,
because the compound multiplier refers to a narrower base (the
autonomous investment alone) while the simple multiplier relates
to a broader base (both autonomous and induced investment).
It is for this reason that governments which deliberately undertake public works investment to alleviate depressions hope that
private investments will be induced and that the consequences
of their original decision will hence be further multiplied.†

---

† Expressed differently, ΔY is k times ΔI_a (the autonomous investment of $1,000
millions) plus k times ΔI_i (the induced investment of $2,000 millions). The induced
investment is δ times ΔY where δ is the rate of induced investment expressed as a
decimal of income change. Symbolically,

Now
$$k_c \, \Delta I_a = k \, \Delta I = \mathrm{k}(\Delta I_a + \Delta I_i)$$

and
$$\Delta I_i = \left(\frac{1}{1 - \delta \cdot k} - 1 \right) \Delta I_a$$

Hence
$$k_c = \frac{\Delta Y}{\Delta I_a} = \frac{1}{\dfrac{1}{k} - \delta}$$

However, the reciprocal of the simple investment multiplier is the marginal propensity to save, and so we have

$$k_c = \frac{1}{\beta - \delta}$$

If β equals δ, k_c tends to infinity, and the economy is unstable.

Investment Multipliers vs. Spending Multipliers

It is probably time to reconcile what we have written about investment multipliers here with what was asserted concerning spending multipliers in Part II.

In Chapter 7 (pp. 97–98) there was an example of firms that suddenly reduced their spending time lag, and in so doing spent $40 billions, with the result that the flow of payments finally increased by approximately $535 billions. In the present chapter we have just analyzed a model in which distributors decided to invest $1 billion on extra inventories, so that national income finally, in the absence of induced investment, increased by $4 billions. How are these two examples related?

Mathematically, the increase in aggregate payments is equal to the extra spending divided by the marginal hoarding rate, while the increase in real income is equal to extra investment divided by the marginal saving rate.

Economically, the principle of the spending multiplier is more general and less significant for economic welfare. Price rises may rob the extra payments flow of any human benefits. The monetary phenomenon of the spending multiplier is so generally true that it almost amounts to a truism.

However, the principle of the investment multiplier is a special case that falls within the first. It is real income, real consumption, and real savings and investment that are considered by the investment multiplier, and not simply their money values. Moreover, instead of lumping all sorts of expenditures together, the theory of the investment multiplier distinguishes between the purchase of resources for investment and their purchase for consumption.

Sometimes the expenditure multiplier and the investment multiplier tend to be identical in practice. For example, if a government spends new money in constructing public works, and the price level remains unchanged, the two systems of multiplication may operate in parallel. The real investment of the economy is then matched perhaps by the extra money hoards, and the increased money income means more real income. However, coincidences of this kind are accidental, and theoretical identities should not be inferred from them. It is only reasonable to suppose that, after a prolonged period of expansion, prices will rise, and the increment in money flow will exceed that of real income (see Appendix C).

The Equilibrium Income

In any economy under given conditions there is only one level of national income that will prevail. Such an income is not necessarily compatible with full employment but is determined by the forces reflected in the economy's intended savings and intended investment schedules. The public, and the economy in general, intends to save a certain amount at each income level. The economy, and especially entrepreneurs, intends to invest a certain amount at each income level. These two sets of intentions will only be equal at one income level. The equilibrium income is that national income at which intended savings equal intended investment.

It is quite possible that the economy's schedule of intended savings against income follows the relationships set down in Table 12.

TABLE 12

INTENDED SAVINGS AND INVESTMENT SCHEDULES
(Dollars in Billions)

National Income Level	Public's Intended Savings	Entrepreneurs' Intended Investment
150	12	9
100	6	6
50	0	3

At high incomes the public wants to save more than entrepreneurs wish to invest and at low incomes entrepreneurs wish to invest more than the public wants to save. Normally the level of national income adjusts so that both intended savings and intended investment are equal. Incidentally, schedules of intended savings and intended investment, as set forth above, are only valid for a given rate of interest.

Figure 6 is based on the data of Table 12. Income is represented along the vertical axis and savings and investment along the horizontal. The income that will prevail is indicated by the intersection of the intended savings and intended investment schedules. Specifically, the equilibrium income is Y_1, or $100 billions. The actual savings and the actual investment are equal

to X_1, or $6 billions.   No change will occur in the equilibrium
income level unless one of the schedules shifts.

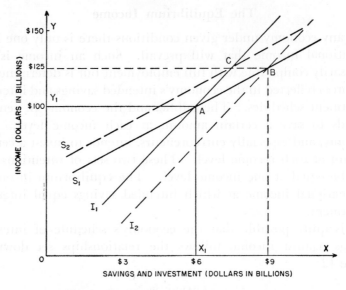

Fig. 6. Equilibrium Income Determination.

The savings line is flatter than the investment line, and so, in
view of our choice of axes, the marginal propensity to save (β)
is greater than delta (δ), the induced investment rate. In the
present case, using linear schedules as we are, it is apparent that,
if national income were $1.0 billion higher, the public would like
to save $.12 billion more but entrepreneurs would wish to invest
only $.06 billion more.   However, at the equilibrium income, the
average rate of intended saving is equal to the average rate of
intended investing, at $6 billions.

There could be no stable equilibrium income if the intended
marginal saving rate (β) did not exceed the intended marginal
investing rate (δ). Expressed differently, the savings schedule
must be flatter than the investment schedule, when income is represented along the vertical axis.   Should the positions of these two
schedules be reversed, the economic system would be unstable,
and any departure from an income of $100 billions would continue
at an accelerating pace.

It should be stressed that the principles determining equilibrium
income are entirely analogous to the operations that determine

price in a commodity market.   In a wholesale carrot market there
are buyers who will purchase a certain amount at a high price and
more at a lower price.   There are also sellers who wish to dispose
of a certain amount at a low price and more at a higher price.   At
high prices, intended purchases would be less than intended sales;
and, at low prices, intended purchases would be greater than intended sales.   Consequently, neither the high nor the low price
is theoretically possible.   The equilibrium price is the price that
equates intended purchases and intended sales and makes them
actual.   In a similar way the equilibrium income brings equality
to intended savings and intended investment and renders them
actual.

Changes in equilibrium income occur if there are new and
autonomous decisions regarding savings and investment.   Such
changes are reflected graphically in shifts in the intended savings
and intended schedules.   For example, an autonomous increase in
investment could be depicted by a shift in the investment schedule
to the right, in which case a higher equilibrium income would
result.   On the other hand induced investment decisions are
represented by the slope of an existing investment schedule.   In
general one can expect national income to rise if, at the
present income level, intended investment exceeds intended saving.   Hence, policies that increase the desire to invest at all incomes, and also policies designed to decrease the desire to save
at all incomes, will tend to raise the national income.

Supplementary Government Investment

The equilibrium income that occurs under *laissez-faire* policies
may fall short of "full employment" income.   "Full employment"
income will not result under *laissez-faire* if the public would
attempt to save more at full employment income than entrepreneurs would care to invest.   Full employment will not occur if
it would lead to oversaving or underinvestment.

It has therefore been suggested that the government—perhaps
through public works—should seek to supplement the inadequate
private investment of businessmen.

Let us suppose that the government undertakes a public works
program of $1.5 billions a year.   We shall also assume that this
program does not encroach upon private investment and so represents a pure addition to the economy's over-all investment.   Such

an autonomous investment decision will require a new investment schedule—always represented $1.5 billions further to the right—drawn horizontally parallel to the original investment schedule. For example, in Fig. 6, I_1 is the original private investment schedule and I_2 represents I_1 plus $1.5 billions of government investment. The intersection (at B) of the new total investment schedule (I_2) and the old savings schedule (S_1) indicates the new equilibrium national income of $125.0 billions.

The magnitude of actual savings and investment increases by $3.0 billions, from $6.0 billions at X_1 to $9.0 billions at X_2. At first glance this may seem paradoxical, considering that the extra investment furnished by the government is only $1.5 billions. The difference is the extra private investment that is called forth as income rises. A higher income means more consumption and a greater derived demand for investment. In this case the public works program of $1.5 billions leads directly to an additional private investment amounting to the same sum. When income-induced investment of this kind develops, the multiplier becomes compound in character.

The final increase in income can quickly be calculated from the formula already given for the compound multiplier. In this case, according to the slopes of the schedule in the figure, the marginal propensity to save is .12 and the induced investment rate is .06. Hence k_c must be equal to the government investment of $1.0/(.12 - .06)$, which is about 16.7. The increase in income will then be $25.0 billions as this is 16.7 times the sustained government investment of $1.5 billions. A check on this is that aggregate savings should increase by .12 of $25 billions, which is $3 billions, and so they do in the diagram.

A serious practical problem is that a public works program may perform services that otherwise would have been performed by private enterprise. Government spending will then reduce entrepreneurial spending. There will consequently be a different new schedule of intended investment. In terms of Fig. 6, the original investment schedule probably shifts to the left and becomes steeper. The leftwards shift means that entrepreneurs will now invest less at all incomes than before, so that the proper multiplicand to use in the formula is the net change in investment that remains after this reduction in entrepreneurial spending has been deducted from the government injection. The steeper slope of the investment schedule means that the induced investment, which is associated with an increased income, is also less than before.

Let us suppose that $1.5 billions of government investment has the twofold effect of reducing private investment by $.5 billion and lowering δ by .02 to .04.   The increase in national real income will then be, in billions,

$$\frac{\$1.5 - 0.5}{.12 - (.06 - .02)} = \frac{\$1.0}{.08} = \$12.5$$

Under these circumstances the net multiplicand is $1.0 billion (instead of $1.5 billions), the net compound multiplier is 12.5 (instead of 16.7), and so the rise in income is only $12.5 billions (instead of $25.0 billions).   Altogether, in this example, it takes twice as large a government investment of resources, as contrasted with private investments, to attain the same increased national income.

In the preceding model it has been supposed that the new government spending was on investments such as a Grand Coulee Dam or new facilities in a National Park.   However a great deal of new government spending may leave no permanent asset behind it.   And actually, from the point of view of income and employment theory, it does not make very much difference whether or not extra government spending is for real capital assets.   As explained in Appendix C, it is possible, when governments are involved, to reformulate our definitions of investment and saving. We can instead think of investment as being all private real investment plus government spending.   Aggregate savings must then be conceived as all private saving plus government taxes. The significance of this modification is that the present section can now be reread, upon the assumption that government "investment" includes some current account expenditures, such as aid to farmers.

Another point worth noting is that the deficit spending theory explained immediately above does not contemplate a cessation of government spending.   The analysis does not suggest that at some stage private enterprise will take over and carry on without the aid of any public investment.   The theory instead presupposes that both government investment and induced private investment continue hand in hand indefinitely.

A Reduction in Intended Savings

The people of an economy may change the rate at which they will save from a given income; as a result, there will be a new equilibrium income, if other forces, such as the entrepreneurial rate of intended investment, remain unchanged.

Let us suppose that an extension of government old age benefits alters the consumption function by reducing the incentive of people to save against poverty during their declining years. Let us suppose this saving reduction is $1.5 billions a year. The intended savings schedule therefore shifts to the left from S_1 to S_2 in Fig. 6. The new intersection of S_2 and I_1, which is at C, indicates a new equilibrium income of $125.0 billions.

It is noteworthy that a reduction in the rate of intended saving of $1.5 billions increases the actual rate of saving from $6.0 billions to $7.5 billions a year. The cause of this seemingly paradoxical outcome is that an autonomous reduction in intended saving increases income, and more induced saving always occurs at higher incomes. A weakening of the will to save by the public increases the investment of the economy!

Summary

The level of income, and hence employment, tends to be determined by the schedules of intended savings and intended investment. National income will remain unchanged if intended investment and intended savings are equal at that income level. If intended investment should exceed intended savings at any given income level, there will be a tendency for national income to rise.

An autonomous increment in intended investment will have a multiple effect on national income. The extent of this multiplication depends upon the consumption function and more especially upon the marginal propensity to consume. Actually the simple investment multiplier (k) is always equal to $1.0/(1 - \alpha)$, where α is equal to the marginal propensity to consume, or alternatively to $1.0/\beta$ where β is the marginal propensity to save. However an autonomous increase in intended investment may bring about induced and intentional investments. In this case the original and autonomous investment will have a compounded effect. The compound investment multiplier (k_c) is equal to

$1.0/(\beta - \delta)$ where δ is the rate of induced investment expressed as a decimal of income increase. The final increment in income will be k_o times the original autonomous investment.

Government spending *may* help to raise *real* income levels. The effect of government spending on money incomes can be the same whether it occurs for real investment goods or not. Actually in these models, investment could mean private real investment plus government deficits. Government deficit spending schemes naturally have a greater effect on income if they occasion induced investments. In all these analyses it is supposed that the new investments, whether autonomous or induced, are sustained period after period. We have not considered cases where extra investment is undertaken during only one isolated year.

Statements for Consideration

1. All estimated values for k are highly theoretical, since they will not be achieved until the infinitely remote future, and hence no practical politician should bother himself about the investment multiplier. *Evaluate*
2. If aggregate private investment is independent of the income level, the compound investment multiplier will equal k in value. *Discuss*
3. The "investment" increment which constitutes the denominator of the k ratio may refer to an increment of government deficit, an increment of private real investment, or both. *Discuss*
4. The private investment schedule may not be independent of government "investment" but may instead shift in the direction opposite from the latter. *Explain*
5. ΔY will be $10 billions when X_a is $1 billion, β is .2, and δ is .1. *Explain*
6. A Presidential election that investors considered "favorable" might so alter private investment propensities at all income levels that government deficit spending, if it existed before, might be terminated without a reduction in national income. *Discuss*
7. The investment multiplier only works upon income in an upwards direction. *Evaluate*
8. An increase in intended saving—at each income level—will very likely lead to reduced actual saving. *Explain*
9. Savings must equal investment just as the number of carrots bought and sold in a given market must be equal. *Discuss*

References

Dillard, D., *The Economics of John Maynard Keynes,* Chapter 5. New York: Prentice-Hall, 1948.

Haberler, G., "Mr. Keynes' Theory of the Multiplier," *Zeitschrift für Nationalökonomie,* VII, 1936. Also in *Readings in Business Cycle Theory.*

Keynes, J. M., *The General Theory of Employment, Interest and Money,* Book III. New York: Harcourt, Brace, 1936.

Morgan, T., *Income and Employment,* Chapter 8. New York: Prentice-Hall, 1947.

Smithies, A., "The Multiplier," *American Economic Review,* May 1948.

10

Inducements to Invest

In view of the importance of extra investment in multiplying income, as outlined in the preceding chapter, it is equally important to understand the reasons that bring people, and especially firms, to invest. All investments inevitably involve some degree of risk, and so there is a general reluctance on the part of firms to purchase capital goods unless some special inducement exists. Moreover, there is always an interest cost—explicit or implicit—attached to investment. Firms must either borrow money (in which case they pay interest) or they invest their own (in which case they forego a return from lending their funds). It is only when expectations of firms and entrepreneurs are sufficiently promising that this normal state of reluctance is overcome and additional investment occurs.

Firms can add to their investments in many ways, some intended and some less intended, some resulting primarily from income changes and others being brought about by movements in interest rates. The main types of investment are in fixed capital, working capital, and finished output inventions. Fixed capital investment, in connection with which the rate of interest may be relatively most important, may be prompted by a desire to obtain more durable equipment, to substitute fixed capital for other factors of production such as labor, or to satisfy an increased demand for output.

Finished Output Inventories

Firms not infrequently discover that the market for their output has declined more rapidly than their curtailment of production, in which event they may find themselves with more unsold output than is either normal or intended. However, once the situation has arisen, a firm can often elect whether to rid itself of its output

139

inventories through cutting prices or to wait in the expectation of better times. The inducement is then the belief in higher prices to come. The deterrent is the implicit interest cost in holding wealth in the form of inventories, for if the output were sold, the proceeds would be available for reinvestment. If the relevant interest rate is 6 per cent, a firm may only be willing to keep its output off the market if it believes that prices will rise at least 6 per cent during the coming twelve months, after deducting costs of storage, spoilage, and so forth. The higher the rate of interest, the greater must be the expected price improvement before firms will deliberately refuse to sell at the prices of the moment, and so in effect decide to invest in output inventories.

Working Capital Investment

Firms may find themselves investing in real working capital for various reasons.

If prices of materials are expected to rise, firms will tend to purchase ahead of their immediate needs, especially if the expected price rise is believed to be considerable or immediate and if the interest cost of hiring money for this purpose is not too great. Naturally, when materials prices are falling, firms tend to disinvest by postponing their purchases. In view of the relatively large fluctuations in materials prices that occur from year to year, the interest consideration is outweighed, in most instances, by the price expectations of managements.

Real working capital may increase because after purchase commitments were made business fell off and output was curtailed. Firms may feel disinclined to work the materials up into a more finished form should this occur. Such reluctance will be increased if the cost of hiring the funds needed to perform this intermediate work is high.

If a firm's operations are expanding, it will need more working capital, quite apart from any expectations it may possess regarding output prices or materials prices. Such an expansion in a particular firm's business may be because it is taking trade away from rivals or because the national income is growing. In this latter event, aggregate national income is probably more of an immediate determinant of the increment in working capital than the rate of interest. Indirectly though, the interest rate still plays a part, for it probably helped to determine the previous and subsequent proportions in which working capital and other factors of production were and are employed.

Fixed Capital Investment

As already indicated, in Chapter 8, firms will tend to invest in extra capital, particularly in extra fixed capital, if the estimated marginal efficiency of capital exceeds the relevant and prevailing rate of interest. Hence it is high time to examine the marginal-efficiency-of-capital concept more closely and then to look behind it. In the background, in turn determining the marginal efficiency of capital, are many complications of everyday business life.

Marginal-Efficiency-of-Capital Mathematics

The earning efficiency of a capital good can be measured just as a gasoline engine can be rated for its ability to convert fuel into power. The earning efficiency of a particular asset is that discount rate which will make the total present value of all its future net income receipts equal to its supply price. In other words, capital efficiency depends upon the shape and height of an asset's income stream, as well as upon its cost of acquisition.

The general formula for calculating the capital efficiency of a particular asset is rather complicated and lengthy to compute. A useful short cut is first to ascertain the present value of the asset's net income stream when discounted, as explained in the following paragraph, by the expected interest rate. It really does not matter that we cannot measure its efficiency exactly without extensive computing. The really important knowledge is whether an asset's efficiency is greater (or less) than the interest rate so that it is a sound (or unsound) investment. An entrepreneur should logically acquire a piece of capital whose supply price is less than the present value of its net income stream when discounted at the expected rate of interest.

The first step then in reaching an investment decision is to calculate the present value of a prospective net yield stream. If the current rate of interest is 5 per cent, the discounted present value of $100 to be received *one* year from now will be $100/(1.05) or $95. The present value of $100 to be received *two* years from now will be $100/(1.05)^2 or $91. And the present value of a $100 receipt n years from now will be $100/(1.05)^n$. The present value of an asset that will yield $100 net a year for n years is given by the expression

$$\$100/(1.05) + \$100/(1.05)^2 + \$100/(1.05)^3 + \cdots + 100/(1.05)^n$$

It can be shown mathematically that this expression simplifies to $100/(0.05)$ in the special case where the income stream is perpetual and constant.

However, let us suppose a more probable case, and assume that a firm is contemplating the purchase of a piece of equipment (A) that will yield a net income of $100 a year for 10 years, at which date it suddenly collapses like the fabulous one-horse shay. The present value of this limited income stream, computed according to the formula set forth in the preceding paragraph, is $772. If the supply price of this asset is $650, as we shall suppose, the firm should acquire the asset. The general rule is that, if the present value of an asset exceeds its cost of acquisition, the efficiency of capital exceeds the interest rate, and investment should take place.

So far we have discussed the efficiency of alternative and unique assets. Sometimes the question is how many *units* of some given kind of asset should be acquired. The answer is that investment should proceed, unit by unit, until the present value of the net income stream of the marginal unit of capital is equal to, or just exceeds, its cost of acquisition.

For example, a firm may need a number of machines of type A, but the exact number it installs is discretionary, depending in part upon the interest rate. The firm's management estimates that, as more and more A assets are added, the net income stream attributable to the "last" additional unit falls lower and lower. The actually estimated net incomes of these marginal capital units are listed in the second column of Table 13. Each machine is expected to have a service life of ten years. If 5 per cent is thought to be the appropriate rate for discounting these future income streams, the present value of the first machine ($100 yearly income) is $772, that of the second machine ($90 yearly income) is $695, that of the third machine ($80 yearly income) is $618, and so on. Presumably the firm will buy two of these type A machines if their supply price is $650, and so invest a total of $1,300. However, if the rate of discount had been 3 per cent instead of 5 per cent, the present values of these successive capital units would have been $853, $768, $682, and so on according to the fourth column of Table 13. At the same supply price of $650 per machine, the firm will now purchase three units, and invest a total of $1,950.

TABLE 13

PRESENT VALUES OF ALTERNATIVE ASSETS
(In Dollar Values)

MACHINE UNIT	TYPE "A" MACHINE			TYPE "B" MACHINE			TYPE "C" MACHINE		
	Yearly Net Income	Present Value		Yearly Net Income	Present Value		Yearly Net Income	Present Value	
		@ 5%	@ 3%		@ 5%	@ 3%		@ 5%	@ 3%
#1	100	772	853	100	830	925	150	1158	1279
2	90	695	768	90	747	833	140	1081	1194
3	80	618	682	80	664	740	130	1004	1109
4	70	540	597	70	581	648	120	926	1026
5	60	463	512	60	498	555	110	849	938

N. B. Type B machines have a service life of 11 years; all others have service lives of 10 years.

The lower the rate of interest, other things equal, the greater the present value of an asset, and the larger the likelihood that more real capital units will be purchased, with the result that investment will increase.

The Economics of Capital Efficiency

So far this discussion of the marginal-efficiency-of-capital concept has necessarily been in terms of mathematics rather than obvious economics. Now we must examine the scheme of commercial circumstances upon which the marginal efficiency of capital depends. Some of the more important determinants are shown in Fig. 7.

As already stated, capital "efficiency" depends upon (a) the cost of acquiring the capital asset either by direct construction or purchase and (b) its estimated future net income stream. The former is probably known but the latter can be estimated only upon the basis of subsidiary conjectures. The estimated future net income stream of an asset depends in turn upon (c) its future gross receipts stream and (d) its future deductions from receipts. Obviously there are many forces at work in determining the gross receipts stream. Some of the more important of these are probably (e) the incomes of buyers and (f) the prices of immediate competitors. On the other hand, deductions from receipts include the cost (g) of labor used directly with the capital asset, (h) of materials processed by the fixed capital, and (i) of the asset's annual depreciation. The above is by no means an exhaustive list of the factors affecting the "efficiency" of a specific asset.

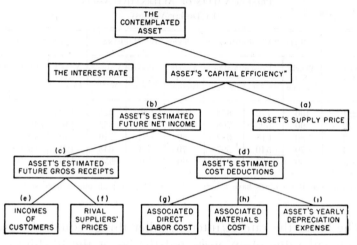

Fig. 7. Factors in Deciding to Invest.

By way of illustration, let us consider the case of a dishpan manufacturer, who is contemplating the addition of some punch presses. He will be more inclined to invest further in this kind of fixed capital if the price of punch presses declines, his competitors' prices rise, household incomes increase, labor cost declines, the prices of aluminum and cast-iron fall, or the depreciation rate is reduced. Some of these developments might operate in more ways than one. A decline in wages might reduce the cost of punch presses, and also reduce deductions from receipts, thus providing a double inducement to invest. On the other hand a general wage reduction throughout the economy might decrease households' income and hence the gross receipts stream.

By way of summary, the efficiency of capital, whether total or marginal, will increase when (1) demand for the product increases, (2) the cost of *other* goods and services used in making the product decreases, or (3) the supply price of the capital good falls. Any one of these changes will normally bring about an increased investment at an unchanged rate of interest. Incidentally, it is difficult for the state to alter the factors that determine the efficiency of capital for firms in general; the rate of interest is probably more susceptible to public policy than most.

How Capitalistic Should a Firm Be?

A given firm can be more or less capitalistic. By this we mean that it can use fixed capital of more or less value, depending upon which course it believes to be most profitable in relation to the value of its annual throughput of inputs and outputs. Thus a firm that "turns its fixed capital over every five years," as some public utilities do, is relatively far more capitalistic than a hamburger stand business that may have a total investment of $500, and yet gross $15,000 a year. When a firm becomes more capitalistic in this sense, it is investing relative to the scope of its operations.

There are a variety of reasons why firms become relatively more capitalistic and thereby invest. They may decide that more durable—and costly—equipment should be installed. They may decide that it would be more profitable to hire less direct labor and instead have the work performed to a greater extent by capital equipment. They may decide that they should enlarge capacity in order to be able to increase sales in periods of abnormally strong demand.

All these decisions will be stimulated by a fall in interest rates. In each case the effect of a lower discount rate is to increase the present value of future money receipts and/or payments and so dictate a reconsideration of managerial policies. In order to illustrate the logic of these principles, we shall now consider examples of investment in extra durability, in extra productivity, and in extra capacity.

Investment in Durability. Most firms can choose between assets having the same use but differing in durability. Naturally, the longer-lived assets usually cost more to construct, and hence to acquire. In these cases firms must estimate the present value of the extra net income obtainable from the additional service years of a more durable asset's life. The lower the rate of interest and discount, the greater the present value of these extra income payments, and the more willing is the firm to pay the extra price exacted for a longer service life.

Let us suppose that the manufacturers of the machine of Table 13 now offer two alternative models. Type *A*, as we have seen, costs $650 and has a service life of 10 years. Type *B*, the new alternative, is priced at $712 and has a service life of 11 years. Our firm previously bought two *A* machines when interest rates were 5 per cent and three *A* machines when interest rates were 3 per cent. How should its management react to this new situation?

Management must compute the present values of successive units of *B* machines. It must decide whether the increase in purchase price of $62 is justified by the present value of the eleventh year's net income. In the case of a second *B* machine, which has a yearly net income of $90, its present value is $747 at 5 per cent discount and $833 at 3 per cent discount. (See the sixth and seventh columns of the table.) Hence, in view of the prices of *A* and *B*, the firm would continue to buy 2 units of *A* if the rate of interest were 5 per cent. However, if the interest rate were 3 per cent, it would purchase 3 units of *B*. In this case a reduction in the interest rate increases investment from 2 units of *A* ($1,300) to 3 units of *B* ($2,136).

Governments may also determine the durability of public works with an eye on the interest rate. For instance, should city sidewalks be made cheaply of wood to last 15 years, or expensively with macadam to last 25 years? Logically this and other similar problems depend in large measure upon the rate of interest.

Investment in Productivity. At any time, given the state of technical knowledge, designers and manufacturers produce equipment items of greater or lesser productivity. Increases in productivity of this kind usually take the form of reducing the amount of direct labor or processed material needed per unit of output. But too much productivity may not pay if it is too dearly bought and the interest rate is too high.

Let us suppose that the management of our firm can choose, when the date for replacement arrives, between installing *A* machines again or *C* machines. The new *C* machines are remarkable, not only for their price of $1,055 each, but because they should yield a net annual income of $150 for 10 years. The higher net income of the more productive *C* model is due to its labor-saving characteristics; it is estimated that, after allowing for its increased depreciation expense, it will save $50 a year in wages. Hence, the yearly net income of the first *C* machine to be installed will be $150, and so on according to the eighth column of Table 13. Again, what should management do?

If the interest rate is 5 per cent, the firm's management will not buy any C machines, because the net gain on two A machines ($167) is greater than the net gain on two C machines ($129). However, if the relevant discount rate is 3 per cent, the firm will buy three units of C (yielding $417 gain) instead of three units of A (yielding $353 gain). It will increase its investment from $1,950 to $3,165 because of the fall in interest rates.

At all times both firms and governments must choose between buying their future labor requirements in advance, and indirectly in the form of capital, or directly and from week to week in the usual way. If the rate of interest is high, the present value of the wages that might be saved in far distant years is not very great, and is perhaps insufficient to justify the extra expense of more productive equipment. The choice is not determined so much by the general level of wages, because these in turn also influence the supply prices of fixed capital, but rather by the interest rate's balancing of present and future payments.

Investment of this kind, undertaken to avoid the future payment of direct labor, will not normally lead to mass unemployment. In fact there are many reasons for expecting the opposite. Labor is now needed at once to produce and process the materials from which fixed capital is made. The immediate supply of jobs of one kind or another should increase. Also, the additional investment may multiply incomes, and occasion substitute, or even additional, jobs for workers.

Investment in Capacity. In many lines of production, operations fluctuate according to a fairly regular pattern. Although annual operations may be fairly constant, certain months of the year are always more active, either because of seasonal demands for output (for example, beer cans) or of seasonal supplies of inputs (for example, meat packing). These fluctuations have little to do with fluctuations in national income, but are instead based on seasonal changes in agricultural production and weather, and hence are roughly predictable.

If a firm's productive capacity is limited to its rate of minimum need throughout the year, some of the profits of peak activity periods may have to be foregone. On the other hand, if capacity is related to peak needs, losses may be incurred in slack seasons. Such a dilemma may be particularly painful if storage is impracticable.

In order to decide this problem logically, the management of a firm should attempt to estimate the amount of net income it will not obtain in certain months because of lack of capacity. The present value of these foregone profits in future years must also be estimated, and this of course involves a consideration of the rate of interest. If the appropriate rate for discounting is low, the present value of these border-line profits will be high.

The Principle of Acceleration

In many lines of economic activity firms do not enlarge capacity, or make other additional investments needed when output increases, until a time of unusually strong demand and high national income is upon them. There are many reasons for this lack of advance planning and the most important explanation is probably that cyclical fluctuations, unlike seasonal variations, are largely unforeseeable. Another consideration may be that, in times of depression, firms may have neither the funds nor the credit to embark upon plant expansion for prosperity even if they so desire.

When a firm is already operating at capacity, and a further increase in demand prompts it to increase output by some percentage, its purchases of equipment and other capital items will very probably increase more than proportionately. The basic reason for this phenomenon, as we shall see, is that fixed capital items have a service life longer than a year. The fact that a given percentage increase in output will, under certain circumstances, lead to a larger percentage increase in capital investment is often called the principle of acceleration.

A simple example of the principle of acceleration is displayed in Table 14. In this table, a firm is assumed to have been producing at a constant capacity rate of 100 output units a year for several years up to and including 1946. Technical factors compel the installation and maintenance of one machine for every 5 annual output units. These machines have a service life of 10 years each. Normally the firm operates 20 machines and on an average replaces 2 of them each year. In 1947, however, the management decides to increase capacity so that production can be raised to 110 output units annually. Hence two additional machines will be required, and as usual 2 old machines must be replaced, so that the firm's purchases of machines will be 4 instead of 2 in 1947. A 10 per cent increase in output has prompted a 100 per cent increase in gross capital investment. Similarly, if output in 1948 is raised from 110 units to 150 units, machinery purchases will increase from 4 units to 10 units. If output is held steady, as it is in 1949, machinery purchases fall back to a replacement rate. And if output is cut in 1950, there may be surplus capacity, and over-aged equipment may not even be replaced, so that gross investment declines to zero. In this last case a 14 per cent fall in output for sale occasioned a 100 per cent fall in machine purchases.

TABLE 14

ILLUSTRATION OF PRINCIPLE OF ACCELERATION
(Single Firm Model)

YEAR	PLANNED OUTPUT	NUMBER MACHINES NEEDED	STOCK OF MACHINES Jan.	STOCK OF MACHINES Dec.	INVESTMENT IN MACHINES Replaced	INVESTMENT IN MACHINES Added	INVESTMENT IN MACHINES Total
1946 and previously	100	20	20	18	2	0	2
1947	110	22	20	18	2	2	4
1948	150	30	22	20	2	8	10
1949	150	30	30	28	2	0	2
1950	130	26	30	28	0	0	0

Note. It is assumed that one machine is needed for every 5 units of output and that each machine has a service life of 10 years.

It should be noted that there is a certain asymmetry in the relation of output sales to equipment purchases as between the upswing and the downswing. During a period of steady and constant sales volume, equipment purchases will be limited to replacement. It is only when original capacity is exceeded that the full force of the acceleration principle operates during the upswing. On the other hand, during a downswing, a relatively small cut in output may render existing equipment redundant, so that when scrapped it is not replaced, and current gross investment in such equipment ceases absolutely. For a particular firm, these changes appear rather discontinuous; for instance, the rate of investment is very different after attainment of capacity operations than before. However, an economy comprises many firms, and different firms reach their respective capacities at different moments during the upswing, so that for an entire economy the principle of acceleration may act more smoothly. But it is still questionable whether, over short periods of time, the relation be-

tween output and fixed capital is the same during the upswing
as during the downswing (see Appendix B).

The principle of acceleration is one of the arguments often
used in support of pump-priming schemes such as that discussed
in Chapter 9. It is often contended that, if government would
keep priming the pump, private investment would be stimulated
to supplement the government spending. The extent to which
private investment may be induced by rising national income depends rather upon the force of the principle of acceleration and
upon whether enough firms reach capacity operations. In general the leverage of the acceleration principle is more pronounced
the longer the service life of equipment. Hence, as there appears
to be a secular tendency for the level of interest rates to fall, and
the economy in consequence tends to invest in more and more
durable capital, greater swings in fixed capital investment appear
more likely.

Which Inducement Dominates?

The foregoing recital of the factors that induce firms to invest
has mentioned price expectations, income changes, and all the
varied circumstances that can affect estimates of future net income
streams. Hence the rate of interest is obviously not the only
determinant of investment. Is it even an important one?

The truth of the matter is that a firm invests because it thinks
it sees an opportunity to profit from so doing. A profit expectation is a necessary prerequisite for investment; if this expectation
of profit is lacking, the rate of interest is inconsequential. However the rate of interest does play a part—small or large as the
case may be—in assessing the possibility of future profits through
investment.

Investment in inventories, whether they comprise materials,
work in process, or finished outputs, is probably governed primarily by price expectations. However, given these price expectations, the rate of interest is not an insignificant factor. If
interest rates are high, firms will buy less ahead of needs when
prices are expected to rise, and will hold off buying even longer
during a price decline.

Investment in plant and equipment is largely governed by the
level of actual or expected national income. High income levels
usually mean high sales volume, and hence high production rates,

and hence an enlargement of capacity. And conversely, if sales are considerably below capacity for most firms, so that they already have redundant plants and equipment, a drop in interest rates will not be very effective in inducing firms to invest in extra fixed capital. During short periods, which are no longer than a single phase of the business cycle, sales volume and national income doubtlessly outweigh the interest rate in the investment calculations of management. However, it is incorrect to assume that the rate of interest has no influence even in these circumstances. If interest rates are high, firms may invest later and more modestly during an upswing, and disinvest sooner and more drastically during a downswing.

In both the matter of inventory investment and fixed investments it is clear that expectations are a vital part of the investment decision. In the case of inventories the relevant expectations concern price, and in the case of fixed capital investment the relevant expectations involve general income levels. Expectations, based as they are on so many emotional subjective factors, tend to be mercurial. If expectations change to a greater relative extent than does the rate of interest—which seems probable—it is reasonable to suppose that interest rates are not the most important determinant of investment over short periods of time.

Nevertheless, there are always some lines of production in which, because of the abnormal importance of fixed capital costs, the rate of interest is always an obvious determinant of investment. In the case of railroads, oil refineries, and electric power generation, for example, a very high proportion of the total cost per unit of output is attributable to interest expense. Thus, if interest expense is 40 per cent of total unit costs, a drop in the applicable interest rate from 4 to 3 per cent will lower unit costs by 10 per cent. Certain large construction projects such as bridges and dams, the subsequent operation of which involves little direct expense for labor and power, may hinge upon the interest rate. Some people believe that in any economy there are many large capital projects poised on the edge of implementation and only awaiting a drop in the rate of interest to push them over into actuality.

It is in the long run that the interest rate is more apt to come into its own. If interest rates are low, firms will tend to purchase capital of greater durability, and so invest more. If interest rates are low, firms will tend to use more capital relative to direct labor, and so invest more. If interest rates are low, firms will be more willing to endure overcapacity during slack seasons in order to produce and sell more during periods of active demand, and so again they will tend to invest more. These tendencies may not be particularly strong in any specific situation, but they operate continuously and universally. Over very long periods of time, the rate of interest may outweigh expectations of income and price in influencing the average level of investment over time, just as the tide prevails over the surf in determining the ocean's edge.

Over moderately long periods of time, income levels and interest rates jointly induce investment, and then it is probably invalid to analyze investment either solely in terms of income levels or solely in terms of interest rates. The intention to invest is then not a two-variable schedule, but a three-dimensional surface, linking investment to interest rates and income levels. This approach is developed in the chapter after next.

Statements for Consideration

1. One need not compute the marginal efficiency of capital if one can estimate the present value of an asset's net income stream and one knows its present cost of acquisition. *Explain*
2. The mathematics of computing an asset's present value are relatively simple: it is knowing the future gross receipts and expenses streams that is difficult. *Discuss*
3. A drop in the price of steel might increase the capital efficiency of some assets in two ways *Explain*
4. The interest rate probably has little effect on working capital, for its influence is swamped by price and business expectations.
   Exemplify
5. The greater expense of more durable assets may be offset in an investor's mind if interest rates fall. *Explain*
6. If firms prepaid all their wages for years in advance, as they do prepay for the services of fixed capital, a change in interest rates might not affect the degree of direct labor productivity they seek in the equipment they buy. *Explain*
7. If interest rates are high, it may often be the better part of business prudence to keep capacity below peak period demand.
   Explain
8. The interest rate probably has a greater effect on investment levels in the long run than it has from one phase to another of the business cycle. *Evaluate*

9. One asset will have a greater capital value than another if it is expected to earn a greater total net income during its service life.

Evaluate

References

Dillard, D., *The Economics of John Maynard Keynes,* Chapter 7. New York: Prentice-Hall, 1948.

Fisher, I., *The Theory of Interest,* Chapter 7. New York: Macmillan, 1930.

Hart, A. G., "Uncertainty and Inducements to Invest," *Review of Economic Studies,* October 1940.

Keynes, J. M., *The General Theory of Employment, Interest and Money,* Book IV. New York: Harcourt, Brace, 1936.

Morgan, T., *Income and Employment,* Chapters 9, 15. New York: Prentice-Hall, 1947.

11

Interest and Liquidity

THE immediate reason for discussing interest rates at this junc-
ture is that the level of interest rates plays a large part, although
no one is sure how large a part, in determining the volume of investment. The gist of the preceding chapter has been that a fall
in the interest rate, unless certain expectations also change adversely, will induce firms to invest. It is therefore of prime
importance that we learn something of the forces that move interest rates up and down.

During the last two decades, the demand of firms and households for liquidity, i.e., the desire to hold some wealth in the
form of money, has been advanced as a theory of interest. The
liquidity theory of interest, so stressed in modern income theory,
involves a special approach to money, an approach that has already
been mentioned. This is the cash balances approach, briefly
described in Part II.

The relation between the demand for wealth in money form
and the national stock of money available to satisfy this demand
is the heart of the liquidity theory of interest. However this
theory is generally recognized to be only a partial explanation of
why interest is paid for the use of money. Supplementary reasons, and a more complete theory of interest, will be advanced
in Part V.

The Demand for Cash Balances

Why don't people spend their cash balances, for either consumer or investment goods, rather than hold money in the form
of demand deposits and legal tender currency?

Before considering motives for holding cash balances, it might
be advisable to ascertain first who it is that holds money. Out of
the $100-odd billions, excluding interest-earning time deposits,
held in the United States of recent years, how much was held by
whom? Approximately 40 per cent was held by corporations, 20

per cent by unincorporated firms, 10 per cent by state and local governments, and 30 per cent by households. These holdings were most unequally distributed in size. Less than one per cent of the holdings exceeded $25,000 but in the aggregate these amounted to about half the total money stock. About four per cent of all holdings were of $5,000 each or more and these in the aggregate accounted for about two-thirds of the money stock. Thus, about 96 per cent of all demand deposits were below $5,000 each, but these altogether contained only one-third of the national money stock.

On the whole, one might generalize by saying that about one-third of the money stock is held by households (in small amounts averaging perhaps only a few hundred dollars each) and about two-thirds by firms (in large amounts averaging fifty thousand dollars or more each). There is hence a cleavage, both in the kind of holder and in the size of the average holding. A different set of motives applies to the holding of small cash balances by households and of large cash balances by firms.

It is customary to specify three motives for holding cash, some of which overlap, and some of which apply more to firms than to households. These three motives are commonly termed the transaction motive, the precautionary motive, and the speculative motive. The same dollars in a cash balance may satisfy more than one motive at the same time.

Transaction Motive

Firms and households make payments that are not exactly synchronized with their receipts. A man who earns $50 a week will probably have to keep an average cash holding of $25. An independent proprietor with a milk route may have to pay cash for his milk supplies but wait an average of two weeks to bill his customers once a month. A man traveling away from home, in an area where he is not known, will have to pay as he goes. "Saving up" funds to buy a car or a security may also be included here.

Precautionary Motive

Households often try to save against an emergency, such as a sickness in the family; if such an emergency occurs, they want money rather than some property or security that they may only be able to sell suddenly at a loss. Firms never know when an unexpected and adverse turn of business will place them under a financial strain; when such times occur, they do not wish to be dependent upon the willingness of a banker to tide them over. During depressions the precautionary motive is stronger than usual. Not only are dangers such as personal unemployment and business failure more evident, but the cost and difficulty of raising emergency funds is also seen to be greater.

Speculative Motive

Many firms and some households, especially during depression periods, have the funds to purchase durable goods and earning assets, but hold off buying in the expectation of declining prices. A corporation may defer the construction of a new factory until building costs come down. A financier, believing that a future increase in interest rates will lower the prices of fixed income securities, may postpone financial investment. The speculative motive obviously tends to wax and wane with periods of falling and rising prices respectively.

It is hard to know which one of these motives is quantitatively most important in explaining the existing cash balances of households on the one hand and of firms on the other. Perhaps, in the case of households, the transaction motive is relatively the strongest and the most sustained over time. People of modest means probably give little heed to the speculative motive, except in periods of marked price decline, but rather spend what they can. Government social security schemes, health and accident insurance plans, and so forth obviously are weakening the precautionary motive as it applies to households. During periods of declining business activity, the speculative motive may swallow up the other two motives, in the sense that the balances that are accumulated in anticipation of price and cost declines might in better times have been held as emergency and transaction funds.

Incidentally, these three motives explain, not so much why firms and households *save,* but why they *hoard* (i.e., hold cash). Presumably, if it were not for the force of these motives, people who saved would make financial investments that would earn them a return, whether as interest, dividends, or profits. The stronger these motives, the greater their cash balances, and the higher the interest rates they will forego.

Interest the Price of Money

The amount of their wealth that people want to hold in money varies for different reasons. It is obvious that people will always keep some money, even though they sacrifice interest and other earnings, because they prefer liquidity to investment. However, the *amount* of money they wish to keep instead of holding other forms of wealth need not be constant. For example, it increases as incomes rise, because people are then buying more expensive goods more frequently. Also, it decreases as the interest rate rises, partly because any preference for liquidity is then being penalized more severely, but also because the likelihood of an imminent fall in interest rates is then stronger.

Accordingly it is possible to conceive of a demand schedule for money, which slopes downwards to the left, assuming that the vertical axis shows the interest rate and the horizontal axis, *stretching from right to left,* represents the total amount of money demanded by all individuals and business units. Such a schedule of demand prices for money relates to a given aggregate income for the economy. Also it is only valid for a prescribed time period (see Fig. 8).

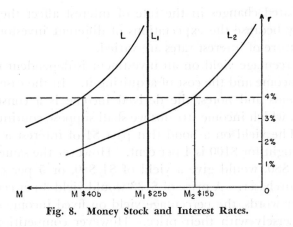

Fig. 8. **Money Stock and Interest Rates.**

The stock of money in the economy (i.e., the value of legal tender in circulation and checking deposits in private banks) is relatively fixed. Of course this money is constantly changing hands, so that one man may hold less money and another more money than before, but the total possession of money can only be altered by the government and the banks. In the absence of bank credit expansion or contraction, or government issuance of new legal tender, the stock of money will not change. It can be represented as a vertical straight line at M in Fig. 8.

The interest rate is the price that equates the demand for money (L) with the available stock of money (M). Accordingly the intersection of the demand and supply schedules in Fig. 8 indicates the rate of interest (4%) that will prevail under the circumstances depicted there. The slope of the demand schedule shows that, *if* the rate of interest could rise, people would want to hold less money than the available stock; however, this would be impossible, unless the stock of money were correspondingly reduced, because there cannot be unowned money in existence.

The onset of a financial panic, with its attendant emphasis on liquidity, may temporarily increase the demand for money through the calling of loans, and so raise interest rates. Action by the monetary authorities to increase the stock of money will shift the vertical supply schedule to the left and initially tend to lower interest rates. In other words, shifts in the demand or supply of money will alter its price of hire.

Interest Expectations and Money Demand

Anticipated changes in the rate of interest affect the demand for money because the expectations of different investors regarding the future of interest rates are varied.

The percentage yield on an investment is dependent upon the derived income and the cost of acquiring it. In the case of interest on bonds and notes, the derived income is a constant sum each year, which income streams we shall suppose continue indefinitely. The yield on a bond that pays $4 of interest a year and can be bought for $100 is 4 per cent. However the same bond, if priced at $80, would give a yield of $4/$80, or 5 per cent, to a current purchaser. A price of $133 would yield 3 per cent.

In other words, the percentage yield on fixed income securities varies inversely with their price. However competition among investors keeps the yield on current purchases equal to the prevailing rate of interest. Hence security prices rise when interest rates fall and *vice versa*.

A single investor, who thinks that interest rates will soon rise, and that current interest rates are therefore unduly low relative to the near future, should sell fixed income securities now, hold cash until interest rates have risen as he anticipates, and then reinvest, possibly in the same kind of security. For example, suppose A now owns a bond which pays $4 interest a year, and which is currently priced at $133, so that the current interest is presumably 3 per cent. Investor A, but not the financial world as a whole, believes that interest rates will soon rise to 5 per cent, in which case the price of securities paying a fixed income of $4 a year should fall to $80. Consequently he sells his bond now for $133 and waits to repurchase it later at $80. If he alone has anticipated the future course of interest rates correctly, he will eventually have the same dollar income, and $53 in money besides.

An investor who expects interest rates to rise will shift from bonds to money while he waits for his predictions to be realized. Conversely, an investor who expects interest rates to fall, which means that the prices of fixed income securities will rise, hurries to shift out of money into bonds before his anticipations materialize. If investors, as a group, are evenly divided in their expectations, the aggregate amount of money which they wish to hold will remain the same.

However, if the preponderant opinion is that interest rates will rise, the shift from bonds into money will be stronger than the movement from money into bonds. The prices of bonds will therefore fall. Such an outcome in effect constitutes a rise in interest rates. Prospects become actualities if most investors believe in the same future.

Investors' expectations regarding the future of interest rates depend in part on their present level. If interest rates are low now, there is a greater likelihood that they will rise in the future. Consequently investors will anticipate a fall in the prices of fixed income securities. In preparation for this event they will want to hold less wealth in investments and more in money. Hence investors try to hold more money when interest rates are low. Conversely, when interest rates are high, so that they are generally expected to fall, investors will prepare for this event by trying to hold more securities and less money.

The speculative motive of investors prompts an attempt to hold more money at low interest rates, and less money at high interest rates, because interest rates are always expected to move away from abnormally low or high levels.

Active and Passive Balances

It is analytically useful to distinguish between two kinds of money balances. The money people hold to facilitate their day-to-day transactions will be termed "active balances" and designated by the symbol M_1. Money held by speculative investors will be called passive balances and represented by M_2. Active and passive balances constitute the sum total of the money stock.

The direct demand for active balances (M_1) is almost entirely a function of income and only remotely a function of the interest rate. The direct demand for passive balances (M_2) is primarily a function of the level of interest rates and is hardly affected by income. Any relation between the demand for active balances and the demand for passive balances is indirect and operates usually by way of a change in the rate of entrepreneurial investment.

However, it is conceivable that there would be no demand whatsoever for passive balances in an economy where the interest rate was expected never to change. There would then be no speculative motive for holding money. All money would then be held in active balances.

Some people, when discussing the income velocity of money (v), consider only the velocity of active balances. The turnover of the passive balances normally tends to be zero and so is disregarded. For example, if M_1 were 25 billion dollars, M_2 were 15 billion dollars, and the national income were 100 billions, they might say that the income velocity (v) was 4.0 (i.e., 100/25) and not 2.5 (i.e., 100/40).

These recent statements need to be reconciled with the analysis of Part II. The money supply (M) was classified as circulating legal tender (M') or bank deposits (M''). Here we have segregated the stock of money into active (M_1) or passive (M_2) balances. These two systems of classification are quite unrelated. A typical active balance will consist of both hand currency and checking deposits.

The Liquidity Function

The over-all demand for money, consisting of the demand for active and passive balances, is expressed by a so-called liquidity function, which embraces three variables.

The three variables are (*L*) the demand for money, (*r*) the rate of interest, and (*Y*) the level of income. The demand for active balances will be denoted by L_1, that for passive balances by L_2, while the total demand for money will be designated by *L*. In equilibrium M_1 will equal L_1, M_2 will equal L_2, and *M* will equal *L*.

Figure 8 shows money and the demand for money on the right-to-left scale and the interest rate on the down-to-up scale. L_1 is shown as a vertical straight line, because the demand for active balances is not directly related to the rate of interest. (It *is* related to income, but this variable is not shown.) L_2 is shown as a curve sloping toward the lower left because the speculative desires of investors to hold funds increases when the interest rate is low. The total demand for money (*L*) is simply the horizontal summation of L_1 and L_2. The entire diagram is valid only for a given income level. If income were to increase for some reason, the L_1 schedule, and hence the *L* curve, would shift to the left, and the over-all demand for money would increase. However L_2 would not shift, since the demand for passive balances is not directly dependent upon income.

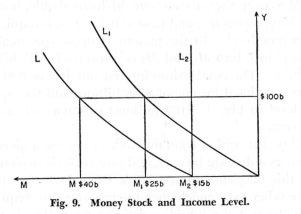

Fig. 9. Money Stock and Income Level.

Figure 9 also shows money and the demand for money on the right-to-left axis. However the *Y* dimension, which runs backwards from the front, now represents the level of income. L_2 is a straight line because the demand for passive balances is not directly related to income. (It *is* related to the interest rate but this last is not included in the figure.) L_1 is shown as a curve toward the upper left because the transactionary desire of the public to hold funds increases with income. L is the horizontal addition of L_2 and L_1. The interest rate is omitted here and assumed to be a constant. If the interest rate should happen to fall, L_2, and hence L, but not L_1, would be directly shifted to the left, and the total demand for money would increase.

The total stock of money is deemed a constant. The division of M into M_1 and M_2 is variable, however, and depends upon the rate of interest and the level of income. Let us suppose that M is \$40 billions. Then, for the level of income subsumed in Fig. 8, it would seem that the equilibrium rate of interest, reading off from the L curve, must be 4 per cent; and, at 4 per cent, the stock of money is divided into active balances of \$25 billions and passive balances of \$15 billions. Similarly, at the interest rate subsumed in Fig. 9, the equilibrium level of income, according to the L schedule in that diagram, is \$100 billions, at which level the total stock of money apparently comprises an M_1 of \$25 billions and an M_2 of \$15 billions.

When the stock of money is constant (for example, \$40 billions), only one level of income is consistent with a given interest rate, and only one rate of interest is compatible with a given income level. Moreover the interest rate in force should instigate the same division into active and passive balance as is required by the actual income level. In the present example the breakdown of the money stock into M_1 and M_2 is respectively \$25 billions and \$15 billions. The equilibrium interest rate in Fig. 8 (4 per cent) subsumes a national income of \$100 billions and the equilibrium income level in Fig. 9 (\$100 billions) subsumes an interest rate of 4 per cent.

The idea that, with a constant stock of money, a given interest rate requires a definite income, and *vice versa,* is depicted in Fig. 10. In this diagram, interest reads from down to up, income along the other axis, and higher interest rates are required with higher incomes if the liquidity demand for dollars is to remain unchanged. If the stock of money were increased, say from \$40 billions to \$50 billions, either interest rates would fall or the income level would rise, or both.

It is best to think of the liquidity function as a surface. A relation involving three variables needs three dimensions if it is to be represented graphically. The addition of an extra dimension transforms the curve of an ordinary figure into a surface.

In this case we shall imagine a three-dimensional model in which money increases from east to west, income increases from south to north, and interest increases from down to up. Each dimension is at right angles to every other one. The relation between interest and money will be shown as a curve by any vertical cut through the surface taken in an east to west dimension (see Fig. 8). The money to income relationship can be obtained by a horizontal slice taken at any altitude (see Fig. 9). The interest and income combinations are revealed by a vertical cut along the south to north axis (see Fig. 10).

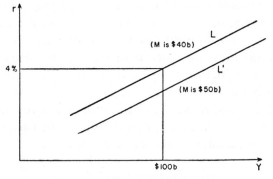

Fig. 10.   Income Level and Interest Rate.

The liquidity surface itself falls to the west (meaning lower interest rates with more money) and rises to the north (meaning higher interest rates with more income). Low interest rates increase the speculative demand of investors for passive balances and high incomes increase the transactionary demand of the public for active balances. One way to avoid higher interest rates when the national income rises is concurrently to increase the stock of money.

Other Aspects of Interest Theory

The liquidity preferences of the public—firms and households alike—are obviously only a partial explanation of why interest is paid for the use of money. The various motives that prompt people to hold cash balances certainly help to explain why they insist on interest as a price for relinquishing some degree of liquidity. However, in practice, it does not explain why most borrowers of funds pay interest.

Governments, firms, and households do not ordinarily pay interest on borrowed funds in order to be more liquid, that is to hold cash balances of greater value. Governments borrow money, and are willing to pay interest, because they are more able and willing to spend than to tax. Firms are willing to pay interest on borrowed funds because they believe that the real capital investments they will undertake can earn a net return over cost. Households are willing to pay interest in order to buy durable goods such as automobiles now rather than later. In each case, those that pay interest have borrowed money, not to hold it, but to spend it.

The time preferences of households and the productivity of real capital investments are just as much part of the whole theory of interest as is the liquidity preference for cash balances. The rate of interest must do more than equate the demand for cash balances with the national stock of money. The rate of interest, together with the level of income, must equate intended saving and intended investment. And the rate of interest must equate the supply and demand for loanable funds. In Chapter 30 these additional considerations are taken up in turn.

Statements for Consideration

1. The demand for active balances and the demand for passive balances depend one upon income and the other upon the interest rate.   *Discuss*
2. A decline in the price of a gilt-edge means that interest rates are rising.   *Explain*
3. People always want money, and so it seems strange to say that, at the equilibrium interest rate, no one wants to be any richer.
                                                                                     Evaluate
4. The liquidity demand for money is really a three-dimensional problem and cannot be depicted adequately by an ordinary two-way diagram.   *Explain*
5. If more people were paid by the day or week, instead of monthly, the interest rate might fall.   *Explain*
6. One test of whether an asset is "money" or only "near money" is whether it earns interest.   *Exemplify*
7. Different sets of motives apply to the holdings of cash by households and to cash holdings by firms.   *Explain*
8. The liquidity theory of interest asserts that interest is a reward for sacrificing liquidity rather than a reward for postponing consumption.   *Discuss*
9. The liquidity theory of interest is a complete theory.   *Evaluate*

References

Dillard, D., *The Economics of John Maynard Keynes*, Chapter 8. New York: Prentice-Hall, 1948.

Hart, A. G., *Money, Debt and Economic Activity*, Chapter 8. New York: Prentice-Hall, 1948.

Hicks, J. R., "A Suggestion for Simplifying the Theory of Money," *Economica*, February 1935.

Keynes, J. M., *The General Theory of Employment, Interest and Money*, Chapters 15–17. New York: Harcourt, Brace, 1936.

Lindahl, E., *Studies in the Theory of Money and Capital*, Part II. London: Allen and Unwin, 1939.

Robinson, J., *Introduction to the Theory of Employment*, Chapters 8, 9. London: Macmillan, 1937.

Robinson, J., "The Concept of Hoarding," *Economic Journal*, June 1938.

Smithies, A., "The Quantity of Money and the Rate of Interest," *Review of Economic Statistics*, February 1943.

Wallick, H. C., "The Current Significance of Liquidity Preference," *Quarterly Journal of Economics*, August 1947.

12

The General Theory

THE MODERN THEORY of income, interest, and money is a general theory, and one which includes a number of special interactions. The first special relation to be analyzed was that among income, the consumption function as reflected in the marginal propensity to save, and investment. Another important relation already discussed is that among investment, a number of considerations affecting the marginal efficiency of capital, and the rate of interest. Finally, we have seen that the rate of interest is in large measure dependent upon the factors that cause people to demand money as a means of achieving liquidity on one hand and upon the national stock of money on the other. These and other ideas can now be integrated into a simultaneous and general theory. Actually, the fitting together of these various parts can best be done if we use diagrams, because the interactions of the subsidiary systems can then be seen most clearly. Moreover, the job of assembly is simplified if we start where economists originally commenced a century ago and then proceed to evolve a more complete theory.

The Classical System

The classical economists concentrated their attention upon the relation among intended savings, intended investment, and the rate of interest. Income was ignored and so implicitly assumed to be at a constant level. Any demand for money as an alternative and preferable form of holding wealth was also disregarded.

The core of the classical system can be readily graphed on a two-axis diagram such as Fig. 11. The interest rate is represented vertically. Intended savings and intended investment are represented along the horizontal axis from left to right. The intended savings schedule shows that people will wish to save more at higher rates of interest and the opposite slope of the intended investment schedule indicates that entrepreneurs will choose to invest less at higher interest rates. The equilibrium rate of interest is that which equates intended savings and intended investment. Actual savings must always equal actual investment, and in the classical theory also, if we adhere to our modern definitions of them.

According to this theory, an increase in thriftiness on the part of the public would shift the intended savings schedule to the right, and so, other things equal, result in a lower rate of interest and increased investment. Or an invention of more efficient machinery might shift the intended investment schedule to the right, and so, other things equal, raise the interest rate and increase the amount saved. In either event, the two schedules are treated as though they were independent of one another; hence, when one of them shifts, the other remains stationary, and is merely intersected at a different point.

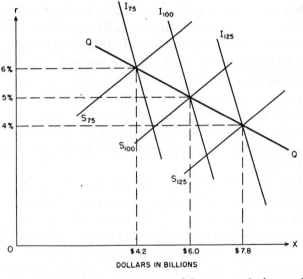

Fig. 11. The Effect of Interest and Income on Savings and Investment.

It has already been stressed that the classical theory subsumed a constant level of income and hence of employment also. Therefore any increase in actual savings and investment by the economy required a temporary sacrifice of consumption for both the individual lender and the economy. It was in part for this reason that the earlier writers used to refer to interest as a reward for waiting and abstinence.

Income Introduced as an Extra Variable

In reality, income is very much a variable, as past records of business cycles reveal. The rate of investment tends to determine the level of income, and this in turn influences the amount people will wish to save. Today we deny that savings and investment are independent, except at a given income, and maintain on the contrary that saving is linked to investment through changes in income.

These more recent ideas can be illustrated rather imperfectly in a two-dimensional diagram of the kind just used. However it is important that each intended savings and intended investment schedule be tagged with the income level to which it relates. For each different income there will be a special savings schedule and a special investment schedule. For example, in Fig. 11, S_{100} is the intended savings schedule, and I_{100} is the intended investment schedule, when the national income is $100 billions. In general, as income rises, both schedules will shift to the right, but the intended savings schedule will shift farther and faster to the right than will the intended investment schedule. Figure 11 shows three pairs of intended savings and intended investment schedules. Each pair is drawn for a different income. The three income levels that have been arbitrarily selected are $75, $100, and $125 billions respectively. Each pair of schedules intersects at a different rate of interest.

It will be noticed that lower income levels are associated with higher interest rates and low interest rates with high income levels. The geometric explanation of this is that the horizontal shift of the savings schedule, which follows a change in income, is greater than the horizontal shift of the investment schedule. The economic reason is that a variation in income, given the interest rate, causes a greater change in intended savings than in intended investment.

The three intersections of these three pairs of schedules are points on a rather special kind of function relating three variables. These three variables are (r) the interest rate, (Y) the income level, and (X) actual savings and actual investment. (The schedule that links these variables will be called the Q schedule.) The relation in the present case is as follows:

Interest Rate	Income Level	Savings & Investment
(r)	(Y)	(X)
6%	$ 75 bs.	$4.2 bs.
5	100	6.0
4	125	7.8

Within limits it should be possible to interpolate along this Q Schedule. For example, an interest rate of $4\frac{1}{2}\%$ would probably increase investment to about $6.9 billions, and this would in turn raise income to approximately $112.5 billions, at which level savings would equal investment. The vital relation stressed here is that, other things equal, lower interest rates are associated with higher incomes and more actual savings and investment.

Influence of the Demand for Money

It has already been shown that the rate of interest under equilibrium conditions is the price that equates the demand for money with the stock of money (see Fig. 8). In the preceeding section it has just been stated that the equilibrium rate of interest is that which equates intended savings and intended investment. Apparently an economy will not be in equilibrium unless the rate of interest equates (1) money demand with money stock, *and* (2) intended savings with intended investment.

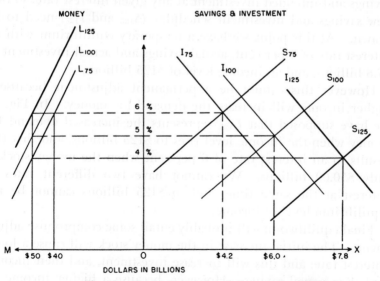

Fig. 12. Money Demand and Income Equilibrium.

These dual conditions are both satisfied in Fig. 12. The right-hand portion of the diagram is the "classical" figure with which we started just above. The left-hand portion is similar to Fig. 8, already employed in the discussion of liquidity preference. Three of the schedules are valid for a national income of $75 billions and so are directly comparable. The stock of money in the economy is then $40.0 billions, and this occasions, in conjunction with the money demand that exists when income is $75 billions, an interest rate of 6 per cent. The intended savings of a $75 billion income (i.e., $4.2 billions) will equal the intended invest-ment of a $75 billion income (also $4.2 billions) when there is a 6 per cent rate of interest. In this case the entire system is in equilibrium because the interest rate determined in the left part is equal to that determined in the right portion of the figure.

What readjustments would follow an increase in the stock of money from $40 billions to $50 billions?

First, the supply of $50 billions will intersect the $75 billion income demand for money at a lower interest rate, perhaps at 4 per cent. Second, a lower interest rate will cause entrepreneurs to invest more even before income changes. Third, more dollars spent on investment will increase incomes in a multiple manner. Fourth, a high income will lead to an increase in the intended savings and intended investment at any given interest rate, so that new savings and investment schedules (S_{125} and I_{125}) need to be drawn. At this point we have a temporary equilibrium with an interest rate of 4 per cent, actual savings and actual investment of $7.8 billions, and an income level of $125 billions.

However this cannot be a permanent adjustment because a higher income will increase the demand for money. In Fig. 12 we have supposed that L_{125} represents the increased demand for money when the income level rises to $125 billions, and that this results in an interest rate of 6 per cent when the money stock is only $50.00 billions. We cannot have two different rates of interest at the same time, and so $125 billions cannot be the equilibrium level of income.

Final equilibrium will probably entail some compromise adjust-ment. The initial increase in the money stock will cause a lower interest rate, and this will increase investment, and then income, and then actual saving. However, because a higher income in-creases the demand for money, this rise in income and saving and investment will be less than one would otherwise expect. Consequently, the outcome of increasing the money stock from $40.0 billions to $50.0 billions may be an interest rate of 5 per cent, actual savings and investment of $6.0 billions, and an income level of $100 billions. At this equilibrium the three relevant schedules shown in the diagram are L_{100}, S_{100}, and I_{100}.

The above description of events has been made to appear a sequential affair, with one development succeeding another in time. It was phrased this way to facilitate comprehension. In reality the entire adjustment is probably simultaneous. As the money stock increases, interest falls, investment rises, and income increases also; the intended investment schedule shifts to the right, the intended savings schedule shifts even faster to the right, and the liquidity demand schedule for money shifts upwards. As these developments proceed, the rate of interest that the savings and investment schedules indicate is proper becomes lower, but the rate of interest that the demand for money indicates is proper becomes higher.

These opposite developments restore equilibrium. The initial stimulus to an over-all readjustment was an equating interest rate for money demand and money stock that was lower than the equating interest rate for intended savings and intended investment. As incomes increase, the former equating interest rate rises and the latter equating interest rate falls, until they are similar.

The effect on income levels of a change in the money stock would be considerably greater if a change in income did not affect the demand for money. A simpler, but rather unrealistic model, would be one in which the theorist assumed that the money demand was independent of the income level, so that there would be a unique money demand schedule valid for all incomes. The more complete theoretical system employed here indicates that the fall in interest rates that follows an increase in the money stock is soon arrested by the increased money demand that follows a rise in income levels. A rising income brakes itself.

Altered Human Attitudes

Superficially, it might appear that the money stock determines the interest rate, savings-investment, and the level of income. However, it is obvious that these three resultants in part depend upon the character of the schedules of money demand, of intended savings, and of intended investment.   Consequently we must next consider the effect of a shift in any one of these three schedules upon some resultant such as income.

Changed Saving Propensities

Let us suppose that the public begins to look upon thrift as a virtue and attempts to practice greater frugality.   In this event the community will try to save a greater sum at each income level and interest rate than it did before.   Such a change in human attitudes toward saving is depicted in Fig. 13.   Schedules $^1S_{75}$ and

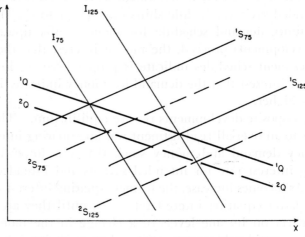

Fig. 13.   Incidence of Altered Saving Propensities.

$^1S_{125}$ show the *previous* rates of intended savings when income was $75 billions and $125 billions respectively.   On the other hand schedules $^2S_{75}$ and $^2S_{125}$ show the *subsequent* rates of intended savings when income is $75 and $125 billions respectively.   The intended investment schedules for income of $75 and $125 billions do not change.   The ^1Q schedule links the actual savings and investments that occurred at different interest rates before the new attitude toward thrift.   The ^2Q schedule links the actual savings and investments that will occur at different interest rates after the community becomes bent on frugality.   There are really two systems of schedules here, but only one is relevant for a given attitude toward thriftiness.

It will be noticed that the ^2Q schedule lies below and to the left of the ^1Q schedule.   One interpretation of this is that a lower income level will be required after the change in order to equate actual savings with actual investment.   An alternative statement would be that actual savings and investment will subsequently be less at any given rate of interest.   The above conclusion that an increase in thriftiness, evidenced by a shift to the right in the intended savings schedule, would actually lead to less saving and investment at a lower income, runs counter to classical propositions.

Changed Investment Intentions

Another possible change in human attitudes is that of entrepreneurs towards investment.   A series of favorable and publicized events may lead to a wave of optimism throughout the business community.   The schedule of intended investment at any given interest rate and income level may shift to the right. In that event the Q schedule will shift upwards and to the right. (The student should draw such a diagram for himself.)   The significance of such a shift would be that entrepreneurs will now invest more at any given interest rate.   A higher rate of investment, savings propensities unchanged, means a higher income. Consequently, a more favorable attitude toward investment will cause a higher income level and more actual savings and investment, even though the interest rate may rise slightly as higher incomes increase the demand for money.

Changed Liquidity Preferences

Finally, perhaps because of institutional changes, the public demand for money at any given interest rate and income level might alter.   For example, a law might be passed requiring all salaried employees to be paid weekly instead of monthly, in which case these persons would not need such a large bank balance to carry on their ordinary day-to-day transactions.   The money demand schedule constructed for a given income level would shift downwards, so that the existing money stock would now be compatible with a lower interest rate.   A lower interest rate will evoke an increased sum of actual investment, even though the intended investment schedule remains unchanged, and this will in turn lead to a higher income, other things equal.

A Three-Dimensional Restatement

The section that follows is not essential. The student who dislikes graphic models can omit it without interrupting the continuity of the exposition. However, a better understanding should follow an attempt to think in terms of surfaces rather than schedules.

The general theory can be represented by two contiguous boxes each containing a pair of surfaces. The left box will be called the Money Box and the right box will be called the Savings and Investment Box.

The Money Box has three dimensions. The stock of money (M) is shown on the axis that runs from the origin out to the *left*. Interest (r) is shown on the axis that rises from the origin upwards. Income (Y) is shown on the axis that goes from the origin backwards. The Savings and Investment Box has three dimensions also. Actual savings and investment (X) is shown along the axis running from the origin to the right. Interest (r) is shown on the axis that rises upwards. Income (Y) is represented along the axis that pushes backwards from the origin. It is obvious that the two boxes have a common wall that shows the relationship between interest and income.

Money Box Surfaces

There are two surfaces in the Money Box. One is the stock-of-money surface and the other is the demand-for-money surface. A great deal of information regarding these surfaces has already been given in Chapter 11.

The stock-of-money surface appears as a vertical straight line, if cut by a vertical right-to-left plane. It appears as a line running straight backwards and forwards, without any left or right deviation, when cut by a horizontal plane (see Figs. 8 and 9 in Chapter 11). The stock-of-money surface is really a plane surface without convexities or concavities. In other words the money stock is constant irrespective of changes in interest and income.

The money demand surface appears as a schedule sloping downwards and to the left when cut by a vertical right-to-left plane, which means that people will want to hold more money at lower interest rates when income is unchanged. A horizontal section would show a schedule tending backwards and to the left, which means that increasing incomes cause the public to demand more money at a constant interest rate. And a vertical backwards and forwards section would show a schedule rising as it went backwards, which means that people will pay more interest when incomes rise in order to hold a constant stock of money.

These two surfaces will intersect one another. The loci of these intersection points will fall along a vertical backwards and forwards section that corresponds to the existing stock of money (see Fig. 10 in Chapter 11). In other words, these intersection points comprise a single schedule, which indicates that higher interest rates will be associated with higher incomes when the economy has the use of a constant stock of money.

Savings and Investment Box Surfaces

There is an intended savings surface and an intended investment surface in the second box, the character of which has already been tentatively revealed in Chapter 10.

The surface of intended savings slopes upwards and to the right when revealed by a vertical left-to-right sectional cut, so that apparently, at higher interest rates, people will save more out of a constant income (see Fig. 11). A horizontal cut shows an intended savings schedule that runs backwards and to the right, which means that higher incomes cause people to save more at a given rate of interest (see Fig. 6 in Chapter 9). And a vertical backwards and forwards section reveals an intended savings schedule that falls as it goes backwards, indicating that a lower interest rate at higher income levels will evoke a constant intended saving. In other words, people will try to save more at higher income levels and higher interest rates.

The intended investment surface appears as a schedule sloping downwards and to the right when cut by a vertical left-to-right schedule, which means that entrepreneurs will seek to invest more at lower interest rates despite a constant income. A horizontal section reveals a schedule moving backwards and somewhat to the right, which indicates that businessmen and others will regard increased income as a sign to invest more at a given rate of interest. A vertical fore-and-aft cut shows a schedule that rises as it moves backwards, so that apparently a higher rate of interest can be obtained from entrepreneurs when incomes increase, if actual investment is to remain unchanged. The character of the intended investment surface states that there will be an increased attempt to invest at higher income levels and lower interest rates.

Increased income will greatly increase the desire to save and somewhat increase the desire to invest. Higher interest rates will increase the desire to save but reduce the desire to invest. The effect of income changes upon intended savings and intended investment is in the same direction, but the effect of interest changes upon them is contrary.

These two surfaces intersect. It is supposed that the path of intersection runs back, to the right, and downwards. The significance of this is that a lower interest rate will be associated with greater savings-investment and with a higher income.

Equilibrium

The system as a whole will be in full and final adjustment when the adjustment in the Money Box is compatible with the adjustment in the Savings and Investment Box.

We know that full equilibrium requires that the demand for money be equated with the stock of money. However, there are a series of combinations of income and interest that would occasion this necessary equation. For example, money demand and money stock might be equal when income and interest combinations are those set forth in the first two columns of Table 15.

TABLE 15
Equilibrium Between Both Boxes

M = L		S = I = X
r	Y	r
4.0 per cent	$ 75 billions	5.5 per cent
4.2	80	5.4
4.4	85	5.3
4.6	90	5.2
4.8	95	5.1
5.0	100	5.0
5.2	105	4.9
5.4	110	4.8
5.6	115	4.7
5.8	120	4.6
6.0	125	4.5

We also know that a complete adjustment necessitates that intended savings equal intended investment. Here also there are several income and interest combinations that will give an equality. Perhaps the possible combinations include those set forth in the last two columns of Table 15.

It should be noticed that under these assumptions there is only one combination of income and interest common to *both* subsystems, and that is $100 billions with five per cent. This is one of many combinations that will equate intended savings with intended investment. This is also one of many combinations that will equate money demand with the stock of money. However, it is the *only* combination of income and interest that will *both* equate intended savings with intended investment *and* equate money demand with the stock of money. Once the four surfaces are given, there is a unique equilibrium for the system as a whole, and particularly for r, X, and Y.

The requirements for a complete and final adjustment, given the surfaces, is that (1) the demand for money equals the stock of money, (2) intended savings equal intended investment, and (3) the former and latter equations involve the same combination of income and interest.

Causes and Effects

The general theory of income permits a useful distinction to be made between underlying causes and resultant effects. The causes are the human and institutional circumstances that are together represented in the four schedules (if we are thinking in two-dimensional terms) or surfaces (if we are thinking three-dimensionally). The intersections of these schedules or surfaces determine the income level, the interest rate, and savings-investment. These last three variables are the resultant effects.

It is simplest in this connection also to start with the classical model. The early theory had two causes, each expressed in an ordinary schedule, and these were intended savings and intended investment. The only two effects were the interest rate and actual savings-investment. An increase in intentions to invest, depicted by a shift in the intended investment schedule upwards and to the right, makes a new intersection farther up on the old intended savings schedule, with the result that the interest price rises and savings-investment increases in value. An increase in intentions to save, depicted by a shift in the intended saving schedule downwards and to the right, makes a new intersection farther down on the previous intended investment schedule, with the result that the interest rate falls and the savings-investment increases. No possible effects on income were considered and the possible influence of money stock and money demand were ignored.

In the general theory, however, there are four causes or determinants:

(1) Intention to invest—represented by the intended investment schedule or surface.
(2) Propensity to save—represented by the intended savings schedule or surface.
(3) Liquidity preference—represented by the money demand schedule or surface.
(4) Effective money supply—represented by the money stock schedule or surface.

The three effects (excluding money stock) are:

(r) the interest rate—the price people pay in order to hold their wealth in money form—represented vertically in the three-dimensional boxes.
(X) actual savings and investment—the dollar excess of income over consumption—represented along the left-to-right scale of the right-hand box.
(Y) the income level—the value of total output—represented along the backwards scale in the three-dimensional boxes.

The subsequent analytical procedure will be to assume an increase in each of the four causes in turn and trace the results this will have on the three listed effects.

Increased Intention To Invest

An increased propensity to invest will cause all the intended investment schedules to shift to the right. The altitude of the curve that relates Y and r with X—the Q schedule in Fig. 11—will go up. X increases. Y will rise. A higher Y increases the demand for M_1 balances and so—although the money demand *surface* does not change—a higher r is indicated with an unchanged M.

Increased Propensity To Save

An increased propensity to save will shift all the intended savings schedules downwards and to the right. The schedule that relates Y and r with X—the Q schedule in Fig. 11—will fall lower. X will therefore become less at the previous r. Therefore Y will fall. At a lower Y the demand for M_1 balances will be slightly less, even though the money demand *surface* remains unchanged, and so there will be a fall in r in the absence of any change in M.

Increased Liquidity Preference

An increased liquidity preference will shift all the money demand schedules in the left-hand box upwards and to the left. (The scale in this box reads from right to left.)   Therefore a higher r is required.   The Q schedule, which relates r with X, will be intersected at a higher point and so X will be reduced. Less X spells a lower Y.   A lower Y will somewhat reduce the demand for M_1 balances, even though the money demand *surface* is unchanged, so that the initial rise in r will actually be less than first expected.

Increased Money Supply

An increased effective money supply shifts the M schedules— in the left-hand box—further over to the left.   There will be a fall in r.   The Q schedule in the right-hand box is intersected at a lower point, so that X increases.   A higher volume of X brings about a multiplied increase in Y.   Higher Y increases the demand for M_1 balances, although the money demand surface is stationary, so that the fall in r is less than originally anticipated.

Comparison with the Classicists

It is not difficult to compare the classical and modern theories of interest, saving, and investment in terms of causes and effects and along the lines of Table 16.

TABLE 16

Causes and Effects According to Classical and Modern Income Theory

Determinants (or Causes)	Determinates (or Effects)	
	Classical	General
(1) Intentions to invest, ↑	r ↑ X ↑	r ↑ X ↑ Y ↑
(2) Propensity to save, ↑	r ↓ X ↑	r ↓ X ↓ Y ↓
(3) Liquidity preference, ↑	(ignored)	r ↑ X ↓ Y ↓
(4) Effective money supply, ↑	(ignored)	r ↓ X ↑ Y ↑

One of the major differences, of course, is that the classicists ignored the effective money supply and what we today term liquidity preference.   Also, they did not specifically include income as a dependent variable, or indeed consider it to be a variable. Hence the general theory of income, interest, and money has added two causes (i.e., liquidity preference and money supply) and at least one effect (i.e., income).

Noteworthy is the fact that the classical and modern theories reach somewhat different conclusions regarding the effect of an increased propensity to save. The classicists supposed that a fall in r and a rise in X would result. Modern theorists agree that r will fall, but assert that X will also fall, so that Y will in turn be reduced by some multiple amount. The older economists ignored the changes in Y that link intended savings and intended investments.

The classical theory is essentially a special case of the more general theory of today. Geometrically, the classical theory can be contained in one plane of two dimensions, comprising part of the two boxes of four dimensions required to illustrate the modern theory. An analogous contrast would be between a one-room cabin and a house that has been built around an original cabin. In view of the inclusion of the classical theory within today's general theory, one cannot say that logically they are in conflict.

However, as we have seen, the two systems do lead at times to different conclusions regarding public policy. Hence a choice must often be made between them when it comes to selecting a tool of analysis for dealing with unemployment problems of the real world. On such an issue there can be little doubt that the more complete theory, the one that also explains more adequately the facts of economic life, must be preferred despite its greater complexity.

Statements for Consideration

1. The classical theory is all right as far as it goes, but it doesn't go far enough.   *Explain*
2. The modern theory of income only added the income variable.
                                                                                        Discuss
3. It is still a moot point whether the intended investment and intended savings schedules are independent of one another; if they are not, the modern and more general theory of today breaks down.
                                                                                        Discuss
4. All schedules representing intended savings and intended investment at different interest rates should bear an income level tag.
                                                                                        Explain

5. The general theory added two causes and one effect to the classical theory of interest, savings, and investment. *Explain*
6. The liquidity demand for money imposes a brake on income changes. *Explain*
7. The fact that an equilibrium income level may be suboptimum from a welfare viewpoint is not the fault of any selfish group but is attributable to the attitudes and institutions of the community.
Discuss
8. Intended investment and intended saving may be equal at some given interest rate and yet not be in income equilibrium. *Explain*
9. The general theory of interest, money, and income is irreconcilable with the classical theory of interest; for example, they are in flat contradiction over the effects of increased public thrift. *Evaluate*

References

Dillard, D., *The Economics of John Maynard Keynes,* Chapter 3. New York: Prentice-Hall, 1948.

Harrod, R. F., "Mr. Keynes and the Traditional Theory," *Econometrica,* January 1937. Also in *The New Economics.* New York: Knopf, 1947.

Hart, A. G., *Money, Debt and Economic Activity,* Chapter 9. New York: Prentice-Hall, 1948.

Keynes, J. M., *The General Theory of Employment, Interest and Money,* Chapter 18. New York: Harcourt, Brace, 1936.

Lange, O., "The Rate of Interest and the Optimum Prosperity to Consumer," *Economica,* February 1938. Also in *Readings in Business Cycle Theory.*

Lerner, A. P., "Savings and Investment: Definitions, Assumptions, Objectives," *Quarterly Journal of Economics,* LIII. Also in *Readings in Business Cycle Theory.*

Lindahl, E., *Studies in the Theory of Money and Capital.* London: Allen and Unwin, 1939.

Morgan, T., *Income and Employment,* Chapter 10. New York: Prentice-Hall, 1947.

Robertson, D. H., "Some Notes on Mr. Keynes' General Theory of Employment," *Quarterly Journal of Economics,* November 1936.

Samuelson, P. A., "The Simple Mathematics of Income Determination," *Income, Employment and Public Policy.* New York: W. W. Norton, 1948.

Tarshis, L., *Elements of Economics,* Chapters 27–31. Boston: Houghton Mifflin, 1947.

13

Government Employment Policy

UNNECESSARY and unwanted unemployment is one of the greatest economic problems of our time and the value of income theory must be assessed in terms of its ability to suggest remedial measures. The diagnosis of the preceding chapters is not an end in itself, but it is an essential first step toward a solution of unemployment. Now that our analysis is largely completed, it is time to suggest government policies that seem to hold some promise of success.

What the Analysis Has Shown

We learned in Part II that the circuit of payments could not be maintained, but would fall, if taxes plus intended private saving tended to exceed government spending plus intended private investment. And in Part III it has been shown that income will fall if intended savings tend to exceed intended investment. Actually, these two statements are alternative ways of describing the same situation, for the aggregate savings and aggregate investment of the economy will be equal at the same national income which equates private saving and taxes with private investment and government spending. (See Appendix C.)

Hence it would seem to appear that the flow of payments, and up to a point real income too, would increase if either of the following occurred in isolation: a greater private inclination to invest rather than save, or lower government taxes relative to government spending at each level of national income. Unfortunately, the private propensities of firms and households to invest and save is something the national government of a country can influence only very indirectly and uncertainly. In this case, the burden of preventing or alleviating mass unemployment falls rather squarely on fiscal policy, that is upon government taxing, spending, and borrowing. Apparently the government must

182

resort—and a politically popular recourse it is, too—to spending more or taxing less.

The same broad conclusions can also be reached by way of the analytical scheme developed in Fig. 5, where the income system, the investment system, and the interest system were displayed.

In the case of the income system (Chapter 9), it was stated that national income would tend to be raised if investment increased or the marginal propensity to save declined. However, the marginal propensity to save can only decline at each income level, thereby raising the value of the investment multiplier, if there is a shift in the entire consumption function. It is conceivable that the government might be able to reduce the community's attempts to save through progressive income and inheritance taxes, but there are several serious dangers attached to such a course, as we shall see. On the other hand, the possible effectiveness of government supplements to spending and investment is considerable, in view of the fact that budget deficits are often akin to private investment so far as multiplier effects are concerned.

The previous description of the investment system (Chapter 10) showed that private investment depended primarily upon the rates of interest and the numerous factors that collectively determine the marginal efficiency of capital. Tax reductions and certain kinds of government spending may serve to raise the marginal efficiency of capital, while the general attitude of government toward private enterprise obviously influences the profit expectations of businessmen. The level of interest rates can also be lowered by the government through having the central bank support the market for low-interest-bearing government securities, and buying them back when necessary with new bank credits.

Our analysis of the interest system (Chapter 11) revealed that the level of interest rates would fall if the liquidity demand for money could be reduced or if the effective supply of money were increased. In this connection, the ability of the government to alter liquidity preferences within a short period of time is probably slight. However, a liberal budget policy of lowering tax rates and increasing disbursements will create deficits, if carried far enough, and so in turn increase either demand deposits or legal tender.

Logically, the above list of remedial opportunities is relevant, not only to underemployment situations that are permanent, but also to the mass unemployment that would occur temporarily and periodically if a regular business cycle existed. Theories of self-generating trade cycles, in which each phase grows out of an earlier one and in turn gives birth to the next swing or turning point, can be fitted into the general framework of income theory as developed here. They are special theories, in that an additional explanation of their regenerative characteristics must be evolved. There may also be special government measures that would dampen the oscillations of business cycles without raising the average level of employment and income over time. Nonetheless, policies that may be presumed effective in countering permanent underemployment can generally be expected to lessen temporary underemployment. In the present chapter, rather than prejudge the existence or nonexistence of periodic business cycles, the argument will run in terms of alleviating more or less permanent underemployment through government action.

The analysis of Parts II and III has shown that there are many factors affecting the flow of payments and the level of national income. Some of these factors are more, and some less, susceptible to government influence. Probably none of them can be controlled precisely by the central government of a free enterprise economy. The government is really only half in the driver's seat. While the government is pushing down on the accelerator, the public, which is the other driver, may be pushing down on the brake pedal. Can the national government really accelerate or retard economic activity under these circumstances?

Soaking the Rich

Certain principles of modern income theory have been seized upon as an additional argument for comprehensive social security schemes and for progressive income and inheritance taxes.

Income theory asserts that, other things equal, full employment income is prevented by the attempts of the public to save too large a fraction of such an income. Why does the public save? Middle-income households save against a rainy day. High-income households save because they cannot consume with enjoyment all that their incomes would permit. Large corporations, which by some are thought to be monopolistic, allegedly reap large profits that they deliberately refuse to reinvest. These various savings could probably be reduced. The motive that prompts households to save against such emergencies as unemployment, sickness, or death might be removed if there were a comprehensive scheme of national health benefits, unemployment benefits, and so forth. The ability of rich firms and households to save would be weakened if they were subjected to high and progressive rate income taxes. Estate and inheritance taxes could also operate to reduce income inequalities and hence lessen the proportion of national income annually saved. Here, it seems, is a happy chance to soak the rich, aid the distressed, and increase employment and income.

It is correct to surmise that, if other things were to remain equal, national income would be augmented by a diminution in the savings function. But other things might not always remain equal. In the present case, if private saving is reduced by income and inheritance taxes, private investment will also diminish, not to mention private consumer spending.

If an extra billion dollars is exacted from well-to-do households, they will save less and consume less, the decline in each case being perhaps about half a billion dollars. Of the half billion dollars previously saved, nearly all may have proceeded into real investment. It would therefore be essential that, to avoid a *fall* in national income, the government spend all its extra tax receipts.

These necessary disbursements might take the form of payments to the unemployed, sick, and aged. It would be best for the employment effect if these security schemes were not real insurance schemes and if "covered" persons did not suffer payroll deductions and the like. Substantial income transfers between rich and poor would probably then result.

However, when all these steps have been undertaken, what has been accomplished for employment? Private saving may be half a billion less and taxes a billion more, so that together they will be half a billion more. On the other hand, private investing will be about half a billion less and government spending about a billion more, so that together they will be half a billion higher. Each side of the equation that maintains a steady circuit of payments—i.e., taxes plus private saving equals private investment plus government spending—has altered by the same amount. Under these assumptions there should be no acceleration in the flow of payments.

The danger that private investment will be reduced by such a program is a very real one. Many corporations invest directly from their undistributed profits. People with wealth will prefer to hold more of their wealth in the form of money rather than in earning assets, if corporate and personal incomes are to be heavily taxed, especially when capital losses can only be partially deducted. Their attempts to disinvest and hold money instead will have two adverse consequences. An increased liquidity preference will raise the rate of interest and further weaken the inducement to invest, while failure to replace investment goods when they wear out will have a multiplied tendency to lower income. The suggestions examined here would redistribute national income but could very possibly render it smaller in the aggregate.

Unbalancing the Budget

Another scheme popular in some quarters, and one that holds more promise of elevating national income if properly conducted, is that of unbalancing the budget. Naturally this can be accomplished without great delay in either of two ways. Government spending can be increased or government tax rates can be lowered. Those who incline toward less public and more private enterprise may favor the latter on political grounds. There may also be some economic grounds for preferring the expedient of tax cuts to spending hikes. Possibly a more important consideration relates, however, to the manner of covering the deficit. Should the government issue legal tender to cover the difference, borrow at low or zero rates from the central bank and banking system, or attempt to tap some of the unlent savings of the public at large by selling them bonds?

Government Spending

It may come as something of a surprise, but the federal government may have some doubts and difficulties in substantially and suddenly increasing its rate of disbursements. In general, there are three obvious ways in which it can inject new money into the circuit of payments. It can make gifts disguised by such names as bonuses, crop loans, and unemployment insurance. It can pay subsidies to firms in order to encourage them to produce more. Or it can underwrite public works projects. In actual fact the federal government might find it necessary, if it wished to increase its spending by very large amounts, to adopt all three methods.

Public Works.   Public works can certainly be costly, and so get rid of government money, but there are relatively few such projects that can escape disbarment on one or more of several counts.

A great many conceivable public works projects would compete with private enterprise to such an extent that government investment would substantially replace private investment.   This would undoubtedly happen if the federal government ever received congressional authority and funds to enter the steel or textile or coal industries as an operator.   To a limited extent this probably occurred when the Tennessee Valley Authority undertook to generate electric power in an area already served less generously by a private utility company.   On the other hand, when the government has invested to produce cheap electric energy, this has sometimes stimulated investment in privately-owned distributing companies.

Actually there are not many economic activities the government can prosecute without competing almost directly with private industry.   In the main, governments are limited to the construction, directly or indirectly, of highways, canals, river dams and bridges, airfields, public buildings, and national defense.   During periods of international tension, large defense expenditures, paradoxical though this may seem, may increase national income by more than their cost.

A large government construction program *may* indirectly reduce private investment by lowering the marginal efficiency of capital.   If the prices of building materials and the wages of construction labor are involuntarily bid up by the government, the cost of plant expansion and other private capital improvements will be raised.   However, in the special case of a severe depression, it is unlikely that such a price effect would develop until substantial recovery had been made.   And an increased national income may seem to promise larger receipts streams for private enterprise and so induce private investments.

Of course, the mere fact that governments are undertaking public works may cause private enterprise to fear that, when the federal government has built, say, a post office at every crossroads, it will invest in more competitive ways such as public utility services, transportation, or urban housing.   It is hard to know how nervous business managements and capitalistic households really are.   Undoubtedly some business groups cry "Wolf" too often and too soon; on the other hand, people who have never had the worries and fears of risking money in private production should not scoff too scornfully at these psychological factors.

Another difficulty about public works projects is that they take time to plan and execute. For example, in building a large suspension bridge, engineers must design the structure, contracts must be let, and parcels of land may have to be acquired for government use before any significant injection of money ever occurs. Delays of this kind are particularly important in the case of a business-cycle depression. To some extent such time lags can be shortened by advance paper work. Governments might complete design and real estate preparations and then hold construction in abeyance until unemployment becomes serious.

Finally, substantial public works only benefit the unemployed very indirectly and tardily, for the government's first payments are to contractors or for materials and skilled labor. During periods of severe depression, it is the urban unskilled worker, the men and women who are usually near the margin of employment, whose plight is the most urgent. Many public works projects are out in the country (for example, Hoover Dam) or require the specialized labor of masons, plumbers, electricians, and so on (for example, any public building). The unemployed and unskilled town worker will benefit only if and when the public works projects have caused a rise in national income and public spending.

Here then is something of a dilemma. There are only a few public works projects that (1) are non-competitive with private enterprise, (2) can be quickly implemented, and (3) will benefit the unemployed urban worker. And yet the government wants to spend a lot of money and help the unemployed immediately. Hence, in practice, it is often driven into less and less productive public works. Bridge building may give way to leaf raking and even eventually to an unvarnished dole.

It has often been asserted in the past that, so far as aggregate national output is concerned, it is better to have the government employ a man in only a semiproductive way than to have him completely unemployed. Cutting trails in national parks, cataloguing books in public libraries, or building monuments by hand all add something to the real national income of the present and future. Hence it has been argued that, if necessary, a government should continue its public-works program during a depression, even after all obviously useful projects have been completed, rather than leave men unemployed and so contributing absolutely nothing to national output.   There would be considerable substance to this argument if the only alternative to semiproductive projects really were complete unemployment.   Actually, as we shall see, there are other alternatives, such as subsidies and cutting taxes, which may provide both employment and additional aggregate output.

Subsidies for Production.   The federal government, and state governments besides, might seek to inject additional money into the circuit of payments, contribute to national output, and provide local employment by subsidizing certain lines of private enterprise.

Housing is one kind of output that governments might subsidize.   They might subsidize private owners, building contractors, the producers of building materials, or even the occupants.   There are pros and cons relating to each possibility.

Let us suppose that a subsidy of $1,000 is made payable to the first owner of every new dwelling unit.   Dwelling units would naturally have to be defined by minimum specifications and to include private apartments as well as houses.   In this way, many entrepreneurial landlords with idle funds might be induced to risk them in housing investments, and the level of rents would presumably fall.   The construction of owner-occupied homes would also be stimulated.   The main disadvantage of such a scheme is that there would be no economic purpose gained in paying a subsidy to the owners of existing dwelling units; hence they would probably be excluded from the scheme, and yet they would suffer a loss in the values of their buildings if a great deal of new construction did occur.

There is, of course, far less danger of discriminating between the suppliers of old and new output in the case of subsidizing goods such as textiles and food, which are obviously less durable than houses.

A new difficulty, then, is to know whether to subsidize all new output or simply additional new output.   For example, if a dairy farmer last year produced 30,000 gallons of milk, and a subsidy of 25¢ a gallon is contemplated, should he be allowed this subsidy on all the current year's output or only on his output in excess of 30,000 gallons.   If the former plan is adopted, the farmer may increase his output only slightly, thus providing little extra employment directly, and yet pocket $7,500 gratis on the output he would have produced anyway.   In the event that only extra output receives a subsidy, it must be realized that extra milk output from all dairy farmers will tend to reduce the price obtainable from buyers and consumers, so that the effect of the falling price is opposed to the effect of the per unit subsidy.   Of course, if the subsidy is only to be paid on additional output, the government could afford a considerably larger subsidy per gallon.

In general, the government should subsidize those commodities for which the demand price falls slowly, and for which the unit production costs rise slowly, as output increases.   When such commodities are subsidized, the increase in output resulting from a given unit subsidy will be comparatively great.   Of course, in the case of commodities that are already taxed, the subsidy can take the form of eliminating the tax.

Various objections can be leveled against even such a limited subsidy program.   The prices that unsubsidized producers must pay for productive factors may be bid up by subsidized producers and this may adversely affect the marginal efficiency of capital of the former.   The base year outputs of established producers become more unsatisfactory as a means of computing subsidy allowances for extra output as time goes on.   Since it is administratively and politically feasible to subsidize only certain lines of production, the composition of the national output may become warped from what it would be if consumers were spending these subsidy funds for the articles they wanted most.   Also, it is historically true that a subsidy, once allowed, can only be canceled with the greatest political difficulty; against this it should be pointed out that if it is permanent underemployment we wish to cure, sustained injections of money are essential, and that this is a reason for preferring subsidies to non-recurring public works projects.

Direct Relief.   A quick way to distribute additional money into the circuit of payments is for the federal government, without further ado, to start mailing out checks to everyone.   However, many people are too conservative to stomach a general wallow in the public trough, and hence some eligibility standards must be set up.   In the United States, the government makes payments under certain circumstances for previous service in the armed forces, for old age, for unemployment, and so on. But obviously the federal government could be more generous. It might make monthly payments to heads of families for each living child—as in Canada today—or it might guarantee each adult a certain minimum annual income.

Transfer payments such as these do not raise real national income directly. If aggregate national output does subsequently increase, it will probably be due to the chain of spending that follows the original receipts, and possibly to induced private investment. Because the first payment by the government is a transfer payment, the value of the government spending multiplier will be less than otherwise.

There can be little doubt that any program of widespread and generous transfer payments would reduce the eagerness of people to earn money and raise the minimum wage that unemployed workers would accept for available jobs. Hence, unless the wages employers would be willing to pay are already below legal minima, one effect of direct relief payments is to raise the cost of labor to firms and perhaps to lower the marginal efficiency of capital for private enterprise. Widespread direct relief would probably weaken one of the major incentives to work which propels our economy.

Reducing Taxes

Every government can quickly unbalance its budget by drastically reducing tax rates or eliminating certain impositions entirely. Administratively this is much simpler than devising public works projects and subsidy schemes. Moreover, business groups as well as workers and consumers may welcome such a program, so that politically it has certain merits also.

In order to analyze this proposal, it is convenient to distinguish between income taxes, domestic excise taxes, and import duties.

If income tax rates are cut, affected firms and households will have more disposable income. Undoubtedly they will save a fraction of this increment, but they will certainly spend part of it, and the recipients of this extra spending will engage in extra respending. Some of this extra private saving will probably become extra private investment. The inducement to invest has been increased in three ways: the public will be spending more on consumer goods, private enterprise is now more willing and able to invest its extra savings, and interest rates may fall because of the larger stock of money now in the public's hands. Eventually, as national income rises, government tax receipts will increase, even though the tax rates remain at their reduced levels, until a new equilibrium is reached. At this new and higher national income, intended private saving plus taxes will again equal intended private investment plus government spending.

A reduction in domestic excise taxes may increase output, profits, and other factor incomes, and lower prices to consumers. The output effect will be greatest in the case of commodities that are sensitive to price changes on both the demand side (that is, people buy them or not depending largely upon the prices demanded) and on the supply side (that is, firms expand and contract their output according to obtainable prices). Where an increase in the net price to suppliers evokes only a slight increment of output, the removal of a tax will give profits to producers, but not necessarily higher incomes to the factors they employ. A cut in an excise tax should raise the marginal efficiency of capital for producers selling the commodity in question (who now obtain a larger gross receipts stream) and for producers who buy it (who now have lower disbursement streams). A positive shift in the intended investment schedule may result.

On the other hand, a reduction in import duties will have a mixed effect. Firms that use the untaxed import will benefit, and they are more likely to invest, but domestic firms that are competitive suppliers of the imported good may disinvest. Where the United States imposes high protective tariffs, over which only a trickle of imports flows, duty reductions may be of questionable value in raising national income. However, when most domestic uses are supplied from foreign sources, so that the tariff is primarily a means of raising revenue, duty reductions may raise national income.

A reduction in tax rates, whether on incomes or commodities, should not occasion a continuous budget deficit. After a while, as pointed out, there will presumably be a higher national income, which will yield almost the same tax proceeds as before. Meanwhile government deficits will occasion an increased national debt, and presumably, if bank loans to the public are not contracted, an increase in the effective money supply.

It is to be hoped that reducing taxes, like extra government spending, will supply a multiplicand upon which the investment multiplier can work. However, reducing taxes is unlike extra government spending in several respects. Reducing taxes is more likely to induce private investment than are public works. Reducing taxes is administratively simpler than subsidy plans. Reducing taxes should eventually result in the government's playing a smaller relative role in the national economy. Reducing taxes is likely to be more universally acceptable, for such a program injures hardly anyone and scatters widespread benefits.

The Government Expenditure Multiplier

When deficit financing by government is under consideration, the value of the government expenditure multiplier, which operates when there is an autonomous increase in the government's net spending, is crucial. It makes little difference in this case whether the government's excess of disbursements over receipts is for current or capital account. It will be assumed that these extra net disbursements—whether due to increased spending or to tax cutting—are the multiplicand. They consist of funds that were previously either idle or nonexistent.

When discussing the pure theory of the multiplier, we stated that the simple investment multiplier was equal to the reciprocal of one minus the marginal propensity to consume. In the United States this propensity has been variously estimated at around .80. Accordingly, the value of k is nominally about 5.0. However, for a number of reasons, the practical value of the government expenditure multiplier in the United States is more likely to be 3.0 or 2.0.

First, the estimate of an 80 per cent marginal propensity to consume refers to the *disposable* income per cent that is not saved. In the United States, because of corporate and personal income taxes, disposable income is considerably less than national income; hence the marginal propensity to consume, in relation to national income, is less than .8 and may be only .6.

Second, as national incomes rises in the United States, the public spends more for everything, including imports, so that the money claims of foreigners on Americans increase relative to those of Americans on foreigners. There is thus a leakage of money claims from domestic residents to foreign residents. The propensity of the American economy to import extra goods and services probably ranges from 5 to 10 per cent of extra national income. Hence the marginal propensity of United States residents to consume *domestic* goods, the propensity upon which the government expenditure multiplier depends, may range from .6 to .5.

Third, the theoretical values previously given for the multiplier referred to its final value, a value it would attain only after an infinitely long wait. Practical politicians cannot wait forever, and so it may be advisable to adopt some arbitrary waiting time, and cite the multiplier effect realized at the end of this time. If a congressional term of 2 years is accepted as a conventional waiting period for assessing the multiplier's value, and if the spending time lag is 4 months, how much extra national income will be occasioned each year by a single government injection of one dollar, assuming that the marginal propensity of the public to purchase domestic goods with extra gross receipts is .5? In the first year, out of the first injection of one dollar, in three successive respendings, there will be an extra 87½¢ of consumer spending. The three respendings, in the second year, of what remains from this initial dollar, will augment consumer spending by 11¼¢ in the second year. However, if the federal government injected an extra dollar each year, say on January 1st of 1950 and 1951, the total increment in national income by December 31st of these same years would be 87½¢ and 98¾¢ respectively. However this supposes that the injected dollar was a gift, and contributed nothing itself to national income, which explains why it has not been counted. If, in fact, the injected dollar was spent each year for real goods and services, then the additions to national income would be $1.87½ and $1.98¾ at the end of the first and second years respectively.

All the above assertions presuppose that the extra government spending does not partially replace other spending by governments, firms, or households, and hence is a net autonomous increase in spending for the economy. A hundred dollars of government unemployment relief will not give us a multiplicand of one hundred dollars if private charities, relatives, or the distressed families themselves would have spent some money they now do not spend.   A more important danger is that government spending for public works of a competitive kind will cause a decrease in private investment.

It appears that the simple government expenditure multiplier is considerably less than the simple investment multiplier of pure theory.   Therefore the federal government, as a matter of practical necessity, would have to rely heavily upon the supplementary effects of autonomous and induced private investment.   Reducing taxes rather than increasing government spending may possibly not only encourage more private investment at each national income level, but also induce larger increments in private investment as national income rises, and so may prove superior.

Financing Government Deficits

It has been asserted above that a government budget deficit is very much akin in its income effects to an increase in private investment.   This assertion was predicated upon the assumption that the deficit money—if we may so call the excess of government spending over receipts—is money that was not previously available to the public for spending.   It is new money, in the sense either that the government has recently created it or that the government has recently decided to dishoard it.   How expansionary this deficit money proves to be will depend in part upon from where it originally came.   In general, the government can obtain funds to cover a budget deficit in the following ways, listed according to their increasingly expansionary effect in normal times:

> Sell securities
>> to the public
>> to the commercial banks
>> to the central bank
>>> bearing interest
>>> interest-free
> Print currency

It is possible that during a depression the public may hold idle balances that it will place in government securities but in nothing else.   In this case government borrowing from the public and immediate spending of the proceeds will increase the economy's effective demand for goods and services.   However, one cannot count on this possibility.   It seems more probable that part of the public's lending to the government will be in lieu of other uses for its money. Also, if the public believes that interest rates may rise within the next few years, a development that could lower the market value of its government securities, it will not invest its idle funds in this way.

Commercial banks may have excess reserves during periods of unemployment, in which case their purchase of government securities will not displace other lending to firms and households. If the banks see no promise of an imminent improvement in business conditions, they will probably prefer obtaining a low rate of return on government bonds to obtaining no return at all. Their willingness to lend to the government will naturally be increased if they believe that the central bank will support the market for government securities when interest rates subsequently rise along with economic activity. But if the government's policy of unbalancing the budget is successful, and employment and income rise appreciably, the commercial banks will probably be unwilling either to *relend* the proceeds of maturing securities or to lend additional funds to cover present and future budget deficits.

Accordingly the Treasury will probably, sooner or later, resort to borrowing from the central bank. In the United States, the Federal Reserve Banks, as we have seen in Part II, are not restricted by the clearing house drain or the currency drain, and excess reserves for them either exist or can readily be created. Moreover the United States' central banks need not concern themselves, at least nowadays, with the international drain that logically could develop when the American people use some of their new money receipts to import goods and services. Foreigners who receive dollar claims do not try to cash in these claims for gold or other national currencies but respend them rather promptly in the United States market.

The Board of Governors of the Federal Reserve System, through the Federal Open Market Committee, can instruct the Federal Reserve Banks to purchase government securities. In the past, these securities have always been interest-bearing, but it has been argued that some of them might be interest-free in the future. Free lending by the Federal Reserve Banks would probably not reduce their financial ability to make other earning loans. The purpose of the government borrowing is to promote national prosperity, which in turn increases the number and attractiveness of loan applications to banks. Also, the payment of interest by taxpayers could be deflationary, since the excess reserves of member banks are reduced when taxpayers' checks on them are deposited in Federal Reserve Banks by the Treasury for collection.

Alternatively, the Treasury might simply print greenbacks, deposit them in the Federal Reserve Banks, and so add to its checking accounts. It would then issue checks to contractors, veterans, and so on, who would deposit them in member banks, thus increasing the latter's excess reserves. The economic consequences of printing greenbacks or compelling the Reserve Banks to purchase interest-free government securities is essentially the same.

It might appear to some people that printing money is preferable to selling bonds, because the latter increases the national debt, but this is not so. Actually the national debt is a rather light burden upon the American people as a whole, for foreign lenders have made few net purchases of United States government securities. It is true that, nominally at least, one group of Americans (i.e., taxpayers to the United States government) are placed in debt to another group (i.e., holders of United States securities), but the first will probably never be called upon to discharge more than a small portion of this indebtedness. When currently held securities mature, they can often be replaced by the sale of new securities to the Federal Reserve Banks or to voluntary lenders.

During a deep depression it may make little difference which method the government uses to finance its budget deficits. However, as general business conditions improve and employment becomes fuller, further increases in national spending may drive prices up rather than expand production. The Treasury now has a choice to make when financing its continuing but shrinking annual deficits. If it borrows from the Federal Reserve, it will be adding to the money supply and so pouring fuel on the inflationary fire. If it attempts to borrow from voluntary lenders, such as the public and the commercial banks, it will not be increasing the money supply, its spending will tend to displace other public spending, and it will have to pay higher interest rates. If the United States government feels that prices are rising too rapidly, and that full employment has been almost attained, it should probably solicit voluntary loans to avoid further inflation.

Statements for Consideration

1. A government can do relatively little about reducing the community's liquidity preferences. *Discuss*
2. A policy of soaking the rich through progressive taxes and giving the proceeds to the poor as "free" benefits, may do little to speed and expand the circuit of payments. *Evaluate*
3. Upon examination, a great many potential public works are seen as rather meager contributors to increased employment and income, although some of them may be quite costly. *Evaluate*
4. The unskilled urban worker receives only the most indirect employment benefits from public works. *Discuss*
5. Government subsidy plans may reduce the marginal efficiency of capital expectations of unsubsidized producers. *Explain*
6. A reduction in income taxes, unaccompanied by a reduction in government spending, might raise income and employment.
Explain
7. There are several reasons why reducing taxes may be the best way for a central government to inject additional money into the economy and so "invest." *Explain*
8. The simple investment multiplier of theory and the government spending multiplier of practice may differ in magnitude. *Discuss*
9. In view of the possibly low value of any actual government spending multiplier, no government can dispense with the supplementary income and employment props of private investment. *Discuss*
10. It makes little difference to income and prices whether the government acquires its "deficit money" from private lenders or by printing greenbacks. *Evaluate*

References

Colm, G., "Fiscal Policy," *The New Economics.* New York: Knopf, 1947.

Dillard, D., *The Economics of John Maynard Keynes,* Chapters 6, 11. New York: Prentice-Hall, 1948.

Ellis, H. S., Anderson, B. M., and Clark, J. M., *Financing American Prosperity.* New York: Twentieth Century Fund, 1925.

Ellis, H. S. (Ed.), *A Survey of Contemporary Economics,* Chapter 5. Philadelphia: Blakiston, 1948.

Hansen, A. H., *Economic Policy and Full Employment,* Parts IV, V, VI. New York: McGraw-Hill, 1947.

Harris, S. E. (Ed.), *Postwar Economic Problems,* Part I. New York: McGraw-Hill, 1943.

Hart, A. G., *Money, Debt and Economic Activity,* Part V. New York: Prentice-Hall, 1948.

Higgins, B., *Public Investment and Full Employment.* Montreal: International Labor Office, 1946.

Meade, J. E., and Hitch, C. J., *An Introduction to Economic Analysis and Policy*, Part I. New York: Oxford University Press, 1938.

Morgan, T., *Income and Employment*, Chapter 16. New York: Prentice-Hall, 1947.

Musgrave, R. A., "Audit Controls, Interest Rates, and Management of the Public Debt," *Income, Employment and Public Policy*. New York: W. W. Norton, 1948.

Samuelson, P. A., *Economics*, Chapter 18. New York: McGraw-Hill, 1948.

Samuelson, P. A., "Fiscal Policy and Income Determination," *Quarterly Journal of Economics*, August 1942.

Tarshis, L., *Elements of Economics*, Chapters 33–35. Boston: Houghton Mifflin, 1947.

Villard, H. H., *Deficit Spending and the National Income*. New York: Farrar and Rinehart, 1941.

14

Money, Income, and Prices

In attempting to stimulate employment and income, a national government, if successful in increasing effective demand, will eventually have to decide how great a rise in the price level is justified by a given increase in employment. For example, if the government pushes on with its program of deficit financing, the time may come when this is expected to increase employment only one per cent while raising prices ten per cent. In explaining how a national government may find itself confronted with this dilemma we can unite some of the ideas of monetary, income, and price theory, and so connect Parts II, III, and IV.

Effective Demand

The immediate object of unbalancing the budget is to increase effective demand. Effective demand is not merely the desire of firms and households to have better real capital or more consumer goods respectively. In periods of depression, goods still have use value but the public is either unable or unwilling to spend money for them. Hence, for there to be an increase in effective demand, one or both of the following must occur. The public must either come to want goods more urgently (and have the financial means to purchase them) or come to have more money to spend (and have previously been prevented from buying for lack of funds).

Firms may want more capital goods for various reasons. Fixed capital, which previously constituted excess capacity, may finally have depreciated to a point where it must be replaced, in which case firms may enter the market. They may decide to make net investments in fixed capital because their expectations concerning future sales volume have become more optimistic. If materials prices seem to have reached bottom, they may fill their materials inventories. Or perhaps their new eagerness to invest has been prompted by a fall in interest rates. In none of these examples would firms spend more simply because they came to hold larger bank balances.

On the other hand, the major limitation on household spending is usually lack of funds. During a depression, households do not refrain from spending because they do not want things. And when households do come to increase their spending, it is not because they have suddenly come to want houses and clothes and automobiles more urgently, but because they now have the financial wherewithal.

Here, then, is something of a contrast. Firms do not spend in a depression because they do not want goods so badly, and not because they lack the means. Households do not spend in a depression because they lack funds, and not because they do not want goods. Naturally this distinction does not hold in all cases, but it is probably valid more often than not.

Money Stock and Effective Demand

To what extent will an increase in the means of payment, achieved perhaps through deficit financing, increase the effective demand of the original recipients? Of course, once the multiplier has gone into operation, the increase in effective demand over a whole year may considerably exceed the increment in money stock, but that is another matter. The present question concerns the willingness of recipients of new disposable funds to respend them.

When firms succeed in accumulating money balances during a depression, they are more likely to place these funds in passive (M_2) balances than in active (M_1) balances. The reverse will tend to be true of households. Who comes to hold newly created money determines the velocity of money and the relative increase in effective demand.

If firms place all additional money holdings in M_2 balances, which have zero velocity, the over-all velocity of the national money stock will tend to fall. If households place all additional money holdings in M_1 balances, which have a positive velocity, the over-all velocity of the national money stock will tend to rise. What happens to money velocity and effective demand will depend in large measure upon whether an increased national money stock comes to be held in passive or active balances and whether by firms or households. If the percentage share of households in the national money stock is greater than before, the velocity of money will probably be greater, and effective demand will prob-ably increase by a greater proportion than has the national money stock.

In Chapter 6 the equation of exchange was defined as

$$P \cdot T = M \cdot V$$

The product $P \cdot T$ in this equation is a reflection of effective de-mand, rising as effective demand rises, and *vice versa*. The M of this equation can be broken down into active balances (M_1) and passive balances (M_2). The velocity of the M_1 balances may be denoted by V_1. Hence we can redefine the equation of ex-change as

$$P \cdot T = M_1 \cdot V_1 + M_2 \cdot V_2$$

The second term on the right-hand side can be disregarded because V_2, the velocity of M_2, is always zero. Any increase in M_1 will probably increase effective demand. Such an increase might come about by a shift of the existing money stock from passive to active balances or by an increase in the national money stock that does not accrue entirely to passive balances.

However, while increases in M_1 will increase effective demand *directly*, barring an equal proportionate fall in V_1, additions to M_2 may *indirectly* increase effective demand. Passive balances are held in response to the speculative motive. If more money becomes available to satisfy this demand, and if the liquidity demand does not increase, the rate of interest will fall. A fall in the rate of interest may eventually stimulate private investment. Thus national income will probably rise, as also will effective demand and $P \cdot T$, so that either the active balances must become enlarged or their velocity must increase. If this leads to M_2's being drained off into M_1, the rate of interest may rise in order to equate the smaller M_2 with the enlarged demand for passive balances, in which case the rate of income increase may be slowed.

The Influence of Supply on Prices

An increase in effective demand, which is reflected in an increase in $P \cdot T$, can take the form of either higher prices or more trans-actions. The deciding factor is what happens to supply. There is probably a tendency, as expansion proceeds, for effective demand to affect T less and P more.

When buyers are spending more money and effective demand has increased, the public will either buy more at present prices or buy present quantities at higher prices. Naturally it would prefer to do the former. However, prices may eventually increase compared with output, owing, among other things, to:

    (1) rising labor costs
    (2) diminishing returns in the short run
    (3) temporary bottlenecks
    (4) monopoly
    (5) full employment.

Rising Labor Costs

As economic activity increases, labor costs are likely to rise, either because wage rates per hour or by the piece are higher, because workers individually work less hard, or because poorer workers are given jobs.

The power of workers to bargain over wages improves as business picks up. Employers are anxious to employ additional men because demand has improved. Employers of organized labor are particularly anxious to avoid a strike during a period of active and profitable demand for their output. Large corporations that are before the public's eye may even be able to use a wage rate increase as an excuse for raising product prices. The employers of unorganized labor find, as unemployment decreases and the first twinges of a manpower shortage come to be felt, that they are increasingly compelled to pay union wage rates.

The productivity of individual workers, particularly of unorganized workers who have no seniority rights or union to enforce them, declines as their fear of the "sack" diminishes. If they are "fired," they now have a better chance of obtaining another job. And the employer knows that he will have more difficulty in obtaining better men. Hence workers tend to "let up" and accomplish less work, so that employers' unit costs of production tend to rise.

As economic expansion proceeds, employers take on additional workers, but these workers are likely to be inferior. Employers would like to pay these new and poorer workers a lower wage, but this is usually impracticable. So here again firms find themselves paying the same wage for less work and experiencing rising unit costs.

Diminishing Returns in the Short Run

A firm is said to be operating in the short run if, during the period for which plans are being made by the management, there is insufficient time to alter the fixed capital appreciably. While the maximum physical capacity of a given plant may be somewhat uncertain, it is very clear that, after some rate of output is exceeded, further attempts to increase output by running three shifts, working more people on all shifts, operating machinery without stopping for maintenance and overhaul, and so forth, will increase expenses proportionately more than output. Unit costs of production will then rise.

Temporary Bottlenecks

The costs of one producer may rise when he is forced to delay production or improvise expensive substitutes because some ingredient or component of his output is in short supply or unavailable. Thus a shortage of platinum may retard the production of ignition distributors and hence cause automobile manufacturers to slow down their assembly lines—without, however, reducing their considerable overhead costs. Or refrigerator manufacturers may have to curtail production despite many other expensive commitments because of a shortage of electric motors. Manufacturers, finding themselves short of a critical good, naturally offer high prices to obtain supplies. Hence the prices of bottleneck goods rise rapidly and many of these prices enter into the cost of other goods.

Monopoly

In most trades and industries, rival producers compete to supply an active demand. Each firm feels that, if it does not at once obtain a share of the existing demand, it will suffer. It fears that rival firms may secure a permanently increased share of the trade if once they obtain a superior sales volume.

These spurs to immediate expansion of output do not apply so sharply in the case of goods produced by a single firm (a monopoly) or by a small group of firms (an oligopoly) that are not in very serious competition. If control of supply is secure and other firms cannot break into the industry for lack of patents or some other reason, the monopoly or oligopoly, as the case may be, will be more likely to raise prices than to expand output.

The reasoning behind this restrictive policy is usually plain. Buyers, despite their eagerness to purchase a monopoly good, cannot resort to alternative sources of supply. If buyers do not purchase at this year's high prices, they may simply be forced to return next year when their need is greater. There seems little profit in expanding capacity today in order to be burdened with excess capacity tomorrow. Firms that enjoy a measure of monopoly power can afford to take a longer view than competitive rivals. They raise prices rather than scramble after business when demand is active.

Full Employment

Eventually, after a long period of increasing economic activity, there may be no idle resources remaining. Most plants may be operating at or near capacity. All healthy adults who want to work may be employed. One firm can then only secure more workers by hiring them away from another firm. More steel can then only be obtained to build automobiles by diverting it from refrigerators, and so on. All temporary bottlenecks have by now been broken by developing new sources of supply. The remaining limitation is the size of the bottle itself. If and when a state of full employment is reached, any further increase in effective demand can only raise prices and cannot increase output.

What's Wrong with Spiraling Prices?

The foregoing discussion has implied that a substantial and seemingly continual rise in price levels, even although coupled with full employment, may not be altogether desirable.

One reason why this is so is that a permanent shift in the price level is socially unjust. As already mentioned, rising prices benefit debtors at the expense of creditors, and conversely. Some people have little sympathy for creditors, conceiving them to consist of a few wealthy men, but actually their ranks include all bondholders, life insurance policy holders, and savings deposit holders, besides many other persons of modest means.

An economic reason for fearing a state of full employment in conjunction with an increasing supply of inflationary money is that the price system will then be unable to function as satisfactorily as usual. Prices are traffic lights that guide goods and services into their appropriate employments. Relative price increases promote extra production and more economical use of goods that are in short supply. The price system can perform these functions more effectively if some prices are falling, if some kinds of output are declining, if some workers are being forced out of expiring firms, and if less capable entrepreneurs are on their way out.

It is probably very hard for any government to arrange the economic environment so that resources are *both* fully employed *and* properly allocated. Too much of one kind of economic efficiency may mean too little of the other. Here indeed is a need for the exercise of economic judgment free from the myopia of special interest pressures.

Statements for Consideration

1. Effective demand of firms and effective demand of households are limited by the same considerations during a depression.
   Evaluate
2. Whether an increase in the national money stock will stimulate income and employment rather than raise prices depends upon whether firms or households come to hold the new money.
   Explain
3. During a business upswing the percentage distribution of the national money stock between passive and active balances normally remains unchanged. *Evaluate*
4. Increases in M_2 balances during a depression may *indirectly* increase effective demand. *Explain*
5. Labor costs remain relatively unchanged from depression to prosperity. *Evaluate*
6. An increase in effective demand will increase output rather than prices. *Evaluate*
7. Full employment may lead to another kind of economic inefficiency. *Explain*

References

Boulding, K. E., *Economic Analysis,* Chapter 19. New York: Harper, 1948.

Dillard, D., *The Economics of John Maynard Keynes,* Chapter 10. New York: Prentice-Hall, 1948.

Ellis, H. S. (Ed.), *A Survey of Contemporary Economics,* Chapter 2. Philadelphia: Blakiston, 1948.

Haberler, G., "The Place of the General Theory of Employment, Interest and Money in the History of Economic Thought," *Review of Economics and Statistics,* November 1946. Also in *The New Economics.*

Haberler, G., *Prosperity and Depression* (Revised Edition). Geneva: League of Nations, 1939.

Hansen, A. H., *Economic Policy and Full Employment,* Parts IV, V, VI. New York: McGraw-Hill, 1947.

Hansen, A. H., "Keynes and the General Theory," *Review of Economics and Statistics,* November 1946. Also in *The New Economics.*

Harris, S. E. (Ed.), *Postwar Economic Problems,* Part I. New York: McGraw-Hill, 1943.

Hart, A. G., *Money, Debt and Economic Activity,* Part III. New York: Prentice-Hall, 1948.

Kalecki, M., *Essays in the Theory of Economic Fluctuations.* New York: Farrar and Rinehart, 1939.

Klein, L. R., *The Keynesian Revolution,* Chapters 2–4. New York: Macmillan, 1947.

Lintner, J., "The Theory of Money and Prices," *The New Economics* (S. E. Harris, Ed.). New York: Knopf, 1947.

Morgan, T., *Income and Employment,* Chapter 17. New York: Prentice-Hall, 1947.

Robertson, D. H., *Money,* Chapter 10. New York: Cambridge University Press, 1948.

Samuelson, P. A., *Economics,* Chapter 18. New York: McGraw-Hill, 1948.

Samuelson, P. A., "Lord Keynes and the General Theory," *Econometrica,* July 1946. Also in *The New Economics.*

Tarshis, L., *Elements of Economics,* Chapter 39. Boston: Houghton Mifflin, 1947.

Villard, H. H., *Deficit Spending and the National Income.* New York: Farrar and Rinehart, 1941.

Williams, J. H., "An Appraisal of Keynesian Economics," *American Economic Review,* May 1948.

PART IV

Price Theory

15

Price Theory Introduction

It is sometimes said that income theory is a study in macroeconomics and price theory a study in microeconomics. Income theory deals with large aggregates relating to the entire economy (for example, the national product), but price theory deals with the operations of a single firm (for example, its own output). However, a free enterprise economy is made up of independently operating firms; and so, just as more can be learned about a forest by examining its trees, so can a study of firms help to explain a whole nation at work. It is now time to put down the telescope through which we have been viewing the economy in general, and reach instead for a microscope with which to observe particular markets, commodities, and producers.

Economic Significance of Price Theory

In the last Part we were concerned with the over-all volume of resource employment, but in this Part we will be concerned with the ways in which employed resources are used. Whereas income theory is concerned with the value of the national product, price theory is concerned with the relative quantities of different sorts of goods produced. Whereas income theory is concerned with total consumption, price theory is concerned with the ways in which an individual household spends its money. In price theory it is more or less assumed that aggregate national output, resource employment, and personal income are all constant, whereas in income theory these are the principal variables.

Price theory supplies the tools to test a particular kind of economic efficiency. In each economy, there are numerous households, with certain needs and desires, and there is a certain quantity of land, labor, and capital to satisfy these wants. In practice, these demands of households somehow become meshed with these supplies of resources, and a national income, comprising some particular assortment of goods and services, comes to be produced. However, the particular assortment of goods and services that actually results may not be the best which is possible. Some other allocation of resources and composition of output might be better, in the sense that it might provide more satisfaction with the same employment, or perhaps the same satisfaction with less employment.

Superficially it may often seem that the central aim of price theory is to explain the relative exchange values of different goods and services. For example, why does a bushel of wheat sell at $2.50 and a pound of wool at $1.00, so that a bushel of wheat can command 2.5 pounds of wool in exchange? However, the real significance of price theory is that, in explaining these relative values, it shows how the differing abilities of the economy to produce wheat and wool come to be reconciled with the varying desires of households for them.

Role of the Firm

In a free enterprise economy the reconciling of households' demands for consumer goods and the economy's supplies of productive resources is indirectly and unconsciously performed by millions of separate producing units. Such producing units, whether legally organized as proprietorships, partnerships, or corporations, and whether engaged in agriculture, manufacturing, or any other industry, will hereafter be called firms. Millions of firms, in attempting to maximize their profits, incidentally determine the allocation of resources, the composition of the national output, and the character of household consumption.

Each firm has an input side on which it buys goods and services and an output side on which it sells goods and services. Every firm employs labor, needs capital funds, and uses natural resources directly or indirectly, besides reprocessing intermediate goods or wearing out capital goods. Every firm has an output of either producer or consumer goods. Even the firms that only make producer goods are indirectly making consumer goods, because the demand for producer goods is derived from the demand for consumer goods. Hence, directly or indirectly, every firm is employing the economy's resources to satisfy the desires of consuming households.

No firm buys inputs of resources and sells outputs of goods in a haphazard and undirected manner. Each firm is conducted with some aim in view. Price theory assumes that the objective of each firm is profits and that every firm is managed competently. In other words, it is supposed that the actions, and especially the output decisions of each and every firm, are calculated to maximize profits. Of course, in the real world, some managers may prefer power or social approval to profits, and the managements of all firms will occasionally make mistakes. Nevertheless, price theory does not attempt to cope with these aberrations and lapses, and how could it?

Three Product Types

The way in which the prices and outputs of different goods and services come to be determined depends in part upon their characteristics.

The character of some goods is almost preordained and the supplier or producer cannot significantly modify their essential character. Examples are iron ore, crude oil, salmon, potatoes, milk, logs, cotton, and eggs. All these goods are either extracted directly from our natural endowment or result from biological processes over which the so-called producer has little control. It is perfectly true, of course, that these goods are usually graded, but sorting after the event is not the same as prescribing beforehand. For example, eggs can be graded for size, but the hen cannot be adjusted to drop cubic eggs containing three green yolks! Admittedly, a farmer can decide whether to grow turnips or potatoes, but the characteristics of each crop are largely predetermined by nature. We shall call goods of this kind "natural goods."

A firm that produces natural goods must decide which of several alternative and predetermined kinds of goods it wishes to produce. After this election has been made, the range of discretion is rather limited. It can decide how much to produce and it can take pains to see that there is no waste of inputs. However, it cannot decide at what price to sell, for this is determined by the market, but only whether to accept or reject the prevailing price. It cannot advertise, or otherwise promote the sale of its own output, because its production cannot be told apart from that of rivals; for example, Farmer Jones cannot profitably advertise Jones Wheat because, grade for grade, no buyer will be able to distinguish it and nobody will believe it to be different. Nor can a firm that produces and sells natural goods alter their essential character.

"Fabricated goods" are in many ways the opposite of "natural goods." The performance characteristics of fabricated goods can in large measure be prescribed. Steel products can be made so that they are flat or round, hard or soft surfaced, brittle or bendable, and so forth. A pen can be made with a nib or a ball point, to write thick or thin, and be given a variety of shapes and colors. Numerous other examples come readily to mind.

Producers of fabricated goods must determine the character of their output in advance. A farmer can produce milk or eggs just by feeding cows or hens, but no firm will just produce something called steel or pens. There is always conscious and deliberate product design in the making of fabricated goods.

Fabricated goods can be subclassified as "specification commodities" or "differentiated products."

A firm that makes fabricated goods must decide whether to make an output that will meet certain standard specifications or an output different from that of any other producer. A firm that operates a sawmill cuts its logs into certain standard shapes (for example, $2'' \times 4''$), and so lumber tends to be a specification commodity. On the other hand an automobile producer, in determining body contours and colors, engine and chassis, and so forth, makes a motor car that is a differentiated product.

The above distinction is an important one. Producers of specification goods subject themselves to a measure of competition from other producers who make goods to meet the same specifications. Producers of differentiated products are in some measure able to acquire a limited monopoly and so a shelter from the full blast of commercial rivalry. Moreover, because differentiated products bear special brand names, it is practicable to promote them by advertising and other means. Promotion, for other producers, is largely an unnecessary and unknown field.

The makers of specification goods cannot easily charge prices that are different, grade by grade, from those of rival producers located in the same market. A higher price will stop all sales and a lower price will either result in retaliatory price cuts or bring more orders than can possibly be filled. Hence specification goods markets usually have a single price for each grade. Such a common price may be due to the ordinary action of pure competition, price leadership, or conventional pricing. A good example of such a situation is afforded by the basic steel industry.

Firms producing goods that have been differentiated, either physically through product design or psychologically by means of advertising, can set their own individual and distinct prices. A Ford does not have to sell at exactly the same price as a Plymouth or Chevrolet, because these rival makes are not physically identical, and hence a modest price differential is possible. When most buyers have brand preferences, there is likely to be some independent pricing by producers, but it is seldom possible completely to ignore rivals' prices either.

Incidentally, some goods are "natural goods" at the time of their original production, and yet they are "differentiated products" at the time of sale. Milk is a natural good, since it comes from the cow, but the housewife receives it as a branded product in a labeled bottle or carton. Oranges and almonds are branded on their way from the orchard to the kitchen. A great deal of modern merchandising, in fact, consists of buying natural products and then packaging them in some special way so that they can be sold as differentiated products.

The distinction between natural goods, specification products, and differentiated products is important for several reasons. One reason is that the ways in which rival producers compete is related to the kind of products they are selling or buying. Another reason is that too many of the economy's resources may be devoted to differentiation.

In general, rival producers are able to compete on the basis of price, promotion, or product quality, or some combination of these three. Firms that supply natural goods (for example, apple growers) are normally limited to a very narrow kind of price competition; they can either sell at the prevailing market price or not, as they choose. Firms that sell specification goods (for example, cement) do not usually compete in price but they may employ salesmen and do a little advertising. Firms that sell differentiated products may compete on all three fronts (for example, manufacturers of television sets), but this is not always the case (for example, cigarette makers).

Degrees of Competition

The man on the street often uses the terms "monopoly" and "competition" and probably imagines he knows what these treacherous words mean. The economist has only been able to make reasonably sure by distinguishing and defining many degrees and kinds of monopoly and competition. Even at the present time, despite improvements in terminology, the economist must pick his way carefully among these slippery concepts.

One of the oldest concepts of price theory is that of pure competition. The essential features of pure competition are that there is no product differentiation and that a homogeneous good is bought and sold by so many buyers and sellers that none of them take into account any of the ways in which they might be able to influence its price. Most natural goods, and some specification goods, are sold in purely competitive markets.

Monopoly has traditionally been looked upon as the opposite extreme of pure competition. Monopoly in Greek means a single seller. A single seller, however, of what? If one wants to split hairs, the Radio Corporation of America is the only producer of RCA radios and phonographs for instance, but that is not what is meant. A firm is a monopolist only if it is the sole seller of some widely conceived type of product. A radio seller, in order to be a monopolist, would have to be the only seller of radio sets. Even such a monopolist would experience some fringe competition from movies and television, but this is usually ignored. In the past there have been few complete monopolies in the case of natural goods, specification products, or differentiated products.

Monopsony is a recently coined term to describe a situation in which there is a single buyer but many sellers. The United States is a monopsonist in the case of newly mined gold. National governments are also monopsonists in wartime as regards combat weapons. Some employers in small towns are monopsonists in the hiring of labor.

Actually a great many employers' associations are almost in the position of monopsonists and many of the unions with which they negotiate are in the position of monopolists. In the case of industry-wide collective bargaining this is especially likely to be true. When such situations arise, the resultant wage agreement is theoretically indeterminate and the outcome may lie anywhere between the wage rates that would arise if there were only a monopolistic labor union or only a monopsonistic employers' association.   Another term for this special circumstance is bilateral monopoly.

Market situations are occasionally encountered in which there are only two sellers but many buyers ("duopoly") or many sellers but only two buyers ("duosony").   The price and quantity outcome in such cases depends upon the special retaliatory behavior patterns that may prevail between the two rivals.   This branch of economic theory is rather fruitless, without the mathematical insight of modern "game theory," and so will be disregarded.

In the modern world a very large number of market situations, perhaps a majority of them, exemplify what the economist calls monopolistic competition.   Monopolistic competition, as the name implies, refers to any situation in which there are elements of both monopoly and competition.   General Motors has a monopoly in the sale of Cadillacs, Buicks, Chevrolets, and other cars, but it must face the competition of other automobile manufacturers. Joe's Giant Hamburgers must face the competition of other hamburgers, but they alone are sold at Joe's stand and served up by Joe himself.   Usually this mixture of competition and monopoly depends in part upon product differentiation by each seller, but it may also result from the fact that there are only a few sellers. If there are only a few sellers, each one of them will realize that the number of units he can sell will depend upon the price he charges.   Within the field of monopolistic competition it is customary to distinguish between polypoly and oligopoly.

In the case of polypoly, there are not so many sellers that they disregard their possible influence on price; actually, these sellers do not accept a market price but determine their own.   However, there are enough sellers in competition so that no one seller, in determining his price, or his promotion, or his product quality, bothers to consider whether his own action will compel his rivals to alter their price, promotion, and product determinations.   The restaurants of a large city are usually in a state of polypoly, for example.

Oligopoly, in contrast to polypoly, refers to situations in which there are a few sellers in such close competition that, in determining their respective prices, product specifications, and promotional efforts, each tries to take into account the possible reactions its decisions will have upon its immediate rivals. For instance, *A* may not cut his price because he fears that this will cause *B* to cut his price too, thus nullifying much of the quantity effect of *A*'s price cut. In some respects oligopoly is like a poker game.

Oligopoly is extremely prevalent throughout the American economy and most other industrial nations. In various parts of the United States there is an oligopolistic situation in the case of cigarettes, steel, cement, automobile tires, and gasoline, to mention a few outstanding cases. Even in small towns one often finds an oligopoly situation among the three or four local movie houses, laundries, and groceries.

In view of all these real and pseudo-Grecian terms, it might be helpful to summarize some of these distinct market situations, as follows:

1. *Monopoly.* Single seller who sets own price independently. Large number of unorganized buyers. May sell natural, specification, or differentiated product.
2. *Monopsony.* Single buyer who sets own purchase price independently. Large number of unorganized sellers.
3. *Bilateral Monopoly.* Monopolist confronted by a monopsonist. Each side of the market negotiating as a single party. Price result unpredictable.
4. *Monopolistic Competition.* Combines elements of monopoly and competition. Monopoly elements come from fewness of sellers and/or differentiation of product. Sellers determine their own prices. Sellers sometimes engage in quality and selling competition also. Includes cases of oligopoly and polypoly.
5. *Oligopoly.* Each seller, whether or not his output is differentiated, considers rivals' reactions to his own price, product, or promotion decisions.
6. *Polypoly.* Enough sellers for each to disregard possible reactions of rivals. Product always differentiated.
7. *Pure Competition.* Sellers and buyers accept market price. The actions or possible reactions of other buyers and sellers ignored. Excludes case of differentiated products.

In the case of pure competition, when there are many sellers of natural or specification goods, it is possible to group the numerous producers of a homogeneous good into an industry. It is for this reason that so much competitive price theory has traditionally emphasized industry analysis.   The entire economy could be subdivided into industries if there were always many buyers and sellers and never any differentiated products.   On the other hand, monopolistic competition logically destroys the concept of an industrial group, at least for most analytical purposes.   Which firms are inside or outside a particular industry may be problematical when each is producing a different good that is more or less a substitute for the output of other concerns.   Classifying firms into groups may prove more arbitrary than assigning the heaven's stars to different constellations.   And counting the number of firms in an industry must be an almost hopeless task when the very confines of the group are uncertain.   Also it is impossible to draw up a significant group demand schedule.   For example, one cannot construct a demand curve for "automobiles" that will have any ordinary meaning, for a buyer does not have a reservation price for motor cars in general, but rather for a Ford sedan, a Buick convertible, and so on.   Price theory can make little use of the group concept when products are differentiated.   A monopoly constitutes a group by itself, in a sense; any competition it experiences is between "its" industry and other groups producing different goods.

The Concept of Final and Temporary Equilibrium

In the last century, price theory tended to stress what was and is described as long-run equilibrium.   Long-run equilibrium is the final outcome that would result if, after some autonomous change took place, a sufficient time elapsed for a complete adjustment to be made by the firm or its industry, and even the entire economy.   During this period of adjustment, it is, of course, necessary to assume that no more autonomous events of a disturbing nature intervene.

It is this last requirement that always prevents the attainment of long-run or final equilibria in the real world.   There is no guarantee that the lapse of a long period of time will automatically bring about long-run equilibrium.   In fact, the longer the intervening period of adjustment, the greater is the likelihood of another and interfering autonomous event.   Firms, industries, and the economy itself may always be heading toward final equilibrium; however, before they arrive, some new development starts them off toward a new destination, which in turn they never reach. Long-run equilibria can never be attained so long as inventions are made, natural resources are discovered or exhausted, populations change their age and size, and taxes, import restrictions, and government regulations are inconstant. Nevertheless, the direction of long-run adjustments may be of current importance, even though they never completely run their course.

Modern price theory is increasingly concerning itself with the temporary adjustments that firms make to current conditions. For instance, while no firm would operate forever at a loss, most firms, so long as they can more than cover their operating costs, will find it less unprofitable to work at a loss for a single season than to close down. The temporary or short-run adjustment, which is to continue production, actually occurs. The final or long-run solution, which is to close down, is only material in the event that the currently unprofitable set of conditions endures indefinitely.

Occasionally there may be no time for adjustment at all. The classic example of such a case is that of a seller who has already produced a perishable commodity that cannot be held over until a later date. Frequently there is nothing left for him to do but accept whatever price is obtainable.

Price theory altogether distinguishes among three degrees of possible adjustment. In the long run, a complete and final adjustment is possible (for example, a producer can decide whether or not to buy or replace his fixed assets and keep his enterprise in being). In the short run, a partial and temporary adjustment is possible (for example, a producer has a plant in being but can decide whether or not to operate it). In the immediate market period, no real adjustment is possible (for example, the entrepreneur has already produced his output). The long-run period and the immediate market period are opposite extremes. In practice, short-run situations are most commonly encountered.

Incidentally, the term "equilibrium" does not connote anything beneficial, but simply means stability until conditions change again. Economic equilibria may coincide with conditions that waste resources or leave people unemployed and miserable. Equilibrium simply means that the dependent variables in some system will not alter further.

Analysis of Particular or General Equilibrium?

In the past economists have been concerned with both particular equilibrium analysis and general equilibrium analysis. These two approaches differ in their employment, complexity, and practicability. Neither is necessarily superior to the other and the valid use of each depends upon the nature of the problem being analyzed.

Particular equilibrium analysis operates with blinkers and usually does not look much beyond two sets of functions containing a common variable. Such a procedure is entirely justifiable if the two functions are not indirectly related, but are in reality the only two independent or determining variables of significance. However, it often happens that the interrelations are more complex. For example, a tax on gasoline might normally tend to raise gasoline prices by a given amount if demand remained unchanged; 'but if the gasoline tax finances highway construction, which makes motoring pleasanter, the demand of motorists for gasoline will increase, and the price increase will be greater. Wider horizons are then required, more variables must be considered, and a less particularized or a more general equilibrium must be considered. In extreme cases the narrowest permissible scope of an investigation is as wide as the economy itself.

General equilibrium theory concerns the simultaneous adjustment of most or all the variables in an economy. Ideally it should embrace all factor and product prices, all inputs and outputs of productive enterprises, the optimum adjustments of all households, and all the major counterflows of money and goods within a single analysis. It includes both the particular equilibrium of a single entrepreneur or industry (for example, the determinants of a single product's price and output) and the aggregates of macroeconomics (for example, income, consumption, and investment relationships for an entire nation).

However, this does not mean that general equilibrium theory can be used to determine a "proper" price and volume and money flow for each of the thousands, or even millions, of goods and services that are annually provided in a capitalistic economy. Who would be capable of simultaneously solving a million equations even if the functions they would try to express were known? The true usefulness of general equilibrium theory is quite different.   It sets up and analyzes simplified models that stress the inter-relation of entrepreneurs, households, and sometimes governments. In this way the logical validity of various concepts can be tested but real world answers are unlikely.

In this book, so far as possible, the more pedestrian but practical alternative of particular equilibrium will be adopted.   Few intellects are capable of mentally handling more than a few variables without the aid of mathematics.   Actually, in the outline of the general theory of income determination in Chapter 12, six variables in four dimensions were included in the analysis.   Students who did not enjoy even this degree of complexity may be pleased to learn that this will not happen again.

Statics and Dynamics

The ways in which producers, consumers, and the owners of factors behave depend in large measure upon their expectations regarding the future.

In static theory the possible effects of future expectations on economic behavior are ignored.   If the price of a good falls, purchasers are supposed to buy more units without stopping to consider the future course of its price.   Static theory assumes implicitly that everyone expects present conditions to continue indefinitely.   Persons who have anticipations of this kind are sometimes said to have an elasticity of expectation of unity.   Naturally conditions never do continue unchanged.   However, when circumstances alter, the new set of conditions is then supposedly thought to be normal by everyone.

In dynamic theory an attempt is made to handle anticipations of change.   For example, under some conditions, a declining price, because purchasers view it as a herald of further price reductions in the future, may in reality cause *less* buying now.   Dynamic theory can obviously become frighteningly complicated. Not only must persons' future expectations be assumed, or tied somehow into the theory, but generally these individual expectations will not coincide but will instead constitute a sort of spectrum of anticipations.

Nonetheless, despite its complexity, dynamic theory is often needed to understand the economic behavior of people in general, and the output decisions of entrepreneurs in particular.   For example, after World War II, some economists claimed that rent ceilings were preventing investors from building houses and apartments for income. Occasionally this may have been true, but it is more than probable that a lifting of rent ceilings would have had little effect. The cost of constructing an apartment house is determined by present costs and conditions, but the receipts earned by the building are earned over a service life that may run from 30 to 50 years. The payment of contractors and the receipt of rents would occur at different dates and price levels. Many potential investors avoided projects that involved V-J Day costs but might never come to command V-J Day rentals. Many economic and business decisions must attempt to take into account just such a time dimension.

In this Part IV, which deals with price theory, the emphasis will be almost exclusively on statics. Analyses will be made of pure competition, monopoly and monopsony, and monopolistic competition, applicable to the immediate market period, the short run, and the long run. The implications of these theories as regards the optimum allocation of resources will be discussed in Chapter 25.

Statements for Consideration

1. A great deal can be learned about the economy as a whole from an understanding of the motives and behavior of individual firms.
   Exemplify
2. The principal object of price theory is to explain why some goods command higher or lower prices than other goods.   *Evaluate*
3. Firms employ resources in a haphazard way and the proportion of the economy's resources that go to make this or that good is largely a matter of chance.   *Evaluate*
4. The basic unit of price theory is the industry.   *Discuss*
5. Coal, refrigerators, and pig iron are all sold under the same market conditions.   *Evaluate*
6. A farmer has far fewer variables to worry about than a retail store operator.   *Explain*
7. The concept of pure competition is in many ways a very special one involving numerous limiting assumptions.   *Discuss*
8. The distinction between polypoly and oligopoly is largely one of whether sellers take into account the probable reactions of rivals to their own price changes.   *Explain*
9. Monopolistic competition logically destroys the concept of an industrial group for many analytical purposes.   *Explain*
10. Long-run equilibrium is probably never attained, but long-run forces are almost constantly at work.   *Explain*

11. The term "equilibrium" connotes something beneficial. *Evaluate*
12. Dynamic theory can be more realistic than static theory.
Exemplify

References

Boulding, K. E., *Economic Analysis,* Chapter 30. New York: Harper, 1948.

Bowman, M. J., and Bach, G. L., *Economic Analysis and Public Policy,* Chapter 15. New York: Prentice-Hall, 1943.

Burns, A. R., *The Decline of Competition,* Chapter 1. New York: McGraw-Hill, 1936.

Due, J. F., *Intermediate Economic Analysis,* Chapter 2. Chicago: Irwin, 1947.

Garver, F. B., and Hansen, A. H., *Principles of Economics,* Third Edition, Chapter 6. New York: Ginn, 1947.

Hamilton, W., *Price and Price Policies.* New York: McGraw-Hill, 1938.

Machlup, F., "Monopoly and Competition: A Classification of Market Positions," *American Economic Review,* September 1937.

Marshall, A., *Principles of Economics,* Eighth Edition, V. London: Macmillan, 1920.

Meyers, A. L., *Modern Economics,* Chapter 10. New York: Prentice-Hall, 1941.

Stigler, G. J., *The Theory of Price.* New York: Macmillan, 1946.

Triffin, R., *Monopolistic Competition and General Equilibrium Theory.* Cambridge, Mass.: Harvard University Press, 1940.

16

Pure Competition

IT IS OFTEN supposed that, if pure competition prevailed, each commodity would be produced and consumed at an optimum rate. In other words, consumers as a whole would not be better satisfied if more of some goods were produced by sacrificing some output of another good. Several of the theoretical grounds upon which the argument has been based will prove useful later on and are worth studying.

Price Determination in a Competitive Market

A market is an area in which demand and supply forces, for a given product, are in such close contact with one another that a common price prevails throughout the area. The common price may change over time, but at any instant it is the same everywhere in the market. A purely competitive market is a special kind of market, characterized by a complete lack of price manipulation by any one buyer or seller. No participant in the market can influence the price by offering or taking more or less quantity; or, if any buyer or seller does have such influence, he ignores this power and behaves as though he did not possess it. In other words, a buyer can either purchase at the market place or not purchase at all; and a seller can accept the market price or not make a sale. The price in a purely competitive market is a *datum* for those who participate in it. Collectively, they have all made the price, but individually the influence of each is so slight as to be ignored.

Some buyers are more eager to purchase than others. In any market the bids of various would-be buyers could be arranged according to a descending order of bid prices. For example, buyers as a whole might be willing to buy 290 bushels of wheat in some market at 125¢ a bushel; 300 bushels at 120¢, 310 bushels at 115¢, and so on. Such an array of bid prices, as set forth in columns 1 and 2 of Table 17, is called a demand schedule.

TABLE 17

MARKET DEMAND AND SUPPLY SCHEDULES

(1) Demand (bushels)	(2) Price (cents)	(3) Supply (bushels)	(4) Demand after 15¢ tax (bushels)
290	125	380	260
300	120	360	270
310	115	340	280
320	110	320	290
330	105	300	300
340	100	280	310
350	95	260	320
360	90	240	330
370	85	220	340
380	80	200	350
390	75	180	360
400	70	160	370

Sellers' asking prices can also be arranged into a supply schedule, which will show how much the sellers are willing to supply
at each one of several different prices. For example, as shown
in columns 2 and 3 of Table 17, the seller might be willing to
supply 380 bushels at 125¢, 360 bushels at 120¢, 340 bushels at
115¢, and so on.

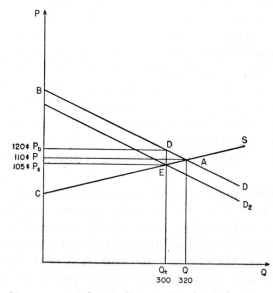

Fig. 14. Equilibrium Price under Pure Competition Including Tax Incidence.

Demand and supply schedules can be charted in the form of a two-dimensional diagram having a horizontal axis representing quantity (bushels in this case) and a vertical axis representing price (in cents). Figure 14 is a purely competitive market diagram based on the data of Table 17. What competitive price and quantity will result from the interaction of these demand and supply conditions? A price of 100¢ could not be a stable and competitive price because buyers would then demand 340 bushels but sellers would be willing to supply only 280 bushels. This excessive demand would lead some buyers to offer a higher price and cause some sellers to hold out for a higher figure. On the other hand, a price of 115¢ is too high, since it would lead to an excessive supply amounting to 30 bushels. The competitive price is that which will equate the quantities demanded and supplied. In the present example, 110¢ is such a price, and everybody will be satisfied to trade 320 bushels of wheat. This price is also the *equilibrium price,* since it will remain stable until there is a change in either the demand or the supply schedule.

However, demand and supply schedules do change quite frequently. The demand for a product may increase because people have acquired a taste for it or because buyers' money incomes have risen. A *bona fide* increase in demand means that buyers will pay more for a given quantity, or will take more at a given price, or some combination of these two reactions. Such a development is called an increase in demand in the *schedule sense*. An increase in sales that results from a cut in price only is an increase in the *market sense* and is clearly quite a different matter. Graphically, a schedule sense increase in demand entails an entirely new curve, located higher or to the right; but a market sense increase in demand merely involves moving along the same curve from left to right.

An increase in demand in the schedule sense will normally result in a higher price and quantity. For example, Fig. 15 shows what happens when there is an increase in demand, as shown by a new demand schedule, D_2. There is a new intersection point (I_2 instead of I_1), a higher price, and a greater quantity. The extent to which price and quantity increase depends in large measure on the slope of the supply schedule (S_1). On the other hand, a decrease in supply, represented by a new supply schedule (S_2), means that sellers will now supply less at a given price or demand more for a given amount. A decreased supply (S_2), in combination with the old demand (D_1) gives a new intersection point (I_3), a higher price, and a reduced quantity. If demand increases and supply decreases, the price will certainly be greater (P_4) but the quantity (Q_4) could be higher, lower, or the same.

The mere fact that the market price of some commodity has changed does not indicate whether the change was brought about by a demand or supply schedule change. For example, if the price of a good falls, its fall might be due to (1) decreased demand, (2) increased supply, (3) a combination of (1) and (2), (4) a small increased demand but a large increase in supply, or (5) a small decrease in supply but a large decrease in demand. Simple inferences are highly treacherous in price analysis.

Price Ceiling Effects

The war period, with its diversion of resources from civilian to military production, gave the United States an object lesson in the forces that operate in approximately competitive markets.

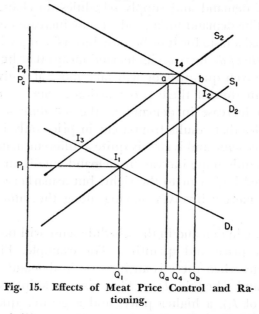

Fig. 15. Effects of Meat Price Control and Rationing.

Some of the civilian markets particularly affected were those dealing in meat, dairy, and textile products. Figure 15 is also helpful in explaining what happened.

Let us suppose that the "meat" market in 1940 is represented by the schedules D_1 and S_1. The enormous government expenditures for the war eventually flowed through to consumers. Families, with more dollars to spend for everything, began to have higher demand prices for meat. (The technical reasons for this are explained in Chapter 18.) By 1942, the demand schedule for meat, as for most other civilian products, had shifted to the right, and might be graphically represented by some such curve as D_2 in Fig. 15. In the meantime, costs of production had been rising; the competition of war plant jobs forced wage rates up and other factors also rose in price. A reduced supply schedule, further to the left, and possibly located as S_2 is in the figure, came into being. Therefore, by 1942, the equilibrium price and quantity were probably P_4 (i.e., higher) and Q_4 (i.e., greater).

These higher prices were politically unpopular, and a fear that allowing prices to rise would bring about inflation became widespread; accordingly, legal price maxima were set for meat commodities by the federal government. These price ceilings were subequilibrium; i.e., they were below what a free market price would have been. If the price ceiling for "meat" were shown by P_c in the diagram, the amount supplied would be Q_a and the amount demanded would be Q_b. In other words, the government, in setting a subequilibrium price maximum, created a "shortage" of Q_aQ_b. More housewives wanted to buy meat than the available supplies permitted. The next step was to prorate the Q_a supply over the Q_b demand by means of rationing. It is noteworthy that this diagrammatic "shortage," which leads to rationing, is a pseudo-scarcity, as the 1942 supply of meat (Q_a) is greater than that of 1940 (Q_1). And, as a matter of fact, the civilian per capita consumption of meat in the United States increased considerably during this period. The empty meat shelves were not the result of a physical shortage but of a rapidly increasing effective demand. Incidentally, if the government had not interfered, and had instead allowed the price to rise to P_4, supply would probably have increased, in the market sense, to Q_4. Is it better to have more but pay a higher price, or to pay a little and partly do without?

Buyers' and Sellers' Surpluses

It has already been explained that a demand schedule consists of a series of reservation prices. In any market, some of the units purchased will have reservation prices in excess of the amount actually paid by the buyer. For example, reverting to Table 17, the market price was $1.10, at which price 320 bushels exchanged hands. However, 290 bushels were valued at $1.25 or more; another 10 bushels at between $1.25 and $1.20; and a final 10 bushels at between $1.15 and the actual price of $1.10. The purchasers of these intramarginal units obtained a surplus in the sense that they received something they valued more than the price they had to pay. This difference is called "buyers' surplus."

The suppliers who make a sale receive an analogous surplus. Table 17 shows that sellers would have been willing to supply 160 bushels at $.70 or less, whereas they actually received $1.10. Other sellers would have contributed some supplies at $.75, $.80, $.85, . . . , $1.05; but they also received $1.10. All the intramarginal sellers would have accepted a lower price than they actually obtained, and this excess is termed "suppliers' surplus."

This notion of a surplus for buyers and sellers must be handled with care. It can best be understood if one first considers the case of an individual. Next one must consider the special problems of attempting to add individual buyer's surplus into collective buyers' surplus.

Let us imagine a motorist buying gasoline. If the price is 20¢ a gallon, he may use 12 gallons a month. But the first gallon, on which he makes his most essential trips, will be worth far more than 20¢ to him. The second, third, and all subsequent gallons, except for the last or marginal gallon, will each be of greater use value to him than they cost him to buy. These surpluses show how much more pleasure he gets in spending his money on these intramarginal gallons of gasoline than he would if he spent 20¢ more on some other commodity instead. The money value the buyer places on the utility he derived from the consumed gasoline depends upon his wealth and income and how much pleasure he could alternatively have procured with 20¢. If he is a rich man, and has so much of everything that 20¢ buys him little enjoyment elsewhere, his buyer's surplus on the consumed gasoline will be rather high in terms of dollars and cents.

There is no way of adding the utility of one man's consumption to the utility of another's, because this is a subjective and psychic affair. It *is* possible to add the buyer's surplus of one consumer to that of another because these surpluses are expressed in money

values. The resultant sum, however, must be interpreted with
care. If the money incomes of buyers decline, buyers' surplus may
also decline, even though each consumer is independently receiving as much subjective use value as before.

Diagrammatically, buyers' surplus is shown as the area below the
demand curve and above the price line, whereas suppliers' surplus
is the area above the supply curve and below the price line. In
Fig. 14, buyers' surplus is the area ABP and suppliers' surplus is
the area ACP. Buyers' and suppliers' surpluses, when added together, are at a maximum when the market price is the natural or
equilibrium one. Also the greatest possible number of units are
then bought and sold.

Commodity Tax Effects

A better understanding of purely competitive price theory can
be had from considering the effects of a commodity tax. Perhaps
the government imposes a 15¢ per bushel tax on wheat and makes
the millers (the only buyers by assumption) legally liable. What
will happen to the market price and quantity?

The millers' reservation prices will decrease 15¢ for each successive unit they buy. The use value of wheat to millers remains
the same (D_1 in Fig. 14), providing the price of flour and other
milling costs are unaltered, but the market price they can afford to
pay will be less by the amount they must pay to the Collector
of Internal Revenue. The buyers accordingly have a new demand schedule (D_2), which is vertically parallel, but 15¢ lower
throughout, than their former one (D_1). Specifically, if we continue to use the data of Table 17, the new demand schedule, after
the tax is imposed, will be $1.10 for 290 bushels, $1.05 for 300
bushels, $1.00 for 310 bushels and so forth.

The market price, after the 15¢ tax is imposed on buyers, is
given in Fig. 14 by the intersection of the S and D_2 schedules.
This will occur at 300 bushels (Q_t) and give a market price of
$1.05 ($P_s$). The market price is in this case both the gross and
net revenue of suppliers, as they have no legal liability for the tax.
But $1.05, the market price paid by buyers, is only the gross cost
borne by purchasers; their net cost is $1.20, because they must
pay 15¢ to the government on every bushel they buy.

Market equilibrium after the imposition of a tax involves two
conditions. (1) The net prices received by sellers and paid by

buyers must differ by the amount of the tax. (2) The new demand at the buyers' net price and the relevant supply at the sellers' net price must be equal. In the present case P_b ($1.20) and P_s ($1.05) differ by the tax of $.15. Also the buyers will take 300 bushels at $1.20 and the sellers will supply 300 bushels at their net price of $1.05.

The effects of a commodity tax can be treated under several heads. (1) *Tax impact,* or legal liability, has nothing to do with economics, but is decided by governments. In this case it is 15¢ a bushel on buyers of wheat. It is probably administratively cheaper to collect from whichever side of the market is less populated—in this case the demand side. (2) *Tax incidence,* or who bears the tax, concerns the changes that take place in buyers' and sellers' net prices. In this case buyers contributed 10¢ a bushel and sellers paid the balance of 5¢. The buyers paid twice as much of the tax as sellers because the demand schedule, for a given quantity change, rises and falls twice as steeply as that of supply. It would be a coincidence if both schedules had the same slope so that both sides of the market bore the tax equally. (3) *Tax burden,* or loss of well-being, relates to reduction in suppliers' and buyers' surpluses. In this case, with the net price received by sellers falling from P to P_s, suppliers' surplus is now P_sEC instead of PAC, a loss of $PAEP_s$. Analogously, the net price paid by buyers has risen from P to P_b. Accordingly, the buyers' surplus after tax is P_bDB, instead of PAB, and this is a loss of $PADP_b$. However, the government has new tax revenues of P_bDEP_s. Tax collections are a partial offset to the losses in suppliers' and buyers' surpluses, because they should result either in new government services or in tax relief somewhere else in the system. Assuming tax collections are a gain, we should deduct P_bDEP_s from the total loss in joint surpluses of P_bDAEP_s, and this leaves an apparent net loss for the economy of ADE. However, any final judgment should take into account the real contribution to welfare of the goods and services acquired with the tax proceeds.

If this tax had been assessed on sellers instead of buyers, there would be a different legal liability. There would then be an S_2 schedule, higher than S by 15¢ throughout, and the relevant demand would be the original D curve. The market price would be $1.20 instead of $1.05. But the net cost per unit to buyers would still be $1.20 and the net revenue per unit to sellers would still be $1.05. The quantity would again be 300 bushels after the tax is imposed. The tax burden, like the tax incidence, will not be affected by the change in legal liability.

The slopes of the schedules are important in any analysis of this type. The flatter the schedule, the more alternative opportunities are open to the people concerned. If the supply schedule is fairly flat, it means that suppliers can grow other crops, or can sell in other markets, or can afford to wait. A flat demand curve indicates that there are substitute commodities that can be used instead. Flat curves show bargaining power and ability to escape, and for this reason the side of the market with the flattest schedule always bears the smallest part of the tax. Governments will find that it does not pay to tax commodities that have very flat demand and supply schedules. A tax will then decrease quantity more than anything else, and few units will be bought and sold and so pay the tax. In such a case the power to tax is indeed the power to destroy; some products have been driven out of existence by the combination of a high tax and buyers and sellers with alternative products and occupations to fall back on.

Parenthetically, the effect of a subsidy paid for a purely competitive commodity is almost exactly opposite to that of a tax. A subsidy of 15¢ paid to suppliers would lower their reservation prices by this amount for each several quantity. Diagrammatically, there would be a 15¢ downward and parallel shift in the supply schedule, a new intersection point with the old demand curve, and hence a new equilibrium price and quantity.

Price Elasticity of Demand and Supply

A demand schedule indicates the relation between the quantity bought and the price charged. A supply schedule shows the relation between quantity supplied and the price obtained. In each case the two variables are quantity and price. Quantity is often regarded as being the dependent variable while price is viewed as being independent.

The relation between quantity and price—whether we are interested in the quantity demanded or supplied—can be expressed in terms of an elasticity coefficient. For example, price elasticity of supply is the proportionate change in quantity supplied divided by the proportionate change in price that ostensibly occasioned it.

Price elasticity of demand is concerned with proportionate changes in the quantity bought rather than in the quantity supplied. Elasticity is a ratio, and the resultant abstract quotient may vary in magnitude from zero to infinity.

Let us suppose that 90,000 tons of some material are demanded at a price of $55 a ton and 110,000 tons at a price of $45 a ton. The *absolute* change in quantity (Δq) is 20,000 tons. However, we want to know the *proportionate* change in quantity, and we shall consider it to be the *absolute* change divided by the *average* quantity (Q). In numbers this will be 20,000 divided by 100,000, or 0.2. The proportionate change in price is similarly the absolute price change (Δp) divided by the average price (P). In numbers this will be $10 divided by $50, or again 0.2. Price elasticity of demand in this case will then be 0.2 divided by 0.2, which is equal to 1.0. Unit elasticity such as this is of course a special case.

Symbolically, price elasticity can be expressed as

$$\frac{\dfrac{\Delta q}{Q}}{\dfrac{\Delta p}{P}} \quad \text{or} \quad \frac{P\,\Delta q}{Q\,\Delta p}$$

In the case of price elasticity of *demand,* the quantity symbols naturally refer to the amount *bought;* and, in a price elasticity of *supply* formula, the quantity symbols of course relate to the amount *offered* on the market.

The elasticity of a given point on a demand or supply curve can be determined graphically by the method employed in Fig. 16. The problem is to determine the elasticity of the point *A* on either the demand schedule or the supply schedule, shown respectively in Diagrams I and II. First, draw a tangent to the point *A,* and extend this tangent line so that it makes an intercept on the quantity axis at *X*. Next, drop a perpendicular from *A* to the quantity axis at *B*. Then the elasticity coefficient will be the linear distance *BX* divided by *BO*. The denominator in this elasticity ratio is always the distance between the axes' origin (*O*) and the perpendicular's intercept (*B*). Point *A* on the *supply* schedule in Fig. 16 obviously has an elasticity in excess of unity, since *BX* is clearly longer than *BO*.

A few minor terminological matters need to be mentioned.

A schedule with an elasticity of less than one is said to be "inelastic," while one with an elasticity in excess of unity is said to be "elastic." A vertical schedule has zero elasticity and is said to be "perfectly inelastic." A horizontal schedule is termed "perfectly elastic" and has an elasticity of infinity.

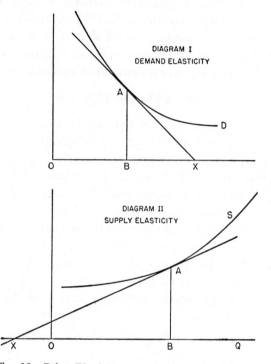

Fig. 16. Price Elasticity of Demand and Supply.

The notion of price elasticity, whether of demand or supply, has various uses. On the supply side, for example, it is an aid in comparing the extent to which a price change will evoke changes in the supply of different goods. If an increase in price of $1.00 will occasion 1,000,000 tons more steel output, or 8,000,000 more barrels of petroleum output, is steel or petroleum more sensitive in its supply responses to price changes? No answer is possible because there is no way of comparing tons of steel and barrels of petroleum directly. The steel supply increase could be made to seem larger by expressing it in pounds instead of tons. Moreover, the price increase of $1.00 may be a relatively large change for petroleum and a relatively small one for steel. The only recourse is to express the price change, and also the quantity change, proportionately rather than absolutely.

On the demand side the concept of elasticity is also essential for comparing the quantity effects of price changes among different commodities. Another significance of elasticity, but only on the demand side, is that it indicates whether a price change will cause buyers to make a smaller or larger total money outlay than before. If demand is elastic, a price decline will cause buyers to spend more money, so that sellers' receipts will increase in the aggregate; and conversely when demand is inelastic.

The Cobweb Theorem

There are some commodities that are produced and consumed, not regularly throughout the year, but spasmodically at certain seasons. Two obvious but not particularly important examples are Christmas trees and Thanksgiving turkeys. In these cases, the supply is provided independently by many producers who do not know of each other's actions, and production is commenced a considerable time before a short selling season, which terminates abruptly. When these circumstances exist, the price is apt to fluctuate considerably from one selling season to another, being high one year, low the next, then high again, and so on.

Figure 17 is supposed to illustrate the normal New York City

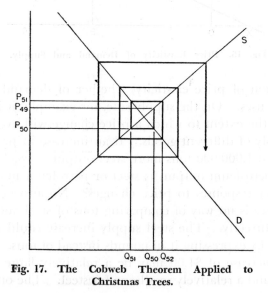

Fig. 17. The Cobweb Theorem Applied to Christmas Trees.

Christmas tree market. The demand and supply schedules remain about the same every year and are supposedly stable over time. If all producers could see the future, the price would probably be determined at the intersection of these two schedules. Actually, each producer is ignorant of the supply being prepared by other producers, so that the total supply is not based on *this year's demand* but on *last year's price*. Hence the 1949 price (P_{49}) is remembered by producers during 1950 and occasions an excessive supply (Q_{50}). By Christmas 1950 the price has fallen to P_{50} but the trees are now in and it is too late for producers to adjust their supply. Next year, in 1951, sellers remember the 1950 price, and so independently bring in only Q_{51} trees. The price rises to P_{51}. In 1952, because of the previous year's high price, the supply is excessive, and the realized price falls. In the diagram, the suppliers, although carrying out their plans independently, collectively miscalculate demand, first over and then under, year after year. Each of them plans according to the last known price and none of them can see the actual demand and imminent supply.

Theoretically, these price oscillations will become ever wider if supply is rather sensitive to price changes while demand is not. On the other hand, these fluctuations in price will tend to iron themselves out if demand is sensitive to price changes and supply is not. A little diagram drawing will demonstrate the geometry of these contentions. The sketching of a few graphs will also show why this theorem is called the cobweb theorem.

The cobweb theorem in its purest form is something of a "sport" in the larger theory of purely competitive markets. But there are numerous situations in which the supply side of the market operates in the manner here described. The production of all agricultural commodities requires that producers make their plans almost simultaneously and independently, and then, after an interval, simultaneously discover whether they have produced too much or too little. However in many of these cases the demand does not suddenly cease on a particular day in the year. People don't want Christmas trees after December 25, but they do eat potatoes all year, for example. Moreover, there are often several opportunities to carry over agricultural supplies to a later market period. In the case of extracting industries, which are often purely competitive, the supply can be adjusted almost continuously throughout the year to changes in demand.

Statements for Consideration

1. In a purely competitive market buyers and sellers do not act as if they could influence the price but accept it as a fact of life.
                                                                    Explain
2. A reduction in price increases demand in the schedule sense.
                                                                    Evaluate
3. More units are exchanged at the equilibrium price than at any other.   *Explain*
4. The elasticity of a demand schedule is indicated by its slope.
                                                                    Evaluate
5. Rationing of meat was rendered necessary during the war by a reduction in meat supplies.   *Evaluate*
6. A specific tax is always paid by the buyers, for even when they are not legally liable the tax is passed on to them by the sellers.
                                                                    Evaluate
7. An increase in price indicates that demand has increased. *Evaluate*
8. A rich man may have a large buyer's surplus and yet receive less extra subjective utility than a poor man does whose buyer's surplus is much less.   *Discuss*
9. Prices may fluctuate violently when natural causes require all producers of a good to make simultaneous but independent output plans that will not mature for some time to come.   *Explain*
10. An equilibrium price in a purely competitive market is one that makes the number of buyers equal to the number of sellers.
                                                                    Evaluate

References

Boulding, K. E., *Economic Analysis,* Chapters 3–6, 8.   New York: Harper, 1948.

Bowman, M. J., and Bach, G. L., *Economic Analysis and Public Policy,* Chapter 17.   New York: Prentice-Hall, 1943.

Due, J. F., *Intermediate Economic Analysis,* Chapter 5.   Chicago: Irwin, 1947.

Ezekiel, M., "The Cobweb Theorem," *Quarterly Journal of Economics,* February 1938.

Garver, F. B., and Hansen, A. H., *Principles of Economics,* Chapters 7, 8.   New York: Ginn, 1947.

Samuelson, P. A., *Economics,* Chapter 19.   New York: McGraw-Hill, 1948.

17

Interdependent Prices

THE PRICE of a single good in a particular market is not always determined independently of its price in another market or of the prices of other goods. The price of wheat at Chicago may be influenced by contemporary prices of wheat at Liverpool and in other markets. And the price of wheat in Chicago today is in part determined by future Chicago prices that are now anticipated. Moreover, the price of wheat is related to the prices of competitive products, the prices of other goods with which wheat may be used, and so forth. The current chapter is dedicated to the theme that few product prices are determined in isolation.

Spatial Interdependence

Political frontiers and geographic obstacles separate the world into a number of different markets for the same product. However, these numerous submarkets are not entirely independent because goods will move from one to another if price differentials are sufficiently wide. The mere fact that prices are unequal in different markets is no evidence that they are unrelated. They are only independent if there is no movement of goods from one market to another and if the different prices fail to rise and fall together.

Suppose that there are two regions in the same country. One is rural (R) and well adapted to butter production; the other is urban (U) and hardly suited for dairying. Figure 18 shows these two butter markets. There is a common vertical scale for price. The horizontal scale represents quantity but reads from right to left in the case of Region R (on the left), although reading from left to right for Region U (on the right). Each regional market has a demand and supply schedule for butter, with the demand schedule in R necessarily sloping downwards toward the left, which is rather unconventional.

If these two markets were completely independent, the price in R (P_r in the diagram) would be given by the intersection of this region's demand and supply schedules. And the price in U would be P_u by the same reasoning. These two prices might be termed "isolation prices," since in each case the other market exerts no influence by assumption.

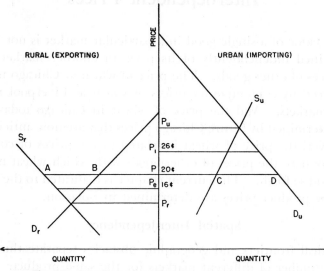

Fig. 18. Interdependent Export and Import Markets.

The opposite case would be if these two markets were in reality one, with no cost obstruction against shipments from one region to the other, in which event there would be a single price. Such a common price would have to equate total demand with total supply in equilibrium. Symbolically, it would be necessary for $S_r + S_u$ to equal $D_r + D_u$, and therefore for $S_r - D_r$ to equal $D_u - S_u$. The latter expression states that the surplus shipped out of R must be equal in quantity to the deficit shipped into U when an equilibrium price prevails. In Fig. 18, such a price is shown as P, and it has been located at 20¢, in order to equate "exports" (AB) with "imports" (CD). A single price that is common to two regions is evidence that *economically* there is only one market, even though they may be nominally distinct.

It is the in-between case of two markets, economically distinct and yet having interdependent prices, that next concerns us. We shall imagine that there is a per unit freight cost, represented by the vertical distance P_iP_e, separating the two regions. Prices in these two regional markets will be dependent if the difference between the "isolation prices" exceeds the freight cost.

If the difference between the isolation prices is 18¢ and the freight cost is assumed to be 10¢, there will be butter shipments from R to U. These shipments will have the effect of raising the price in R above P_r and lowering the price in U below P_u. However, this tendency will cease when the price difference has narrowed to the amount of the freight cost per unit.

When equilibrium has been established, what will be the exporting price in R (i.e., P_e) and the importing price in U (i.e., P_i)? The two conditions for equilibrium are that (1) exports equal imports in quantity and (2) the price in the exporting region be less than that in the importing region by the amount of the unit freight cost. We shall suppose the situation is stable when P_e is 16¢ and P_i is 26¢.

The reader will notice that the freight cost of 10¢ is being borne unequally, with 4¢ bearing on R and 6¢ on U. What determines which market will bear most of the freight cost burden? The region that has the flatter demand and supply schedules, when these are taken together, will have a smaller part of the freight cost shifted on to it. And the region with the steeper schedules, again taken together, will bear a larger share of this transportation expense. Figure 18 has been so drawn that the combined quantity response to a unit price change is slightly greater in the rural region.

During World War II, so-called "ceiling" prices, below the equilibrium price, were placed on commodities such as butter. Let us pretend that the Office of Price Administration in those days set a price ceiling of 14¢ in R and one of 24¢ in U. The supply in R is above the local demand there, and so some butter is normally exported; however, competition will always compel an equality between the net price received on exports to U and the prices paid by consumers in R. The net price on exports to U must be 14¢ because the real freight cost is 10¢ and the legal maximum in U is 24¢. However, at a 14¢ price in R, production will be decreased and consumption will be increased, and less butter will remain over for export. Shipments into U are now less; and, at a lower 24¢ price, production there will be down and consumption up. However, while prices are subequilibrium in both markets, and hence over-all supply is below demand, only the importing region (*U*) feels this artificially created shortage. The final paradox is that consumers in *R* have in effect been encouraged to eat *more* butter despite an over-all shortage in the market sense.

A little consideration reveals that within a single country there are a great many spatially related markets for any one of a number of commodities. Nearly all agricultural commodities are produced in rural areas, but used primarily in urban areas, and because of transportation costs these areas often constitute different markets. Hence it is often essential that government regulations which keep prices below their equilibrium level be supplemented by rationing. In these cases the rationing is particularly needed in what is normally the export area, so that an available surplus for export can be maintained, which will be forced out to the usual import areas.

Temporal Interdependence

There are different markets at different times for a single product always being sold at the same place. The U. S. market for wool in April of any one year (before most domestic shearing takes place) is a different kind of market from that in August (after shearing). And yet these two markets—separated only in time—are linked together by speculative dealings.

Figure 19 represents the August and April markets respectively.

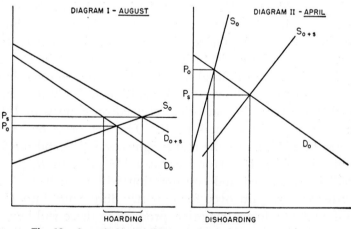

Fig. 19. **Speculative Linking of Future and Past Markets.**

The ordinary textile demand is about the same from one month to another and is identified by a subscript "o" for "ordinary." The wool supply coming from sheep ranches is heavy in August and light in April. The ranch supply schedules also have the "o" subscript. It is evident that, if each market worked out a price independently of other months' markets, the August price would be very low and the April price would be high. However, speculators, anticipating a price rise from August to April, buy in the previous summer and sell in the coming spring. Accordingly there is an additional demand from speculators in August that must be added to the ordinary textile demand. (The total demand for August bears the subscript "o + s" in Diagram I.) On the other hand, speculators add to the normal ranch supply of wool in April. (The total April supply is shown in Diagram II by the subscript "o + s.") In this case speculation smooths out most of the price fluctuation that would otherwise result. The price in August does not fall far, since it is supported by speculative purchases; and the price in April does not rise sharply, because it is kept down by speculative sales. The prices in these two markets will differ, but only by the cost of storage and risk, if speculation is in volume and past experience offers a guide to the future.

Temporal interdependence of markets is especially useful in promoting price stability when changes in supply are periodic and demand is fairly constant. Seasonal variation of this kind is notable in many agricultural and retail markets. Under these circumstances, speculative dealings, often undertaken by the subsequent processors, lead to a steadier rate of manufacture and use.

The shadow of future shortages is often cast by speculators over present markets. Imagine that a government stops the production of all liquors because it is waging a war and the alcohol is needed for explosives. Initially, manufacturers and distributors have stocks on hand, but these will be exhausted within a year or two if consumers continue to drink at the present rate. For a while they will be consuming too rapidly and then they will suddenly have to stop.

Speculation, if permitted, would provide a shock absorber. Liquor stocks would be hoarded, present prices would rise, and this would cause more economical use by consumers in the immediate future. Inventories would be exhausted less rapidly.

And, in the more distant future, when prices are reaching a scarcity level, a new supply would appear as speculators begin selling their hoards. The speculators may profit, but only to the extent that they originally underestimate the ultimate severity of the coming shortage, and they will lose if whisky production is resumed sooner than they had expected. In any event, there is expert warning of coming shortage, and the economy can begin adjusting in advance. Naturally these results are prevented when legal maxima prohibit a speculative rise in prices.

Speculation may not be so beneficial for the economy, however, when even experts have no grounds for deciding what the future will bring. Under these circumstances speculation becomes gambling, price fluctuations may be aggravated rather than dampened, and supplies may by mistake be carried over from periods of relative shortage into periods of relative abundance. Yet even in such extreme cases the speculator may not be without his uses. Many businesses seek, through hedging, to avoid the risks that are always present when the future is uncertain, and there could be no hedging without speculators. The existence of a class of people who will risk money on their estimates or guesses of the future is of service at least to commerce.

Substitutes and Complements

The price of a given good is influenced by the prices of other goods when they can be substitutes for it or are complements to it. A linkage of this kind exists under conditions of (1) rival supply, (2) rival demand, (3) joint supply, and (4) joint demand. The word "rival" denotes possibilities of substitution and the term "joint" indicates a complementary relation.

Rival Supply

Two or more products are often in competition to satisfy the same general want. Examples are butter and margarine as cooking fats and beer and wine for social drinking. In this case substitution establishes a price link.

Diagram I of Fig. 20 shows two markets, one for building bricks, the other for lumber. The subscript "1" always indicates an initial equilibrium and the subscript "2" is used to show the final result. We shall suppose that the original adjustment is upset by a strike of logging crews, which shifts the lumber supply schedule to the left, and consequently raises its price.

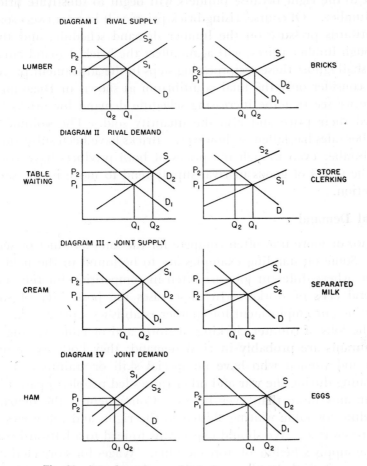

Fig. 20. Interdependence of Substitutes and Complements.

Bricks are now *relatively* cheaper, although sold at the same price, because lumber prices have gone up. Accordingly there is a greater demand for bricks. However, this increase in the demand for bricks is of the schedule kind (being prompted by a rise in lumber prices) and not of the market type (as would follow from a decline in brick prices). Demand and supply schedules are normally constructed on a *ceteris paribus* assumption, and so, when the prices of other goods change, at least one schedule of the given product *may* have to be redrawn, especially if the other goods are substitutes or complements of the given product.

In the present instance the demand schedule for bricks will shift to the right because builders will begin to substitute bricks for lumber. Of course, rising brick prices will in turn exert some rightwards pressure on the lumber demand schedule, and this, through lumber prices, will again affect the brick demand curve. We shall ignore these reciprocating steps in the adjustment process and consider only the final equilibrium as shown in Diagram I. Here we see that the increasing schedule demand for bricks has raised their price and also the quantity sold. The volume of lumber sales has fallen off however. Bricks have been substituted for lumber even though the prices of both products have risen.

The prices of goods in rival supply tend to move in the same direction.

Rival Demand

Two or more uses often compete for the same product or service. Some outstanding examples are to be found in the field of labor, where different jobs are often in competition for the same general class of worker. In these cases the possibility of substituting one employment for another establishes a price link.

The jobs of counter clerking in stores and of table waiting in restaurants are probably in rival demand; they both use young girls and women who have no special skill or training. Food rationing during the war and other causes led people to patronize restaurants more than ever before. Consequently, the demand schedule for table waiting shifted to the right, and the wages of waitresses rose. We should expect this to lead to a leftward shift in the supply schedule of store clerking. Wages for store clerking are now relatively low because waitresses' wages have risen. Eventually the reduced supply schedule of store clerks will force a rise in their wages. The theoretical outcome is shown in Diagram II.

The prices of things in rival demand tend to move in the same direction.

Joint Supply

Two or more goods are often produced involuntarily by the same act. The slaughtering of cattle also yields hides, the threshing of wheat for grain incidentally provides straw, and refining petroleum for gasoline produces asphalt. Goods are said to be in joint supply when natural conditions inevitably lead to their simultaneous production.

Diagram III is concerned with cream and separated milk. We shall suppose that being slim ceases to be fashionable and that women's demand for cream increases in the schedule sense. The price of cream rises, and so, if dairy farmers were previously maximizing profits, they will now be induced to produce a little more cream. However, one cannot obtain more cream of a stated butterfat content without separating more whole milk from the cow, and this necessarily results in an increased supply of the residual, which is separated milk. The demand for cream is linked to the supply of separated milk. Accordingly the supply schedule of separated milk shifts to the right and its price declines.

The prices of joint supply goods tend to move in opposite directions whenever there is a change in the demand for one of the products in question.

Joint Costs

Joint costs include all the costs of making joint supply products. The costs of buying and feeding and milking cows are all joint costs of producing cream and separated milk. If the separated milk is subsequently "homogenized," this is a special cost and not a joint cost, but our initial statement is still valid, for homogenized milk is a different product from merely separated milk.

Joint costs are not overhead costs. Joint costs may vary considerably as output is changed. An increase in the production of separated milk and cream will increase the dairy farmers' outlays for cows and feed and help. Overhead costs are constant despite considerable variation in volume of business. The "overhead" incurred for building, heating, and insuring a large department store is the same at Christmas when sales are high as in February when they are not. Ordinarily overhead costs are incurred in other than joint supply operations. For example, reverting to a department store, sales of ladies' gloves and men's slacks are not in joint supply. However, it is true that *some* joint costs are constant and hence overhead costs, an example being a dairy farmer's trade association fees. Joint costs include an element of overhead, but overhead costs are more often than not unrelated to joint costs, and the two concepts are certainly not identical.

Joint costs cannot be broken down into special costs for goods that are strictly in joint supply and produced in fixed proportions. It is next to impossible to discover the real cost of supplying cream as distinct from that of producing separated milk. However, this does not prevent ambitious cost accountants from attempting to allocate joint costs, and some complicated "methods" have been evolved. (See Appendix D.)

Joint Demand

Two or more goods are often used together by reason of either necessity or preference. The motorist who runs an automobile has a joint demand for gasoline, tires, lubricating oil, spark plugs, license plates, and so forth. The demand for a single good that is necessarily in joint demand depends upon the rate at which its associated products are bought.

Diagram IV of Fig. 20 depicts the case of ham and eggs—two products often in joint demand on American breakfast tables. Reduced costs of feeding hogs may cause the supply schedule for ham to shift to the right and so reduce its price. Consequently, the cost of eating ham and eggs is lower, and more people will cook or order this dish. The demand for eggs then increases in the schedule sense and the price of eggs should rise.

The prices of goods in joint demand tend to move in opposite directions when there is a change in the supply of one of the products.

The demand for a single good that is necessarily in joint demand tends to have a very low price elasticity. We have just pointed out that the demand for motoring can only be satisfied by purchasing all sorts of constituent goods and services. Refusal to replace one part (for example, tires) renders all the other jointly demanded goods worthless, and hence motorists will continue to buy tires at almost the same rate even though their price increases markedly. Demand also has a low elasticity in the case of price reductions. A 50% reduction in tire prices will only reduce the total cost of motoring by a few per cent, and hence the number of cars, their annual mileages, and tire purchases will only increase slightly percentagewise.

Cross-Elasticity and Product Interdependence

When there is no interdependence between two kinds of products, a change in the price of one will not affect the sales of the other, and *vice versa*. However, when there is interdependence, the amount sold of one commodity depends in part upon the prices of other goods with which it may be in rival demand, rival supply, joint supply, or joint demand. For example, if the price of lumber rises owing to a supply shortage, we have seen that the quantity of bricks that are sold will probably increase. Such a phenomenon is usually called cross-elasticity. Coefficients of cross-elasticity can be employed to gain an impression of the degree of interdependence between two goods.

Let us see how to measure the cross-elasticity of bricks on lumber. Perhaps, when some index of lumber prices rises from $45 to $55 per thousand board feet, brick sales increase from 950 tons to 1,050 tons a week in some city. A 20 per cent rise in the price of lumber has apparently occasioned a 10 per cent increase in brick sales. The cross-elasticity of bricks on lumber is then 10%/20%, or 0.5. In general terms the cross-elasticity of B (bricks) on A (lumber) is $(P_a \cdot \Delta Q_b)/(Q_b \cdot \Delta P_a)$.

Caution must be taken however in applying this measure. If the demand for housing were increasing, the price of lumber would rise, the sale of bricks would rise, but the sale of lumber and the price of bricks would also rise. In such a case the increased brick sales are not due to any substitution of bricks for lumber. In the case of rival supply goods, cross-elasticity coefficients can only be used to measure interdependence when there is no general change in demand for both goods. Similarly, in rival demand situations, the aggregate supply of the good or service for which there is competition must be unchanged.

Apart from this, the greater the degree of substitution, the higher will cross-elasticity coefficients tend to be. If two goods are perfect substitutes, their cross-elasticity will be infinite. Zero cross-elasticity implies no interdependence.

The cross-elasticity of B on A may differ from that of A on B. Perhaps, in a rival supply situation, A has only one use whereas B has this use and one other employment besides. Then, in this common use, A quantity changes may be rather small proportionately despite proportionately large changes in *B* prices. The cross-elasticity of *A* on *B* may be lower than that of *B* on *A*. In the real world of commerce it is sometimes surprising to find how many substitute and complementary relations there are between different products. Sometimes this link exists on the demand side and sometimes on the supply side. A symptom of such interdependence is usually to be found either in associated price changes or in associated quantity changes. Cross-elasticity coefficients make use of these symptoms to measure interdependence.

Statements for Consideration

1. A low price ceiling imposed upon two spatially interdependent markets may make rationing necessary. *Discuss*
2. If prices in different geographic markets are dissimilar, the markets in question are independent of one another. *Evaluate*
3. In a way speculators perform a service somewhat analogous to that performed by transportation companies. *Discuss*
4. The shadow of future shortages is often cast by speculators over today's markets. *Explain*
5. Speculators usually make a great deal of money. *Evaluate*
6. High customs duties may render markets independent which were previously interdependent. *Explain*
7. Joint costs are synonymous with overhead costs. *Evaluate*
8. An increase in demand for gasoline may lead to a fall in the price of fuel oil. *Explain*
9. The demand for one product that is in joint demand with several others tends to be inelastic. *Discuss*
10. The price behavior of goods in rival supply or rival demand is usually similar. *Discuss*
11. Coefficients of cross-elasticity measure the interdependence of firms. *Explain*

References

Garver, F. B., and Hansen, A. H., *Principles of Economics,* Chapters 11, 13. New York: Ginn, 1947.

Lerner, A. P., *The Economics of Control.* New York: Macmillan, 1944.

Samuelson, P. A., *Economics,* Chapter 25. New York: McGraw-Hill, 1948.

18

Forces of Demand

CRITICS have likened an economist to a parrot who has learned the trick of repeating "supply and demand" whenever confronted with a problem. Occasionally there has been merit in this criticism. It is not enough to know that a purely competitive price is fashioned from the intersection of a demand and a supply curve. Schedules of supply and demand are a surface phenomenon. It is far more important to understand the forces that determine demand and supply schedules. In this chapter we shall explain the influence of consumers upon market demand schedules.

The demand of the public for a good is based on the demands of individual buyers. The prices a buyer is willing to pay for each successive unit of a good are his demand for that good. The level of these demand or reservation prices depends upon both the amount of wealth or income he has to spend and the extent to which he desires each unit.

In actual fact there is no absolute measure of a person's desire for a good or service. However, one can logically employ the idea of want if it is always thought of in a relative sense. One can measure a man's desire for a unit of A in terms of how many units of B he is willing to forego. The whole theory of demand can be based directly upon the rates at which a person is willing to trade or substitute one good for another. This indifference curve approach to demand theory is developed in Appendix D.

If one were to carry on experiments with an individual, one might be able to ascertain his substitution rates between commodities A and B, between B and C, and so on. Perhaps, given his present holdings of A, B, and C, he is willing to give up three units of B for two of A, and four of C for three of B. In such event it is convenient and not difficult to establish some single *numeraire* or measuring unit, which might be one of the actual

251

commodities involved or might be quite artificial. For instance we might say that to this individual the marginally held units of *A*, *B*, and *C* are respectively worth $6x$, $4x$, and $3x$. Also, in order that the *significance* of this *numeraire* may not be forgotten, we might pretend that the x units are called "utils" and that they measure something called utility.

However this procedure involves a danger and a disability. The danger is that, if a person's sets of substitution rates are not in conformity with the relative satisfactions the goods give him, the *numeraire* that depends upon these rates cannot reflect relative use value either. The disability is that there is no way of comparing the *numeraires* of different persons. Hence, although we may discuss the utils of satisfaction enjoyed by one person, we cannot compare these with the utils experienced by some other person, for utils as a unit for measuring utility are peculiar to each individual.

The utility approach to demand theory that is developed in this chapter—in contrast to the indifference approach developed in Appendix D—has certain advantages that seem to balance its defects. Some ideas can be expressed more quickly in utility language, even though conclusive proof of their validity requires the aid of indifference curves. The utility curve approach ties in more directly with market demand schedules, which are in turn an essential part of most theories concerning price determination and profit maximization.

The Summing of Individuals' Demands

A market demand curve is a collective schedule. It is the sum of the demand schedules of all the individuals who have reservation prices on units of the commodity in question. Some of these individual demands will come from producers and others from consumers. However, this distinction makes no difference so far as the summation process is concerned.

In Table 18 we are assuming only five buyers of the good. (This is obviously too few if there is to be no price influence on the part of purchasers.) At any given price, each prospective buyer will be willing to purchase a certain number of units. For example, at $1.00 *A* may want to buy 3 units, *B* 6 units, *C* only 1 unit, *D* 4 units, and *E* 2 units, making a total demand at $1.00

of 16 units. This gives us one point on the collective demand curve. Similarly, at $.90, we find that the total demand is 24 units, and so on. The various points that are determined in this way can then be connected to make up a market demand schedule.

TABLE 18

AGGREGATING INDIVIDUAL DEMANDS

Price	Mr. A	Mr. B	Mr. C	Mr. D	Mr. E	Market Demand
$1.10	2	4	0	1	0	7
1.00	3	6	1	4	2	16
.90	4	8	1	7	4	24
.80	5	10	2	10	6	33
.70	6	12	2	13	8	41
.60	7	14	3	16	9	49

It is important to remember that individual demands are summed horizontally and not vertically. That is to say, the various quantities at a given price are added together. It would be an error to add the various prices that different buyers would be willing to pay for the same quantity.

The Determination of a Consumer's Demand

An individual consumer is in the market for a great many different goods. Unfortunately his limited financial income prevents him from purchasing all the goods he would like in the quantities that would satisfy him. He must attempt to balance his consumption so that he gets the greatest possible satisfaction from the outlays he makes.

Diminishing Marginal Utility

It seems to be an established biological fact that, as the rate of consumption of a good is increased, a point is reached where additional units provide less and less utility. Eventually additional units afford less satisfaction. For example, one may buy a suit that gives a great deal of satisfaction. A second suit will occasion less extra satisfaction. A third suit may give almost no satisfaction and lack of closet space might even render it a nuisance.

No way has ever been devised of measuring the amount of utility a good affords in consumption. A strap cannot be placed around a man's arm and attached to a meter, which will indicate the number of utils given by a slice of apple pie or a close-up of Lana Turner. However, we shall pretend that utility *can* be measured in utils, and this scientific hypocrisy may not be so invalid as one might first suspect.

TABLE 19

INDIVIDUAL UTILITY AND QUANTITY CONSUMED

Quantity (Q)	Total Utility (U)	Change in Utils (Δ U)	Change in Quantity (Δ Q)	Marginal Utility (MU)
1	8 utils	8 utils	1	8 utils
2	17	9	1	9
3	24	7	1	7
4	28	4	1	4
5	28	0	1	0
6	23	—5	1	—5

Table 19 shows the total utility and marginal utility obtained by Mr. *A* as he consumes different quantities of Good Z. Utility schedules are highly personal affairs and always pertain to a particular individual. And naturally they must also refer to a specific good. Marginal utility is the additional total utility occasioned by consuming an extra unit of some good. Consequently it is derived by subtracting successive total utilities and dividing this difference by the change in quantity consumed. Symbolically *MU* is equal to $\Delta U/\Delta Q$. It should be noticed that total utility is at a maximum when marginal utility is zero. If marginal utility is negative, then total utility must be declining.

Figure 21 is a graph of Table 19.

The principle of diminishing marginal utility is sometimes unfairly ridiculed because it is misunderstood. It is stupid to declare it vitiated by the fact that people may acquire a taste for a good as they use it over time. The tenth avocado I ever ate in my life was far more enjoyable than the first one I ever tried several years ago. The real point is that a tenth avocado eaten at the same meal would not have been so appreciated. The idea of diminishing marginal utility refers to a very short space of time.

The practical importance of this principle is that marginal utility schedules eventually begin to fall as consumption is increased. If it were not for this negative inclination, a consumer would spend all his money on one kind of good, the first unit of which provided more satisfaction than that of any other good. Actually, marginal utilities do decline, and so, after a few units of the most prized good have been consumed, a buyer turns to the first units of less important products.

Budgeting Outlays

A consumer has a limited amount of money to spend. Therefore he should attempt to budget his outlays in such a way that a
maximum of utility is obtained in return. If he is to succeed, he

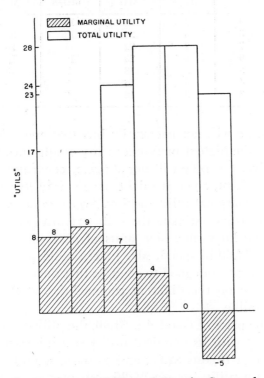

Fig. 21. Personal Utility and Quantity Consumed.

should have some idea of the marginal utility that successive units
of various goods afford him; also, he should know the prices
charged for each of these products. Armed with this knowledge
he can proceed to act intelligently according to the following
prescription.

Let us suppose that Mr. Jones is interested in only three commodities, Good *A*, Good *B*, and Good *C*. He knows his marginal
utility schedules for these goods, and they are as set forth in
Table 20. Their retail prices—$1.00, $2.00, and $5.00 respec-
tively—are also known to him. If these data refer to a period of
one week, and he has only $14.00 to spend during this time, how
should he apportion this money among the three goods?

TABLE 20

OPTIMUM ALLOCATION OF CONSUMER OUTLAYS

Number of Units Used	Good A (P = $1.00)		Good B (P = $2.00)		Good C (P = $5.00)	
	MU	MU/$	MU	MU/$	MU	MU/$
1	9	9	26	13	30	6
2	8	8	24	12	25	5
3	7	7	22	11	20	4
4	6	6	20	10	15	3
5	5	5	18	9	10	2
6	4	4	16	8	5	1
7	3	3	12	6	0	0

Naturally, he will not necessarily buy that good the first unit of which has the highest marginal utility of all, since it might be very expensive. Also he will not at first necessarily buy the good that costs the least, since it might have a very low utility. He must balance marginal utility against monetary outlay. In other words, he must first estimate the utility return per dollar he obtains when he buys successive units of different goods. Then, armed with $14.00 to spend, Mr. Jones should purchase unit by unit, transferring from good to good, so that the utility return per dollar obtained on the different commodities, at the margin, is as high as possible.

Because the price of Good A is $1.00, the utility return per dollar is identical with its marginal utility schedule (see Table 20). However, Good B costs $2.00, and so the first unit of this commodity gives a utility return of 26 utils over 2, or 13 utils per dollar. And the first unit of Good C, which costs $5.00, gives a utility return of 30 utils over 5, or 6 utils per dollar. The order of purchase should be first unit of B, second unit of B, third unit of B, fourth unit of B, first unit of A, and fifth unit of B, second unit of A, and sixth unit of B. No units of C are purchased at all. At this point $2.00 has been spent on A, $12.00 on B, nothing on C, and the entire $14.00 has been expended.

The formula for maximizing total utility from a given outlay of consumer funds is to allocate expenditures so that

$$\frac{MU_a}{P_a} = \frac{MU_b}{P_b} = \cdots = \frac{MU_n}{P_n}$$

so far as is possible. Another expression of this rule is that the marginal utilities of goods should be kept as nearly proportional to their prices as possible. If B costs twice as much as A, the utility of the last purchased unit of B should be about twice as great as that of A.

Of course it is not always possible to approach a close equality among these ratios. Items such as automobiles come in rather expensive units and the number used cannot be so easily adjusted as can the number of packs of cigarettes. Moreover, wartime rationing programs often make it legally impossible for families to budget their incomes, and so utilize their country's resources, as efficiently as possible. Also, consumers cannot always accurately predict the utility that various goods will afford them. The economist therefore does not say that consumers do equalize exactly the ratios of marginal utility to price for all consumed goods. He merely states that consumers should try to follow this rule.

Marginal Utility of Money

Indirectly, money has utility, since it is the means by which want-satisfying goods are obtained. In the above example, in which the buyer had $14 to spend in a week, the last dollar he put out bought goods providing 8 utils. If Mr. Jones had one dollar stolen from him, the aggregate utility of all the goods he could afford to purchase would be 8 utils less. Accordingly, we say that the utility of money (i.e., of a dollar) to Mr. Jones is 8 utils when he has $14 to spend.

Individual Demand for a Single Good

It is possible to calculate Mr. Jones' demand schedule for any specific good, providing we know the utility of money to him and also his marginal utility schedule for the good in question. How much should Mr. Jones be willing to pay for the first unit of Good A? This first unit provides him with 9 utils of satisfaction and his "last" dollar will in general buy 8 utils of satisfaction. Consequently, he should be willing to pay 9/8 of a dollar (i.e., $1.125) for the first unit of Good A, $8/8 (i.e., $1.00) for the second, $7/8 (i.e., $.875) for the third, and so forth. A series of reservation prices such as these constitutes a demand schedule.

An individual's demand schedule should properly tell us how many units of a good he will buy at a stated price. In the previous example we have supposed that Good *A* was priced at $1.00. In the preceding paragraph we calculated that Mr. Jones' reservation prices on the first, second, and third units of Good *A* were $1.125, $1.00, and $.875 respectively. Consequently, he will buy the first and second units, but not the third. Our earlier budget calculation, that Mr. Jones should buy two units of Good *A*, is thus confirmed.

Income Changes and Individual Demand

Other things equal, the quantity of a good that a man purchases is dependent on his income. If his income increases, he presumably has more money to spend on consumer goods, and he will buy a greater number of units and a wider variety of goods. The theoretical route by which we arrive at this obvious conclusion is not without importance.

Let us suppose, continuing with the example of Table 20, that Mr. Jones now has $23.00 a week to spend instead of $14.00. He will then proceed to buy a seventh unit of *B*, a third and fourth unit of *A*, and finally the first unit of Good *C*. The entire amount is then expended. The utility return on the marginal dollar is now 6 utils instead of 8 as hitherto.

A new marginal utility of money necessitates a recomputation of all Mr. Jones' demand schedules. In the case of Good *A*, if a dollar at the margin is worth only 6 utils, and the first unit of *A* offers 9 utils, Jones should be willing to pay $9/6, or $1.50, for it. Similarly, Jones will have higher reservation prices for all other units of Good *A*, now that his income has increased to $23 a week. His previous and subsequent demand schedules for *A* are shown in Table 21. Jones will buy 4 units of *A* now that his income is $23, instead of 2 units as he did when his income was $14. An

TABLE 21

INCOME EFFECT ON INDIVIDUAL DEMANDS

Unit of	Reservation Prices of Jones' Income	
Good A	Income $14.00	Income $23.00
1st	9/8 = $1.125	9/6 = $1.50
2nd	8/8 = 1.00	8/6 = 1.33
3rd	7/8 = .875	7/6 = 1.17
4th	6/8 = .75	6/6 = 1.00
5th	5/8 = .625	5/6 = .83
6th	4/8 = .50	4/6 = .67
7th	3/8 = .375	3/6 = .50

increase in income and practicable consumer outlays has the effect of raising an individual consumer's reservation prices and thereby shifting his demand curve to the right.

In order to be able to calculate an individual's demand schedule for a stated good, it is necessary to know his marginal utility schedule for the good in question and also his marginal utility for money. However, we cannot ascertain the marginal utility of money unless we know how he spends his last dollar of income. In other words, we must know the results of the budget problem. And, in order to solve that, we had to know the individual's total possible expenditure, his marginal utility schedules for all relevant goods, and the prices of these commodities.

Declining Marginal Importance of Money

Additional dollars of income have a declining importance for most individuals. They cannot buy more and more units of the same good. A twentieth suit of clothes or a tenth car may almost be a nuisance rather than a pleasure. Of course, the enjoyment of extra money can be sustained for a while in the purchase of a greater variety of goods; few of us would shun a generous financial gift. However, the fact remains that extra dollars for expenditure do afford us less and less additional satisfaction, and this phenomenon has a number of repercussions in practical life.

The rationale of progressive income tax rates is based on the belief that the last dollar of a rich man's income occasions him less extra enjoyment than that provided by the last dollar of a poor man's income. Perhaps Mr. Rich gets 2 utils of satisfaction from his last and 50,000th dollar of income whereas Mr. Poor gets 10 utils from his last and 2,000th dollar. In this case, if Mr. Rich pays a marginal income tax rate five times as great as does Mr. Poor, each will be sacrificing the same number of utils of real enjoyment from his last dollar of income. The real tax burden is then the same at the margin of income. Whether interpersonal comparisons of this sort are valid can hardly be settled here.

The declining importance of extra income to an individual explains why many successful professional people, who are in a position to decide their hours of work, may reach a point where they prefer extra leisure to earning additional fees. The enjoyment to be obtained from a few more dollars may be so slight that the harried dentist or lawyer decides to take fewer cases and go fish-ing. His decision to escape his professional duties will be made all the easier if the government is imposing a high tax rate on his marginal income.

There would be no logical reason for people to insure against loss from civil suits arising from accidents if it were not that the disutility of paying damages may be disproportionately greater than the disutility of paying the premium. Let us suppose that the actuarial risk during one year of having to pay \$10,000 because of injury inflicted on a third party due to negligent driving is 1 in 150. The actuarial premium should then be \$10,000 divided by 150, or \$67. Normally the premium charged by an insurance company will be greater than this, since the company must provide for administration expenses, selling commissions, and perhaps a profit. Let us suppose it sets a premium of \$100 a year for public liability arising from driving a car. Why would a motorist in his right mind pay a premium so much higher than that warranted by the actuarial risk? The answer is that the utility he has to forego, because paying a premium leaves him with \$100 less a year to spend on consumer goods, is presumably less than one-hundredth of the utility he would lose if he had to sacrifice \$10,000 worth of consumer goods in a year owing to an accident.

Demand, Price, and Income

The quantity of a consumption good that is bought in a market depends upon a number of elements. Two of the most important determinants are the price at which the good is sold and the incomes of the buyers. Quantity is the dependent variable; price and income are the two independent variables.

A conventional demand schedule, which indicates the relationship between price and quantity, is drawn up on the assumption that incomes are constant. If this should not be true, and incomes have perhaps increased, then a new demand schedule, further to the right, will normally come into being. The price to quantity relation is customarily described by a coefficient known as price elasticity of demand.

It is also possible to construct and graph an income demand schedule that is altogether analogous to the more familiar price demand curve. Figure 22 shows two income demand schedules. The horizontal axis represents the quantity demanded at each several income. The vertical axis represents the income of buy-

ers in the market.   The curve D_1 is drawn on the supposition that
the price of the commodity is held constant.   As buyers' incomes
rise, more units of the good are purchased, but at a decreasing
rate.   The other schedule (D_2) lies below and to the right, which

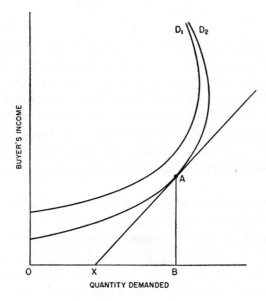

Fig. 22.   **Buyer's Income and Demand at a Constant Price.**

means that people will buy more at each income level; clearly,
then, this second curve must be graphed on the assumption of a
lower price for the commodity.

Occasionally, as incomes rise to a higher level, the demanded
quantity may begin to diminish.   An example of this is margarine, which a family usually replaces with butter as its income
increases.   Goods of this type are sometimes called "inferior"
goods.   The commodity depicted in Fig. 22 may be such a commodity, since D_2 begins to curve back to the left at the highest
incomes shown.

The relation between quantity change and income change,
when price is held constant, can be summarized by a ratio which
is altogether analogous to that employed in describing price and
quantity changes.   The coefficient of income elasticity of demand can be defined as the proportionate change in quantity

divided by the proportionate change in income. Symbolically this can be expressed as

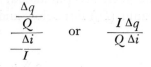

$$\frac{\dfrac{\Delta q}{Q}}{\dfrac{\Delta i}{I}} \quad \text{or} \quad \frac{I\,\Delta q}{Q\,\Delta i}$$

where I indicates average income and Δ_i the absolute income change. Thus, if a 10 per cent change in incomes alters the quantity demanded by 15 per cent, income elasticity is 1.5.

Income elasticity of demand can also be determined graphically in a manner similar to that already described in connection with price and quantity changes; for example, the income elasticity of point A on D_2 (see Fig. 22) is BX/BO, where AB is a perpendicular and AX is an intercept on the quantity axis of a tangent drawn to A.

The concept of income elasticity of demand has become generally familiar only during the last few decades. The sales of very large corporations, which dominate their particular industries, often depend more upon the incomes of prospective buyers than upon the prices charged by the company. The number of new automobiles sold in the United States in any one year probably depends more on the level of national income than on the price policies of the major producers. A government, attempting to raise tax revenue and anxious to estimate the total yield, must often consider income levels rather than tax rates.

"Needs" and "Luxuries"

There is always a temptation to look upon certain goods as "needs" and upon others as "luxuries." One often hears people objecting that some family they know has no business buying some "luxury" while it still lacks some "essential." Or instead it is perhaps stated that so-and-so cannot "afford" some purchase and that he should have used his money for something else. Government officials are rather prone to expatiate on the subject of "essential" and "nonessential" products. Such judgments are often arbitrary and without definite economic meaning.

In economics there is an acid test for deciding whether a good or service is useful in satisfying a human want. That test is whether would-be users are willing to pay money, exchange other goods, or supply labor to gain the good in question. The greater the willingness of an individual to do one or all of these things to acquire a good, the more useful to this man does the economist consider the good to be, irrespective of whether or not its use is moral or understandable to others.

The word "luxury" does not really have a place in the economist's lexicon. The only "luxury" a buyer cannot "afford" is one that gives him a lower utility return per dollar of outlay than other goods he might have acquired instead. In this sense, many consumers undoubtedly purchase goods they cannot "afford," because of ignorance of alternatives, habit, or lack of thought. However, the "luxury" in this case may not be a high-priced gadget, as the term normally implies, but a cheap good that does not work properly or a redundant unit of a product that in smaller amounts is a sound buy.

It seems probable that different goods may possess different relative usefulness for different people. Some people don't smoke and consider the production of cigarettes a waste of resources. Some people live in cramped quarters in order to own expensive automobiles. The apportionment of every household budget reflects the character, health, status, age, and sex of its members. It is for this reason that a rationing scheme which attempted to allot equal quantities of each kind of good to each family would distribute goods inefficiently. The inefficiency would be revealed by households' subsequently trading rations they did not especially want.

Superficially, and particularly in wartime, it often seems that some goods are "essential" and others are dispensable. In most cases, however, it does not make much sense to attempt the almost impossible task of ranking products according to essentiality. There are normally some uses of supposedly "nonessential" goods that are more important by most tests than some uses of supposedly "essential" goods; one can imagine uses of paint that are more important than some uses of gasoline, and conversely. The aim of wartime curtailment programs should be to restrict the availability of goods to consumers so that the marginal uses of each are, having regard to their cost of production, of about equal importance.

How does one ascertain the relative importance of different goods to consumers? We have seen that, for any single individual, the buyer's demand prices provide the answer. However, what if one is anxious to determine the relative importance of different goods to a whole market of buyers, many of whom are poor and a few of whom are very rich? For instance, even though the per pound price of butter is twice that of margarine, we must be careful in making statements about their relative utility, because poor people buy margarine rather than butter. It is likely that the utility of a dollar to poor people is much higher than its utility to rich people, and so the low price poor people offer for margarine may understate its relative utility, which may be much more than one-half that of butter. Of course, this sort of problem does not arise when considering the use values of goods that rich and poor people buy in rather similar proportions.

A free enterprise economy gears its production to the demands of the market place. Market demand is a reflection of relative want plus relative income or wealth. The demand curve for *A* may lie above and to the right of the demand curve for *B*, either because *A* has greater use value, or because the people who want *A* have more money, or for both reasons. It is as though consumers voted their dollars in favor of having *A* or *B* produced but that some people had more votes than others.

How much of a bias the existence of income inequality imparts to the proportions in which an economy produces different goods it is impossible to say. Undoubtedly this distortion is most serious in the case of so-called "inferior" goods that people cease to buy at high incomes (for example, hamburger), and in the case of "superior" goods that people begin to buy at high incomes (for example, squab). Many people might retort, though, that this bias is desirable. A free enterprise economy is powered by incentives. People would not struggle to acquire more income, and in most cases produce more as a consequence, if the possession of more income did not permit them to gratify other wants, however unimportant these may seem to poorer people.

Statements for Consideration

1. It is not enough to know that price equates demand and supply in a purely competitive market.   *Discuss*
2. A collective demand schedule is computed by adding together all the prices people will pay for each given quantity of the good or service.   *Evaluate*
3. The principle of diminishing marginal utility states that a person

will be worse off with more units of a good—but this is clearly untrue. *Evaluate*

4. Consumers should allocate their expenditures so that the utility return per dollar, obtained from the last unit of each kind of good, is about the same. *Explain*

5. The marginal utility of money probably declines with income. *Discuss*

6. The principle of diminishing marginal utility cannot be valid because a second shoe has more use value than one shoe of a pair. *Evaluate*

7. An individual's demand for a good depends not upon his income but upon its price. *Evaluate*

8. A person's demand for a good can be determined if we know its price and its marginal utility for him. *Evaluate*

9. An income elasticity of demand of 3.0 means that three more units will be purchased for each extra dollar of income. *Evaluate*

10. A good that is priced too high for a man to be able to afford is a luxury good. *Discuss*

11. Market demand is a reflection of relative want plus relative income or wealth. *Explain*

12. The dollars of consumers are sometimes likened to the votes of citizens except that in elections each citizen votes only once. *Explain*

13. A good is an "inferior" good if it costs less than the average of consumer goods prices. *Evaluate*

References

Bain, J. S., *Pricing, Distribution and Employment,* Chapter 2. New York: Holt, 1948.

Boulding, K. E., *Economic Analysis,* Chapters 29, 33. New York: Harper, 1948.

Bowman, M. J., and Bach, G. L., *Economic Analysis and Public Policy,* Chapter 16. New York: Prentice-Hall, 1943.

Due, J. F., *Intermediate Economic Analysis,* Chapter 3. Chicago: Irwin, 1947.

Garver, F. B., and Hansen, A. H., *Principles of Economics,* Third Edition, Chapter 9. New York: Ginn, 1947.

Marshall, A., *Principles of Economics,* Eighth Edition, III. London: Macmillan, 1920.

Meyers, A. L., *Elements of Modern Economics,* Chapters 5, 6. New York: Prentice-Hall, 1948.

Robinson, J., *The Economics of Imperfect Competition,* Chapter 2. London: Macmillan, 1938.

Samuelson, P. A., *Economics,* Chapter 20. New York: McGraw-Hill, 1948.

Stigler, G. J., *The Theory of Price,* Chapters 5, 6. New York: Macmillan, 1946.

19

Forces of Supply

THE COLLECTIVE supply schedule that exists in a purely competitive market is based on the costs of the numerous enterprises engaged in supplying it. The supply schedules of individual enterprises are determined by physical input-output ratios and the prices that must be paid for factors. Only costs that vary with output influence supply and hence market price in turn. These and other points will be explained in the present chapter.

Collective and Individual Supply Schedules

The Collective Supply

The collective supply schedule is the sum of the supply schedules of all the separate enterprises that are producing for the market. At any given price, say $1.43, Firm A may be willing to supply 155 units, B 45 units, C 201 units, and so on, and these and other firms together may in the aggregate be willing to supply 25,000 units. At another price, perhaps $1.67, A may supply 185 units, B 90 units, C 300 units, and so on, and the whole industry 33,000 units. In this way two points on the collective schedule have been obtained; namely, 25,000 units at $1.43 and 33,000 units at $1.67. Other points on the market supply schedule can be found by adding the various quantities that all the firms will supply at, say, $2.00, at $2.50, and so on. Here also, as in the case of determining a collective demand schedule, it is the *quantities* that are added at each price, and not the prices each firm must receive if it is to supply a stipulated quantity.

A Firm's Supply Schedule

Presumably every enterprise is anxious to maximize profits and will supply the market in the quantities that seem to do just that; and, under normal circumstances, a firm will produce and sell at

about the same rate, for otherwise it will create inventory difficulties for itself. An enterprise will then profit itself most if
output and sales are adjusted so that the "last" unit made and sold
renders the same contribution to total receipts as to total costs.
The general rule is that profits are maximized if output is adjusted
so that marginal (i.e., additional) costs are the same as marginal
(i.e., additional) receipts.

In the case of pure competition, a firm's marginal revenue is
equal to the price obtained in the market. Marginal revenue can
be defined as the addition to an enterprise's total revenue resulting
from the sale of an extra unit. If the going price on the market
is $1.67, then the sale of the first unit adds $1.67 to receipts, the
sale of a second unit adds another $1.67, and the sale of an nth
unit will also add another $1.67 to receipts. If, under pure com-
petition, the marginal revenues of sellers are equal to the market
price, a firm will maximize profits when it adjusts its output so
that its marginal costs are finally equal to the *price*.

Let us consider the case of Firm A as set forth in Fig. 23. We
shall assume that the price used to be $1.43, and that Firm A then
produced 155 units per time period. The market price now
rises, for reasons entirely outside of A's control or even understanding, to $1.67 per unit. How should A adjust his output in
view of the new price?

Firm A will clearly be sacrificing potential profits if it does not
expand its output. For example, the 156th unit adds only $1.43
approximately to costs, but realizes $1.67 additional receipts; a
156th unit would therefore improve A's profits position by almost
24¢. A 170th unit would add less to profits. A 184th unit will
add almost $1.67 to costs and exactly $1.67 to receipts. However,
the expansion of output should cease at 185 units, at which point
marginal costs ($1.67) are then equal to marginal receipts, and
hence to price also.

Figure 23 shows the adverse effects upon A's profits if, with a
market price of $1.67 a unit, it produces at some rate other than
185 units. For example, if only 155 units are produced, this
negative change in output will bring a large decrease in total
receipts (represented by the area Q_1BCQ_2) and a smaller decrease
in total costs (represented by the area Q_1ACQ_2). A larger decrease in receipts than in costs means a worsened profit position;
the loss is represented by ABC. On the other hand, if the price

is still $1.67 but output is expanded to 210 units, Firm *A* will not be so well off as if it were producing the appropriate 185 units. Marginal costs at an output rate of 210 units are $2.00, according to the figure, and so the last units of output are evidently adding

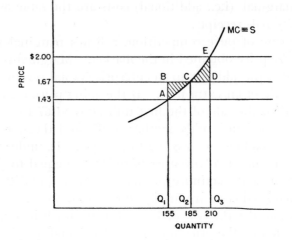

Fig. 23.   Marginal Costs and Supply Price.

more to costs than to receipts.   An expansion of output from 185 to 210 units, the price being $1.67, would increase total receipts by only Q_2CDQ_3, but total costs would rise by as much as Q_2CEQ_3; accordingly, the firm's profit position would deteriorate by a sum represented by *CDE*.

If the market price rose to $2.00, Firm *A* should expand output to 210 units, since marginal costs would then be equal again to price, whereas a price of $1.43 dictates an output of 155 units if marginal costs are to be equated to price.   In other words, given any market price, one can read off, from the marginal cost curve (*MC*) depicted in Fig. 23, the output that will maximize profits and hence will supposedly be produced and put on the market. The *MC* curve of Firm *A*, therefore, functions as a supply schedule, for it shows the quantity this firm will offer on the market at any one of several different prices.   Therefore, this *MC* curve is also an individual supply schedule, and it has accordingly been so labeled with an *S*.

Marginal costs and market supply schedules are only identical if we make the common assumption that firms maximize profits and produce at the same rate as they sell. There are two additional and more special qualifications. One is that the firm be supplying a purely competitive market so that price and marginal revenue become two aspects of the same thing. The other amendment is that the firm be producing beyond the point of diminishing returns. These last two points will be explained later.

Marginal Costs Vital

The management of a firm cannot know the output rate that will maximize profits unless it can estimate not only the firm's marginal revenue but its marginal costs of production as well. In contrast, overhead costs, which remain fixed when output changes, need not be known for this purpose, and neither do total costs or costs per unit. How are marginal costs determined?

Marginal cost is the addition to the so-called variable costs that occurs when the rate of production is increased by one unit. In order to produce one more unit of output each period, an enterprise always incurs expense for a little more labor, materials, power, depreciation, and so on. These extra costs are termed marginal costs. It is not necessary to know overhead costs because, being fixed, they cannot increase and thereby enter into marginal costs.

Let us suppose a fixed plant that is now combined with some extra units of various kinds of inputs. An expenditure of $50.00 for various inputs raises output from 210 to 235 units per period. Inasmuch as output has increased 25 units, the marginal cost over this output range is roughly $50/25, or $2.00.

The Production Function

Most producing enterprises are engaged in transforming various goods and services, which we shall call inputs (which occasion expenses), into one or more other goods and services, which we shall call outputs. These inputs are remarkable for the fact that more of them are required or used up whenever output is increased. Normally these inputs are combined with various fixed factors of production, which last give rise to expenses that are independent of the output rate for the time being, although eventually they may need replacement if output is to be maintained. In the following analysis we shall suppose there is a fixed factor, a single kind of output, and two kinds of inputs. The interactions between these two inputs and the single output are sometimes termed the production function (see Appendix D.)

In order to give these factors names, we shall suppose that the fixed factor occasioning overhead expense is a farm property (which we shall loosely call Land), that one of the variable inputs is fertilizer (which we shall call Capital), and that the other input is some grade of Labor. In this case the farmer's production function has various facets. First, he can worry about the physical consequences of changing the proportions in which he uses Capital and Labor. Second, he can worry about the output effects of using more Capital *and* Labor with his fixed Land factor. And thirdly, some day in the future when he can perhaps alter his Land holding, he can worry about the production effect of altering the scale of the entire operation, and perhaps adding to all three factors.

If the farmer adds a little Labor, he can probably dispense with a little Capital and yet maintain his output. If he is employing a great deal of Capital relative to Labor, a little more Labor will usually be equivalent to quite a lot less Capital, for normally the productivity of an extra unit of a factor is greater when it is employed with other factors in relatively small quantities. Actually, the proportions in which a farmer employs Capital and Labor should depend on their relative prices, as well as upon their relative productivities at the margin. If a day's labor costs as much as eight sacks of fertilizer, the farmer should combine the two in such proportions that a day's labor more or less will have the same effect on output as eight sacks of fertilizer more or less. If the price of labor increases, the farmer will probably decrease the proportion in which Labor is combined with this kind of Capital, so that the last day of labor is now more productive in comparison with the last eight sacks of fertilizer.

Given the price relation between Capital and Labor, the most economical proportions in which to combine them will often depend upon the intensity with which the fixed factor is being used, which is another matter to be settled. If, as more variable inputs are combined with the fixed factor, it becomes more economical to employ extra Capital in relation to Labor at given prices for them, it means that, apart from the marginal units, Capital is a better substitute for Land than is Labor. Sometimes, however, the most economical proportion in which to combine

Capital and Labor may remain the same, as more and more of them are combined with the fixed Land factor. When this occurs, we can think of the input proportions as being locked and think in terms of homogeneous packets of variable inputs, each one of which always contains the same amount of each input. In the future this is what we shall assume.

A fixed factor, Land in this example, can be used more intensively by applying more inputs to it. When this occurs, the rate at which inputs occasion outputs will almost certainly be affected. In economics, this observed phenomenon is sometimes called the principle of varying returns, and the output rate at which these variable returns stop increasing and begin to decline is often called the point of diminishing returns.

However, it is important to distinguish between marginal returns and average returns. As inputs are added, an output point will finally be reached at which the ratio of *extra* outputs to *extra* inputs ceases to rise and begins to fall; this is the point of diminishing *marginal* returns. On the other hand, the point of diminishing *average* returns, usually reached at a somewhat higher output, is when the total output divided by the total input (i.e., the output *per* input) is at its maximum.

These various input and output relations are a physical affair and they do not provide a guide to maximum profits except under certain price and cost conditions. No firm would rationally produce at or before the point of diminishing marginal returns. If the demand for a firm's output seems to be perfectly elastic (i.e., it can sell all it has to supply at a constant price), it should never produce below the point of diminishing average returns. The most profitable output is that at which the cost of the extra inputs has risen to equality with the addition to total revenue occasioned by the sale of the extra output thereby produced. The logic of this equal marginal costs and marginal revenues maxim has already been explained.

So far we have supposed that there is a fixed factor (Land) involved in the production function and that the only way the farmer can expand his output is to apply more units of variable inputs (Capital and Labor). If this occurs to any considerable extent, a point will be reached where a given expenditure on extra Capital and Labor will increase output more if spent instead for extra Land. Often there may be some specific obstacle that prevents any immediate additions to the fixed factor. However, in time, it may become possible to add or subtract from the fixed factor, in which case Land becomes a variable input. When this occurs, the farmer will probably take steps to reduce the lopsided proportions in which he has been employing the three factors. He will probably try to adjust the quantities in which he employs these three factors until the output contribution of the "last" unit of each is proportional to its cost. When a producer wishes to alter his output it is normally true that the subsequent output can be produced at a lower per unit cost if he can vary the quantities in which he uses *all* employed factors. If there are one or more fixed factors, a new output will customarily be produced at a higher per unit cost.

Under ideal circumstances, when all employed factors are variable as regards quantity and cost, a producer may experience what are called returns to scale. That is, as output is expanded and all factors are kept in balance, so that each several output is produced at the lowest of all possible unit costs, a proportional increase in inputs may occasion a greater or lesser proportionate increase in output. In the former case, if inputs can be secured at constant prices, the per unit cost of output will decline. The firm is then said to be experiencing increasing returns (per input unit) and decreasing costs (per output unit). Some further aspects of increasing returns will be explained in the section on the long-run planning curve.

Four Cost Curves

Primarily a firm needs to know its marginal cost curves in order to determine the best output adjustment to the demand for its product. Occasionally it is also important to know the cost per output unit of all the variable inputs, because—as we shall see in the next chapter—it will be better to suspend operations if the selling price falls below this cost. Also, it is naturally a matter of interest to know whether a firm is making a profit or not, and this can be ascertained by comparing the total cost per output unit with the price obtainable for output.

Altogether there are four cost relations which, for purposes of economic analysis, it is often helpful to understand conceptually. These relations can be graphed in the manner shown in Fig. 24, p. 276. When graphed they are given the following names:

Marginal Cost Curve—addition to total variable cost or to total cost of producing one output unit more or less.

Average Variable Cost Curve—total cost of all variable inputs divided by output.

Average Fixed Cost Curve—the fixed or overhead cost divided by output.

Average Total Cost Curve—the total cost, variable and fixed, divided by output.

It is conventional to graph these curves with the output along the horizontal axis and the costs along the vertical axis.

These cost curves cannot be drawn until there has been a division of costs into fixed and variable. Fixed costs can be conceived in various ways that probably amount to almost the same idea. Fixed costs can be defined as the total expense of all items that are not used in greater or lesser amounts when output is changed, or they can be defined as total costs when output is zero. There are a number of other cost terms, such as overhead costs and supplementary costs, which are similar in meaning to fixed costs. Variable costs can be defined as the total expense of all items that are used in greater or lesser amounts when output is changed, or as the excess of actual total costs above the total costs of zero output. Operating costs and prime costs are synonomous terms for variable costs.

In segregating all costs into either variable or fixed, and all costs are one or the other in any given situation, it is necessary to classify expense items very narrowly. For example, all labor costs cannot be thrown into either the fixed or the variable group; it is necessary to distinguish between night watchmen (fixed), foremen who might be kept on during a temporary shutdown (fixed), janitors who are unnecessary during a shutdown (variable), and direct shop labor (variable), and so on. Depreciation of equipment is a fixed cost if a function of time and a variable cost if a function of output. The fuel for heating the front offices is a fixed cost, but that for operating the machinery is a variable cost. The accuracy of cost curves depends upon the care with which this segregation of all cost items is conducted.

With these preliminaries in mind, we shall examine the cost curves of a hypothetical company producing one kind of output, and employing a single fixed factor and variable amounts of inputs in fixed proportions.

TABLE 22

FIRM COSTS AND FIRM OUTPUT

(1) I	(2) O	(3) O/I	(4) ∮	(5) TVC	(6) MC	(7) AVC	(8) AFC	(9) ATC
1	35	35.00	35	$ 50	$ 1.43	$1.43	$2.86	$4.29
2	80	40.00	45	100	1.11	1.25	1.25	2.50
3	120	40.00	40	150	1.25	1.25	.83	2.08
4	155	38.75	35	200	1.43	1.29	.64	1.93
5	185	37.00	30	250	1.67	1.35	.54	1.89
6	210	35.00	25	300	2.00	1.46	.48	1.94
7	230	32.85	20	350	2.50	1.54	.43	1.97
8	245	30.60	15	400	3.33	1.66	.41	2.07
9	255	28.40	10	450	5.00	1.73	.39	2.12
10	260	26.00	5	500	10.00	1.92	.38	2.30

I (col. 1) is number of inputs (given)
O (col. 2) is number of units of output (given)
O/I (col. 3) is average output per input (O/I)
ϕ (col. 4) is marginal physical productivity $(\Delta O/\Delta I)$
TVC (col. 5) is total variable cost (I times given price of one input)
MC (col. 6) is marginal cost (Δ in TVC divided by ϕ)
AVC (col. 7) is "average" variable cost (TVC/O)
AFC (col. 8) is "average" fixed cost (Assumed fixed cost divided by O)
ATC (col. 9) is "average" total cost $(AVC + AFC)$

N.B. "Average" here means "per unit of output."

In Table 22, column 1 gives the number of units of input and column 2 the number of units of output. Column 3 gives the output-over-input ratio. It is worth noting that there is variation in the output return obtained from investing in more input units. With 1 input, one gets 35 outputs per input and with 3 inputs the return is 40 outputs per input; but then it declines, until 10 inputs realize only 26 outputs per input. Declining average returns occur at around 2 to 3 inputs.

Column 4 indicates the increment in output occasioned by applying one extra unit of input. This change in total output is often termed the marginal physical product. In the present example it rises to 45 units and then falls. The marginal physical product is equal to the output per input (here 40 units) when the latter is at its maximum. The first four columns of the table refer exclusively to physical relationships and by themselves tell us nothing about the enterprise's costs.

The most significant costs, because they alone directly determine output, are those costs incurred for units of input. Column 5 shows the total cost of all applied inputs and hence is captioned "total variable cost." These magnitudes are calculated by multiplying the price of an input by the number of inputs used. In this example we are still supposing that each input cost $50.

Column 6 gives the marginal costs (*MC*), which are equal to the change in total variable cost divided by the change in output. For example, variable costs increase from $150 to $200 when output is raised from 120 to 155 units; that is to say, an increase of $50 in costs is associated with an increase of 35 units of output. The approximate increase in costs occasioned by producing *one* extra unit is therefore about 1/35 of $50, and $50/35 is $1.43. Marginal costs are naturally lowest when marginal physical productivity (ϕ) is highest.

Column 7 indicates the variable cost per unit of output. These average variable costs (*AVC*) are naturally least at the point of diminishing returns where output per unit of input is a maximum. *AVC* and *MC* are equal at the earliest output stage. Another interesting relationship is that *AVC* is declining with output when *MC* is less than *AVC;* and, when *AVC* is increasing, *MC* will be found to exceed *AVC*. From this it follows that *AVC* and *MC* will be equal when *AVC* is at a minimum and hence neither declining nor increasing.

Any change in the price of factors, or in the technological rate at which inputs produce outputs, will naturally alter the total variable cost necessary to realize a stated output. Accordingly *AVC* and *MC* would be altered. Finally, this change will affect the output at which marginal cost and marginal revenue are equal, and therefore a different output will maximize profits and be produced.

The fixed factor, which in our example has been dosed with varying quantities of inputs, also involves a cost, which is supposedly unaffected by the rate of output. Column 8 (*AFC*) shows the fixed cost per unit of output that would prevail if the constant cost incurred for the fixed factor were $100 per time period. The average fixed cost naturally declines at a decreasing rate with increasing output. The notion of "spreading the overhead" by greater production is a familiar one.

Average total cost (*ATC*) is given in column 9. *ATC* can be obtained by summing *AVC* and *AFC*. Total costs per unit reach a minimum at an output slightly greater than that which minimizes *AVC*.

Figure 24 is based on Table 22. The following items are worth noting. (1) *MC* and *AVC* originate together. (2) *MC* intersects *AVC* and *ATC* at their lowest points. (3) The lowest point on *ATC* is to the right of the lowest point on *AVC*. (4) *AFC* declines at a decreasing rate, and approaches, but never

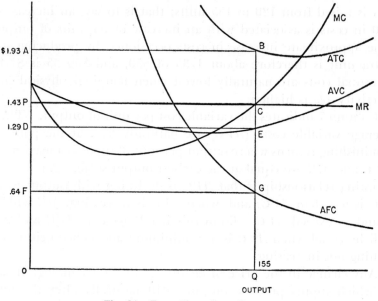

Fig. 24.   Four Firm Cost Curves.

reaches, the horizontal axis. (5) The vertical distance between *ATC* and *AVC* is always equal to the height of *AFC*.

Knowledge of a firm's costs alone does not tell us whether it will in fact produce, what its output should be if it does produce, or what its profits will be at the financially optimum output. Profits, the maximization of which is commonly supposed to be the goal of every enterprise, are equal to total receipts minus total costs. Hence we must have data from the revenue side, in addition to knowledge of the cost side, before we can determine the policy that will maximize profits.

The Planning Curve

The four cost curves described in detail above might be termed plant curves because they refer to an actual firm that is in being and that has, for a while, certain fixed costs. Eventually, as time rolls along, some of the cost items that are now fixed may become variable. The scrapping date for equipment will inevitably arrive and when it does the replacement may be of larger or smaller capacity. Theoretically, given enough time, most fixed costs will become variable costs, and so it is intellectually possible to imagine a case in which the producer has complete freedom of decision and can combine *all* factors in any proportions he wishes. In this case we could draw up a planning curve.

It is reasonable to suppose that, for any given output, a plant could be specially designed to produce that output more cheaply than any other plant. Thus Plant #1 might be designed to produce 12,000 units per week, Plant #13 to produce 54,000 units, and some other hypothetical plant to produce 84,000 units. And, in the long run, if 12,000 units were the most profitable output to produce, the enterprise, having an indefinitely long time to adapt to this situation, would in time find itself with a productive organization designed along the lines of Plant #1.

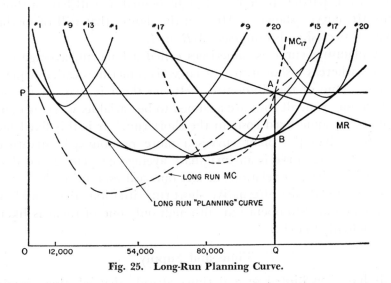

Fig. 25. Long-Run Planning Curve.

It is conceivable that an entrepreneur might work out the *ATC* curve for each of numerous hypothetical plants. In Fig. 25 these have been graphed for Plants 1, 9, 13, 17, and 20. The long-run planning curve is then obtained by fitting it tangentially to these and other possible plant cost curves. If a great many different plant curves were available, the planning curve would be continuous and smooth. It should be emphasized that the planning curve does not refer to a particular plant but shows the average costs that could be obtained if the most economical plant were put into operation for each different output. The planning curve is an "average curve," since it shows per unit costs; consequently, after first obtaining successive total costs, it is possible to calculate a long-run marginal cost relation. Long-run MC is shown as a dotted line in Fig. 25 and of necessity it intersects the planning curve at the latter's lowest point.

The significance of the long-run MC and ATC schedules is that they reveal the best long-run output to produce, and the best specific plant to operate, given a marginal revenue schedule. In Fig. 25, long-run MC intersects the price line (assuming pure competition) at A or intersects MR (assuming monopolistic competition) at A. Therefore, Q is the appropriate long-run output. The proper plant to produce Q output is #17, as its ATC (at point B) determined the planning curve at this output range. When this particular design of plant is used, it will have a short-run MC curve (shown as MC_{17} in the figure) that will of mathematical necessity also intersect MR at A.

A planning curve is sometimes called a long-run average cost curve, whereas a short-run cost curve is sometimes called a plant curve. One of the differences between them is that, in the so-called long run, all costs are assumed to be variable, whereas there are always some fixed costs in the short run. It is this fixed factor that gives the plant curves a more pronounced curvature. The planning curve is an imaginary average cost curve and does not depict the cost relations of any one real establishment. The plant curves depict alternative short-run situations that could actually be put into operation, although only one of them is likely ever actually to exist.

Time and Supply

It has been hinted several times already that whether certain cost items occasion fixed or variable costs depends upon the time available for a firm's management to rearrange the operation. Over any given time period there will be certain agreements, technical combinations, and productive operations that give rise to costs. Those which can be modified, deferred, or eliminated at the discretion of the management can be considered voluntary or variable costs. Those which have already occurred, are legally binding, or cannot be altered are historical and involuntary and are fixed costs. In general, the more time there is available for adjustment, the more cost items will be variable costs and the fewer will be fixed costs.

A great many costs that are fixed, according to the above definition, during a short time may become variable in a longer time. And over a very long period all contracts will lapse, and whole factories will come up for replacement, so that in a sense every cost item becomes a variable expense. On the other hand, when there are only a few days or weeks to make adjustments, the management may have very little discretion over expenses and outputs, and hence most costs are in effect fixed.

Usually the period of time for which an enterprise is analyzed is of such a duration that there are both variable costs and fixed costs. We shall call such a period a *short-run period*. An *immediate market period* is one so brief that no costs are variable and all are fixed. A *long-run period* is one so extended that all costs are variable and none are fixed. A period of calendar time, such as a year, might be "long run" for a man who takes the peanut concession at the Yankee Stadium by the season, but would be almost an "immediate market" for a dam-owning hydroelectric utility. The immediate market period and the long-run period are in the nature of extreme and limiting concepts. A large majority of practical problems involve short-run situations that possibly tend toward being immediate market or long-run cases.

The fact that, in a given enterprise, more costs become fixed as the time period is shortened means that costs then have even less influence upon the market price. For example, at the beginning of the lettuce-growing season a man may plan to lease land and plant out seedlings, cultivate them, and have the grown lettuce picked, crated, and shipped to market. The cost per lettuce of each successive step in the production process is given in the first numerical column of Table 23; the total variable costs that remain before each operation are shown in the next column; and the fixed costs, now "sunk" after each step, in the last column.

At the very beginning of the season the grower still has complete discretion and is in a long-run situation. All his costs, amounting to 5¢ a head, are variable in this sense. He therefore will not undertake lettuce-growing unless he expects the final pay-off price at the market to be at least 5¢ a head. Later in the season, when the lettuce is full grown but not yet picked, the producer is in a short-run situation. The remaining variable costs are $1\frac{1}{2}\not\!c$ a head, and he must anticipate a market price of at least this amount or he will allow the lettuce to rot in the field. If the price is $1\frac{1}{2}\not\!c$, or better, he will proceed to have the lettuce picked, even though such a price will fail to cover the $3\frac{1}{2}\not\!c$ of fixed costs already incurred. Finally, the grower ships all his lettuce to a market where no refrigerated storage is available. He is now in an immediate market period, since all his costs of $5\not\!c$ a head are past history and no discretionary costs remain. Since lettuce is perishable, he will accept *any* price at all. If he refuses to sell, he is out $5\not\!c$ a head; but if he accepts a price as low as $\frac{1}{4}\not\!c$, his losses will be reduced to $4\frac{3}{4}\not\!c$ a lettuce.

TABLE 23

TRANSFORMATION OF COSTS FROM VARIABLE TO FIXED

	Cost of Process	VC (before)	FC (after)
Renting land and planting out	$1\frac{1}{2}\not\!c$	5 $\not\!c$	$1\frac{1}{2}\not\!c$
Cultivating and plants	2	$3\frac{1}{2}$	$3\frac{1}{2}$
Picking grown lettuce	$\frac{1}{4}$	$1\frac{1}{2}$	$3\frac{3}{4}$
Crating lettuce	$\frac{1}{2}$	$1\frac{1}{4}$	$4\frac{1}{4}$
Shipping to market	$\frac{3}{4}$	$\frac{3}{4}$	5

The moral of this is that discretionary or variable costs influence price to some extent. Supply is one of the determinants of price and the quantity supplied is in large measure based upon whether producers believe the price will cover their variable costs. Where variable costs are relatively unimportant, producers will keep on supplying the market even though the price is low and leaves them with a loss, so long as these variable costs are covered by sales receipts. In the immediate market period, there are no variable costs, and therefore any positive price on existing output is acceptable. In the long run, all costs are variable, and hence the price must cover them if supply is to be continued indefinitely. Fixed costs have no immediate price influence, and, in a sense, are hostages to fortune.

Concluding Comment

In this chapter we have listed some of the forces that determine supply. The amount of output that firms will supply buyers depends not only upon the strength of demand but also upon costs of production. Costs of production depend for the most part on two considerations. One of them is the production function, i.e., the extent to which inputs can be converted into outputs at different rates of operation.   It is in this connection that industrial engineering, productive know-how, and technological invention are so important.   The other consideration is the cost of additional input units.   If a new invention enables a firm to use 10 per cent less of some input, but in the meantime the price of this input has increased 10 per cent, the firm's costs and willingness to supply output may on balance remain unchanged.   The prices of productive factors in turn reflect their usefulness in other employments and their lack of supply.

Statements for Consideration

1. Total costs per unit of output are of little use in helping managers to determine the most profitable output.   *Discuss*
2. Marginal cost is the addition to total costs—but not to total variable costs—occasioned by producing an extra unit of output.
                                                                 Evaluate
3. The "point of diminishing returns" is a rather ambiguous concept, one that may have several alternative meanings.   *Explain*
4. Knowledge of the production function is sufficient to decide how intensively the fixed factor in a productive combination should be worked.   *Evaluate*
5. A firm has no individual supply schedule under any circumstances.
                                                                 Evaluate
6. Depreciation can be both a fixed and a variable cost.   *Discuss*
7. All labor expense is always a variable cost.   *Evaluate*
8. Fixed costs have little influence on price in the immediate market period and are simply hostages to fortune.   *Explain*
9. A year can be "long run" in one business and "market period" in another.   *Explain*
0. If average costs are falling, marginal costs must be falling too.
                                                                 Evaluate
11. Average fixed costs only rise at high outputs.   *Evaluate*

References

Bain, J. S., *Pricing, Distribution and Employment,* Chapter 3.   New York: Holt, 1948.

Boulding, K. E., *Economic Analysis,* Chapters 23, 24.   New York: Harper, 1948.

Bowman, M. J., and Bach, G. L., *Economic Analysis and Public Policy,* Chapters 18–22.   New York: Prentice-Hall, 1943.

Chamberlin, E. H., *The Theory of Monopolistic Competition,* Chapter 2.   Cambridge, Mass.: Harvard University Press, 1938.

Clark, J. M., *Studies in the Economics of Overhead Costs.*   Chicago: University of Chicago Press, 1923.

Due, J. F., *Intermediate Economic Analysis,* Chapter 4. Chicago: Irwin, 1947.

Garver, F. B., and Hansen, A. H., *Principles of Economics,* Chapters 5, 10. New York: Ginn, 1947.

Marshall, A., *Principles of Economics,* Eighth Edition, Book IV. London: Macmillan, 1920.

Meyers, A. L., *Modern Economics,* Chapter 9. New York: Prentice-Hall, 1941.

Samuelson, P. A., *Economics,* Chapter 21. New York: McGraw-Hill, 1948.

Stigler, G. J., *The Theory of Price,* Chapters 7, 8. New York: Macmillan, 1946.

Viner, J., "Cost Curves and Supply Curves," *Zeitschrift für National-ökonomie,* III, 1.

20

Equilibrium of Firm and Industry

WE HAVE now learned that demand and supply are adjusted to one another in a purely competitive market through the attainment of a single and uniform price. We have also examined some of the forces that lie behind the demand and supply schedule of such markets. It is now time to analyze the manner in which the profit seeking of firms provides a supply of goods in the most economical manner and adjusts this supply to changes in demand. How complete and efficient these adjustments are depends in part upon the length of time that elapses before some new circumstance dictates a new kind of adjustment. However, even though complete long-run equilibrium may never be attained in practice, it is important that we know its theoretical characteristics, so that we can sense the direction in which long-run forces are pulling the economy.

Competitive Firm Equilibrium

A purely competitive firm is characterized in various ways. For one thing it does not differentiate its product, and its management has no problems of promotional effort or product design. The firm does not and cannot decide the price at which it sells its output, for this price is determined impersonally by the market, and the firm is only left with the choice of accepting this price or not selling. At the market price there is a demand for all the firm's supply, and its management assumes that the firm can in no way influence the price. It is because of these circumstances that a firm's marginal revenue is equal to the market price.

$MC = MR$

It is axiomatic, in price theory, that firms seek to maximize their profits, which means that they attempt to make their total revenue minus total cost as large as possible. Logically, this means that a firm will strive to adjust its output so that its marginal costs are brought into equality with marginal revenue, which last is the market price under conditions of pure competition. However, this rule is subject to the proviso that the total revenue is equal to or greater than total variable costs, for if this condition is not satisfied the firm will be better off financially if it closes down, at least temporarily.

The logic of these statements can best be grasped by an examination of the short-run equilibrium attained by the firm described in Table 22 and pictured in Fig. 24. In this case it is assumed that the competitive market price is $1.43. The output that equates MC to MR, or in this case makes it $1.43, is 155 units.

One way of explaining why Q is the most profitable output is as follows. Profits, which the firm attempts to maximize, are equal to total revenue (TR) minus total cost (TC). TC is the sum of variable costs (VC) and fixed costs (FC). FC is a constant by definition. Hence profits are at a maximum when TR minus VC is at a maximum. This excess of TR over VC, which when maximized incidentally yields maximum profits, is the operating surplus, sometimes called quasi-rent (QR). Now the area under the marginal revenue schedule, up to Q, represents total revenue and the area under the marginal cost schedule, up to Q, stands for total variable costs. Hence the first area minus the second area represents the operating surplus or quasi-rent (QR). Obviously, as output is increased, QR can only be increasing if MC is less than MR, and QR can only be decreasing when MC exceeds MR. Hence QR will be greatest when MC and MR are equal. As profits are equal to quasi-rent minus fixed costs, and fixed costs are constant, profits will also be at a maximum when marginal revenue and marginal costs are equal.

Once the price (P) and the output (Q) are known, one can calculate a number of important financial magnitudes and represent them graphically as shown below in Table 24.

The total revenue of $221.65 is obtained by multiplying the price ($1.43) by the output (155). The profits in this case are "negative," and hence are really losses. However, total revenue exceeds total variable cost by $21.70, and this surplus is the "quasi-rent." All these magnitudes are predicated on an output of Q. Another price would entail an entirely different equilibrium output for this firm.

TABLE 24

Minimizing Short-Run Losses

Item	Value	In Figure 24
Total Revenue, (i.e., $P \times Q$)	$221.65	*PCQO*
Variable Cost	$199.95	*DEQO*
Fixed Cost	$100.00	*FGQO* or *ABED*
Total Cost (i.e., $VC + FC$)	$299.95	*ABQO*
Profit (i.e., $TR - TC$)	—$ 78.30	*—ABCP*
Quasi-Rent (i.e., $TR - VC$)	$ 21.70	*PCED*

The extent of the fixed costs ($100) has no influence on the output. If fixed costs were $200, the marginal costs, which are calculated from changes in total cost *or* in total variable cost, would remain unchanged. Hence the output that equates marginal revenue and marginal cost will remain the same. Also, if fixed costs doubled, the quasi-rent, which is based on total revenue and total variable cost, would not change.

Minimizing Losses in the Short Run

In the short run—a situation in which there are both fixed and variable costs—a firm often finds itself suffering a loss if it continues in production. And yet the most profitable course of action is often *not* to shut down. The decision whether or not to keep operating depends upon which action will minimize losses. After all, in a rather unhappy way, minimizing losses is one aspect of maximizing profits.

Firm A, in the present example, makes a loss of $78.30 per time period. However, if it shut down, it would be worse off. Admittedly, if it ceased producing, it would "save" the variable costs of $199.95; but it would also have nothing to sell, and would hence also be without $221.65 of total revenue. Its losses would then be equal to its fixed costs of $100.00 per period. By remaining in production, this firm obtains total revenues that exceed variable costs by $21.70, and this "quasi-rent" goes at least a small way toward paying the fixed costs. In this way the total loss is cut from $100.00 to a minimum of $78.30. Production should be continued whenever it is possible to earn a positive quasi-rent. If the price should fall a little below $1.25, the lowest to which

AVC descends, there would be no quasi-rent, and hence no pro-duction.   Output is zero at prices below $1.25.

Therefore the MC curve is only a supply schedule for prices exceeding minimum AVC and for outputs beyond the point of diminishing average returns.

Concept of Quasi-Rent

Quasi-rent can be viewed as the income of the fixed factor to which inputs are being applied.   For example, suppose there is a mining property, which is being "worked" with inputs of labor, power, and dynamite.   What rental could a sensible operator af-ford to pay for a lease on the mine?   The answer is the excess of total revenue over variable costs that would result if he worked the mine.   The financial value of the mine would be the sum of all the present discounted values of its future quasi-rents.   If no quasi-rents are expected, the mine will have no present worth at all.   Land that is left unused, oil wells that are no longer pumped, and steamers that are indefinitely moored are presumably unable to yield a quasi-rent at the moment.   Therefore, unless conditions are expected to become more favorable in the future, they probably have no commercial value as productive assets.

The Industry's Adjustments

The many firms that make a common and undifferentiated product in competition with one another comprise an industry. Collectively, all the apple growers who supply a similar market are an industry, even though popularly they would not be called an industry.   A given industry usually comprises large and small firms, old and new firms, and profitable and unprofitable firms.

Short-Run Adjustments

The price that confronts the firms of a purely competitive in-dustry is likely to change from time to time.   Each time this price alters, the industry's firms must adjust as soon as possible. For the moment, all firms will have some fixed costs, and so their first adjustment will necessarily be limited to the attainment of a new short-run equilibrium.   Eventually, if no further demand or cost changes were to occur, they should be able to complete their adjustment and reach a long-run equilibrium position.

Meanwhile other firms will also be entering or leaving the industry.

Figure 26 illustrates the short-run equilibrium of three firms

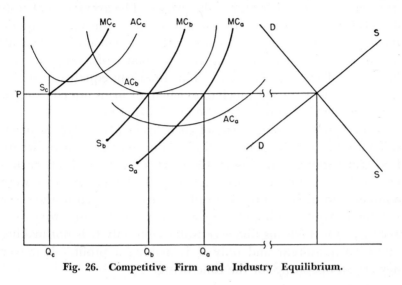

Fig. 26. Competitive Firm and Industry Equilibrium.

in an industry of many firms.   The price is determined by the industry or market demand schedule (based on the preferences and incomes of buyers) and the industry or market supply schedule (based on the production functions and factor costs of the sellers).   Naturally, if this is a purely competitive market, there must be far more than three firms, and the collective supply must be many times that provided by these firms.   This is indicated, in the figure, by the break in the quantity scale and price line, which must be imagined to represent a yard or two perhaps of horizontal distance.   The three firms shown are designated A, B, and C.

Firm A is making a profit at the going price, as indicated by the fact that the price line (P) lies above its average total cost curve (AC_a), and for this reason it might be called a "superior" firm. Firm B is breaking even financially, as evidenced by the tangency of P and AC_b, and may accordingly be described as a marginal firm.   Unfortunately, Firm C is experiencing a loss, for P lies below AC_c, and this firm can be described as "inferior" or "sub-marginal."

The outputs of these three firms are represented by Q_a, Q_b, and Q_c respectively.   In each case this is the most profitable output for the firm in question under the circumstances.   We can see that this is so because in each case the output is such that the firm's marginal cost is equal to the price.   The average total costs of each firm are indicated by the abutment of the vertical quantity line with each firm's AC curve.   It is worth noting that, although each firm has different average total costs, they all have the same dollar marginal costs.   This interfirm equality of dollar marginal costs is indeed inevitable, when all firms are confronted by the same price, and if they are maximizing profits.

In the figure, only that part of each firm's MC curve is shown which lies beyond the point of diminishing average returns, where AVC is at a minimum.   Hence these MC curves are also firm supply schedules and have so been labeled.   If the market price were to fall ever so slightly, Firm C would close down, even in the short run, for it would be unable to cover its variable costs from total revenue.   Of the firms under consideration only C is not making a positive quasi-rent and only A is making a profit.   However they are all operating for the time being.

Long-Run Adjustments

Unless the price rises, the situation shown in Fig. 26 cannot endure indefinitely.   The day will sooner or later arrive when Firm C, faced perhaps with the necessity of replacing a large fixed capital item or closing down, will refuse to invest further funds to incur fixed costs it does not expect to recover.   The disappearance of Firm C from the industry scene means that the upper portion of the market supply schedule will shift very slightly to the left.

In the long run, if there were no intervening price changes, all the inferior or submarginal firms in the industry would be weeded out.   There would be no firms with average cost curves lying above the price line.   The loss of all these firms, which contribute temporarily to supply in the short run, means that the long-run supply of the industry will tend to diminish, unless this tendency is offset by the entry of new and more efficient firms into the industry.

Actually, if more firms leave the industry than enter it, so that the market supply schedule shifts to the left, the price will rise slightly in the absence of demand schedule changes.   In this case some of the firms that were submarginal at the old price may become marginal at the new price. If these firms can survive long enough, they can perhaps survive indefinitely.

It is occasionally argued that, in the long run, the average cost curves of the superior firms would rise until they were tangential with the price line. Supposedly this is due to a revaluation of employed factors by the superior firms. For instance, if Firm A's short-run profits were due to the efforts of a manager who was worth far more to this firm than he was paid, in time he might obtain a proper salary increase. Or, if Firm A is depreciating a lot of equipment that it acquired cheaply, but which is really worth more to it than its accounting value, an accurate reassessment of its depreciation expense might raise the firm's average cost curve to the price line. Of course, the reverse argument can sometimes be made, to the effect that a revaluation of the assets and expenses of many apparently submarginal firms might show them breaking even on profits. For example, a firm might be suffering losses as a result of excessively high fixed interest charges; in the long run, if a reorganization occurred, these charges might be reduced to a point where the firm could escape further current losses. However one must not carry this argument too far. If all the expenses of firms were adjusted for profits at actual prices, apparent profits would always be zero, and all firms would appear "marginal." All that this procedure would accomplish would be to eliminate current profits and losses by converting them all into realized capital gains or losses. Such an approach does not alleviate the loss of people squeezed out in a reorganization. It tends to lose the baby with the bath water.

The theoretical rule that all firms must make zero or positive profits in the long run is compatible with the more general rule that firms must secure zero or positive quasi-rents in order to continue operations. In the long run there would be no truly fixed costs. Hence $TR - TC$ (which is profits) is equal to $TR - VC$ (which is quasi-rent) in this special case.

The main distinction between short-run equilibrium and long-run equilibrium is that, in the short run, changes in market supply arise from changes in the output and marginal costs of a given set of firms. Part of the long-run adjustment in market supply to a new price would come from this same source. However, part of a long-run contraction in supply would probably come from the exit of submarginal firms, and part of an expansion in long run supply from the entry of firms.

If the price in a competitive market is high enough to provide most of the existing firms with profits, this will naturally encourage other entrepreneurs, who learn about these profits, to enter the industry. If existing firms, possessing no special advantages, can make profits, why might not a new concern do likewise? Naturally, profits, if expected to be relatively permanent, will provide a greater encouragement to new firms than profits that are generally viewed as transitory.

During any given period of time, even when the market price is constant and general conditions remain unchanged, the population of the industry will be turning over. As we have seen, the exit of firms shifts the market supply schedule to the left, and the entry of new firms naturally has an opposite effect. When price is declining, the exits will probably outnumber and outweigh the entries, and hence the short-run supply schedule of the kind shown in Fig. 26, that is to say one that is the summation of all the supply schedules of all the independent operating firms, will move upwards and to the left. Conceivably one might take these shifts in the short-run market supply schedule into account and thereby construct a long-run schedule. The long-run schedule would be flatter than the short-run schedule for this reason.

Industry-Wide Economies

Mention was made, in the preceding chapter, of returns to scale, and this referred to the fact that, up to a point, most firms experience a reduction in unit costs as they expand output. These are sometimes referred to as internal economies because they are internal to the firm and do not depend upon any developments outside the firm. It has been alleged in the past that an *industry* may also experience certain economies or diseconomies as the scale of its operations changes.

The level of the cost curves of the firms of an industry depends upon a number of things that may be a function of the industry's scale of operations. If, as industry output expands, particularly suitable factors become available, or if their price for some reason falls, or if conditions in general become more favorable for that industry, the cost curves of its firms may fall. Such economies have been termed external economies because their origin lies outside the individual firms.

It is not difficult to imagine circumstances that might give rise to external economies. The expansion of a new industrial area may cause special transportation facilities to be constructed. The existence of a growing demand for special kinds of equipment to be used by an expanding industry may lead to improved design and increased supply of such equipment. As an industry grows, it may be able to afford more powerful lobbies, and so obtain special and favorable legislation. Industry advertising and industry-subsidized research may become more practicable.

On the other hand, industry size may bring external diseconomies. The greater the employment the industry offers, the greater the likelihood that its labor, which may have been non-union, will be organized. If the value and volume of an industry reach a considerable magnitude, the taxing authorities may be tempted to impose excise taxes. However, while it is not difficult to imagine various sources of external diseconomies and economies, it is not easy to know whether they inevitably occur when industry output changes, so that no general principle can be enunciated.

Interaction of Demand and Supply

Prices equate demand and supply. However this is a very superficial view of what prices do. Prices fundamentally provide a means whereby all the forces of demand can interact with all the forces of supply.

On the supply side of a market there are many elements that must be taken into account. Some of the important elements are the production functions of firms and the prices of factors, the demand for joint supply products (if they exist), and the strength of the demand for substitute uses. On the demand side of the market there are many elements that are equally relevant. These include such things as the utility functions and money incomes of buyers, the supply of joint demand products (if they exist), and the availability of rival supplies. Figure 27 illustrates in schematic form the main forces at work on the demand and supply sides of a market.

Let us consider the price of butter as sold in retail stores primarily for household use. The immediate but superficial determinants of the price are the demand and supply schedules of the market. These in turn depend upon the demand schedules of individual buyers and the supply schedules of individual sellers.

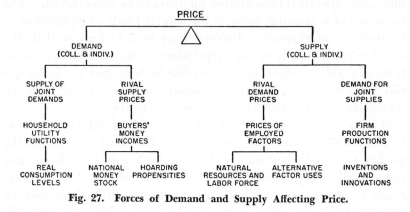

Fig. 27. Forces of Demand and Supply Affecting Price.

However, the demand for butter is affected by joint demand considerations on the one side, and by rival supply considerations on the other. A reduction in the price of bread, buns, and other products used with butter will increase the demand for butter. An increase in the prices of substitutes, such as margarine, will also increase the demand for butter. On the supply side, an increase in the price of cream, from which butter is made, will reduce the supply of butter. And a reduction in the demand for milk, which is in joint supply with cream, will reduce the supply of cows' milk and butter.

The demand for butter depends upon buyers' utility functions; that is, upon the rate at which marginal utility declines with quantity consumed, and upon the extent to which the utility of butter depends upon the holdings and utility of other goods that are in joint demand or rival supply. Given the utility functions of buyers, the larger their money incomes, the higher the price they will offer for a unit of butter having a given utility. In the present case, we shall suppose that the real consumption of buyers is constantly improving, so that more and more of them are substituting butter for margarine. Moreover, buyers' money incomes are increasing, not only because the national stock of money is being expanded but also because of a propensity to hold a smaller fraction of income as cash.

The supply of butter depends upon suppliers' production functions and the prices of factors. The production function depends upon the state of the arts and the extent to which improved techniques are developed. The prices of factors indirectly depend upon the natural endowment of the country and the size of the labor force. If a nation has relatively little land suitable for grazing or raising fodder, the supply of butter will be more restricted on this account. If alternative employments compete more strongly, so that perhaps rural labor is going to the cities, the falling supply of agricultural labor will tend to reduce the supply of butter.

The price of butter must weigh all these elements of supply against all the elements of demand. If demand is becoming heavier relative to supply, the price will have to shift to keep the two opposing forces in balance. In the above case, the price of butter will have to rise, and this will accomplish the important task of preventing some uses and purchases while occasioning some outputs and sales that otherwise would not have been made.

The economic world is always changing and the forces that affect a particular market do not remain the same. Each change must be absorbed through a readjustment by other elements in the situation. The stimulus that prompts these readjustments is usually a price change. For instance, if Good A and Good B are in rival demand for Factor X, and Good B and Good C are in rival supply for Use Y, an increase in the demand for A will lead indirectly to an increased production of C. Sometimes the adjustments to an autonomous change that affect one factor or product will cause extremely far-reaching readjustments. The original impulse is transmitted through the effect of price changes on the profit-maximizing calculations of firms and the utility-maximizing calculations of households. The price mechanism is an extremely supple but powerful system for reconciling the conflicting wants and dislikes of producers and consumers, not only with each other, but also with the economic realities of the world we live in.

Statements for Consideration

1. Purely competitive prices are impersonal prices.　　*Discuss*
2. Profits plus fixed costs equal quasi-rent.　　*Explain*
3. In order to maximize profits a firm should adjust its output so

that marginal costs equal not marginal receipts but price.

Evaluate

4. A firm will minimize losses by shutting down if it cannot operate at a profit. *Evaluate*

5. An asset that has no prospects of earning quasi-rents will have no value. *Explain*

6. The three time periods of supply are distinct categories that fail to merge into one another. *Discuss*

7. Different firms in the same industry can be assumed to have always the same marginal costs but not always similar average costs. *Discuss*

8. Expansion of an industry may lead to lower factor prices for firms and other external economies. *Exemplify*

9. The price of a commodity is a sort of fulcrum point that balances numerous demand considerations against numerous supply factors. *Explain*

10. If the price of butter rises, any one of a dozen things may have caused it. *Exemplify*

11. The price system is an extremely supple method for reconciling consumers with producers and with economic reality. *Discuss*

References

Bain, J. S., *Pricing, Distribution and Employment,* Chapter 4. New York: Holt, 1948.

Boulding, K. E., *Economic Analysis,* Chapter 7. New York: Harper, 1948.

Bowman, M. J., and Bach, G. L., *Economic Analysis and Public Policy,* Chapters 23, 24. New York: Prentice-Hall, 1949.

Ellis, H. S., and Fellner, W., "External Economies and Diseconomies," *American Economic Review,* September 1943.

Garver, F. B., and Hansen, A. H., *Principles of Economics,* Third Edition, Chapter 12. New York: Ginn, 1947.

Knight, F. H., "Cost of Production and Price over Long and Short Periods," *Journal of Political Economy,* 1921.

Marshall, A., *Principles of Economics,* Eighth Edition, V, Chapters 3–5, 12, 13. London: Macmillan, 1920.

Meriam, R. S., "Quasi-Rent," *Explorations in Economics.* New York: McGraw-Hill, 1936.

Meyers, A. L., *Modern Economics,* Chapters 12, 13. New York: Prentice-Hall, 1946.

Robinson, J., *The Economics of Imperfect Competition,* III. London: Macmillan, 1937.

Samuelson, P. A., *Economics,* Chapter 22 (A) New York: Mc-Graw-Hill, 1948.

Stigler, G. J., *The Theory of Price,* Chapters 9, 10. New York: Macmillan, 1946.

21

Monopoly and Monopsony

A PURELY competitive market has been defined in Chapter 16 as a market in which there were so many buyers and sellers that no one of them was able to influence the going price. However this is not the case in many market situations. When there is only one seller (a monopolist), but many buyers individually without price influence, we say the situation is one of monopoly. On the other hand, when there is only one buyer (a monopsonist), but many sellers individually without price influence, we speak of monopsony. What special considerations are important in monopoly and monopsony?

The Concept of Monopoly and Monopsony

By way of introduction, it may be useful to examine the meaning of monopoly and monopsony, and whether they really exist in a pure form. A monopolist is a single seller, but a single seller of what, where, and when? Similarly, a monopsonist is a single buyer of what, where, and when? If we consider the monopoly case in some detail, conclusions for monopsony can then be drawn from analogy.

Let us suppose that some company is the only producer and supplier of aluminum in the country at the moment. This company is then a pure monopolist if the what is aluminum, if the where is the United States, and if the when is now. However, if the what were not aluminum but the broader classification "light metals," this company would not be a monopolist unless it also controlled the supply of magnesium. Also, if the where were not just the United States, but included other national markets in part supplied by rival aluminum producers, this company would not have a complete monopoly. Moreover, while this company may be the only supplier in some market at the moment, new discoveries and inventions, or even its own prices, may be preparing rival sources of supply. A firm has a complete and perfect long run monopoly only if, in addition to being the only seller of a specific good at the moment, it controls all rival supply goods in all markets in which it sells, and if there is no obvious threat to the continuance of this situation.

Monopsony in any pure form is also rare. Most actual monopsonists are governments, which have made themselves such through legislation. The United States Treasury is the sole buyer of newly mined gold in this country. Foreign governments that exercise exchange control usually compel their residents to sell to them any and all foreign exchange they may acquire either from exports or in any other manner.

Price Policies of a Pure Monopolist

A pure monopolist, in seeking profits, is faced by certain special circumstances. The demand for his output is not infinitely elastic and he must determine his own price. Also, so long as he acts with restraint, he may not need to fear the long-run competition of new rival firms.

Demand as Seen by the Monopolist

The demand schedule that confronts a monopolist will normally be negatively inclined; that is to say, he can always sell more units of his product if he will quote a lower price to buyers. For example, a monopolist might be able to sell 850 units at $10 each, 1,050 units at $9, or 1,250 units at $8 apiece, and so on. This is in contrast to the situation of a purely competitive seller, who always receives the same market price whether he sells one unit or his entire output.

The monopolist is concerned with the marginal revenue that he obtains when he lowers his price and thereby manages to sell a larger quantity. Marginal revenue is defined as the addition to total revenue occasioned by selling an extra unit. In the above case, what is the monopolist's marginal revenue when he lowers his price from $10 to $9? The extra 200 units that can be sold at $9 realize a gross addition of $1,800 in total revenue. However, there is a partially offsetting loss of $850, because the 850 units which could have been sold for $10 are now each sold for one dollar less. The net increase in total revenue is therefore $1,800 minus $850, or $950, when 200 more units are sold through cutting price from $10 to $9. The addition to total revenue, occasioned by selling *one* extra unit, is therefore approximately $950/200, or $4.75.

TABLE 25

MARGINAL REVENUE DERIVATION

(1) P	(2) Q	(3) TR	(4) ΔTR	(5) ΔQ	(6) MR
$10	850	$ 8,500			
			$ 950	200	$ 4.75
9	1,050	9,450			
			550	200	2.75
8	1,250	10,000			
			150	200	.75
7	1,450	10,150			
			−250	200	−1.25
6	1,650	9,900			
			−650	200	−3.25
5	1,850	9,250			
			−1,050	200	−5.25
4	2,050	8,200			

Table 25 exemplifies the derivation of a marginal revenue schedule (column 6) from a demand schedule (columns 1 and 2 taken together). Column 3 gives the total revenue obtained at each price, column 4 the change in total revenue, and column 5 the change in quantity sold. The demand schedule in this example is of a rather special kind since it would appear as a straight line if graphed; and, because of this, the marginal revenue schedule will also be rectilinear. It will be noticed that marginal revenue is zero near $7 and becomes negative when the price is reduced still further. The demand has unit elasticity at the quantity that yields zero marginal revenue, the reason being that zero marginal revenue means a momentarily constant total revenue, and a constant total revenue requires that the proportionate change in price and quantity be equal. The demand is elastic for quantities less than 1,450, for the positive marginal revenue indicates that total revenue is then increasing with quantity, and this could only occur if the proportionate change in quantity were greater than the proportionate change in price. The demand for quantities greater than 1,450 is inelastic by converse reasoning.

However, a difficulty still remains to be considered. Is marginal revenue the change in total revenue that occurs when one sells a little more or when one sells a little less? For example, reverting to Table 25, when 1,450 units are sold at $7.00, is the marginal revenue $.75 or –$1.25?   Actually it is neither.   All we know is that the *average* marginal revenue is $.75 between 1,250 and 1,450 units and –$1.25 between 1,450 and 1,650 units.   So long as we have such large discontinuous jumps along the price and quantity scales, we shall never know the exact marginal revenue at 1,450 units.   One expedient would be to average $.75 and –$1.25, but the result would be only an approximation at best. Another imperfect method is to adopt an arbitrary convention and pretend that marginal revenue is the change in total revenue *either* between N and $N + 1$ units *or* between N and $N - 1$ units. The harsh but simple truth of the matter is that the marginal revenue is ideally the *rate* at which total revenue increases when physical sales increase infinitesimally.   There is no precise means of ascertaining this from discontinuous data, although approximations of the kind described above are derivable.

Marginal revenue can be ascertained graphically after the manner outlined in Fig. 28.   What is the marginal revenue associated with the price and quantity indicated by point A on the demand schedule shown in this diagram?   First, draw a tangent to A and have it intercept the vertical axis at Y (and perhaps also the horizontal axis at X).   Second, drop a perpendicular to the vertical axis at P and to the horizontal axis at Q.   Third, bisect the line AP at B.   Fourth, draw a line from Y through B such that it intersects the perpendicular AQ at C.   The marginal revenue at P price and Q quantity is then represented by the length of the line CQ.   A marginal revenue *schedule* can be graphically obtained by carrying out this same process for other points on the demand curve.   For example, C' could be shown to be the marginal revenue associated with a demand of A', C'' to be the marginal revenue of the demand A'', and so on.

The student may wonder about the relationship among price, marginal revenue, and elasticity.   The degree of elasticity (ε) is equal to price divided by price minus marginal revenue; symbolically,

$$\varepsilon = \frac{P}{(P - MR)}$$

Or, in terms of the diagram letters, QX/QO (which Chapter 16 showed to be a measure of elasticity) is equal to AQ/AC.   Geometricians may care to prove this after the manner of Euclid.

The difference between price and marginal revenue—AC in Fig. 28—is the increment in buyers' surplus that purchasers obtain at this point in the price range. The distance AQ represents the worth of the marginal (or Qth) unit to buyers. QC represents the

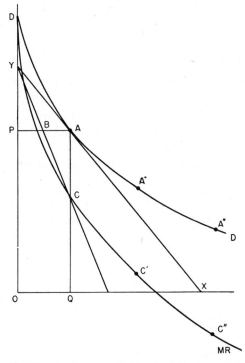

Fig. 28. A Monopolist's Marginal Revenue and Demand Elasticity.

addition to the seller's total revenue from selling this Qth unit. Therefore the difference (AC) is a surplus for the purchasers. Elasticity is accordingly equal to price over marginal buyers' surplus. Also, what is true at one marginal point, such as that of the Qth unit, will also be true of all other units.

If we sum successive increments, we obtain aggregates. Therefore, for a quantity of OQ units, the total use value of all purchases to the buyers is represented by the area $DAQO$, the total revenue of the seller by $DCQO$, and the aggregate buyers' surplus by DAC. We also know from Chapter 16 that sellers' revenue can be shown by $PAQO$ and buyers' surplus by DAP.

Short-Run Pricing

A monopolist, no less than an entrepreneur in any other type of market situation, presumably attempts to maximize profits. He knows that, as he produces and sells more, his total costs will increase, while his total revenues will increase up to some output and then decrease. Therefore the problem of the monopolist is to ascertain the output at which his total revenues cease to increase as rapidly as his total costs when he expands output. He must estimate the selling price that will equate marginal cost and marginal revenue. In general this is always true. However, the solution of this problem involves special considerations, depending upon whether the relevant supply period is immediate market, short-run, or long-run.

In the short-run the monopolist has both variable and fixed costs by definition. He will therefore have four distinct cost relations to consider—*MC, AVC, AFC,* and *ATC*—and these we shall assume are as set forth in Fig. 29. The *MR* schedule is calculated

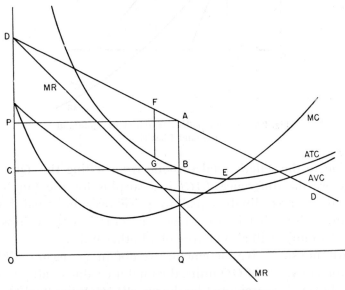

Fig. 29. Maximizing Monopoly Profits.

on the supposition that any given output is always sold at the highest price it will bring on the market. In this case the most profitable quantity is *Q,* because the *MR* and *MC* curves intersect at that output, and this can be sold at a price P, according to the demand schedule.   Hence, the monopolist can be theoretically expected to announce a price of P.   His per unit profit will be CP and his total profit will be the rectangle $PABC$.

Some of the alternative possibilities that are open to the monopolist, but which he should *not* adopt, are worth noting.   (1) He does not charge the highest possible price (D).   Theoretically, such a price would only sell one unit.   Only an infinitesimal fraction of the overhead would be covered and his losses would certainly be enormous.   (2) He does not produce and sell the output that gives him lower total per unit costs than any other (E).   Such an extended output realizes a depressingly lower price as well as reduced unit costs.   Marginal revenue may now even be negative, and the last part of his production has obviously added more to costs than to receipts.   (3) He should not seek to produce and sell the output that yields the greatest per unit profit (FG).   It is *total* profit and not *unit* profit that should be maximized.   Marginal revenues will still exceed marginal costs at the output that maximizes per unit profits.

In the past, there has been some controversy whether a monopolist can pass on or must absorb a specific or an ad valorem excise tax on each unit of output.   It used to be sometimes argued that, inasmuch as the monopolist was presumably charging a price that maximized his profits before the imposition of any such tax, he would continue to charge the same price after a tax levy.   This view is incorrect.   A specific excise tax can be thought of as an addition to the monopolist's marginal cost curve, in which case he will alter his price so that "old" marginal revenue and "new" marginal cost will again be equal at a new and lower output.   An ad valorem excise tax can be analyzed as though it were a constant proportional deduction from the monopolist's demand schedule, so that his marginal revenue schedule is shifted, and so that a higher price and lower quantity are now required to equate marginal cost to marginal revenue.   In general a monopolist will pass on part of an excise tax.   However, the final price increase will probably be less than the tax, so that part of the tax, but only part, is absorbed by the monopolist.

Another point of interest is that there is no individual supply schedule when we come to deal with a monopolist.   There is no one curve from which, knowing the price, one can read the quantity supposedly supplied.   The reason for this is that a monopolist, unlike a purely competitive supplier, does not adjust his marginal costs to *price.*

Market Period Pricing

An immediate market period was defined as one in which all costs are fixed and none are variable.   When such an extreme situation is encountered, *MC* and *AVC* are always both zero and hence do not bother the entrepreneur.   The *AFC* and *ATC* relations to output are identical.   Figure 30 depicts this uncommon case.

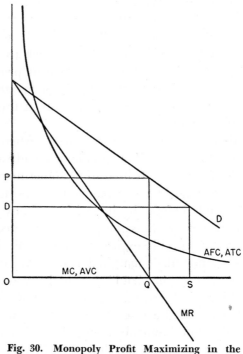

Fig. 30.   Monopoly Profit Maximizing in the Market Period.

The diagram shows that the enterprise has completed the production of *OS* units and brought them to market.   It has *OS* units available for immediate sale and we shall suppose that there are no storage alternatives.   If *OS* units were dumped on the market, they would only bring a price of *OD*.   The question therefore arises whether this monopolist would not realize greater profits if he withheld part of his supply and allowed it to go to waste.

Chapter 20 stated that profit maximization required the same policies as maximizing quasi-rent. Quasi-rent is equal to TR minus TVC. In the market period TVC is always zero. Consequently, the maximization of quasi-rent is reduced in this simple instance to a maximization of total revenue. TR is at a maximum when MR is zero. MR is zero when Q units are sold. Q units can be sold when a price P is demanded. Hence P is the price the monopolist charges, and he destroys QS, which is the unsold balance of his supply.

The simultaneous maximization of profits, quasi-rent, and total revenue that profitably occurs in the market period involves an equation of MR and MC, as always. A price is deliberately chosen which renders MR zero. And MC is also zero, since there are no variable costs in the market period.

If the total supply brought to market were less than the quantity that renders MR zero, all produced units would be sold, and the output-sale point that might equate MR and MC would never be reached. Monopoly in the market period does not inevitably require that some of the available supply be thrown away. After all, when the supply is too great to be disposed of at the optimum price, the monopolist has invested money in producing units from which he obtains virtually no return, and he has miscalculated to his own loss.

Pricing by a Monopsonist

A monopsonist, as the only buyer in a market, will normally be confronted by a positively inclined supply schedule, which means that he will have to pay higher prices in order to obtain a greater quantity. For example, he may be able to obtain 100 units at $1, but will have to offer $2 before 150 units will be offered. Under circumstances such as these the monopsonist will distinguish between average purchase cost (APC) and the marginal purchase cost (MPC).

Table 26 exhibits the way in which marginal purchase cost is derived from average cost of purchasing in the case of a monopsonist. Column 1 gives the various price offers of the monopsonist, column 2 gives the quantities that will be offered to him at these prices, and so the two columns together constitute a supply schedule. Column 3 gives successive total costs. Column 4 is the change in total cost. Column 5 is the change in quantity.

Column 6, which is column 4 divided by column 5, approximates the addition to total cost occasioned by purchasing an extra unit (i.e., *MPC*).

TABLE 26

MONOPSONY CALCULATIONS OF MARGINAL PURCHASE COST

(1) P = APC	(2) Q	(3) TC	(4) ΔTC	(5) ΔQ	(6) MPC
$1	100	$ 100			
			$200	50	$ 4
2	150	300			
			300	50	6
3	200	600			
			400	50	8
4	250	1,000			
			500	50	10
5	300	1,500			
			600	50	12
6	350	2,100			
			700	50	14
7	400	2,800			

The monopsonist's price is also his average cost of purchasing. If he buys 150 units at $2, the total cost is $300, and the average or cost per unit is equal to the price of $2. The marginal purchase cost is always greater than the average purchase cost when the supply schedule is positively inclined. The reason for this is simple. In order to buy 150 units instead of 100, the monopsonist must offer a price of $2 instead of $1. The addition to his total costs is then not only $100 (the extra 50 units times the purchase price of $2) but actually $200 (because the 100 units that could have been obtained at $1 now cost one dollar each more than before). In the above example, *APC* is a straight line, and therefore *MPC* is also rectilinear.

The price elasticity of supply can be calculated from the formula

$$\varepsilon = \frac{P}{MPC - P}.$$

At a price of $2.50 the elasticity is approximately .71 [i.e., 2.50/(6.00 — 2.50)]. It is interesting that, at another price, the elasticity will differ, even though the slope of the supply schedule is the same in each instance.

A monopsonist is human and wishes to extract the greatest possible gain in his buying policies. He may have a series of maximum reservation prices that express the use value to him of each successive unit, as shown by *D* in Fig. 31. (The manner in which this use value schedule is determined need not detain us here.) He can also calculate the marginal cost of purchasing

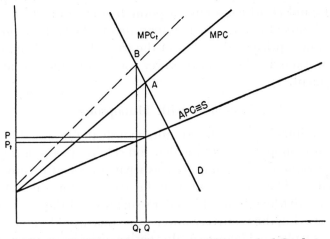

Fig. 31. Incidence of a Tax upon a Monopsonized Good.

(*MPC* in Fig. 31) providing that he can first estimate the supply schedule (curve *S*) that confronts him. The most advantageous rate of purchasing will be that which equates the marginal use value (*D*) and marginal cost of buying (*MPC*). Such a quantity is *Q*. He attempts to purchase this amount at the lowest possible price (*P*).

In this manner the monopsonist maximizes buyer's surplus. The area under the demand schedule represents the aggregate use value to him of different quantities. The area under the marginal cost curve represents the aggregate cost of making pur-- chases. The difference in area—i.e., the space above *MPC* but below *D*—is greatest at *Q* quantity for the reason that *MPC* and *D* intersect at *A*.

What would be the effect of a payroll tax of 20 per cent if the supply situation confronting this monopsonist constitutes the labor of potential employees measured in man-hours? The imposition of the tax does not alter the use value of labor to the employer (the *D* schedule) or the willingness to work of prospective and actual employees (the *S* schedule). The immediate significance of the payroll tax is that the enterprise has an additional tax expense of $2 for each extra $10 in aggregate payroll cost. Accordingly there will be a new marginal purchase cost schedule (MPC_t) that will always have a vertical height 20 per cent higher than that of the previous marginal purchase cost curve (MPC in Fig. 31). The employer will now be concerned with the equation of MPC_t and D, which occurs at point B, and results from taking Q_t man-hours of labor. Such a quantity of labor can be obtained for the lower price of P_t. Part of the payroll tax has been shifted to the workers in the form of lower wages, and there is also less employment.

Monopoly with Monopsony

It sometimes happens that simultaneously the supply side of the market is monopolized *and* the demand side is monopsonized. In this case value theory cannot tell us what price and turnover will eventuate. The monopolist will be striving for the relatively high price that maximizes his seller's surplus and the monopsonist will be seeking the relatively lower price that would maximize his buyer's surplus. These two alternative prices are theoretically determinate and together they mark the extreme limits to which the price might rise or fall. The actual price in such a case will probably be a negotiated and intermediate one. A compromise price, which arises from bargaining, will only equate market supply and demand by accident (see also Chapter 28).

Long-Run Considerations

Private monopolies and monopsonies do not set prices in quite the ruthless and exacting manner some people seem to believe. They frequently refrain from making the maximum short-run profit from fear of long-run repercussions. There are two important explanations for this restraint. One is the lack of anonymity enjoyed by monopolists and monopsonists. The other is that their monopoly or monopsony is often conditional upon their own behavior.

The identity of a monopolist is known; its behavior now will attach ill will or good will to itself in the future. If there is a sudden increase in demand in the short run, the exaction of a full monopoly profit from the situation may lead to future boycotting when the need for the monopolist's output has declined. If the monopolist becomes too unpopular with too many people, it may find itself the subject of a government investigation or of special and unfriendly legislation.

This is all in marked contrast to the situation of a purely competitive producer and seller. Farmer Jones can exact the full market price during a wartime period of extreme demand for wheat and yet remain protected. Buyers do not know him or remember him in the future. Moreover, he is one of so numerous a company that they can collectively influence legislation in their favor.

In many cases a monopolist knows that its own behavior can upset its current monopoly situation. If prices are set too high, supplies may be imported from other areas, despite transportation expense or customs duties. If prices remain too high, new sources of supply may be produced from operations that at lower prices would be submarginal, and hence have not yet been developed. When a monopoly of the moment depends upon some patent, the monopolist must always remember that at certain prices the use of inferior and unpatented processes may become profitable. Sometimes there is a single producer and seller in the area, even though entry is free, because the current monopoly established itself first, and there is not enough business to provide profits for more than one seller at present prices. However, at higher prices, a share of the present business volume may promise sufficient profits for newcomers to provoke their entry.

In short, the monopolist, and no less the monopsonist, must either exercise enough restraint in his profit-seeking or else occasion hostile government investigation or regulation, the establishment of neighboring rival concerns, or imports from distant markets or exports to them. Monopolies and monopsonies cannot profitably forget that they exist in a social and political milieu.

Statements for Consideration

1. A monopolist charges the highest price buyers will pay.   *Discuss*
2. A lower price increases total receipts if more units can be sold.
   Evaluate
3. There is no such thing as a pure monopolist in the real world.
   Discuss
4. The United States government is a monopsonist in some respects.
   Explain
5. The marginal outlay of a monopsonist is different from the price per unit it pays for purchases.   *Exemplify*

6. A monopsonist can never shift any part of a tax per unit of input.
Evaluate

7. Long-run equilibrium for a firm also involves short-run equilibrium.
Explain

8. A monopolist may under certain circumstances follow a different pricing policy in an immediate market period situation than might a purely competitive seller.
Discuss

9. A long-run planning curve represents the average total costs of the plant a firm should actually build and operate in the long run.
Evaluate

10. During a period of sudden emergency demand it is the purely competitive sellers who often gouge the public more than the monopolists.
Discuss

References

Bain, J. S., *Pricing, Distribution and Employment,* Chapter 5.   New York: Holt, 1948.

Boulding, K. E., *Economic Analysis,* Chapters 25, 26, 32.   New York: Harper, 1948.

Bowman, M. J., and Bach, G. L., *Economic Analysis and Public Policy,* Chapter 25.   New York: Prentice-Hall, 1949.

Garver, F. B., and Hansen, A. H., *Principles of Economics,* Third Edition, Chapter 14.   New York: Ginn, 1947.

Marshall, A., *Principles of Economics,* Eighth Edition, V, 14.   London: Macmillan, 1920.

Meyers, A. L., *Modern Economics,* Chapter 15.   New York: Prentice-Hall, 1946.

Robinson, J., *The Economics of Imperfect Competition,* II, VI.   London: Macmillan, 1937.

22

Non-Price Competition

A DISTINCTION has already been made (see Chapter 15) between those goods the character of which is determined largely by nature (for example, coal, apples, and meat), those that are fabricated but sold largely by specification (for example, sheet steel, lumber, and plate glass), and those that are differentiated from one another (for example, Buick cars, Philco radios, and Rogers silverware). The last class of goods were called *differentiated* goods. The makers of differentiated goods, which always carry brand names, may or may not compete on a price basis, but they must almost inevitably engage in what is often termed non-price competition. Non-price competition comprises product rivalry (for example, better quality, more service, flashier appearance) or promotion rivalry (for example, more advertising, extra salesmen, better public relations). The production and sale of consumer goods is especially characterized by non-price competition.

Price, Product, and Promotion

A monopolistic competitor, selling a product that has been differentiated, either physically or psychologically, has three weapons to use in the struggle to win profits. He can cut his price, and so filch clients away from those rivals who do not cut their prices in retaliation; he can make his product better or more attractive, and so divert custom; and by clever promotional campaigns he can vest his product with greater utility power in the minds of buyers, and so increase their demand for it. Price cuts, improved product quality, and intensified promotional effort are highly strategic variables in commercial rivalry.

Price, product, and promotion are related to output, and also to one another. Six of the most important relations are as follows: output and price (negative), product and price (positive), product and output (positive), product and promotion (negative), promotion and price (positive), and promotion and output (positive). A negative relation means that a change in one variable is associated with an opposite change in the other variable. Figure 32 depicts these relations.

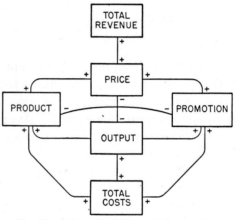

Fig. 32. Price, Product, and Promotion.

Ultimately it is, of course, the effect of changes in these four variables upon total revenue and total cost, and hence upon profits, that concerns the businessman. An expanded output will only increase revenues if demand is elastic, whereas it will always increase total costs. An improved product and intensified promotion are negatively related and serve as substitutes. Intensified promotion or product improvement will indirectly increase total revenue, through either a higher price or greater output, and will raise total costs directly.

Promotion or Product as a Variable

Promotional selling effort is expensive, and obviously it would not be undertaken if there were no way of exploiting the enhanced consumer acceptance that it normally creates. In general (see Fig. 32), the advertiser can recoup his expenditures and presumably make a profit, by selling more units, raising his price, or deteriorating his product. Some of these ways to maximize profits through promotion or product change will now be examined.

When Price and Quality Are Fixed

Occasionally a producer has a price and product that are constant for all practical purposes so that only the sales element is free to vary. For example, sellers of soft drinks know that the public accepts the "nickel" price as traditional, and therefore they don't alter prices, say, from 4 cents to 6 cents a bottle; also, if the bottle has a special shape and size, it may be difficult to alter the product itself without scrapping a large bottle investment. How will a producer make use of promotion to maximize profits in this simple case where sales vary but price and product are constant?

If the producer did not undertake any promotion, he would be able to sell some given number of units (Q) at some conventional price (P), as shown in Fig. 33. He can sell no more units at this

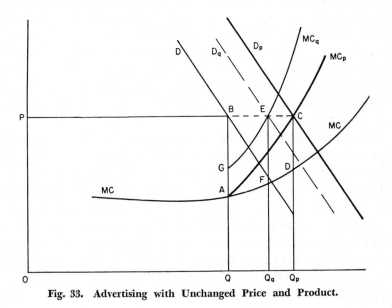

Fig. 33. Advertising with Unchanged Price and Product.

price because he has reached the demand curve (D) that normally exists for his unchanging product. His marginal costs of *production* are shown by the MC schedule and are actually AQ for Q units of output. His marginal receipts curve is PB if price is constant in practice. Accordingly the producer can hardly be maximizing profits if his marginal costs at Q output are so much inferior to his marginal receipts. He should produce and sell more units, but, under our assumptions, he can only increase sales through promotion, for price and product are unalterable.

However, promotion involves an expense, and so the marginal cost of *producing and selling* some output beyond Q will be higher than the marginal cost of producing it alone; consequently, in the diagram, MC_p (the marginal cost of producing *and* selling) lies above MC (the marginal cost of only producing) for all outputs to the right of Q. What this means is that the producer, by spending money on promotion, can shift the demand curve for his product over to the right, and hence sell extra units of a given product at the traditional price. He should pursue this policy until MC_p is equal to marginal revenue, which last, under our assumptions, is always equal to the price.

The most profitable arrangement is to produce and sell Q_p units of output, for MC_p and the price line intersect at C. The sales curve confronting the firm has been shifted from D over to D_p so that sales at P price have expanded from B to C or from Q to Q_p. It now costs DQ_p to *produce* the "last" unit and CD to *sell* it. Resorting to promotion has increased the enterprise's receipts by BCQ_pQ, production costs by ADQ_pQ, selling expense by ACD, and profits by ABC.

Parenthetically, it will be recalled that product improvement and intensified promotion are alternative means for gaining sales at a constant price. This can also be shown in Fig. 33. The schedule MC_q shows the marginal cost of selling different outputs of varying quality at a constant price and with no promotion.

If the management arbitrarily decided to vary the product, instead of promotion, it would add quality until the demand schedule had shifted over from D to D_q. Sales would then be Q_q at the constant price. Gross receipts would increase by BEQ_qQ, costs of producing a changing product by GEQ_qQ, and profits by GBE. In the present case it is clear that the profits can be increased more by intensified promotion (a gain of ABC) than by product improvement (in which case profits increase only by GBE). However this need not always be so.

When Sales and Quality Are Fixed

Sometimes an enterprise does not wish to increase its sales for the time being. It may temporarily be at capacity production and so be unable to sell more units. However, the producer can still undertake promotion, if he wishes to exploit its effect by increasing his prices.

The financial effect of using promotion solely to increase price can best be understood if we construct a diagram that represents total revenue and total cost on the vertical axis and the extent of promotion along the horizontal scale. The extent of promotion must be measured physically, and not financially; for instance, newspaper advertising might be measured in terms of column inches.

Figure 34 shows a case in which the only promotion is news-

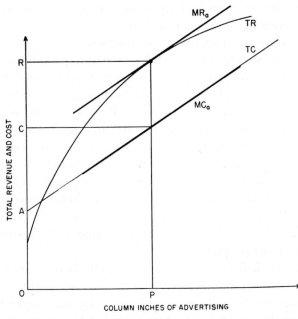

Fig. 34. **Advertising with Unchanged Quantity and Quality.**

paper advertising and the charge for space is a uniform sum per column inch. Hence the total-cost-of-advertising schedule (TC) is a straight line. The amount of total cost with zero advertising (OA) shows the expense of producing the given output. Figure 34 also shows that total revenue (TR) increases as more newspaper space is bought. The explanation of this is that, with more press advertising, it is possible to sell a given output at a higher price and hence for a greater total revenue. The volume of output and sales is assumed equal and constant. It would be possible, but not particularly helpful, to convert the vertical scale into average cost and average revenue, simply by dividing the constant output into total cost and total revenue.

The number of column inches of newspaper advertising that will maximize profits is that which finds the total revenue curve most above the total cost schedule. It would be unwise to carry on *no* advertising. As the figure shows, not only would no advertising cause a loss, but, as promotion is started from zero, total revenue increases faster than total cost increases. We know this from the fact that TR is steeper than TC for small quantities of advertising. Actually, the additional revenue to be obtained from buying an extra column inch of newspaper space is shown by the slope of a tangent drawn to the TR curve; and the addition to total cost, similarly occasioned, is represented by the slope of a tangent drawn to the TC schedule. (In this particular case the marginal cost of advertising is constant and equal to the average cost of a column inch because we are assuming that the newspaper makes a uniform charge for space.) Profits will be maximized when the marginal receipts (MR_a) and marginal costs (MC_a) of advertising are the same; that is to say, when the slopes of TR and TC in the figure are similar for the same amount of advertising space. Tangents drawn to TR and TC are parallel at P rate of advertising. The total revenue is then R, total cost is C, and profits $(R - C)$ are at a maximum. The price charged for each unit of the product will be the total revenue (R) divided by the fixed quantity of output.

Incidentally, it is possible to show the effects of changing product quality upon total receipts, total costs, and profits by means of a diagram wholly analogous to Fig. 34. Quality might be made the horizontal variable and advertising held constant, instead of the other way around as we have just assumed. Of course, "quality" is too vague a concept to use as an independent variable, and it is necessary in practice to concentrate attention on a single characteristic of the product. For instance, in the case of gasoline, octane rating is an important product attribute, and so might be used as the quality variable. The profit maximizing producer should provide just the amount of quality that renders total-revenue-of-quality most in excess of total-cost-of-quality when output is held constant. Changes in total revenue are then due to the fact that a higher price can be charged for a better product.

Sales and Price Effects of Promotion

So far we have considered the amount of promotion that maximizes profits when a producer is free to vary either his sales *or* price, but not both. We shall now take up the case of how to adjust price *and* sales to maximize profits when a given promotional undertaking has already been decided upon and the expenses incurred. The product's quality is temporarily impounded in *ceteris paribus*.

The predetermined selling effort shifts the demand schedule for the enterprise's output upwards and to the right (see Fig. 35).

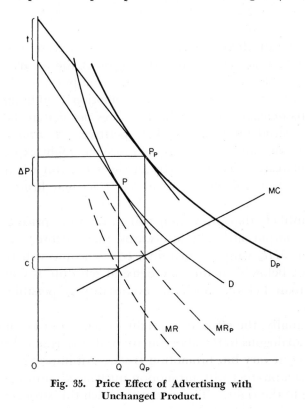

Fig. 35. Price Effect of Advertising with Unchanged Product.

A new marginal revenue schedule (MR_p) is derivable from this new demand schedule (D_p). The marginal cost schedule shows only the addition to total cost of *producing* an extra unit of output, and so is presumably unaffected by the selling activity that has already been decided upon. Figure 35 shows that the most profitable output after promotion (Q_p) equates MR_p with marginal costs and can be sold for a new price (P_p).

The relation between the new and the old price is definite. The price after promotion (P_p) will be greater than the prior price (P) if either marginal costs are higher at the new output *or* if the new demand schedule is less elastic than the old demand at the old price. In Fig. 35, c is the marginal cost at Q_p output minus the marginal cost at Q output, and t is the intercept made by a tangent to D_p at Q_p output minus the intercept made by a tangent to D at Q output. We now have the formula:

$$P_p - P = \frac{c + t}{2}$$

Promotion can therefore be expected to increase price unless either c or t is sufficiently negative to offset the other. In some enterprises, marginal costs may fall with output, and then c will have a minus value. However, a promotional undertaking that only shifts demand to the right, and does not flatten the demand schedule considerably, will make t positive. *A priori* estimates are dangerous, but in a majority of cases one might expect promotion to increase price, especially in the short run when there is insufficient time for higher prices to attract new firms into competition.

It is unlikely that promotion will so raise the price that fewer units of output are sold afterwards than before. The intersection of MR_p with the marginal cost schedule will only be at an output below Q if the new demand schedule is considerably steeper than before. Such an eventuality is possible but not probable.

Incidentally, the effect of a product change can be shown in a manner analogous to the above analysis, if it is assumed that price and sales can vary but promotion is set. An improvement in the quality of a product will, promotion unchanged, shift the demand schedule to the right. The extent to which this stronger demand will be exploited through selling more units or raising the price depends again upon the elasticities of the demand schedule and the effect on marginal costs of changing the product. In almost all cases a better product, in the sense of a more acceptable product commercially, will involve an upwards shift in the marginal cost curve. The probability of a higher price is therefore considerable. Sales may also increase in quantity.

Controversies over Advertising

The most outstanding example of promotion is of course advertising, and advertising has always, since its inception, been the center of controversy. It has been praised and blamed for many reasons. It has been given the credit for spurring men and women on to greater productive efforts so that they will have extra income to buy goods that advertising has made them want. On the other hand, the low birth rate of American families has been attributed to the fact that many parents can only indulge in the semiluxury consumption that advertising especially promotes through the economies of having fewer children. More frequently, however, the argument concerns the price effect of advertising, and here the layman encounters many fallacious propositions. Some of these will now be considered. Also a more basic economic evaluation of promotion will be suggested.

Mass-Production Economies Argument

It is often argued (1) that advertising increases sales, (2) that a higher output realizes mass-production economies, and (3) that the resultant lowering of unit costs is passed on to the consumer in a lower price. Each of these three links in the chain of argument should be separately tested. First, we have seen that expanding output is only one way of exploiting the enhanced consumer acceptance that results from successful advertising; the management might decide instead to raise the price or adulterate the product. Second, not all enterprises have equilibrium outputs, without advertising, below the volume that minimizes total costs; and, even if the average cost of producing is still falling, the expense of advertising may be greater than the production economy obtained in this manner. Third, even if we grant these first two points for the sake of argument, we have every reason for doubting that any cost reduction per unit will be passed on in lower prices. Producers do not deliberately set their prices according to unit costs. The owners of the enterprise would surely prefer to pocket any cost economies as profits. Of course, it is conceivable that competition might compel the management in certain cases to pass on these economies despite its wishes, but successful advertising usually has the effect of reducing competition and investing each producer with limited monopoly powers. The short-run effect, before other firms come into the group, need not be the effect that is suggested by the apologists for advertising. In a longer-run period, the possibility of attaining lower unit costs with a larger plant is greater, but will the advertising firm prefer to exploit this possibility?

Consumers-Pay-the-Cost Argument

It is often argued that advertising costs money, that producers do not ordinarily make outlays which they cannot recover, and that buyers therefore pay for the advertising in the selling price. Such a case cannot logically be made against advertising unless one assumes that output cannot be expanded. No one will deny that the cost per unit of a given output is greater when there is advertising, or that in the long run producers expect to cover all their costs. However, advertising may cause an increase in sales, and the unit costs with advertising of a higher output may be lower than the unit costs of merely producing a smaller output. Nevertheless, as we have seen, it is still questionable whether any such unit cost saving will cause lower prices. This argument also ignores the possibility of quality change. And, whereas the argument which favored advertising suggested that the only possible reaction was a change in sales, the hostile argument implies that the volume of output cannot be varied. In both cases it is more reasonable to expect a combined price and output effect from promotion of all kinds (see Fig. 32).

Economists' Approach to Evaluating Promotion

An economist should never attempt to judge the desirability of advertising, or of any other kind of promotion, according to its effect on price. The injury inflicted on a consumer by a higher price may be offset by a gain for the enterpriser or the factors that he employs. Any analysis that stops at the price effect is altogether too superficial to be useful.

A fundamental evaluation of promotion must be related to questions of adequate resource employment and proper resource allocation. Does advertising so whet consumers' desires that they will work harder and the economy will produce more? It is extremely difficult to say anything conclusive on this score and it is even questionable whether economic activity is desirable *per se*. Could the resources that are employed in promotion—equal in value to 3 or 4 per cent of the national income of the United States —be used for other purposes that would contribute more consumer satisfaction? In a great many instances there can be little doubt that promotion does not invest the product with any extra utility and that the labor and materials that it requires are being wasted. Humans are suggestible animals, however, and in other cases the user may enjoy attributes that exist only in his mind; if advertising has convinced a woman that she can be more successfully feminine by using "Allure" perfume, have the resources used by the promoter and the extra price she paid really been a waste for the economy or for herself?

Even a socialist economy might advertise cosmetics and other such goods. There is limited advertising in the Soviet Union. If the same value of economic resources can produce $100x$ units of unadvertised goods *or* $96x$ units of highly advertised goods, and if the latter arrangement provides more total utility, then this advertising opportunity would seem to be economically worth while. The same sort of test in other cases might, of course, indicate that promotion was economically wasteful.

Why is Non-Price Competition so Prevalent?

During the present century the trend in the United States has been in the direction of more and more promotion and product competition. Price competition in many markets has ceased or has become relatively unimportant. Why is product differentiation becoming so strenuous and prevalent?

One reason is probably that fifty years ago a much smaller fraction of the national product consisted of goods that lent themselves to differentiation. There were few or no automobiles, refrigerators, vacuum cleaners, or radios produced. Most women bought yardage materials or wool and made or knitted their clothes. More households were more self-supporting as regards food, partly because rural families found it harder to get supplies from town, and partly because women were prepared to spend more of their lives in their kitchens. Nowadays a new car may be preferred to improving the home, many women's clothes are nationally advertised, and soup comes from a can. It is impossible for goods bought at retail not to be differentiated, if only because of the location of the store or the personalities of the sales people, and the relative decline of household production has naturally meant that more goods flow to consumers through retail outlets.

Another important reason is that differentiation has repeatedly been found to pay. The branding and advertising and packaging of such commonplace goods as oranges, milk, bread, soap, and even coal, to cite a few familiar examples, has permitted the enterprisers in question to make a profit. The profit has tended to come from mass production economies, from higher prices, or from adulteration of the product. In some cases the result is economically beneficial and in others it is not.

In many lines of industry and trade, production has become concentrated among a few sellers, whereas previously it was dispersed among a greater number. Such a transition to oligopoly from polypoly may alter the attractiveness of non-price competition versus price competition. When a firm is one seller among many, and enjoys only a small share of the market's sales, it may appear that price cutting will greatly increase sales and total revenue, for cross-elasticities of demand are generally high. However, when a firm is one of a few sellers, it is likely to become rather nervous and self-conscious about price cutting. From its superior vantage point, such a firm can see that its price reduction may cut so painfully into the sales of its rivals, and be so obvious to them in turn, that they will reduce prices in retaliation. If price cutting is seen to be too dangerous, rivalry must take other forms. As it happens, product differentiation, through promotion, probably becomes more practical and profitable when production and sales are concentrated among a few firms. The cost of advertising per unit of output may then be less because more units are sold. Also it may cost less money in the aggregate to *keep* a brand in public favor than to *raise* it from the ruck of numerous brand names; buyers are more likely to remember a brand that many of them already buy from habit.

Non-price competition seems to be both an effect and a cause of increasing oligopoly. One effect is to make price competition less attractive for the established majors. Also product differentiation, together with new forms of capital that place a premium on volume operations, has helped to concentrate production of many goods among a handful of firms.

Statements for Consideration

1. A product improvement can be exploited in the short run by the producing firm in three different ways. *Explain*
2. Advertising is an aid to economic efficiency if it at least occasions lower prices. *Discuss*
3. Promotion must lead to a higher price if the quality of product is not altered. *Evaluate*
4. A rational socialist economy would never employ advertising. *Evaluate*
5. Product differentiation has probably increased during the last half century. *Discuss*
6. Product and promotion competition is sometimes less dangerous to those concerned than open price competition would be. *Explain*
7. There is at least one circumstance in which a firm should equate its marginal cost of producing *and* selling to the price. *Explain*
8. Under certain circumstances it may pay a producer to adulterate his product. *Discuss*
9. There is often some uncertainty whether various kinds of advertising expense should be treated as fixed or variable costs. *Discuss*

References

Arlsburg, C. L., "Economic Aspects of Adulteration and Imitation," *Quarterly Journal of Economics,* November 1931.

Bain, J. S., *Pricing, Distribution and Employment,* Chapters 6, 7. New York: Holt, 1948.

Bowman, M. J., and Bach, G. L., *Economic Analysis and Public Policy,* Chapters 26, 27. New York: Prentice-Hall, 1949.

Burns, A. R., *The Decline of Competition,* Chapters 3, 7. New York: McGraw-Hill, 1936.

Chamberlin, E. H., *The Theory of Monopolistic Competition,* Chapters 4, 6, 7. Cambridge: Harvard University Press, 1938.

Ellis, H. S. (Ed.), *A Survey of Contemporary Economics,* Chapter 4. Philadelphia: Blakiston, 1948.

Enke, S., "Profit Maximization under Monopolistic Competition," *American Economic Review,* June 1941.

Meyers, A. L., *Modern Economics,* Chapter 16. New York: Prentice-Hall, 1946.

Stigler, G. J., *The Theory of Price,* Chapter 11. New York: Macmillan, 1946.

23

Monopolistic Competition

MARKET situations are neither purely competitive nor purely monopolistic in the case of differentiated products. As already explained, the Ford Motor Company, for example, experiences a measure of competition from Plymouth, Chevrolet, and others, but it does have a monopoly in the production and sale of Ford automobiles. We might call such a situation competitive monopoly, imperfect competition, or monopolistic competition. Actually, the last term is the one customarily used in the United States, while imperfect competition is favored in the United Kingdom. Monopolistic competition almost inevitably involves non-price competition, which usually takes the forms described in the previous chapter. In the present chapter we shall examine the output equilibria that occur under monopolistic competition. It will be found that these equilibria resemble those of pure monopoly in some ways and those of pure competition in others.

Interdependence Among Firms

Under monopolistic condition, each firm is confronted with rivals, some of which are "close" and some of which are "far." A "close" rival is one making a product that appears to most buyers to be almost a perfect substitute. A "far" rival is one making a good or providing a service that is at best only an imperfect substitute in the view of a few buyers. There is not always a definite group, as was once thought, within which all firms are equally close competitors and outside which all firms can be disregarded.

Measures of Interdependence

Conceptually, there are a number of ways in which firm interdependence might be defined and measured if the required data were available.

One possible definition of interdependence is the measure of cross-elasticity (see Chapter 17) between the products of Firms *A* and *B* as measured perhaps by the ratio of the proportionate change in *A*'s physical sales to the proportionate change in *B*'s price which occasioned it. However, instead of considering the effect of a change in *B*'s price upon *A*'s physical sales, one might consider its effect upon *A*'s total revenue from sales, or again upon *A*'s profits. Or one might try to evolve a measure of interdependence that would take into account the extent to which large current profits attract new firms into the same line of business so that future profits are reduced. Fundamentally, the notion of interdependence implies that the sales, revenues, or profits of one firm are rather directly affected by the actions of another.

However, this sort of interdependence may exist, and yet be imperceptible in practice, because it is lost to view in all the other changes that occur in markets. In this case, firm interdependence may be ignored by all and sundry, with each firm pursuing its own policies without thought of the consequences for other firms or the possibility of retaliation. We have given the name polypoly to such a situation of blithe disregard.

On the other hand, the interdependence of certain firms is all too obvious to them. Then it may be that they never reach a price decision without worrying about the reactions of immediate rivals. We then have a self-conscious and nervous state of affairs and a condition of oligopoly.

It is important to realize that the existence of firm interdependence may be more marked on some flanks than on others. *A*'s decision to cut prices may always prompt *B* to cut prices also, and yet a decision by *A* to increase promotional outlay may not cause *B* to intensify its promotion. Hence, in a sense, one may have oligopoly in price policies but polypoly in promotional policies. The trend in business is to cease active competition in those matters that are characterized by oligopoly and to continue rivalry in those respects that continue to be characterized by polypoly.

Price with Oligopoly and Polypoly

The shape of the demand schedule for a firm's product under monopolistic competition depends upon the price policies of rival producers, the character of the partially competitive group, and the preferences or brand attachments of buyers. Obviously, if all rivals cut their prices when *A* cuts its price, the quantity of *A*'s sales will not increase by as much as they would if the prices of *A*'s rivals remain unchanged. In examining this question, we shall first of all suppose that each buyer in the market has his own particular scale of brand preferences; for example, Brown may prefer brands *E, B, D, A*, and *C* in that order while Jones's scale reads *B, A, D, C*, and *E*.

Let us imagine a monopolistically competitive industry in which each firm sells a single branded product. However, while these firms are relatively interdependent, there is no significant degree of competition between these firms and those outside the group. An example might be the household refrigerator field.

TABLE 27
DEMAND UNDER OLIGOPOLY AND POLYPOLY

P	*d*	*D*	MR_t	MR_c
$120	10,000	40,000		
			$110	$+35
115	20,000	42,500		
			100	+25
110	30,000	45,000		
			90	+15
105	40,000	47,500		
			80	+ 5
100	50,000	50,000		
			70	− 5
95	60,000	52,500		
			60	−15
90	70,000	55,000		
			50	−25
85	80,000	57,500		
			40	−35
80	90,000	60,000		

In Table 27 it is assumed that Firm *A*, which produces brand *A*, is now selling 50,000 units a month at a price of $100. The *P* and *d* columns taken together indicate the changes in sales volume that will occur when *A* changes its price but rivals' prices remain unaltered. The *P* and *D* columns show the demand schedule for *A* when competitors retaliate in order to match all *A*'s price changes and retain their proportionate share of the market. Figure 36 illustrates Table 27. It will be noticed that the *dd'* schedule is much flatter than the *DD'* schedule.

Different groups have different traditions regarding price policy. If *A*'s group is accustomed to independent pricing by its members,

A will consider its *dd'* schedule relevant, whereas its *DD'* schedule will seem irrelevant. On the other hand, if the group normally follows retaliatory price policies, the relevant demand schedule for *A* will obviously appear to be *DD'* from the outset.

The price and output combination that *A* considers most profitable for itself will naturally depend in part upon its marginal revenue schedule. In Table 27 and Fig. 36 MR_i is the relevant

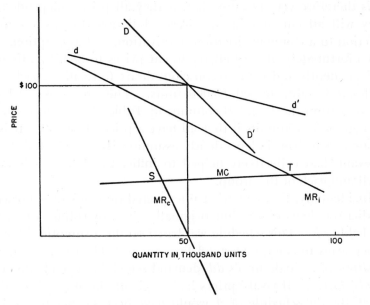

Fig. 36. Demand under Oligopoly and Polypoly.

marginal revenue schedule for *A* if independent price policies are the rule within the group and isolated price changes occur. On the other hand, MR_c is *A*'s marginal revenue schedule if common price changes always result because each firm is watching and matching the lowest price charged by any other. It will be noted at once that MR_c lies considerably below MR_i at each given quantity.

Figure 36 shows *A*'s marginal cost schedule. It intersects MR_c at an output of 41,250 units and a value of $35 ($S$) while intersecting MR_i at an output of 85,000 and a value of $40 ($T$). Superficially, it therefore seems that *A* will set one of two possible selling prices depending upon the expected price policies of the group. If independent pricing occurs, *A* will set a price of about $82.50 and hope to sell 85,000 units. Conversely, if common and dependent pricing occurs, it seems that A will sell only 41,250 units at a price of approximately $117.50.

Something has been overlooked however. The other firms in rivalry with A are confronted with rather similar factor supplies, cost functions, and product demands. If it pays A to cut prices when it supposes nobody will retaliate, will not B, C, D, and others independently reach the same conclusion and act similarly? It is therefore very possible that, if they all price independently, they will all cut, not in conscious retaliation, but as a similar reaction to a common situation, motivation, and assumption.

Unfortunately, if they all try to cut prices to $82.50, although independently and with no conscious desire to retaliate, each firm will *not* be able to sell 85,000 units. The group as a whole, judging from the P and D columns in Table 27, can only sell an average of 58,750 units if they all have a price of $82.50. It is as though each firm, independently assuming its dd' schedule to be relevant, had collectively helped to inflict the DD' schedule on itself and each of the group.

Incidentally, this somewhat unexpected outcome does not contradict the demand schedule originally given by columns P and d in Table 27. This schedule was based on the assumption that all other firms in the group stood firm at the $100 price. Now the *position* of a single firm's dd' demand schedule depends upon its *rivals' prices.* If rivals' prices had originally been $90 instead of $100, the dd' schedule of A would have been farther to the left, so that it could not have sold 50,000 units at $100. Conversely, if rivals' prices had originally been $110, A's dd' schedule would have shown that more than 50,000 units could have been sold by it had it charged only $100.

If a series of dd' schedules are constructed for A, one when other firms charge $110, another when they charge $100, still another when they charge $90, and so forth, we can begin to see what really happens when all firms adopt the same prices, independently and unconsciously. Then, when Firm A drops its price from $100 to $90, it does not simply travel down its dd' schedule, which is appropriate for rivals' prices of $100, but it has to shift on to the dd' schedule appropriate for rivals' prices of $90, if all the competitors make the same independent price cuts. The DD' schedule is then revealed to be a loci of points, each one of which

is on a distinct *dd'* schedule.   Also, on each *dd'* schedule, there is
one point that is also on the *DD'* schedule.

It seems that *A* will in the end remain located on a *DD'* schedule whether it assumes conscious retaliation or independent pricing.   However, the assumption *A* makes regarding the group's
pricing policies does make a difference and hence is important.
If *A* and all its rivals expect retaliation, they will never cut prices
in the independent expectation of moving down the *dd'* schedule, which intersects *DD'* at the initial price, and the original price
will very often remain unchanged for long periods of time.   If
independent pricing is practiced, *A* travels down the *DD'* schedule,
along with its rivals, but each of them independently expects to
find the original *dd'* schedule relevant.   The outcome is unexpected and contrary to the wishes of the firms involved.

Attachments of Buyers

The character of a firm's sales curve also depends in large measure upon the preference patterns and brand attachments of buyers.

It is possible to distinguish between many kinds of buyers according to their brand preference systems.   Some buyers, hereafter termed *preference buyers,* rank all available brands according to preference.   One such buyer might prefer *A* above all
others, after which he would take *B*, then *C*, and so forth.   If he
cannot obtain *A*, he does not buy just any alternative brand, but
instead seeks out *B*.   At the other extreme are *unattached buyers,*
who have no preferences and consider all the competing brands
equally satisfactory, despite all the efforts of advertisers and others
to make them think differently.   Between these extremes are buyers, who might be called *one-preference buyers,* who prefer one
brand to all others, but thereafter do not discriminate between
rival brands; for example, a buyer may prefer *A*, but be indifferent about *B, C, D,* and *E*.   Theoretically, of course, one might
also distinguish *two-preference buyers;* for example, some buyer
might prefer *A*, then *B*, but have no preference among the remaining *C, D,* and *E* brands.   One could go on in this way forever.   In the following analysis, however, we shall only consider
preference buyers and *unattached buyers.*

If all competing brands are sold at the same price, *A* will be
sold to a number of buyers, not all of whom will have the same

attitude toward it. Some of these purchasers will be preference buyers and their attachment to A may be strong enough to stand a price differential. The remainder of those who purchase brand A may be unattached buyers, who have bought A by accident rather than design, and who would not buy A in the future if it came to be sold at a higher price than rivals' outputs.

In this case A's *ceteris paribus* demand schedule (dd') will be very different than we previously supposed when assuming all purchasers were preference buyers. Now, if the price of A rises, but the prices of all rival brands remain unchanged, A will shake out only a few preference buyers but will lose *all* its unattached buyers. And now, if the price of A is cut, other things equal, A will pick up a few preference buyers and *all* the unattached buyers of the entire group's output. The dd' schedule of a single firm will be discontinuous, and in two parts, when there are both preference and unattached buyers in the market.

A numerical example may make this more evident. Let us suppose that there are 5,000 preference buyers and 5,000 unattached buyers of a group's output. Each buyer normally buys one unit per time period. The unattached buyers are scattered equally and in a random manner among the various brands. Each firm has the same number of preference buyers at the outset.

Initially, if there are only 5 rival firms, each will have 1,000 preference buyers and 1,000 unattached buyers. There will be some preference buyers on the margin between A and B, between A and C, between A and D, and between A and E. We shall suppose that a change of one dollar in the price of A, other prices unchanged, will shift 100 buyers across each of these four margins. Under these circumstances, a one dollar raise by A will lose it 400 preference buyers and all its 1,000 unattached buyers, or a total of 1,400 buyers and sales units. However, a one dollar price cut by A will add 400 preference buyers and all the other 4,000 unattached buyers, or a total of 4,400 buyers and sales units. The sales response is far more violent in the case of a price reduction.

The above phenomenon is even more pronounced if we suppose that the group comprises A and nineteen other rival sellers. Perhaps each firm enjoys the custom of 250 preference buyers and 250 unattached buyers. A small price raise by A will then lose it 250 unattached buyers, but a small price cut will add 4,750 such purchasers.

The above contrast points a moral. If there are many rival firms in a group, and each is physically and profitably able to expand output considerably, price reductions tend to be determined independently, with each firm reducing prices to increase sales rather than to win back lost customers. However, where there are only a few rival firms, the gains from one's own price cutting are not so disproportionately great and the losses suffered from the price cutting of others are not so disproportionately small.

Where there are relatively few rival sellers, and a relatively high proportion of unattached buyers among the customers, no one firm will permit others to sell at lower prices than itself. For example, the major oil companies would never allow one of their number continually to sell gasoline to motorists at a cent less than that charged by the other companies, for eventually the sales inroads made by the price cutter would become seriously large. In these cases the price weapon cuts so painfully that it is "outlawed" by common agreement.

The practice of price leadership is one way in which the effects of price competition can be allayed. A single firm, usually either the largest or the oldest seller in the group, publicizes its price changes, sometimes in advance, and other firms follow its lead. The above procedure usually becomes reinforced by tradition after a period of time. Price leadership does not necessarily entail consultation and collusion on what the price shall be. Neither is the resultant price necessarily the price that the leader itself would prefer.

Neutralization of the price weapon naturally tends to emphasize other forms of business rivalry. The two major kinds of nonprice competition, as already indicated, are promotional effort and product improvement, one of which may be stressed more than the other in certain cases. An outstanding example is the cigarette industry, which competes primarily through advertising.

Long-Run Equilibrium

Even under conditions of monopolistic competition, there are in operation long-run forces that tend to squeeze the profits of individual firms, if not perhaps to zero, at least below what they may often be in the short run. The way in which this "squeeze" takes place is through the arrival on the scene of new and rival firms that have been encouraged to enter the trade by the earnings of already established concerns. Hence, in the long run, there is a tendency for the price and average costs of each firm to approach equality, and for each firm's demand schedule to be pushed up against its average cost curve.

To the extent that profits are eliminated in the long run, the price and output of each firm depend not only upon its average cost curve, but upon the slope and position of its demand schedule. Specifically, if the firms in a group follow independent price policies, so that what we have called the dd' demand schedule is relevant, tangency of dd' and AC will tend to occur toward the bottom of each firm's AC curve. On the other hand, if DD' is relevant, its tangency with AC will tend to occur at a higher price and lower output.

Profits in this analysis refer to what are often termed economic profits. Economic profits, described in Chapter 31, are smaller than the accounting profits of businessmen because our average cost curve includes various costs that most accountants would not include as expenses. For instance, if the proprietor participates in the affairs of the firm, and is exceptionally able, so that the firm's accounting profits are largely due to his activities, it is supposed that the value of his services is estimated and included as an expense, on the grounds that he always has the alternative of hiring himself out to another firm as an employee.

Long-Run Profits

The monopoly elements possessed by a monopolistic competitor may be relatively unimportant and limited to a peculiar brand name and the special associations with which promotion has invested it. He can legally prevent a rival from marketing an identical product, but usually he cannot stop a potential competitor from making and selling a close substitute. For example, Coca Cola can sue any concern that passes off a perfect imitation of its product, but it cannot exclude Royal Crown Cola, Pepsi-Cola, and others from the same group.

In many instances the fact that an established firm is continually making substantial profits may serve to attract other companies into the field. The honey one bee enjoys may attract others. Of course, the profits of an existing firm are not a guarantee that a prospective company will obtain similarly generous returns on its investment. However, to the extent that old and new concerns have access to the same productive factors and techniques, continued profits of present firms will probably attract new rivals into a trade. The advent of these additional firms will drive the demand schedules of established companies downwards and to the left, while the prices of factors may be bid up, in which case cost curves will rise. These two reactions will exert a squeeze on profits.

If this squeezing action is complete, so that all profits are extinguished, the final long-run equilibrium will entail equality between average revenue (price) and average total costs *and* an equality between marginal costs and marginal receipts. The per unit cost curve will lie above the demand curve at every output save one, at which point they will be tangent, and profits will be maximized while losses will be minimized. Financially the enterprise "breaks even." So-called "tangency equilibria" of this kind are depicted in Fig. 37. Complete adjustments of this kind probably only *tend* to occur.

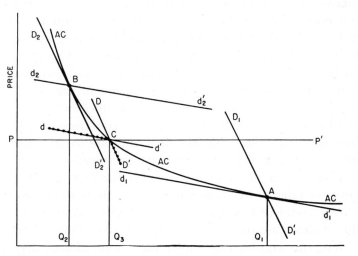

Fig. 37. Effect of Price Policies upon Long-Run Equilibrium.

Long-Run Output

The output that would be produced if long-run equilibrium ever came to be established depends on the possibility of long-run profits. In this section we shall assume, for the sake of discussion, that the entry and exit of firms into and out of the group is so easy that long-run profits are always zero. We shall also assume, again to simplify the analysis, that the entry and exit of firms affects the demand schedules rather than the cost curves of the remaining firms in the group. Moreover, we shall suppose that each existing firm shares equally in the total sales of the group. Finally, it is supposed that the long-run planning curve of a typical firm resembles the AC curve in Fig. 37.

The long-run output of a representative firm within the group will then depend upon the price policies pursued. These alternative policies are (1) independent price setting with each firm acting on the basis of its dd' schedule; (2) deliberate common pricing, based on common retaliation or price leadership so that the DD' schedule is relevant for each firm; and (3) oligopolistic price constancy, due to fear of price change, especially when there are large numbers of unattached buyers.

Independent Price Setting. If all purchasers are preference buyers, and there is independent pricing, the dd'_1 schedule is relevant and will become tangent to AC at A in the figure. If it lay above AC at A, there would be temporary profits, other firms would presumably be attracted into the group, and so the share of each firm in the groups' sales would be reduced, as evidenced by a sliding to the left of all firms' dd' schedules. The DD'_1 schedule here has no direct importance, but it does show what sales the firm in question would have if all the firms in the group raised or lowered their prices. Long-run equilibrium also requires short-run equilibrium, and so the long-run output (Q_1) must equate marginal costs with marginal revenue for the firm (not shown) as well as average cost with average revenue (at A).

Deliberate Common Pricing. In this case DD'_2 is relevant and can only be tangent to AC at B in Fig. 37. If DD'_2 never touched AC there would be losses, and if it intersected AC there would be profits at some outputs, neither of which conditions is compatible with long-run equilibrium under our assumptions. Hence the point of tangency (B) indicates the long-run output (Q_2). The dd'_2 is of academic interest only, since the individual firm does not dare to invite retaliation by price cutting on its own initiative. The marginal revenue schedule, which might be derived from DD'_2, would cut this firm's marginal cost schedule at Q_2 output, because the firm must be in short-run equilibrium when it is in long-run equilibrium.

Oligopolistic Price Constancy. Under certain oligopoly conditions, each firm may fear either to raise or lower its price, so that in practice existing prices tend to remain unchanged. This fear is based on two beliefs. Each firm believes that rival firms will duplicate its price cuts—thereby leaving it with only slightly more sales and a lower price. Also each firm believes that rival firms will not follow a price rise—thereby leaving it with far fewer sales and only a slightly higher price. In other words, each firm believes that its relevant demand schedule is dd' for price increases and DD' for price cuts. This composite or kinked demand curve —which is dd' above and DD' below the current price—is represented by the dotted dD' lines in Fig. 37. If these suppositions of the firm's management are really correct, a price cut will reduce total revenue, and a price hike will also reduce total revenue. Hence, it may be thought, the only way to maintain revenue is to adhere to the current price.

In Fig. 37 this constant and equal price is shown by the line PP'. In the long run, the tendency for profit elimination, discussed above, might lead to an abutment of dD', which is the composite kinked demand schedule, on AC at C. The long-run output would then be Q_3.

Price constancy of this kind is especially probable when there are numerous unattached buyers in the market. The slightest price rise, unless others follow, will then immediately sacrifice all sales to unattached buyers, and for this very reason rivals will refrain from following, in the absence of collusion. The slightest price cut will then strip every rival of all their sales to unattached buyers; and this they will not let pass without retaliation. In the absence of collusion, or of a tradition of price leadership, it is difficult to imagine how an established price would ever come to be changed.

When a given price is perpetuated, perhaps for the reasons given above, average costs adjust to price rather than the other way around. For instance, if all average cost curves were to fall, including the AC curve in Fig. 37, the resultant profits might instigate new entries; these might in turn push all firm demand schedules, such as dotted dD', to the left, and into a new abutment with AC. The final effect of the fall in average costs might be not a fall in price but a reduction in output per firm.

Gasoline service stations exemplify this tendency. Their retail "margins" are relatively permanent and their operating costs per gallon depend largely upon gallonage. The number of service stations owned and operated by independent retailers, and hence the gallonage per station also, probably adjusts with time so that costs per gallon become equal to the allowed retail margin. If a local government were forcibly to reduce the "margin," the final outcome, after temporary suffering, might be fewer stations with larger individual gallonages and contracted unit costs. Naturally the motoring public would find that fewer service stations sometimes caused them inconvenience.

Firm Numbers and Price Policy

For several reasons one tends to find deliberate common pricing in groups that include only a few firms and to discover independent price setting in groups including many firms. If there are only a few firms, it is simpler for each firm to watch the prices of rivals, and a price cut by a rival will occasion a more obvious loss of sales when there are only a few firms within the group. Conversely, if there are many firms in the group, ignorance of rivals' prices is greater, and the increased sales volume that any one firm can gain by price cutting is much larger compared to its previous sales. Hence industrial groups that are well populated with firms are more likely to carry on aggressive price policies (and operate according to dd' schedules), whereas groups that include only a few member firms are more likely to carry on price leadership (and operate according to DD' schedules). Where there is no outstanding firm to act as leader, and yet the number of firms is small enough so that the firms are aware of the dangers of price cutting and can watch each other, there may be a general reluctance to alter prices at all from some conventional level. In these ways, the number of sellers in the group may indirectly affect long-run price, output, and unit costs.

Composite Nature of Monopolistic Competition

In most respects monopolistic competition lies between pure competition on the one hand and pure monopoly on the other. The truth of this assertion is most clearly revealed by comparing and contrasting these three degrees of monopoly and competition. A partial summary of modern price theory is also gained thereby.

Substitutability of Rivals' Outputs

The outputs of rival firms are perfect substitutes under pure competition in that all buyers are unattached. The dd' of a single firm is then horizontal and the DD' of a single firm is simply a miniature reproduction of the public's demand for the commodity produced by the trade or industry. For example, a wheat farmer has an infinitely elastic demand schedule for his output, and the public has a sloping demand for wheat as a whole.

In the case of pure monopoly there are no obvious substitutes to bother the single producer who comprises the entire industry. Hence the dd' and DD' schedules of a pure monopolist are identical. All the purchasers of its output are preference buyers.

Under monopolistic competition each firm in the group will sell to preference buyers and to unattached buyers. Its dd' schedule slopes instead of being horizontal, except that, due to unattached buyers, it may be flat over a limited quantity range. Its dd' and DD' schedules are distinct. Which schedule is relevant will depend in part on the number and price policies of firms in the group.

Entry and Profits

Additional firms are perfectly free to enter into the production of a good in the case of pure competition, and so long-run profits should be zero. On the other hand, entry is restricted in the case of monopoly, and thus long-run profits are quite possible on theoretical grounds, although they are not inevitable. Under monopolistic competition it is usually possible to make a very close physical substitute, which may be more or less profitable than the imitated forerunner, but exact duplication is prohibited by trademark, copyright, or patent laws. The cola drink business is an obvious example and has already been mentioned. Profits tend to be zero in the long run, but in certain instances persistent long-run profits are conceivable.

Firm Supply Schedules

The marginal cost curve of a pure competitor, at least for outputs exceeding its point of diminishing returns, is a supply schedule, because price is then tantamount to marginal revenue. Knowing the price, one can read off from the marginal cost curve the amount the pure competitor will supply.   Under monopolistic competition and pure monopoly, price and marginal revenue are seen to be distinct, and there is no supply schedule for the individual firm.

Output Formulae for Maximizing Profits

Output should always be adjusted—whether the situation is one of pure competition, monopolistic competition, or pure monopoly —according to certain formulae if profits are to be maximized. In elaborating on this statement it is necessary to distinguish between the immediate market period, the short run, and the long run.   Altogether there are nine possible situations of which monopolistic competition in the short run is probably the most general.   They are shown in the price theory summary at the end of the chapter.

Immediate Market Period.   In the case of pure competition the seller should dump all that he has at the going price.   The pure monopolist should sell the quantity that will make marginal revenue equal to zero and destroy any remaining surplus.   The monopolistic competitor will usually act like the monopolist unless he fears that too high a price will create ill will against his brand, and so reduce the demand for his "make" in later markets.   If he does fear this, he may act moderately in seeking to maximize profits over time.   The pure competitor, but not the pure monopolist, can usually escape identification through a brand name in this way, and hence can usually disregard public opinion in this respect. In all cases total revenue must exceed or equal zero.

Short-Run Period.   All sellers attempt to equate marginal costs and marginal receipts through output adjustments.   In the case of pure competition it superficially appears that marginal costs are in this way equated to price.   Total revenue must exceed or equal total variable costs for sellers to remain in production.

Long-Run Period.   All sellers will strive, as in the short run, to equate their marginal revenues with the marginal costs of their actual plants.   All sellers will also attempt to match these marginal revenues with the marginal cost schedule derivable from their long-run planning curves.   Plant marginal costs and planning marginal costs should be equal both to each other and to long-run marginal revenue for full equilibrium and profit maximization.   Of course marginal revenue is identical with price in the case of pure competition. Total revenue must exceed or equal total cost if producers are to remain in business.

Quasi-Rents Crucial. It will be noted that the decision whether to continue or cease operations depends upon quasi-rents. An entrepreneur will continue in production if quasi-rents (i.e., total revenues minus total variable costs) exceed or equal zero. The reason for this in the short run has already been explained (see Chapter 20). However, this is also true in the market period (when there are no variable costs), and in the long run (when all costs are variable costs). Hence quasi-rents are equal to total revenue in the immediate market period and to total profit in the long-run period. After all, total revenue is simply the sum of a series of marginal receipts, and total variable costs are simply the sum of a series of marginal costs. Hence, the equation of marginal costs and marginal receipts maximizes quasi-rents, and in turn profits, since profits are quasi-rents minus some constant value for fixed costs.

Variables To Be Determined by the Management

The manager of a purely competitive enterprise, accepting the market price as a datum over which he has no control, adjusts output so that marginal costs equal the going price. He has no influence over price and can only decide to take it or leave it. Selling a homogeneous and unbranded product, the manager of a purely competitive enterprise has no opportunities to advertise or to undertake the more usual kinds of promotion. And, if he is producing a natural commodity, he does not determine the design and performance characteristics of his product. Efficient production and adjustment of output are his only ways of maximizing profits.

A pure monopolist has in addition to formulate a price policy. He may determine promotion and product variables also. Selling a product that is sold by no other firm, and which is usually identifiable, a monopolist is not precluded by circumstances from promoting his output; however, inasmuch as there are no close substitutes for a monopolist's product, the profitability of promotion is often limited. A monopolist is also likely to be more restricted than a monopolistic competitor in the matter of product determination, for the monopolized product may be a natural commodity; or, if manufactured, its specifications may in effect be limited by the terms of some patent grant.

Monopolistic competition, by way of contrast, gives management wide discretion. A definite price decision must be reached and announced. There is full scope for all kinds of promotion. The product, instead of being preordained, must be planned by the firm's technical advisers. The management of a monopolistic competitor has the most variables to perplex it and the most opportunities to make mistakes.

PRICE THEORY SUMMARY

Immediate Market	*Short Run*	*Long Run*
PURE COMPETITION		
Dumps output for what it will bring	$MC = P \equiv MR$	$P \equiv MR = MC = AC$
MC curve a supply schedule	MC curve a supply schedule	MC curve a supply schedule
		No profits
Perfect rival substitutes	Perfect rival substitutes	Perfect rival substitutes
$TR \geqslant 0$	$TR \geqslant TVC$	$TR = TC$
MONOPOLISTIC COMPETITION		
Sets price so that MR equals zero unless fears future ill will toward brand	$MC = MR$	$MC = MR$
	No supply schedule	No supply schedule
No supply schedule		Demand curve shifts to reduce profits
Partial substitutes	Partial substitutes	Partial substitutes
$TR \geqslant 0$	$TR \geqslant TVC$	$TR \geqslant TC$
PURE MONOPOLY		
Sets price so that MR equals zero unless fears ill will	$MC = MR$	$MC = MR$
		No supply schedule
No supply schedule	No supply schedule	Demand curve independ· ent of profits
No close substitutes	No close substitutes	No close substitutes
$TR \geqslant 0$	$TR \geqslant TVC$	$TR \geqslant TC$

Statements for Consideration

1. Firms are either in full competition with other firms or independent of them. *Evaluate*
2. The degree of monopoly a firm enjoys tends to vary with interfirm independence. *Discuss*
3. The curvature and position of a firm's demand schedule depend on the current prices and future price reactions of rivals. *Explain*
4. The simultaneous presence of preference buyers and unattached buyers in a market tends to occasion a kink in the *ceteris paribus* (*dd'*) demand curve of a firm. *Explain*
5. Long-run profits only tend to be zero under conditions of monopolistic competition. *Discuss*
6. Unit costs adjust to the price when, for any one of several reasons, the price of a good is inflexible. *Discuss*
7. A firm attempts to maximize quasi-rents in all time periods. *Evaluate*
8. Each firm has a supply schedule, whether or not it has a monopoly. *Evaluate*
9. Under certain circumstances a firm may fear either to raise or to lower its price. *Explain*
10. The variables that have to be determined by management are always the same in at least one respect. *Discuss*

References

Bain, J. S., *Pricing, Distribution and Employment,* Chapter 8. New York: Holt, 1948.

Boulding, K. E., *Economic Analysis,* Chapters 27, 28. New York: Harper, 1948.

Bowman, M. J., and Bach, G. L., *Economic Analysis and Public Policy,* Chapter 25. New York: Prentice-Hall, 1949.

Burns, A. R., *The Decline of Competition,* Chapters 4, 5. New York: McGraw-Hill, 1936.

Chamberlin, E. H., *The Theory of Monopolistic Competition,* Chapter 5. Cambridge: Harvard University Press, 1938.

Due, J. F., *Intermediate Economic Analysis,* Chapters 6, 7. Chicago: Irwin, 1947.

Garver, F. B., and Hansen, A. H., *Principles of Economics,* Third Edition, Chapter 15. New York: Ginn, 1947.

Machlup, F., "Evaluation of the Practical Significance of the Theory of Monopolistic Competition," *Quarterly Journal of Economics* November 1940.

Nicols, A., "The Rehabilitation of Pure Competition," *Quarterly Journal of Economics,* November 1947.

Stigler, G. J., *The Theory of Price,* Chapters 12–14. New York: Macmillan, 1946.

Triffin, R., *Monopolistic Competition and General Equilibrium Theory.* Cambridge: Harvard University Press, 1940.

24

Price Discrimination

PRICE discrimination can be defined as the sale of different units of a homogenous product at different net prices. There are two noteworthy points in this definition. The product must be of uniform quality and sold under identical conditions of packing and credit and so on. The provision regarding net prices is a reminder that the cost to the purchaser is often greater than the price retained by the seller, the difference being due to freight charges; in this case, it is differences in the effective f.o.b. prices at the factory that constitute price discrimination. The usual purpose of price discrimination is to increase profits. As will be demonstrated below, a given output will realize a greater total revenue for the seller, except in one special case, when it is sold according to discriminatory principles rather than at a uniform price. However, the total cost of producing and marketing a given output is seldom affected, at least to any appreciable extent, by the existence or absence of discrimination. Consequently, as profits are equal to total revenue minus total costs, a given output can usually be made to yield a greater profit, or smaller loss, if discriminatory prices are charged.

Examples of Discrimination

An extreme instance of price discrimination—sometimes termed "perfect" discrimination—would be if the seller could estimate the maximum reservation price that every prospective buyer had placed on each unit he contemplated purchasing and then had the ability to demand that price. In this case the seller would charge as many prices as the number of units he sold. If the demand curve started at $19.00 for the first unit, $18.50 for the second, $17.75 for the third, and so on, "perfect" discrimination would entail the charging of $19.00 to the purchaser of the first unit, $18.50 to the purchaser of the second unit, and so on. The marginal revenue in this case would be, unit by unit, $19.00, $18.50, $17.75, and so on. In other words, in this extreme case, the demand curve becomes the marginal revenue schedule of the seller. The average revenue schedule—which has no direct significance under discrimination—would be above the demand curve. Graphically, the entrepreneur would extend output until his marginal cost schedule intersected the demand curve, and his quasi-rents would be represented by the area lying above the marginal cost schedule and below the demand curve. There would be as many prices as units sold. It is remarkable that there is no buyers' surplus in this extreme instance. It has all been converted into seller's revenue.

Most discrimination encountered in practice is of a much milder sort. A great deal of it takes the form of offering what is in effect a lower price per unit if the customer will increase the size of his purchase. A familiar example is the sign in "dime stores" announcing "10¢ each—3 for 25¢." In this case the first unit sells for 10¢, the second also for 10¢, but the third really sells for 5¢. The seller realizes, of course, that the demand schedule of any buyer is negatively inclined, and that therefore the third unit often cannot be sold for 10¢, but could for 5¢. It is still worth while to sell this third unit at 5¢ providing its marginal cost is not greater than this amount. However, the seller does not wish to dispose of the first two units at 5¢ each, since he would then only realize 15¢ for all three units. His solution of "10¢ each—3 for 25¢" enables him still to sell three units and increases his total revenue by 10¢ over what he would realize from a uniform price of 5¢. Slightly more complex examples of this same principle are to be found in the practice of selling packets of different size at disproportionate prices. The "Individual Size" (8 ounces) may sell at 40¢, the "Family Size" (16 ounces) at 64¢, and the "Economy Size" (32 ounces) at 96¢. The effective prices per ounce in these three cases are respectively 5¢, 4¢, and 3¢. A great majority of public utilities charge lower rates for electricity, gas, and water as the customer increases his use. For example, the first thousand cubic feet of gas may be sold at 7.0¢ per 100 cubic feet and the next thousand at 6.0¢ per 100 cubic feet, with even lower prices for succeeding "blocks." All these cases are forms of discrimination based on quantity.

Price discrimination is often geographic. A Boston producer

of shoes may sell at the same price throughout the United States; and because freight costs on sales to Salt Lake City will be greater than to New York, it follows that the *net* price received by the manufacturer is higher on sales to New York and lower on sales to Salt Lake City.   In a sense, the local buyers are being discriminated against, because they cause lower costs and might therefore expect a lower price.

Discrimination is often based on income.   A familiar instance is that of a surgeon who perhaps charges $500 to a rich patient for a tonsillectomy, but only $25 to a poor man who requires the same operation.   Discrimination that depends on income differences is found most frequently in the case of professional services. The poor man cannot resell the tonsillectomy to the rich man.

It is much more difficult to sell a *commodity* at different prices to rich and poor people because of the possibility of resale.   In this case it is customary to market two different models.   A refrigerator company may market a "standard" model, which costs only $80 to make and distribute, and sells at $95.   It may also sell a "de luxe" model, identical except for the addition of numerous chromium fittings, which costs only $85 to make, and sells for $115.   High-income customers, who place a lower utility valuation on a dollar, can afford to pay $20 more for a little eye pleasure and so buy the "de luxe" model.   Middle-income buyers budget their outlays, can only afford to purchase the essential service of refrigeration, and so purchase the standard model.   In this way the refrigerator company is able to charge a higher effective price to rich people and make a large profit on the de luxe model; but, in addition, it succeeds in retaining the broader market by the offer of a "standard" model at a more moderate price.   (This refrigerator illustration is not strictly a case of price discrimination, as we have defined it, because the two products are not quite identical.)

Discrimination between Already Separated Markets

Frequently a monopolistic seller finds that his total demand comes from a number of different markets, which are not separated by his own action but are distinct by reason of government regulation, sex differences, color prejudices, and the like.

Let us suppose that there is a radio manufacturer, with a large factory at Schenectady, who sells a given model in the United States and Canadian markets.   The demand schedule for each market is given in Fig. 38, the quantity scale for the Canadian market appearing on the left-hand side of the diagram, reading from right to left. The United States has higher per capita incomes and this

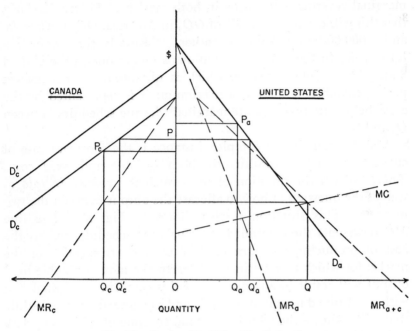

Fig. 38. Geographic Price Discrimination.

possibly explains the higher initial prices that can be obtained in the domestic market. A marginal revenue schedule has been derived for each market from its own demand schedule. Assuming a market period problem, in which the company has already manufactured 1,000,000 radios on speculation and no longer considers historical costs, how should it allocate the million units between the two markets?

It would be a great mistake to charge the same price in both markets if they have different elasticities of demand. For example, it might be possible to dispose of the million units at $60 each by selling Q'_a units in the United States and Q'_c in Canada. However, at $60, the demand in the Canadian market might be more elastic than in the American, as evidenced by a marginal revenue of $45 in Canada and $25 in the United States. In this event, the radio company can increase its total revenue by $20, and hence its quasi-rents and profits by the same amount, through diverting a unit away from the American market (a gross loss of $25) and toward the Canadian market (a gross gain of $45). Relocation of output in this direction should be continued until marginal revenue is the same in both markets. Figure 38 shows that this will occur with a sale of OQ_a in America, OQ_c in Canada, and 1,000,000 units sold altogether. Naturally this compels a lower price in Canada (P_c) and allows a higher one in the United States (P_a). Total revenue, which is quasi-rent in this market period example, is then at a maximum; it is represented by the areas below the two separate marginal revenue schedules between Q_a and Q_c.

A more realistic but complex instance is the short-run case of current production resulting in both variable and fixed costs. There is then the question of how much to produce *in toto* as well as the question of how to allocate the output between the two markets. This situation is also shown in Fig. 38. The line MC represents the combined marginal cost schedule, that is the cost of producing an extra unit of output, irrespective of the market for which it is destined. Clearly, the most profitable total output will result in an equation of this combined marginal cost with a combined marginal revenue, and so we need a new schedule that will indicate the addition to total revenue of selling an extra unit. Here it is important to make a distinction, for the amount of additional total revenue from selling an extra unit will vary depending upon whether it is sold in a discriminating manner (equal marginal revenues but different prices in each market) or in a "simple" manner (equal prices but different marginal revenues in each market).

The combined marginal revenue schedule (MR_{a+b}) that results from discrimination is obtained by horizontally summing the two market marginal revenue schedules. The combined curves of marginal revenue and marginal cost intersect at an output of OQ. In order to maximize profits, prices of P_a and P_c should be charged in the United States and Canadian markets respectively, because these prices equate the marginal revenues of the two markets.

A minor refinement may now be added. Perhaps the American radio company, with its factory at Schenectady, must pay a $5 per unit duty before its product can enter Canada. There will then be two Canadian demand curves. D'_c is the demand of Canadian buyers in Canada and indicates the prices that will actually be charged to them. D_c represents the effective demand as seen by the company, is \$5 lower throughout, and shows the net prices the company receives for different quantities sold in Canada. Hence, MR_c is derived from D_c, which is derived from D'_c.

It is possible to contrast a discriminatory monopolist and a simple (i.e., non-discriminating) monopolist on the score of prices, output, and profits.

Prices. The discriminating monopolist charges more than one price. A reduced price will be charged in the more elastic market, and the less elastic market will have a raised price. Discrimination causes a lower price in at least one market.

Output. For a discriminating monopolist, the total and discriminatory marginal revenue schedule (DMR), as already depicted in the figure by MR_{a+b}, is obtained by horizontally summing the marginal revenue schedules of the different markets. However, a single monopolist does not recognize the distinct marginal revenue curves, or even demand curves, of the constituent markets. All he notices is a combined demand curve from which he derives, in the accustomed mathematical manner, a single marginal revenue schedule. This simple marginal revenue schedule (SMR) shows the addition to total revenue of selling an extra unit at a price that is the same in every market. The discriminating monopolist sets output to equate DMR with MC. The simple monopolist settles on the rate of production that equates SMR with MC. In most cases DMR will lie above SMR over the quantity range where they might intersect MC. Consequently, discrimination usually yields a higher output, although there are exceptional cases where the reverse might hold true.

Profits. Unless discrimination unduly increases the costs of producing and selling, a *given* output will always yield a greater total revenue, and hence profits, if sold at discriminating prices rather than at a single quotation. A discriminating monopolist will then make a larger profit even at the output that is most profitable for the simple monopolist. His profit superiority is therefore even greater when he produces and sells the (usually larger) output that is most profitable under discrimination.

Discrimination between Markets Separable at Will

It is conceivable that a monopolistic seller might be able to divide the total market into a number of submarkets at will.

For example, a monopolist might be in the business of installing and servicing a patented water filter and softener in family homes. In any given city, there is usually an undesirable neighborhood (in some hot converted swamp perhaps) and a desirable neighborhood (on some hill with a view and cool breezes). As one ascends Hillside Road, from West First Street in the undesirable district to West 160th Street at the top of the hill, there is likely to be a fairly even gradation upwards in both the size of family income and the amount families are willing to pay each month for the proposed service. The management of this monopoly can charge different prices to different families—so long as it doesn't make such a policy seem too personal—since they can hardly resell its service or remove its installed water units. The company might charge $2.00 a month to all customers between West First Street and West 50th Street and $3.00 to all service subscribers west of that; or the dividing line might be made at West 60th Street, or any other street for that matter.

In Fig. 39 we shall suppose that the demand curve (D) indicates

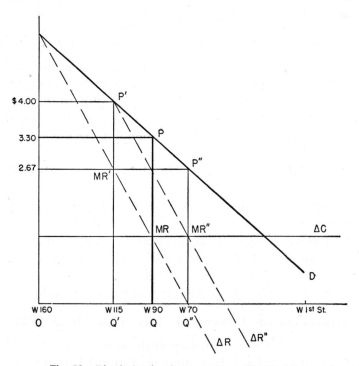

Fig. 39.   Discrimination between Separable Markets.

the maximum monthly service fees that families will pay, from the high reservation prices of people living as far west on Hillside Road as West 160th Street, to those living down at the bottom at West First. The ΔC curve represents marginal cost. A simple monopolist would equate ΔC with ΔR (at MR on the figure) and charge $3.30 a month, and every family west of West 90th Street would become a customer, but the families east of this rubicon would be unwilling to take the service. There is an evident opportunity, however, to increase profits by charging a higher price to those further up the hill, and to offer a lower price that will attract additional subscribers from further down the hill.

Assuming the discriminating monopoly wishes to divide its total market in *two*, it should divide it so that the marginal revenue in the first and higher market (MR') is equal to the price obtained in the second and lower market (P''); moreover, so that the total output is optimum, the marginal revenue in the second and lower market (MR'') should equal the marginal cost of supplying the entire output (ΔC). Let us suppose that the monopoly achieves this goal, on the first attempt, when it decides to divide the total market at West 115th Street and to charge $4.00, which is the maximum possible. This leaves a potential but untapped market east of West 115th Street. Graphically, it is as though we had a new vertical axis of $P'Q'$, instead of the ordinary one, and that we now measure quantity to the right from Q'. Consequently, the marginal revenue schedule of this second and lower market commences at P', where the demand curve of this market also starts. This second marginal revenue schedule intersects the ΔC curve at a quantity Q'', which, by interpolation, is estimated to be at West 70th Street. Therefore the monopoly should charge the highest price that the people at this level on the hill will pay, which appears to be $2.67. The increase in profits due to discrimination is represented by the quadrilateral $P'MR''MR\ MR'$. It should be noted that this arrangement satisfies the two conditions listed at the outset of this paragraph.

It might be that the monopolist desires to divide the market into three parts. Then MR_1 should equal P_2, MR_2 equal P_3, and MR_3 equal MC for the entire output. This formula can be adapted to cases of 10, 20, or n submarkets. The greater the number of submarkets, the greater will be the success of the monopoly in turning erstwhile buyers' surplus into profits for itself. A very large number of properly divided submarkets approaches the situation of perfect discrimination.

Basing Points and "Freight Absorption"

A geographic type of price discrimination is evident in a number of industries that do not sell at a factory door price, but deliver to the buyer at a price based on some selected point plus freight from it. Familiar examples of basing-point industries in the past have been afforded by steel, cement, and asbestos. The customer cannot buy at the mill or factory, and then himself arrange for subsequent transportation; instead, he pays a single price per unit, which includes the service and expense of delivery to his door. Delivered price systems, as contrasted to f.o.b. price systems, are practiced in industries where the commodities are homogeneous.

In the last century all steel was sold in the United States, irrespective of where it was actually produced, on the basis of "Pittsburgh plus." The customer was charged the announced price at Pittsburgh plus the freight cost from that point to his door. More recently, other places, such as Gary (Ind.) and Birmingham (Ala.), have also been basing points. In 1948, the U. S. Supreme Court eliminated many features of the old basing-point system in cement, and hence indirectly in steel. However, because of its historic interest, its current parallel in other industries, and its possible return, the economics of steel basing points deserve study.

Let us investigate the price discrimination that may arise in the simple and imaginary case of a Company A steel mill at Pittsburgh and a Company B steel mill at Gary. These two points are about 500 miles apart and we shall suppose that the freight on a specific steel product is $5.00 per 100 ton-miles. We shall further suppose that this product is selling in Pittsburgh at $50.00 a ton and in Gary at $60.00 a ton. At what point along the route between Pittsburgh and Gary will we pass over the "shed" that separates one market territory from the other?

In Fig. 40, the delivered price is shown to rise, from an initial level of $50.00, by $5.00 per hundred miles, the further away from Pittsburgh and toward Gary the customer happens to be located. Delivered prices also rise away from the Gary basing point, where they start at $60 a ton. Most basic steel products are identical, the output of Company A being no different in quality from that of Company *B,* so customers purchase on a price basis without reference to good will or advertising. In the present hypothetical case, one might expect all customers located within 350 miles of

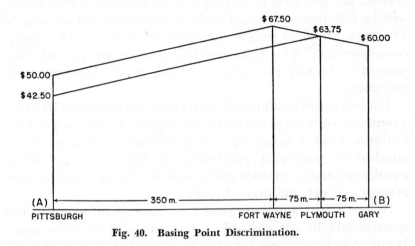

Fig. 40. Basing Point Discrimination.

Pittsburgh to buy from *A* (which we are pretending is the only steel company there) and all those within 150 miles of Gary to purchase from *B* (the only company supposedly at Gary). Fort Wayne would be approximately the dividing point. In the absence of price discrimination this would in fact be the result.

Steel plants enjoy lower per unit costs in the short run as output increases. Consequently steel companies are particularly anxious to increase sales, which, in view of the homogeneous nature of rivals' products, cannot be had unless a delivered price as low as competitors' prices is quoted. Company *A,* at Pittsburgh, might hanker after the 75 miles of territory between Fort Wayne and Plymouth; however, to compete in Plymouth, *A* would have to meet the price of $63.75 quoted there by Company *B* of Gary.

A very unattractive possibility for *A* would be to lower its Pittsburgh price to $42.50, add $21.25 freight, and quote $63.75 in Plymouth. Company *A* would then get the business between Fort Wayne and Plymouth, but it would be realizing $7.50 less a ton on the sales it already had "in the bag" between Pittsburgh and Fort Wayne. The net effect could be a reduction in *A*'s total revenue even though it sold a greater steel tonnage.

A more profitable alternative would be to maintain the $50 Pittsburgh price and absorb freight in the Fort Wayne to Plymouth territory. This means that Company *A* will quote a delivered price of $63.75 in Plymouth (as it must), and $67.50 in Fort Wayne (as it did before). The mill net at Pittsburgh—i.e., revenue per unit after deducting freight—on sales in Fort Wayne will be $50 (the announced basing-point price) and on sales to Plymouth $42.50 (a freight absorbtion of $7.50). Such a policy constitutes geographic price discrimination on the part of Company *A* as its mill net varies according to the location of the customer.

The practice of quoting delivered prices and absorbing freight is a means of lowering prices to distant buyers, in order to win their business, while keeping up prices to those customers already attached by geographic proximity. In this way, other things equal, a given steel tonnage can be sold for a higher total revenue, average mill net, and over-all profit.

However, basing-point systems do not always increase the steel tonnage sold by any company. Two can play the same game. While *A* is penetrating into the Gary market, *B* is doubtlessly absorbing freight to enter the Pittsburgh territory. *A* is delivering on the Gary side of Fort Wayne and *B* is delivering on the Pittsburgh side of Fort Wayne. This cross-hauling keeps the railroads busy but often represents an economic waste.

Economic Desirability of Price Discrimination

The term "discrimination" has nefarious associations for the layman. Large companies have in the past attempted to destroy financially weaker and smaller companies by charging abnormally low prices in common markets and recouping these losses by high prices in those areas that the strong company already monopolized. Predatory and temporary discrimination of this kind is as bad or good as the monopoly end to which it is a means. However, many of the examples of price discrimination that we have considered are continuous in character, and are not motivated by a desire to gain a stronger monopoly through destroying competition. How can we evaluate these last?

The outstanding result of discrimination is that total revenue, and usually net income in turn, are greater than under a uniform price policy. In many cases a firm would experience losses if it could not discriminate, and therefore would not survive in the long run. The existence of many such sustained enterprises is thoroughly justified and desirable.

A simple example is that of a small-town physician. Perhaps he charges rich patients $10.00 and poorer ones $2.00 for a house call. In this way he earns more money a year than if he charged a uniform fee of $5.00 per house call. Rich people have only a slightly elastic demand for this service (since they call the doctor as often as they feel sick and ignore the cost), while poor people have a much more elastic one (since they weigh the apparent severity of the illness against the probable fee). A doctor levying flat $5.00 fee would make very few more house calls to the rich but far fewer calls to the poor. He might earn so little that he would be compelled to quit his practice and the town would then lack his necessary services.

The railroads provide a more complex example. Economic ignorance might lead to legislation requiring rail carriers to make a uniform charge per 100 pounds per 100 miles. It is inevitable that this rate would be too high to permit long hauls or the movement of heavy goods of low value such as coal. At a uniform charge light objects of high value (for example, clothing) would relatively be traveling free. The volume of goods that could pay the price would be insufficient to cover the costs of railroading. Rolling stock would not be replaced and much trackage would be abandoned. The transportation industry would wither away, to the detriment of the entire economy.

On the other hand, discrimination, by raising their total revenue, may enable too many firms, collectively employing too many resources, to continue their existence in an industry. A group of nine firms, each having rather high overhead costs per unit and unduly small plant, is perhaps enabled to continue because discriminatory pricing yields a sufficiently large total revenue on even a small output per firm. A uniform price, charged by all firms in the group making a fairly homogeneous product, might evoke about the same total industry output, but would probably extract a smaller aggregate outlay from all buyers. In this case there would not be "financial room" for nine companies, and perhaps the number of concerns would fall to six, in which case, if overhead costs are important, typical per unit costs might fall. *If* industry output were about the same, then fewer and less valuable resources would be tied up in this line of production.

In nearly all cases, discrimination, because it yields more total revenue for the sale of a given output, has the effect of keeping more entrepreneurs in existence than would otherwise be the case. When this enables one doctor to keep in practice, where otherwise there would only be enough illness to support half a doctor, we are inclined to welcome discrimination. But in industries populated by firms with large overheads, and selling homogeneous products, the usual view is that resources are being wasted. Is it not possible to develop a reasonably objective yardstick that will tell us whether or not the extra subsidy effect of discrimination is economically desirable?

One possible approach to this problem is to attempt an estimate of the ratio of the monetary value of the users' surplus provided by a good to the total value of the resources employed in making it. We might call this relationship of users' value to resource value the *economic ratio*. This ratio will obviously vary from firm to firm and from industry to industry. Theoretically, there will be an average economic ratio for the economy as a whole, which we shall assume is 1.6. The more desirable enterprises will be those for which the economic ratio is above the average of 1.6, and the less desirable will be those with ratios below this value.

The existence of a high economic ratio is no guarantee that an enterprise will be financially practicable. What we might call the *financial ratio,* defined as total revenue over total cost, has no necessary relationship to the *economic ratio* already discussed. If the financial ratio is less than unity, the firm is making a loss, and will not continue in the long run if privately financed.

It is of passing interest to note that if a business were able to practice perfect discrimination it would have the same economic ratio and financial ratio.

Enterprise A might have an economic ratio of 1.9 (and therefore be economically desirable) but have a financial ratio of .9 (in which case private capitalism will not sustain it). A change from simple to discriminatory pricing policies might raise the financial ratio from .9 to 1.1. However, the economic ratio will remain the same if output is unchanged. In this case discrimination is apparently desirable as an economically worth-while enterprise is rendered financially practicable and hence continued in being.

On the other hand, Enterprise *B* might have an economic ratio of only 1.2 (below the average of 1.6), and a financial ratio of .8 with a uniform price and 1.2 under discrimination. Discrimination is not economically desirable in this second case, because, although it makes the concern financially profitable, Enterprise *B* has a subnormal economic ratio and is consequently an undesirable firm.

These and other theorems regarding the contrasting nature of economic efficiency and financial profit will be developed in Chapters 25 and 32. However, the present analysis is enough to reveal the disparity between legal attitudes toward discrimination and the lessons of economic theory. And this can hardly be otherwise so long as significant economic concepts remain statistically indeterminate.

Statements for Consideration

1. Price discrimination occurs whenever a producer sells at different delivered prices.   *Evaluate*
2. Import restrictions may encourage price discrimination on the part of sellers located in the protected nation.   *Discuss*
3. Price discrimination is unprofitable when the elasticity of demand in different markets is similar at a uniform price.   *Explain*
4. Discrimination is economically undesirable because it is sometimes a weapon of predatory competition by large companies. *Evaluate*
5. Our nation would not have an adequate railroad system if freight rate discrimination were outlawed.   *Discuss*
6. When rivals sell a bulky and homogeneous product, such as steel, basing-point systems of pricing are almost inevitable.   *Discuss*
7. Price discrimination cannot occur under conditions of pure price competition.   *Explain*

References

Burns, A. R., *The Decline of Competition,* Chapter 6. New York: McGraw-Hill, 1936.

Meade, J. E., and Hitch, C. J., *An Introduction to Economic Analysis and Policy,* Part II. New York: Oxford University Press, 1938.

Pigou, A. C., *The Economics of Welfare,* II, Chapter 17. London: Macmillan, 1946.

Robinson, J., *The Economics of Imperfect Competition,* V. New York: Macmillan, 1933.

25

Private Profit and General Welfare

THE ECONOMIST should have no special loyalties to labor or
capital or agriculture but should seek to ascertain and represent
the public interest so far as this is possible. General welfare requires not only that the national product be no less than is desirable (income and employment theory), and that it be distributed
in some way that seems equitable and encourages output (primarily distribution theory), but also that the national product comprise the proper goods in the best proportions (price theory).
Naturally these three fields of theory overlap. However, one
cannot study everything at once, and so in this chapter we shall
dwell on the problem of national product composition and resource allocation. More specifically, we shall see what price
theory can tell us regarding the likelihood that a free enterprise
economy will of itself produce this and that good in the most
useful amounts, rather than employing too many resources to
make this and hence producing too little of that. Such a study
inevitably leads us to the question of public control of monopoly
and unfair competition.

A free enterprise economy would tend to produce the right
things, in the right proportions, and in the right way, if the private
interests of entrepreneurs coincided with the public interests of
the economy. This would tend to occur if, when firms succeeded
in maximizing their profits, their marginal revenues corresponded
to some incremental social gain and their marginal costs corresponded proportionately to some incremental social cost. One of
the tasks of government in regulating business should be to render
this correspondence as great as possible.

There are several major reasons why private net product (i.e.,
profits) are often not in correspondence with social net product
(i.e., increased economic welfare). One of these reasons is that
the money costs of a firm may differ from the real cost of produc-

tion to the economy.   This disparity may be positive or negative. In other words, it may cost the economy more or less to produce some good than the money costs of the producing firms indicate. Similarly, the revenues of a firm may differ from the use value to the economy of its output, the difference again being either positive or negative.   A second reason for disparities in private and social product is that inequalities in income size prevent the demand prices of different households from always reflecting the relative urgencies of desire for different goods.   A third reason is that monopoly prevents a firm from producing as much of a good as the economy should use, while monopsony prevents a good from being used as extensively by the buyer as it should.   Each of these causes of resource malallocation will now be considered in more detail.

Real and Money Costs and Revenues

Some firms are able to escape many of the real costs that they occasion, not through fraud, but because of the nature of our social structure.   For instance, fish canneries inevitably foul the air with stench and adjoining rivers with waste, and as a consequence nearby families must install air conditioners and downstream plants cannot use river water economically.   Some of the true costs of production in this case are not being borne by the producer.   As a consequence, probably either the price of the product is too low or the profits of the producer are too high; hence there is probably a greater output and use of the product in question than would occur if the producing firm's money costs included all real costs to the community.   Accident-prone industries are also likely to employ too many resources and produce too much output, if the true cost of their accidents is not borne by their member firms, through the payment either of compensation benefits or of accident insurance premiums.   Some motion picture theaters make it difficult for nearby residents to park in front of their homes.   City bars and saloons do not have to pass on to their patrons the extra police department costs they create.   It is very simple to think of many examples of firms that do not bear all their real costs and so in a sense receive a hidden subsidy that distorts the character of the national output.

On the other hand, there are firms that perhaps bear more than their real costs.   All firms producing goods that are heavily taxed are likely to have either their profits reduced or their prices raised, with the result that output and employment may be contracted below an economically desirable level. Long distance telephone calls, most forms of entertainment, and cigarettes afford other obvious examples. The railroads claim that, relative to the air lines and truck lines, they pay an undue amount of taxes, and if this is so the economy is probably moving too few of its passengers and freight by railroad.

Not all firms collect the full measure of revenue to which their output might seem to entitle them, and when this occurs they are also likely to be undersized. For instance, the sort of athletic events the public sees depends partly on the ability of sports promoters to collect from the public. One would see more regatta crew-racing and fewer tennis matches if it were possible to prevent people from lining a river bank and seeing much of a rowing race at no cost. Because this potential revenue is lost, promoters organize stadium events instead.

However, some resources are used to make things that are perhaps wanted less by the public than the revenue obtained from them might indicate. The renting of billboard space yields revenues from firms that wish to advertise. And yet these billboards are an annoyance to many persons who might be willing to pay not to have them erected. However, there is no established procedure whereby the people who dislike billboards can cast a money vote against them. Similarly, jukeboxes have no "silence" selection, so people who like to eat and converse simultaneously cannot express this preference in an effective manner.

All of us have at one time probably thought of some business that would cater to an obvious need only to have some friend tell us "there's no money in it." Sometimes—but certainly not always—this may be because there is no way of collecting revenue from those who really would enjoy the output or because the enterprise would have to bear taxes or other costs in excess of its real cost to the economy. Occasionally, of course, when the need is too obvious to be denied and no means of collecting from beneficiaries exists, the government supplies the need *gratis;* examples are lighthouses at sea and public health inspectors.

Many of the examples cited above may seem too trivial to mention in a discussion of so large a subject as the proper allocation of a nation's productive resources. However, there are many thousands of similar instances in the real world. Some of these cases exemplify overemployment of resources and excess output. Others exemplify the opposite. In the aggregate, if they were all known and listed, their rectification might involve a very large shift in resources and a significant change in the composition of the national product.

In the literature of welfare economics, the term private net product has often been used to describe what we have thought of as profit, and the term social net product to designate the excess of real revenue over real cost. Whichever term is used, one fundamental difficulty always remains, however. It is to define real costs and real revenues, i.e., social net product, in a world where money values are known and comparable but the feelings of individuals are not.

Interpersonal Utility Comparisons

There is no way of knowing whether A or B wants good X more urgently. Of course, we can quickly discover that A will pay $100 for X while B will only offer $45, but this may simply mean that B has a much lower income. Undismayed, we may then discover that A will pay $50 for good Y whereas B will offer $60 for it. However, this information only tells us that, as compared with B, A prefers X to Y. We still don't know whether a unit of X and Y would contribute more satisfaction to A or B. And we never will know positively, for the very simple reason that there is no precise yardstick.

We can still conjecture, however. What are the various reasons that might prompt A to offer more for X than B does? One possible reason, already mentioned, is that A may have more disposable income. Another is that A may have fewer dependents and family responsibilities. And still another is that A's individual tastes may be such that he greatly appreciates X. As a short cut we shall refer to these differences as income, responsibility, and taste differences.

In general, we should like taste differences to be reflected in different price offers so that the economy can be better guided into the ways that gratify them most precisely. However, a man with many dependents will clearly not be able to gratify any single taste, other things equal, as adequately as a man with no responsibilities to others. Whether or not this fact is to be regretted is debatable, but we shall adopt the view that the size of families is deliberate and that sickness and old age can be covered by social insurance.

Whether a rich man should have a louder voice in determining the output and subsequent commodity distribution of an economy is often questioned.   One view might be that inequalities which are the result of unequal productive contributions should be so rewarded.   The enjoyment of money is a strong incentive to work, train, invent, invest, and otherwise contribute to output.   However, income inequalities that are not based on personal economic contributions of the past may be another story.

If, perhaps quite unreasonably, we decide that we do not wish income inequalities to be reflected in the composition of the national product, what still can be said regarding resource malallocation?   Presumably goods that comprise a large percentage of rich families' budgets, as compared to those of poor families, are overproduced, and vice versa.   However, there are still many products that are neither markedly superior nor markedly inferior in this sense, but rather occupy roughly the same relative place in rich as in poor household budgets.

In the event that both X and Y were such goods, and the prices at which consumers were buying them were \$100 and \$80 respectively, one might not be far wrong in assuming that another unit of X would provide about 1.25 the utility of another unit of Y. Such a contention is not logically correct under all circumstances, and it might very well be incorrect in the case of any pair of buyers such as A and B.   But the attributes of individuals do tend to concentrate around public averages, so that more people have almost normal tastes than have very abnormal tastes.   Hence, so long as goods are not typically poor men's goods (for example, beer) or rich men's goods (for example, champagne), their market prices may roughly reflect their relative contributions to economic welfare.

The Monopoly Problem

There would still be a disparity between private and social net product, even if income inequalities were unknown and money costs corresponded to true costs, if monopolies and monopsonies existed side by side with purely competitive firms in an economy. The markets of an economy relate the forces of demand to the forces of supply. The manner in which these forces finally interact and the proportions in which different goods are actually produced depend upon the extent of monopoly and monopsony, both of which cause suboptimum employment and output in the affected trades. The distorting influence of monopoly and monopsony can best be understood in contrast to the supply and demand interactions of pure competition.

Resource Allocation under Pure Competition

A purely competitive economy would be one in which all prices are determined impersonally by markets populated with many buyers and sellers. There is supposedly a preordained set of products in the economy and the character of no single good can be changed by man. All units of the same good are identical and their actual producer remains unknown. There is no deliberate product differentiation. Under pure competition the problem of resource allocation resolves itself into whether the firms of one industry (for example, coal mining) should have resources transferred to them from another (for example, cordwood).

Let us suppose that the industries that supply coal and cordwood are purely competitive, are located in the same area, use many of the same productive factors, and provide alternative fuels with which consumers can heat their homes. Let us further suppose that the final equilibrium price for coal is $12 a ton and that for cordwood is $6 a cord. The ratio of these prices (i.e., P_c/P_w) is 2.0. Now one of the essential features of a purely competitive equilibrium is that each producer, accepting the market price of his output as a datum, expands production up to the point where his marginal costs are equal to price. Hence we can expect the cost of producing an extra ton of coal to be $12 for each and every mine operator and the marginal cost of cutting an extra cord of fuel wood to be $6 for each producer. The ratio of these marginal costs (i.e., MC_c/MC_w) is therefore 2.0 also. In Chapter 18 we learned that rational consumers will always adjust the rate at which they use different goods so that the ratio of these goods' marginal utilities will be equal to the ratio of their prices.

Accordingly we have the following equations:

$$\frac{MC_c}{MC_w} = \frac{P_c}{P_w}; \qquad \frac{P_c}{P_w} = \frac{MU_c}{MU_w}; \qquad \frac{MU_c}{MU_w} = \frac{MC_c}{MC_w}$$

The first equation is due to the profit-maximizing attempts of purely competitive producers. And the second equation is due to the utility-maximizing ambitions of all rational consumers. Prices are the connecting links that render the ratio of marginal utilities equal to the ratio of marginal costs.

The rate at which consumers will be willing to substitute wood for coal at the margin will be 2 cords for 1 ton if the price of wood is $6 and the price of coal is $12. If the price system were suddenly eliminated, and consumers began bartering their fuel inventories, 2 cords to 1 ton would be the swapping rate and would reflect the relative use value of these two products when only a few units are being exchanged. We might call this 2-to-1 ratio the "marginal substitution rate of consumers."

The producers' marginal rate of substitution is shown by the ratio of marginal costs. An extra dollar's worth of productive resources will produce either an extra $\frac{1}{12}$ of a ton of coal or an extra $\frac{1}{6}$ of a cord of wood. Therefore, under certain assumptions, the cost to the economy of producing an extra ton of coal is two cords of wood and that of producing an extra cord of wood is half a ton of coal.

Costs calculated in this way are called "opportunity costs" and were discussed in the first chapter. The necessary assumptions are: (1) there is a constant employment by the economy of each productive resource; (2) the relative amount of resources needed for an extra ton of coal or cord of wood is shown by the ratio of the marginal costs of coal and wood producing; and (3) it is possible to transfer resources from one use to another, either directly or indirectly.

Productive resources are supposedly allocated in an optimum manner between coal and wood producing when the marginal rate of substitution among consumers is the same as that among producers. The truth of this statement will be more evident if we imagine a government ordering more coal production at the expense of a smaller cordwood output. The price of coal will have to fall if consumers are to buy the larger output, and the price of cordwood will rise as it becomes scarcer. We can normally suppose that the marginal cost of producing coal will be forced up, while that of cordwood will fall. Users of coal and wood adjust their rates of consumption to the new prices. It may be that

MU_c/MU_w is now 1.8 whereas MC_c/MC_w is now 2.3 instead of both ratios' being 2.0 as hitherto. This novel situation can hardly constitute an optimum allocation of resources, for while it is really costing 2.3 cords to produce an extra ton, consumers only want to give 1.8 cords of wood for a ton of coal. The economy is getting a poor bargain unless the marginal rate of substitution among producers (i.e., the ratio of marginal costs) is the same as that among consumers (i.e., the ratio of marginal utilities).

The above analysis implicitly assumes that a given consumer will buy both coal and wood. Only if this supposition is realistic can we say categorically that the marginal utilities of consumers are in the same ratio as the going prices. Occasionally it might happen that one group of people uses coal and another group uses cordwood. If each group has about the same income—both as regards average and dispersion—this mutually exclusive division of consumers does not seriously affect our conclusions regarding the allocation of resources. The dollar value of the derived consumer utility may then be roughly equal for both groups. However, if the coal users are rich and the wood burners are poor, or vice versa, our results have a more limited significance. We can then only say that pure competition fits resources to *effective demand* as closely as possible. The allocation of resources in terms of human needs may not be optimum. But when rich and poor are to be found equally in both markets, the distinction between effective demand and human need has no relevance, and pure competition can be expected to provide an optimum allocation of resources in the fullest sense.

Malallocation of Resources with Monopoly

Any economy usually includes a number of enterprises that are purely competitive, some of which are monopolies or monopsonies, and even more of which are monopolistic competitors. Such a variation in the degree of monopoly or competition threatens a malallocation of resources. However, we shall see that monopoly is not injurious *per se* in this connection, but only when existing side by side with more or less competitive firms.

We shall suppose in this analysis that there is a purely competitive copper industry made up of numerous concerns and a single thoroughly monopolistic producer of aluminum. The purely competitive price of copper is 30¢ a pound, and so this will also be the level of each copper producer's marginal costs. The selling price of aluminum charged by the monopolist is 10¢ a pound. The marginal costs of producing aluminum will certainly be less than the selling price, because of the demand schedule's negative inclination and the monopoly situation, and we shall arbitrarily suppose them to be 5¢ a pound initially. The ratio of P_c/P_a is therefore not equal to that of MC_c/MC_a. The marginal rate of substitution among users will therefore be incompatible with the "opportunity costs" of production.

The allocation of resources could be improved if we began transferring a few units of them from copper to aluminum producing. The prices of copper and aluminum are such that the users are willing to give up one pound of copper for three pounds of aluminum. However, the ratio of marginal costs shows that only a half a pound of copper need be sacrificed in order to produce an extra three pounds of aluminum. The opportunity cost of producing extra aluminum is only one-half the real price that consumers are willing to pay.

The economy will therefore experience a gain if resources are shifted from copper to aluminum production until P_c/P_a equals MC_c/MC_a. Expressed differently, copper production should be contracted, and aluminum output expanded, until P_c/MC_c (which is now 1.0) is equal to P_a/MC_a (which is now 2.0). A contraction in copper production will occasion a higher scarcity price for copper, and in purely competitive industries a slight reduction in output below the normal equilibrium will lower marginal costs. An expansion in aluminum production will have to be accompanied by a falling price and probably a rise in marginal costs. Eventually, as resources are transferred and outputs change, a point will be reached at which the price-to-marginal-cost ratio is the same for both commodities. We shall suppose that an equal ratio of 1.5 occurs when P_c is 36¢, MC_c is 24¢, P_a is 9¢, and MC_a is 6¢. Users are then willing to pay a real price of four pounds of aluminum for a pound of copper and this is also the opportunity cost of producing copper. Employing all the assumptions of the preceding section—except that of universal pure competition, of course—we can say that resources are now being allocated between copper and aluminum in an optimum manner.

Reallocation by Government

The administrative possibility of bringing about such a transfer of resources in an ostensibly free enterprise economy is an important problem.

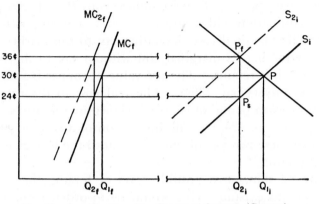

Fig. 41. Specific Tax To Contract Output (Copper).

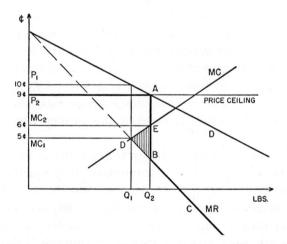

Fig. 42. Price Ceiling To Stimulate Output (Aluminum).

Total copper output might be reduced by a tax in the manner shown in Figure 41. There the quantity scale is broken, so that the widely divergent outputs of a single producer and his industry can be shown together. The firm in question was previously supplying Q_{1f} of the industry's Q_{1i} supply and equating its marginal costs to the competitive price of 30¢. The imposition of a 12¢ tax per pound of copper on producers, represented by the vertical distance P_bP_s in the diagram, will raise marginal cost schedules of producers and the collective supply schedule of the industry by 12¢ throughout. The industry now produces Q_{2i} and the buyers pay the 36¢ price indicated by P_b. The single firm under examination will produce Q_{2f}, at which output it will be equating its marginal costs including tax to the market price of 36¢ *and* equating its marginal cost without tax to the net price of 24¢, which it retains. The use value of copper is indicated by the prices buyers pay (36¢). The real cost to the economy of making an extra pound of copper is shown by the firm's marginal costs without tax (24¢). The imposition of a specific tax of 12¢ has spread these two magnitudes apart until the former is now 1.5 times the latter.

Figure 42 shows two possible ways of forcing the aluminum monopolist to expand. One would be to order a relatively low maximum selling price of P_2 (i.e., 9¢); this would establish a marginal revenue schedule for the monopoly represented by P_2ABC. (If selling above 9¢ is illegal, the price and marginal revenue coincide at this figure until the demand schedule is encountered at A, after which the relevant marginal revenue is based on the normal market demand schedule.) The closest the monopolist can come to equating MR and MC (at E) is to produce an output of Q_2. The price-to-marginal-cost ratio should now be 1.5 if the government has ordered the proper legal maximum price.

Another possibility would be for the government to offer a sliding scale subsidy, starting when output is pushed beyond the *laissez-faire* equilibrium of Q_1, and amounting to a little more than the excess of MC over MR for higher outputs. The subsidy would vary unit by unit. The absolute minimum that the government could offer and still achieve its purpose is shown by the shaded area DEB in Fig. 42.

The same principles apply where there are a great number of different enterprises. The best allocation of resources in terms of effective demand is the one that results when the ratio of price to marginal cost is the same for every firm and industry. Accordingly, interfirm comparisons of the P/MC ratio constitute a useful measure of resource malallocation. Any excess over unity indicates the degree of monopoly power being exercised. When this formula indicates that a firm is following more monopolistic price policies than are average for the economy, the firm should employ more resources and expand its output. Contraction of production is indicated for those firms which have abnormally low monopoly measures.

It must also be pointed out that the above analysis has assumed the existence of a single layer of enterprises situated between factor markets below and final product markets above. However, an economy is more likely to have a market structure resembling a multiple-decker sandwich, and in this case serial monopoly distortion will result. A final product (y) may be produced by an enterprise monopolizing to an extent of 1.4 and processing an intermediate good (x) that is sold by a concern having a monopoly of 1.2. The serial degree of monopoly that has been pyramided in this manner is 1.4×1.2, or 1.68. If the economy's average degree of monopoly, calculated over the whole span from primary factors to end products, is 1.5, then the monopoly being exercised in making y and x should be adjusted so that their serial monopoly effect is not over 1.5.

Examples of monopsony are also to be found in most economies. In this case there is a varying gap between the supply price (or average cost) of the purchased article and its marginal use value (because the monopsonist deliberately equates the *marginal cost* of buying to the marginal use value). Ideally, resources should be transferred from user to user until the ratios of marginal use value to supply price are universally equal. In numerous instances serial monopsony distortion will have to be taken into account.

The existence of monopoly or monopsony prevents a coincidence of private interest and public welfare. The exercise of monopoly power has the effect of preventing the specific employment of as many resources as are really needed to satisfy adequately a given demand. Hence other less urgent wants are relatively oversatisfied. The exercise of monopsony power leads to underuse of a good by the monopsonist and its relative overuse by others. The presence of either monopoly or monopsony elements is likely to cause a relative underemployment of inputs and a relative underproduction of outputs. In comparison, the goods used and made by purely competitive industries will be respectively employed and produced in too great volume. This is essentially the problem of monopoly as seen by the economist.

Government Antimonopoly Policy

The man in the street is likely to think of the monopoly problem in political rather than in economic terms. He probably believes that monopolies gain their position by the predatory means that are usually collectively described as unfair competition. He also probably believes that monopoly is dangerous because commercial dominance can lead, through influence and corruption, to political power. He may feel that monopolies are lazy about technical progress and slow to innovate. He may dislike monopolies because they make richer men than himself still richer. Hence he is opposed to monopolies, and this opposition has caused Congress in the past to legislate against monopolies and unfair competition. It is probably true to say that the aim of more efficient production of goods in more desirable proportions has been a secondary objective of government administrators, the law makers, and the public. The provisions of the law do not deal directly with these matters.

The popular imagination often thinks of a monopoly as some giant firm that supplies 85 per cent, 95 per cent, or even 100 per cent of the country's demand. Do these facts necessarily indicate that the situation is so economically undesirable as to permit and require improvement through government action? We have seen that one of the main economic objections to monopolies is that they underproduce. The seriousness of this can be gauged in part by comparing price with marginal cost. One theoretical measure of monopoly power is $(P - MC)/P$, which tends, when a firm is maximizing profits, to be the reciprocal of its price elasticity of demand. Hence, if a monopoly has a relatively elastic demand, its monopoly power measure will be low, and the evil effects of the monopoly may be slight. In fact, it is quite conceivable that the single hotel of many a small town has a higher $(P - MC)/P$ ratio than would a large national monopoly. Of course, the mere size of the latter makes it conspicuous, and its larger aggregate profits make it a better political target.

Public policy must always think of alternatives. If a large monopoly, supplying perhaps 95 per cent of the national market, were to be dismembered, what then? Would the resulting oligopoly engage in active price competition? Would the new group of firms produce much more output in the aggregate? Would these new firms be able to produce the previous monopoly output at no greater aggregate cost in employed resources? Would the new firms have large costs for rival advertising that was not incurred by the previous monopoly? Naturally it is impossible to answer these questions in the abstract. However, in any particular case, they should be carefully considered, especially by government officials armed with antimonopoly powers.

It may sometimes be the wiser course, especially if a monopoly owes its position to greater efficiency, to permit its continuance. However, steps should be taken to ensure that this efficiency is at least shared with the public, perhaps through higher wages, but preferably through lower output prices. If the monopoly is sheltering behind a tariff, the relevant customs duty should be repealed. If it seems that some violation of law can be proved, it might be advisable to reach an agreement with the company which would cause it to charge a lower price, for the reasons explained in the preceding section. It does not matter much that a company remains a monopoly, in the sense that it continues to be the only seller in a national market, if it is no longer behaving like a monopoly but instead is selling at a price that approaches marginal cost.

Of course, a very pertinent question is whether a monopoly owes its position to efficiency or to unfair competition. A large company can often eliminate rivals in ways that depend, not upon its economic efficiency, but upon its financial or commercial power. It may be financially strong enough to lower prices temporarily in the local market of a smaller rival and so drive it out of business. The large company may be able to bludgeon its suppliers into charging it a price that is not only lower than that paid by smaller rivals but is also lower than any price warranted by possible economies of large-scale purchasing. Naturally, small firms always raise the cry of unfair competition when a larger rival cuts its price below theirs, and unfortunately it is often impossible to know the motivation and future price policies of the larger firm. In theory, there is no particular economic objection to a firm's growth if this increase is based on efficiency; but growth due to unfair competition is unlikely to lead to economies of production and distribution, besides suggesting that the management is bent on future exploitation.   However, this conceptual distinction between growth due to efficiency and growth due to unfair competition is very hard to draw in practice.

Actually, although it occasions less public concern, oligopoly is probably more of an economic problem than monopoly pure and simple.   In the United States, there are more instances of oligopoly than of monopoly, and the resources employed by oligopolies are more valuable in the aggregate.   Many oligopolies engage in such limited price competition that their prices are not very different from those that might prevail if they were combined in a single firm.   Such oligopolies may waste resources more than would a monopoly.   Several large firms may engage in a lot of unnecessary cross-hauling throughout the country.   Rival oligopolists may undertake expensive promotional competition that is of little advantage to the public.   They may be in a better position to obtain price supports through import tariffs.   Oligopolists have been known to indulge in unfair competition as well as monopolists, not so much against each other, but as "majors" against "independents."   All in all, oligopoly is more of an economic problem than monopoly, but because more than one firm is involved the public often remains unperturbed.

It is extremely difficult to know how economic principles could be translated into applicable controls against oligopoly.   It would be quite impracticable to pass a law that made some government agency responsible for bringing the P/MC ratio of all firms into equality, if only because marginal costs are often statistically indeterminate.   No agency in peacetime is ever going to be given authority to determine prices and excise taxes or subsidies for individual firms.   Advertising and other forms of promotion will remain unregulated for a long time to come.

What then can the federal and state governments do?   They can continue to prevent unfair competition whenever possible and slowly evolve a code of fair competition through superior efficiency, but they must be careful not to allow measures against unfair competition to be perverted into a program against ordinary price competition.   They can make certain detectable situations and actions illegal and give them legally defined names such as "monopoly" and "restraint of trade," even though these situations and actions are not always economically undesirable.   The fact of illegality can be used by the government to bargain with those companies which, in addition to being in violation of the law, are acting in an economically undesirable manner. Out of the negotiations, and with the approval of a court, a consent decree may be entered, which will in effect eliminate the undesirable aspects of the previous "monopolistic" situation.

This brief prescription is a caricature of government monopoly control today. It is a pity that so much discretion must be left to officials, and that the true objectives of government policy cannot be written into antitrust and fair trade laws directly, so that businessmen would know better where they stood. Unfortunately the relevant economic concepts seem to defy legal definition in a way that renders them administratively useful, so that sensible economic ends must be approached through legislation that often seems to have less relevance to economics than to popular emotion.

Statements for Consideration

1. The special interest of the economist is the general economic interest of the community. *Discuss*
2. The money costs of a firm may differ from the real costs of production for the economy. *Exemplify*
3. A firm that does not bear all the real costs it occasions may distort the character of the national output. *Explain*
4. Some very useful goods and services are not privately supplied because there is no profit from supplying them. *Evaluate*
5. The prices at which different kinds of goods sell indicate their relative contribution to economic welfare. *Evaluate*
6. Households with large incomes or few dependents should not be placed in a favored position from which they can bid away goods and services needed by poorer or larger families. *Discuss*
7. It is not the fact of monopoly, but differences in the degree of monopoly, that occasion a mallocation of resources. *Explain*
8. Universal pure competition would cause an optimum allocation of resources among firms and users. *Discuss*
9. There is no way short of government operation by which private monopolies can be induced to expand their output. *Evaluate*
10. The extent to which a monopoly underinvests is in part dependent upon the elasticity of demand for its output. *Explain*
11. A large company can often eliminate rivals in ways that depend, not upon its economic efficiency, but upon its financial or commercial power. *Exemplify*
12. In the United States oligopoly may be more of an economic problem than relatively pure monopoly. *Discuss*

References

Bain, J. S., *Pricing, Distribution and Employment,* Chapter 9. New York: Holt, 1948.

Bowman, M. J., and Bach, G. L., *Economic Analysis and Public Policy,* Chapters 33, 40–42. New York: Prentice-Hall, 1949.

Ellis, H. S. (Ed.), *A Survey of Contemporary Economics,* Chapters 1, 3. Philadelphia: Blakiston, 1948.

Garver, F. B., and Hansen, A. H., *Principles of Economics,* Chapters 16, 17. New York: Ginn, 1947.

Kahn, R. F., "Some Notes on Ideal Output," *Economic Journal,* March 1935.

Lerner, A. P., *The Economics of Control,* Chapters 2–4. New York: Macmillan, 1945.

Mason, E. S., "Price Policies and Full Employment," *Public Policy.* Cambridge: Harvard University Press, 1940.

Meyers, A. L., *Modern Economics,* Chapter 11. New York: Prentice-Hall, 1941.

Pigou, A. C., *The Economics of Welfare,* II, Chapters 2–4, 9, 15. London: Macmillan, 1946.

Robinson, J., *The Economics of Imperfect Competition,* IV, X. New York: Macmillan, 1933.

Tarshis, L., *Elements of Economics,* Chapter 22. Boston: Houghton Mifflin, 1947.

U. S. Temporary National Economic Committee Monograph 32, *Economic Standards of Government Price Control.*

PART V

Distribution of Income

26

General Principles of Income Distribution

WHAT determines the money income of each family or person is a question that interests everyone. The reason for this concern is of course the fact that the potential share of each consuming unit in the net national product varies with the size of its income. Hence we shall consider some general principles of real and money income distribution.

Some Alternative Principles

There are many possible and actual schemes of distribution and the contrasting nature of some of these alternatives places our own economy in clearer perspective.

The communist formula for production and distribution, enunciated a century ago, was "from each according to his ability, to each according to his need." In large measure this is the principle adopted within any ordinary American family, with the breadwinner earning what he can, old parents and young children consuming without producing, and the housewife spending the pay check on the needs of the family as a whole. In the past there have also been several attempts by groups of families to establish utopian communities that would practice this supposedly ideal kind of economy. However they failed, probably because, among other reasons, a severance of the connection between personal production and consumption leads to slack work and low output; also, most men and women are unwilling to share goods, according to need, with other people, unless they are close relatives. The principles of pure communism in this connection are of little practical interest and it is significant that no attempt to put them into operation has been made by any socialistic government in the world.

The government of a completely socialized economy, in which the state owned all the natural resources and capital goods, would have the power to distribute the national output according to any scheme it favored. It *might* issue ration books based on the height, weight, or other irrelevant characteristics of the individual recipient; however, such a distribution of goods could not be justified on the grounds of equity or expediency, and would of course be quite arbitrary. Or the state might attempt exact equality in distribution, with each person, subject to slight modification according to sex and age and work, receiving precisely the same amount of each good as everyone else. In fact, necessities are distributed rather in this way by countries at war, whether socialist or not. However, even though no ration book is issued to persons who will not report for work, it has been found, in the Soviet Union for example, that equalitarian distribution provides an insufficient incentive to work harder and produce more.

The kinds of income that can be earned must depend upon the laws of each land and hence any actual distribution of income depends upon the institutions of the country. Interest on money loans has run counter to religious edict in the past, is socially taboo among many primitive peoples even today, and is often considered inadmissible by socialists. Rent on natural resources is lessened or prevented if subsurface minerals are deemed to belong to the state, private ownership of land is illegal, or entrepreneurs are not allowed to sell privately the produce of land. Entrepreneurial profits are limited if no man is allowed to hire another as his employee, and they are eliminated if no one may produce for sale.

However, in the absence of special limitations of the kind mentioned above, most economies unconsciously evolve distributive schemes which, although never planned deliberately, tend to be fashioned in a like manner by the same natural forces of self interest. A combination of free enterprise, the right to employ others, the lending and borrowing of money, private ownership of natural resources and capital goods, and property and inheritance laws has always resulted in the kind of economy still possessed by the United States. The distribution scheme of such an economy is often called the productivity principle, although such a term is really only half a description.

It would be more accurate to say that economies of free enterprise and private capitalism, such as that of the United States, have a market price system of income distribution. The income of each subfactor of labor, for example, is the product of its wage rate and the number of hours of employment. These are in turn dependent upon the supply and demand of this particular kind of labor. The supply is based upon numerous and varying sociological and economic conditions. The demand comes directly from entrepreneurs and is derived ultimately from the demand for the goods they make and sell. These same principles also operate in the case of capital funds and natural resources.

In general, an entrepreneur will never pay more for a unit of a factor than it is worth to him. For example, if each additional unit of output will increase the entrepreneur's total receipts by $5, and if the employment of one extra worker will increase his total output by 2 units, then the entrepreneur might pay this worker as much as $10 a day after deducting other additional costs. Or, if the use of an extra acre of land would increase output by half a unit a day, the entrepreneur might pay rent as high as $2.50 a day for it. It will be noticed in this instance that the entrepreneur's reservation wage is four times his reservation rent because the extra worker was four times as productive as the extra acre when measured in units of output.

One should be very careful not to infer that the end results of a market price system of income distribution are perforce equitable, simply because entrepreneurs' reservation prices for factors are based largely on physical productivity. For one thing, an entrepreneur need not, under certain circumstances, pay each employed factor the full value of its net productive contribution; such a situation is termed exploitation, and it is analyzed in some detail in the final section. The factor incomes that result from a market price system of distribution have at times been criticized on the following moral grounds.

First, the price of a factor depends upon its supply as well as upon a productivity-determined demand. The supply of factors has nothing to do with equity. For example, the supply of untrained labor is always greater than the supply of professional labor, because only a few people can afford to defer earnings during years of study; and so the children of poor parents tend in turn to earn low incomes. The owners of natural resources in an overcrowded country obtain high rents, because of the low land-to-labor ratio, but they can hardly claim credit for the excessive population. Workers in a poor country, which has not the capital to equip its labor properly, are less productive and receive low wages, but they are no less deserving because they had the misfortune not to be born in another land.

Second, outlays for land and capital are paid, not to the factors themselves, but to their owners, and the property rights of these last may not always be in accord with popular ideas of justice. Land ownership in some parts of the world is based on earlier conquests. Income earned on inherited property is not earned by the individual recipient, even though his assets contribute to output.

Third, employees who earn high salaries or wages usually do so because of superior intelligence or strength, which attributes are due in large measure to heredity. Some people might claim that a man who has inherited strength is no more entitled to higher earnings than a man who has inherited blue eyes. Would personal effort rather than productive results be the basis of income determination in a more perfect world?

Entrepreneurial Outlays for Productive Factors

However, we actually live in an economy where single entrepreneurs use factors as an incident to earning profits. Accordingly, the employers of factors are interested in physical output and the extra sales revenue to be derived from selling it. Hence, as a practical matter, we must learn how an entrepreneur relates factor prices and inputs, and so helps to determine the income of each subfactor that he employs. The total of such outlays by all entrepreneurs gives the total money income of each kind of employed factor.

Entrepreneur's Demand for a Single Factor

Every enterprise must combine a number of productive factors in order to operate. Certain kinds of labor, land, and capital will be in joint demand. Some of these factors may be supplied by the entrepreneur himself, but most of them will be hired; in either event, there are certain principles that should be observed by the operator if he is to maximize profits.

Each successive unit of a given productive agent that is set to work by an entrepreneur has a definite value to him. This value is the maximum reservation price he should place on that particular unit. We shall call this maximum reservation price the *marginal revenue product* of the factor and designate it by *MRP*. The *MRP* of a specified kind of labor, or land, or capital, will normally vary from unit to unit. For example, the 17th employed man-hour of mason's skill will have a different marginal revenue than the 18th or 19th.

The marginal revenue product of a factor can be defined as the addition to total revenue resulting from the sale of the extra output occasioned by the use of an additional factor unit. It is assumed that the number of employed units of other factors remains unchanged. The determination of *MRP* rests upon the "last" unit's physical productivity and the extra revenue that this increased output will realize when sold.

Let us consider the imaginary case of a stenographic service bureau, which now employs four girls, turns out a total of 200 pages of typing a day, and charges customers 20¢ a page. Perhaps a fifth girl of the same skill applies for work. The employer asks himself what will be the increase in total receipts if he employs her. Let us suppose that possibly, because of increased crowding and noise, the output will only jump from 200 to 240 pages a day, in which case her marginal physical productivity is 40 pages. *If* this extra output can also be disposed of at 20¢ a page—which means that the original four girls alone are incapable of satisfying the entire demand at 20¢—then the *MRP* of a fifth girl is 40 times 20¢, or $8.00. If the prevailing wage was $5.00 a day, and this is also demanded by the fifth girl, she will presumably be taken on, and the bureau will improve its profit position by $3.00.

One simplification in this case is that we have supposed that all other expenses are in the nature of a fixed or overhead cost. But probably there will be contingent variable costs, such as the depreciation of an extra machine and desk and the increased use of paper, which should not be ignored. If these contingent expenses amounted to $1.50 per girl per day, the *net MRP* would be $8.00 minus $1.50, or $6.50.

It is rather unlikely that there would be an infinitely elastic demand for stenographic service of this sort. And one would normally suppose that the management of the bureau would always charge the maximum per page that would just dispose of the entire output. Accordingly, if there is a demand for 200 pages a day at 20¢ a page, it is improbable that the 240 pages can be disposed of at the same charge. Perhaps the public can only be induced to use the bureau to this greater degree by dropping the charge per page to 18¢. In this case we must reconsider the marginal revenue occasioned by employing a fifth girl. The *gross* change in total revenue is (240 × 18) cents minus (200 × 20) cents, or $3.20. However, after the contingent variable expense of $1.50 has been deducted, the net *MRP* is only $1.70. Evidently she would not be employed by a rational manager at the assumed wage rate of $5.00 a day.

TABLE 28

Derived Demand of a Firm for a Productive Factor

1	2	3	4a	4b	5a	5b	6	7a	7b
I_f	O_p	MPP	P_p	P_p'	TR	TR'	CVC	MRP	MRP'
1	50	50	20¢	26¢	10.00	13.00	1.50	8.50	11.50
2	105	55	20¢	24¢	21.00	25.20	3.00	9.50	10.70
3	155	50	20¢	22¢	31.00	34.10	4.50	8.50	7.40
4	200	45	20¢	20¢	40.00	40.00	6.00	7.50	4.40
5	240	40	20¢	18¢	48.00	43.20	7.50	6.50	1.70
6	275	35	20¢	16¢	55.00	44.00	9.00	5.50	—.70
7	305	30	20¢	14¢	61.00	42.70	10.50	4.50	—2.80

Table 28 reveals the significant relationships. Column 1 (I_f) is the number of units of input, in this case stenographers. Column 2 (O_p) is the output in pages per day. Column 3 (MPP) is marginal physical product, the change in total output caused by using an extra unit of input. Column 4a (P_p) is the price of the product, in this case a typewritten page; this price remains constant, indicating an infinitely elastic demand for the product. Column 5a (TR) is the total gross receipts obtained from customers, and it is the product of O_p and P_p. Column 6 (CVC) is the total of contingent variable costs, in this case the extra expenses of typewriters, paper, and the like. Column 7a (MRP) is the *change* in gross total revenue *minus* the *change* in contingent variable cost. It shows the net worth of an extra unit of input to the employer. Under the circumstances, when the demand is infinitely elastic at 20¢ a page, it is the demand schedule of the entrepreneur for the productive factor. At a prevailing wage of $5.00 a day, the bureau should hire 6 girls, but not a 7th.

We have asserted that a *less* than infinitely elastic demand for the product is more than likely. Such a demand schedule for typewritten pages is indicated by column 4b, and designated P'; for example, 50 pages can be disposed of at 26¢ each, 105 pages at 24¢, and so on. Column 5b (TR') is the product of columns 2 (O_p) and 4b (P'). Column 7b (MRP') is equal to the change in TR' *minus* the change in CVC. Consequently, the net addition to the employer's total revenue, after paying extra contingent expenses, is $11.50 for the first girl, $10.70 for the second, and so on.

It is noteworthy that the net marginal revenue is *negative* for the sixth and seventh girls despite their positive physical contribution. Thus the seventh girl increases the output of the bureau by 30 pages a day. However, these extra pages can only be disposed of at a price reduction of 2¢ a page, which must also be deducted from the 275 pages turned out by six girls. Hence the total receipts from customers decline from $44.00 to $42.70, a negative change of $1.30, to which must be added the increase of $1.50 in contingent variable costs, making MRP' equal to $-$2.80. In this case column 7b is the demand schedule of the employer for stenographers, and therefore, at a prevailing wage of $5.00 a day, the bureau should only hire three girls.

The demand schedule of an entrepreneur for a factor is, therefore, the change in output times price, minus the change in contingent variable costs. Symbolically,

$$MRP = \Delta(O_p \cdot P_p) - \Delta(CVC)$$

Marginal revenue product, if one can assume no contingent variable costs, is approximately equal to marginal physical product multiplied by marginal revenue from the sale of the output.

In reality, of course, the marginal physical product (MPP) of a particular factor depends upon the quantity of other factors with which it is employed. In the above stenographic bureau example, the size of the room was assumed to be always the same, so that it perhaps became overcrowded as more girls were added; if they had suddenly been given a larger room, the entire MPP schedule for stenographers might have shifted upwards, especially over the higher employment ranges. This notion of the interdependence of the MPP schedules of productive agents that are employed together is developed in the chapter on land rent.

Supply Elasticity of an Employed Factor

In some factor markets a single employer has an infinitesimal influence on the price of the productive agent in question. Under such circumstances the employer views the factor supply schedule as a horizontal line located at the level of the prevailing price. He can then obtain 1, 5, or 75 units of input without having to offer a higher price. Previously we have supposed just such an infinitely elastic factor supply.

However, an employer is often in the position of a monopsonistic competitor in the hiring of his labor and of other factors. Perhaps he can only obtain another unit of input by offering a higher wage rate, since extra workers may have to be recruited from other firms or towns. In most situations he will be unable to pay different workers unequal wages for the same kind of a job. In the absence of discrimination, the higher price will have to be offered not only to the "last" unit of input but to all the other intramarginal units as well. Therefore, the increase in the total cost of the factor (MC_f) will have to exceed the factor price (P_f), when the factor supply is less than infinitely elastic (i.e., when its schedule is positively inclined).

TABLE 29

EMPLOYER'S LABOR DEMAND WITH MONOPOLY AND MONOPSONY

1	2	3	4	5	6	7	8
P_f	I_f	O_p	P_p	TC_f	MC_f	$TR - CVC$	MRP
$4.00	1	50	26¢	$4.00	$4.00	$11.50	$11.50
4.25	2	105	24¢	8.50	4.50	22.20	10.70
4.50	3	155	22¢	13.50	5.00	29.60	7.40
4.75	4	200	20¢	19.00	5.50	34.00	4.40
5.00	5	240	18¢	25.00	6.00	35.70	1.70
5.25	6	275	16¢	31.50	6.50	35.00	−.70
5.50	7	305	14¢	38.50	7.00	32.20	−2.80

A situation of this kind is shown in Table 29. Columns 1 and 2 together constitute a supply schedule of stenographers hired by the day. The addition to the total payroll (MC_f) occasioned by hiring a second girl is $4.50, even though the wage rate will only have to be raised to $4.25. The explanation is that the extra 25¢ a day, which is required to attract a second girl from some other occupation, must also be given to the first girl, assuming no discrimination by the employer among his hires.

What will be the number of employees, the wage rate, and the total payroll, when the basic data are those of the first four columns of Table 29? Columns 1 and 2 indicate a rising supply schedule for the factor, columns 3 and 4 show a falling demand schedule for the product, and columns 2 and 3 give the input-to-output ratio. We are confronted perhaps with a situation of monopsonistic competition in the hiring of labor and one of monopolistic competition in selling the product. The entrepreneur should attempt to equate MC_f and MRP, which aim is most nearly realized when he hires 3 stenographers. He can be expected to offer the lowest daily wage that will attract this number of girls into his employ; this wage, as the supply schedule shows, will be $4.50 a day. The daily payroll is $13.50.

The entrepreneur decides on the factor price he will pay when he is in the position of a partial monopsonist. There is no single and prevailing market price for the entrepreneur to accept or reject. Being confronted by a positively inclined supply schedule, he distinguishes between P_f and MC_f, and estimates the wage and input combination that will maximize his profits.

Pure Competition, Monopoly, and Monopsony

An entrepreneur is active in a number of markets. He may sell a number of different products and he uses a number of different factors. Competitive conditions will not be the same in all these markets. In one of his product markets he may be a competitor, in another a monopolist, and so on. In one factor market he may be a pure competitor, in another a partial monopsonist, and so on. We shall simplify by supposing he has only one product to sell and one factor to hire. In this case there are four possible situations in which the entrepreneur might find himself. In every case he will add units of the factor until $MC_f = MRP$. However, this profit-maximizing formula can be expressed more specifically in the first three of the four following cases.

Case 1. Pure competition in both the sale of the product and the hire of the factor. The factor supply schedule and the product demand schedule are infinitely elastic. The entrepreneur logically need not distinguish either between P_p and MR or between P_f and MC_f. The entrepreneur has no price policy in either the input or the output market. This case is the most special one possible and is emphasized to a dangerous extent in most elementary textbooks on economic theory. The entrepreneur hires extra units of the factor until $P_f = \phi \cdot P_p$, where ϕ (phi) is the marginal physical product.

Case 2. Pure competition in the factor market and partial monopoly in the product market. MRP will now only be positive, irrespective of the marginal *physical* productivity of any factor, if demand for the product is elastic over the relevant output range. The general equation of MC_f and MRP can be rephrased more specifically as $P_f = MRP$. The entrepreneur has a price policy only in the product market.

Case 3. Partial monopsony in the factor market and pure competition in the product market. The entrepreneur rightly distinguishes between MC_f and P_f because the supply schedule of the factor is positively inclined. The most specific rule for maximizing profits is for him to equate MC_f with $\phi \cdot P_p$. This is equivalent to equating MC_f and MRP. The entrepreneur has a price policy only in the factor market.

Case 4. Partial monopsony in the factor market and partial monopoly in the product market. The concern should equate MC_f with MRP. The entrepreneur will have a price policy in both markets. This formula for maximizing profits is, of course, the most general of all. It is the one that should be stressed.

Another Practical Example

It is sometimes remarked that we write prose all our lives without knowing it. Some businessman or farmer, reading the above analysis, might snort and assert that he had never thought in such terms in his life. Of course some entrepreneurs do operate by guess and by God for a short while. But most successful businessmen and farmers do use this line of reasoning as much as possible, although they might be surprised to learn that they were engaging in the incremental comparisons of marginal analysis.

In fact it is hard to imagine any other rational procedure. If a sheep rancher is contemplating the lease of an extra section of grazing land, what else can he do but ask himself the extra costs and revenues its use may occasion? Knowing the land, he can estimate how many more sheep he can keep on it, and he must turn this into lambs and wool, and then into *extra* total revenue on the basis of assumed prices. More sheep may mean an extra herder, more salt, and a little more expense at shearing time, and so he estimates the *extra* contingent costs. Whatever gross surplus is then foreseen must be set against the cost of the lease. Some decision whether or not to take up the lease is now indicated.

The rancher, in going through these steps, roughly estimated *MPP* (the extra lambs and wool), P_p (the prices of lambs and wool), *CVC* (the extra expense for herders and materials), and *MRP*. The MC_f (annual lease rental) was known. Incremental analysis is just logic, and most managers try to be as rational as possible.

Optimum Outlays for Productive Factors

An entrepreneur uses more than one agent of production in making his output. Consequently he has the task of combining different factors in the proportions that he estimates will prove most profitable. In reality he has at least two problems to solve. One is to secure the greatest possible gross financial return for any given outlay of capital funds. The other is to invest in productive resources at an over-all rate that maximizes his profits.

The entrepreneur will obtain the greatest posible output for a given expenditure of capital if he can keep the ratio of marginal physical productivity to marginal purchase cost the same for every factor he uses. An extra dollar of capital funds will hire $1/MC_f$ units of input (for example, $1.00 will buy two units of a factor if its marginal cost is 50¢). An additional unit of input will occasion an extra output of ϕ units (for example, 3 pounds). Consequently, an extra dollar spent on this factor will bring a marginal physical return of $(1/MC_f)\cdot\phi$, or about 6 pounds in the present case. Moreover, inasmuch as the marginal physical return on an extra dollar spent for labor (subscript r) should be the same as that obtained on an extra dollar spent for land (subscript d),

$$\frac{\phi_r}{MC_r} \quad \text{and} \quad \frac{\phi_d}{MC_d}$$

should be equated whenever possible. It will then be impossible for a reallocation of funds to increase output. P_f can be substituted for MC_f when the factor in question has an infinitely elastic supply.

Another problem is what total investment on all factors an entrepreneur should make. Should he expand or contract his inputs and outputs and rate of operations? The general principle he should follow is to invest capital funds in additional inputs— always hiring the different factors in order to maintain the equation given immediately above—until he is just able to recover the last dollar laid out.

It is evident that the selling of one extra unit of output will occasion some change in total revenue. This change will be symbolized by MR. It will then be approximately true that one extra unit of input will bring about a change in total revenue (MR) equal to its marginal physical product (ϕ) times the extra revenue resulting from the sale of an extra unit of product (MR). Now one extra dollar spent on a factor buys $1/MC_f$ more units of it for use. And each extra unit of input employed realizes $\phi \cdot MR$ extra revenue. Therefore the marginal gross revenue obtained from one dollar invested in extra units of a factor is

$$\frac{\phi \cdot MR}{MC_f} \quad \text{or} \quad \frac{MRP}{MC_f}$$

The value of this ratio will of course be unity when the numerator and denominator possess the same magnitude. In other words a dollar of investment will bring back a marginal *gross* revenue of one dollar when the marginal cost and the marginal revenue of a specific factor are equal. The marginal *net* revenue occasioned by the investment will then be zero and at this point the entrepreneur should stop expanding.

What of the rate of interest in this connection? The reality of interest rates can be taken into account in the above equations by including the cost of money in MC_f as one of the expenses of investment. A zero marginal net revenue on outlays for factors will then signify that the investor is earning exactly the normal rate of return at the margin.

One application of these principles is of financial importance. Let us suppose a normal rate of return is generally supposed to be 4 per cent and that the profits of a particular firm have been at a rate of 10 per cent for many years. Should that firm obtain more funds to expand its operations? Not necessarily, because, although the *average* net revenue from its operations may be 6 per cent, after allowing for a normal 4 per cent opportunity cost on money in general, the *marginal* net revenue may already be at zero. Expansion and contraction of operations should depend upon the net return obtained at the margin rather than on an average.

New Inventions and Marginal Productivity

The "state of the arts" is always advancing. New machines may be invented that alter the productivity of land and labor and capital goods investments used in some particular employment. And management is continuously finding new methods that are more efficient. These innovations alter the productivity of some kinds of factors relative to that of others. As a consequence, entrepreneurial demands for productive resources vary also, and the relative size of factor incomes becomes altered.

Let us suppose that a new biochemical discovery now makes it possible at negligible cost to raise a given bushel crop of rice when using .40 times as much land and .67 times as much labor as before. Such an innovation apparently makes the average physical productivity of land 2.5 times, and that of labor 1.5 times, as great as before. What may happen to the incomes of the landowners and workers who are involved?

The demand for land on the part of rice growers may decline. Each acre, for example, may in general be 2.5 times as physically productive as before, but the extra output can probably be sold only at a lower price. If the elasticity of demand for rice by the public were absolutely zero, only 40% of the land and 67% of the labor previously used for rice growing would remain in that employment. On the other hand, if three times as much rice could be sold without depressing the price, 1.2 times as much land and 2.0 times as much labor would be required. However, these are extreme assumptions.

Let us suppose instead that in actuality the rice crop is doubled, that the price of rice is halved, and that rice growers sell in a purely competitive market. Hence they view the price and marginal revenue of rice as being identical. The demand schedule of a typical rice grower for land will then become about 1.25 times as high as before because the new productivity of 2.5 times outweighs the new price of .5 times. A typical rice grower's demand schedule for labor will become .75 times as high as before because the new productivity of 1.5 times is overbalanced by the new price of .5 times. Therefore the employment of rice land will rise and the employment of rice labor will fall.

However, while the owners of rice land will receive larger incomes, one cannot estimate the extent of this increase without making additional assumptions. If other kinds of land can readily be used for rice, and if rice has replaced the crops this other land used to grow, then the supply of land for use in rice may be so elastic as to prevent any appreciable increase in rents. Conversely, if rice land is of a special kind and limited in supply, or if alternative demands for agricultural land are unaffected, rice land rents will rise and so will the incomes of its owners. Similar reasoning indicates that the earnings of rice workers will fall only to the extent that those who are laid off experience difficulty in obtaining alternative employments.

In general, an innovation will increase the earnings of directly employed factors only if the demand for the produced output is so elastic that the decline in marginal revenue is less proportionately than the increase in factor productivity. However, each factor within the employing firm must shift for itself, and so the specific effect on particular factors must also be considered, as in the above manner. The availability of alternative supplies will check an income increase if the physical demand rises and the possibility of substitute employments will check an income decrease if the physical demand falls.

Substitution of Factors

Most factors of production are, within certain limits, in rival supply; that is to say they are substitutes, and in competition with one another. A fairly slight change in the relative prices of two competitive factors may cause a firm to substitute the factor that is now comparatively cheaper for that which is now comparatively dearer. As we have seen, ignoring cases where the employing firm possesses monopsony power, entrepreneurs will adjust the quantities in which they use different factors until their respective marginal physical products are in accord with their respective prices. It follows that, if one factor becomes relatively more abundant, and hence comparatively cheaper, it will tend within limits to be introduced into firms as a substitute for other factors with which it is in rival supply.

Let us imagine a country, which has long excluded foreign workers and where wages are high, that suddenly permits unrestricted labor immigration. In agriculture, to take one example, farmers who previously employed one man for each 25 acres may now alter this ratio to one man for each 20 acres. In this case the new laborers do not drive the land out of employment, and are not *absolute* substitutes; they are *relative* substitutes in that the ratio of labor to land has altered so that *comparatively* more labor is now employed.

The extent to which these new laborers can penetrate into established producing units, and be taken into employment in combination with other factors, depends upon the extent to which the marginal physical productivity of the added factor alters when recombined in new proportions. As a general rule, the physical productivity of the marginal unit of the factor that is now combined in smaller relative amounts tends to rise, and that of the factor now combined in larger relative amounts tends to fall. For example, if new labor is penetrating into established firms, so that the ratio of labor to land within them is increasing, the marginal physical product of labor will be falling relative to that of land.

If a fairly small change in the labor-to-land ratio brings about a comparatively large alteration in the ratio of their marginal physical products, workers will find it requires a larger reduction in wage rates in order to gain employment within productive combinations. Their eventual employment will mean higher land rents per acre and lower earnings per worker. On the other hand, if the marginal physical productivities of different factors are rather insensitive to changes in the proportions in which they are combined, workers should succeed in securing employment at wage rates only slightly below their previous levels. Such ease of substitution usually means that factor prices tend to be more stable than they would be if altered factor proportions drastically affected marginal physical productivities.

Various formulae have been developed in the past to yield coefficients expressing ease of substitution. One possible approach is to say that substitution is "easy" if, in *relation* to the total income of all factors employed by the firm or in the economy, the aggregate income of the penetrating factor tends to become greater. For instance, if A enjoyed 30 per cent of national income before, and 35 per cent of a larger national income after additional supplies of A have been combined into firms, substitution for A has been simple. It would then be said that its elasticity of substitution exceeded unity.*

Exploitation

It is sometimes claimed by labor and its sympathizers that employers exploit their workers. Also some economists have held that monopoly and monopsony necessarily lead to an exploitation of factors if producers attempt to maximize profits. The theoretical possibility and significance of such factor exploitation need to be examined.

Exploitation can be defined in various ways. Many people would hold that exploitation exists when an entrepreneur pays a factor less than its worth to him when employed. If a factor is paid its full use value, it should be able financially to buy back from the employer what it has produced, and it will have escaped exploitation. Of course, the use value of a factor cannot be computed unless, in addition to the selling price of the product, the peculiar contribution of the specific factor toward the employer's total output is known. In the past, economists have defined the exploitation per unit of factor input as the excess of marginal physical product times selling price of the output above the factor price.

Although any kind of factor is theoretically as likely to suffer from exploitation as any other, most thinking has concerned the exploitation of labor, and in the succeeding analysis we shall follow this tradition. First we shall consider the possible exploitation of a single gifted employee, who is in a class by himself, because then the two possible definitions of exploitation provide the same answer. Subsequently we shall consider both the marginal and average definitions when many similar workers are employed.

---

* In general, the elasticity of substitution of factors states the proportionate changes in the relative employment of both factors divided by the proportionate changes in their relative prices; symbolically this might be expressed as

$$\left(\frac{Q_b \cdot \Delta P_a}{Q_a \cdot \Delta P_b}\right) \quad \div \quad \left(\frac{P_b \cdot \Delta Q_a}{P_a \cdot \Delta Q_b}\right)$$

where Q and P are an average of $ex\ ante$ and $ex\ post$ quantities and prices respectively.

Possible Exploitation of a Gifted Employee

It may serve as an engaging introduction to the entire subject to consider the possible exploitation of outstanding artists and athletes who possess great drawing power with the public and make commercial appearances.

Let us suppose that Alberto Pirelli is a famous basso. He is offered $50,000 for a season by the Cosmopolitan Opera Company and finally accepts because the next best offer he receives is $5,000 less. The Cosmopolitan, before making the offer, estimated that a less outstanding basso would cost it $30,000 in any case, and that the inclusion of Pirelli in the company would result in box office receipts $45,000 higher than would be realized if another basso were used. In other words, $75,000 is the Cosmopolitan's maximum price and $45,000 is Pirelli's minimum price. The contract for $50,000 that they sign gives Pirelli a kind of rent surplus of $5,000 and permits the Cosmopolitan to obtain an exploitation surplus of $25,000.

However, this exploitation surplus will not all be profit. Perhaps the Cosmopolitan is able to outbid other organizations because it has the largest opera house and alone can accommodate all the people who will pay to hear Pirelli. Such a large theater naturally costs more to acquire and maintain. Also Pirelli can be presented more effectively in the company of other superior singers who of course must be paid higher salaries too. It may even be that, if the Cosmopolitan were unable to sign Pirelli at less than he is worth to it, the company would suffer a loss on the season's operations. An exploitation surplus is like a quasi-rent that may lessen losses without providing an absolute profit.

Exploitation of this kind arouses little interest. The victims are well-to-do and instances are relatively infrequent. Accordingly we shall pass on to the exploitation of ordinary workers who are relatively similar to one another.

Ordinary Workers' Exploitation

The circumstances that may give rise to exploitation, as variously defined, should be understood. Marginal exploitation occurs whenever the wage (W) is less than the value of the *marginal* physical product $(\phi \cdot P)$. Average exploitation occurs whenever W is less than the value of the *average* physical product, which last can be written $\theta \cdot P$, when *theta* is the average physical product.

Marginal exploitation, assuming firms attempt to maximize profits, will result from partial monopoly in selling the product, partial monopsony in hiring the factor, or both. If the demand for the firm's output is less than infinitely elastic, MR is less than P, and so $\phi \cdot MR$ (i.e., MRP) will be less than $\phi \cdot P$. Assuming no monopsony, W is equal to the marginal cost of hiring the factor, and this will be equated by firms to $\phi \cdot MR$. If there is some monopsony, W will be less than MC_f, which last is then equated to $\phi \cdot MR$, and exploitation at the margin will be even greater than if there had only been monopoly without monopsony.

Marginal exploitation, as here defined, does not necessarily benefit the employing firm. The marginally employed unit adds to costs what it adds to receipts. Moreover, even though there may be exploitation at the margin, it is quite possible that the firm obtains no aggregate surplus from all the intramarginal units it employs. Actually, the difference between $\phi \cdot P$ and $\phi \cdot MR$ is the addition to buyers' surplus occasioned by adding an extra factor unit. And the difference between MC_f and W, which emerges under monopsony conditions, is extra suppliers' surplus for the intramarginal factor units that were available at lower reservation prices. The persons who do inevitably gain from exploitation, in the marginal sense as defined here, are intramarginal product buyers and factor suppliers, and not the employing firm.

One would think that the workers would themselves object to this marginal definition of exploitation. Surely, it is the value of their average physical product that they will normally consider their due, and not the value of their marginal physical product. An employer, by adding extra men, can eventually reduce the marginal physical product of a factor very rapidly, even though its average physical product remains high. The use value of a typical employee is not the use value of the "last" worker employed.

We are now confronted with the average conception of exploitation again. The practical difficulty here, as already mentioned, is that there is usually no way of accurately estimating the net physical contribution to output of a particular kind of factor. Dividing the total output by the total number of employees may give a quotient, but the spurious output per man that results is also due in part to the cooperative use of other factors employed along with the workers. There are several rather unrealistic routes of escape from this dilemma. One way is to suppose that the entrepreneur is, for some reason, unable to vary the quantity of any of the other factors, so that their expense may be treated as a fixed cost. Another is to suppose that the most profitable way to combine factors, for all outputs, is in some set ratio, so that all these factors can be lumped together and treated as a single conglomerate factor.

There will be exploitation, in the average sense, if W is less than $\theta \cdot P$. Such an occurrence may or may not be due to monopoly or monopsony conditions, the existence of which is now largely irrelevant to the problem at hand. If average exploitation occurs, it will be because the use value of the factor to the employing firm is greater than the disbursements made to it. Such a differential may be due to either of two circumstances. One is that the exploiting firm is able to make greater use value of these factors than other firms. The other is that the exploiting firm is able to obtain these factors at an abnormally cheap rate.

If there is no monopsony power on the employer's side, W will be the same for all firms in rival demand for the desired kind of labor, and no single firm can obtain labor at specially low rates. If only one employing firm makes profits, indicating the existence of exploitation, it will probably be because that firm is more efficiently operated. Any attack on this kind of exploitation surplus is an attack on the profits that are normally held to reward superior entrepreneurial efficiency.

If all, or most, of the firms in the group experience profits, and so appear to be practicing exploitation in the average sense, it may be due to restrictions on entry into this industrial field. The profits may be monopoly profits. Naturally, the factors that are employed by these firms would like to share in these monopoly advantages, but their moral claim is no greater, and may be less, than that of other groups, such as consumers and governments.

If the employing firm has monopsony power, and finds itself confronted by a positively sloping individual supply schedule of labor, it does not have to accept any wage rate, but must determine W simultaneously when determining the scale of operations that will maximize its profits. The profits, which measure exploitation in the average sense, may then be due, not to outstanding management or product design, but to the discovery, perhaps in some remote spot, of a supply of cheap labor. However, this supply schedule of remotely located labor is a datum for the entrepreneur and is seldom caused by him. At worst, the exploiting entrepreneur is then guilty, not of depressing the economic lot of the workers, but of utilizing their misery without helping them. However, there is no more moral obligation on employing firms unnecessarily to pay higher prices for factors than there is on consumers unnecessarily to pay higher prices for the goods they buy.

General Summary

There are various ways in which national income might be distributed among individuals. In a free enterprise economy the incomes of factors depend upon their prices and the extent of their employment, and superficially it often seems that these are in turn determined by entrepreneurs in the course of their profit-making. However, the entrepreneur appears as a rather passive being when viewed in his more fundamental context. He stands between product demands and factor supplies over which he has little control. If the demand for his product declines, he will in turn reduce employment and indirectly lower factor prices. Many of his other actions are also in response to exterior forces. In a sense, he must act as an agent of the buyers in his dealings with suppliers, and vice versa. He serves as a front man for each and a buffer man for both. If the pressure on him from the two sides is too great, he suffers losses.

It is often claimed that in this process the entrepreneur makes his middleman's profit by exploiting the factors he uses. The epithet of exploitation can be defined in various ways. The marginal definition tends to make it identical with buyers' and suppliers' surplus. The average definition is usually inapplicable because the net physical contribution of each kind of factor is ordinarily indeterminate. The extent of exploitation of all factors employed by a firm tends to be equal to its profits. These conclusions suggest that the term "exploitation," though frequently employed, has little practicability, significance, or usefulness.

A free enterprise system may not distribute income in the most perfect manner. Some of the resultant imperfections might be remedied through an amendment of property laws rather than by changing the fundamental characteristics of a free economy. However, no other system of combining resources for output has yet been demonstrated its superior in terms of over-all economic efficiency.

Statements for Consideration

1. Economic Communism is practiced within most American homes.
   Discuss
2. Distribution should not be based upon productivity in view of the importance of inherited traits.   *Discuss*
3. The income of factors depends upon law as well as upon economics.   *Exemplify*
4. Doctors receive good incomes, not because of their productivity, but because of the high cost of training them.   *Discuss*
5. Even though we grant that land is productive, it does not follow that the landowner, who receives rent, is particularly productive or deserving.   *Discuss*
6. The marginal revenue product of a factor is the contribution of that factor to the net profits of the employer.   *Evaluate*
7. A marginally employed unit of a factor may have a positive physical product but a negative revenue product.   *Explain*
8. A monopsonistic employer equates the marginal revenue product of labor to its wage rate.   *Evaluate*
9. A firm, in its use of different productive factors, should in some ways follow a similar rule to that adopted by consumers, assuming both are rational.   *Explain*
10. A new invention, adopted by some firm, may increase the income of one employed factor while reducing the income of another.
    Explain
11. Only low-paid employees are ever exploited.   *Evaluate*
12. When exploitation of a factor occurs, it is often the eventual buyers, rather than the employer, who are doing the exploiting.
    Discuss

References

Bain, J. S., *Pricing, Distribution and Employment,* Chapters 10, 13. New York: Holt, 1948.

Boulding, K. E., *Economic Analysis,* Chapters 11, 12. New York: Harper, 1948.

Bowman, M. J., and Bach, G. L., *Economic Analysis and Public Policy,* Chapters 28, 29, 32. New York: Prentice-Hall, 1949.

Cassels, J. M., "On the Law of Variable Proportions," *Explorations in Economics,* 1936. Also in *Readings in the Theory of Income Distribution.*

Chamberlin, E. H., *The Theory of Monopolistic Competition,* Chapter 8. Cambridge: Harvard University Press, 1948.

Clark, J. M., "Distribution," *Encyclopaedia of the Social Sciences*, V, 1931. Also in *Readings in the Theory of Income Distribution*.

Due, J. F., *Intermediate Economic Analysis*, Chapter 8. Chicago: Irwin, 1947.

Garver, F. B., and Hansen, A. H., *Principles of Economics*, Chapters 28, 29. New York: Ginn, 1947.

Henderson, H. D., *Supply and Demand*, Chapter 5. London: Pitman, 1932.

Hicks, J. R., *The Theory of Wages*. London: Macmillan, 1935.

Hicks, J. R., and Hart, A. G., *The Social Framework of the American Economy*, Chapter 17. New York: Oxford University Press, 1945.

Lange, O., "A Note on Innovations," *Review of Economics and Statistics*, vol. XXV, 1943. Also in *Readings in the Theory of Income Distribution*.

Lerner, A. P., *The Economics of Control*, Chapters 13, 14. New York: Macmillan, 1945.

Machlup, F., "On the Meaning of the Marginal Product," *Explorations in Economics*. Also in *Readings in the Theory of Income Distribution*.

Machlup, F., "The Common Sense of the Elasticity of Substitution," *Review of Economic Studies*, II, June 1935.

Marshall, A., *Principles of Economics*, Eighth Edition, Book VI, Chapters 1, 2. London: Macmillan, 1920.

Meade, J. E., and Hitch, C. J., *An Introduction to Economic Analysis and Policy*, III. New York: Oxford University Press, 1938.

Pigou, A. C., *Income*, Chapter 7. New York: Macmillan, 1946.

Pigou, A. C., *The Economics of Welfare*, IV, Chapters 3, 4. London: Macmillan, 1946.

Robinson, J., *The Economics of Imperfect Competition*, VII.

Robinson, J., "The Classification of Inventions," *Review of Economic Studies*, V, 1937–1938. Also in *Readings in the Theory of Income Distribution*.

Samuelson, P. A., *Economics*, Chapter 22 (B). New York: McGraw-Hill, 1948.

Stigler, G. J., *The Theory of Price*, Chapter 15. New York: Macmillan, 1946.

27

Earnings of Employees

A MAJOR PORTION of the labor performed in an economy is contributed by employees. The self-employed labor of entrepreneurs is of minor importance except in the case of farm and retail proprietorships. Hence the subject of employees' earnings covers most of the topic of labor's rewards.

Wages, Earnings, and Payrolls

The pay received by employees can be described in various ways that need to be distinguished at the outset. The term *wage*, in the following analysis, will refer to the average money rate of pay, per hour or per piece, received by an individual worker. The term *earnings* will refer to the money pay received by a single worker over some prescribed time period such as a week, a month, or a year. The term *payroll* refers to the total money payments made by an enterprise to all its employees over a stated time period. The terms *real wage, real earnings,* and *real payrolls* correspond to the above definitions, except that an allowance is made for changes in consumer goods' prices. For example, if earnings and the cost of living both double, real earnings remain unchanged. Altogether we have six distinct concepts here and several of them have important relationships.

Some Important Relations

Clearly there are some definite mathematical relations among wages, earnings, and payrolls. An employee's earnings are equal to his wages times the amount of work he performs. A firm's payroll is equal to the sum of all the earnings of its employees during the same period of time. An enterprise's labor cost is equal to its payroll divided by its output. The total income of all employees in the economy is the sum of all the payrolls of all the firms in the economy.

Incidentally, it is always important to distinguish between the rates of pay that are determined for each job classification in a plant and the average hourly wages of its workers. During World War II average hourly wages rose far more rapidly than job pay rates for two reasons. First, many employees worked overtime, for which they received time and a half, or even double time. Second, many firms classified their employees more generously, so that they were filling more highly paid jobs, even though they were doing the same work in reality. One cannot infer that job pay has changed because average hourly wages alter.

During a long upswing in economic activity there tends to be an increase in wages, hours worked, and numbers employed. At the commencement of an upswing, when there are still reserves of unemployed labor, the increase in employed man-hours is probably greater than the rise in hourly wage rates, although later this relation is likely to be reversed. In any event, so long as wages, hours of work, and numbers employed are all increasing, it follows that factory payrolls must be increasing more rapidly than individual earnings, and that these in turn must be increasing more rapidly than average hourly wages.

These relations are nicely illustrated by Table 30, which contains data for production workers in United States manufacturing industries from 1933 to 1946, a period of almost continuous expansion except for the recession of 1937–38.

The latter stages of an upswing are usually characterized by rising prices for all kinds of goods. Until a decade or so ago, it was supposed by most economists that consumer goods' prices increased more rapidly than wage rates, with the result that real wages fell. On the other hand, more recent statistical investigations seem to indicate that oligopolistic and institutional elements, at least as regards consumer goods' prices, prevent them from rising as rapidly as wage rates do. If this is generally true, it means that, during the upswing, real wages, real earnings, and real payrolls also increase, but not as rapidly as their money counterparts. The data of Table 30 seem to bear out this contention for at least one long period of expansion.

Prosperity, Employment, and Labor Costs

When business conditions are improving and a firm is expanding, a newly hired employee may not be so productive as the

TABLE 30

PAYMENTS TO EMPLOYEES IN MANUFACTURING: 1939–44

(1939 = 100)

YEAR	AVERAGE HOURLY EARNINGS		AVERAGE WEEKLY HOURS	AVERAGE WEEKLY EARNINGS		NUMBER OF PRODUCTION WORKERS (000 omitted)	WEEKLY PAYROLLS		REAL AV. HOURLY EARNINGS*	REAL AV. WEEKLY EARNINGS*
	¢	Relative		$	Relative		($000,000 omitted)	Relative	Relative	Relative
1939	63.3	1.00	37.7	23.86	1.00	8,192	180	1.00	1.00	1.00
1940	66.1	1.05	38.1	25.20	1.08	8,811	207	1.14	1.03	1.05
1941	72.9	1.17	40.6	29.58	1.26	10,825	302	1.66	1.09	1.17
1942	85.3	1.37	42.9	26.65	1.13	12,617	443	2.44	1.15	1.31
1943	96.1	1.55	44.9	43.14	1.84	14,560	604	3.32	1.22	1.45
1944	101.9	1.61	45.2	46.08	1.96	14,126	624	3.44	1.28	1.53

* Deflated by Consumer Price Index.

Source: *Handbook of Labor Statistics*, published by United States Bureau of Labor Statistics.

397

regular employees. However, this relatively inferior worker is accepted and paid the same wage as the superior employees. The result is analogous to wage discrimination and is, in its way, as profitable as other kinds of price discrimination. One alternative open to the employer would be to attract new employees, of the same quality as the regular employees, by paying a higher wage for each job classification. If this higher wage were paid only the new employees, there would almost certainly be trouble with the former employees; but if the new and higher wage were paid to both new and old workers, the employer would have to meet a very much larger payroll. Accordingly, most employers maintain the same job pay as before, accept the higher labor cost which results from taking on poorer workers at the same job pay, and by means of what is in effect a hidden sort of wage discrimination, prevent their payrolls from rising as rapidly as they otherwise would do.

The labor costs of an expanding firm, especially if there is a general upswing in economic activity, rise for several reasons. The payroll rises more rapidly than the number of employed man-hours because of higher wage rates and the increasing occurrence of overtime. The physical output eventually rises less rapidly than the number of employed man-hours because the new employees are poorer workers, because the same productive effort cannot be maintained over long hours of overtime, and because each plant's ratio of labor to capital equipment is rising, with a consequent fall in the marginal productivity of labor. These developments combine to raise labor costs per unit of output.

However, despite the rising labor cost of output that characterizes an expanding firm during a business upswing, an enterprise may still be able to increase its total profits, and even its profit per unit of production. An imaginary example is given in Table 31. The firm used to produce 50,000 units priced at $10 and now sells 100,000 units at $15. The overhead of $250,000 is the same after expansion as before. The materials input doubles, and, at an assumed 50 per cent higher price, the total materials cost increases three times. The payroll increases five times, partly because we assume that, because of lower physical productivity, it takes 2.5 times as many man-hours to produce double the output, but also because average wage rates have doubled. Profits per unit rise from zero to $2.00 and total profits

increase from zero to $200,000. This result occurred even though
product prices rose only 50 per cent in contrast to the 100 per
cent increase in wage rates. Such an outcome may be quite general because (1) revenue per unit is always greater absolutely
than labor costs per unit, (2) overhead per unit normally declines
with a short-run expansion of output, and (3) the physical ratio
of materials to output remains fairly constant with output changes.
The significance of this example lies in its ability to explain why
firms will expand production despite rising real wages and mount-
ing labor costs per output unit.

TABLE 31

INCREASING PROFITS WITH RISING LABOR COSTS

	BEFORE EXPANSION (50,000 units)		AFTER EXPANSION (100,000 units)	
	Total	Per unit	Total	Per unit
Revenue	$500,000	$10.00	$1,500,000	$15.00
Overhead	250,000	5.00	250,000	2.50
Materials	100,000	2.00	300,000	3.00
Labor	150,000	3.00	750,000	7.50
Cost	500,000	10.00	1,300,000	13.00
Profit	0	0	200,000	2.00

Economics of Overtime

A rather similar analysis explains why entrepreneurs are often
willing to pay time and a half for overtime work even though the
productivity of these extra hours is known to be inferior.

We shall suppose that all the costs of a firm can be classified as
either overhead (which does not vary with output changes), materials cost (which varies proportionately with output), or payroll
(which may increase proportionately more than output). It is
also assumed that all prices and wage rates always remain constant.
What will happen to profits, in view of these suppositions, if a firm
lengthens the work week from 40 hours to 48 hours, so that a
worker is paid the equivalent of 52 hours (30 per cent more) and
produces the equivalent of 44 hours (10 per cent more)?

Profits will increase if total revenue minus materials cost increases by more dollars than does the payroll (overhead can be
ignored because it is a constant). In the present case total revenue minus materials cost increases to 1.10 of its former value because output has risen 10 per cent. The payroll is now at 1.30 of

its former value, since weekly earnings have risen 30 per cent. Hence there can only be an increase in profits if the previous payroll was less than 10/30 of the previous value of total revenue minus materials cost.

Of course, a firm will be less likely to pay overtime wages if additional output can only be sold at a lower price. However, where the price of the product is not noticeably affected, overtime operations are frequently profitable for the employer. It is best if the payroll is not too large relative to the overhead, because he can then make more intensive use of his plant and equipment.

Wage-Rate Differences

It is a commonly observed fact that wage rates vary tremendously within a firm and among trades. What is the explanation of this variation? It is primarily due to (1) wage compensation for other job aspects, (2) non-competition among workers of different race, sex, and competence, (3) the uneven demand of the economy for different services, (4) union restrictions on labor supply, and (5) government wage and hour laws.

Compensating Wage Differences

A job has many aspects and the wage rate is only one of them. The steadiness and volume of employment are probably as important. Other considerations are working conditions, various types of benefits, social attitudes toward the job, and the living costs, climate, and amenities of the area where the job is located.

A worker is probably more concerned with his annual earnings than with his hourly wage rate. A steady job always pays a lower rate than an irregular one when other things are equal. High wages may be both an effect and a cause of interrupted employment. The wage may be high because work is uncertain. Or the high wage may attract and hold such a large pool of job seekers that the annual income of each may be similar, or even lower, than that in other trades hiring the same skills.

Blind-alley jobs have to pay a higher starting wage than ones that offer reasonable assurance of steady promotion. In some trades the worker is through at 45 years of age, whereas in some professions this age may mark the beginning of high earnings. However, everyone does not have the foresight or financial staying power to disregard hourly wage rates and instead maximize lifelong earnings.

The employer may or may not provide certain benefits such as paid vacations and sick leave, pensions, and severance pay. Employer practices in the same industry and area often differ in this respect. Consequently many so-called wage comparisons are invalid.

An employee spends most of his adult life on the job. Noise, dirt, bad ventilation, uncomfortable temperatures, uncongenial associates, dangerous work or unhealthy surroundings, and abnormal strain of all kinds must normally be compensated by higher pay.

Certain jobs carry a degree of social prestige (for example, teaching), whereas others have at times been looked down upon by the public (for example, slaughtering). Generally, indoor white collar jobs have been considered more respectable than outdoor overall jobs. However, these social distinctions are less clearly drawn in the United States than in Europe, so that in many cases the pay compensation may have gone too far in this country.

One must live near one's job, and so area living costs and climate become relevant. Wages for a specific kind of job are usually higher in New York City than elsewhere because rent and food are expensive there. Pay scales in San Diego would be higher than they are if that city had Boston's climate.

Employers who are in rival demand for workers from the same segment of the labor force do not need to pay the same wages. Economists, for instance, frequently transfer between government and university posts, even though the salaries of these positions may differ by several thousand dollars a year. Compensating pay differences, such as those outlined above, are necessary to equalize the over-all attractiveness of alternative jobs.

Non-Competing Groups within the Labor Force

The labor force comprises many segments that are not in competition with one another. Certain jobs can only be filled by persons who, in addition to possessing native ability and acquired training or experience, belong to an approved race, sex, and religion. Social prejudice may erect barriers to employment that are more insuperable than competency requirements. An uneducated Negro woman and a white college alumnus will never be in the same labor market. Geographical distance further subdivides workers into distinct supplies of labor.

Men and women do not compete for many jobs. Social conventions have prevented women, except in wartime, from being employed as bank tellers, cab drivers, and traffic policemen, although they may be equally capable. Lack of physical strength bars women from many jobs (for example, mining and riveting), although this factor is becoming ever less important. On the other hand, young women will take many jobs having no future, and which are largely ignored by men, because the former anticipate marriage and withdrawal from the work force.

In the past (as in the present) women often received less pay than men for the same work. The explanation is that the supply of female job seekers, relative to that of male workers, was greater than the number of jobs for which women were considered suitable. The relatively keen competition among women forced them to accept lower pay and so employers were able to discriminate between them and men on the same job. This still occurs in Europe, where poverty drives married women into the labor force, and where lack of mechanization places more of a premium on the muscular strength of men.

The American Negro is in the same kind of predicament as women generally, but to a far more exaggerated extent. White employees and white customers—rather than employers—will only permit the Negro to perform certain types of work. The supply of Negro workers outside the old South is very great relative to the number of unwanted jobs as porters, washroom attendants, and so on, open to them. Consequently they are driven to accept low pay. A legal requirement of equal pay for equal work would accomplish less for Negroes than is often believed because there are not many job classifications in which white and colored help work shoulder to shoulder. The employer could always evade the law's intent by classifying the work of white and colored employees a little differently.

Professional employment is only open to people who possess both native intelligence to learn and enough financial resources to postpone earnings during what is often a long period of training.

Also, ambition, discipline, and responsibility are usually necessary to some extent. The combination of all these things is not encountered so very frequently, and thus the supply of competent engineers, accountants, surgeons, and lawyers is limited enough to provide them with more than sufficient income to repay what might be termed their "cost of production."

Finally, in every economy, there are a few stellar roles to be filled by rare persons. The outstanding performer, whether in sports, the arts, or the professions, has a monopoly based on natural ability. A Joe Louis, a Caruso, or an Edison all require some training, but all the training in the world could not transform an ordinary man into such a boxer, singer, or inventor. Each person of this sort is a class unto himself.

Theoretically, if we were to divide the total labor force into its various compartments, the wages paid to workers within a given class should all be the same, except in so far as variation is required to compensate for other job aspects.

Derived Demand

The wage of a job is based on demand as well as supply. The salary of a mathematical statistician in Somaliland is low, not because of the excessive supply of such persons there, but because of the slight demand. No employee can earn a substantial income unless his job is essential to the provision of some good or service for which there is in turn a market demand. Over periods of time, changes in prosperity, techniques, and taste may advance or withdraw the demand for a certain service; and this change in demand may occur more rapidly than the supply can be adjusted, especially in a complex culture in which qualifications tend to be more narrowly specialized. For example, during World War II, the demand for engineering draughtsmen multiplied almost overnight. Under such special circumstances, a rapid increase in demand tends to occasion special earnings for scarce training which are akin to quasi-rents; conversely, a very rapid decrease in demand may unduly depress the annual earnings of those people who will only take jobs requiring the skill they struggled to acquire. Sudden and widespread shifts in demand, coupled with specialized training, may widen wage differences.

Union Restrictions on Labor Supply

Most union contracts limit the employer's selection of workers to some extent and in this way constitute a restriction on the supply of labor available for jobs offered by the employer.

The practice of seniority, which of course may be observed in unorganized shops also, is perhaps one of the most universal supply restrictions. If strictly enforced, it limits the employer, when expanding after a contraction, to the rehiring of those workers whom he previously laid off. Otherwise he might pick outside men who were younger and stronger or willing to accept lower-paid jobs.

Whether a union shop agreement (which requires a new employee to join the union upon employment) constitutes a labor supply restriction depends on the entrance requirements of the union. If the union imposes difficult tests, high joining fees, or a long trial period of employment at low wages, the supply of labor will be reduced unless there exists a pool of unemployed unionists. Probably the employer will have to pay higher wages to recruit extra workers and give these increases to former employees also, unless he resorts to the subterfuge of overrating the new employees.

Closed shop arrangements can become outright labor monopolies and have in some instances. The employer may then only hire the workers sent to him by the union. Higher wages and more frequent payment of overtime can often be exacted by limiting the union's membership. However, a greater opportunity for increasing the worker's real reward, and incidentally raising the employer's labor cost, is the performance of poor and slow work.

Wage and Hours Laws

A great many employers, and an even larger proportion of employees, are covered by federal or state laws that set minimum wages, maximum hours, or both. However the scope of these laws is by no means complete, for they often exclude agricultural workers, firms employing only a few workers, and domestic servants. These statutes may also operate to restrict competition between alternative labor supplies for a reason essentially similar to that presented immediately above.

Let us assume for the sake of argument that the federal government sets a high minimum wage to be paid by employers in certain kinds of interstate commerce. A number of workers who were employable at a lower wage will now be unemployable at the high wage. It should never be forgotten that workers in the same trade vary greatly, not only in such obvious things as their individual skill and output, but also as regards lack of absenteeism and tardiness, cooperation with the employer, and influence on their fellow workers. Some workers are barely employable at a given wage while others may be worth more to the employer than they receive.

A legal minimum wage high enough to have any real effect will stop inferior workers from securing jobs covered by the statute. It will also, unless seniority rules prevent it, occasion a screening out of poorer workers already employed by firms affected by the act. It will raise the wages of better workers whose superior qualities were not rewarded previously.

Minimum wage laws both increase and decrease various wage differentials. Some workers who retain their employment may get higher wages, whereas excluded workers may eventually secure jobs at lower wages. The wages of the better workers are now more akin to the wages of good workers elsewhere and the wages of the poorer workers are now more akin to the wages of poor workers elsewhere. Such an outcome seems altogether fair on productivity grounds, since the wages of the better and poorer workers are now less similar.

Many persons believe that minimum wage laws raise wages generally. It is probably true that raising the wages of the lowest-rated jobs in a plant will eventually compel the employer to give similar raises to other employees; but this is irrelevant to laborers who lose their jobs as a result of the law. It is true that some employers not covered by the law will raise their wages, if they are in rival demand with covered employers for the same kind and grade of labor; but this does not help the poorer workers whom the covered employers no longer want. It is true that, in a period of manpower shortage, *all* employers are in rival demand for labor; but in slack times workers are in rival supply for jobs. It is also true that, if the coverage of the law were made complete, poorer workers would not have to accept lower wages; but in this case inferior workers might never hold jobs and so they would earn nothing. The crux of the matter is that a government can force an employer to pay a certain wage, but it does not determine what workers, and how many, he must employ.

However, a partial exception must be noted in the case of employers who possess monopsony power in the labor market and have been exercising it. Recognizing that their supply schedule of available labor is positively inclined, these monopsonistic employers probably distinguish between the price of labor and its marginal purchase cost. They have presumably offered a wage that will evoke a supply such that the marginal cost of labor is equal to its net marginal revenue product to the firm.

For example, in terms of Figure 43, the depicted firm may have

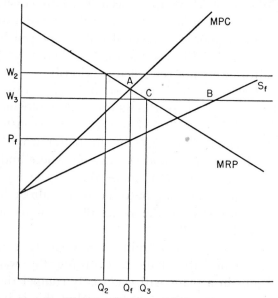

Fig. 43. **Minimum Wages and Labor Monopsony.**

been paying P_f, and hiring Q_f labor, because marginal purchase cost (MPC) intersects marginal revenue product (MRP) at A. A legal minimum wage may or may not help workers in such a case. If it is much higher than the old wage (say W_2 in the diagram), employment will decline (to Q_2), and the payroll will vary depending upon the elasticity of the employer's labor demand (MRP). If the legal minimum wage is slightly higher than the old wage (say W_3), the employer will look upon the new wage as his new marginal purchase cost of labor, for the old supply schedule below B is no longer relevant if he observes the law. Hence he will hire the amount of labor (Q_3) that equates (at C) his demand for labor (MRP) with the marginal purchase cost of labor (W_3). In this case the workers secure more employment, a higher wage, and larger earnings. The practical difficulty is that, even though some monopsonistic employers exist, a minimum wage law applies uniformly to all employers in covered industries. It is naturally not determined specifically for each individual employer. Hence a given minimum wage law may improve matters for monopsonistically employed workers in some cases while rendering matters worse for them in others.

How Real is Technological Unemployment?

Working-class people have feared that new machines would take away their jobs and livelihood since the earliest days of the Industrial Revolution. The very term "sabotage" refers to the wrecking attempts of French workers who threw their wooden shoes (*sabots*) into factory machinery in the hopes of jamming and breaking it. Nowadays such overt wrecking attempts are not the fashion, but the same fear of what has come to be known as "technological unemployment" remains. And for certain workers in certain localities this fear has proved to be well founded. On the other hand, some economists have correctly shown that labor in general, in the long run, should look upon new capital equipment as a friend rather than an enemy, for it acts to lighten toil and raise the community's standard of living. Actually, although these two views may appear contradictory, they can be reconciled.

The reality of local short-run unemployment, attributable to technological innovation, can be realized from any hypothetical example such as the following. Let us suppose a good has been manufactured, until recently, at a cost of $1.00 per unit, and that of this 80¢ per unit was for direct labor. A new type of machine now cuts the direct hand-labor needs in half so that, at the same wage rates as before, the direct labor cost per unit is now 40¢. Of course the firm does not experience so large a reduction in total unit cost. The new machines incur new expenses. Perhaps the new and extra depreciation, interest, and maintenance expense, plus extra power requirements, is 30¢. The new total unit cost is hence 90¢.

The burning question, so far as the workers who supply the direct labor are concerned, is whether these cost reductions will double sales and output and so preserve their jobs.

If the producing firm is a monopolistic competitor, it may produce a little more and drop its price a trifle, so that the new and probably lower marginal costs can be equated with marginal revenue. If the firm is part of a purely competitive industry, all firms will probably be encouraged to produce rather more, until the price declines. In either event there will probably be a rather lower price that will somewhat increase sales. Of course, there is no way of knowing how great this price decline will be, but if we make the simplifying assumption that price is always equal to unit cost, then the price will fall from $1.00 to 90¢. The demand elasticity must be roughly 20, which is high indeed, if output is to double and employment remain unchanged.

Naturally, by changing the assumptions, we can make the lot of the directly employed workers apparently better or worse. If the *extra* depreciation, interest, and maintenance expenses amounted to 10¢ per unit, instead of 30¢, then the price might fall to 70¢, and a demand elasticity in the neighborhood of 7, instead of 20, would preserve the jobs of the directly employed hands. On the other side, if direct labor has been responsible for a smaller proportion of total unit costs, demand elasticity would probably have to be even higher than originally supposed.

It is to be hoped that some of the displaced hand workers can transfer to new jobs within the same firm. The new machines will need maintenance, for example; it is questionable, however, whether the previously employed workers can and will be trained for this work. Many of the original workers may have to seek employment elsewhere. If there is no adequate substitute employment, their best course of action is probably to move, although it is by no means certain that they will. In either event they are victims of technological unemployment.

However, the innovation of the new-type machinery will probably not reduce the total demand for labor in the country. Machines represent congealed labor, as it were. Machines have to be designed and built, which requires labor. They have to be serviced and supplied with power after they are installed, which requires labor. We are all familiar with stories of wonderful new machines that perhaps "will do the work of twenty-five men,"

and although this may mean that 25 men will be at least temporarily looking for jobs, there will not be 25 fewer jobs in
the economy.   The introduction of machinery means that labor
is being used in other forms and not that less labor in general is
being used.

Unfortunately, the use of labor in other forms usually means
the use of some other people's labor, and this shift in demand is
of little solace to the man who finds himself no longer needed.

A practical example may serve to stress the distinction between
the specific short-run *unemployment* and the general long-run
employment caused by new machinery.   For some time now mechanical cotton pickers have been slowly introduced and have
inevitably reduced the demand for field labor.   The reduction in
the total unit cost of cotton is not great, and the price of cotton
is a very small part of the cost of cotton products, such as shirts
and sheets, so that little if any extra cotton will be raised and
picked as a result.

The sort of people who traditionally pick cotton will seldom
be trained and given jobs on machine picker maintenance or as
oil company salesmen.   Of course, the production of mechanical
pickers provides many jobs in the Great Lakes region, but that
is a thousand miles away and often seemingly in another world.
It is too much to expect that the man or woman who cannot find
jobs picking cotton will arrive at the gate of the factory making
mechanical pickers and secure employment.   The best that can
be expected is that the man who takes a newly created job making
pickers will leave a job, which will be taken by a man who leaves
another job, which will be taken by someone leaving another job,
and so on, until the last vacated job is taken by the erstwhile field
hand.   The chain of job substitutions could be very long and
tangled and yet still not stretch far enough.   Of course, in the
long run, the use of mechanical pickers probably reduces the
aggregate need for all kinds of labor in supplying cotton, so that
somebody's labor, perhaps that of the next generation, becomes
available for making additional goods of different kinds.   In this
way the national product ultimately becomes larger and more
varied.

In many lines of enterprise the first impact of mechanization is
now over, and the new and superior machinery more often dis-
places old and inferior machinery.   The reduction in directly-

employed labor on the spot is then less drastic than when machinery was first introduced in place of hand labor. Nevertheless, it is important to remember that, even though the aggregate demand for labor remains unchanged, the people who no longer have the old jobs may not live long enough to find the new ones.

Statements for Consideration

1. Real wages tend to fall during an upswing in business.   *Discuss*
2. Labor costs to employers tend to rise during a long upswing and hence firms tend to lay off workers until labor costs begin to decline.   *Evaluate*
3. Firms pay workers overtime as a compensation to workers who work extra hours and not because employers profit from this more intensive use of their plant.   *Evaluate*
4. Wage differences are due to demand differences as well as supply differences.   *Exemplify*
5. Costs of training may become either a barrier that separates non-competing groups or a basis for compensating differences in earnings.   *Discuss*
6. The mechanization of many jobs may have reduced the earnings differential between men and women in the United States.   *Discuss*
7. Frequently it is not the employers who object to hiring Negro labor; under other circumstances they would be very glad to, as occasionally it can be obtained for lower wages.   *Discuss*
8. A combination of rigid seniority and high wages may often be quite enough to protect present employees from outside competition.   *Discuss*
9. An increased minimum wage may serve to discriminate between relatively productive and non-productive labor.   *Evaluate*
10. The introduction of machinery may create specific short-run unemployment while creating general long-run employment.   *Explain*
11. Increased minimum wages may prove beneficial to all affected workers in those trades in which employers exercise monopsony power.   *Discuss*

References

Bloom, G. F., "A Reconsideration of the Theory of Exploitation," *Quarterly Journal of Economics,* vol. XV, 1940–1. Also in *Readings in the Theory of Income Distribution.*

Bowman, M. J., and Bach, G. L., *Economic Analysis and Public Policy,* Chapter 30. New York: Prentice-Hall, 1949.

Due, J. F., *Intermediate Economic Analysis,* Chapter 11. Chicago: Irwin, 1947.

Garver, F. B., and Hansen, A. H., *Principles of Economics,* Chapter 23.   New York: Ginn, 1947.

Hicks, J. R., *Theory of Wages,* Chapters 1, 3–6.   London: Macmillan, 1932.

Marshall, A., *Principles of Economics,* Eighth Edition, Book VI, Chapters 3–5.   London: Macmillan, 1920.

Meyers, A. L., *Modern Economics,* Chapters 19, 21.   New York: Prentice-Hall, 1941.

Pigou, A. C., *Lapses from Full Employment.*   London: Macmillan, 1945.

Pigou, A. C., *The Economics of Welfare,* III, Chapters 9, 15–18.   London: Macmillan, 1946.

Robbins, L., "On the Elasticity of Demand for Income in Terms of Effort," *Economica,* vol. X, June 1930.   Also in *Readings in the Theory of Income Distribution.*

Robertson, D. H., "Wage Grumbles," *Economic Fragments,* 1931.   Also in *Readings in the Theory of Income Distribution.*

Robinson, J., *Introduction to the Theory of Employment,* Chapter 6.   New York: Macmillan, 1947.

Robinson, J., *The Economics of Imperfect Competition,* VIII, IX.   New York: Macmillan, 1933.

Rolph, E., "The Discounted Marginal Productivity Doctrine," *Journal of Political Economy,* vol. XLVII, 1939.   Also in *Readings in the Theory of Income Distribution.*

Samuelson, P. A., *Economics,* Chapter 9.   New York: McGraw-Hill, 1948.

28

Union Leaders and Wage Rates

IT MAY WELL BE that the primary concern of a union leader is the security and growth of his union. Considerations of power and politics may override those of economics and finance when these two are in conflict. A union is more likely to go out on strike over the dismissal of a union steward than over the failure of an employer to grant vacations with pay. However, apart from sudden crises, when the security of the union appears to be threatened, a union's officers and membership are probably more continuously concerned with questions of pay than with any other.

One important point must first be made by way of preface. Each union leader represents only a small fraction of the labor force. Out of a total labor force of slightly over 60 million, and an employed force of slightly less than this same figure, only approximately one-quarter are organized at all. The Congress of Industrial Organizations, which in general seems to possess more cohesiveness than the American Federation of Labor, has a total membership of only about one-tenth the country's employed labor force. The largest single union—the Teamsters—includes about one-fiftieth of the employed labor force. However, the largest independent unions do not make a single contract for the whole economy. The most important single union contract, in terms of the number of workers covered, is probably that negotiated from time to time by the United Mine Workers, but even in this case considerably less than one per cent of the nation's employed labor force is involved.

A vast majority of contracts obviously relate to far smaller fractions of the economy. Consequently, a union officer, during negotiations, is presumably interested in advancing the financial welfare of his own rank and file, rather than that of all working people. Another important consequence of the fractional nature

412

of union negotiations is that the techniques of particular equilibrium analysis are relevant to most questions of employee pay.

Wages or Employment?

Any union leader, who stops to think about the matter, must realize that in negotiating with employers he may be seeking incompatible benefits for the rank and file. High wage rates may result in less employment than otherwise and more employment may be obtainable only at the cost of lower wages than might otherwise be secured. There is a dilemma here, although many working men and some labor economists may not perceive it. In the end, possibly because the rank and file know a wage increase when they get one, but do not see its employment effect, the union leader may be forced to act as though wage rate increases and worker welfare were one and the same thing.

In any given situation it is difficult to know what the relation between wage rates and employment may be. There may be no layoffs the first week or month after a new union contract providing for higher wages has been signed, for a firm's demand for labor is probably rather inelastic in the very short run. And this may encourage unionists to believe that wage rate increases have no employment repercussions.

Eventually, but not immediately, higher wage rates may reduce employment below what it would otherwise have been, in various ways that may seem unrelated because of the delay between cause and effect. First, new methods may be introduced that dispense with direct labor; the innovation of these methods may have awaited higher wage rates, but superficially it may seem that these new methods came along in the normal course of progress. Second, previously expanding enterprises may not lay men off, but instead grow more slowly or not at all. Third, firms that might have become established may now fail to enter the trade. Fourth, some firms may years later be forced to close down, by which time this may be attributed to the inefficiency of the management or some other cause. Fifth, with higher marginal costs, firms may tend to charge higher prices than they otherwise would, whether in periods of boom or depression, in which case their sales and output will be somewhat less, but this may be supposedly due to business conditions. The point is that a year or two can bring so many new circumstances that the relation between wages and employment is lost from view.   Nevertheless, unless the deductions of economic theory are quite incorrect, that relation exists.

The link between wages and employment can often create a difficult political dilemma for a union and its leaders.   On the one hand, fewer hours of employment in the aggregate are now offered, and on the other more people wish to work at the new and more attractive wage rates.   Either fewer employees must remain employed or more employees must individually work a great deal less.   If the first policy is pursued, there is the unpleasant necessity of making some of the present workers unemployed.   If the second policy is pursued, there is the difficult task of deciding how to share the limited available employment.   Essentially the union must decide whether to adopt "closed" policies (which restrict entry and limit membership) or "open" policies (which permit anyone to be a union member).   Naturally, the less inelastic the employees' demand for labor, the more pointed this dilemma becomes.

A great many "closed" labor organizations effect a concentration of employment through seniority provisions in the unions' contract.   As the wage is forced up, those with "seniority" stay and those with "juniority" go.   Sometimes where there is a union shop or closed shop contract, the usual seniority provisions are supplemented by high joining fees and competency tests that are seldom passed.   The original membership will then gradually age and contract and the reduced employment that goes with a higher wage may be effected with fewer layoffs.   Normally, despite various exceptions, the gains of those who retain their employment at a higher wage are usually associated with losses suffered by those who must now obtain other employment.   There will often be a period of idleness and low income before those who are actually laid off are able to secure a new job.   More important still is the fact that the competition of the displaced worker will tend to depress earnings in those occupations where employment is both unrestricted and available.   The principal exception is when, during a period of full employment, the rival demands of firms for labor compel unorganized plants to provide wages and working conditions as satisfactory as those in organized firms.

In the case of "open" unions, with an unrestricted membership, a large pool of partially employed workers develops whenever the wage is forced above the competitive level. If one industry or firm pays unusually well for some kind of work, all the workers in the area will want to work in that industry or firm, and will prefer to work part-time there for the same weekly or annual take-home pay. The resultant labor pool may far exceed the needs of the industry or firm. An outstanding example of such a development is the motion picture industry around Los Angeles. Actually, the creation of a large labor pool often leads to some hiring hall or other means of rotating employment. Economically, unless workers obtain other jobs when not employed by the industry or firm, a partially employed pool is undesirable because the output of the community is reduced. In most instances the interests of the economy would be better served by concentrating employment upon a favored few. Then the residual labor force, which has been rendered "surplus" by the high wage, will be forced, from lack of income, to seek and take employment elsewhere.

The union leader, in pressing for higher wages, must often consider what the employer *can* pay, although, of course, ability to pay is not a valid economic criterion of what an employer *should* pay. In the long run, labor earnings must be paid out of sales receipts, and so the farsighted union leader must consider the output demand curve confronting the employer. He probably realizes that the ability of a single firm to pass a wage rate increase on to its customers through higher prices is much less than that of a group of employers supplying the same product or service. Hence industry-wide organization and bargaining is to the advantage of the union, and possibly to some of the employers, although certainly not to the customers. Then, if a wage rate increase is obtained from all firms in the industry, a general price increase can follow, and the total reduction in employment will be primarily influenced by the industry's loss of sales. If the demand for the industry's product is inelastic, and the employing firms are numerous and in active competition, the union may be able to push them along as a buffer in front of it, and reap monopoly profits. Essentially this is what has happened in the bituminous coal industry. The more general effect of industry-wide bargaining, however, is, neglecting monopsony cases, to reduce the unemployment cost that actual or potential workers must usually pay when unions raise wages.

Of course, if the union has sufficient strength, it may be able to win higher wages without causing reduced or partial employment, by dictating work rules and generally telling the management how and where to employ labor.   If the management is relatively helpless or heedless, unions may be able to prevent it from using new labor-saving equipment, materials, or methods, so that the firm has to employ the same amount of labor as before.   The construction trades are notorious for such practices and "featherbedding" has seldom been confined to the railroads.   In these cases, until the whole industry eventually begins to slip in competition with others, organized labor comes remarkably close to having and eating its cake.

Some Union Wage Arguments

Wages are generally determined, in the absence of legal intervention, by demand and supply forces and the relative bargaining strength of the employer and the representatives of his workers. However, rather than issue a blunt wage ultimatum, many union leaders prefer to argue that wages be determined according to some formula that currently suits their purpose, or that higher wages will benefit other groups in the economy as well.   Of course, unions have no monopoly on invalid arguments, but most of the more ingenious theories have originated with them because they have taken the initiative in proposing wage changes.

Employee Purchasing Power

Union leaders sometimes argue that a higher wage rate will increase employee purchasing power and so benefit the employer in turn.   Under extremely unrealistic and favorable circumstances, such as a simultaneous wage rate increase by all employers financed from inflationary bank credits, it might be possible for *money* wages to be raised generally without inflicting losses upon the entrepreneurial class.   However, this is not quite the result envisaged by proponents of the purchasing power argument, and all firms actually do not alter wages together.

No single employer can profitably finance his customers.   Let us suppose, for the sake of argument, that General Motors raises wages without reducing employment or output, so that its employees earn $1,000,000 more a year than before.   If the employees of General Motors annually spend two per cent of their extra income on General Motors products, and if the company can keep

10¢ of each sales dollar as profit after taxes, General Motors will recapture $2,000 of its $1,000,000 greater payroll in the first year, and so impair its disposable profit position by only $998,000!

Of course General Motors' employees will spend their extra earnings on food and clothing and housing, and so farmers and garment workers and construction workers, and many others, will come to buy more cars and refrigerators, some of them made by General Motors. However, if the company's profits are only 0.2 per cent of all personal incomes, the national income would have to be increased about $500,000,000 before General Motors would begin to meet the increased payroll. Now, other things equal, how long would it take and how much would it cost, for General Motors, through payroll injections of new credit, to raise the national income by this amount? Theoretically, if there are no leakages from hoarding, it would eventually cost General Motors about $250,000,000, and the final consequences would be approximated within 25 years or so.

The conclusion must be that, if a large corporation cannot lift itself by its own bootstraps, an ordinary employer, who constitutes an even smaller fraction of the economy, certainly cannot. Moreover, in the above example, it was supposed that General Motors had access to unlimited funds with which to finance its experiment, and that this introduction of new money eventually raised the national income to a point where sales revenue was increased $1,000,000 a year too. It is difficult to imagine that many firms could or would finance such a foredoomed experiment.

Ability To Pay

During periods of prosperity it is often suggested that an employer should raise wages when he has high profits. Sometimes it is stated, by way of excuse, that an employer with profits has ability to pay. However, if ability to pay is to become the basis of money transfers between all persons, whether the donor is an employer, acquaintance, or someone accosted on the street, we would all be left with uniformly low incomes.

Such a scheme would prove most undesirable if it meant imposing a definite ceiling on each employer's permissible profits, with all excess being disbursed either as a belated bonus to last year's employees or as higher wages next year. The firm would have no incentive to increase efficiency beyond a certain limit.

Unfortunately, no one can say with finality what reasonable expenses are, what reasonable value the firm has, or what is a reasonable rate of return in view of the risks of the industry. Moreover, while this plan would tend to raise wages during prosperity phases, it does not provide for reducing wages during a depression phase. A proposal of this kind would be a one-way street to bankruptcy.

It is barely conceivable that a plan might be evolved whereby a basic wage at zero profits was adjusted up or down according to the profits or losses revealed by the last quarter's accounts. Business earnings would then be less of a feast or famine proposition for the owners. An effective wage rate that adjusted itself to business conditions might prevent the employer from expanding and contracting his work force so drastically. On the other hand, workers who are secure in their jobs would be subject to fluctuations in income and in a degree would be shouldering some of the risks of entrepreneurship. Also, all employees would unfairly suffer in the short run from inefficient management.

However, this latter plan is not really a formula for wage determination, since the basic wage rate, and the extent to which it should be modified by profits or losses, would still have to be negotiated.

Productivity of Labor

Many unions have requested higher wages on the grounds of alleged increases in worker productivity. They have pointed to (1) higher value of output per man-hour, (2) higher value added per man-hour, or (3) higher physical output per man-hour. The first may obviously be due to higher selling prices, proves nothing regarding worker productivity, and may even be associated with reduced profits because of disproportionate increases in materials and other costs. The second may be a good indication of increased ability to pay but that is another argument the validity of which has been evaluated above. Actually it is higher physical output per man-hour that is usually cited.

A statistic of physical output per man-hour is obtained from dividing total physical output by the total number of production man-hours worked. It is important to realize, though, that there is no necessary causal relation between the numerator and the denominator of this ratio. The output per factory window might be similarly calculated, but an increase in this figure could not be made an argument for giving the owners of the plant a larger share in the sales revenue.   It is more than probable that, when output per man-hour rises, so does output per machine, output per square foot of floor space, output per company president, and so on.

The crucial question is who or what is responsible for the increased output.   In industry the output per production worker can usually be increased by equipping him with more modern and costly kinds of equipment.   Sometimes management evolves more efficient factor combinations.   A production worker is hardly entitled to higher pay if his increased output is attributable to the use of new capital goods purchased out of investors' funds or to the performance by management of its proper function.   If a firm launches a program of intensive mechanization, the output of its directly employed labor probably increases, owing to its extra payments for labor previously employed in making the machines. However, when working conditions and equipment within a plant are unchanged, and the ratio of labor to other factors is also constant, it can usually be presumed that the workers are themselves responsible for any increased output per man-hour.   In general, it is only fair that they should be paid more for working harder and faster.   Worker productivity is not an unreasonable basis of wage determination over short periods of time when output changes attributable solely to employees can be ascertained.

In practice, it is extremely difficult, if not impossible, to determine what fraction of increased output is due to labor, rather than to capital or management.   Hence the productivity formula will always lead to uncertain results of doubtful validity.   Or some constant fraction of changes in output per man-hour may be accepted as a compromise figure.   Consistent application of such a formula will yield harmful or ludicrous results.   Directly comparable jobs will pay different rates if one is in a new and expanding industry and the other is in a declining trade.   This would be unfair to employees in these trades.   It would also mean that one job would have too many applicants and the other too few.   Another economic defect is that if all, or an undue fraction, of increased output per man-hour is paid to employees, the price of the product will not be reduced to the extent that it otherwise might have been.   Moreover, the employer will not have the same incentives to introduce improved methods and equipment. Would management and capital have helped to triple the productivity of industrial labor during the twentieth century if wages had throughout been based on man-hour output?

Over long periods of time, taking industry as a whole, the benefits of increased productivity are distributed to consumers in lower prices and to all workers in higher money and real wages.

Comparable Wages for Comparable Jobs

Whether this principle is economically acceptable depends upon what jobs are considered comparable by its advocates. Does it mean the same wage for the same sort of job (1) in a given industry throughout the country, (2) in a given area irrespective of the industry, or (3) in a given industry within a given area? And who decides whether jobs offered by different employers, even though in the same industry and area, are really similar or not?

Payment of a uniform industry-wide wage throughout the nation is economically unsound. The amenity and cost of living vary so greatly within the country that the payment of an industry-wide wage would create real differences in the welfare of employees. Another objection is that a uniform industry-wide wage would interfere with desirable shifts of labor and capital within the nation. The old South, as contrasted with the Great Lakes area, has too much labor and too little capital. The higher wages in the North help to pull labor out of the South and the low wages in the South attract capital from the North. Equal wages would slow this adjustment.

Payment of an equal wage by all industries employing the same kind of labor in an area is also unacceptable on economic grounds. Different industries do not provide the same stability of employment throughout the year, working conditions may be more or less pleasant, and physical danger may vary. Driving a city bus and driving a long distance truck are not really the same job. A carpenter in the building trades is in a different context than a carpenter in a furniture factory. A more fundamental objection, perhaps, is that there are always some expanding and some declining industries. Uniform wages for similar jobs in an area would check the introduction of new inventions and products and so hinder the steady improvement in living that consumers can normally expect.

Payment of a similar wage rate by different employers in a given industry in a given area is less objectionable. However, it should only be attempted if all the major aspects of different jobs—for example, vacations, working conditions, labor relations—make the alternative employments reasonable substitutes in the judgment of most workers.   If the job content offered by different employers is equal in attractiveness, a comparable wage will also be the competitive wage, and it will possess the latter's usual merits.

One of these economic virtues is that a prevailing wage imposes standards of efficiency on each firm. It usually compels each entrepreneur to maintain normal rates of technological progress or go bankrupt, just as deep water forces a swimmer to continue his exertions or drown.   Occasionally this economic discipline is allayed when the employees of an inefficient firm accept lower wages to avoid being laid off.

Actual surveys of wages for similar jobs in a given industry and area usually reveal a wide range of rates. And in practice the demand for comparable rates naturally comes from those groups of employees who are being paid less than the average.   When and if the principle of comparable wages is acceptable, it should be applied consistently, and entail a reduction of all rates currently above the average. A sound principle should cut both ways.

Bargaining Power in Wage Negotiations

Much of the preceding analysis may be objected to by some on the grounds that either the demand for labor of an employer is almost completely inelastic or that most unions have insufficient bargaining power to raise wages significantly.   In support of the analysis it is contended that the labor demand of every employer must become zero in the long run above a certain wage rate and that the bargaining power of organized workers often exceeds that of the employer.   The following hypothetical case may illustrate these points.

Let us suppose Company *XYZ* operates a plant employing 1,000 production workers at $10 a day and producing an output of 5,000 units.   The labor cost per unit of output is then $2.00, since each worker produces an average output of 5 units in a day.   We shall suppose that the overhead per unit is $3.00, the materials cost per unit also $3.00, and the price $8.00.   In terms of totals, the revenue is $40,000, the payroll $10,000, materials $15,000, overhead $15,000, and pure profits zero dollars per day.

The employees are organized and possess a union shop contract with the company. The local area has a number of different industries and plants, and there is, except for a few unemployables and seasonally idle, no real unemployment in the region. Heartened by these conditions, the union demands a doubling of the daily wage from $10 to $20 and an undertaking by the company not to introduce new methods or machinery in order to economize on labor.

What is the bargaining strength of the company and the organized employees? If labor is well organized in the area, there is little possibility of the company's being able to replace its entire work force. It cannot transfer its plant to another area, although smaller pieces of equipment may be movable at a cost or salable at a sacrifice. If the company shuts the plant down, it will sustain a loss, from the continuing overhead, amounting to $15,000 a day or about $5,500,000 a year. If the union closes the plant down, its membership will immediately lose $10,000 a day in wages, but if the period is one of full employment, the workers will in time find other work, in the same area or some other. They will be put to an inconvenience and loss of seniority but for a while they may in some localities be able to draw unemployment benefits. Under the assumed circumstances both sides will suffer a loss if the plant is closed down, but the company can probably least afford a cessation of operations.

If the company accedes to the union demands, and if in the short run its demand for labor is rendered virtually inelastic by its inability to introduce labor-saving methods or equipment, its daily costs per unit will now be $4.00 for labor, $3.00 for materials, and $3.00 for overhead. With total costs of $10.00 a unit, a selling price of $8.00, and an output of 5,000 units, it will sustain a daily loss of $10,000. However, in the short run, because the price more than covers the variable costs per unit incurred for labor and materials, it probably will prefer continuing in operation at a loss of $10,000 a day to shutting down and losing $15,000 a day. Of course exceptions can be imagined. The company may be run by a management group who have no significant ownership stake in it. Or the front office may become so emotional over the union's demands that it disregards cold calculations of profit and loss in its desire to "teach those fellows a lesson." However, in the abstract, we can suppose that the company will still operate and temporarily accept a minimum loss.

Eventually the time will arrive when various physical assets become so worn out that continued repair and maintenance will not keep them in operation and they must be replaced.   If these assets are few in number, are relatively inexpensive to buy and install, and are essential to the continued operation of the plant, they will probably be replaced.   However, when it becomes necessary to replace a number of expensive assets, the company will close down the plant if the prospective quasi-rent, that is the excess of total sales revenue over total variable costs, is insufficient to cover the depreciation of new physical assets.   In our example the company would certainly close down when major replacements could no longer be postponed.

An employer will always have some demand for labor in the short run, provided his labor cost per unit of output is not forced so high as to render quasi-rents negative.   However, in the long run, the labor cost must not be so high that it renders profits negative.   Many wage demands will be paid in the short run that will not be met in the long run.

Herein lies a grave danger for the worker and the economy alike. The union membership may sincerely believe that an employer can pay a certain wage scale indefinitely because he is paying it now.   Or the union leadership may realize that the high wages they have obtained must be temporary, but counts on being elsewhere when, as an ultimate consequence of its acts, the employer closes down, lays off all his workers, and stops supplying goods to the economy.   In the short run, a union worker can usually get more; in the long run, he may often have to accept less. A wise and conscientious union leader should on occasion decide to make more moderate wage demands than the moment permits.

Summary

Employee pay is probably the main concern, after union security is assured, of most union leaders.   However *pay* may mean hourly wage rates, weekly earnings, or total payroll.   And over time, although the connection may not always be obvious, the total volume of employment provided by a single firm or industry is to some extent dependent upon the wage rate.   Hence the union leader must decide which kind of pay should be maximized and how much unemployment for somebody he is incidentally willing to occasion. In carrying on negotiations, the union leader may have more bargaining power than is usually suspected, especially where a corporation's large overhead renders any cessation of production extremely costly. Most unions usually supplement their bargaining power by advocating the adoption of some formula favorable to themselves. Certain of these formulas have grave implications for economic progress and so it is just as well that they are often advanced without serious conviction.

It is extremely difficult for employees to increase their real income at the expense of others because the employees' share in aggregate national income is ordinarily 60 to 70 per cent of the population's. Employees are a majority group within the economy, and consequently the possibility of greatly advancing their economic lot by giving them a larger share of a given national income is very limited. (Conversely, a relatively small group, such as those who received interest and dividends, can be immensely benefited by receiving a larger share.) Therefore, if employees were represented by a single union, which they are not today, they should be primarily concerned with raising the national output.

However, in the United States, and in most other countries for that matter, the decision to employ and produce and expand lies with millions of separate entrepreneurs, who act only when they anticipate a profit. They do not look upon outside pressures to pay higher wages as an incentive to further risk-taking and output. Employees as a whole are therefore in a difficult dilemma, naturally wanting higher real income, being really unable to secure it by their own direct actions, and having to wait impatiently for technological and other events to provide it. If all labor ever became organized, its leaders would have to exercise great restraint and statesmanship, more so probably than the representatives of any other special interest group in the economy.

Statements for Consideration

1. Since workers are consumers, farsighted employers realize that high wages that increase purchasing power will also raise their profits.
   Evaluate
2. The bargaining power of employees is always less than that of their employer.
   Evaluate
3. Seniority is very nice for those who have it; but its obverse is

"juniority," and so it is questionable whether seniority really benefits all workers as a class.   *Discuss*

4. A higher wage rate may result in a smaller total payroll but higher earnings for all the employees of a firm.   *Explain*
5. An increase in output per man-hour indicates that directly employed labor has become more productive.   *Discuss*
6. A very low wage may create additional job opportunities in a plant but reduce the number of workers employed there.   *Explain*
7. The methods of partial equilibrium analysis are applicable to most analyses of wage contracts between a single firm and its employees.   *Discuss*
8. The mere fact that the unemployment effect of rising wages may be obscure does not deny its existence.   *Discuss*
9. A prevailing area or industry wage often enforces certain standards of efficiency on each employer.   *Explain*
10. The employees of a profitable firm have more right to share in these profits (through higher wages) than do its customers (through lower prices).   *Discuss*
11. A union leader would never press for higher wages if he did not implicitly assume that the employer's demand for labor was inelastic.   *Evaluate*

References

Bronfenbrenner, M., "The Economics of Collective Bargaining," *Quarterly Journal of Economics*, August 1939.

Bowman, M. J., and Bach, G. L., *Economic Analysis and Public Policy*, Chapter 31.   New York: Prentice-Hall, 1949.

Dunlop, J. T., *Wage Determination under Trade Unions*.   New York: Macmillan, 1944.

Dunlop, J. T., "Wage Policies of Trade Unions," *American Economic Review*, Vol. XXXII, Supplement, 1942.   Also in *Readings in the Theory of Income Distribution*.

Ellis, H. S. (Ed.), *A Survey of Contemporary Economics*, Chapter 7. Philadelphia: Blakiston, 1948.

Fellner, W., "Prices and Wages under Bilateral Monopoly," *Quarterly Journal of Economics*, August 1947.

Garver, F. B., and Hansen, A. H., *Principles of Economics*, Chapter 27. New York: Ginn, 1947.

Hicks, J. R., *Theory of Wages*, Chapters 1, 3–6.   London: Macmillan, 1932.

Lerner, A. P., "The Relation of Wage Policies and Price Policies," *American Economic Review*, vol. XXIX, Supplement, 1939. Also in *Readings in the Theory of Income Distribution*.

Lester, R. A., "Shortcomings of Marginal Analysis for Wage Employment Problems," *American Economic Review*, March 1946.

Lindblom, C. E., "The Union as a Monopoly," *Quarterly Journal of Economics*, November 1948.

Meyers, A. L., *Modern Economics,* Chapter 20.   New York: Prentice-Hall, 1941.
Pigou, A. C., *The Economics of Welfare,* IV, Chapters 5, 7, 8.   London: Macmillan, 1946.
Robertson, D. H., "Wage Grumbles," *Economic Fragments.*
Slichter, S. H., *The American Economy,* Chapter 2.   New York: Knopf, 1948.
Tarshis, L., "Changes in Real and Money Wages," *Economic Journal,* vol. XLIX, March 1939.   Also in *Readings in the Theory of Income Distribution.*

29

Rent on Land

ONLY approximately one-third of the aggregate national income of the United States is paid out to the owners of natural resources as rents, to owners of capital funds as interest, or to entrepreneurs as profits. However, incomes from these sources tend to be high, per recipient, because relatively few people participate in these three distributive shares. Because persons with large incomes usually receive them from these sources, and because no great personal effort appears to be involved in contrast to labor earnings, many social reformers have attacked the payment of rent, interest, and profits as economically unnecessary and morally unjustifiable.

Economic rent—allegedly "unearned" income—is paid for use of the indestructible powers of nature. It does not include payments for the use of farm buildings, machinery, improvements such as irrigation or drainage systems, or large capital constructions such as a hydroelectric dam. However, it is, of course, often difficult to separate the elements of pure or economic rent from the total use value of a piece of agricultural property or real estate.

Theoretically, ignoring this problem, the economic rent of a particular land holding arises from both the general scarcity of natural resources and its own comparative productivity.

Rent of Land in General

The only basis of land rent and value, if all land were of uniform quality and character, would be the scarcity of natural resources relative to other productive factors, such as labor and capital, and to population. It is normally true that the productive contribution of a marginal unit of some factor is high when that factor is combined in low proportions with other factors. And the productive significance of another unit of a factor, already being employed in high proportions, is normally low. This phenomenon is somewhat analogous to a college dance, which is being attended by 10 fellows and 50 girls; the advent of another fellow (fellows being combined in low proportions) will then contribute more to the success of the dance than the arrival of another girl (girls being combined in high proportions). It also follows that, as the combination ratio of a factor (or of fellows to girls) becomes higher, an extra unit (or fellow) becomes less significant. In economics, this phenomenon is called the *principle of varying proportions*, when productive factors are being considered.

Varying Factor Proportions

Land rent arises when the ratio of land to other factors falls below some critical figure, the magnitude of which depends primarily upon the state of the arts.

Let us imagine a country in which the land area consists of 10,000,000 acres of uniform quality. The inhabitants grow only one kind of crop and seem to survive on their monotonous diet. Moreover, agricultural experiments have demonstrated that a factor combination of 3.0 acres to one man, or of .33 men to 1.00 acre, yields the greatest output per man. Now, if the population of this country were so low that the number of available agricultural workers was only 2,000,000, only 6,000,000 acres would be cultivated, and the remaining 4,000,000 acres could be had free for the asking.

Alternatively, if a little more land were used, the land-to-labor ratio would be less favorable, the output per man would decline, and hence the total output also. The marginal productivity of the newly cultivated acres would be negative and the output contribution of the 6,000,000th acre would be zero. Hence the economic rent of the used land, which is assumed no better or worse than the unusued land, would be negative.

On the other hand, if 5,000,000 workers were employed, the optimum supply of land would be 15,000,000 acres, which is 5,000,000 more than actually exist. In this case a small increase in the available supply of land would increase output, always keeping the same number of men at work, and so the marginal productivity of land would be positive. The land would then earn rents.

The principle of variable proportions, particularly as it applies to land and labor, is exemplified in Table 32, the data of which

TABLE 32

LAND RENT AND VARIABLE PROPORTIONS

Stage	Land-to-Labor Ratio	No Workers (000,000)	Total Bushel Output (000,000)	Per Acre Output (bu.)	Per Worker Output (bu.)	Last Worker Output (bu.)	Rent Per Worker (bu.)	Total Bushel Rent (000,000)
	10.00	1	10	1.2	10	10	0	
1st	5.00	2	22	2.2	11	12	-1	
	3.33	3	36	3.6	12	14	-2	
	2.50	4	44	4.4	11	8	3	12
2nd	2.00	5	50	5.0	10	6	4	20
	1.67	6	54	5.4	9	4	5	30
	1.43	7	56	5.6	8	2	6	42
	1.25	8	56	5.6	7	0	7	
3rd	1.11	9	36	3.6	4	-20	24	
	1.00	10	0	0	0	-36	36	

have been graphed in Fig. 44. In this example, the land-to-labor ratio is constantly declining as more men are set to cultivating the

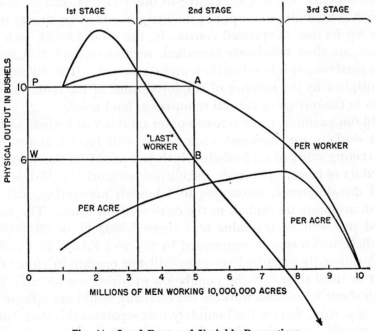

Fig. 44. Land Rent and Variable Proportions.

constant land acreage of uniform quality. The important series in this case are the output per acre, the output per worker, and the marginal product of labor.

Three Distinct Stages

The relationship of these three series to one another defines two important boundaries that separate three distinct stages. In the first stage there is no land rent, and in fact the marginal product of land, although not shown, is negative. The boundary between the first and second stages is determined by the equality of the average and marginal output of labor; this is the point of diminishing returns, a concept that has played so large a part in the history of economic doctrines. In the second stage land has a positive marginal product and earns rent. The second stage merges into the third at the point where total output is a maximum and the marginal product of labor becomes zero. In the third stage land is at a premium, and too many men are working, so that "firing" a man would raise output.

In practice, no economy operates beyond the second stage, and so it is in this stage only that land rent normally arises. Then land is sufficiently scarce, relative to other factors such as labor, that it contributes to output at the margin, and so producers will pay for its use. Expressed conversely, the other factors, such as labor, are then sufficiently abundant, relative to land, that their marginal output is less than their average output. The difference, multiplied by the number of employed units of the other factor, goes to the owners of natural resources as land rent.

In our example, if the acre-to-worker ratio is 2 to 1 when 5,000,-000 workers are employed, each worker will receive as pay the marketing value of six bushels, which last would be the marginal product of labor. However, the output per worker is 10 bushels, and this difference, amounting to 4 bushels per worker, will be paid, assuming no capital, to the owners of the land. The total land rent will be the value of 4 times 5,000,000, or 20,000,000 bushels, which sum is represented by the area $PABW$ in Fig. 44.

A rationally organized economy will not operate in either the first or third stage. If the population provided considerably less than about 3.5 million workers, the economy would not operate in the first stage, but on the boundary that separates this stage from the second, combining about three acres with a man and leaving some land area unused. Or, if there were over 7.5 million workers available, the economy would not operate in the third stage, but would allow the excess workers to remain unemployed. The reason for these assertions is that the marginal output of land is negative in the first stage and the marginal output of labor is negative in the third stage.

Comparisons of Efficiency

Is some combination of land and labor within the second stage more economically efficient than any other? In general, the best combination is that which entails the fullest possible employment of all the available land and labor without crossing the boundary into either the first or third stage. Ideally, the ratio of land rents to labor wages will then conform to the ratio of their marginal outputs, when both factors are fully employed. A capitalistic economy that succeeds in maintaining this equality will normally be more efficient than one that does not. Total production, from which the public's consumption must come, will then be at a maximum.

Intereconomy comparisons of output per acre or output per worker indicate little or nothing regarding economic efficiency. Output per cultivated acre is low in the United States as compared with Europe, but output per farm laborer is low in Europe as compared with the United States. Actually, it is quite impossible to infer from this whether agriculture is more efficient in one region than in the other. All that we can infer from these comparisons is that the land-to-labor ratio must be higher in the United States.

It would be folly to advocate public policies directed toward maximizing output per acre or output per worker. Output per acre can only be at a maximum if labor is employed as lavishly as though it were a free good. Output per worker can only be maximized if land can be combined in such quantities that its marginal output falls to zero, and this can happen only in the rather exceptional case where land, relative to other factors, is so abundant in supply that it is free. A more reasonable assumption is that all factors will be economic goods, rather than free goods, in which case the most economical use of *one* factor will prevent the most economical use of *all* factors in combination.

Specific Land Rent

In reality there are different qualities of land and the rent of each depends in part on its comparative productivity.

Let us suppose that there are four grades of land—A, B, C, and D—in a country where the population and supply of labor and capital are steadily increasing. Originally, there may have been enough Grade A land, relative to demand, for there to have been no rent. However, as population increased, all the Grade A land became employed, and, as soon as it was cultivated beyond the point of diminishing average physical returns, it began to exact rents. A little later a point was reached where producers had to pay such high rents for Grade A land that they began to use free Grade B land, because experience showed that the value of the crop raised on this inferior land just paid for the labor and capital used in its cultivation. Later on, as the need for land increased even further, all the Grade B land began to be cultivated beyond the point of diminishing returns, and so began to pay rent. Finally, as population expanded still more, agriculturalists began to use Grade C land, which just repays cultivation at zero rent, as an escape from paying moderate rents on B land and very high rents on A land. At the present time we shall suppose that D land is submarginal, C land is marginal, and that B and A land, especially the latter, are cultivated intensively and provide rents.

These effects of population increase on land use have been traced in detail because the basis of rent has sometimes been misunderstood.

A few writers appear to explain the existence of rent by reference to the cultivation of land of marginal quality. For instance, if C is marginal, and produces *x* bushels, they would measure the rent on B land by subtracting the value of *x* bushels from the value of the crop obtained from B land when similarly cultivated. Sometimes this explanation is called the *differential productivity theory* of land rent.

Actually, although this is a minor point, the better B land would be cultivated more intensely than the marginal C land; hence, if some more labor and capital are combined with B than C, a simple comparison of the value of their crops will not measure the better land's rent.

Unfortunately, and this is more serious, many readers infer that it is the *existence* of the poor marginal land that *causes* rent on the better land. Such a view is quite contrary to the truth. If the D, C, and B land were all suddenly flooded and hence no longer available for use, the A land would have to be cultivated more intensively than ever and would earn even higher rents. Actually, producers turn to the cultivation of poorer land to escape the payment of exorbitant rents for the use of the best land, which is in inadequate supply. Fundamentally, a piece of superior (B) quality land does not pay rent because it is more fertile than marginal (C) land, but because it is not too inferior in fertility to the use value of the very best (A) land.

The ultimate explanation of economic rent is the scarcity of first-class land. If there were so much of the best land available that it never had to be cultivated beyond the point of diminishing returns, there would be no rents. It is only because there is an insufficiency of the best land that poorer land is used. It is then approximately possible to *measure* the rent of a particular piece of land by comparing its output with either the best land or the marginal land. However, the kind of land that is marginal depends on the rents earned by the best land, which in turn depends on its relative scarcity.

Urban Site Rents

The rent theories of the classical economists ran in terms of agricultural land, but in the modern world the economist must supplement these earlier principles with an explanation of urban site rent, for it is in the cities that land is at a premium and rents may be a hundred dollars per inch of frontage a year.

In reality, agricultural and urban rent theories are not contrasting, but comprise part of a whole. It was always recognized that, as between two pieces of land of equal size and fertility, the one which lay closest to the market, in terms of freight costs, would earn the higher rent because its crop would command a higher net price per unit. Fertility is simply a special kind of productivity, when productivity means ability to command a stream of money receipts. Proximity to market is another form of productivity that may be more or less important than fertility in any given instance.

Commercial rents in a city are largely based on "closeness to market." However, the "market" is not an exchange but simply buyers passing up and down outside with money to spend. Hence, in a northern city, the pieces of land on the north side of downtown streets are "closer to the market," because people prefer to walk on the sunny side of the street. Site rents along Park Avenue are higher than on Seventh Avenue, two blocks away, not because more people walk up and down on Park Avenue, but because those that do have more money to spend. The concessions that rent space in Grand Central Station are very close to the market indeed because a Niagara of people goes by twice a day.

The important point about commercial site rents is that a given business, in a given kind of store, with a given collection of merchandise and salespeople, will be able to sell more, and at higher prices, at one location than another. The net income stream, before deducting site rent, may be $25,000 a year at the location where demand is stronger and $10,000 a year at some other location. In this event there will probably be a difference of $15,000 in the economic rent. And the capital value of the more desirable site, vacant, without improvement or construction, will be about two and a half times as great.

Naturally, a hundred and one circumstances affect the size and future, and hence the value, of the economic rent stream of each lot of urban land. In the case of retail stores, it is not only the number and affluence of people who pass by, but also the sort of people they are and the mood they are usually in. A soda fountain won't do on a street frequented by seamen and stevedores. People going through Grand Central are in a hurry, and so will not linger to buy a suit, but will stop momentarily for cigarettes.

It is important to realize that one site is not equally superior to another site for all sorts of businesses. A hat shop can be in the middle of a block but a drug store needs to be on a corner. The hat shop cannot afford the rents of the corner site and the drug store cannot afford the loss of not being on the corner. A dentist does not have to be on the ground floor and fronting the street, and hence never pays such rents, but a florist who saved expenses by setting up in a back office on the fourth floor would soon be out of business. Site rents help to sort different firms out and locate them at different places.

An old chestnut of an examination question in rent theory is whether a firm charges high prices because it has to pay a high rent or pays a high rent because it can charge high prices. For instance, a downtown parking lot may charge $1.00 an hour, and you may remonstrate, only to be told that the site rent is $90,000 a year and that an hourly charge of a dollar just permits the operator to break even. However it does not follow that prices are rent-determined. The parking lot business charges a dollar an hour because it can get enough desperate motorists to pay this price. The truth is that, while motorists must pay enough to pay the rent, the highest rent the parking lot operator will pay is based upon what motorists will pay. Prices are more rent-determining than rent-determined.

Occasionally, in built up areas, one sees a vacant and unused lot flanked by tall buildings on either side. Whoever the owner is, he must be having a thin time of it, what with taxes and no gross income, and one may wonder what he thinks he is doing. Logically, if affairs were always static, it would be most irrational for any real estate owner to withhold his land from use. However, when a city or area is developing rapidly, such speculative action may be profitable. A piece of land might make a profitable apartment house site in five years' time, but if the apartments were built today they would operate at a loss. On the other hand, even though a store building might be profitable today, its existence five years from now will prevent the building of the apartment. It is seldom worth while to erect one kind of building only to tear it down soon after. If building were less specialized, and if cities did not develop rapidly, owners would not withhold land from use. As it is, if the development is not as rapid as they anticipated, they may suffer losses on their speculation.

Of course, a great deal of urban land is not used for business but for residence. The value of such land is not based upon productivity but upon utility. Commuting time and distance, proximity to stores and schools, and perhaps a view are important aspects of utility for the householder. Suburban land is in joint demand with housing, and so, if the cost of lumber and hence of house construction goes down, the value of home sites may rise, other things remaining equal. The size of suburban lots also depends on several factors. The tract owner who plans a subdivision naturally wishes to realize the largest possible receipts. If gardeners' wages and water rates are rising, the subdivider knows that people will want smaller gardens. He also knows that the better-to-do spend relatively more on grounds than houses. Hence, if the tract is in an unfashionable district, flat, without a view, and near a gas works, upper income families will not be interested, and the lots had better be as small as practicable.

The Rent Concept

One reason why land rent was originally explained by a special theory was that the completely inelastic supply of land supposedly rendered land and its rent quite distinctive from the income of any other productive agent. This view has become substantially modified. It is now recognized that the supply of land for any particular use is not absolutely inelastic because the supply of land in general is. It is now also recognized that in many short-run situations some other productive asset may be in inflexible supply.

Land is obviously not homogeneous but heterogeneous. Different pieces have different uses. For example, nearly all arable land is suitable for grazing but not for mining, whereas a great deal of mining country is suitable for grazing but not for cultivation.

Let us suppose that A, B, and C are three uses for land, and that their alphabetical order is the order of their current financial value. Some of the existing land is suitable only for C, some for C and B, and the rest for C, B, and A. At the moment all the C and B land is in B use, and all the C, B, and A land is in A use. However, the demand for the output of the land in C use increases enormously, and hence the demand for C-use land does also. As the rent obtainable by land in C use rises, the B- and C-use land will be put to C use, but only when the rents paid by C users equal or exceed the rents paid by B users. And later, if the rent of land in C use rises further, the B-, C-, and A-use land will be put into C use, but again only when the rents paid by C users equal or exceed those paid by A users. In this case, the supply schedule of land for C use is not vertical but is positively inclined.

The early economists thought of land as having a zero supply price and a zero elasticity of supply, but this is only logical if land has only one use or is uniform in character. If the attributes of different pieces of land differ and there are various competing uses for different pieces, each piece of land has a minimum supply price, based on its most profitable alternative use of the moment.

Hence the supply curve of land, for a given use, is not vertical but positively inclined, because extra land for this use can be bid away from more and more profitable alternative employments.

Some economists of today have gone so far as to define the rent of land in a particular use as the surplus it obtains over what it would obtain in its next most profitable use. Land rent is then tantamount to the per acre suppliers' surplus of land owners. The earlier view was that land rent was identical with the net earnings per acre. Here is a case where either or both concepts can serve so long as they are always properly defined.

The next question is whether land alone earns a rent in either one of these senses. The actual operations of any firm include certain fixed costs. Sometimes the fixed element in the situation is the land being used, but sometimes it is the building and equipment of a plant, or it may even be the management. If the demand for the firm's output increases, the fixed elements earn a sort of rent, because the increase in total sales receipts will exceed the increase in the total cost of the variable elements. Consider the case of an automobile toll bridge, such as the San Francisco Bay Bridge, located in an area of increasing traffic density. As the stream of automobiles across the bridge lengthens and widens, more toll takers are added and more revenues are collected, but no more bridges spring up. The existing bridge earns a sort of rent because of its fixity of supply. However we call this a quasi-rent—"quasi" means "seeming"—because it is best to reserve the term "rent" for the earnings of land.

Should Rents Be Paid for Using Land?

Social reformers are fond of pointing out that there is no economic necessity to pay rent for the use of land. In a limited sense they are perfectly correct. If all the land owners died tonight in their sleep—and this is a better fate than some reformers would admit they deserve—the indestructible powers of the economy's natural resources would still be available for use tomorrow. The land is there, physically available for use or enjoyment, irrespective of ownership or owners.

Explicit land rent depends in part upon the institution of private property. The power of an owner to control the use of his land or dispose of it as he sees fit is not a natural right but one that has been accorded him by custom and law. No one would pay for the use of land if there were no such thing as private ownership of land.

It is sometimes said that rent is an unearned income because the land owner does not contribute anything personally to the services of his land. The crop sprouts from the land and not from its owner, and the location of a site does not depend on the location of its owner, so why should he receive a reward for nothing. Such a criticism would have weight if most land had originally been acquired gratis, by legal trickery, armed invasion, and the like. However, the present owners of most natural resources bought their land as an investment. Presumably they obtained the purchase price honestly. Some people have acquired land out of savings from wages and salaries. The purchase price of a piece of land, like that of any other asset, tends to be the capitalized value of the estimated income stream. Investors in bonds and stocks should not receive interest and dividends if investors in land ought not to receive rent. If the receipt of rent is ever unjustifiable on moral grounds, it is not because the owner can collect while lying in bed, but because, in some instances, the land was acquired improperly.

It is frequently forgotten that land rent performs a most useful function in a free enterprise economy. If land is scarce, rents are high. If rents are high, producers will not use land for less essential purposes and householders will build their homes on smaller lots. As land becomes scarcer and rents become higher, the more frivolous uses of land tend to be abandoned. The existing rent structure allocates land among different uses just as the pricing system in effect rations other goods and services in a rough and ready manner.

Even if a government prevented the payment of *explicit* rent by declaring such payments illegal, it could never eliminate *implicit* rent. The cultivation of superior land will always yield a surplus, after the other factors have been paid, law or no law. Superficially this surplus would appear as profits, if the use of land never legally costs anything, but actually it is attributable to the land rather than the entrepreneur, and so it is really implicit rent.

A socialist economy, in which all the land was publicly owned, would obtain extra production by using good land rather than bad land. Moreover, it would soon find that a given piece of superior land might have a more valuable surplus when put to one use than to another. If it were a wise socialist government, it would record the higher of the two implicit rents as a cost of production in its accounting books, in order to guard against the land's being used in less satisfactory ways. Economically the payment of rent is unnecessary to obtain the service of land, but it is most useful as a guide to its optimum use.

Statements for Consideration

1. Under certain circumstances it would be more economical to leave some land, although of similar fertility to employed land, out of cultivation. *Discuss*
2. One aspect of land productivity is "closeness to market." *Exemplify*
3. American wheat land is less fertile than European as evidenced by its lower yield per acre. *Evaluate*
4. The existence of low-grade but cultivated land reduces the rents on the best land. *Explain*
5. Land use is essential to production, but the land owner is not, and hence the payment of economic rent to present owners is morally unjustifiable. *Evaluate*
6. An intelligent farmer who is employing two scarce factors of production should combine them so that the output per unit of one of them is at a maximum. *Evaluate*
7. The theory of urban rent is essentially different from that of agricultural land rent and the two cannot be reconciled. *Evaluate*
8. Firms that pay high land rents must necessarily charge high prices. *Evaluate*
9. The existence of vacant and unused lots in downtown city sections cannot be explained or justified on economic grounds. *Evaluate*
10. The modern concept of rent is akin to that of suppliers' surplus based on alternative earnings opportunities. *Discuss*
11. It is perhaps the manner in which land owners acquired their property, rather than their individual contributions to output, that should determine their moral eligibility to receive rent. *Discuss*

References

Boulding, K. E., "The Concept of Economic Surplus," *American Economic Review,* December 1945. Also in *Readings in the Theory of Income Distribution.*

Buchanan, D. H., "The Historical Approach to Rent and Price Theory," *Economica,* vol. IX, June 1929. Also in *Readings in the Theory of Income Distribution.*

Due, J. F., *Intermediate Economic Analysis,* Chapter 9. Chicago: Irwin, 1947.

Enke, S., "Space and Value," *Quarterly Journal of Economics*, August 1942.
Garver, F. B., and Hansen, A. H., *Principles of Economics*, Chapter 24. New York: Ginn, 1947.
Marshall, A., *Principles of Economics*, Eighth Edition, Book VI, Chapter 9. London: Macmillan, 1920.
Meade, J. E., and Hitch, C. J., *An Introduction to Economic Analysis and Policy*, IV. New York: Oxford University Press, 1938.
Meyers, A. L., *Modern Economics*, Chapter 24. New York: Prentice-Hall, 1941.

30

Interest on Capital

IT USED to be said that interest was the income of capital and was a reward of waiting. More recently it has been said that interest is the price people demand as compensation for sacrificing liquidity when they loan money. The existence of interest has been explained in terms of time preferences, liquidity preferences, and the superior productivity of certain roundabout methods of production. Superficially these theories seem to be in conflict, and in the aggregate they tend to be confusing. However, despite the use of different terms and alternative viewpoints, most of the theories that have been accepted at different times are reconcilable, and in fact constitute most useful supplements to one another. The three blind men, each separately feeling the elephant's trunk, leg, and side, may have thought that it resembled a rope, a tree and a wall, as the case might be; and, in a limited way, they were all correct. So it has been with each economist, bent on discovering the basis of interest, who may have sensed one, but not all, of its numerous facets.

Who Pays Interest?

Interest is supposed to be a price. Who pays interest to whom and what exactly changes hands as a result? It is probably accurate enough to say, as a first approximation, that interest is the price paid for the use of another's money. Loanable funds is another term for money that is temporarily placed in the control of someone else. Interest is paid on loanable funds by borrowers to lenders.

Borrowers are of various kinds. Some borrowers are consumers who wish to consume at a higher rate than their incomes permit. Some borrowers are producers who want to invest additional funds in increased materials inventories or enlarged plant facilities. Some borrowers may simply wish to hold more money, perhaps

441

because they expect goods and security prices to fall, and this group may comprise consumers and producers. On the other side of the loanable funds market are the lenders, some of whom are consumers who prefer to save part of their incomes, producers who feel that inventories and plants are unjustifiably large, and people who find themselves with more money than they need for transaction purposes and would prefer to hold this wealth in the form of an interest-bearing loan.

The interest rate must, among other things, equate the supply of loanable funds with the demand for them. Their demand comes from dissavers of consumer income, producer goods investors, and hoarders of money. The supply comes from savers of consumer income, disinvesting producers, and dishoarders of money stocks.

Motives of Borrowers and Lenders

Borrowers and lenders may have a variety of motives. Time preference and the special productivity of most capital goods are motives that have long been recognized. The modern income theory school has emphasized liquidity preference.

Time Preference

A consumer might prefer to have the spending of $100 now to the spending of $110 one year from today. He would then be said to have a time preference of 10 per cent. Such a time preference may depend on several circumstances. His income today may be very low (in which case his marginal utility of a dollar will be high) and he may expect to be earning a good salary or to inherit an estate very soon (at which time the utility of his marginal dollar will be comparatively low). On the other hand, some people may have a time preference that is low, or even negative, examples being people who anticipate a sudden fall in income or the acquisition of new family responsibilities. A man is likely to borrow funds if his time preference exceeds the interest rate and to lend funds if the interest rate exceeds his time preference. There is always a tendency for time preferences to be lower in the case of wealthy people with large incomes, because they are not particularly anxious to increase their current consumption, and so they find it easier to save and are more likely to lend. If all loans were directly related to the rate of consumption and were not used for productive investing or cash hoarding, the rate of interest would approximate the average time preference rate of the community. The community's time preference is probably positive, because of a psychological predilection toward over-weighting the present relative to the future, a bias that is particularly strong among those groups whose low and uncertain incomes force them to live from hand to mouth.

Productivity of Capital

Most efficient methods of production are roundabout. In the long run, a producer of cotton cloth, for instance, finds it both cheaper and quicker to produce a large output if he first subdivides the various operations and then acquires complex and costly machines to perform them with the help of a little direct labor. In other words, he proceeds indirectly.

It is not the fact of their roundaboutness that makes capitalistic processes more productive. The famous Rube Goldberg contraptions are extremely roundabout but hopelessly unproductive. However, in a well-conducted economy, one only sees in operation plants and processes that are so specially productive that they justify their extra roundaboutness.

Roundabout methods of production involve large outlays of capital funds. In fact the ratio of fixed capital to gross receipts might be used as a measure of roundaboutness. The producer may spend millions of dollars for plant and equipment and materials in process before he receives a cent from sales. He will only invest in these things if, in addition to recovering the principal, he can obtain a rate of return at least as great as the rate of interest. The rate of return on the marginally invested dollar is of crucial importance and will normally differ from the average rate of return on the entire investment. A producer will usually invest additional funds if the marginal rate of return promises to be greater than the interest rate. Conversely, if it is expected to be less, the producer may not fully replace depreciated assets, and so partially disinvest. The marginal rates of return of all producers should equal the interest rate and so be equal to one another; but the average rates of return, which is the concept most often considered in the financial world, will usually differ.

Liquidity Preference

Several considerations that lead people to hold some of their wealth in the form of liquid money instead of investments have already been given (see Chapter 11). Most people, for example, find it necessary to hold certain minimum average amounts of money, simply because of the impossibility of exactly synchronizing receipts and expenditures, and this is often termed the transactionary motive. People who have a fairly low liquidity preference will normally be glad to relinquish their cash and balances if a borrower will pay them a high enough interest rate. Theoretically, one may expect everyone, individuals and corporations, to adjust their cash holdings until their marginal liquidity preference is matched by the rate of interest.

The Demand and Supply of Loanable Funds

Since the interest rate is a price, it must equate the demand and supply of one or more things. Actually the rate of interest is an equilibrium price in three different senses. One of these equations is that of the demand and supply of loanable funds.

Equations of an Individual

These matters can best be understood if we first consider the monetary equations of an individual. A person receives, during a given time period, a certain factor income (y), which he may consume (c), invest in productive assets (i), add to his money holdings, pocket money, or bank balances (h), or loan out to others (l). Symbolically then,

$$y - c - i - h = l.$$

This can be abbreviated a little by substituting savings (s) for $y - c$.

Obviously this relation can be restated in the form of alternative equations; for example, $s - i = h + l$; which means that the excess of a man's sumptuary savings over his direct productive investments must either be banked away or loaned out.

Each one of these terms has an opposite, of course. If c exceeds y, there will be dissaving and s will be negative. The opposite of investment is disinvestment $(-i)$. The opposite of hoarding bank balances and pocket money is dishoarding $(-h)$; and the opposite of lending is borrowing $(-l)$.

We can now define a lender and a borrower. A man loans money if $s - i - h > 0$ and he borrows money if $s - i - h < 0$. This can be verbally paraphrased in many ways. For instance, a man will lend if his uninvested saving $(s - i)$ exceeds his rate of hoarded bank balances (h); and a man borrows if his rate of dissaving $(-s)$ exceeds his rate of combined disinvestment $(-i)$ and dishoarding $(-h)$.

These equations are valid for a single household or firm or local government. In the case of a corporation, y is profits and c is dividend payments. Corporate saving must either be reinvested, hoarded, or loaned out.

The Loanable Funds Market

In every economy there are lenders and borrowers. However, the entire economic population need not fall into one or the other of these two classifications, and in practice there are bound to be many people for whom $s - i - h$ equals zero. Moreover, a man who may be a borrower when interest and income are low may switch roles and become a lender when interest and income are high. Presumably, for the whole economy, there is one interest rate which, given the general level of incomes, will equate the dollar value of the funds supplied by lenders and demanded by borrowers.

The market for loanable funds can be charted, after the manner of Fig. 45, if we disregard income changes for the time being. The vertical axis represents the rate of interest and the horizontal axis the number of dollars lent or borrowed, and so on. L is the schedule of loanable funds that lenders will supply, and B is the schedule of loanable funds that borrowers will demand, at different interest rates, given the income level.

The L schedule is the sum of three subsidiary elements: the net savings of would-be lenders (S); the net real disinvestment of would-be lenders, which is represented by $S + Di$ when algebraically added to S; and the net dishoarding of would-be lenders (which is represented by L minus $S + Di$). In the figure, the three schedules that relate to would-be lenders (i.e., S, $S + Di$, and L) all diverge from one another horizontally as the interest rate rises, which means that we have assumed a higher rate of net saving, net disinvestment, and net dishoarding at higher rates of interest. This is not an unreasonable assumption. It is usually supposed that people are encouraged to save more at high interest

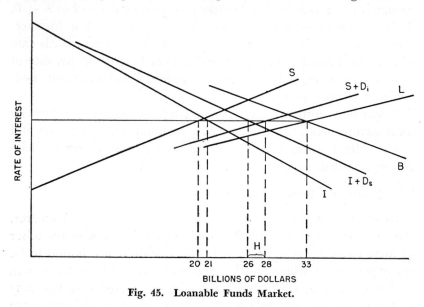

Fig. 45. Loanable Funds Market.

rates. Also at relatively high rates of interest, it is more difficult to find direct investments that will pay a rate of return commensurate with the interest rate, in which case people will make fewer direct investments and may deliberately undertake more disinvestment; in the figure it has been assumed that would-be lenders, as a group, disinvest rather than invest. Similarly, in the case of hoarding and dishoarding, it is generally supposed that people will wish to keep a smaller stock of money under their control at high rates of interest, and it has been supposed that would-be lenders, as a group, dishoard rather than hoard, although perhaps by only a small margin. Briefly, while *some* lenders may dissave, or invest, or hoard, it has been supposed that, on balance and *as a group*, would-be lenders occasion net savings, net disinvestment, and net dishoarding.

On the other hand, it has been supposed that, *as a group*, would-be borrowers occasion net investment, net dissaving, and net hoarding, although naturally some borrowers may disinvest, or save, or dishoard. However, no person could do all three and still be a borrower, of course. The *B* schedule is also composed of three elements. One of these is the net direct investment of the borrowing group (I), another is the net dissaving of borrowers (shown in the figure as $I + Ds$ when added algebraically), and the remaining element is the hoarding of borrowers (which is the horizontal distance of B minus $I + Ds$).

The equilibrium rate of interest (r) naturally equates lending (L) and borrowing (B) in the market sense. However, so long as part of the economic population are neither lenders nor borrowers at this interest rate, there is no necessity for the savings of lenders to be exactly equal to the investments of borrowers, and so on. For example, in the diagram, the savings of lenders are $20 billions while the direct investments of borrowers are $21 billions, lenders' disinvestment is $8 billions while borrowers' dissaving is $5 billions, and the dishoarding of lenders is $5 billions while the hoarding of borrowers is $7 billions. These various discrepancies must cancel each other out in the aggregate, at the equilibrium rate of interest, for otherwise the total demand and supply of loanable funds would not be equal.

Loanable Funds and Aggregate Investment

We already know that, for the economy as a whole, investment and saving are not only equal but virtually identical by definition. However, it has just been stated that the savings of lenders do not need to equal the investments of borrowers when the loanable funds market is in equilibrium. In order to understand this superficial paradox it is necessary to investigate further the relation of loanable funds to other economic aggregates such as total investment.

The economic population can be classified at any moment as lenders, borrowers, or neither. Everyone must fill one of these roles, and only one, at the same time. Hence, because investment and saving for the economy are identical, it follows that any discrepancy between the combined saving and combined investment of lenders and borrowers must be canceled by an opposite discrepancy on the part of those who are neither one nor the other.

Table 33, which is based on the equilibrium situation in the loanable funds market shown in Fig. 45, shows that the combined savings of lenders and borrowers ($15 billions) exceeded their combined investments ($13 billions) by $2 billions, which they collectively hoarded. However, the rest of the economic population invested $2 billions more than it saved, which it could only do through dishoarding. The economy as a whole had an income that exceeded its consumption by $17 billions and so this is necessarily the value of its aggregate savings and investment combined.

TABLE 33

SCHEDULES OF BORROWERS AND LENDERS

	Net Income (Y)	Net Consumption (C)	Net Saving (S)	Net Investment (I)	Net Hoarding (H)	Net Lending (L)
Lenders	90	70	+20	− 8	−5	+33
Borrowers	80	85	− 5	+21	+7	−33
Lenders and Borrowers	170	155	+15	+13	+2	0
All Others	30	28	+ 2	+ 4	−2	0
Economy Net Total	200	183	+17	+17	0	0

Note: A minus sign denotes dissaving, disinvestment, dishoarding, or borrowing if it refers to saving, investment, hoarding, or lending respectively.

It is worth noting that the $33 billions loaned and borrowed during the period under review is a far larger sum than the value of the economy's net investments. Examination of the table shows that lenders not only saved but undertook direct disinvestments. Also it can be seen that borrowers not only invested directly but dissaved. The exchange of loanable funds was swollen even further by the fact that lenders were assumed to be dishoarding while borrowers were hoarding.

The net hoarding of the economy is zero in the table. Unless there is a change in the total stock of money, there can be no net hoarding or dishoarding for the economy as a whole. The available stock of money is always held by someone.

The situation is a little more complicated if we think of an economy in which the banking system or the central government is creating or destroying legal tender and checking balances. The equation for the Treasury and for each commercial bank contains one more term than that of an individual household, firm, or local government, being $s - i - h + m = l$, where m is the amount of newly created money. Then, summing for the economy as a whole, and using upper case letters to denote these aggregates, we have

$$S - I - H + M = L$$

If there has been an increase in the economy's money stock, M will be positive and also equal to H. The reasoning is as follows. For the entire economy, there can no more be net lending than there can be net selling, and so L must be zero when the lending and borrowing operations of all households, firms, governments, and banks are lumped together. The economy's savings equal the economy's investments. Hence $M = H$. In other words, the net increase in checking balances and pocket cash is equal to the increase in the effective money stock during the period.

It is noteworthy that the magnitudes of S, I, and H depend on a different set of facts and motives. Saving and dissaving depend on time preference, investment and disinvestment on the productivity of roundabout methods of production, and hoarding and dishoarding on liquidity preferences.

Full Equilibrium and the Interest Rate

An economy will not be in full equilibrium unless the prevailing rate of interest and level of income permits an equation of (1) the demand and supply of loanable funds, (2) the demand for money to hold with the existing stock of money, and (3) the intention to invest with the intention to save.

There is probably only one level of income which, for a given economy at a given time, will permit one and the same rate of interest to perform all the three equations cited immediately above. It has already been shown, in Part III, that a rising income normally increases the demand for money to hoard, and so raises what may be termed the liquidity interest rate. It was also shown that a rising income permits an equation of intended investment and intended saving at what may be termed a lower investment interest rate. How does a change in national income affect the interest rate that will bring equilibrium to the loanable funds market?

Lenders and borrowers will together tend, as national income rises, to save considerably more and invest somewhat more. Hence, the combined group will have more funds available for hoarding or lending. The interest rate tends to fall if this increase in funds is greater than the increased demand to hold money.

The market for loanable funds provides a nexus, within the

economy, between equated savings and investment on the one hand and equated money stock and aggregate private holdings on the other. It is a sort of battleground where people who wish to invest more with borrowed funds can struggle for them against people who wish to hoard more through borrowing. It is also a place where people who wish to lend their savings must compete against people who wish to loan their dishoardings. The competition is rendered no less real for the *individuals* involved because of the fact that savings must equal investment and that money hoards cannot change unless the economy's stock of money is altered.

In periods of disequilibrium, the lending interest rate probably lies between the investment interest rate and the liquidity interest rate. In full equilibrium all three interest rates should be identical. The attainment of equilibrium is due largely to adjustments in the income level resulting from transactions in the loanable funds market.

Function and Justification of Interest

Is it fair that people should earn interest on money they loan and does this practice perform any useful economic function?

No economy can produce at a high rate unless it uses roundabout methods of production. This is a technological fact; it is divorced from all such issues as free enterprise *versus* state socialism. The U.S.S.R., for example, is straining every nerve to become more capitalistic, in the sense of adopting more roundabout productive methods.

It is quite conceivable, of course, that an economy might become so capitalistic that the addition of a little more capital, in the form of some still more complex and capitalistic plant or process, might add nothing net to output, in which case that economy would have reached what we shall term the capital saturation point. However, it is most unlikely that any actual nation has reached that point yet. Meanwhile every economy is confronted by two important problems. How shall it decide which of many alternative roundabout methods to adopt? How fast shall it proceed toward capital saturation?

The rate of interest selects the more efficient capitalistic processes and rejects the less efficient. No producer in a free enterprise system will rationally and knowingly invest in capitalistic or roundabout methods of production that do not offer marginal rates of return greater than or equal to the interest rate. Under state socialism there may be no explicit interest rate, but it is just as important, albeit perhaps more difficult, that the more efficient equipment and methods be adopted first.

It is evident that an economy would proceed more rapidly along the path leading to capital saturation if loanable funds were available in sufficient amounts at almost zero rates of interest. The producers of a free enterprise economy would then adopt more roundabout methods of production and it would pay to construct such assets as buildings and public works so that they would be more durable. However, all these changes are likely to reduce current consumption, if an increasing volume of resources is being devoted now to providing future output, shelter, and the like. The marginal time preferences of individuals are likely to rise as their consumption levels fall. Eventually this should cause higher interest rates again and this would deter direct investments. It is approximately true that the rate of real capital accumulation (i.e., investment) is a compromise between producers (who anticipate a marginal rate of return from more roundabout methods) and the consuming public (which wants to be satisfied now rather than later).

It would seem that the rate of interest is an economic regulator of great importance. It performs functions that are not provided by any other institution of a free enterprise economy. A socialist economy regulates these matters in other ways, which may be better or worse in their effects.

However, the question still remains, "What does interest reward?" Wages reward the work of labor and rents supposedly reward landlords for the use of natural resources. Interest must reward somebody for something.

Interest is only obtained by a person if the sum of his lending and investing is positive. Algebraically, this requires that his income exceed the sum of his consuming and hoarding, or that his saving exceed his hoarding. Savings will not earn interest if they are hoarded. Dishoarding will not earn interest if hoarded funds are dissaved through extra consumption or less income. Saving alone is not enough, and dishoarding alone is not enough to earn interest. What is required is saving without hoarding or dishoarding with saving. Interest is the reward for resisting *both* time preferences and liquidity preferences.

It does not necessarily follow that the *actual* recipients of interest payments are morally entitled to them. People enjoying large incomes and possessing great wealth tend to lend or invest because they have low rates of time preference and liquidity preference relative to others. If they are not morally entitled to their income and wealth, they may not be able to justify their receipt of interest. In this connection one should perhaps distinguish between income from inherited wealth and income that has been directly or indirectly earned by the recipient. Interest obtained on loans or investments saved from wages and salaries cannot justifiably be stigmatized as unearned.

Statements for Consideration

1. Some economists say that interest is the reward for waiting, others that it is the reward for sacrificing liquidity; since it cannot be a reward for both, it is time the economists made up their minds.
Evaluate

2. Young men who are still receiving professional training quite properly have high time preferences as a rule.   *Explain*

3. All roundabout methods of production are more efficient than less roundabout techniques, but their extra productivity may be insufficient to warrant their innovation at current interest rates.
Evaluate

4. There would be no lending or borrowing if there were no such thing as liquidity preferences.   *Evaluate*

5. Whether one can justify interest income depends rather upon whether one can justify the existing distribution of wealth.
Discuss

6. Only borrowers have liquidity preferences and only lenders have time preferences.   *Evaluate*

7. Anyone can enjoy interest income who will consume less than his earnings and consequently save.   *Evaluate*

8. The net savings of lenders must equal the net investments of borrowers because actual saving and actual investment must be equal for the economy as a whole.   *Evaluate*

9. Time preference is only an economic consideration in capitalistic countries, but it is economically irrelevant in the Soviet Union.
Evaluate

10. The liquidity theory of interest concerns stock concepts but the time preference theory of interest concerns flow concepts.
Explain

References

Bain, J. S., *Pricing, Distribution and Employment*, Chapters 11, 12. New York: Holt, 1948.

Due, J. F., *Intermediate Economic Analysis*, Chapter 10. Chicago: Irwin, 1947.

Garver, F. B., and Hansen, A. H., *Principles of Economics*, Third Edition, Chapter 25. New York: Ginn, 1947.

Hicks, J. R., "Mr. Keynes and the 'Classics'; A Suggested Interpretation," *Econometrica*, vol. V, 1937. Also in *Readings in the Theory of Income Distribution*.

Keynes, J. M., "Alternative Theories of the Rate of Interest," *Economic Journal*, June 1937.

Keynes, J. M., "The Theory of the Rate of Interest," *The Lessons of Monetary Experience; Essays in Honor of Irving Fisher*, 1937. Also in *Readings in the Theory of Income Distribution*.

Knight, F. H., "Capital and Interest," *Encyclopaedia Britannica*, vol. IV, 1946. Also in *Readings in the Theory of Income Distribution*.

Lerner, A. P., *The Economics of Control*, Chapter 25. New York: Macmillan, 1945.

Lerner, A. P., "Alternative Formulation of the Rate of Interest," *Economic Journal*, June 1938. Also in *The New Economics*.

Lerner, A. P., "Interest Theory—Supply and Demand for Loans or Supply and Demand for Cash," *Review of Economics and Statistics*, May 1944. Also in *The New Economics*.

Lindahl, E., *Studies in the Theory of Money and Capital*, Part II. New York: Farrar, 1940.

Marshall, A., *Principles of Economics*, Eighth Edition, Book VI, Chapter 6. London: Macmillan, 1920.

Meyers, A. L., *Modern Economics*, Chapter 23. New York: Prentice-Hall, 1946.

Taussig, F. W., *Principles of Economics*, Chapters 38–40. New York: Macmillan, 1939.

von Hayek, F. A., "The Mythology of Capital," *Quarterly Journal of Economics*, L, February 1936. Also in *Readings in the Theory of Income Distribution*.

31

Profits of Entrepreneurship

THERE IS general agreement among economists to apply the name profits to the income that rewards entrepreneurship. However, not every writer has the same concept of entrepreneurship in his mind when he seeks to explain the origin and magnitude of profits, and it is therefore not surprising that writers frequently offer different profit theories. In general, we shall take the view that entrepreneurship comprises all the functions not usually supposed to pertain to the other three productive factors.

The Functions of Entrepreneurship

Logically, if all income from production can be classified as wages, rent, interest, or profits, it follows that entrepreneurship comprises all those productive functions that are not thought to be rewarded by wages, rent, or interest. The entrepreneurial function is then conceived as including all productive contributions that are not routine human effort, do not involve the use of indestructible natural resources, and do not entail the provision of capital funds. Entrepreneurship according to this view is a residual function, just as profits are often described as residual income.

Up to a point it is a fairly simple matter to say what functions are not included as entrepreneurship and hence are not rewarded by profits. Profits are not a payment for the use of the indestructible power of natural resources, even when the land is owned rather than leased by the producing unit. Profits are not a payment for the labor of a manager, who carries out a business plan of campaign drawn up by a higher authority or simply handles familiar problems in a manner that is both prescribed and routine. The acid test of whether a management's functions are those of labor or entrepreneurship is where its responsibility is limited or complete. As compared with this test, it makes little difference

454

whether a manager is employed at a fixed salary or participates in residual net income, either by way of a bonus or as the right of a part owner. Profits are not a payment for the use of capital funds when the loan is well secured and the risk of financial loss for the lender is slight. The owner of a bond, which has valuable and liquid assets as specific security, has relatively little risk of losing his principal, and in this example the payment is interest. However, the owners of common stock, and also of preferred stock in most instances, bear too much risk just to be investing for pure interest. Naturally there are many borderline cases, but the relatively riskless provision of capital funds, especially when the manner in which they are to be used is determined by others, is not an entrepreneurial function.

A more positive attempt to define what entrepreneurship is, rather than what it is not, would certainly include such things as risk taking, originating, and the combining of factors.

The risk-taking element involved in entrepreneurship is obvious enough. Profits are what is left after every other factor of production has been rewarded. Although the other factors may bear some degree of risk, their rewards are relatively certain, and so any untoward development is borne primarily by the entrepreneurial group, although naturally it seeks to pass its misfortunes on to other factors if it can. However, profits bear the first impact of an adverse change, and so it is sometimes said that the entrepreneurial group assumes the "front-line trench risk." In this connection it is worth remarking that profits are the only productive factor income that ever becomes negative.

If there were no new products, no new ways of making them, and no possibility of creating new profit opportunities, there would be no need for businesses to be conducted by imaginative, experimental, and venturesome people, and those who provided capital funds could escape many actual risks. Each business would be run in the same way; routine-minded managers could be hired at fixed salaries and needed capital borrowed for interest. In a stationary economy, where technological progress was absent, even business owners would have no entrepreneurial functions to perform.

No producing unit can begin to operate until land, labor, and capital have been brought together. The other productive factors have to be organized by entrepreneurship before goods and services can be supplied. No other factor attempts to perform this function of combining productive resources.

Entrepreneurship performs all three functions of risk taking, originating, and combining, and possibly more besides. However, an entrepreneur is not anyone who does just one of these three things. For example, a speculator in grains takes risks, but he does not innovate or combine factors and does not function as an entrepreneur. An inventor may originate a new process, but this is not entrepreneurship unless he risks funds in making or using the new method. A man may be asked by his government to produce a specified good under a cost-plus-fixed-fee contract, in which case there is no real risk, originality, or entrepreneurship.

Up to this point, there has been frequent mention of "entrepreneurship," but the term "entrepreneur" has rarely been used in this chapter. The reason for this is that the entrepreneurial function may be performed, not by one man, but by several men, and some of these may simultaneously be providing land, labor, and capital also. Historically, of course, and especially during the earlier part of the industrial revolution, the new manufacturing firms were usually financed and managed by their owners. Many economists consequently have identified ownership with entrepreneurship. However, in the case of a large modern corporation, while the stockholders are legally the owners, it is the directors and officers who originate and determine business strategy, generally with little financial risk to themselves. Thus the entrepreneurial function has become diffused among many persons. It is invalid to suppose that *one* man will always and necessarily perform *all* the entrepreneurial functions and *none* of the functions of the *other* three productive factors.

Determining Economic Profits

It is extremely difficult to estimate the exact magnitude of pure profits with any accuracy. Part of the interest of bondholders and part of the salaries and bonuses of top officials may be economic profit as here defined. Part of the dividends of shareholders and part of the net income of proprietors may not be profits. The economic concepts of entrepreneurship and profits are not recognized in the contracts and business relations of the commercial world.

A simple illustration may indicate some of the ways in which ordinary accounting statements must be modified in order to isolate pure profits. Let us suppose that a man owns and operates a store. For a given year his sales revenue was $50,000 and the cost of merchandise sold was $28,000, leaving him a gross profit of $22,000. Cost of doing business, which includes such things as wages, utilities, depreciation, and taxes, totaled $18,000, leaving the proprietor an apparent profit of $4,000. However, the proprietor cannot determine his profits until he has computed the income he should pay himself for the land, labor, and capital he has devoted to the business. He might have had the opportunity of earning an alternative income of $3,600 a year as the salaried store manager of a large grocery chain. He might have been able to lease the store for $5,000 a year. He may have invested, as a working capital fund, about $6,000, and on this investment, assuming a basic and safe interest rate of 4 per cent, he should receive $240 a year. Altogether his opportunity costs, that is the alternative income he could have obtained from the productive factors he devoted to the business, are $8,840. His economic profits are minus $4,840. The significance of these negative profits is that he would be $4,840 better off if he had let others use the productive factors that he devoted to his business. Meanwhile, as a result of his ineffectual proprietorship, he and his family have a net income of $4,000 a year to live on.

Under competitive conditions, with no producers enjoying permanent advantages, pure profits would tend toward zero if there were always sufficient time for all firms to make all necessary adjustments to each new circumstance. There would no longer be any entrepreneurial functions left to perform by the time full equilibrium was finally reached. However, this does not mean that active proprietors would starve toward the end of the adjustment period, because they would still be able to live off implicit and self-paid wages, interest, and rents.

Single Firm Profits

It is very evident that the profits or losses of a *single* firm in any *one* year are largely due to circumstances beyond the control of the producer. Examples are an unexpected change in demand, a strike that interrupts shipments or supplies, a new fiscal policy, tariff changes, a higher legal minimum wage, new freight rate charges, and so on. The economic weather of the year—i.e., business conditions throughout the country—can occasionally provide the most inefficient firm with profits or the most efficient firm with losses. The financial showing of a single year has little to do with entrepreneurial policies or personalities. Much of the profits of exceptionally good years are windfalls even if the management does preen itself on the results. There is little difficulty attached to explaining the causes of one year's profits or losses.

A more difficult matter is to explain how some firms earn substantial annual profits with fair regularity. All the really large corporations in the United States have had many years of large profits and only a few years of small losses. No one needs to be told that such firms exist, but not everybody can tell the source of these sustained and average profits.

Cheaply Acquired Assets

It is clear that a firm can make a profit if in some way it acquires assets at a cost that is far below their actual or subsequent real value to the concern. Mineral lands may be obtained from previous owners who did not understand their real worth. Tariff protection may be obtained in return for very modest outlays on lobbying and political campaigns. A valuable patent monopoly may be established because an unworldly inventor was hired as an employee at low salary. Profitable companies usually enjoy advantages or possess assets that they obtained for far less than their use value. Some of these advantages and assets may give the owning firm a legal or effective monopoly. However, it is not the possession of a partial monopoly that leads to profits. The real requirement is that the monopoly power be more valuable than its cost of acquisition.

Run of Luck

One rather agnostic theory of how some firms repeatedly earn profits is that these concerns experience a prolonged run of luck. After all, there are several million firms in the country, and so, if we think of each year as a gamble having an even chance of bringing either profits or losses, probability theory alone could explain the growth and emergence of a few giant corporations as well as the eventual demise of most of the remainder. Probability theorems of this kind are unfortunately both irrefutable and undemonstrable. They are interesting and deserve more attention than they are usually given, but they leave one with an unsatisfied urge to find more specific sources of long-run firm profits.

Lack of Room

Sometimes, in a market of limited size, there may be enough business to give one firm profits but not enough to support two firms if they existed side by side. For example, in a small town, there might be a need for one good modern hotel, whereas two hotels would experience losses. In this case the first hotel to become established will be able to make profits secure from competition. Potential rivals will not construct a competing hotel whenever some existing hotel is profitable, but will carefully consider the consequences of overbuilding hotel accommodations in a town of limited size. Profits, in cases of this kind, arise from the combination of an inflexible demand and a technology that causes a discontinuous supply. In each line of production there is a minimum practical scale of operations below which soaring unit costs eliminate all profits. It would be an accident if the demand were an exact multiple of the minimum practical output per firm.

Special Entrepreneurial Rents

There are still a fair number of nonconformists in the world. Some of these individualistic people would rather be their own bosses than take employment and have to follow the methods of other men. Some of these "square-peg" entrepreneurs are extremely imaginative and more efficient when running things than when taking orders. In time, unless plagued with misfortune, some of them may earn large incomes for themselves, not as implicit wages but as profits. These large incomes are not implicit wages, because these nonconformists would not be offered such sums as wages by another firm, and indeed would not be worth such an amount to an employer. It is not hard to imagine circumstances in which a man might be worth only $10,000 a year as an employee, implementing conventional policies, and yet be worth $25,000 to himself when putting his own ideas into practice. The difference of $15,000 is a profit attributable to the peculiar talents and nature of the proprietor. It is a sort of entrepreneurial rent or surplus. One of the great advantages of a free enterprise system, especially in those sectors of the economy where capital requirements are not too great, is that a man who cannot convince an employer to adopt his views on how to do things can start his own business and try them out.

Originating

Not all firms and their entrepreneurs are particularly original. In fact some of them, through either inertia or a desire to minimize risk, may always prefer to do things in the customary way. Safety and repose may be sought, but not always found, in habitual imitations of the past. On the other hand, there are entrepreneurs that either want or have to do things in a new fashion. New circumstances beyond their control may compel an adjustment—as when a wartime regulation cuts off the supply of a stock in trade— or the proprietor may be an opinionated man who insists on his own unusual views. Originating, whatever its cause, constitutes a gamble.

Firms that try out new ideas can never be sure in advance that they will prove satisfactory and profitable. If it were generally obvious that some innovation was going to be profitable, it would be universally and immediately adopted, and this in itself would extinguish much of the opportunity for gain. An individual entrepreneur may, of course, be convinced that his idea will be profitable, but he can never really know in advance whether he is right or wrong. Time and the market alone can prove his point.

Originating, or innovating as it is often called, is more than having a new idea. Innovation consists of putting a new idea into effect. An inventor may design a new machine, but there is no original economic contribution until someone has had the machine built and put into operation. The blueprint must be converted into substance and put to work. Money is needed, and must be risked, when a new idea is put into effect. One man may design the new machine, another may have the vision to see its commercial applications, and yet another may advance funds to realize these potentialities. All three men have participated in the innovation and all should be rewarded with part of the profits.

When an innovation is no longer novel and patented, and all the advantages and disadvantages of an idea that was once new are now well known, so that the probable gain or loss of using the innovation is almost a certainty in each possible application, it will no longer occasion profits. The capital value of the machines that incorporate the new inventions will be equal to their prices and full costs of production. Capital used to purchase and operate such machines will no longer bear special risks and will instead tend to earn only pure interest. Plant managers who decide to use such machines will not be experimenting but merely be making routine purchases in imitation of others. The new idea will have become accepted and incorporated into the circular flow of everyday economic life, and the end of novelty and peculiar risk probably marks the end of large economic profits.

The notions of risk taking and originating are obviously tied up together in the case of a single firm. However, certain distinctions can be drawn. The special risks of innovating are *avoidable*. On the other hand, there are certain kinds of risk—for example, that new government policies may incidentally reduce profits—that are *unavoidable* so long as a firm stays in business.

Obviously, firms would never deliberately incur the risks of innovation if successful originating did not yield special profits over and above the expected level of profits that some firms may require to continue incurring the ordinary run of unavoidable business risks. Excess profits taxes and graduated income taxes reduce the net gains of successful innovation without reducing the losses of unsuccessful innovation to the same extent. The provision of venture capital (funds that are hazarded on new ideas) is thereby discouraged. It is true that, as a result, fewer of the economy's resources are wasted on trying new ideas that are not worth while, but unfortunately it is also true that fewer new ideas are tried out.

General Long-Run Profits

Another problem in the field of profit theory, and one that is quite distinct from what occasions the profits of a single firm over time, is to determine whether all firms in general must expect profits as a condition of continuing long-run operations. Whether these expectations are realized in practice is, of course, another matter. The question is whether profits are a necessary price that the economy must at least appear to promise entrepreneurs in order to induce them to incur the *unavoidable* risks of business.

What is the nature of some of these unavoidable risks? First, there are competitive risks. There is no guarantee that rival capitalists may not enter an already populated industry, or that another industry may not develop a new and competitive product, or that an existing firm in the industry may not commence price cutting or aggressive advertising. Second, there are technical risks. There is no guarantee that recently installed equipment may not shortly be rendered obsolete by some new process or machine. One reason why firms are often hesitant to invest in fixed capital in any one year is that they wonder whether next year's fixed capital will not be radically improved. Third, there is the risk of uncontrollable cost and price changes. There is no guarantee that some government action may not have the effect of raising costs or lowering product prices. Firms whose labor is organized seldom know from year to year what wages they will have to pay as a price for continuing operations. Fourth, there is no guarantee against downswings in general business conditions, which leave customers with reduced incomes to spend. Fifth, there is no guarantee against losses from enemy action, a danger that may exist even in the United States if there is another war.

These risks are not only unavoidable, in that the individual firm can do little if anything to aggravate or allay them, but they are for the most part uninsurable. Many business risks, such as loss from fire or from a company driver's killing a pedestrian, can be covered by insurance. In a few cases the risk of an adverse price change can be shifted, at a slight cost, onto a speculator through hedging. However, there are always a great many risks, such as those mentioned in the preceding paragraph, that no insurance company will normally cover, and which the entrepreneurial group must bear itself.

Profits have therefore sometimes been explained as a self-paid insurance premium. It is as though the profits of years in which nothing untoward occurred are banked away in a sort of premium fund out of which the occasional losses of unfortunate years are paid. However, is the fact that each firm expects its occasional losses will be offset by its occasional profits enough of an incentive to attract an investor to enter a business and continue reinvesting in it?

It seems unlikely, for reasons given immediately below, that individual householders would ever become and remain entrepreneurs if they only expected the good and bad years of the future to cancel evenly. Profits are known to be the most fluctuating of all factor incomes and most people prefer a steady income to a fluctuating income of similar eventual magnitude. Because of the diminishing utility value of extra income, entrepreneurs, who are consumers like everyone else, enjoy a given financial gain less than they suffer from an equal financial loss.

Let us suppose a man is asked to invest $10,000 in some project. Analysis of the venture leads him to conclude that there is 1 chance in 5 of his losing the entire investment and 4 chances in 5 that he will get his money back plus another $2,500 to boot. Mathematically, the chances of potential gain and loss exactly cancel each other, and so one might suppose that he would only have to toss a coin in order to reach a decision.

Actually it is most unlikely that he will make the investment. If he is like ordinary people, successive dollars of income will bring him less and less utility, and so the utility of his last dollar if he had $10,000 fewer would be greater than the utility of his last dollar if he had $2,500 more. Hence the disutility of losing $10,000 is more than 4 times the utility of profiting $2,500.

The reasoning that underlies this proposition is shown in Fig. 46. The U line, which in the real world is probably convex

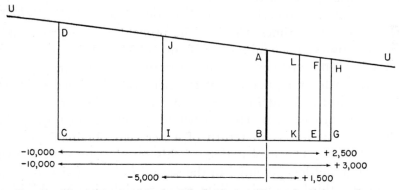

Fig. 46. The Subjective Worth of Probable but Uncertain Gains or Losses.

when viewed from beneath, is the marginal utility schedule of a potential investor, and the horizontal scale represents the number of dollars added or subtracted from his wealth or income. The loss of $10,000 ($BC$) would occasion a disutility of $ABCD$, and a gain of $2,500 *(BE)* would occasion a utility of *ABEF*. If *CB* is four times *BE,* and it is by construction, *ABCD* must be more than four times *ABEF*.

Consequently, before a man will even seriously consider investment, there must be a mathematical *probability,* but of course no *certainty,* that he will make money. Let us change the previous example and now suppose that, as an offset to a 1 in 5 chance of losing all the $10,000 invested *(CB* in the figure), there is a 4 in 5 chance of recovering his investment and making $3,000 *(BG)* besides. In the diagram the negative inclination of the marginal utility schedule *(U)* is such that the disutility of the possible loss *(ABCD)* is 4 times the utility of the possible profit *(ABGH)* and exactly offsets it. The probable return in this case is 4 times $13,000 over $50,000, or 4 per cent on the investment of $10,000. Even so, under the circumstances, he will be indifferent toward the investment.

If the project is somewhat amended so that, upon a $10,000 investment, analysis estimates a 1 in 5 chance of losing $5,000 or 4 in 5 chances of recovering the capital and making $1,500 to boot, the investor will be glad to venture his money. Retaining the same marginal utility schedule, and still employing Fig. 46, the disutility of losing $5,000 will be *ABIJ* and the utility of making a clear $1,500 will be *ABKL*. It is not hard to prove by geometry that *ABIJ* will be less than four times *ABKL* if *ABCD* was exactly four times *ABEF*. The probable net return in this case is 4 times $1,500 minus $5,000, or $1,000, and this represents, on a $50,000 investment, a rate of return of 2 per cent.

It is worth noting that an entrepreneur would be glad to invest in this third and last instance when the probable but uncertain rate of return is 2 per cent but would be indifferent toward the probable but uncertain return of 4 per cent obtainable in the second case. The explanation of this seeming paradox is that the profit and loss potential in the second case was twice as great as in the third example. The extra possible loss would have worked a relatively greater hardship and the extra possible profit would have occasioned relatively less enjoyment. No one would seriously consider the first investment opportunity, in which the mathematical chances of profit and loss were equal.

Of course human beings do not always go through all these cal-culations very consciously or exactly. They do not always under.

stand the full import of the odds against them. Commercial gamblers usually exploit this fact by offering the public a disproportionately small opportunity to make a very large gain. For example, a $1 sweepstake ticket may carry a 1 in 1,000,000 chance of winning a $500,000 prize, and people gladly buy the ticket because their minds are too occupied in spending the prize to consider the odds. However, no gambling syndicate has ever tried to attract the public's fancy by offering it a good chance to make a small gain, all in return for a slight risk of suffering a large loss. Business risks are usually of this latter type, carrying a good probability of a moderate profit and a small possibility of losing the investment. In other words, business risks are in some ways the opposite of gambling risks. Everyone who stops to think knows that gambling is irrational. Actually, it is also irrational to incur business risks unless the odds are more than somewhat in one's favor, but almost everyone senses this because the cost of an investment is so much more than the price of a ticket.

The above analysis provides a deductive proof of the theory of necessary profits, if first one grants the assumption that a typical entrepreneur considers a dollar of loss to outweigh a dollar of profit. The conclusion is that an expectation of moderate profit is necessary if entrepreneurs are to invest at the outset and then continue to invest. These so-called necessary profits arise from the fact that there are uninsurable risks.

It may appear that this statement is inconsistent with the oft-repeated assertion that competitive profits in the long run would likely be zero. If long-run equilibrium were ever attained, it would be in an economy quite ignorant of autonomous changes, and the economy would be in a stationary state. There would be no new products, no new markets, no new inventions or methods, no new supplies of factors, no new government regulations, and no additional population. The economic activities of last year would be repeated without variation this year. Everyone could count upon the fact that the economic actions of this year would be duplicated next year. The only risks attendant upon production would be acts of God, such as droughts, fires, and floods, all of which would be insurable with companies organized to bear them. The use of capital funds would be rewarded with interest, rather than profits, since there would be no uninsurable risks. Such a stationary state of long-run equilibrium is, of course, never actually attained but remains an extreme theoretical concept. We have only stated that an *expectation* of profit is necessary to induce entrepreneurs to invest. It does not follow that entrepreneurs do enjoy profits on an average over long periods of time. Strictly speaking, it is the *ex ante* expectation, and not the *ex post* reality of profits, that is important, except in so far as these are dependent on one another.

Are Profits Useful?

Many reformers feel that profits are in some way objectionable and should be either prevented or taxed away by government authority. What functions do profits perform? Are those entrepreneurs who actually receive profits more entitled to them than those who do not?

Over short periods of time, profits are probably unnecessary to the continued operation of the economy; as we have seen, it is the expectation of profits, rather than their actuality, that induces continued investment by entrepreneurs. However, despite the saying, hope may not spring eternal in business affairs, and it seems unlikely that the entrepreneurs of a country could long be prevented from earning some profits without their expectations' becoming pessimistic. In fact, entrepreneurial profit expectations, being inevitably based on conjecture, hunches, and straws in the wind, tend to be volatile and often unduly affected by the news and happenings of the moment. Hence, over longer periods of time, some unknown volume of profits is probably necessary if continued reinvestment is to occur. Without continual reinvestment, through capital replacements, free enterprise would start slowing down to a stop. The economy would then have to have production carried out by government and households rather than by firms.

It has been pointed out that most of the risks of innovation can be avoided by adhering to the rut of custom. New ideas will not be tried so readily, especially if large capital sums must be staked on their success, unless special profits can be expected to follow successful innovation. An economy that did not permit such profits could not expect private innovation except in fairly rare cases. Then, unless the government proved to be an imaginative pioneer, technical progress, in some or all directions, would probably cease except for occasional accidental discoveries.

It does not follow, however, that those innovators who are successful and do obtain profits *always* deserve such a reward more than those innovators who lose their money. Innovators sometimes do the right thing for the wrong reason and occasionally stumble onto opportunities more or less by chance. But also it is often not a matter of blind chance that some innovators are successful and others are not. The possession of judgment and insight differs among individuals. Moreover, the institution of profits means that the successful innovator, who secures profits, is then in a financial position to innovate again, while the innovator who is not successful may never again acquire the financial means to risk his economy's resources.

Finally, and this cannot be overemphasized, profits act as a director of resources, except where freedom of entry is barred by some monopoly practice or possession. Entrepreneurs who perform their functions in a way that benefits the economy will tend to make profits. Entrepreneurs who innovate and make profits tend to be imitated by other entrepreneurs, who invest additional resources in providing rather similar goods and services according to similar methods. In a progressive economy, which is kept boiling, as it were, by a constant fire of innovations, the existence of persistent profits shows that the entrepreneurial group is performing one of its most vital functions, namely the introduction of novel ideas that are worth while.

Statements for Consideration

1. An active proprietor will have no income to live on in the long run if his pure or economic profits are zero.   *Evaluate*
2. In every firm there is one man performing all the functions of entrepreneurship.   *Evaluate*
3. An inventor is an entrepreneur because he has discovered a new way of doing something.   *Evaluate*
4. Most of the uninsurable risks of enterprise arise from the fact of innovation.   *Discuss*
5. It is somewhat egotistical for a proprietor to preen himself on the profit showing of his business during any single year.   *Explain*
6. In some respects business investment is the opposite of ordinary gambling.   *Explain*
7. The fact that some firms have made profitable decisions in the past does not prove that they are more efficiently managed.   *Discuss*
8. The earning of profits consists in acquiring assets more cheaply than their use values indicates they are worth.   *Explain*
9. Innovation increases uncertainty.   *Explain*

10. The profits of good years have sometimes been looked upon as self-paid insurance premiums.   *Discuss*
11. The most unfortunate characteristic of all investment opportunities is that, although they promise a mathematical probability of profits, all probabilities are uncertain.   *Explain*

References

Bain, J. S., *Pricing, Distribution and Employment*, Chapter 14. New York: Holt, 1948.

Boulding, K. E., *Economic Analysis*, Chapter 21. New York: Harper, 1948.

Crum, W. L., *Corporate Size and Earning Power.* Cambridge, Mass.: Harvard University Press, 1939.

Due, J. F., *Intermediate Economic Analysis*, Chapter 12. Chicago: Irwin, 1947.

Garver, F. B., and Hansen, A. H., *Principles of Economics*, Third Edition, Chapter 26. New York: Ginn, 1947.

Gordon, R. A., "Enterprise, Profits, and the Modern Corporation," *Explorations in Economics*, 1936. Also in *Readings in the Theory of Income Distribution.*

Gordon, R. A., "Short Period Price Determination," *American Economic Review*, June 1948.

Hall, R. L., and Hitch, C. J., "Price Theory and Business Behavior," *Oxford Economic Papers*, No. 2, May 1939.

Hart, A. G., "Risk, Uncertainty, and the Unprofitability of Compounding Probabilities," *Studies in Mathematical Economics and Econometrics*, 1942.

Henderson, H. D., *Supply and Demand*, Chapter 7. New York: Harcourt, 1922.

Knight, F. H., *Risk, Uncertainty and Profit*, Chapters 8–11. Boston: Houghton Mifflin, 1921.

Knight, F. H., "Profit," *Encyclopaedia of the Social Sciences*, vol. XII, 1934. Also in *Readings in the Theory of Income Distribution.*

Marshall, A., *Principles of Economics*, Eighth Edition, Book VI, Chapters 7, 8. London: Macmillan, 1920.

Meyers, A. L., *Modern Economics*, Chapter 25. New York: Prentice-Hall, 1946.

Schumpeter, J. A., *The Theory of Economic Development.* Cambridge, Mass.: Harvard University Press, 1934.

Triffin, R., *Monopolistic Competition and General Equilibrium Theory.* Cambridge: Harvard University Press, 1940.

PART VI

Political Economy

32

Economic Aims and Political Alternatives

POLITICS and economics have a way of getting mixed up with one another. The way in which the people of any nation undertake production and distribution is a political question as well as an economic one. The settled economic policy of the government may be socialism with planning, or it may be private capitalism under *laissez-faire,* or it may be some compromise between these two. However, the basic economic problems of all nations are very similar and so are many of their less fundamental economic aims. This similarity of underlying economic ends is extremely important because it provides a common denominator for comparing the efficiency of different political schemes for organizing an economy's resources. In Part VI we shall enumerate what these rather universal economic goals tend to be, describe the major political alternatives for using economic resources to achieve them, and then try to evaluate the comparative economic efficiency of socialism and capitalism.

Our Economic Aims

Many people would perhaps casually agree that the economic aim of a national policy should be the greatest good of the greatest number. However, this is not a policy prescription by itself because its meaning is ambiguous. Most government policies do not provide economic advantages to everyone, but tend rather to benefit some while injuring others. Is there any way of deciding, under these circumstances, whether a particular program of government is, on balance, beneficial or injurious, particularly in view of the fact that the utilities and disutilities of different people are incomparable?

One conceptual way around this dilemma is to establish the principle that a government policy or action is "good" if those who benefit could fully compensate those who suffer and still be better

471

off. Then those who receive compensation are neither worse nor better off afterwards, those who pay the compensation are better off notwithstanding, and so the community as a whole has presumably improved its economic situation. It is not necessary, from a conceptual viewpoint, that this full and adequate compensation actually be paid. The important point is that, if it were paid, those who paid it would remain better off than before. If we adopt this approach, we can say that an economy is organized in almost the best possible manner if no further change would leave the community better off after the payment of compensation.

This general rule can be understood better if it is restated as a series of more specific rules for households, firms, and the markets of the economy.

Households

There are a number of requirements each household should observe if the general welfare of the economy is to be as great as possible. One set of these rules applies to the consuming or buying side of households, another to their producing or selling side, another to their decisions to consume now or later, and still another regarding how much they earn and work. The economy's institutions and government policies should be such that the household, apart from ignorance, is able to observe these rules.

In buying consumer goods, each household should be able to purchase each kind of good and service it enjoys so that their marginal utilities are proportionate to their prices (see Chapter 18 and Appendix D). This means that, if the price of shirts is one-fifteenth that of suits, a man should buy shirts and suits until the last suit is worth fifteen times the last shirt. The marginal dollar spent on any good will then return the same utility as it would if spent on any other extra goods.

A household will not be able to observe this rule if goods it wants to buy at the prevailing prices are not available in the stores. A government policy of low price ceilings will make this adjustment impossible for most households. A specific rationing system, under which each kind of good is distributed more or less equally *per capita,* renders this adjustment illegal except by accident.

On the producing side, the members of a household can obtain income in various ways, by working as an employee, loaning money, renting land, or acting as an entrepreneur.   Logically, the household should avail itself of these various opportunities in such a way that any given income is obtained at the least possible real cost or disutility to the household.   The utility calculations that concern entrepreneurs have just been described in the previous chapter.   In the case of land rent, a household normally experiences no real cost from the use of the natural resources it owns, and so we shall simply assume that it always maximizes its income possibilities in this direction.   However, the provision of labor and the lending of money do involve real costs, which must now be considered.

The breadwinner of any household is probably only able to take a fraction of the total number of jobs in his area.   If he has no monopoly power, the extra money he earns by working an extra hour is the wage rate of his job.   Hence a typical breadwinner should compare the disutility and wage of alternative employments and then select that which seems to involve the least real cost of acquiring a given sum of money.   The observance of this rule might mean that, depending upon the amount of money he wished to earn altogether, the breadwinner would have to take several different jobs.   If he wishes to earn more salary than one job provides, he might work on several jobs, a regular daytime one, an "after hours" gardening job, and paid work in his home at night.   If his working conditions are flexible, so that he can work whatever number of hours he wishes at each job, he might allot his time so that the disutilities of the last hour on all jobs were proportionate to the jobs' wages.

The greater the range of jobs over which workers can exercise this sort of discretion, the better for the community, so long as our compensation rule is observed.   The jobs that any single worker can take are often limited by such things as location, competence, race, sex, and union rules (see Chapter 27).   If the labor force is not distributed according to the job pattern of the country, an informed migration of workers is in order.   If competence can be acquired at slight cost through training, it may often be worth while to provide such training at either government or worker cost.   Racial and sexual limitations on job opportunities that are based solely on prejudice exact a toll from the economy.

Households can usually acquire more income if they will lend money.   The lending of money involves two self-denials: the conveniences of holding a stock of cash and the pleasures of immediate consumption. The reward is interest income. A rational household will lend money up to the point where the last dollar of interest is worth the temporary denial of these liquidity and time preferences (see Chapters 11 and 30). No household will be able to make this adjustment unless there are relatively riskless securities available for purchase and lending in this way is legal.

One important household question still remains; namely, how many sacrifices should a family endure to acquire income? Presumably a household should seek an aggregate income, adjusted by having extra members of the household working or lending more, so that the utility in consumption of an extra dollar is brought down to the disutility of earning the same marginal dollar. For, if the sumptuary utility of the marginal dollar exceeded its acquisitory disutility, the household would be better off in real terms by contributing more to production for extra income. If a household cannot make this perfect adjustment, the real value of a dollar will normally be based on the utility of the marginal dollar spent on consumption, for it is more common to find a household with a suboptimum than a supraoptimum money income and expenditure. There are probably more families that would be better off, in terms of maximizing consumption utilities and minimizing production disutility, by working more rather than less.

Obviously, cultural values suggested by the environment are most important in this connection. A materialistic culture, in which advertising causes every bride to hanker after a diamond, will have a higher optimum adjustment of work and money by each household than a tranquil culture, which views everything above subsistence as redundant, and where a doubling of a day's wage may only halve the number of days worked.

The three basic principles that households should follow in order to maximize subjective utility income, are these:

(1) the marginal utility of different consumer goods should be in proportion to their prices;

(2) the marginal disutility of different employments should be kept proportionate to their wages;

(3) the marginal dollar should have the same utility when spent for consumption as it occasions disutility when being earned.

One important assumption that runs throughout this book should be noted. This supposition is that households are sovereign. Consumers, so long as they are informed of alternatives, know what they want and what is good for them. Workers, again so long as they know the alternatives open to them, know better than any government official or Great Leader how hard to work and what sacrifices of leisure and home life are warranted in order to possess more goods and services. Such a view flies in the face of all paternalistic notions. The socialist planners of the U.S.S.R. and the people of the United States would certainly split on this issue.

Firms

In any economy, whether socialistic or capitalistic, the task of production and distribution will have to be divided among a number of operating units, possibly several hundred thousand, which we have rather loosely called firms. The operations of these firms should follow certain rules, just as those of households should, or the efficiency of the economy will suffer. The observance of these rules will ensure a proper allocation of resources among firms and uses.

Naturally it is important that all firms use as little of each resource as possible in the course of production. However, we know that different factors are often substitutes for one another, so that if a firm uses less of one resource, it must use more of another if output is to be maintained. The proportions in which each firm employs different factors of production is hence extremely important. The socially desirable rule to be followed is that the factors employed by a given firm should be used in such quantities that their marginal physical productivities are proportionate to their unregulated supply prices. Such a rule will not maximize all profits in a capitalist economy, because some firms have monopsony power over factors of production, but it will tend to maximize welfare (see Chapter 25). Such a rule cannot readily be followed in a socialist economy, unless the managers of firms are instructed by the state to follow this rule, and unless they are allowed considerable discretion with regard to procurement and operations.

Another important consideration is the share of industry output that different firms in the same industry produce. There will be one plan for allotting production quotas which will be less of a drain on the resources of an economy than any other. This optimum allocation of production will be achieved if all firms making the same good adjust outputs so that their comparable marginal costs are equal, always assuming they follow the input rule of the preceding paragraph. The purely competitive markets of a free enterprise economy bring this about. Deliberate socialist planning might strive to duplicate these more automatic results of capitalism. However, it is almost inconceivable that either of these last two rules can be observed unless the managers of firms can control the amounts of each factor that they use, rather than having to await the resource allocations of some central authority (see Chapter 20).

A third important consideration is that different kinds of commodities are produced in the right proportions. If households are following their purchasing rule, consumer goods prices will indicate the relative utility of different consumer goods, unless distorted by severe income inequalities. Each kind of resource should then be distributed among different firms, possibly each making a different product, so that its marginal value product in each use is the same. The marginal value product incidentally is equal to the multiplication of marginal physical product by the selling price of the output made (see Chapter 26).

An ideal arrangement of resources would be one where the marginal value products of all factors in all employments were in the same relation to one another as their supply prices. It would then be impossible to improve economic welfare by having one firm substitute factors, by having the firms of some industry substitute outputs, or by having households substitute products. The private firms of a free enterprise economy will tend to observe this rule only if they do not possess and exercise any monopoly or monopsony power. The planners of a socialist economy, even if they recognize the validity of this goal, will probably find it very difficult to achieve, unless they make it an officially established goal and allow plant managers a great deal of discretion in working toward it. The world's rather limited experience with socialism suggests that it is too centralized and authoritarian to permit sufficient delegation of responsibility for this task.

The Economy's Markets

The above rules for households and firms cannot be observed by them if they respectively consume or employ goods and services at some uniform or standard rate. On the contrary, the observance of these rules will normally result in each household's consuming various goods at different rates, and in each firm's employing factors in different proportions while producing at various rates of output. Such variation in the character and intensity of household behavior and firm operations may very well depend upon their being able to buy and sell at will. It must be possible for all buyers to buy at will and all sellers to sell at will, neglecting cases of monopoly and monopsony, if prevailing market prices are to equate demand and supply. Such an equilibrium price will result without the intervention of government under purely competitive conditions. Under other circumstances government may deliberately have to establish a price or wage that will succeed in matching demand to supply. All the same, price ceilings and price floors, which respectively create deficits and surpluses, will make it impossible for all households and firms to follow our stated rules.

A corollary of this is that there should be a single equating price in each market, and not two prices, such as one net price to buyers and another net price to sellers. Government excise taxes violate this rule and have the same distorting effects on resource allocation as monopoly, for the resulting equilibrium leaves buyers' marginal demand prices considerably in excess of net marginal costs of supply. Government subsidies to promote output also cause distortion, but in the reverse direction, causing the use values of marginally produced goods to fall below their costs of provision (see Chapter 16).

A number of reasons are forever being advanced in favor of abrogating this rule in one or another specific instance. For example, it is often asserted that liquor should be heavily taxed, milk production should be subsidized, the price of wheat should be supported, apartment rentals should be limited, and so forth. Sometimes it may be true that the price mechanism functions so imperfectly that its actions must be supplemented by direct government intervention. However, it is important to remember that everyone has some special economic interest that he wants the government to pamper, and that the special interest of one group is usually the special "disinterest" of some other. The number of cases that merit government intervention must be a very small fraction of those that are pressed.

Distribution of Income

The supplies of goods that are evoked by effective market demand depend in part upon the distribution among households of the national income. A very unequal income distribution means that some resources of the economy may be used to gratify a whim of a rich man rather than some elemental need of a poor man. Perhaps we cannot quarrel with this outcome though, when it is caused by differences in the degree to which living persons have contributed to output.

There would be no incentive for people to acquire more income if its possession did not enable them to gratify additional wants. And it is certainly not the fault of "well-to-do" people that their marginal wants seem so unimportant to others. However, income differences that are based on inheritance of great wealth may be unnecessary to encourage productive contributions. It may be that some reduction in income taxes, countered by an increase in taxes on bequests, would intensify existing incentives to work, invest, loan money, hire natural resources, and innovate, without reducing government receipts.

Of course, even if remaining income inequalities did accurately reflect differences in individual contributions to output, a question of equity would remain. Some people are more or less productive through no fault of their own except that they had parents who were respectively healthy and intelligent or sick and stupid. The philosophy of a welfare state is essentially that income inequalities based on differential productivity should be modified in extreme cases. Fortunately we do not need to attempt an assessment of this belief here. The main point is that a production pattern which is unduly dependent upon inherited wealth may not be ideal in composition.

Fixed Capital Accumulation

Capital equipment and facilities reduce the labor and unpleasantness of producing a given output; they also make it possible for future national products to be greater. Those who possess political and economic power must always be asking themselves whether it would not have been better to produce the current national output in a more roundabout manner with more fixed capital. They must also wonder whether consumption should not be reduced so that more production might take the form of capital accumulations.

The same problem can be expressed in another way. Most people would agree that the greater are the future increases in output made possible by new and extra capital, the more rapidly should an economy seek to accumulate more of the right kind of fixed capital. However, if community time preferences are high, should the rate of fixed capital accumulation be slow? Should liquidity preferences, which also help to raise interest rates where loanable funds markets exist, be allowed to retard capital accumulation? Perhaps most people would agree that the existence of time preferences is a more valid reason than that of liquidity preferences for limiting the rate of fixed capital accumulation. Perhaps the government of a free market economy could and should lessen liquidity preferences by making it simpler for firms and households to hypothecate assets for money, so that the risks and disadvantages of being caught with wealth but without money would be lessened.

In any event, in every economy where the government is the servant rather than the master of the people, it must create or permit some mechanism that will weigh productivity against time preferences and occasion a desirable rate of capital accumulation. The interest rate, fashioned by a loanable funds market, may accomplish this in so far as households and firms are free to lend and borrow at will. Also the existence of loanable funds markets mitigates the tendency for liquidity preference to deter accumulation.

All the alternatives to the interest rate mechanism are likely to be arbitrary and paternalistic. Under socialism the planning officials make their decisions and presumably know what is best. In a free enterprise economy the aggregate decision is made piecemeal by millions of people.

National Income and Aggregate Employment

That reasonably full employment should be maintained is of equal or greater importance than that employed resources should be properly allocated. However, the rules that have been stated for households, firms, and markets will not suffice to prevent the waste of resources that unemployment can occasion. There are also certain rules, applicable to the nation's monetary authorities, that need to be observed, whether the economy is organized along socialistic or capitalistic lines.

The economy's monetary authorities (the national treasury and the central bank) should seek to maintain effective demand at such a level that employment continues full *and* prices in general remain steady. It is doubtful whether the government, by becoming an employer and large-scale public works producer, can increase net employment by more than a limited amount. Hence, at times, the government will have to vary the national stock of money. Flexible tax rates and planned budget deficits and surpluses that alter the value of total demand deposits are possible means. Also the government, through its banking controls, can usually induce a contraction of credit and sometimes induce an expansion. Of course, the government cannot control spending time lags of firms and households, and so a change in the national money stock does not necessarily occasion a similar change in effective demand.

A difficult problem in connection with national income policy is for the government to know how to balance leisure and consumption against employment and production. It is to be expected, and experience seems to confirm this, that workers will always want to enjoy some of the fruits of technical progress in the form of leisure and recreation rather than in the production of extra goods they do not have time to enjoy. There are not many workers who would wish a ten-hour day even if their take-home pay were correspondingly increased. Government policy must seek to avoid both involuntary unemployment (which entails insufficient income to enjoy leisure) and overemployment (which entails insufficient leisure to enjoy income).

However, so long as different people vary, the proper adjustment between work and leisure cannot involve a similar work week for everyone. The problem is not whether every employee should work 40 hours or 48 hours but how many hours each individual employee should work. The aggregate outcome must be determined for each individual.

An employed person will presumably consider himself underemployed and seek more work if the disutility of earning extra pay is less than the utility of subsequently spending it. He is also underemployed from the viewpoint of the economy if a job can be found for him in which his net marginal value product is equal or greater than his pay. Unless both these conditions are satisfied, it will not be worth both the individual's and the economy's while to have him work more.

So long as the government is maintaining effective aggregate demand, it seems consistent with our other recommendations to suggest that extra employment be provided only when both these conditions are met, for then the estimated money value of the worker's extra disutility will always be exceeded or equaled by the money value of his extra output. Such an outcome will be less likely if workers cannot determine how long they are to work and plant managers cannot determine whom they shall employ. On the other hand, the fact of worker and manager choice in these respects will not suffice to occasion reasonably full employment unless aggregate effective demand is being maintained by the government.

The Political Alternatives

People might still disagree regarding political means even if they agreed that the various internal relations that have just been outlined were desirable economic ends. Some people might feel that these ends would be approached more certainly and closely through socialism. Others might argue that unrestricted free enterprise would guarantee their achievement most assuredly. However, there are alternative and intermediate political ways to attain these economic ends. What would these political schemes mean in terms of economic freedom?

It is not always clear what socialism would entail in any particular place and time, but the following are probably some of its essential characteristics. First, the ownership and operation of natural resources and capital equipment is vested in the state, with the exception that households may be permitted to produce goods for their own use. Second, private employment of others is prohibited. Third, there is a deliberate attempt to control the outputs of different firms and industries according to some supposedly integrated plan.

At the other extreme one can conceive of a system of *laissez-faire* capitalism in which government did little more than provide for the mails, a currency, the enforcement of order and contracts, and certain public works such as highways and canals. In such a country the role of social security schemes would be undertaken instead by private savings and charity. Income inequalities would be extreme and become accentuated through inheritance. The prevention or alleviation of mass unemployment would not be a responsibility of the government. Monopolies would arise whenever profitable.

We have learned enough in the course of this book to know that such *laissez-faire* capitalism would be economically inefficient. Resources would be underemployed for long periods of time and their allocation would be distorted by monopolistic conspiracies and by income inequalities unrelated to productivity. Actually none of the major industrial powers of the world possesses such a political economy today.

In the next chapter we shall show some of the reasons why socialism as we know it will also not perform satisfactorily. The central planners may be unable to achieve the economic ends recommended here because workers and consumers do not have sufficient choice to guide the planners in their task. Even if a socialist economy were to permit workers to select their jobs and spend their wages at will, it would not follow that resources would be properly and adequately employed.

Fortunately there are other alternatives remaining. It is possible to conceive of a system that would permit private enterprise, consumer choice, and worker choice and yet hold some promise of economically desirable results. The government would not indulge in *laissez-faire* but instead would intervene when necessary to bring what we have called social and private product into closer accord. The government would seek to arrange the business environment in such a way that what benefits an entrepreneur would also benefit the economy, and what is a charge against the economy would be an entrepreneurial cost, more or less commensurately. Within this governmentally arranged environment, private capitalism would enjoy free scope; we shall call such a system regulated private capitalism.

Statements for Consideration

1. The dilemma of political economy is that the incidence of government economic regulations upon different persons and classes is often opposite. *Explain*
2. So long as government economic regulations injure some while benefiting others it is impossible to say whether any given state policy is in the general welfare. *Evaluate*
3. Inflexible working hours make it more difficult for breadwinners to work out their economic salvation as happily as they might. *Explain*
4. According to one test an individual may be unemployed, but according to another economic test his employment is not worth while. *Discuss*
5. In theory, households should seek to maximize utility and firms should seek to maximize profits, but the interests of these two groups are hard to reconcile. *Discuss*
6. The fact that competitive firms in the same industry tend to have similar marginal costs is a matter of social consequence. *Explain*
7. The absence of free markets, in which households can buy consumer goods at will and sell their services at will, does not affect the ability of households to attain an optimum adjustment of their affairs. *Evaluate*
8. The bid prices of households for goods indicate the relative importance of those goods to the community. *Discuss*
9. The existence of strong liquidity preferences on the part of the public is a legitimate reason to allow interest rates to rise and so retard the rate of capital accumulation within a nation. *Discuss*
10. Technological progress should be used to provide more output for the poor instead of, as in the past, leisure for the rich. *Discuss*
11. There may be more than one political method of organizing resources to achieve certain economic ends. *Discuss*

References

Boulding, K. E., *Economic Analysis,* Chapter 20.   New York: Harper, 1948.

Henderson, A., "Consumers' Surplus and the Compensating Variation," *Review of Economic Studies,* February 1941.

Hicks, J. R., "The Foundations of Welfare Economics," *Economic Journal,* December 1939.

Hotelling, H., "The Relation of Prices to Marginal Costs in an Optimum System," *Econometrica,* April 1939.

Kaldor, N., "Welfare Propositions and Interpersonal Comparisons of Utility," *Economic Journal,* September 1939.

Lerner, A. P., *The Economics of Control*, I, Chapters 15–18. New York: Macmillan, 1945.

Morgan, T., *Income and Employment*, Chapter 13. New York: Prentice-Hall, 1947.

Phelps Brown, E. H., *The Framework of the Pricing System*, Chapter 4. London: Chapman and Hall, 1936.

Pigou, A. C., *The Economics of Welfare*, Fourth Edition, I. London: Macmillan, 1942.

Reder, M. W., *Studies in the Theory of Welfare Economics*, Part I. New York: Columbia University Press, 1947.

Samuelson, P. A., *Economics*, Chapter 26 (A). New York: McGraw-Hill, 1948.

Stigler, G. J., *The Theory of Price*, Chapter 3. New York: Macmillan, 1946.

33

Problems of Socialism

It is not simple to analyze the economic problems of socialism in very concrete terms because no nation at the present time exemplifies all the socialistic situations that might arise. The Soviet Union does have a professed socialist economy. However, it would not be fair to judge socialism according to the economic failures and successes of the U.S.S.R., a country that has had to cope with the backward technological tradition of Czarist Russia and the ruthless German occupation of the last war. It is possible to conceive of socialist economies that would have neither the natural advantages nor the disadvantages peculiar to the Soviet Union and which might handle their economic affairs in both wiser and stupider ways than its political leaders have done. Moreover, the U.S.S.R. engages in many practices that some people might consider smacked too much of capitalist economies to permit our taking the Soviet Union as an example of socialism in action. The U.S.S.R. is neither the first nor the last word on socialism. Accordingly, it has seemed best to analyze an abstract socialist economy, one that is operated with varying economic sophistication at different times. The essential characteristics of all these socialist arrangements are that the government owns and operates the means of production, that private entrepreneurship and employment are negligible, and that the central government tries to integrate the national output according to a master plan.

Crude Socialist Planning

The crudest type of socialist economy is one that has no money and no freedom of personal choice. The state controls and owns all capital goods and natural resources. Workers are told where to work and what jobs to perform. Each person receives a ration book as a reward for working. The state announces to what each ration stamp will entitle the holder upon presentation at his government store.

A National Planning Board periodically decides what it considers to be proper and possible economic goals. It may decide that next year the public should have x boots, y stoves, and z light bulbs. The technicians then start calculating back from these goals to discover how much leather, steel, and glass will be required. Production to provide the necessary last-stitching machines, stove-part molds, and glass-blowing equipment must be calculated.

The over-all planning group may also decide what investment to undertake. Its plans may call for a new hydroelectric power plant and for double-tracking a main railroad line. The productive resources that will be needed for these projects must also be estimated and a check made to see whether such investment will clash with the consumption goods program. There will be no common yardstick to settle such a conflict scientifically.

The National Planning Board will quickly discover that each new decision vitiates some earlier decision. Today's plan to generate more electric power may amend yesterday's decisions by increasing the number of lamp bulbs that will be needed, reducing the industrial demand for coal, and substituting electric ranges for conventional stoves. The planners *should* make their thousands of decisions simultaneously so that they will all be compatible. Being human, they cannot possibly satisfy this ideal and must instead make a series of amended plans, in the hope that each is less inconsistent than the last.

The state probably administers the economy through operating combines and allocating boards. There will doubtless be a Manpower Board, which will attempt to classify workers according to their skills and peculiarities and allocate them to the different combines according to the National Production Plan. Each industry will probably have a combine in charge of it and agriculture will probably be organized in the same way.

There will have to be numerous allocating boards. For example, somebody must decide how much of the Steel Combine's output is to go to the Automobile Combine rather than to the Shipbuilding Combine. Also, when there is no money and price system at work, somebody must decide what proportion of the Grain Combine's output is to go for feeding animals and what proportion to the millers for bread flour. Some official group must decide how much of the coal output is to be retained as a

producer good and how much shall be allowed to the public for
heating and cooking.   A great many goods can be used as producer
or consumer goods and each producer good has many alternative uses.   Such a basic division must be made more or less arbitrarily.   Allocation of the portion to be used as producers' goods
will normally be according to some complicated priority system.

The managers of each combine are probably under pressure to
get output.   Consequently, they will use every trick to procure
all the labor and materials possible from the various allocating
agencies.   The proportions in which managers combine different
factors will naturally depend upon how many units of each they
can wangle.   And if, at times, they are long on certain factors,
they will hoard their surplus materials and work their laborers
slowly, rather than return them and risk being hamstrung by
critical shortages later on.

In a crudely conceived socialist nation, there is no ready way
of ascertaining whether the planning board, operating combines,
and allocating commissions do their work ill or well.   The Manpower Commission might lengthen the work week in mining and
shorten it in textiles, but there will be no respective quits or layoffs to indicate the wisdom of these orders.   And if the planning
board is prejudiced in favor of bread and against beer, and so
has more bread baked and less beer brewed, this dogmatic error
will not show up in a bread glut.

It is important to understand why maladjustments, in a crudely
organized socialistic state, will not be revealed by labor unemployment and commodity surpluses as they sometimes are in a
capitalist economy.

There can be no voluntary or involuntary unemployment.
Every adult must report for work because he cannot eat and live
without a ration book.   He will be assigned to a farm or factory
and given a task.   If there are no local jobs that seem important
enough to perform, he may be transported to another part of the
country where supposedly he is needed more urgently.   Occasionally he may be ordered to an enterprise that already has too
much labor, in which event he will have little to do even though
he is nominally employed.   However, in primitive economies,
which have little capital and operate inefficiently, it is usually not
difficult to find hard physical labor for everyone.

The public stores will never find unsold goods accumulating

on their shelves under a system of crude socialism.   Each worker
is in possession of ration stamps that entitle him to specific products.   Perhaps red stamp #13 is good for a pair of boots if presented before the end of the year.   The worker can get these shoes
if he will just bother to walk to the store.   He need not spend
money or perform extra work when he collects the boots.   Consequently, and especially if the general plane of living is low,
everyone presents this boot stamp as soon as it becomes valid.   If
the state produces more boots than previously, it disposes of them
by the simple device of more frequently making a new stamp valid
for boots.   All goods will be distributed because all specific rations will be presented.

Living in a socialist state of this extremely crude type would be
rather like army life.   Everybody performs the ordered tasks and
draws the rations issued at the official store.   One has no choice
of jobs as a worker or selection of goods as a consumer.   A system
of this kind must be inefficient in ways that are detailed below.
It will be noticed that the elimination of these inefficiencies leads
in the direction of a freely operating price system with individual
worker and consumer choice.

Individual Consumer Choice

The simplest conceivable kind of socialist regime would entail
a specific rationing system.   For example, if an economy of 100
million people is annually producing 75 million boots, 400 million bars of soap, and 600 million razor blades, these quantities
will be distributed on an aliquot basis.   One designated ration
stamp will become valid for a pair of boots every 16 months, another for a bar of soap every 3 months, and another, found only in
the ration book issued to adult males, will become good for a
razor blade about once a month.   Stamps probably cease to be
valid at the end of announced periods.   Buying and selling or
trading different stamps is illegal.

A specific rationing system can certainly distribute the national
output equally but not according to need.   There are very few
average consumers.   People are of different ages and sexes.   In
each section of a large country, differences in climate and other
geographical conditions dictate a different way of living.   Different jobs give rise to different diet and clothing needs.   Of
course, most specific rationing systems will attempt to allow for

these different needs in part.   Adults will get ration books different from those of children and males will have books different from those of females.   Supplementary food rations may be allowed coal miners and nursing mothers, for example.   The people of some notoriously cold and northern province may be allowed an extra clothing ration.   However, these concessions to the obvious do little to lessen the essential rigidity of the system and painfully duplicate what households would decide for themselves if given enough choice.

Specific rationing is wasteful because a given quantity of any one good could be redistributed in some other manner that would provide a greater total utility.   Razor blades are an example. Some men have heavy beards, work in city offices, and have wives who borrow their razors.   Other men are light-bearded, are single, work in the woods with a logging crew, and are shaved once a month when they come to town.   A razor blade will not have the same marginal utility to these two types of men.   On the other hand, the logger, leading a strenuous life and out in all sorts of weather, will wear out his boots more rapidly than the white collar worker in the city.   The logger receives too many razor blades and too few boots as compared with the clerk.   Part of the resources used to make these blades and boots have really been wasted, since the same over-all satisfaction could have been provided by a smaller output of both goods had they been distributed more sensibly.

Frequently these workers may be more realistic than their government and so swap blades for boots.   However, barter deals of this kind are clumsy and hard to arrange, for A must find another man who wants what A does not *and* does not want what A does. Realization of such a double coincidence is all the more unlikely when private deals are illegal and hence must be conducted secretly.

A socialist government that will sacrifice doctrine for efficiency can overcome this waste to some extent by introducing point rationing.   Ration books then contain coupons of different denominations and the various goods in the government stores carry point prices.   Epicures can then indulge their taste for fancy foods so long as they are willing to deny themselves in other ways. People who don't smoke will have more "point money" to spend on things they really want.   No one is then forced into a standardized way of living and everyone is allowed at least some personal expression.

The allocating boards must attempt to set point prices so that market demand is equal to the previously determined output of each good. Perhaps the National Planning Board has had a certain quantity of soap produced. The point price charged in the government stores for soap must not be too high (in which case some of it will remain unsold and unused) or too low (in which case there will be shortages to annoy unsatisfied shoppers). Moreover, point prices for *all* goods together must be at a level that will exhaust all the points consumers wish to spend.

A point rationing scheme does not mean that consumers *as a whole* receive goods in the proportions they would like. The National Planning Board still decides how much of each good to produce. However, the national output, whatever its composition, is distributed in a way that maximizes consumer satisfaction. One might say that point rationing makes the best of a bad job.

Naturally the introduction of point rationing does not detract from the National Planning Board's power to determine the rate of investment of the economy. Perhaps 90 billion points have been issued in rations to workers engaged in maintaining equipment and producing the output of consumer goods. And possibly 10 billion points have gone to persons adding to investment. Consumer goods prices must then be set high enough to absorb all the 100 billion points that workers will want to spend. If the National Planning Board raises the economy's investment rate, say to 20 per cent, the general level of point prices will have to be raised accordingly. Consumer goods prices must always be high enough to sop up all issued ration points that households attempt to spend on consumption.

Incentive Incomes

There is very little personal incentive to work harder or increase one's productive ability when one knows in advance that this will not increase one's income and consumption. In a system that makes a doctrinal virtue out of equal wages and incomes, the normal human urge to better one's lot operates toward securing appointment to "cushy" jobs and escaping detection for "slacking"; for obviously, if one cannot increase one's right to consume, all that remains is to render one's working life as pleasing as possible. Moreover, in a crude socialist economy, where the worker is shifted between jobs and localities by the state, the individual can do no more to influence his future than make suggestions to his immediate superiors. He is likely to become fatalistic and live from day to day without plans. A system that gives each worker the same number of ration points, irrespective of his efforts and capabilities, is not likely to get the total possible output from and for the economy. Promotion to posts of minor authority, ceremoniously presented medals, and organized worker competitions are only a partial substitute for ordinary money incentives.

Human nature and common sense will eventually compel the introduction of a scheme that in part rewards workers in any plant according to their productivity. Two prizes might be regularly offered: a large prize to workers who produce over 120 per cent of their average output, and a less valuable prize to workers producing between 100 and 120 per cent of their average. (Those turning out less than the average output would receive no prize and merely draw the standard ration book.) If these suggestions are put into effect, the economy will, in reality, have a wage scale that varies with productivity.

Shall the wage scale vary in strict *proportion* with output? In a free enterprise system, the competition of entrepreneurs for workers tends to bring this proportionality about, but there is no necessity for such a result when the state is the sole employer. And such a rigid connection between output and wage cannot be proved the most equitable. For example, in coal mining, physical strength may determine each worker's output, but physical strength is inherited in large part. It may be no more moral or equitable to pay people more because they have been born strong than to set a penalty wage for people born with red hair.

In a free enterprise system, but only very roughly, each worker takes from the national output the equivalent of what he has contributed. When such a situation prevails, the rest of the economy is indifferent to whether a person is productive or not. Only the worker himself is concerned. In contrast to this, part of the communist ideal is that each person should contribute to national income according to his ability, even though he may be paid a standard wage common to all. There is much to be said for this ideal, in the abstract; but unfortunately, human nature being what it is, such a scheme would sacrifice output.

A socialist state could compromise between extreme capitalism and extreme communism by varying individuals' point rations less than proportionately with output. It might permit a superior worker to "keep" *half* his "excess" output. All workers might receive a basic ration of 100 points a month whatever their job. In coal mining the average output is perhaps 50 tons a month. The mean pay is therefore 2 points a ton. A superior miner, who cuts 80 tons, would then receive a bonus of 30 points, giving him a total wage of 130 points for the month. The better miner, as compared with his fellow miners as a whole, is then making a gift of 15 gross tons to the economy. The final effect would be similar to that achieved more usually by income taxes.

Limited Worker Choice

The introduction of wages that vary less than proportionately with output in each occupation does not of itself give workers liberty to choose their jobs. Under our present assumptions, the number of men and women on each job depends upon the orders of the Manpower Commission and not upon the preferences of the workers themselves. The same basic ration book will be issued to those workers in each occupation who produce at or below the average rate. The unpleasant and dangerous jobs presumably pay no more than the pleasant and safe ones.

However, one of the real costs of production is the disutility of labor, and this naturally differs from job to job. Sewer cleaning involves a far greater real cost of production than spray painting. Consequently, under a system that pays all average workers the same basic wage, the person who is assigned unpleasant and dangerous work is forced to sacrifice more for the economy than a man who holds a desirable assignment. The incidence of labor disutility is arbitrary and inequitable when workers are directed to their jobs and paid the same basic wage.

It would be impracticable, however, to allow people to select their own jobs and occupations, at a common basic wage, because everyone would choose the desirable tasks and localities, and no one would present himself for work at sewer cleaning or in remotely located mines. Of course, those government combines that offer preferred employment opportunities might attempt to cope with the flood of applicants by establishing waiting lists or qualification tests. And the second possibility would have the merit of fitting workers to jobs where testable qualities are necessary. But it would still be true that those workers who did secure preferable jobs would be making a smaller real contribution to the economy and so being unfairly favored.

A socialist economy that wanted to equalize the real sacrifice of each worker would have to pay different basic wages in different occupations. Garbage collectors would have to be paid more than delivery men. Wage differentials would have to be adjusted so that the number of people who applied for each job corresponded to the number of workers the government wished to employ. The National Planning Board would establish production goals, the labor requirements in each occupation would be calculated from this over-all economic blueprint, and then wage relations would be modified from time to time so that workers presented themselves at the different government firms in exactly the required numbers. Too many applications should cause the responsible authorities to lower the wage at that firm and vice versa. The workers as a whole would not determine the relative amount of employment in each occupation, for this is still done by the National Planning Board, but each worker would be able to decide, after weighing different jobs against their varying wages, the kind of work that he would do.

Interacting Consumer and Worker Choice

Originally we supposed a very crude form of socialist economy in which consumers draw specific commodity rations and workers are told what kind of work they must do. Subsequently we pointed out that the predetermined national output would provide more total utility if distributed by means of point rations that consumers can spend as they will. And we have just shown that the incidence of work can be most fairly apportioned if workers are allowed to choose their jobs from a range of occupations that pay different point wages.

If these modifications are introduced, the authorities must juggle commodity prices so that demand in the market sense equals the product supplies in each case. And wages must be arranged so that the supply of labor for each job equals the demand for it in the market sense.   The question that now confronts us is the relationship of product prices to wage rates.

Let us concentrate our attention on the production and distribution of coal and wood fuels.   We shall suppose that the National Planning Board has somehow decided that the proper output quotas are 5,000,000 tons of coal and 12,500,000 cords of wood a month.   Experience has perhaps shown that these are constant cost industries and that a miner normally produces 50 tons a month (or 2 tons a day, assuming 25 working days) and a wood worker 100 cords a month (or 4 cords a day).   Consequently 100,000 miners and 125,000 wood workers are needed to meet these production goals.   A crude socialist economy would forcibly recruit these workers and distribute coal and wood as specific rations.   Each consumer would be allowed, assuming a population of 100 million, $\frac{1}{20}$ of a ton of coal *and* $\frac{1}{8}$ of a cord of wood each month.   In a limited sense this would be an equilibrium position, since all jobs are filled and all output distributed, but the production goals might be quite uneconomic.

The National Planning Board can readily test the validity of its coal and wood production goals if it dares to do so.   The consumption side test is to give users a choice of either $\frac{1}{10}$ of a ton of coal (double the former *coal* ration) *or* $\frac{1}{4}$ of a cord of wood a month (double the former *wood* ration).   It is most unlikely that exactly half the population would select one alternative and the remaining half would prefer the other.   We shall suppose that, at the government's offer price of $2\frac{1}{2}$ cords for 1 ton, there is a run on coal, the stocks of which approach exhaustion while wood supplies keep piling up.   The employment side test is to give all coal and wood workers a choice of transferring or remaining at their present jobs.   It would be a sheer coincidence if the number of wood hewers who transferred to mining exactly equaled the number of miners who elected to become wood hewers.   We shall suppose instead that there is a net transfer out of coal mining into wood cutting.   Altogether, the National Planning Board now finds itself in an impossible position, for coal production is below consumption and wood production exceeds consumption.

The National Planning Board may nevertheless cling obstinately to its production goals of 5,000,000 tons of coal and 12,500,000 cords of wood.   And yet, for political reasons, it may wish to give consumers and workers individual choice within limits.   Hence it may pay point wages and charge point prices. It perhaps raises its coal wages to 120 points a month, leaving wood wages at 100 points, so that 100,000 miners and 125,000 wood cutters present themselves. It may set coal prices at 2.70 points a ton and wood prices at .90 points, so that at this higher 3–1 price ratio, consumers demand the 5,000,000 tons of coal and 12,500,000 cords of wood that will be produced by these workers. Given these official wage rates, each worker has chosen the job he wants. Given these official prices, each consumer has chosen the fuel he wants. And the National Planning Board, by juggling wages and prices, has produced the quantities it wanted while keeping physical demand and supply in equality.

TABLE 34

ALLOCATION OF RESOURCES BETWEEN COAL AND WOOD

	COAL		WOOD	
Monthly production	5.0	m tons	12.5	m cords
Output per man-month	50	tons	100	cords
Employment	100,000	workers	125,000	workers
Price of coal	2.70	pts. per ton	.90	pts. per cord
Worker's monthly wage	120	pts.	100	pts.
Total monthly revenue	13.50	m pts.	11.25	m pts.
Total monthly cost	12.00	m pts.	12.50	m pts.
Monthly profit (or loss)	+1.50	m pts.	−1.25	m pts.

N.B. m represents millions.

The above sleight of hand is likely to lead to financial profits and losses. Table 34 summarizes the data and shows that the coal combine makes a profit of 1.50 million points a month, whereas the wood combine suffers a loss of 1.25 million points a month. In this simplified example the total cost of each combine is identified with its payroll; and, in order to neglect the cost of capital goods, we shall suppose that those required in each industry are fairly rudimentary and made directly by the employed workers on the spot.

The real significance of these profits and losses is not financial but economic. Financially, a socialist government can always set the losses of one combine against the profits of another; and, if there are still net losses, these can be eliminated by taxes, raising the general level of product prices, or lowering all workers' wages. Economically, profits in coal, taken together with losses in wood, strongly suggest too little coal and too much wood output. Perhaps the arbitrarily determined output goals of the National Planning Board are invalid after all.

Let us consider some of the effects of transferring one worker from wood to coal production upon (1) physical output, (2) consumer utility, and (3) worker disutility.

Physically, we shall suppose that the output-over-input return in each industry does not vary with the volume of operations. Consequently the average and marginal physical productivity of a worker will be the same. The marginal productivity of a worker (ϕ) is hence 50 tons a month in coal and 100 cords a month in wood.

Transferring a worker increases the marginal utility of the thing he no longer produces. The shifted worker used to produce 100 cords a month, valued at .90 points a cord, which put the monetary value of the utility he provided through wood production at 90 points. The same worker now produces 50 tons of coal, valued at 2.70 points a ton, which means he is providing 135 points worth of utility through coal production. The consumer utility has increased by a net 45 points per month. Against this must be set the greater disutility of coal mining over wood production. The difference of 20 points in the basic wages in these two industries is probably a monetary expression of this greater disutility. The transfer of one worker thus adds 45 points worth of consumer utility and 20 points worth of worker disutility. There is a net gain, since the greater satisfaction afforded by coal as a fuel more than offsets the greater danger and dirt of mining it.

Transfers of workers from wood to coal should continue until the following relationship obtains:

$$\frac{P_c \times \phi_c}{P_w \times \phi_w} = \frac{W_c}{W_w}$$

Initially, before transfers began, the values of these ratios were

$$\frac{2.70 \times 50}{.90 \times 100} = 1.50 \quad \text{and} \quad \frac{120}{100} = 1.20$$

As transfers continue, the price of coal will fall relative to that of wood, because coal is becoming more abundant and wood is becoming scarcer. Also, it will be necessary to keep increasing the coal wage relative to that of wood, because it will now be necessary to attract men into coal mining who really dislike it. We are assuming that the marginal physical productivity of labor in coal mining (50 tons) and wood production (100 cords) remains constant. An optimum allocation of resources will be obtained when and if $P_c = 2.5$, $P_w = 1.00$, $W_c = 125$, and $W_w = 100$ points. The two ratios set forth above will then both equal 1.25. The relatively greater utility of coal over wood production during a month is equal to the relatively greater disutility of coal mining. This is as it should be.

It is worth noting that, under our assumption of constant physical returns, average rate of profit will be the same in both industries when workers are allotted between them in the optimum manner described above. The financial rate of return, which can be calculated from the formula $(P \cdot \phi)/W$, when ϕ is the physical productivity of a man-month of work, will be the same when all necessary labor transfers have been made. A socialist government should allocate resources, when there is no difference between average and marginal physical productivity, in a way that will equalize the rate of profit among all industries.

An efficient economy is one that is directed in accordance with consumer wants (expressed in their product demand schedules) and with worker dislikes (expressed in their labor supply schedules). Somehow these two sets of schedules should be meshed together. A good that occasions much disutility to produce should be sold at a high price so that it will only be used where it is most necessary. And products that provide little satisfaction should only be produced if their making entails little disutility.

A socialist government may not mesh these product demands of consumers and labor supplies of workers. Socialism does not of itself guarantee any such meshing. In fact, we have seen that a planning board can produce goods in any proportions it wishes, and then juggle product prices (so all goods are sold) and wages (to obtain the needed labor). These arbitrary decisions are likely to lead to differential profits and losses from combine to combine unless the Board's output goals conform to consumer wants and worker dislikes.

How will a socialist government know whether it should expand in certain lines and contract in others in accordance with expressed consumer and worker preferences? If physical returns are constant with variations in output, so that average and marginal physical productivity of labor in any given employment coincide, the National Planning Board should adjust resources so that the profit rate of return is universally the same. It should calculate its total point investment (incurred entirely for wages in our simple case) and divide this into the total number of points received from sales by the same industry. Any industrial combine that shows an abnormally large quotient, according to this calculation, should have its operations expanded at the expense of labor and other resources in combines yielding a lower profit rate.

However, we cannot expect constant physical returns in each industry, and so the marginal physical productivity of labor (ϕ) is likely to differ from average productivity. In this case the Board should continually be estimating the point value of a marginal worker's output in each industry ($P \cdot \phi$) and comparing this with the wage being paid (W). The aim should then be to see whether a small transfer of workers, at the prices and wages existing before the shift, would yield a point profit. For example, if $P_c \cdot \phi_c$ is 135, $P_w \cdot \phi_w$ is 90, W_c is 120, and W_w is 100 points, we have seen that a transfer of one worker from wood to coal will increase sales receipts by 45 points while only increasing wage expenses by 20 points. In this case the Board would make a profit of 25 points *if* prices and wages did not have to be altered.

However, only a few workers should be shifted at one time as in reality there will have to be a slight alteration of prices (to sell the new outputs) and of wages (so that workers will voluntarily transfer). Subsequently another calculation must be made, using the second set of prices and wages, to see whether an additional transfer would yield a point profit, assuming again that the new prices and wages will not have to be altered again. Adjustments of this kind should continue until the differences among $P \cdot \phi$ for all industries are proportioned to the differences among W.

Why should the National Planning Board, in making these calculations, adopt the unrealistic assumption that prices and wages will not have to be altered in order to sell the new outputs and recruit the new labor needs? The answer comes as a syllogism. We know from Part IV that pure competition probably gives the best allocation of resources except where income inequalities are very great. Purely competitive entrepreneurs bring about this desirable result because they attempt to maximize profits on the supposition that product demands and labor supplies are infinitely elastic.   Therefore the Board can be expected to achieve the same optimum allocation of resources if it will proceed to maximize point profits under the assumption that product demands and labor supplies are infinitely elastic.

We have now seen that consumers' preferences will remain unknown to the central planners unless they have points to spend as they will.   Moreover, workers' preferences cannot be known unless they are paid point wages and allowed to choose their jobs. A socialist economy will not be operating efficiently unless the various product prices and labor wages are fitted together through the same profit calculations as are carried on by private businessmen in a purely competitive system.

The Rate of Investment

The rate at which a socialist economy invests rather than consumes should not be decided in an arbitrary or accidental manner. It would be arbitrary, for example, if the National Planning Board gave orders entailing a net investment rate of 10 per cent, quite regardless of the public's desires.   Such an investment rate would require that only 90 per cent of the nation's economic activity be for current consumption, with 10 per cent for investment.   Perhaps this would compel more denial of consumption than the public would choose for itself.   How can the socialist authorities determine the public's preferences in this respect?

First of all, it would be necessary for the government to ascertain the average rate of time preference among the public.   A National Loan Corporation might be established, which would borrow point money from individuals who wanted to invest and also lend point money to consumers faced with an emergency or overly eager to consume more now.   The N. L. C. would pay interest on point money deposited with it while charging interest on its loans to consumers.

The N. L. C. might try to equalize the volume of private deposits and consumer loans through adjustments in the official interest rate.   Most normal people would rather consume now than later, but some are especially impatient, whereas others are less unwilling to wait.   A man who is so impatient now that he will give up 108 points worth of enjoyment a year later in order to increase his current consumption by 100 points worth, has a time preference approaching 8 per cent.   A more restrained man might be willing to give up 100 points worth of sumptuary pleasure now for 103 points worth of consumer purchases a year from now. If the official rate of interest set by the N. L. C. were 5 per cent, the impatient man would borrow 100 points, the restrained man would deposit 100 points, and the government would function as an intermediate administrator.

Individuals will also have moderate liquidity preferences because of the need always to have small sums on hand when spending is continuous and wage payments are received only at intervals. However, the transactionary motive for wishing to hold active balances can be minimized by the state's extending store credits which, if exercised, are then deducted from pay checks at the end of each week. There would be little or no speculative demand for inactive balances, since presumably there would be no market in securities, real estate, or other valuable assets.

We can expect that the N. L. C. will be confronted by a private supply schedule of deposits (positively sloping) and a private demand schedule for overdrafts (negatively sloping). The intersection of these two schedules will indicate the equilibrium interest rate when all lenders and borrowers are private consumers. If all deposits with the N. L. C. are treated as loans and accorded interest although drawable on demand, the effect of liquidity preferences will be almost nil. These demand and supply schedules will then depend primarily upon time preference.

However, the N. L. C. may also wish to make loans to state enterprises, so that they can make real investments and thereby add to their efficiency and capacity. These point loans, for reasons explained below, had best come from point deposits made by the public with the N. L. C. However, if there is to be an excess of private deposits over consumer loans, an excess that is available for lending to industrial combines, it will be necessary for the interest rate to be raised. Perhaps a rate of 8 per cent will encourage private savers to raise their deposits from 7 billion to 8 billion points while choking off borrowing consumers from 7 billion to 6 billion points. There will then be 2 billion points a year available for industrial lending to state firms.

The N. L. C. should charge the going interest rate when it lends to industrial combines, even though they are also state-owned and -operated. The reason for this is that many managers probably want loans for expansion and modernization. However, managers who might see their way to paying back 105 points after a year for every 100 they borrow may not feel capable of paying back 108 points. The N. L. C., by raising interest rates, can always cut down the number of serious applications for industrial loans to a value equaling available deposits.

The managers of state enterprises will estimate the rate of interest they can afford to pay much in the same manner as do private entrepreneurs in ordinary economics. If the present earning value of a contemplated asset, computed by discounting its expected future income stream at prevailing interest rates, is more than its supply price or purchase cost, the plant manager should acquire it. An asset should be purchased, with borrowed funds if necessary, when its marginal efficiency exceeds the going interest rate.

The N. L. C. should attempt to equalize the public's apparent time preference with the marginal efficiency of new investment through the official interest rate. Each consumer will lend or borrow until his marginal time preference is equal to the official interest rate. The industrial managers will apply to the N. L. C. for loans until the marginal efficiency of capital in their plants has fallen to the official interest rate. The official rate should be such that net deposits made by the public equal outstanding industrial loans in point value. The regulating effect of the official interest rate will be greater if all lending and borrowing goes through the N. L. C. It might be made illegal for ordinary persons to lend to one another or for plant managers to reinvest profits at their own discretion. Then the economy, by virtue of the profit calculations of plant managers and the scrutiny of loan application examiners, will only invest in additional capital if it provides a rate of return greater than the indicated time preference of the general public.

It would not do for the N. L. C. to *create* new point money to loan to plant managers and thereby avoid the necessity of first borrowing from ordinary consumers. The people would then have no direct way of checking excessive industrial loans and investment. The requirement that loans be made from savings deposits vests the public with a relatively direct control over the rate of investment.

Socialist authorities could test their views on over-all investment if they would establish a state lending authority such as has been suggested here.   If an earlier decision has set the investment rate too high, so that too many capital goods and too few consumer goods have been produced, time preferences will have been forced up above the marginal efficiency of capital.   Cold and hungry men will demand a high interest rate on loans to the state.   Plant managers who have been forced to overequip will only be able to find remaining investment opportunities at a low rate of return.   The authorities will then find that their National Loan Corporation cannot continue the same excessive investment allocation of resources *and* make both ends meet financially.   In order to continue this too rapid investment, the N. L. C. would have to offer a higher interest rate to private depositors than to plant managers, and so entail an operating loss.

A socialist economy that did not limit itself to making real investments out of borrowings from the public would likely press on toward technical improvement and capacity expansion at a pace unwelcome to the public.   Rapid investment involves a temporary denial of consumption and can be carried to dangerous extremes.   An economic democracy should allow the people as a whole to exercise their wishes in this matter.

Decentralized Managerial Decisions

Old-fashioned planners may be surprised at the degree of independence that should be allowed to plant managers.   Managers certainly should be permitted to reorganize their "command" to improve output-over-input ratios.   But should they also be allowed, within limits, to determine output, prices, and even wages?

In industries that are organized into numerous plants, so that no single plant produces more than a fraction of the output or hires more than a fraction of the workers, each manager should be given full authority to maximize profits, measured in point money.   This will make for the best allocation of resources among plants.

The situation is more difficult where technical considerations favor unified control of an entire industry.   A large combine will have monopoly power in the product market and probably monopsony power in the labor market.   Managers will tend to restrict output if simply enjoined to maximize profits.   Instead, they should be instructed to adjust output, and prices and wages if necessary, so that the ratio of the value of a marginal worker's physical product to his wage, calculated for the industry in question, is equal to a yardstick ratio furnished them by the central authorities. Such a yardstick ratio would be the calculated average of the marginal-value-product-to-wage relation for the economy as a whole. Adherence to such instructions would often cut into a state enterprise's profits, and so possibly be resented by a manager who wanted to make a financial record for himself. A national planning board might therefore have to check the marginal-product-value-to-wage ratio in different firms from time to time and possibly order a different output. Obviously, the central authorities would outrank local managers and could occasionally intervene to countermand the latter's decisions. However the aim should be decentralization, if only to simplify administration.

It might be more dangerous, though, to leave investment decisions to independent managers, for they would only expand capacity when demand for their products was great, and, by so expanding, increase the effective demand of other producers. A generalized investment decision might feed on itself and create unnecessary fluctuations in economic activity. However, these ups and downs would not have the amplitude of capitalist booms and busts if new investment had to be borrowed from *deposited* savings, rather than from new bank credits.

Leisure and Unemployment

Presumably it is not a matter of indifference to people whether they work and are paid for a very few or a great many hours a day and weeks a year. Leisure is important to a man's welfare, providing he has sufficient consumer goods with which to enjoy it. On the other hand, involuntary unemployment, with its attendant poverty, is undesirable. Socialist planners should therefore guard against two dangers. One of them is overwork, with each person laboring for long hours, and no one having time to appreciate the consumer goods they have toiled to make. The other is involuntary unemployment.

A crude type of socialist economy, as we analyzed at the outset, could avoid the ordinary form of unemployment. Officials would simply assign everyone to a job, and, by either good luck or good management, the labor force might be kept usefully occupied. However, a directed work system, which provides no place for individual choice, could easily result in excessive hours. An average person will pay a higher price for leisure, in terms of sumptuary denial, as his plane of living rises. Therefore, a socialist economy, assuming that it succeeds in producing a high per capita income, should guard against sacrificing leisure and take care to provide flexible working schedules.

Each state enterprise might give its employees a choice, within limits, of how many hours they wished to work a day and how many weeks a year. The short-time workers would be used during peak load periods of the day and year. A worker who elected to work less than the maximum amount would receive less take-home pay. Such a pay adjustment would not necessarily be proportional to the length of time worked. In some enterprises shorter hours might cause a worker to increase his hourly productivity. In other jobs the dislocation caused by working a short schedule might be so great that a heavy pay deduction would have to be made. Presumably there should be some relation between productive contribution and total pay. Under this system individuals having little interest in consumption could work less and have sufficient time to develop their talents, knowledge, and culture. And less developed types, who must use up consumption goods at a great rate in order to enjoy themselves, would have to work longer as a consequence.

A sophisticated socialism might occasionally be threatened with involuntary unemployment. Plant managers might independently slow their usual rate of investment or lay off more men than they took on. Managerial independence and consumer direction, while necessary in order that the composition of the national income be properly determined, may sometimes result in workers' being unable to find jobs and so experiencing privations.

A socialist government could always attack an incipient depression by various spending schemes, however. A public works program could be kept in reserve during periods of great activity and then be started when the approach of depression was detected. The state could lower all prices or raise all wages. In either case there would be an injection of money into the economy. Widespread unemployment of capable workers need never be an actuality in even a sophisticated kind of socialist economy if the government will act decisively to influence effective demand.

However, even though widespread unemployment is avoided, some workers at any given moment will always find themselves without a job and hence without current income.   The state, as the only employer, might consider a small interest-bearing loan to tide each of them over; it would run less risk than usual in doing so.   A second resort might be temporary unemployment relief on a sufficiently ungenerous scale that the desire for employment would not be inhibited.   Perhaps, in the case of workers of below average mental and physical capacity, the state might be able to find unskilled work within their capabilities that would make them less of a charge on the economy than they would be under a system of indoor relief.   Every economy, socialist and capitalist, includes persons of limited employability within its population.

Concluding Comment

Socialism poses many dilemmas but one is particularly pointed. A socialist economy need never suffer from widespread and involuntary unemployment if it is willing to put people to work with little or no thought to the importance of what they are doing. There is always plenty of work to be done in the world.   Moreover, modern technology tends to make workers so physically productive that, even if most of them are engaged in doing relatively unimportant things, the total national product should be sufficient to maintain the population in some bearable fashion. Economic inefficiency, in the sense of badly allocated resources, becomes more and more tolerable as physical technique improves. On the other hand, the more worker and consumer choice is permitted under socialism, the more difficult it becomes to keep everyone employed at all times.   Any government that cares about the composition of the national product will always be contracting one industry and expanding some other, and there will probably always be some unemployment as a result of these transitions. There are no theoretical reasons to suppose that an economy, simply because it is socialist, will automatically have full employment *and* proper employment of all its resources.

Statements for Consideration

1. There need be no formal unemployment under socialism.   *Discuss*
2. Inefficient use of labor may be as wasteful as involuntary unemployment.   *Discuss*
3. There need be no overproduction with consequent market gluts under socialism, whereas goods that cannot be sold in free enterprise economies are usually destroyed.   *Evaluate*

4. Decentralized production control may improve the composition of the national product, but the danger of partial unemployment may thereby be increased. *Discuss*

5. The granting of free consumer choice is sufficient to occasion a satisfactorily constituted national product under state socialism. *Evaluate*

6. Socialism promises steady output of the wrong goods, whereas capitalism produces the right collection of goods but in fluctuating quantities. *Discuss*

7. The conditions that give rise to sloping demand schedules in a free enterprise economy—for example, product differentiation—would not occasion monopoly distortions under any socialist scheme for organizing the nation's resources. *Evaluate*

8. Opportunity costs do not need to be considered by socialist planners. *Evaluate*

9. State socialism inevitably involves adoption of the communist rule governing personal contributions toward and deductions from the national income. *Evaluate*

10. Under socialism incentive schemes are unnecessary because all workers know that they are indirectly laboring for themselves. *Evaluate*

11. A price system can play no useful part in a socialist economy. *Discuss*

References

Ellis, H. S. (Ed.), *A Survey of Contemporary Economics,* Chapter 12. Philadelphia: Blakiston, 1948.

Garver, F. B., and Hansen, A. H., *Principles of Economics,* Third Edition, Chapter 30. New York: Ginn, 1947.

Hayek, F. A. (Ed.), *Collectivist Economic Planning.* London: Routledge, 1935.

Lerner, A. P., *The Economics of Control,* Chapters 5–7. New York: Macmillan, 1945.

Lippincott, B. E. (Ed.), *On the Economic Theory of Socialism.* St. Paul: University of Minnesota Press, 1938.

Meyers, A. L., *Modern Economics,* Chapters 36, 37. New York: Prentice-Hall, 1946.

Pigou, A. C., *Socialism versus Capitalism.* London: Macmillan, 1937.

Samuelson, P. A., *Economics,* Chapter 26 (B). New York: McGraw-Hill, 1948.

Sweezy, A. R., "The Economist's Place Under Socialism," *Explorations in Economics.* New York: McGraw-Hill, 1937.

34

Why Not Capitalism?

After considering all the problems inherent in socialist planning, and the need to employ the price system and profit calculations of a free enterprise economy in order to achieve efficient production and distribution patterns, an obvious question to ask is "Why not capitalism?" The nature of the answer must depend upon the kind of capitalism that is contemplated as an alternative. It is not evident that the worst sorts of capitalism would be preferable to the best sorts of socialism. However, it is possible to conceive of a regulated capitalist economy that would be preferable to any socialist economy and that would possess some of the characteristics described hereafter.

Three Necessary Reforms

Laissez-faire capitalism, as briefly described above (Chapter 32), is economically unsatisfactory for a great many reasons. Three of the more important defects of such a system are its tendency toward (1) occasional periods of mass unemployment, (2) increasing inequalities in income distribution that are unrelated to current productivity differences, and (3) monopolistic and monopsonistic behavior on the part of firms and factors of production. A free enterprise economy which, with government help, could reform itself in these particulars, might compromise economic efficiency and personal freedom more satisfactorily than any other economic system.

Recurrent Mass Unemployment

All industrial economies have, sometime in the past, experienced periods of widespread business depression coupled with mass unemployment. These experiences have had a twofold effect upon many small proprietors and especially upon the vast majority who work for a living. Their affection and loyalty toward unregulated free enterprise have been shaken. Their willingness to accept government control schemes that promise financial security has increased. In some countries the belief has spread that socialism and planning can alone prevent mass unemployment. Apparently no form of free enterprise capitalism is sure to remain popular and secure unless government fiscal policies, appropriate to prevent mass unemployment, are part and parcel of it. The survival of private capitalism in the long run may well depend upon the possibility of combining it with such fiscal policies. Socialism can be expected tomorrow if the day ever arrives when the entire public becomes thoroughly convinced that effective action against depression and unemployment within a free market economy is impossible.

It is not surprising that many people should be willing to exchange some measure of personal freedom for financial security. Industrialization has meant that each part of every economy has become more specialized and interdependent than before. Each unit is helpless to provide for itself. The urban worker, if he is thrown out of work, cannot raise his own food or cut his own fuel. Even the farmer, now that mixed farming is largely a thing of the past, is dependent on some distant market. After a long period of depression and unemployment, it is natural that some workers are ready to let the government determine their jobs so long as it guarantees a job, and that some farmers are willing to let the government select their crops so long as it stands ready to buy them.

Because of these developing attitudes a burning question of our times is whether *all* forms, or only *some* forms, of free enterprise capitalism are prone to recurrent depression and unemployment. Socialists would have us believe the former. However, in view of the causes of general depression, and the possibility that fiscal policy might prevent or remedy unemployment, it seems very premature to abandon the ship of capitalism.

There are many theories of business cycles that seek to explain why a general business upswing turns into a downswing and then eventually into an upswing again. These various theoretical explanations tend to be conjectural and would alone suffice to fill a book. However, the forces that *continue* a downswing or an upswing are more obvious and certain.

A large part of the national product during normal times consists of durable producer and consumer goods. Most durable goods can usually be made to last a little longer, or a little less long, if necessary. The timing of their replacement is not preordained but is somewhat under the control of their owners. An additional characteristic of durable goods is that they tend to be rather expensive. Their cost may be a sizable fraction of a household's or a firm's annual budget. Accordingly, when incomes begin to fall, replacement of durable equipment is deferred, and the downswing is accentuated. Conversely, when incomes are rising, these extra funds are usually employed to replace aging durable goods, and the upswing is pushed higher as a consequence.

These accentuating tendencies are enormously exaggerated by the principle of acceleration (see Chapter 10). During bad times, not only is capital replacement deferred, but capacity may be allowed to shrink. And in good times, not only may replacement be advanced, but more units of capital will be wanted to expand each firm's capacity.

An increased purchase and production of durable goods of all kinds means more income for the factors of production that supply these goods. Households then have more to spend, and much of this will go for durable consumer goods, which will increase the demand for durable producer goods to help make them. Higher incomes again result. Conversely, a reduction in durable goods production reduces the incomes of productive factors, so that households spend less, especially on durable goods, and the demand for producer goods declines in turn. Appendix B shows how these influences can produce self-generating fluctuations in a simply conceived economy.

Severe economic depressions are due to the isolated decisions of millions of households and firms. Each firm naturally fails to replace aging equipment when capital goods are falling in price and declining sales already have rendered some of its capacity surplus. And yet from the viewpoint of the economy, this is an ideal time, when labor and other resources are idle, for the firm to replace capital. One can blame neither the individual firm for aggravating the depression nor the numerous households that unavoidably spend less when their incomes fall. The misfortune in this case is that the private interest of each firm and the public interest of the economy are for the moment in opposition.

What can the government do to sustain the expenditure stream of households and firms? Part III, especially Chapter 13, gives

some of the answers in detail. Several of the conclusions are
briefly restated here.

A firm is unlikely to replace capacity unless it seems to be
needed. Essentially, this means that effective demand throughout
the economy must in general be maintained, although naturally
there will always be some declining trades and firms that must
accept their fate. The effective demand of households and firms
can probably be influenced, although never precisely controlled,
by the taxing, spending, and credit policies of the government.

The spending of households depends largely upon their incomes
and cash holdings. The bulk of the consuming public, neglecting
the voluntary savings of the better-off families, are limited in their
spending by the money they have in their possession. The sales
of consumer goods industries and trades will respond fairly
promptly and proportionately to increases in household disposable
income. Public works may provide many households with some
additional money to spend. Households in the lower income tax
brackets will spend on consumption most of any tax reductions
that the government might allow them. A reduction of federal
excise taxes would leave households with more money to spend
on other things. If the federal monetary authorities would finance part of the deficits of state and local governments in depression emergencies, they could probably be induced to cut their tax
rates and so further increase households' spending on goods and
services produced by private enterprise. Regulation of consumer
credit should not be overlooked, because households are always
ready to use such credit, and most durable consumer goods are
bought on installment plans.

The spending of firms does not depend to the same extent upon
their liquid wealth position or their ability to borrow. In depressions, firms will not maintain or create surplus capital capacity
unless they feel convinced that it will soon be needed or unless
they feel that the present cost of doing so is unusually and temporarily low. The spending of firms depends upon their current
sales and the expectations that their managements entertain.
Consequently governments can influence the spending rate of
firms only very indirectly, if at all. One rather remote and uncertain way might be, during periods of full employment, to limit
the credit available to firms for expansion, so that, if a depression
begins to develop, more firms will eventually be compelled by

lack of capacity to replace worn-out equipment sooner. A more obvious but indirect means is to have government increase household spending in order to increase firm spending.

It is only in the last decade or so that public opinion in most countries has come to feel that governments have a responsibility to prevent depressions. During the great depression of the 'thirties, few governments took concerted and vigorous fiscal and monetary action or acted according to any definite and articulated plan. Unemployment relief and public works were designed to keep people alive. Government budget deficits were often involuntarily incurred and arose from declining tax proceeds and not reduced tax rates. Governments have had little practice in putting modern income theory to work against depressions and economists have thus had little experience with which to test their theories. It is because of this uncertainty that many people today are still doubtful whether the governments of regulated but capitalistic economies can evolve successful fiscal and monetary techniques for preventing prolonged and severe unemployment.

Extreme Monopoly Distortion

In some trades a vigorous enforcement of existing laws against monopoly and unfair competition could provide an adequate remedy of the monopoly problem. However, in other lines of production, modern technology links size and efficiency inseparably together, so that if unit costs of production are to be low it is inevitable that only one or a few firms can exist. Government intervention in these circumstances is essential.

The government has a choice of economic remedies, although at the moment they are not all legally permissible. It can set ceilings below the prices of monopolies and floors above the prices of monopsonists. Alternatively, in both cases, it can provide a subsidy per unit of output or input, and then prevent undue profit from accruing to the firms by imposing some special tax that does not directly affect the scale of operations. In other cases, it may seem best for the government to subsidize competitive firms or even go into the business itself, in order to set a more competitive pace for the private firms.

Perhaps more novel techniques of control lie just over the future horizon. Perhaps the day will come when, in the case of incurably monopolistic situations, the government will participate in managerial policy.   For example, the government might appoint some of the directors of firms that have been convicted of violating the revised anti-monopoly laws, and require that price decisions receive the approval of such men.   The government, having in effect participated in determining the policies of such firms, should then be estopped from prosecuting them for monopoly violations, although, of course, the government's director might have to be replaced by another man if he lost sight of the public interest.

An arrangement of this kind might also remove a great deal of current uncertainty.   At the present time, except where consent decrees are entered into, firms are often uncertain whether the agencies of the federal government will consider a particular policy legal or illegal and whether, in the latter event, they will move against it.   Moreover, some of these legally questionable policies may not run counter to the public interest; for instance, they may envisage cooperation with rival firms to eliminate certain real costs of advertising, storage, or procurement.   Arm-length competition is not always a virtue, but any other course often runs the risk of federal prosecution.

One must also recognize that some of the worst monopoly distortions in the economy may arise from industry-wide bargaining by strong labor unions.   When the wage paid by some trade for some particular labor skill is forced far above a competitive level, as indicated by the eagerness of outside labor to take jobs in that trade when they are available, the output of that labor is likely to be less than a proper allocation of resources would occasion. Logically, the government must then attempt either to bring all other wages up or to set a lower wage ceiling on the monopoly labor.   Of course, output could also be kept up by subsidizing the employers of the monopoly labor; however, if employers are competing actively for labor, these subsidies will become monopoly wages, and it is not desirable that the incomes of these workers should depend upon organization rather than upon their relative productivity.

At the other extreme from monopoly, there are some trades that seem to invite everyone to try his entrepreneurial luck, so that there are usually too many resources employed at any given time, and too many being employed by inexperienced and hence usually inefficient proprietors who last a season and then pass on. It may sometimes be as important to bring a little stability and contraction to such overinvested trades as to open up monopolized industries to new competition.   Various possibilities suggest themselves.   The government might levy a specific excise tax on sales. It might establish fees for new firms.   Or it might permit only a given number of firms to operate and sell these permits to the highest bidders, rather than have them issued according to influence.

The object of all these remedies of undue monopoly and undue competition is to reorder the allocation of resources in a way that will bring the economic contribution of the marginally employed resources in every trade into greater equality.   The purpose of these government devices is not to moralize or punish.   There is little rationality in becoming emotional and suggesting that the proprietor of a monopoly is a "bad" man because his prices exceed his marginal costs.   The monopolist and the farmer are both just as selfishly motivated when they seek to maximize profits through an equation of marginal cost and marginal revenue.   In fact, relative to the monopolist, the farmer is "guilty" of employing too many resources.   The real social need is not to punish monopolists of the past through fines or imprisonment but to deter future monopoly behavior by means of government actions already described.

Unproductive Income Inequalities

It has already been explained how wide inequalities in income affect the composition, as well as the distribution, of the national product.   However, when these inequalities are based on differences in the economic contributions of individuals and their assets, they are at least partially desirable as incentives.   Even if we can agree thus far, two difficult questions remain, to which perhaps there is no answer.   One of these is whether income differences should be proportional or less than proportional to differences in economic contribution.   The other question is whether income differences that are due to gifts or inheritance inhibit economic productivity, and if so, what as a practical matter can be done about them.

Let us suppose that Jones and Smith both work in the same law office, Jones receiving $12,000 a year and Smith $6,000 a year, the difference being due, not to nepotism, but to their respective values to the employing firm.   So long as employers are free to make their own salary bargains such differences in gross income will always tend to arise.   However, should a similar difference in net income be permitted, or should Jones be taxed proportionately more than Smith?   If Jones pays a higher tax rate than Smith, he is sharing more of his productivity with the community.   The ethical rights and wrongs of such a result are debatable. Actually, in most countries, most voters are in favor of taxing higher incomes more heavily, possibly for the very simple reason that more families have small than have large incomes!

Suppose we complicate the situation a little more, and suppose that Smith's wife has inherited an estate that brings her $6,000 a year, so that the Smith household altogether receives the same income as the Jones household.   Should these two families be left with similar incomes after taxes?   Is it "fair" that Smith should live as well as Jones?   Will Smith's incentives to become as good a lawyer as Jones be lessened by the fact that his wife has $6,000 a year?   Or will Smith improve as a lawyer, and secure a higher *per diem,* but work only three days a week?   In the latter event the inheritance has lost the economy the potential output of the two weekdays Smith can afford to take off.

What steps might the government take, assuming it did wish to prevent any individual from receiving a large inheritance, perhaps on the grounds that this would otherwise permit him to consume out of all proportion to his relative economic productivity? Logically, in view of its purpose, the government should not tax large estates but only large bequests to individuals.   If a millionaire leaves $10 to each of the 100,000 people who live in his home town—perhaps hoping his memory will at least receive a monument in consequence—the economy has no complaint.   However, taxing large individual inheritances is not the end of the problem. Rich men may, while still alive, make large gifts to sons and daughters, and will in fact be encouraged to do so if estate or inheritance taxes exist.   The usual recourse is to impose a gift tax on sums given a single person within a year which exceed a certain limit.

The danger that inheritance taxes will inhibit the incentive of people to earn income, either by working themselves or by hiring their natural resources and capital funds to the economy, must always be borne in mind.   However, an inheritance tax should be less of a deterrent than an estate tax.   Some rich men and women either have no natural heirs or dislike them and would prefer to leave their money to a non-profit cause they believe in. An inheritance tax would not deter such people in the way that an estate tax would. Moreover, inheritance and gift taxes do not affect the desire to acquire income very directly. Most people don't think much about leaving their money until they are well along in years, and meanwhile they hanker after income for themselves. Income spent on self-enjoyment is unaffected by inheritance taxes. To some extent the natural desire of parents to do something for their children can be gratified, especially in the case of sons and sons-in-law, by investing *in* them rather than *for* them, perhaps through supporting them during professional training. In this way the wealth of the parents increases the productivity of their children, whereas an expected inheritance might have tempted the heirs into a life of sloth.

It is not enough that a government should prevent people from enjoying income they have not produced for themselves. Government also has the more positive responsibility of seeing to it that behavior that contributes to the national product is still rewarded even after taxes. If entrepreneurs are to continue innovating, which before the event is usually something of a gamble, the government should not, through income tax laws, reduce the profits of success without alleviating the losses of failure. At present the odds against realizing a net return after taxes are lengthened by the government. Past corporate losses cannot be fully offset against subsequent profits, and past personal capital losses cannot be fully offset against later capital gains. Venture capital, which is invested by corporations, may be taxed twice, first as corporate income and then as personal income, if the enterprise is successful. If the aim of policy is to relate disposable income, although not necessarily proportionately, to the national product contributions of individuals, the present taxation of income should be amended considerably.

The Philosophy of Regulation

Government regulation of a capitalist economy should be along liberal lines so far as possible. The entrepreneur, the worker, the consumer, and all other private units in the economic scheme should be left free, save in the most exceptional cases, to determine their own conduct. The government should limit itself to modifying the economic environment, perhaps through taxes and subsidies and price limits, so that the individual entrepreneur will tend to act, from self-interest, in the public interest.

A police state is more likely to regulate private economic affairs through specific orders. Farmers are told what crops to raise. Workers are directed to their jobs as in an army. Manufacturers throughout an industry may be told how many units they shall each produce. In such cases, if the individual does not behave as ordered, he runs the risk of punishment.

A regulated capitalistic economy could probably achieve the same results by softer means. If more wheat is wanted, a high price or subsidy for wheat, set by the government, will not only shift farmers into wheat growing but also increase the output plans of existing wheat growers. Workers can be drawn from one job to another by wage differentials, which ensure that the men who are most willing to change will do so, and that those who are most settled need not have to transfer jobs. The output of an industry can always be influenced by government-set prices, taxes, and subsidies, and the extra output will come from different firms within the industry, in part according to their marginal costs.

One of the arts of political economy is to obtain desirable economic results with a minimum restraint of private self-interest. Self-interest is the motive power of all but the most collective and planned economies. Without the self-interest of the entrepreneur, of the worker, of the consumer, and of other suppliers of productive factors, there would be little production in a capitalist economy. Governments may have to channel this self-interest at times, but they should always impede it as little as possible. A doctor does not cure his patient but, through prescription or treatment, attempts to bring the natural forces of health into play. Government officials should, by analogy, set the stage so that self-interest is more likely to bring forth socially desirable results and is free to function.

Self-interest provides the administrator with one of the most practical of all controls. By changing some aspect of the economic environment, perhaps through establishing a high price floor, thousands of producers will expand output in the most economical manner from self-interest. The alternative of direct controls would require government officials to determine how much extra each firm should produce and which new firms should start producing where, and then to enforce these plans upon all concerned. Inspectors and policemen would be needed everywhere. Antagonisms would develop between the people and the government.

Perhaps we can learn something about regulating free enterprise from the manner in which psychologists train animals. If we had a rat in a maze, and wished it always to travel through one corridor and never through another, what might we do? We might forcibly push and pull the resisting animal through the maze, by the desired route, and every time we wanted it to repeat the trip we should have to be on hand to renew the struggle. Alternatively, we might provide prizes along the right corridors and penalties along the wrong corridors, so that, after some experience of each, the animal would select the desirable route and reject the undesirable route. Hereafter, it will behave in the intended manner from self-interest, and in the absence of supervisors. In the economic sphere, profits and losses are the prizes and penalties that train entrepreneurs, consumers, workers, and others to behave in economically desirable ways.

How desirable economic self-interest is as a means of powering and regulating the economy can best be realized by considering the alternative. Most governments that dispense with economic self-interest as a *modus operandi* are likely to resort to fear instead. The fears with which they may prod people to behave as prescribed are many and varied. Fear of the concentration camp and fear for one's family are two compelling examples. Governments cannot employ these fears to good purpose and still retain the usual guarantees of civil liberty. If governments are to central economic life, and if civil liberty is to be retained, it is almost essential that regulation and incentives act through the economic self-interest of individuals.

Perverted Regulation for Special Interests

Inherent in all government regulation of economic affairs is an actual danger against which the citizen should always be on guard. The danger is that controls will be used to favor special interests and will thereby sacrifice the general interest. The purpose of regulation should be to bring private and public interest into greater accord wherever possible. When these interests do not coincide, as may often be the case, it is a terrible perversion of controls to use them in the service of special private interests. And yet this can and does happen very easily and frequently.

The tax system is a good example of how a control device can be improperly employed. The tax policy of the past has been to raise revenue in such a way as to minimize political repercussions. Corporations seem impersonal things, so their income is taxed as well as dividend income, with little thought of what this does to investment. The rich are relatively few, and always unpopular with the poorer majority, so their incomes are taxed very disproportionately, with little consideration of the economic effects. Capital gains and losses are handled in such a way that risky ventures become even more unattractive to entrepreneurs and innovation is consequently slowed.

Agriculture furnishes another example. High support prices for agricultural products serve no purpose in peacetime except to provide farmers with extra income. The government must take a loss on the surplus. Agricultural products that are raised by relatively few farmers do not get subsidized, but the economic cause for this is not as apparent as the political reason.

Tariffs on imports provide yet another instance. The prices and supplies of many goods on the domestic market depend upon the level of individual customs duties. These duties exist because of special interest pressures. As a result the allocation of our resources is rendered uneconomic to some degree. Unfortunately, there is no Washington lobby dedicated to the proper allocation of American resources, and there probably never will be.

The history of peacetime rent controls also illustrates how economic considerations can be swamped by those of politics. In the nation as a whole the normal housing situation was not suddenly and appreciably worsened. Increasing rents were due primarily to a doubling of household money incomes, although population shifts within the country considerably aggravated the situation in some areas, and the baby boom placed a premium on certain types of accommodation. By 1947, as compared with 1939, the prices of all major consumer goods and services had on an average doubled, except for rents, which remained partially controlled. The man who supplied labor was allowed to collect

a double wage, the farmer who supplied food was allowed to collect a double price, but the man who supplied a place to live was
restricted.   It is, of course, conceivable that this anomalous situation was due to the political fact that workers, farmers, and
renters are more numerous groups than landlords.   The economic result was that rents did not rise enough to force renters
to economize in the use of living space.   It lessened mobility of
labor and population within the country because a newcomer
could not force his way into a dwelling through rent bidding.
Historical precedence rather than relative need, apart from income
differences, determined who lived where.   The economic consequences of this political policy were probably unfavorable on
balance.

One particularly alarming aspect of government regulation of
economic affairs is that the over-all economic consequences of
each action are seldom considered.   The usual object is to help
the consumer, or to help the farmer, or to help labor, or to help
the textile industry, and so on.   Legislative action tends to be
piecemeal.   Moreover, as Congress can only take up one thing
at a time, hearings are always on a particular bill, and the economic interaction of a great many potential statutes cannot be
considered simultaneously.   Hearings on specific bills naturally
tend to attract the attentions of the special interests directly
affected.   The general interest tends to go by default.

It is not the upshot of these remarks that economists should be
given authority to determine how the economy should be regulated.   The economist is only a technician and all social problems involve questions that the economist is no better qualified
to judge than anyone else.   For example, every new government
regulation involves equity considerations, and economists have
no monopoly on justice.   Technicians are often too single-
minded, and hence should never be given unbridled power to
affect the lives of others; if dieticians were given authority to pre-
scribe what people were to eat, we might all be healthier, but
would we be happier?   No, the real point to be labored here is
that the advice of technicians should be given great weight, and
should only be disregarded if the public in general does not wish
to follow it.   The initiative for proposing government controls
should not lie with some special group that wants help, possibly
to the disadvantage of others, but with economists who feel that

some policy can advance the general economic welfare. The elected representatives of the people would and should make the final decisions.

Government today possesses many powers of control over economic life. A fundamental question that confronts any democratic people is whether these powers shall be exercised in the general economic interest or to grant favors to special interest groups. Unfortunately, these two interests are often antagonistic, and then the problem is very real. What we must all remember is that the founding fathers did not establish political democracy so that the power of government might be enlisted by each special financial interest in its struggle against the general economic interest. Our political processes permit this to happen, but they were not designed with that purpose in mind.

The future prospects of private capitalism would seem to depend upon the political responsibility and maturity of voters, legislators, and officials. We have a regulated private capitalist economy now, but our private capitalism is not always regulated in the right way and for the proper reasons. Yet resistance to socialism depends in large part upon the quality of such regulation and the sovereignty of the public interest. It is accordingly the duty of the economist to perfect his techniques of control and that of voters to make the general welfare paramount.

Statements for Consideration

1. The only kind of private capitalism that is economically possible is *laissez-faire* capitalism. *Discuss*
2. The advent of industrialization has increased the economic insecurity of many people. *Explain*
3. Upswings and downswings in economic activity might not be so pronounced if households and firms used fewer durable goods. *Explain*
4. There is no way in which the government can increase the spending of *firms* in the bottom of a depression, but it can augment *household* spending quite readily. *Discuss*
5. Large-scale economies in production invite government intervention. *Discuss*
6. Competition at arm's length is not always a virtue. *Discuss*
7. Industry-wide bargaining by strong labor unions can occasion monopoly distortions. *Explain*
8. All income inequality is economically undesirable. *Evaluate*
9. A government tax on bequests may inhibit incentives less than a tax of equivalent weight on income. *Discuss*

10. Economic regulation should regulate the environment rather than the individual. *Explain*
11. Self-interest of others provides the administrator with one of the most practical of all control media. *Discuss*
12. All economic controls of government are inevitably in the general interest. *Evaluate*
13. In the political scuffle the general economic interest tends to go by default. *Explain*

References

Garver, F. B., and Hansen, A. H., *Principles of Economics,* Chapter 31. New York: Ginn, 1947.

Jones, E., "In Praise of Competition," *Explorations in Economics.* New York: McGraw-Hill, 1937.

Lerner, A. P., *The Economics of Control,* Chapters 21, 22, 24. New York: Macmillan, 1945.

Lundberg, E., *Studies in the Theory of Economic Expansion.* London: King, 1937.

Marshall, A., *Principles of Economics,* Eighth Edition, Book IV, Chapters 12, 13. London: Macmillan, 1920.

Meyers, A. L., *Modern Economics,* Chapter 38. New York: Prentice-Hall, 1941.

Morgan, T., *Income and Employment,* Chapter 14. New York: Prentice-Hall, 1947.

Samuelson, P. A., *Economics,* Chapter 3. New York: McGraw-Hill, 1948.

Schumpeter, J. A., "Capitalism in the Postwar World," *Postwar Economic Problems.* New York: McGraw-Hill, 1943.

Wright, D. M., "Income Redistribution Reconsidered," *Income, Employment and Public Policy.* New York: Norton, 1948.

Appendix A

Total Cost and Revenue Functions

A MAJORITY of the diagrams used in describing the profit-maximizing decisions of firms, and in analyzing value theory problems generally, have traditionally employed average and marginal curves. The explanation is probably that the first diagrams, involving demand and supply schedules, featured price along the vertical axis. Consequently, when the adjustment of purely competitive firms to the market price came to be investigated, the same vertical scale was employed, and curves of marginal and average cost were added to that of average revenue or price. If monopoly cases had been graphed before those of pure competition, it is not unlikely that the vertical scales would have referred to total revenue and total cost, rather than to revenue and cost per unit, for many relationships can then be more readily grasped. For this same reason the following analysis of total revenue and total cost functions of output is included.

Figure I has physical output along the horizontal axis and dollars along the vertical axis. TC is the total cost curve of a firm. Apparently a short-run situation is depicted here, for there are costs of OA at zero output, and these must therefore be a fixed cost. The variable costs in any case are the excess of total costs over the fixed cost, which is OA. The TC curve shows that total costs always increase with output. However, at point B on TC, which is the so-called "point of inflection," the direction of curvature changes. In economic terms, this means that total costs increase with output at a falling rate from zero to Q_1 output, and subsequently increase at a rising rate. Marginal costs will be at a minimum at OQ_1 output; this is confirmed by the fact that a tangent drawn to TC at B will be flatter than any other tangent drawn to the total cost function. The output that will yield minimum *average* cost can be determined by finding the point on TC to which a line, drawn from O, will be tangent.

TR represents the total revenue when different outputs are sold. It starts at O, as of course there is no revenue when there are no units to sell, and then rises. If the depicted situation were one of pure competition, TR would be a straight line sloping upward and to the right, indicating a constant price, always equal to a constant marginal revenue. Actually a case of monopolistic competition is shown in Fig. I, as evidenced by a total revenue curve that rises, at a falling rate,

523

to a peak at *C*, and then declines.   A tangent drawn to *TR* at *C* would be horizontal, indicating a zero marginal revenue.   In other words, the demand is of unit price elasticity at Q_3, is elastic from *O* to Q_3, and is inelastic thereafter.

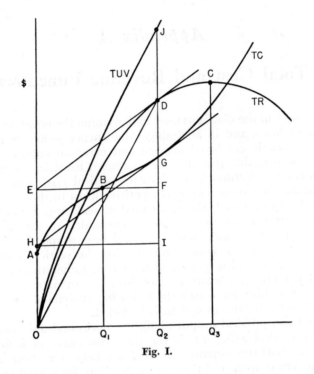

Fig. I.

The diagram illustrates very clearly that a marginal value will always be less than an average value when the latter is falling.   For example, at OQ_2 output, the price is falling, as evidenced by the fact that lines drawn from *O* to the *TR* curve at successively higher outputs will be decreasingly steep; consequently, at *D*, marginal revenue is less than average revenue.   This can superficially be seen by the fact that *ED* is less steep than *OD*.   More precisely, marginal revenue is *DF/EF*, and average revenue is DQ_2/OQ_2; now *EF* is equal to OQ_2, so marginal revenue must be less than average revenue, since *DF* is only part of DQ_2.

The profit obtained at any output is represented by the vertical excess of *TR* over *TC*.   So long as *TR* is rising more rapidly than *TC*, marginal revenue exceeds marginal cost, and profits must be increasing with output.   When an output is reached at which a tangent to *TR* has the same slope as a tangent to *TC*, marginal revenue has become equal to marginal cost, and the vertical distance of *TR* over *TC* is no longer widening and will soon begin to narrow.   Profits are then at a maximum.

In Fig. I an output of Q_2 maximizes profits of DG. Marginal revenue equals marginal cost at Q_2 output because the tangent at D has the same slope as the tangent at G: a check will show that DF/EF is equal to GI/HI. The price charged, that is the revenue per unit, is the total revenue divided by the output, or DQ_2/OQ_2. The average cost is the total cost divided by the output or GQ_2/OQ_2. And the per unit profit—not a very significant magnitude—is DG/OQ_2.

It is worth noting that a firm which possesses some monopoly power over its selling market, as evidenced by the curving total revenue function, will always maximize profits at an output corresponding to an elastic demand. The TC curve is always rising, and so the optimum quantity must be one where TR is also rising; but a rising total revenue indicates a positive marginal revenue, which in turn denotes an elastic demand. Analytically it is incorrect to state that a monopolist will favor inelastic demand situations.

At times there has been a question raised concerning the possibility of a firm's being in output equilibrium with falling marginal costs. Falling marginal costs mean that total cost is increasing with output, but at a decreasing rate, and that the total cost curve would rise but be concave when viewed from below. A cost function of this kind may not be as uncommon in some industries as is sometimes supposed. And theoretically it is not incompatible with equilibrium. A unique output determination will still maximize profits so long as the increase in total revenue declines at an even faster rate than the retardation in the rate of increase in total cost. Graphically, equilibrium requires that the total revenue curve be even more concave from below than the total cost curve. Where monopoly elements are present, this requirement will frequently be satisfied; for sooner or later the demand is likely to lose elasticity, and then the TR curve turns down, in which case the concavity of the TR curve will certainly be more pronounced than that of the TC curve. However, where there is pure competition in the sale of the product and the TR curve is a straight line rising from the origin, equilibrium would be impossible within an output range where marginal costs were falling.

Industrial managers sometimes prepare "break even" charts for their businesses; these charts consist of two straight lines. One is a so-called total revenue line originating at the axis intersection. The other line starts from an intercept on the vertical axis. The distance from the origin to the intercept is the overhead or fixed cost. An absolutely straight total cost line implies variable costs per unit that are equal to a constant marginal cost. It is possible, but not very likely, that such cost characteristics are encountered in situations where there are large sunk costs; for example, once the cost of setting type for a book has been met, extra copies involve a small and fairly constant outlay for ink, paper, and running the presses. "Break even" charts fall further under suspicion because, although they are usually prepared for firms with quasi-monopoly powers, they employ what are superficially straight line TR curves. If a firm sets its own selling price, its total revenue curve cannot be linear but will be concave viewed from below. The revenue line on most "break even" charts, especially when prepared for large manufacturing companies, is not a total revenue function at all, but simply one of many possible lines, like OD in Fig. I, which terminate at the true total revenue curve.

A kind of total use value, measured in money, is shown in Fig. I. This curve represents the total value to buyers, in money terms, derived from using each several quantity of the good. The TR curve is related to such a total use value (TUV) curve and in fact can readily be derived from the latter. For example, at the price that occasions OQ_2 output and use, the slope of TUV must be equal to the slope of OD, because buyers will purchase up to the amount where the marginal use value coincides with the price. Also, when OQ_3 is sold at a price represented by the slope of a line from O to C, this slope will also represent the use value of the "last" unit. Now we can understand why it is that TR may eventually decline with additional output despite the use value of these marginal units and the continued rise of the TUV curve.

One possible representation of buyers' surplus is very straightforward, when TUV and TR schedules are employed, since then it is simply the vertical distance between them, or JD when the monopolistic firm maximizes profits with an output of OQ_2. The maleconomic effects of monopoly power are also rendered evident by a simultaneous examination of a firm's TUV, TR, and TC schedules. *A priori,* the economy desires, in each case, to maximize the difference between total use value and total cost, whereas the private entrepreneur wishes to maximize the difference between total revenue and total cost. These two objectives must be in conflict when the producer senses that his TR curve is not identical with the TUV schedule. More specifically, TUV-TC will be greater at some output above OQ_2, which last maximizes TR-TC. It is possible that a true consumer cooperative, which sought to maximize its members' profits *and* buyers' surplus, might be able to resolve the usual conflict of interest and operate even a monopolistic concern in a manner compatible with the general economic welfare.

References

Ellis, H. S. (Ed.), *A Survey of Contemporary Economics,* Chapter 13. Philadelphia: Blakiston, 1948.

Enke, S., "Consumer Cooperatives and Economic Efficiency," *American Economic Review,* March 1945.

Appendix B

When Saving and Investment Plans Differ

Elements of Instability

A FUNDAMENTAL CAUSE of instability in any economy characterized by both free enterprise and mechanized production—such as that of the United States—is what may loosely be termed the *capital-income-sales* cycle. Commodity inventories are a further source of alternating expansion and contraction in the economy. These two phenemona together offer a partial explanation of the economic fluctuations that are sometimes called business cycles.

The capital-income-sales cycle repeats itself somewhat as follows: (1) The production and installation of additional machinery and equipment involves the payment of newly erected or released money to productive factors; this is especially significant if capital goods are complex and costly. (2) The extra income received by the owners of productive factors leads in turn to increased sales of final goods to consumers; however, if the propensity to consume falls markedly below unity, the sales effect will be geared down from that of income. (3) Producing the extra output for sale will require additions to capital equipment, if no surplus capacity exists; and these additions may prove considerable, in percentage terms, if capital goods are relatively long-lived. And then again, to repeat the cycle, the production of this extra capital produces additional income for consumers.

A sudden change in any one of these three elements—i.e., in capital, income, or sales—will have repercussions on the other two elements and then in turn upon itself. It is altogether conceivable that these adjustments might go on forever, generating one business cycle after another, or even perhaps continue indefinitely in one direction. However, given the conditions of the real world, it is very possible that any autonomous change in one of the elements will, after a number of induced fluctuations, become absorbed into a new state of dynamic equilibrium.

Three Simple Models

Let us imagine a simple economy that produces only one kind of consumer good (called "outputs") with the aid of only one kind of machine (called "capitals"). One unit of capital can produce output at a rate of 200 a year. The price of an output always remains constant at one dollar.

527

Businessmen normally produce each year the quantity of outputs *demanded* during the preceding year. For example, if they produced *x* outputs during the first year, but could have sold *x* plus *y* units, they will produce *x* plus *y* units during the second year; or, if they produced *x* plus *y* units in the first year, but only *x* were demanded, they will produce *x* in the second year, and the preceding year's surplus has presumably spoiled. In other words, there are no inventories to absorb differences between the rate of production and sales.

A breakdown of the per unit costs reveals an indirect capital cost of 40¢ per unit and a direct labor cost of 60¢ per unit. Hence the total per unit cost is $1.00, which is equal to the price, and there are zero profits.

The initial equilibrium involves an annual production of one million outputs, no surplus capacity, and an income for the economy of $1,000,000 a year. The original cause of disturbance in each case is an *autonomous* decision on the part of businessmen to increase output by ten per cent for *one* year. We shall now analyze what transpires if (1) the marginal propensity to consume (*C*) is unity and the service life of capital (*E*) is one year or 200 units of output, (2) the marginal propensity to consume is .50 for all income in excess of "normal" and capital has a one-year service life, and (3) the consuming propensity is once again unity but capital has a service life of five years or 1,000 outputs.

Case One: $C = 1.00$, $E = 200$ units or 1 year

The autonomous decision by businessmen to expand output by 10 per cent to 1,100,000 units for one year will require a stock of 5,500 instead of 5,000 machines. Hence the production of capitals will have to be expanded by 10 per cent or by 500 machines. The cost of a machine must be $80 if the capital cost per unit of output is 40¢ and if a machine produces 200 units of output in its one year of service life. Hence an additional 500 times $80, or $40,000 extra, is spent on the purchase of capitals. Businessmen also make an extra direct outlay of $60,000, for they are producing 100,000 more outputs and the direct cost per unit is assumed to be 60¢. Altogether income is increased by $100,000. Hence the public, because of the unit marginal propensity to consume, will demand 100,000 extra units in the first year.

Then, in the second year, businessmen will be induced to make 1,100,000 outputs, since this was the demand in the first year. The total income made available by businessmen in the second year will again be $1,100,000, for they will again buy 5,500 machines at $80 each and have a total direct expense of $660,000. And again, in the second year, the public will spend every dollar of income and demand 1,100,000 outputs. Hence businessmen repeat their operations during the third, fourth, and ensuing years.

Under our assumptions, any autonomous decision by businessmen to raise or lower output, in the first year, will subsequently induce them to maintain the new level. The entire adjustment process is completed in one year.

Case Two: $C = .50$; $E = 200$ units or 1 year

In this case we assume that the average propensity to consume is one at the normal income of $1,000,000 a year but that the marginal propensity to consume is .50. For instance, if the income made available by businessmen is $1,100,000, the public demand for outputs at one dollar each will be 1,050,000 units, whereas the demand would be for 950,000 units at an income of $900,000. The latter result will be possible if consumers drew on savings or the government provides unemployment relief. In Case Two we shall find that an autonomous decision by businessmen to increase output for one year by ten per cent will have no effect in the very long run.

TABLE I

$C = .50$; $E = 200$ UNITS OR ONE YEAR

	Output	Capitals	INCOME FROM PRODUCING Capitals	Outputs	Total	Demand
Before	1,000,000	5,000	$400,000	$600,000	$1,000,000	$1,000,000
1 yr.	1,100,000	5,500	440,000	660,000	1,100,000	1,050,000
2	1,050,000	5,250	420,000	630,000	1,050,000	1,025,000
3	1,025,000	5,125	410,000	615,000	1,025,000	1,012,500
4	1,012,500	5,062	405,000	607,500	1,012,500	1,006,250
5	1,006,250	5,031	402,500	603,750	1,006,250	1,003,125

The above result is suggested by Table I. The autonomous decision in the first year to produce 100,000 more units increases income by $100,000. However, the demand only increases by 50,000 units. Hence in the second year businessmen are induced to make only 1,050,000 units. This pays out an income of $1,050,000, but at this income level the public demand is only for 1,025,000 units. In each ensuing year the output produced, the income paid out, and the public demand all fall toward the initial one million dollar mark.

An autonomous decision to reduce output ten per cent below normal to 900,000 units would not cause an equivalent reduction in demand, and so, year by year, businessmen would be induced to raise their output to the preceding year's demand, until they were once again at the normal output, income, and demand level of one million dollars and units respectively.

A marginal propensity to consume of less than one, when capital does not survive beyond one year, will slowly induce an economy to return to the normal level, at which demand equals income, and the average propensity to consume is again unity.

Case Three: $C = 1.00$, $E = 1,000$ units or 5 years

We shall now recognize the durability of capital by making the more realistic assumption that a machine has a service life of five years or 1,000 units of output. However, we shall revert to the earlier supposition that the marginal propensity to consume is always one. An autonomous decision by businessmen to increase output in one year will subsequently induce an accelerating expansion.

The reason for this is that a 10 per cent increase in output will necessitate a 50 per cent increase in capital production if the service life of a machine is 5 years and no idle capacity exists. The total stock of capital needed to produce 1,000,000 units of output is still 5,000 if a machine's annual capacity is 200 outputs a year. However, if the service life of a machine is 5 years, only 1,000 machines will need, on an average, to be replaced in any one year. But it will take a capital stock of 5,500 machines to produce 1,100,000 units of output a year. Hence the decision to increase output by 10 per cent, or by 100,000 units of output, means that 1,500 machines will have to be purchased and made, because 500 extra machines will be needed in addition to the normal 1,000 for replacement. This demand is 50 per cent above the normal production of capitals. Incidentally, if the average service life of a machine were 8 years, a 10 per cent increase in output would immediately require an 80 per cent increase in capital production, and so on.

The accelerating expansion of the economy under our present assumptions is shown in Table II. This second table is far more complicated than the first because machines are no longer used in a single year and hence the capital production in any year is no longer 1/200 of the output. It now takes five columns to determine the number of new machines that businessmen will have to acquire each year.

We must first—as before—determine how many machines must be kept in operation during the current year; this will always be 1/200 of the currently planned output and is shown in column 2. Next we must check back and learn the number of machines available for use sometime during the preceding year; this figure is placed in the third column, and it will always be equal to the number of capitals needed in the preceding year (given in column 2 one line above). Then we must determine the number of machines worn out during the preceding year, and this depends upon the service life of a machine and last year's output; for example, if a machine has a service life of 1,000 units, and last year 1,000,000 outputs were produced, 1,000 machines will have been worn out (see column 4). Now we can find the number of machines available at the start of the current year, since this will be equal to the number of machines operated last year minus the number worn out last year; for example, taking the first or any other line, the third column minus the fourth column gives us the fifth column. However, the number of machines that will be purchased by businessmen will be equal to the number currently needed minus the number capable of use at the start of the present year; consequently column 2 minus column 5 gives us column 6 in any year.

It is now a simple matter to calculate the income paid out by entrepreneurs incidental to their operations. They spend money in purchasing machines and they make direct outlays in producing outputs. We are now assuming that the price of a machine is $400, so that the capital cost per unit of output can still be $.40, and hence the income resulting from machine purchases will be 400 times the number of capitals currently acquired; in the table, column 7 is therefore equal to column 6 times the assumed cost of a machine. The direct outlays for producing output are equal to the number made times the direct cost, here assumed to be $.60 a unit of output, so that the total cost per unit will equal the price of $1.00; hence, in the table, column 8 is equal to column 1 times the direct cost per unit of output. The total income paid out from all current production (column 9) is equal to outlays for machines (column 7) plus direct outlays for final consumer goods (column 8).

The current demand (column 10) is based on current income (column 9) and the propensity to consume. In this case we are supposing that C is 1.00 and therefore the current income and demand are equal and the entries in columns 9 and 10 are identical.

The first cross row in Table II shows the repeating events that continually occurred during the preceding equilibrium. Then, in the year marked "1st," businessmen suddenly decide, because of circumstances outside our model, to increase output by 10 per cent to 1,100,-000 units during that year. Consequently they need 500 extra machines in addition to the 1,000 machines replaced, and buy 5,500 machines, valued at $600,000, in all. Direct outlays are up 10 per cent to $660,000. Total income is thus swollen from two sources and becomes $1,260,000.

In the second year after the old equilibrium came to an end (line 3 in the table) businessmen once again plan their production according to last year's demand. Hence they plan to produce 1,260,000 units. They will need the use of 6,300 machines to produce this larger output. Only 4,400 machines are now available, because, while 5,500 machines were in use during the preceding year, 1,100 were worn out in the course of last year's operations. Consequently businessmen must currently acquire 1,900 new machines valued at $760,000. Income in the second year after the old equilibrium, made up of $760,000 for new machines plus $756,000 of direct outlays, rises to $1,516,000.

The incomes of the next few years are $1,925,600 in the third year, $2,580,960 in the fourth, $3,629,536 in the fifth, and $5,307,258 in the sixth. A check will reveal that $Y_6 = 2 \cdot 6Y_5 - 1 \cdot 6Y_4$. Similarly $Y_7 = 2 \cdot 6Y_6 - 1 \cdot 6Y_5$. (See the Mathematical Note at the end of this appendix.)

In this model, because of our assumption of relatively durable

TABLE II

$C = 1.00$; $E = 1,000$ Units or 5 Years

		CAPITAL					INCOME FROM PRODUCING			
	Output (1)	Required (2)	Avail-able Y_1 (3)	Worn Out Y_1 (4)	Start of Y (5)	Purchased (6)	Capital (7)	Output (8)	Total (9)	Demand (10)
Before	1,000,000	5,000	5,000	1,000	4,000	1,000	$ 400,000	$600,000	$1,000,000	$1,000,000
1 yr.	1,100,000	5,500	5,000	1,000	4,000	1,500	600,000	660,000	1,260,000	1,260,000
2	1,260,000	6,300	5,500	1,100	4,400	1,900	760,000	756,000	1,516,000	1,516,000
3	1,516,000	7,580	6,300	1,260	5,040	2,540	1,016,000	909,600	1,925,600	1,925,600

TABLE III

$C = .5$; $M = 2.00$; $D = .8$; $L = 2$; $N = \$100$ Billions
(Dollars in Millions)

		CAPITAL				INCOME FROM PRODUCING			
	Output (1)	Cap. Req. (2)	Stock Lt. Yr. (3)	Dep. Lt. Yr. (4)	Now Available (5)	Capital (6)	Outputs (7)	Total (8)	Demand (9)
Before	100,000	200,000	200,000	80,000	120,000	80,000	20,000	100,000	100,000
1 yr.	110,000	220,000	200,000	80,000	120,000	100,000	22,000	122,000	111,000
2	111,000	222,000	220,000	88,000	132,000	90,000	22,200	112,200	106,100
3	106,100	212,200	222,000	88,800	133,200	79,000	21,220	100,220	100,110
4	100,100	200,200	212,200	84,880	127,320	72,880	20,020	92,900	96,450
5	96,450	192,900	200,200	80,080	120,120	72,780	19,290	92,070	95,535
6	96,335	192,070	192,900	76,160	116,740	75,930	19,207	95,537	97,773

capital goods with a consuming propensity of one, any upward movement, once started, will not stop. The earlier equilibrium was precarious and unstable. It needed only one autonomous decision by entrepreneurs to produce an explosion.

These three models afford some interesting contrasts. In the first, when machines lasted one year and all incomes were spent, any sudden change immediately induced a new level stability. In the second, when machines were still nondurable but people did not alter their spending by the full change in their incomes, a new business decision, taken one year, eventually worked itself out and the old equilibrium was in time restored. In the third model, when machines were durable and people always spent their entire incomes, an autonomous decision by entrepreneurs led to a cumulative disequilibrium. From these results we can tentatively infer that restoration of equilibrium is hindered by the use of durable producers' goods and helped by any public tendency to alter spending by less than the amount its income changes.

General Theory of Capital Acceleration

The foregoing ideas can now be generalized. We shall consider a whole economy using various kinds of capital goods to produce various kinds of consumption outputs. And we shall no longer limit ourselves to simple cases where either the marginal propensity to consume is unity or capitals have a one-year service life.

In each case it will be necessary to assume definite values for five different elements:

C, the marginal propensity to consume, is the ratio of a change in consumer spending to the change in consumer income that occasioned it.

M, the value of the stock of real capital needed to produce a dollar's worth of consumption output.

D, the depreciation in the value of the capital stock occasioned by producing a dollar's worth of consumption output.

L, the direct cost, for labor and so forth, involved in producing a dollar's worth of consumption output.

N, the "normal" level of income before the autonomous events that upset the prior equilibrium.

It will be noticed that we are no longer concerned with the number of machines, the number of outputs, or the annual capacity and service life of machines measured in physical units of output.

In the following analysis we no longer assume that the price of an output is necessarily one dollar, but we do suppose that there are zero profits. "Normal" income is always held to be a 100 billion dollars. In each year entrepreneurs deliberately produce what they *could* have sold in the preceding year. If they produce more than they do sell, we shall suppose that the surplus is thrown away or spoiled. If they produce less than they could sell, they now plan to make, next year, what they might have sold rather than what they did. The income paid out is always made up of gross capital acquisitions plus direct costs in making consumer outputs. It is supposed that all income is spent on consumption when the income level is "normal," and that consumers change their *demand* from "normal" by the marginal propensity to consume times any difference in *income* from "normal."

In Table III, we have a case where the marginal propensity to consume (C) is .5, the direct cost of output (L) is $.20 per dollar's worth, the depreciation in capital per unit of output (D) is $.80 per dollar, and value of capital needed per dollar's worth of output (M) is $2.00. The original equilibrium income, output, and demand were $100 billions. Suddenly, as shown by the second row of the table, businessmen make an autonomous decision to produce an output of consumer goods valued at $110 billions. The resultant shock to the economy causes a series of dampening fluctuations above and below normal.

The calculations in Table III may need explaining, so let us examine the second row, which relates to the year of impact. Column 1 shows the value of output arbitrarily determined by the entrepreneurs. Column 2 is the value of the capital stock needed to produce the planned output, and so is equal to column 1 times M. Column 3 gives the value of the capital stock operated during the preceding year, and so is identical with column 2 one line above. Column 4 states the depreciation cost of the preceding year's operations and so is equal to column 1, a line above, times D. Column 5 indicates the value of capital available for use at the start of the current year and is equal to column 3 minus column 4. Column 6 reveals the gross capital formation that will be necessary to produce the currently planned output and is equal to column 2 minus column 5. Column 7 is the direct outlay occasioned by the current output and is equal to column 1 times L. Column 8 is the total income paid out to productive factors (Y) and is the sum of columns 6 and 7. Column 9 is the demand of the public for outputs and is equal to $N + C(Y-N)$. This last value is equal to the planned production of the *next* year as given in the first column of the line below. All subsequent values are computed in the manner explained above.

Given the assumed values for $N, C, L, M,$ and D, we can compute the income of any year if we know the incomes of the preceding two years $(Y_{-1}$ and $Y_{-2})$. In the present case the formula for finding the current year's income (Y) is

$$Y = 50,000 + 1 \cdot 1Y_{-1} - .6Y_{-2}$$

In this way the incomes of successive years, starting with the third year following the year of autonomous change when output was suddenly increased by $10 billions worth, can quickly be found if the incomes of the first and second years have already been computed. These values, rounded to the nearest tenth of a billion dollars, are given in Table IV. It will be noticed that the series fluctuates around "normal" in ever narrowing oscillations.

TABLE IV

$C = .5; \ M = 2.00; \ D = .80; \ L = .20; \ N = \$100$ Billions

Year (from "Impact" Year)	Income (Dollars in Billions)	Year (from "Impact" Year)	Income (Dollars in Billions)
3rd	$100.1	12th	$99.1
4th	92.9	13th	99.0
5th	92.1	14th	99.4
6th	95.5	15th	100.0
7th	99.8	16th	100.3
8th	102.5	17th	100.4
9th	102.8	18th	100.2
10th	101.6	19th	100.0
11th	100.1	20th	99.9

N.B. $Y = 50,000 + 1.1Y_{-1} - .6Y_{-2}$

On the other hand, with alternative values for C, M, D, and L, we might not have had a slow and fluctuating return to the original income level of N. If we had set C at .75, D at .40, and L. at .60, we would have had a prolonged series of oscillations. The actual income values, calculated to the nearest tenth of a billion dollars and dated from the year of autonomous change, are set forth in Table V.

TABLE V

$C = .75; \ M = 2.00; \ D = .40; \ L = .60; \ N = \$100$ Billions

Year (from "Impact" Year)	Income (Dollars in Billions)	Year (from "Impact" Year)	Income (Dollars in Billions)
1st	$126.0	21st	$ 47.5*
2nd	134.7	22nd	78.5
3rd	136.5	23rd	121.0
4th	129.5	24th	166.8
5th	113.7	25th	205.1
6th	91.4	26th	224.7
7th	66.7	27th	217.1
8th	45.5	28th	178.7
9th	35.5*	29th	113.0
10th	31.0*	30th	65.8*
11th	42.8	31st	44.6*
12th	71.3	32nd	35.1*
13th	112.7	33rd	39.9
14th	159.2	34th	60.6
15th	200.2	35th	95.4
16th	224.3	36th	138.3
17th	222.2	37th	180.1
18th	189.1	38th	210.4
19th	127.1	39th	219.0
20th	72.2*	40th	200.0

N.B. $Y = 1.95Y_{-1} - 1.20Y_{-2} + 25,000$, or $.45Y_{-1} + 25,000$ when asterisked.

One noteworthy feature of this series is that, when income and output are falling rapidly, there may be no need for any capital production. Such will be the case when the amount of capital needed to produce the planned output is less than the stock of capital inherited from the preceding year. In other words, the decline from last year to this in the stock of capital needed for operations is greater than the depreciation of capital resulting from the output of the year before. (The years when there was no capital production have been marked in Table V with an asterisk.)

However, so long as there is any output, capital depreciation will continue, until the stock of capital has fallen so low that some replacement is essential if the expected demand for output is to be supplied. Once capital production is renewed, incomes are rapidly augmented, and demand increases in turn. Moreover, as the stock of capital fell to very low levels during the depression, any substantial increase in demand enormously increases capital production. Boom conditions set in for a time. Eventually, however, the percentage of capital production that is for *replacement* increases, so that the income paid out begins to rise more slowly and perhaps even begins to fall. Also a marginal propensity to consume of less than unity exercises a braking effect on both rises and falls in income.

TABLE VI

$C = .25$; $M = 1.50$; $D = .40$; $L = .60$; $N = \$100$ BILLIONS
(Dollars in Millions)

	(1) 11_{-1}	(2) -13_{-1}	(3) $1 + 2$	(4) 3×1.5	(5) 4_{-1}	(6) $3_{-1} \times .4$	(7) $5 - 6$
YEAR	q	i	O	$O \cdot M$	$O_{-1} \cdot M$	$O_{-1} \cdot D$	$\dfrac{O_{-1}}{(M-D)}$
Before	100,000	0	100,000	150,000	150,000	40,000	110,000
1	110,000	0	110,000	165,000	150,000	40,000	110,000
2	105,250	−4,750	100,500	150,750	165,000	44,000	121,000
3	97,512	−7,738	89,774	134,661	150,750	40,200	110,550
4	94,494	−3,018	91,476	137,214	134,661	35,910	98,751
5	98,337	+3,843	102,180	153,270	137,214	36,590	100,624
6	103,489	+5,152	108,641	162,962	153,270	40,872	112,398
7	103,937	+448	104,385	156,578	162,962	43,456	119,506
8	99,926	−4,011	95,915	143,873	156,578	41,754	114,824
9	96,649	−3,277	93,372	140,058	143,873	38,366	105,507
10	97,644	+995	98,639	147,958	140,058	37,348	102,710

Still other models can be constructed, and other results obtained, by varying the assumed magnitudes of *C, M, D,* and *L*. The formulae that facilitate the computation of successive annual incomes are given in the mathematical note and the reader may wish to construct models for himself. Some of the oscillating series that he can thus obtain for himself will closely resemble the economic fluctuations experienced by capitalistic nations.

Capital Acceleration with Commodity Inventories

A further refinement is to introduce commodity inventories into our model economy. If entrepreneurs produce more outputs than consumers buy, then inventories are increased, and conversely. A surplus supply is now carried over to the next period and a surplus demand is met from outputs of a preceding year.

Various assumptions might be made regarding the inventory levels that entrepreneurs attempt to maintain. Perhaps entrepreneurs try to keep inventories at some constant percentage of past or expected sales or output. In this section, however, we shall suppose that each producer attempts to keep commodity inventories at the same absolute level year in and year out. In practice this assumption induces less violent fluctuations in income than would many other suppositions.

Some special problems arise when we have a case of capital acceleration with commodity inventories. Each year entrepreneurs plan to produce a certain amount for sales (enough to meet last year's demand) plus or minus a certain amount for inventories (enough to bring them back to the arbitrarily determined norm). However, the income paid out to the public in the course of producing this planned output is usually such that the public buys more or less than entrepreneurs

TABLE VI (Cont'd)

(8) $4-7$	(9) $3 \times .6$	(10) $8+9$	(11)	(12) $3-11$	(13) $13_{-1}+12$	(14) $10-11_{-1}$	(15) $10-11$
$O \cdot M-$ O_{-1} $(M-D)$	$O \cdot L$	$Y=O(M$ $+L)+$ $O_{-1}(M-D)$	$S=N+C$ $(Y-N)$	$O-S$	$\Sigma(O-S)$	$II=Y-S_{-1}$	$IS=Y-S$
40,000	60,000	100,000	100,000	0	0	0	0
55,000	66,000	121,000	105,250	+4,750	+4,750	+21,000	15,750
29,750	60,300	90,050	97,512	+2,988	+7,738	−15,200	−7,462
24,111	53,864	77,975	94,494	−4,720	+3,018	−19,537	−16,519
38,463	54,886	93,345	98,337	−6,861	−3,843	−1,145	−4,988
52,646	61,308	113,952	103,489	−1,309	−5,152	+15,617	+10,465
50,564	65,185	115,747	103,937	+4,704	−448	+12,260	+11,812
37,072	62,631	99,706	99,926	+4,459	+4,011	−4,234	−223
29,049	57,549	86,600	96,649	−734	+3,277	−13,328	−10,051
34,551	56,023	390,576	97,644	−4,272	−995	−6,075	−7,069
45,248	59,183	104,429	101,108	−2,469	−3,464	+6,787	+3,323

N. B. $Y = 1.050Y_{-1} - 1.075Y_{-2} + .275Y_{-3} + \$75$ billions, or $.30Y_{-1} - .15Y_{-2} + \$30$ billions, whichever is the larger.

expected. In this case inventories will still not be normal at the end of the year.

In Table VI we have supposed that C is .25, M is 1.50, D is .40, L is .60, and N is \$100 billions. Let us now examine the various column entries for the tenth year after the producers' autonomous decision to increase output by 10 per cent. Column 1 is the value of output produced for expected sales, and is normally column 11 of the line above. Column 2 is the value of output which will presumably bring inventories back to normal and is equal to column 13 of the line above when the sign is changed. Column 3 is the value of the total output and is the sum of columns 1 and 2. Column 4 is the value of the capital stock required to produce the planned output and is equal to column 3 times M. Column 5 is the value of capital in use during the preceding year and is column 4 of the line above. Column 6 is the value of capital depreciation during the preceding year and is column 3 of the line above times D. Column 7 is the value of the capital stock left over from the year before and is column 5 minus column 6. Column 8 is the value of the new capital production and is column 4 minus column 7. Column 9 is the direct outlay occasioned by current output of consumer goods and is column 3 times L. Column 10 is total income paid out and is the sum of columns 8 and 9. Column 11 is the sales of output to the consuming public and is N plus C times the excess of column 10 over N. Column 12 is the change in inventories and is column 3 minus column 11. Column 13 is the cumulative rise or fall of inventories from normal and is the algebraic sum of column 13, one line above, and column 12.

The income of years further into the future can be computed by means of a short-cut formula. Given our assumed values for C, M, D, L, and N, knowing the incomes of the three immediately preceding years, and providing there is never surplus capital capacity at the beginning of the year,

$$Y = 1.050Y_{-1} - 1.075Y_{-2} + .275Y_{-3} + \$50 \text{ billions}$$

The annual incomes computed in this way until the twentieth year are shown under the heading "Alternative No. 1" in Table VII. It will be noted that there is a gentle fluctuation of slightly decreasing amplitude around the "normal" income of $100 billions, with a duration of about five years. Here is a model that will continue to oscillate over a prolonged period. (See Mathematical Note.)

However, contrasting income results would have followed from the adoption of alternative values for C, M, D and L. In order to save space, only three alternatives will be compared by way of illustration. Alternative No. 1—set forth in Table VI and already described— assumes that C is .25, M is 1.5, D is .40, L is .60, and N is $100 billions. Alternative No. 2 has the same assumed constants except that C is assumed to be .50. Alternative No. 3 also supposes that C is .50 but takes M to be 2.0. The annual incomes computed for these three alternatives, up to the twentieth year of disequilibrium where possible, are given in Table VII.

Alternative No. 2 is more fluctuating than No. 1 because the marginal propensity to consume has been raised from .25 to .50. Consequently there is less "slip" between income and sales in No. 2, and

TABLE VII

	Alternative No. 1		Alternative No. 2		Alternative No. 3	
C	.25		.50		.50	
M	1.50		1.50		2.00	
D	.40		.40		.40	
L	.60		.60		.60	
N	$100.0	billions	$100.0	billions	$100.0	billions
Before	$100.0	billions	$100.0	billions	$100.0	billions
1 yr.	121.0		121.0		126.0	
2	90.0		112.1		125.6	
3	78.0		91.3		107.2	
4	93.3		67.2		65.2	
5	114.0		56.6		37.0*	
6	115.7		74.5		42.8	
7	99.7		121.8		106.3	
8	86.6		176.7		231.7	
9	90.6		200.3		378.5	
10	104.4		157.6		447.2	
11	111.1		64.5*		300.4	
12	104.3		21.4*		76.1*	
13	93.8		43.0		(−1.4*)	
14	91.9		129.8			
15	99.3		241.8			
16	106.3		302.5			
17	105.1		236.6			
18	98.4		81.2*			
19	94.6		7.8*			
20	97.5		21.8			

* No capital production apart from possible investment in inventories.

increased capital production gives a greater boost to current sales and next year's output. In certain years during the downswing, indicated by an asterisk in the table, the drop in income, sales, and output is so considerable that no capital production is undertaken. The oscillations of this second alternative are becoming wider over time.

Alternative No. 3 is even more violent in its fluctuations than No. 2. The explanation of this is that M has been raised from 1.5 to 2.0 and so changes in the rate of capital production have a larger income effect. In the third alternative model the fluctuations become so great that, by the 13th year, the formula yields a negative income! Apparently in the twelfth year sales fell below output, and commodity inventories were built up to such an extent that the accumulated inventory exceeded sales; hence in the thirteenth year producers planned to produce nothing and met demand out of heldover stocks.

These three alternatives indicate two highly important facts. A low marginal propensity to consume contributes to stability. And a low ratio of capital to output also contributes to stability.

Investment and Saving

One condition of full equilibrium is that intended investment (II) and intended saving (IS) be equal not only to each other but also to actual investment and saving (X). Hence we cannot expect equilibrium in our models if II is not equal to IS or if X is not equal to both II and IS. Here is an equilibrium requirement that can be better understood with the help of the acceleration and inventory model set out in Table VI.

The value of X can be ascertained by computing either actual saving or actual investment, because these two elements are really alternative aspects of the same event and hence in essence an identity. Actual saving in any year is simply the excess of income (Y) over sales (S). Actual investment is, of course, the algebraic sum of the change in the capital stock plus the change in inventories. This statement, rephrased in symbols, can be simplified to $Y - S$ also, as shown in the mathematical note. Hence X is equal to $Y - S$.

However, intended investment (IS) is not equal to actual investment and saving (X). At the beginning of each year entrepreneurs plan a total output (O) that is the sum of output intended for sale (q) and output intended for inventories (i). Now entrepreneurs always *expect* current sales (S) to be equal to last year's sales (S_{-1}). Actually, because current income will differ from last year's income, S and S_{-1} will not be equal during a state of disequilibrium. If S exceeds S_{-1}, actual investment will be less than intended investment, the amount of the difference being the output which, intended for inventories, had to be sold instead. In other words,

$$II = X + (S - S_{-1})$$

but

$$X = Y - S$$

so

$$II = Y - S_{-1}$$

Intended investment is equal to current income minus last year's sales. (The proof of this statement is also given in the mathematical note.)

The definition of intended saving in our present example must be based on the assumption we made that consumers' expenditures are a function of current income. Therefore consumers actually spend what they intended to spend. Intended saving is hence $Y - S$, which is also actual saving, because of the assumption underlying the model. It is not always necessary that intended saving should equal actual saving, however.

Inasmuch as sales are a direct function of income, it follows that S can only increase if Y rises; hence $Y - S_{-1}$ will be greater than $Y - S$ when income is rising. In other words, an increasing income occurs when intended investment $(Y - S_{-1})$ is greater than intended saving $(Y - S)$. And from this it follows that income falls when intended saving exceeds intended investment.

Figure II charts the values of Y, S, and q given in Table VI. The fluctuations of S around the "normal" value of $100.0 billions are only one-fourth of the fluctuations of Y around this sum because C was assumed equal to .25. Y and S consequently always intersect at N. Output for sales (q) is always equal to the sales of the year before

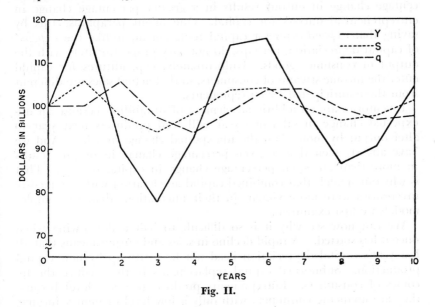

Fig. II.

(S_{-1}), so that the q line lags the S line by one year. The economy is actually disinvesting and dissaving when the Y line lies below the S line, which happens, because of our assumed consumption function, whenever Y and S are below "normal." Intended investment exceeds actual investment whenever q, which is always equal to S_{-1}, lies below S; in this case the depletion of inventories will be represented by the vertical distance separating the S and q lines. Intended saving is represented by the amount the Y line lies above the S line. It will be noted that income is increasing in those years that experience declining inventories and for which intended investment exceeds intended saving.

However, no causal sequence should be inferred from this particular association of intended investment, intended saving, and income. For example, government action to stimulate or deter sales, so that S equaled S_{-1} some one year, would not of itself eliminate all subsequent fluctuations. Such an equality between intended investment and intended saving is a necessary but insufficient condition of stability.

Concluding Comments

These model economic systems would not exhibit such fluctuations if there were no flexibility in bank credit or variations in the hoarding rates of individuals. There must be a change in the stock of money or in its velocity. Otherwise producers and consumers could not simultaneously increase their outlays.

These models throw light on the workings of a real economy. The use of equipment lasting more than a year means that a given percentage change in output results in a greater percentage change in entrepreneurial outlays for capital. One might paraphrase this by saying that *expenditures* for capital replacement, unlike the *expense* of capital depreciation, perhaps, do not vary proportionately with the output of consumer goods. Unfortunately, expenditures for capital enter the income streams of consumers, so that actual sales are different from those anticipated by entrepreneurs.

Inventories are an additional element of instability, because an unexpected change in sales one year will lead producers next year to alter output by more than the unexpected change in sales. And we have already seen that a given percentage change in output results in more than an equal percentage change in capital outlays. That is why our models that combined capital acceleration with commodity inventories were more violent in their fluctuations than the simpler models we first examined.

We can now see why it is so difficult to halt a downswing when once it has started. A rapid decline in sales and output means that all last year's capital depreciation need not be made up by new capital production. Subnormal capital replacements further reduce the incomes of consumers. Entrepreneurs produce at a low level because they are financing consumers with only a low level of money income. And consumers are receiving low incomes because entrepreneurs are making low outputs. It is this vicious circle that invites government pump priming.

On the other hand, a low marginal propensity to consume, so that the public does not alter its purchases by the amount its income changes, is an important element of stability. Moreover, the government can render the marginal propensity to consume lower than it naturally is by taxing away a smaller or larger percentage of the national income, depending upon whether it is running abnormally low or high. This will occur automatically, to some extent, if the tax structure has progressive rates. Here is an argument for government deficits during depressions, surpluses during prosperity, and a balanced budget over time.

Economic fluctuations seem to be a natural but not inevitable characteristic of any economy that combines highly capitalistic methods of production with private control of the means of production. The entrepreneur then adds to his real capital, and so contributes extra income for the public, at the very time that consumer purchases are running high enough to strain his plant capacity. Or he fails to maintain income from capital goods production when consumer purchases are low. And, if extremely roundabout methods of production are employed, a small change in output will occasion a large change in income derived from capital replacement or additions. Hence, very capitalistic techniques of production, which permit a high level of real income, also contribute to income instability and an occasional prolonged depression.

Mathematical Note

The validity of some of the statements and calculations appearing above can best be demonstrated by employing a little symbolic logic.

Capital Acceleration *without* Commodity Inventories

Given values for C, M, D, L, and N, Y can be determined from Y_{-1} and Y_{-2} as follows, where O is the value of the current output of consumer goods, P is current capital production, and A is the stock of capital left over from last year:

$$Y = O{\cdot}L + P$$
$$= O{\cdot}L + [O{\cdot}M - A]$$
$$= O{\cdot}L + [O{\cdot}M - (O_{-1}M - O_{-1}D)]$$
$$= O\,(L + M) - O_{-1}\,(M - D)$$

But O is equal to last year's consumer demand or $N + C(Y_{-1} - N)$. Similarly O_{-1} is $N + C\,(Y_{-2} - N)$. Substituting, we have

$$(N + CY_{-1} - CN)\,(L + M) - (N + CY_{-2} - CN)\,(M - D)$$

which resolves into

$$C[Y_{-1}\,(L + M) - Y_{-2}\,(M - D)] + N\,(L + D) - CN\,(L + D)$$

But $L + D$ must equal unity because the capital depreciation expense and the direct labor expense represent the total cost of producing consumption outputs. This leaves us with

$$(1)\ldots{.}Y = C\,[Y_{-1}\,(L + M) - Y_{-2}\,(M - D)] + N\,(1 - C)$$

However, there is an important condition attached to this formula: P cannot be negative, for no economy would deliberately smash up its capital if $A > O{\cdot}M$. If $A > O{\cdot}M$ in practice, P must be considered zero, in which case

$$(1^{A})\ldots Y = O{\cdot}L$$
$$= (N + CY_{-1} - CN)\,L$$
$$= L\,[Y_{-1}{\cdot}C) + N\,(1 - C)]$$

The proper choice between formula (1) and formula (1^{A}) is that which yields the higher positive value.

Capital Acceleration *with* Commodity Inventories

It is again true that

$$Y = O\,(L + M) - O_{-1}\,(M - D)$$

However, the total output of consumption goods (O) is equal to their production for sale (q) plus their production to restore inventories to normal (i). Current production for sale (q) is equal to last year's sales (S_{-1}). Current production for inventories (i) is equal to $(S_{-1} - q_{-1})$ because inventories can only be below normal at the start of the current to the extent that last year's actual sales exceeded last year's expected sales. Otherwise i_{-1} would have been the amount needed to restore inventories to normal last year. However, q_{-1} is S_{-2} and so $i = S_{-1} - S_{-2}$. Hence $O = q + i = 2S_{-1} - S_{-2}$ and similarly $O_{-1} = q_{-1} + i_{-1} = 2S_{-2} - S_{-3}$. Now S, under our assumptions, is $N + C(Y - N)$, so $O = C(2Y_{-1} - Y_{-2}) + N(1 - C)$ and $O_{-1} = C(2Y_{-2} - Y_{-3}) + N(1 - C)$. Substituting for O and O_{-1}, and then simplifying, we have

$$(2) \ldots Y = C[Y_{-1}(2L + 2M) - Y_{-2}(L - 2D + 3M) + Y_{-3}(M - D)] + N(1 - C)$$

Once again P must be considered zero if $A > O \cdot M$. Then

$$(2^A) \ldots Y = O \cdot D = CL[2Y_{-1} - Y_{-2}] + NL(1 - C)$$

Formula (2^A) should be used during a severe depression if it gives a higher positive value than formula 2.

Investment and Saving

Actual investment is equal to the algebraic sum of changes in the capital stock plus changes in the commodity inventory. The change in the capital stock is $P - O \cdot D$; but P is equal to total income minus direct outlays for labor, and so forth or, in symbols, $P = Y - O \cdot L$. The change in inventory is $O - S$. Hence actual investment is equal to

$$(Y - O \cdot L - O \cdot D) + (O - S)$$
$$= Y - O(L + D) + O - S$$

but $L + D$ must equal unity, so actual investment is

$$Y - S$$

Actual saving, of course, is also $Y - S$, since actual investment and actual saving are two aspects of the difference between income and consumption.

Intended investment is the algebraic sum of its change in capital stock plus the change in inventories necessary to restore the latter to normal. Intended investment in capital stock is again $(Y - O \cdot L - O \cdot D)$. Intended investment in inventories is i, which is equal to $O - q$ or $O - S_{-1}$ because producers deliberately make q equal to S_{-1}. Hence intended investment is

$$(Y - O \cdot L - O \cdot D) + (O - S_{-1})$$
$$= Y - S_{-1}$$

There is clearly a close relationship between actual investment $(Y - S)$ and intended investment $(Y - S_{-1})$, the former being smaller than the latter by $(S - S_{-1})$.

References

Boulding, K. E., *Economic Analysis,* Chapter 18. New York: Harper, 1948.

Ellis, H. S. (Ed.), *A Survey of Contemporary Economics,* Chapter 10. Philadelphia: Blakiston, 1948.

Lundberg, E., *Studies in the Theory of Economic Expansion.* New York: King, 1937.

Appendix C

More on Savings and Investments

A RECONCILIATION of certain of the ideas contained in the chapters on the "Circuit of Payments" (in Part II) and on "Multipliers of Income" (in Part III) may be of interest. In our discussion of the circuit of payments, it was said that the equilibrium rate of payments is that which, when the money stock is constant, equates private saving plus taxes with private investment plus government spending. In the discussion on multipliers of income, it was said that the equilibrium level of income was the level that equated intended savings with intended investments. Can these statements be reconciled?

In order to examine this question let us provisionally ignore the existence of banks, assume the stock of money to be constant, and suppose that the economy comprises governments on the one hand and firms with households on the other. We shall further assume that the latter, that is the non-bank public, lends funds to government and receives gift handouts from government. We might as well be as realistic as possible!

What do the payments and receipts of the non-bank public look like? The non-bank public has factor earnings (Y), receives gifts from government (g), pays taxes (t), spends money on consumption (c), lends money to government (l), invests in real capital (i), and hoards the balance (h). The payments of the non-bank public can be summarized by the equation

$$Y + g - t - c - l - i - h = 0$$

What do the payments and receipts of the governments look like? The governments collectively receive taxes (t), borrow from the public (l), make transfer payments to the public (g), spend money in providing current goods and services for the economy $(\overline{c})$, spend money on real investments for the economy $(\overline{i})$, and perhaps add to their money holdings $(\overline{h})$. These government transactions can be summarized by the equation

$$t + l - g - \overline{c} - \overline{i} - \overline{h} = 0$$

At this point we can check on the frequently made assertion that, for the economy as a whole, savings from income (S) must equal real investment (I). If the economy is populated by governments, firms, and households, there being no banks, then the sum of the two pre-

545

ceding equations will give us a payments equation for the economy as a whole. This will be

$$Y - (c + \bar{c}) - (i + \bar{i}) - (h + \bar{h}) = 0$$

The gifts, lending, and taxes all cancel out. If the money stock is constant, $(h + \bar{h})$ is zero. The aggregate real consumption of the economy (C) will be $(c + \bar{c})$, and hence $Y - (c + \bar{c})$ is S, the savings of the economy. The aggregate investment of the economy (I) must be $(i + \bar{i})$. Hence $S - I$ is zero and Savings equal Investment.

It was stated in Chapter 7 that private saving plus taxes must equal private investment plus government spending. The term "private" here is synonymous with the term "non-bank public." We are now in a better position to understand why this is so. Private saving, for one thing, is a summary term for $Y + g - c - t$. Government spending is $g + \bar{c} + \bar{i}$. Hence the original equation, namely that private saving plus taxes equals private investment plus government spending, can be written as

$$(Y + g - c - t) + t = i + (g + c + i)$$

Elimination leaves us with

$$Y - c = i + \bar{c} + \bar{i}$$

Subtracting $\bar{c}$ from both sides leaves

$$Y - (c + \bar{c}) = (i + \bar{i})$$

or

$$Y - C = I$$

Hence, whenever savings for the economy equal investment for the economy, as they always must, private saving plus taxes must equal private investment plus government spending.

Parenthetically, if we wish to take changes in the money stock into account, this can be done with little extra complication. The source of new money, apart from minting operations, tends to be the issuance of dollar currency (d) and bank loans to firms and households (b) or to governments $(\bar{b})$. Hence

$$d + (b + \bar{b}) = (h + \bar{h})$$

If these available sources of funds are taken into account, the grand equation that summarizes the transactions of governments and the non-bank public is

$$Y - (c + \bar{c}) - (i + \bar{i}) = (h + \bar{h}) - d - (b + \bar{b})$$

And, as we have seen, the right-hand side of this equation sums to zero. Hence $Y - C = I$.

In many statements of income theory, especially the earliest ones, it was usually postulated that intended aggregate saving and intended aggregate investment are each related to national income, which must be such that they are equal. However, aggregate saving and aggregate investment are very summary concepts. For many purposes, especially for fiscal policy analysis, it is useful to distinguish at least between the actions of private firms and households and those of governments.

It may be better, then, if we think of private saving and taxes as being each separately related to income, and of the possible individual relations of private investment and government spending to income. The equilibrium income level will then presumably be the one that equates intended private saving plus taxes with intended private investment plus government spending. Alternatively, inasmuch as government spending minus taxes equals the government deficit, we might say that the national income will be that which equates intended private saving with intended private investment plus government deficits.

It seems fairly reasonable to suppose that both intended private saving and public tax payments are individually related to national income in some fairly stable way. Households and firms seem to save more as national income rises. Taxes on personal and corporate income, and excise taxes also, are levied in such a way that aggregate tax yields increase with national income even though tax rates remain unchanged. However, there are grounds for wondering whether intended private investment is related in any definite way to national income. And, judging by the past at least, government spending, if it follows any principles, obeys laws of its own. Hence, while analytically it may be possible to imagine, against national income, schedules of intended private saving plus taxes, some economists have doubted the reality of any schedule representing the sum of intended private investment and government spending against national income.

Another disquieting possibility is that these two composite schedules may not be independent. For instance, a new old age pension plan may increase government spending and reduce intended private saving, at one and the same time; or, to give another example, a new tax may discourage private investment. The mathematical necessity for private saving plus taxes to equal private investment plus government spending does not necessarily mean that we can always predict the income effect of an alteration in any one of these four variables. Considerations of this kind do not mean that modern income theory is invalid. They do mean, however, that public policy must proceed with caution. "Forewarned is forearmed!"

Appendix D

Indifference Curves

INDIFFERENCE CURVES were developed, and are extensively used, by economists of continental Europe. There are many kinds of indifference curves; we shall consider three kinds in this appendix. A consumer's iso-utility curve shows the different combinations of two goods that will always yield the same utility. A producer's iso-quant curve may show the different combinations of two factors that will always yield the same physical output. Or one might construct an iso-cost curve that shows the various proportions in which two joint supply products can be obtained from a constant expenditure by the producer. In all these cases an indifference curve represents alternative combinations of two variables that are related to a constant value of some third element.

Indifference Curves and Consumer Demand

Indifference curves are especially helpful in any analysis of consumer demand. For example, they make it possible to distinguish between two different effects, the substitution effect and the income effect, of a change in the price of a purchased good. Also, indifference curves circumvent our inability to measure utility and relieve us of dependence on the necessarily hypothetical character of marginal utility analysis.

The Iso-utility Map

A diagram of a consumer's indifference curves is not unlike a contour map of a hill. However, the vertical axis of the diagram represents, not north and south, but the physical quantity of some kind of good; and the horizontal axis represents, not east and west, but the physical quantity of some other kind of good. In Fig. III, for example, pounds of butter are shown going up the vertical scale and number of cigarettes is shown going to the right on the horizontal scale.

The indifference curves tend to slope diagonally between the upper left and lower right. In most cases they are convex when viewed from the origin of the axes. These indifference curves will never intersect, but they usually will not be exactly parallel to one another.

An indifference curve is more precisely an iso-utility curve. Every point on a given indifference curve gives the same satisfaction to the

548

consumer, even though each point represents a different combination of two consumer goods. For example, the indifference curve I_1, shown in Fig. III, is constructed to represent the indifference schedule set forth in the first two columns of Table VIII. It is therefore a matter of indifference to this consumer whether he has .1 lb. of butter and 141 cigarettes, .2 lb. of butter and 128 cigarettes, or 2.0 lbs. of butter and 30 cigarettes, and so on.

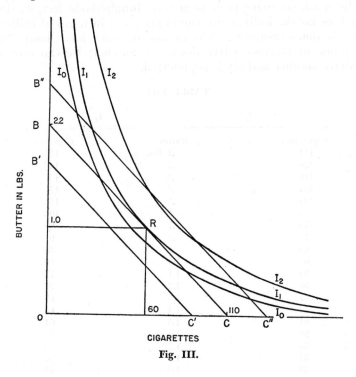

Fig. III.

However, the utility experienced anywhere on one indifference curve must be more or less than the satisfactions enjoyed anywhere on another indifference curve. The pleasures obtained on two separate indifference curves cannot be the same in intensity. In almost every case we can suppose that, in choosing between two indifference curves, a consumer will always prefer that curve which lies to the right and above the other curve. In Fig. III, the consumer will prefer the curve I_2 (based on the last two columns of Table 1) to the curve I_1 (based on the first two columns), for the simple reason that the combinations on I_2 always involve more units of one or both goods; for example, on I_1 1.0 lb. of butter is combined with 60 cigarettes, but on I_2 1.0 lb. of butter is associated with 80 cigarettes, or more cigarettes with the same amount of butter. We can therefore refer to indifference curves that lie upwards and to the right as being "higher" because they represent more utility and are preferable.

A consumer's indifference diagram can be likened to a contour map of a hill of pleasure. Every point on a given indifference curve involves the same amount of pleasure just as every point on a given contour line represents the same elevation above sea level. Consequently, as one progresses from lower left to upper right, one is ascending in terms of altitude or pleasure, as the case may be. The only discrepancy in the analogy is that while the contour lines of a hill are spaced equally apart, occurring perhaps at every hundred-odd feet, we do not know how far the indifference curves are apart in terms of utility, for utility is non-measurable. We cannot measure how many "utils" higher one indifference curve lies above another; we can only rank one above another and say it is preferred.

TABLE VIII

I_1		I_2
Cigarettes	Butter	Cigarettes
141	.1 lbs.	151
128	.2	148
116	.3	136
105	.4	125
95	.5	115
86	.6	106
78	.7	98
71	.8	91
65	.9	85
60	1.0	80
55	1.1	75
50	1.2	71
47	1.3	67
44	1.4	64
41	1.5	61
38	1.6	58
36	1.7	56
34	1.8	54
32	1.9	52
30	2.0	50
29	2.1	49
28	2.2	48

Consumer Efficiency

A rational consumer, according to our lights, is one who efficiently converts financial outlay into sumptuary satisfactions. Theoretically, the aim of the consumer is, by purchasing goods in appropriate combinations, to obtain the most utility from a given outlay or to purchase a given utility at least outlay. Actually the principles that must be followed in order to maximize utility or minimize outlay are the same, and the two objectives are really alternative facets of consumer efficiency.

Maximizing pleasure from a fixed outlay. Let us suppose that a consumer has $2.20 to spend per time period, and that butter costs

$1.00 a pound and cigarettes cost 2¢ each. He could then purchase 2.2 lbs. of butter if he did not buy any cigarettes (*OB* in Fig. III), or 110 cigarettes if he did not want any butter (*OC*), or he could buy some other combination such as 1.2 lbs. of butter and 50 cigarettes. Assuming the outlay and prices that we have supposed, the line *BC* indicates the alternative combinations of butter and cigarettes that our consumer can afford to buy, for every point on this line will require an expenditure of $2.20.

The line *BC* will hereafter be called an "outlay line," for it shows all the various combinations of the two goods that would cost $2.20 to purchase. The slope of this line is determined by the prices that prevail on the market and so is a datum for the consumer over which he has no control. If the outlay line were steeper, it would mean that the price of butter had fallen relative to that of cigarettes and that the price of cigarettes had risen relative to that of butter. The *position* of this line, as contrasted with its *slope,* is determined by the sum of money the consumer intends to spend, a shift to the right and up indicating a larger outlay and a shift to the left and down indicating a smaller outlay.

In the present case, we are assuming that *BC* is the relevant constant line, and so the question is "How should this consumer spend his $2.20 between butter and cigarettes?"

The simplest solution to this problem is found graphically. Figure III shows the $2.20 outlay line (*BC*) and a series of indifference curves. Such an outlay line intersects a number of indifference curves (for example, I_0), just touches one curve (I_1), and does not reach the other indifference curves at all (for example, I_2). In other words, I_1 is the "highest" indifference curve the consumer can attain with an outlay of $2.20, and he can just reach this curve at the point *R* if he buys 1.0 lb. of butter and 60 cigarettes.

The rule for a consumer who intends to spend a given sum of money is to purchase different goods in the combination that is indicated by the point of tangency between his outlay line and the highest indifference curve he can afford.

Marginal Rate of Substitution. The same answer can be obtained by arithmetic computation rather than by graphic inspection. The procedure then requires determination of the consumer's marginal rate of substitution between butter and cigarettes. Subsequently, it is necessary to find, by trial and error, the combination of butter and cigarettes that occasions a marginal rate of substitution equal to the exchange ratio of these two goods that prevails in the market.

A consumer's marginal rate of substitution is the ratio at which a consumer can exchange a very small amount of one commodity for a very small amount of the other without affecting his over-all utility. Let us suppose that a consumer is neither better nor worse off if he exchanges 5.0 cigarettes for .1 lb. of butter. The marginal rate of substitution of cigarettes to butter is then 5.0 divided by .1, or 50.0.

Marginal rates of substitution between cigarettes and butter can be calculated from the first two columns of Table VIII. It will be noticed that the marginal rate of substitution varies with the absolute amount of butter and cigarettes enjoyed by the consumer. When he has approximately 1.9 lbs. of butter and 32 cigarettes, the marginal rate of substitution of cigarettes to butter is 2.0 cigarettes divided by .1 lb. of butter, or 20. And when the consumer has approximately .2 lb. of butter and 128 cigarettes, the marginal rate of substitution of cigarettes to butter is about 12.5 cigarettes to .1 lb. of butter, or 125.

It is clear, from the three marginal rates of substitution computed from this single indifference schedule, that substitution rates vary considerably according to the absolute proportions in which butter and cigarettes are held. The marginal rate of substitution of cigarettes to butter is high when the absolute ratio of butter to cigarettes held by the consumer is low. The existence of this relationship is illustrated by the convex shape of indifference curves.

Marginal rates of substitution can be determined graphically from the slope of a tangent drawn to an indifference curve. For example, BC is tangent to I_1 at R, and values of the two intercepts of this tangent are 110 cigarettes (horizontal axis) and 2.2 lbs. of butter (vertical axis). The marginal rate of substitution of cigarettes for butter is therefore 110 over 2.2, or 50, which figure can readily be obtained by computation from the schedule. The diagram reveals that tangents will be steeper, which means that the marginal rate of substitution of cigarettes for butter will then be lower, for combinations involving more butter and fewer cigarettes.

It has already been stated that the most satisfactory combination of cigarettes and butter for a consumer is the one that equates the marginal rate of substitution with the market exchange rate. The market exchange rate between two goods is the ratio of the number of units of each good that can be purchased with a given sum of money. Under our assumptions a dollar will buy 50 cigarettes (at 2¢ each) and 1.0 lb. of butter (at $1.00 a lb.) and so the market exchange rate is 50 to 1, or 50.0. The market exchange rate between cigarettes and butter is necessarily the reciprocal of the ratio of the price of cigarettes to the price of butter. The consumer should find a combination of cigarettes and butter that gives the same marginal rate of substitution as the market exchange rate. Such a combination will be an optimum one for the consumer because the relative use value of the goods to him will be equal to their relative values in the market.

Minimizing outlays for a given total satisfaction. A consumer might be interested in purchasing a given amount of satisfaction at the lowest possible cost. We shall suppose that he wishes to obtain an over-all satisfaction equivalent to that obtainable from any one of the combinations set forth in the first two columns of Table VIII and depicted by the curve I_1 in Fig. III. Which combination will cost least?

The combination that costs least will depend upon the price relations in the market. We shall continue to suppose that butter costs $1.00 a pound and that cigarettes cost 2¢ each. A combination of .1

lb. of butter and 141 cigarettes will then cost 10¢ plus 282¢ or $2.92 to buy, a combination of .2 lb. and 128 cigarettes will cost $2.76, the final combination of 2.2 lbs. and 28 cigarettes will cost $2.76, and so on. Trial and error will reveal that, at the assumed prices, 1.0 lb. of butter and 60 cigarettes will cost only $2.20, which is a smaller outlay than that required to purchase any other combination yielding equivalent utility. At this combination the marginal rate of substitution is, of course, equal to the market exchange rate.

The same result can be obtained graphically from Fig. III. I_1 is based on the first two columns of Table VIII again. The diagonal straight lines $BC, B'C', B''C''$, and so forth are alternative iso-outlay lines. All these lines are parallel, since their slopes are commonly determined by the price of butter and cigarettes in the market. Lower lines to the left involve a smaller total outlay than higher lines to the right. The cheapest combination of cigarettes and butter on I_1 will be shown by the point on this indifference curve that touches but does not intersect some exchange line. Actually, the "lowest" or cheapest exchange line reached by I_1 is the line BC, and the point of tangency is R, which combination again involves 60 cigarettes and 1.0 lb. of butter.

The slope of the exchange line and the slope of the indifference curve I_1 at R are, of course, the same. In other words, the market exchange rate and the marginal rate of substitution are similar. It is this equality that always characterizes the optimum adjustment by the consumer in his purchasing of two or more commodities.

Consumer's Adjustment to Price Changes

A consumer always adjusts to a change in commodity prices by altering the proportions in which he purchases goods. He will buy relatively more of a product if it becomes relatively cheaper; this reaction is sometimes termed the substitution effect. However, there is also another effect, the income effect, which depends upon whether the consumer tries to hold his satisfaction or his outlay constant.

Constant Satisfaction Case. Let us suppose that a consumer attempts to keep his over-all utility constant. In other words, he absorbs the income effect of altered prices by changing his outlays. What will happen then if the price of cigarettes falls from 2¢ to 1¢ each while the price of butter remains at $1.00 a pound?

In Fig. IV the former equilibrium is shown by the tangency of the market exchange line BC with the indifference curve I_1 at R. (This situation is already familiar to us from Fig. III.) However, the final adjustment under our new price assumption will be at S, where DE is tangent to I_1, for the reasons now given.

If cigarettes were halved in price, and so cost 1¢ each, the minimum cost combination will be different from what it was with the former price relationship. Since one hundred cigarettes now exchange for one pound of butter on the market, the minimum cost combination will be one that involves a marginal rate of substitution of cigarettes to butter of one hundred. Such a substitution rate prevails in the proximity of .4 lb. of butter and 105 cigarettes (the difference between 116 and 95 cigarettes is 21, the difference between .3 and .5 lb. of

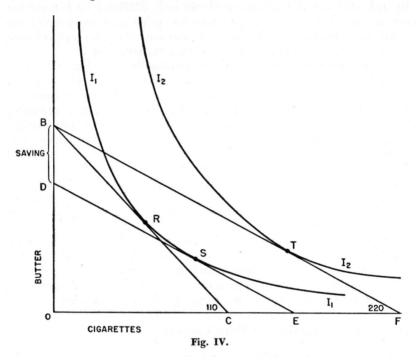

Fig. IV.

butter is .2, and 21 divided by .2 is 105). The cost of this combination is about $1.45 and is less than the outlay that would be required to purchase any other combination of equal satisfaction.

A halving in the price of cigarettes means that twice as many can now be bought for the same outlay. Accordingly, a person with $2.20 can now buy 220 cigarettes instead of 110 cigarettes. Hence the outlay line relevant to a $2.20 expenditure is now BF, instead of BC, since the distance OF is drawn twice as long as OC. The outlay line BF will now touch an indifference curve higher than I_1, and so it is clear that the consumer does not need as much as $2.20 to reach I_1, which supposedly represents an adequate level of utility for him. What smaller sum need he now spend?

There must be some outlay line, parallel to BF but lying below it, that will just touch I_1. DE is such an outlay line and has a slope that reflects the new price relationship. Hence the consumer will buy cigarettes and butter in the quantities indicated by the tangency point of DE with I_1 at S. Interpolation on the axis reveals that these quantities will be approximately 80 cigarettes and .65 lb. of butter. The cost of these will be 80¢ and 65¢ respectively, or a total of $1.45, so that the saving in terms of money is 75¢, although the level of utility enjoyed is the same as before.

The saving in outlays can also be obtained from Fig. IV. The new minimum outlay line *DE* makes an intercept on the vertical axis equal to *OD*. We know that *OB* lbs. of butter cost $2.20. Therefore, the cost of *OD* lbs. of butter will be *OD/OB* of $2.20, or $1.45, since the price of butter has not changed. Therefore, the cost of purchasing the *S* combination at the new prices must also be $1.45, for *S* and *D* are on the same outlay line. In other words, the distance *BD* represents the 75¢ saving that results from a lower cigarette price.

Constant Outlay Case. On the other hand, a consumer might decide to maintain a customary outlay, even when some prices fall, and so benefit from an increase in utility instead of from a reduction in outlay.

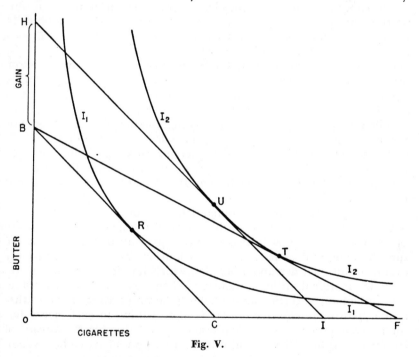

Fig. V.

Let us again suppose that the price of cigarettes is halved, from 2¢ each to 1¢ each, and use Fig. V to analyze the outcome. The new $2.20 outlay line is again *BF,* for reasons explained above, and the highest indifference curve that it can touch is I_2, the tangency point being at *T*. Perpendiculars to the vertical and horizontal axes would indicate the number of units of butter and cigarettes respectively that will be purchased.

The consumer is obviously better off in real terms at *T* on I_2 than at *R* on I_1. It is possible to express this real income addition in money terms by discovering how much more money would be needed to climb from I_1 to I_2 at the former price relationship. Diagramatically the answer can be found by constructing a line that is *both* parallel to the former exchange line *(BC) and* tangent to the subsequent indifference curve (I_2). Such a line is *HI*, with a point of tangency at *U* and an intercept at *H* on the vertical or butter axis. The price of butter is still $1.00. Hence *OH* represents the sum of money which, if spent efficiently at the former prices, would be needed to attain the real income level represented by I_2. Consequently *BH* represents the monetary value of the additional real income made possible by a price reduction in cigarettes.

Buyer's Surplus

The concept of buyer's surplus has already been encountered in connection with demand schedules. The same notion can be graphically represented with indifference curves. In Fig. VI, the vertical axis represents money, the horizontal axis stands for Good *X,* and I_1, I_2, and so forth are attained indifference curves at successively lower prices. The tangency points between successive indifference curves and outlay lines are T_1, T_2, and so on. The buyer has OY_1 dollars to spend.

When the price of *X* is prohibitively high, so that the buyer does not purchase a single unit of the good, X_1 is located at the origin *O,* T_1 is located at *Y,* and the relevant indifference curve (I_1) joins the vertical axis at *Y.* When the price falls, so that the outlay line becomes an extension of Y_1T_2, I_2 is attained at T_2. What is the buyer's surplus in this case?

It depends a little on the adopted definition of buyer's surplus. We have previously described it as the excess of the maximum outlay the buyer would be willing to make for the quantity purchased over the sum he actually does pay. Such a definition was satisfactory in the case of traditional demand schedules, which implicitly assume an unchanging marginal utility of money. When we use indifference curves we can be more realistic, however, and take into account the fact that a man with more effective dollars is more willing to exchange a few for a given product. The significance of all this for the theory of consumer surplus is that the adjustment that would have to be made in a buyer's income, in order to offset exactly his buyer's surplus, will depend upon whether the original reference situation is taken to be one in which he buys no units and has no surplus or the one that he actually adopts in adjusting to the market price.

Figure VI may help to clarify these points. Let us suppose the price is such that the buyer, with OY_1 income to spend, can just attain I_2 at T_2. The vertical distance between T_2 and *A* represents the money spent on Good *X.* Now, if the price had been prohibitively high, so that the buyer purchased zero units of *X,* he would have spent no money on *X* and been at T_1 on I_1. Therefore, *if* the buyer had had to spend *AB* dollars to purchase OX_1 units of *X,* he would still be on I_1, no better or worse off than before. But in actuality he has to spend only AT_2 dollars on OX_2 units of X. Hence he has a surplus of BT_2, in the sense that he spends this much less than he would have been willing to *if he had started at T_1 with no purchases of X at all.*

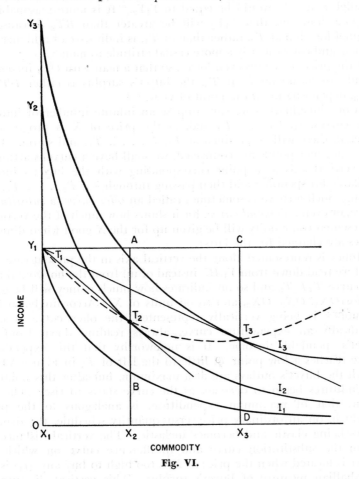

Fig. VI.

However, it is entirely hypothetical to suppose that he starts at T_1 on I_1. In reality, the market price and his income being what they are, the buyer is really located on I_2 at T_2. We might therefore attempt to measure the "surplus" he thus enjoys by ascertaining the additional income he would need to maintain the same real income if the price of X became so prohibitively high that he did not purchase any. The amount of such necessary compensation is shown by the distance between Y_1 and the tangency of I_2 with the vertical axis at Y_2.

The contrast is now clear. If we suppose that the buyer is originally located at T_1 and then moves to T_2, BT_2 could be subtracted from his income and he would be as well off in real terms as before. On the other hand, if we suppose him originally at T_2, he would need to be compensated by Y_1Y_2 in order not to suffer in well-being when the price of X becomes prohibitive. *If* the buyer's marginal utility of money were constant, all the indifference curves would be vertically parallel, and BT_2 would be equal to Y_1Y_2. It is more reasonable to suppose, however, that Y_1Y_2 will be greater than BT_2, because an original location at T_2, rather than at T_1, is indicative of a higher real income and consequently a more casual attitude to money.

If the price of X falls even lower, so that a man with OY_1 income to spend can locate on I_3 at T_3, the buyer's surplus is either DT_3 or Y_1Y_3, depending upon the point of view.

In our imagination we can suppose an infinite number of indifference curves, I_1, I_2, . . ., I_n, and, as the price of X is progressively lowered, these will be attained at T_1, T_2, . . ., T_n, and so on. If all these tangency points are connected, we shall have a curve, starting on the vertical axis at a point corresponding with the buyer's income available for spending and then passing through T_1, T_2, . . ., T_n, and so on. Such a curve is sometimes called an *offer curve*, a *substitution curve*, or even a *demand curve*, for it shows how much of the vertically represented commodity will be given up for the X good when different prices are charged for the latter.

Money is represented along the vertical axis in the present case, and so, if we read down from Y_1AC, instead of up from the horizontal axis, the curve $T_1T_2T_3$ and so on indicates how much money will be given up for OX_1, OX_2, OX_3, and so on units of X. Accordingly, so long as money is being vertically represented, the offer curve is more specifically an expenditure curve, always reading down from the buyer's spendable income. It is noteworthy that this expenditure curve reaches a low point (a little to the left of T_3 in Figure VI), at which the buyer's outlays are at a maximum, but after this point his expenditures begin to decrease as the curve starts to rise. The low point, that of maximum expenditure, is analogous to the point at which, on an ordinary price-versus-quantity schedule, the demand ceases being elastic and becomes inelastic. The vertical distance between the substitution curve and indifference curve on which the buyer is located when the price of X is too high to buy any (I_1) is the Marshallian measure of buyer's surplus. This vertical distance increases as the price falls and more units of X are purchased.

Measuring the Welfare Effect of a Price Change

A change in the price of a good habitually purchased by a consumer will normally affect his material well-being. He may spend more or less and the utility he derives from his purchases may be more or less. Statisticians have long attempted to measure and express numerically the changes in consumer well-being that follow a price change.

There are several different ways in which the change in well-being might be measured, and each method will give a slightly different answer. Two alternative approaches have already been employed and an additional two possibilities will now be indicated. Indifference curves of the iso-utility kind readily illustrate at least four alternative ways to measure welfare effects of price changes.

We shall suppose the problem is to express in dollars the change in a consumer's cost of living when there is a cut in the price of one product he customarily buys.

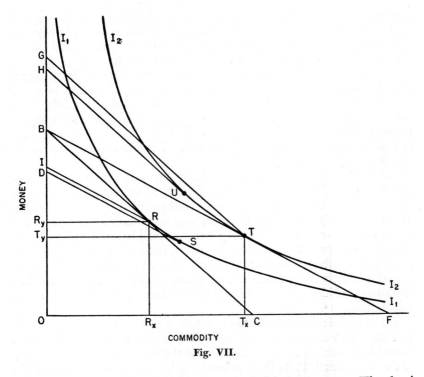

Fig. VII.

Fig. VII maps the iso-utility curves of this consumer. The horizontal axis represents Good X; the vertical axis again represents money, rather than some other product. OB stands for the total outlay that the consumer will spend on *all* goods. We shall suppose that Good X experiences an alteration in price. Initially, its price was such that the consumer's total outlay would just buy OC units; but later, when its price is lowered, this same outlay will buy OF units. Accordingly, the quantity of X that is bought at the high price (OR_X) is shown by a perpendicular from R to the horizontal axis while, OT_X will be bought at the lower price. The sum of money spent on X will be the vertical distance BR_Y when the price is high and BT_Y when the price is low. The consumer attains the iso-utility curve I_1 (at R) during the high price and I_2 (at T) during the low price on X. In both cases the consumer's total outlay on all goods is OB.

A dollar expression of the consumer's gain when X falls in price can be obtained by comparing his actual total outlay (OB) with the aggregate sum he would have to spend in certain hypothetical situations. More specifically, how much would he have to spend in order to:

(1) buy the prior collection of goods at the subsequent prices;
(2) attain the prior real income level at the subsequent prices;
(3) buy the subsequent collection of goods at the prior prices; and
(4) attain the subsequent real income level at the prior prices?

("Prior" and "subsequent" here refer to the periods when X was priced high and low respectively.) The differences between each of these four necessary sums of money and OB, the consumer's actual total outlay, are four possible and alternative answers to our question.

(1) The prior collection of goods at the subsequent prices would now require an outlay of OI. The non-X goods, the prices of which have not changed, would cost OR_Y both before and afterwards. The outlay for OR_X units of X at its lower price will be R_YI if IR is drawn through R so that it is parallel to BF. It used to cost the consumer OB to buy the prior collection of goods. Therefore the difference, or "saving," is BI dollars.

(2) The prior real income at subsequent prices will cost at least OD dollars. The consumer is equally well off in real terms anywhere on I_1, which is the iso-utility curve he had attained at the prior prices. We have already shown that the minimum cost of attaining a given real income at a new price relationship is determined by the Y-axis intercept of a tangent drawn at the new slope to the old curve. Accordingly DS is supposed to be constructed tangent to I_1 and parallel to BF. If the actual outlay was OB, and the necessary outlay in the hypothetical situation considered is now OD, the consumer's gain might be put at DB dollars.

(3) The subsequent collection of goods at prior prices would cost OG dollars. The cost of OT_X units of X is T_YG, because TG is drawn through T parallel to BC. The cost of the non-X products is actually OT_Y, and, inasmuch as their prices have not changed, this would also be their total cost in the prior situation. Hence, if there were a return to prior prices, it would cost the consumer BG more dollars to live as he does in the subsequent price period.

(4) The subsequent real income level would cost OH dollars at prior prices. We know this because a line drawn tangent at U to I_2 and parallel to BC will make a vertical axis intercept at H. Actually, at subsequent prices, it costs the consumer only OB dollars to attain the I_2 iso-utility curve. Therefore, yet another estimate of the gain to our consumer of a price cut in X would be BH dollars.

A priori, and without having a definite purpose clearly in mind, one cannot state that any one of these four answers is "right" or "wrong." The change in income and outlay a man would need in order to be neither worse nor better off than before in utility terms is either BD or BH. On the other hand, if he is to continue to buy the same collection of goods, there must be an addition or subtraction of BI or BG

to his income and outlay. The appropriate measure also depends upon whether the prior or the subsequent state of affairs is held equitable. If the earlier period is considered "normal," then the change in income and outlay will have to be BI or BD, whereas it will be BH or BG if the later period is taken as a standard. Which method to use depends on whether the aim is maintaining a constant real income level or a constant set of purchases and whether the situation ex-ante or ex-post the price change should be viewed as normative.

Regularly maintained price level series, such as the Bureau of Labor Statistics' cost-of-living index, are based on the changing total cost of purchasing some historic collection of goods. The "market basket," which is repriced each period, is supposedly representative of the kind of goods purchased by some income group in a stated past period. Price index series of this type become out of date when families alter their consumption patterns and the relative prices of goods change. On the other hand, it would be just as arbitrary to compare the cost at two different periods of buying the collection of goods that people typically purchase after prices have changed. Indices that periodically reprice a "market basket" representative of prior consumption patterns are sometimes described as Laspeyres-type indices and those that use subsequent consumption patterns are often named after Paasche. In terms of Fig. VII, the numerical value of a Laspeyres-type index would be OI/OB, whereas a computation of a Paasche-type formula would yield OB/OG as an answer. The magnitudes of these two results will be only approximately the same.

Certain economic groups in any nation make political demands to the effect that their incomes should be adjusted from time to time in accordance with price level changes. For example, some labor unions have claimed that wages should be modified so that take-home pay changes by the same percentage as the cost of living rises. Irrespective of the merits of such a demand, it is worth noting that such a policy, if put into effect, would increase real income of workers. Suppose a worker is located on I_2 at T during some period when prices are low. The price of Good X increases—so that an outlay that would have bought OF units of X will now only buy OC units. The total cost to the worker of purchasing the same collection of goods as he used to buy will now be OG instead of OB. Accordingly, he or his union might demand an increase of BG dollars in take-home pay, or a multi-plication of his pay check by OG/OB. However, with increased money income, he can attain a higher indifference curve if he will act like an efficient consumer and adjust his purchases so that marginal rates of substitution accord with market exchange rates. Actually, an increase of BH dollars in income will enable the worker to stay on I_2, which he can just attain at U. In other words, the worker can maintain the same real income, if he will follow the usual principles of maximizing utility from a given total outlay, with a smaller increase in dollar income than would be needed to purchase the old collection of goods at the new prices. And in the opposite case, when prices are falling instead of rising, a worker's take-home pay could be cut by more than the cost reduction of purchasing the original set of goods without reducing his real utility income. Under a policy of adjusting take-home pay, whether up or down, in accordance with a Laspeyres-type cost-of-living index, such as is used by the Bureau of Labor Statistics, the income recipient is usually enabled either to raise his real income or to act irrationally and waste the nation's resources.

Only one theoretical qualification of this statement is necessary. If the prices of all purchased goods change by the same per cent, there will be no substitution effect: the prior and subsequent consumption patterns will be identical, and the change in money needed to continue purchasing the old collection of goods will be exactly the same as that required to maintain the prior real income. However, as an empirical fact, a change in the general price level is always characterized by disparate price movements of individual goods.

Consumer's Adjustment to Income Changes

A typical consumer will vary the proportions in which he buys different goods, even though their price relations remain unaltered, when he experiences a change in income.

Let us suppose that a consumer's appreciation of different goods does not change, but that, in fairly rapid succession, his monetary income is doubled and then trebled from its initial level, and that he spends all his income in the same period as he receives it. Prices are unchanged. His highest possible exchange line in each successive period will be represented in Fig. VIII as BC, $B'C'$, and $B''C''$ respectively. At each income and outlay level there will be one indifference curve tangent to but not intersecting the outlay line. These indifference curves are I_1, I_2, I_3, and so on and the points of tangency T, T', T'', and so on.

It will be noticed that, in Fig. VIII, while this consumer buys more butter and cigarettes as his income rises, he increases his purchases of butter more considerably than his purchases of cigarettes. A doubling of income results in the use of more than twice as many pounds of butter but less than twice as many cigarettes. The income elasticity of butter is in excess of unity and that of cigarettes is less than unity.

A curve, originating at the axes intersection and drawn through successive tangency points, may be called a pattern-of-living curve. In Fig. VIII, OL is such a curve, for it passes through T, T', and T'', and it shows the different proportions in which two goods will be used as income changes. If this curve were a straight line, starting at O, the proportions would be constant and the income elasticity of both goods would be unity. However this is unusual. Normally, there will be some curvature, indicating that the pattern of consumption is becoming more heavily weighted with one good and less heavily weighted with the other.

Occasionally, in the case of "inferior goods" used by poorer people as substitutes for more expensive goods, such as margarine for butter, the pattern-of-living curve will bend back upon itself, reflecting an absolute decrease in consumption as income rises. Other examples

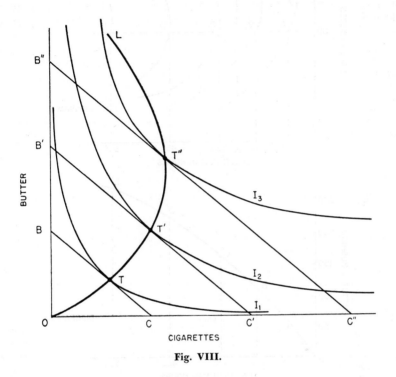

Fig. VIII.

of "inferior" (or "poor man's") goods are bus fares, beer, and linoleum, which tend to be replaced by private automobiles, liqueurs and wines, and carpets, respectively. In Fig. VIII, the rather improbable assumption has been made that cigarettes, replaced perhaps by cigars, eventually become an inferior good and have a negative income elasticity of demand.

Iso-Quant Curves and Producer Demand

A producer buys factors of production in order to obtain outputs, whereas a consumer buys goods in order to obtain utility. Hence an analysis of producer demand involves iso-quant curves, instead of iso-utility schedules of the type employed in the preceding section. Any point on an iso-quant curve involves the same physical output of product as any other point on the indifference curve, just as all points on a given iso-utility curve involve the same satisfaction. However, in the case of iso-quant schedules, the horizontal and vertical axes represent inputs of two particular factors of production (see Fig. IX).

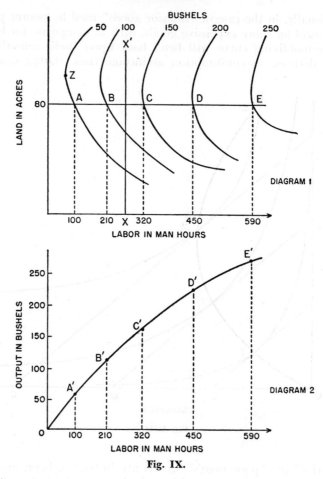

Fig. IX.

Determining the Marginal Productivity of a Factor from Iso-Quants

Since physical output, unlike utility, can usually be measured, precise numerical values can be given to successive iso-quants. For example, in Fig. IX, where the vertical and horizontal axes represent land and labor respectively, another iso-quant is drawn for each additional 50 bushels output. These indifference curves are therefore exactly like evenly spaced contour lines on an ordinary topographical map.

The marginal productivity of a particular factor, when used in combination with a fixed quantity of some other factor, can be derived from an iso-quant map.

For example, let us determine the marginal productivity of labor, measured in bushels, when labor is combined with 80 acres of land. First, it is necessary to discover the relationship between labor input and total bushel output when 80 acres are cultivated. A horizontal straight line, drawn across diagram 1 in Fig. IX, will intersect the 50-bushel iso-quant at A, the 100-bushel iso-quant at B, and so on; then, by referring to the horizontal axis, we find that a 50-bushel output requires 100 man-hours, 100 bushels requires 210 man-hours, and so on. In other words, from the $A, B, \ldots$ points where the "80 acre line" crosses the iso-quants, we can learn the relationship between bushels of output and man-hours of labor input when 80 acres are cultivated.

Diagram 2 of Fig. IX graphs this relationship; from it can be derived the marginal productivity of labor. For example, the increment in output obtained by employing an extra 320th man-hour is given by the slope of the curve at C'. The slope at C' is somewhat flatter than the slope at B' and so the marginal product of a 320th man-hour is less than that of a 210th man-hour. The average marginal productivity of labor, between 210 and 320 man-hours, is $(150 - 100$ bushels) divided by $(320 - 210)$ man-hours, or .55 bushels per man hour.

Of course, the marginal productivity of labor, man-hour by man-hour, would be different if the number of cultivated acres were other than 80. If, for example, a "100 acre line" were drawn across diagram 1, it would reach the 50-bushel iso-quant before 100 man-hours were employed, the 100-bushel iso-quant before 210 man-hours were employed, and so on. In other words, with more land cultivated, a given output can usually be realized with less labor. Graphically, if drawn into diagram 2, this would appear as a total-bushel-to-total-man-hour curve lying above the one drawn for 80 acres.

However, if more and more land were used, a stage might be reached where the land-to-labor ratio became so topheavy that, when more land was added, more labor had also to be added in order to maintain a given bushel output. Thus, the 50-bushel iso-quant turns back on itself at Z, which means that extra land will thereafter have a negative productivity. These results are in accord with an earlier discussion of the principle of variable proportions, in which three stages were distinguished and it was shown that if too much land were combined with a little labor land had a negative marginal productivity. (See Chapter 29.)

Another way of determining the relationship between bushels of output and acres of input would be to take a vertical line, such as XX', across the iso-quants, and then note the number of acres associated with each successive output datum. The marginal productivity of land can then be computed from the total-bushel-to-total-acres relation in the way indicated above for labor. Obviously, the marginal productivity of land so determined will depend upon the constant quantity of labor combined with it.

The Most Profitable Combination of Factors

The most profitable combination of two factors can be determined with the help of iso-quants if the relative prices of the factors and the intended total outlay of the producer are known or assumed.

Let us suppose that the producer expects to spend $1,000 a month for the use of land and labor and that an acre leases for $50 a month while a man's monthly wage is $200. The $1,000 outlay could then hire 20 acres, or 5 man-months, or some combination of the two as shown by the outlay line *BC* in Fig. X. The highest iso-quant curve that the outlay line can attain is I_3, which it touches at *T,* and which involves a combination of 12 acres and 2 man-months.

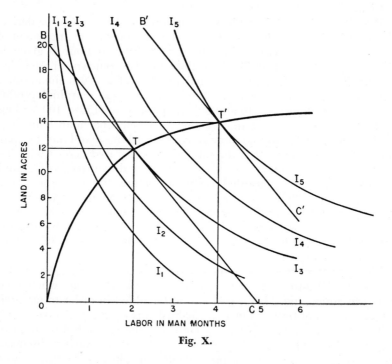

Fig. X.

The slope of I_3 at *T* indicates the marginal rate of substitution of labor to land when the output is unchanged. The slope of I_3 at *T* is the same as the slope of *BC,* and so must be 20 acres to 5 man-months or about 4 acres to a man. Hence, when the producer is using 12 acres and 2 man-months, the marginal productivity of each factor is such that he would be just about willing to exchange one man for 4 acres or vice versa. Now it is worth recalling that the wage of one man for a month is 4 times the lease cost of one acre for a month. Hence the marginal rate of substitution is equal to the reciprocal of the prices of the factors. These results confirm our earlier analysis of consumer efficiency.

It is most important to realize, however, that the optimum combination of two men and 12 acres depended not only on the price relationship but also on the assumption of a $1,000 outlay. If a larger scale of operations were undertaken, and 50 per cent more money spent for factors, we cannot assume that 50 per cent more men and 50 per cent more acres would be used. It is true that, *if* only *two* factors were required for production, they would always be combined in the same proportions so long as prices remained unchanged; then, if the optimum combination ratio were 6 to 1 in land to labor, we would find 18 acres and 3 men, or 24 acres and 4 men, and so forth. However, to be realistic, in the short run there are usually a number of fixed productive agents, whose quantities cannot be continuously adjusted as changes are made in the variable factors. For example, as men are hired or laid off, an enterprise cannot immediately adjust the extent of its capital equipment. And, in the long run, when capital can be adjusted, some people would say that entrepreneurship still remains as a fixed factor of production.

In constructing Fig. X it was supposed that some third fixed factor, perhaps an installed irrigation system, is in fact used along with the land and labor depicted in the diagram. If the producer intends to expand his operations by spending $1,500 instead of $1,000, he will have little use for extra land he cannot irrigate and will instead concentrate on hiring additional men. Accordingly the $1,500 outlay line in Fig. X becomes tangent to the highest attainable iso-quant (I_5) at a point representing 14 acres and 4 men. The optimum combination ratio of acres to men is now $3\frac{1}{2}$ to 1, instead of 6 to 1 as previously.

Apparently there are some complementary (joint demand) and substitution (rival supply) influences between land and labor and some "other" factor at work here. We shall simplify matters by supposing that all productive agents other than land and labor can be lumped together and designated by "O." These other outside factors will include agents that cannot be continuously adjusted in quantity, and so we shall suppose that "O" is in the nature of a fixed factor. Now, if an expansion of operations involves a disproportionately small percentage addition to land, it must be because land is a complement of "O" that is relatively fixed in supply. Also, if increasing outlays to $1,500 results in a disproportionately large percentage increase in labor, it must be because labor is a substitute of "O" that is comparatively fixed in supply. Hence, because reversibility holds, "O" tends to be a complement of land and a substitute of labor. We use the word "tends" because we do not know whether land and labor together are a substitute or a complement of the other fixed factor. Perhaps a more accurate statement would then be that the relation between "O" and land is more complementary, or less substitutable, than the relation between "O" and labor; and labor and "O" are less complementary, or more substitutable, than are land and "O."

In summary, the optimum combination ratio of two factors depends upon the scale of operations, because they work with other comparatively fixed factors, as well as upon the price relationship of the two variable factors.

Bilateral Trading and Commodity Rationing

Different users—whether producers or consumers—do not need or desire a similar kind of good with the same degree of urgency. Therefore, if several users are given a certain quantity of X and a certain quantity of Y, they will very sensibly begin trading X and Y among themselves. This rather obvious fact is usually ignored by government allocation and rationing schemes.

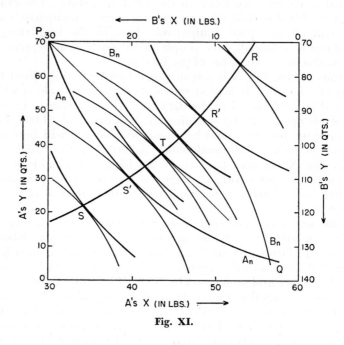

Fig. XI.

Let us suppose that A and B are each allowed 30 pounds of X and 70 quarts of Y. This ration of X and Y is represented by P in Fig. XI. In this bilateral trading diagram, A's possessions of X and Y are represented as usual, but B's possession of X is shown to the left along the top horizontal axis while his possession of Y is shown going down the right vertical axis. Hence, the diagram represents a closed system, embracing only A and B, and when we show A gaining X we automatically show B losing X by the same amount. Our double diagram enables us to show A and B trading X and Y.

The allowed ration, indicated by P, places A on one indifference curve (A_n) and B on one of his own indifference curves (B_n). It would be a most remarkable accident if A_n and B_n were tangent to one another, since this would mean that they each had exactly the same marginal rates of substitution between X and Q when separately possessing 30 pounds of X and 70 quarts of $Y;$ consequently, they would not wish to trade at an exchange rate acceptable to both.

The probable situation, as shown in Fig. XI, is that A_n and B_n are not tangent at P, but intersect; in this case there is "room to trade," because the relative values that each places upon the marginal units of X and Y will differ.

Any combination of X and Y that can be represented by a point lying between the curves A_n and B_n and between the points P and Q will be preferred by both A *and* B to the official allocation of 30 pounds and 70 quarts each. We can imagine, within this bargaining area, a great many indifference curves, all of which are not shown; the ones belonging to A will be convex from below and those belonging to B will seem concave from below. Each of these convex indifference curves (A's) will be tangent to some concave one (belonging to B) and vice versa. The various points of tangency lie along a curve passing through R and S. Any position on this RS curve, *if once attained*, will be stable, since A and B will then have the same marginal rates of substitution between X and Y.

The original position is P. Hence, since A is already on A_n, he will not be willing to move on to RS anywhere between S' (which is also on A_n) and S. Similarly B will not move from P (on B_n) to anywhere on RS between R' (also on B_n) and R. A distribution of X and Y such as the one represented by the point R' would of course be far preferable to A but indifferent to B.

The final equilibrium arrangement must afford equality among the following: (1) A's marginal rate of substitution between X and Y (as shown by the slope of A's indifference curves), (2) B's marginal rate of substitution between X and Y (as shown by the slope of B's indifference curves), and (3) the mutually agreed upon barter terms of trade (shown by the slope of a line drawn through P and intersecting RS). Only one point along RS (shown as T in the figure) will give similar slopes for A's indifference curve, B's indifference curve, and an exchange rate line passing through P.

Restated more succinctly: (1) P cannot be a stable position, since A and B are on intersecting indifference curves and so can improve their well-being by trading; (2) Any point along RS will be stable, if once attained, because A and B will be on tangent indifference curves and so have the same marginal rates of substitution; (3) If A and B start at a position off RS, only one point on RS can be attained, namely the point that permits an exchange line from the original position to be tangent simultaneously to an indifference curve of A and one of B.

The economic moral of the geometry is that an aliquot rationing or allocation scheme distributes goods in a suboptimum manner. The practical proof of this is that individuals often swap their rations in an attempt to increase their satisfactions. Such behavior, which is rational economically, is usually declared illegal by the allocating authority. If the rationing scheme is enforced, there is a waste of resources, for an uneconomic distribution requires a larger output in order to realize a given over-all level of satisfaction.

Joint Supply Products and Iso-Cost Curves

Joint supply products are goods simultaneously produced by a single process or act. Examples are the refining of crude oil (which yields gasoline, fuel oil, and other petroleum derivatives), the separating of whole milk (which yields cream and separated milk), and the threshing of wheat (which yields grain and straw). In certain cases the proportions in which the end products are obtained are variable (cream and separated milk) while in others they are predetermined (for example, grain and straw).

Invariant joint supply products relieve the entrepreneur of many perplexities. He need not concern himself with producing the end products in the most profitable proportion because this ratio is beyond his control. He need not bother about the specific costs of end products that are in joint supply because there is nothing specific about them to give them special costs. Invariant joint supply products only have joint costs and the only possible entrepreneurial decision is whether or not to turn out the predetermined product mix.

Variable joint supply products do occasion entrepreneurial decisions, however. The most profitable proportions must be determined. And, in searching for this answer, the opportunity cost of different end products can be discovered.

Let us imagine a dairy farmer who sells cream and separated milk. He can vary the relative yield of these two end products by changing the type of cow in his herd and the amount and kind of feeding. Experiments might give sufficient data to estimate iso-cost curves as shown in Fig. XII.

The vertical axis of the figure represents quarts of separated milk, and the horizontal axis represents quarts of cream. Any one iso-cost curve shows the various combinations of cream and separated milk that can be obtained for the same expenditure on cows, grazing, fodder, milking, separating, and so forth. The farmers total outlay is the same for all points on a single curve. Higher curves, upwards and to the right, involve great expenditures, since the output of one or both of the end products is always larger. It is as though there were a third dimension, rising up off the page, representing dollars, and the iso-cost curves were contours measuring a hill of expenditure. The iso-cost curves are concave when viewed from the origin because, as the percentage recovery of a specific product becomes greater, extra recoveries occasion disproportionate effort and expense.

The *real* cost of producing one extra quart of milk is the quantity of cream that will have to be sacrificed if the producer's total outlay is to be kept constant. For any total scale of output this information can be had from the appropriate iso-cost curve. For example, if the dairy farmer is producing the R combination of cream and separated milk, the real cost of either cream or separated milk can be learned from the slope of a tangent drawn to I_3 at R. Let us suppose that such a tangent has a 1 to 3 slope as shown by the distance from O to the tangent's points of interception at X and Y on the cream and milk axes respectively. The real cost of 1 more quart of milk is then the loss of $\frac{1}{3}$ quart of cream and the cost of 1 more quart of cream is the loss of 3 quarts of milk.

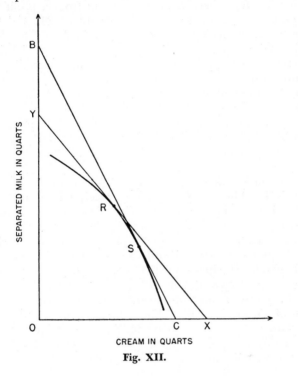

Fig. XII.

However, the dairy farmer may want bookkeeping costs in dollars and cents rather than real costs expressed in quarts of an alternative product. Actually, the money opportunity cost of producing one more quart of milk is merely the revenue lost from producing $\frac{1}{3}$ fewer quarts of cream. Consequently, so long as the market prices of the two end products are shown, the problem is simple. Let us suppose that separated milk sells for 20¢ a quart and cream for $1.00 a quart, and that the real opportunity ratio, as we have seen, is 1 cream to 3 milk. The money opportunity cost of one more quart of milk is hence $\frac{1}{3}$ of $1.00 (or 33¢) and that of cream is 3 times 20¢ (or 60¢).

What use are such cost figures? These cost figures can be used to determine, like marginal costs, the financially optimum proportion of end products. It was explained that an entrepreneur will maximize profits if he adjusts his output so that marginal costs are equal to marginal revenue, or, more specifically in the case of pure competition, are equal to price. Analogously, if the price of milk is 20¢, the quantity ratio of cream and separated milk should be adjusted so that the money opportunity cost of milk is 20¢. Similarly, if the price of cream is $1.00, adjustments should be made so that the money opportunity cost of cream is $1.00. After all, the prices are data beyond the control of a single dairy farmer, and hence he must adjust his costs to prices rather than prices to his costs.

Combination R is therefore not optimum from a profit viewpoint. Taking milk, the market price is assumed to be 20¢ and the money opportunity cost to be 33¢, so apparently milk should be produced in relatively smaller quantities. The output of cream should be relatively increased as the price of cream is currently exceeding its money opportunity cost.

The optimum combination will be such that the marginal rate of substitution is a reciprocal of the price ratio between the two end products. The ratio of the cream price to the milk price is $1.00 to 20¢, or 5.0, and the reciprocal of this is $\frac{1}{5}$. The dairy farmer should therefore seek a marginal substitution rate of cream to milk of $\frac{1}{5}$ or .20.

The combination that maximizes profits can readily be determined from Fig. XII. The line BC is a sales receipts line and its slope reflects the 5 to 1 relationship in the price of cream to that of separated milk. Any point on this line will yield the producer the same sales revenue whether he sells four quarts of separated milk and .2 quarts of cream, 2 quarts of separated milk and .6 quarts of cream, and so on. The highest sales receipts line that iso-cost curve I_3 can touch is BC at S. Also, any tangent drawn to I_3 at S must have the same slope as BC, and hence the money opportunity cost of separated milk is 20¢ and that of cream is $1.00. These money opportunity costs then coincide with the prevailing prices for the two end products. Therefore, for a given expenditure such as is represented by the iso-cost curve I_3, the S combination is the most profitable.

Concluding Comments

Indifference curves are a rather rough and ready way of analyzing three elements by means of a two-dimensional diagram. The curves are a device to represent the third dimension, which we cannot draw. If this third element is measurable, as in the case of iso-quants, the indifference curves become analogous to known altitude contours on a topographical map. If the third element is not measurable, as in the case of utility, the iso-utility curves can only denote the ranking of higher and lower preferences. The essential characteristic to be found in all these examples is that three variables are being depicted on two dimensions in a rather clumsy way. If we were more skillful in constructing and interpreting three-dimensional models, made perhaps with clay or strings, the more pedestrian use of indifference curves would not be necessary. Even so, indifference curves can handle many problems that tend to be passed over by two-dimensional schedules, and so they represent an intermediate technique, inferior to a three-dimensional model, but superior to the ordinary schedule.

References

Bain, J. S., *Pricing, Distribution and Employment,* Chapter 7. New York: Holt, 1948.

Boulding, K. E., *Economic Analysis,* Chapter 34. New York: Harper, 1948.

Hicks, J. R., *Value vs. Capital,* Chapters 1–3. New York: Oxford University Press, 1939.

Meyers, A. L., *Modern Economics,* Chapter 7. New York: Prentice-Hall, 1941.

Appendix E

Symbols Appearing in Text

α	(alpha) Marginal propensity to consume
β	(beta) Marginal propensity to save
Δ	(Delta) Change in value of a variable
δ	(delta) Ratio of extra induced investment to extra income
ϕ	(phi) Marginal physical productivity of a factor
θ	(theta) Average physical productivity of a factor
C	Consumption (aggregate)
c	Individual's consumer expenditure
GNP	Gross National Product
H	Hoards (aggregate)
h	Individual's hoards
I	Investment (aggregate)
i	Individual's investments
k	The investment multiplier (no induced investment assumed)
k_c	The compound investment multiplier
L	Liquidity demand for money
L_1	Demand for M_1 balances
L_2	Demand for M_2 balances
M	National money stock; public ownership of demand deposits and legal tender
M_1	Active balances
M_2	Passive balances
M'	Publicly owned legal tender
M''	Publicly owned demand deposits
m	Ratio of eventual increase in periodic payments to periodic government injections
MEC	Marginal efficiency of capital
NFI, NI	National income (at factor cost)
NNP	Net National Product
O	Net National Output
P	The price level of all goods and services
p	Price level of finished goods
PI	Personal income

r Rate of interest

S Savings (aggregate)

s Individual's saving

T Physical quantity of transactions during a year

t Ratio of induced tax leakage to extra public spending

V Transactions velocity of money: the number of times it changes ownership in a stated period, such as a year

v Income velocity of money.

X Actual savings and/or actual investment

Y Income (aggregate)

y Individual's income

Index

A

Acceleration, principle of, 148–150
Accumulating, defined, 111
Accounting, national income, 28–45 (*see also* National income: accounting)
Adjustments, industry's, 286–291 (*see also* Industries: adjustments of)
Advertising:
  controversies over, 317–319
    approach to evaluating promotion, 318–319
    consumers-pay-the-cost argument, 318
    mass-production argument, 317–318
  with unchanged price and product, 311–312
  with unchanged quantity and quality, 313–314
Agriculture:
  and government regulation, 518
  in Europe and America, compared, 431
  in police state, 516
Allocating boards, under socialism, 486, 487, 490
Allocation of resources, under pure competition, 359, 361
American Federation of Labor, 412
Analysis, economic, elements of, 3
Arts, state of the, 11
Assets:
  alternative, 142
    present values of, *table,* 143
  cheaply acquired, 458–459
  unique, 142

B

Bank credits, 98–99
Bank loans, 53–54
Banks:
  Federal Reserve (*see* Federal Reserve Banks)
  households and, 20
  governments and, 23–26
Bargaining power of unions, 216, 421–423
Basing point discrimination, 348–350
Billboards, 356
Bills, treasury, 67
Borrowers:
  and loanable funds market, 445–447
  and rise of national income, 449

Borrowers (*Cont.*):
  motives of, 442–444
  schedules of, 448
  types of, 441–442
Borrowing by firms, 51, 52, 139
Bottlenecks, temporary, 204
Brand names, 309, 320, 330
Break-even charts, 525–526
Budget of United States:
  deficit, 99
  unbalancing, 186–195
Budgeting consumer outlays, 255–257
Business cycles, 148, 184
Business depressions (*see* Depressions, business)
Buyers:
  attachments of, 327–329
  one-preference, 327
  preference, 327
  surplus, 229–231
    indifference curves, 556–558
  two-preference, 327
  unattached, 327

C

Capacity, investment in, 147–148
Capital, 527
  acceleration:
    general theory of, 533–536
    with commodity inventories, 537–539, 543–544
    without commodity inventories, 543
  and labor, proportions to combine, 270–271
  concepts of, 7–8
  efficiency of:
    economics of, 143–145
    marginal, 116–117, 141–143
    mathematics of, 141–143
    when it will increase, 144–145
  fixed (*see* Fixed capital)
  fixed accumulation of, 478–479
  funds, 8
  goods, 8
    nature of, 9
  private fixed, 47
  private working, 47
  productivity of, 443
  values, 8
  varying, taxes on, 515
  venture, tax on, 515
  working, 139
    investment in, 52
    private, 47

Capitalism, 507–521
 firms under, 475–476
 government regulation under:
  perverted, for special interests, 517–520
  philosophy of, 515–517
 laissez-faire, 481–482, 507
 necessary reforms:
  extreme monopoly distortion, 511–513
  recurrent mass unemployment, 507–511
  unproductive income inequalities, 513–515
 private, future prospects of, 520
Capitalists, 8
Cash balances approach, 77, 154
 demand for, 154–156
 precautionary motive, 155–156
 speculative motive, 156
 transaction motive, 155
Ceilings:
 price, 241–242, 472, 477
  effects of, 228–229
  to stimuate output, 363
 rent, 222–223
Changes:
 dynamic, economic welfare and, 57–60
 in business taxes, 59
 in investment, 59–60
 in national product, 58
 in population, 60
 in productivity, 60
 in quality, 59
Circuit of payments, 77, 91–106
 graph, 96
Classical system, 166–167
Classical theory, compared with modern theory, 179–180
Clearing house, drain on Federal Reserve Banks, 69–70
Cobweb theorem, 236–237
Collective bargaining, 216, 421–423
Combines, operating, under socialism, 486–487
Commercial banks, 24
 legal service requirements amended for, 72–73
Commodities:
 produced in right proportions, 476
 rationing, bilateral trading and, 568–569
Commodity inventories:
 capital acceleration, 537–539, 543–544
 without commodity inventories, 543
Commodity tax, effects, 231–233
 tax impact, incidence, burden, 232
Commodity theory of money, 76, 79–81
 evaluation of, 81
 original theory, 79–80
 qualified version of, 80–81
Communism, formula for production and distribution, 373

Competition:
 degrees of, 216–219
 firm equilibrium, 283–286, 287
 imperfect, defined, 322
 monopolistic, 322–339 (*see also* Monopolistic competition)
 non-price, 309–321, 329
 reasons for prevalence of, 319–320
 pure, 216, 218, 225–238
  buyers' and sellers' surpluses, 229–231
  cobweb theorem, 236–237
  commodity tax effects, 231–233
  income distribution, 381–382
  price ceiling effects, 228–229
  price determination in competitive market, 225–228
  price elasticity of demand and supply, 233–236
  price theory, 338
  resource allocation under, 359–361
 unfair, monopoly and, 367
Competitive risks, 462
Concentration camps, 517
Congress of Industrial Organizations, 412
Consumer demand:
 determination of, 253–259
 for single good, 257–258
 income changes and, 258–259
 indifference curves and, 548–563
 summing of, 252–253
Consumer goods, household stocks of, 47
Consumers:
 adjustment:
  to income changes, 562–563
  to price changes, 553–556
 efficiency, indifference curves, 550–553
 marginal substitution rate of, 360
 outlay of:
  budgeting, 255–257
  optimum allocation of, 256–257
 spending of, 47
Consumption:
 average propensity, 113
 defined, 4, 111–112
 function, 112–113, 114, 115
 household, 91–92
 marginal tendency, 112–113
 short-run national income, 50
Corporations:
 and national income accounting, 36
 large, 184
Cost curves, 272–276
 types of, 272–273
Costs:
 and output, of firm, 274
 factor, 42, 43
 joint, 247–248
 marginal:
  and supply price, 268
  defined, 269
 opportunity, 9–10, 360
 real, 355–357
  firms that bear more than, 355–356

Costs (*Cont.*):
  real (*Cont.*):
    firms that escape, 355
    total, and revenue functions, 523–526
    transferred from variable to fixed, 279–280
Credits, bank, 98–99
Cross-elasticity, measurement of, 249–250
Currency, drain on Federal Reserve Banks, 69, 71
Cyclical fluctuations, 148, 184

D

Decentralization under socialism, 503
Deficits, government, 99–104
Deficit spending theory, 135
Demand:
  as seen by monopolist, 296–299
  consumer (*see* Consumer demand)
  forces of, 251–265
  income, price and, 260–262
  joint, 248
  rival, 246
  supply and (*see* Supply: and demand)
  under oligopoly and polypoly, 324
  utility approach to theory of, 252
Department of Commerce, national income estimates by, 38–40, 46, 49
Deposits, time, 67
Depressions, business, 24
  and budget deficits, 197
  and income taxes, 92
  household spending during, 201
  of 1930's, 91, 511
  precautionary motive during, 156
  severe economic, 507–511
  theories of, 109
Discrimination:
  meaning of term, 350
  price (*see* Price: discrimination)
Dishoarding, 93–96, 446, 450, 451–452
  active, 97–98
Disposable income:
  defined, 92
  personal income not, 38
Distribution, production and, communist formula for, 373
Dollar, devaluation of (1933–34), 81
Duopoly, defined, 217
Duosony, defined, 217
Durability, investment in, 145–146
Duties, import, reducing, 191, 192
Dynamic theory, 222–223

E

Earnings:
  of employees, 395–411
  overtime, 399–400
  payrolls, 395
  wages (*see* Wages)
Economic aims, 471–481
  and political alternatives, 481–482

Economic ratio, 352
Economics, defined, 3
Economies, industry-wide, 290–291
Economists, single-mindedness of, 519–520
Elasticity:
  price:
    marginal revenue, and, 297, 298–299
    of supply, 304
  supply, of employed factor, 380–381
Emergency funds, 155–156
Emergency savings, 185
Employees:
  and wages:
    ability to pay, 417–418
    purchasing power of, 416–417
  earnings of (*see* Earnings)
  gifted, exploitation of, 389
Employers (*see* Entrepreneurs)
Employment:
  full, 205
    through large-scale government expenditures of new money, 99
  government policy, 182–199
  prosperity, and labor costs, 396–399
  under socialism, 485, 487, 488
  wages or, 413–416
Enterprise, 8–9 (*see also* Entrepreneurship)
Entrepreneurs:
  and income taxes, 515
  demand for single factor, 376–379
  earnings of, 395
  outlays for productive factors, 376–385
    optimum, 383–385
  pure competition, monopoly, monopsony, income distribution, 381–382
  "square-peg," 459
  supply elasticity of employed factor, 380–381
Entrepreneurship:
  combining element in, 455–456
  functions of, 454–456
  originating element in, 455, 456, 460–461
  profits of, 454–468
    general long-run, 461–466
    single firm, 457–458
  risk-taking element in, 455, 456
  single firm profits:
    assets cheaply acquired, 458–459
    lack of room, 459
    run of luck, 458
    special rents, 459–460
Equation of exchange, 83–85
Equilibrium, 176–177
  defined, 220
  final and temporary, concept of, 219–220
  full, and interest rate, 449–450
  income, 131–133
    changes in, 133
    under *laissez-faire* policies, 133

Equilibrium (*Cont.*):
  long-run, 219, 220
    monopolistic competition, 329–330
  market, after imposition of commodity
    tax, 231–232
  of firms, 283–290
    competitive, 283–286, 287
  particular or general, analysis of, 221–
    222
  price, 226–227
  short-run, 220
  tangency, 331
Estate taxes, 514–515
Excess profits taxes, 100
Exchange, equation of, 83–85
Excise taxes, 100, 513
  domestic, reducing, 191, 192
  government, 477
Exploitation, 388–392
  average, 388, 389–392
  defined, 388
  marginal, 388, 389–390
  of gifted employee, 389
  of ordinary workers, 389–392

F

Factor costs, 42, 43
Factors:
  of production:
    optimum outlays for, 383–385
    substitution of, 386–388
  supply elasticity of employed, 380–381
Farmers, as monopolists, 513
Fear, and government regulation, 517
Featherbedding, 416
Federal Reserve Banks, 24, 68 ff.
  central banks, 71–75
  deposit creation by member banks, 69–
    71
  ownership of, 68
Federal Reserve System, 68–76
  and U. S. Treasury, 68
    rival goals, 75–76
  discount rates, changes in, 72, 74–75
  financing of government deficits, 196–
    197
  influence on money supply, 72–75
  investment, 73–74
  membership in, 68–69
  open market purchases, 74
  organs of, 68
Financial ratio, 352
Financial risks, 458
  kinds of, 461–462
  reluctance to take, 12–13
  unavoidable, 461–466
Finished output inventories, 139–140
Firms, 20–23
  and general welfare, 475–476
  and national money stock, 93–96
  borrowing by, 51, 52, 139
  defined, 16, 20–21
  degree of capitalism, 145–148
  equilibrium of, 283–290, 291

Firms (*Cont.*):
  expanding, labor costs of, 397–399
  future labor requirements of, 147
  government, and expenditure stream
    of, 509–511
  government purchases from, 47
  gross value added, 21–22
  households and, 16–18
  interdependence among, 322–329
    attachments of buyers, 327–329
    measures of, 322–323
    price with oligopoly and polypoly,
      323–327
  investing by, 111
    examples, 145–148
  investments and saving, 50–54
    classes of investment, 52
    government and, 54–56
  money stock held by, 155
  net value added, 22
  new, and profits, 335
  numbers of, and price policy, 334
  reinvestment of profits by, 51
  rivals, substitutability of outputs, 335
  role of, 212–213
  single firm, profits of, 457–461
  supply schedules, 335–336
  why they borrow, 164
Fixed capital, 139
  investment in, 52, 139, 141–148
Fluctuations, economic, 24
Free enterprise:
  economy (*see also* Private profit):
    land rent in, 438
    unrestricted, 481
Free goods, 5, 19
Free services, 5
  from governments, 19
Funds:
  capital, 8
  emergency, 155–156
  loanable (*see* Loanable funds)

G

Gains, probable, 463–464
General theory, 166–181
  and human attitudes, 171–180
  classical theory and, 166–167, 179–180
  demand for money and, 169–171
  income, as extra variable, 168–169
Gift taxes, 515
Gold:
  and paper money, 80
  and value of money, 79–80
  as commodity, 79–81
  standard, 80, 81
Goods (*see also* Products):
  capital, 8, 9
  circulation of, 91
  defined, 5
  differentiated, 309
  economic, defined, 5
  essential, 262–264
  fabricated, 309

Goods (*Cont.*):
  free, 5, 19
  inferior, 261
  joint costs of, 247–248
  joint demand for, 248
  joint supply of, 246–247
  nonessential, 262–264
  rival demand for, 246
  rival supply of, 244–246
Governments:
  and banks, 23–26
  and national money stock, 93–96
  antimonopoly policy of, 366–369
  capital transactions of, 42
  deficits, 99–104
    financing, 195–197
  employment policy, 182–199
  firms, and households, national income, 54–56
  households and, 18–20
  investment, 47
  participation in managerial policy, 511–512
  policy, alternatives to, 366–367
  reallocation by, 363–365
  regulation by, 41
    consequences seldom considered, 519
    of prices, 241–242 (*see also* Prices: ceilings)
    perverted, for special interests, 517–520
    philosophy of, under capitalism, 515–517
  spending by, 133–135, 186–189
    multiplier, 193–195
    of new money, 99
  subsidies (*see* Subsidies)
  supplementary investment by, 133–135
  valuing contribution of, 40–42
  why they pay interest, 164
Gross value, added, 21–22

H

Hedging, 244
Hoarding, 91, 446, 450, 451–452
  active, 95
  and dishoarding, 93–96 (*see also* Dishoarding)
  differentiated from saving, 96
  motives for, 156
  passive, 95
  rate of, average and marginal, 98–99
Home production, 47 (*see also* Households)
Hoover Dam, 188
Householders as entrepreneurs, 462–463
Households, 15–20
  accumulations of, 53
  and banks, 20
  and consumption, 91–92
  and firms, 16–18
  and general welfare, 472–475
  and governments, 18–20

Households (*Cont.*):
  and national money stock, 93–96
  characteristics of, 15–16
  cultural values and, 474
  experienced income, 47
  free government aids to, 47
  government, and expenditure stream, of, 509–511
  high-income, 184
  income, how obtained, 472–473
  investment and saving, 50–54
    government and, 54–56
  lending of money by, 473–474
  maximizing subjective utility income, 474–475
  money stock held by, 155
  purchase of consumer goods, 472
  receipts and expenditures, *table*, 17
  sacrifices, to acquire income, 474
  savings plans of, 111
  sovereignty of, 475
  why they borrow, 164

I

Import duties, reducing, 191, 192
Incentive incomes, 490–492
Income:
  as extra variable, 168–169
  changes in:
    and individual demand, 258–259
    consumer's adjustment to, 562–563
  defined, 111–112
  demand, price and, 260–262
  disposable (*see* Disposable income)
  distribution of, 373–394
    alternative principles, 373–376
    and general welfare, 478
    new inventions and marginal productivity, 385–386
    substitution of factors, 386–388
  equilibrium (*see* Equilibrium: income)
  exploitation, 388–392 (*see also* Exploitation)
  extra, declining importance of, 259–260
  incentive, under socialism, 490–492
  inequalities, unproductive, under capitalism, 513–515
  level:
    interest rate and, 163
    money stock and, 161–162
  multipliers of, 122–138
    equilibrium income, 131–133
    investment (*see* Investment: multiplier)
    supplementary government investment, 133–135
  national (*see* National income)
  personal (*see* Personal income)
  real (*see* Real income)
  system, 118–120, 183
  taxes, 100, 478, 517
    business depressions and, 92

Income (*Cont.*):
taxes (*Cont.*):
  rates, progressive, 259
  reducing, 191–192
theory, 109–121
  consumption function, 112–113, 114, 115
  contrary saving and investing plans, 110–111
  "investing" in, 110–111
  investment multiplier, 115–116
  liquidity theory of interest rates, 117–118
  marginal efficiency of capital, 116–117
  relations, 118–120
unearned, 427, 438
Indifference curves, 548–573
and consumer demand, 548–563
Industries:
adjustments of, 286–291
  long-run, 288–290
  short-run, 286–288
industry-wide economies, 290–291
Inheritance taxes, 478, 514
Innovations:
and profits, 455, 456, 460–461
risks of, 466
Inputs, 269–272
Instability, elements of, 527
Insurance, reason for, 260
Interest:
and liquidity, 154–165
and price of money, 157–158
expectations, and money demand, 158–159
function and justice of, 450–452
motives of borrowers and lenders:
  liquidity preference, 444
  productivity of capital, 443
  time preference, 442–443
nature of, 441
on capital, 441–453
  loanable funds (*see* Loanable funds)
rate of:
  and investment, 150, 151–152
  full equilibrium and, 449–450
  income level and, 163
  liquidity theory of, 117–118
  money stock and, 157–158
system, 118–120, 183
who pays, 441–442
why it is paid, 163–164
Inventions, new, and marginal productivity, 385–386
Inventories:
commodity (*see* Commodity inventories)
finished output, 52, 139–140
Investing:
and saving, 540–541, 544
defined, 110–111
Investment(s):
aggregate, loanable funds and, 447–449

Investment(s) (*Cont.*):
and national income, 114–115
and saving, 50–57, 540–541, 544, 545–547
  firms and households only, 50–54
  governments, firms and households, 54–56
  nature of, 50
and savings box surfaces, 175–176
autonomous, 127, 129
deciding to invest, *chart*, 144
defined, 111–112
effect of interest and income on, *graph*, 167
ex ante, 110
ex post, 110
Federal Reserve System, 73–74
government, 47
inducements to invest, 127, 139–153
  finished output inventories, 139–140
  fixed capital, 141–148
  principle of acceleration, 148–150
  which dominate, 150–152
  working capital, 140–141
in inventories, 150
in plant and equipment, 150–151
intention to invest:
  autonomous investments, *table,* 123
  changed, 173
  compound, 127–129
  increased, 178
  multiplier, 115–116
  simple, 122–126
  vs. spending multipliers, 130–131
of firms, 139
  classes of, 52
  in capacity, 147–148
  in durability, 145–146
  in productivity, 146–147
plans, and saving plans, when they differ, 527–544
private, and soaking the rich policy, 185–186
rate of, under socialism, 499–502
system, 118–120, 183
types of, 139
variability, and welfare, 59–60
Iso-cost curves, joint supply products and, 570–572
Iso-quant curves:
and producer demand, 563–564
determining margnial productivity of factor from, 564–565
Iso-utility map, 548–550

L

Labor, 6–7
and investments of firms, 147
costs:
  of expanding firm, 397–399
  prosperity employment, 396–399
  rising, 203–204
disutility of, 11–12

Labor (*Cont.*):
  force, non-competing groups in, 401–403
  kinds of, 9
  land and, comparisons of efficiency, 431
  productivity of, and wages, 418–420
  supply, union restrictions on, 404
  unions (*see* Unions)
  untrained, supply of, 375
Laissez-faire attitudes, 110, 133
Laissez-faire capitalism, 471, 481–482
  necessary reforms, 507–515 (*see also* Capitalism: necessary reforms)
Land, 7
  elements of, 9
  grades of, 432–433
  marginal product negative, 430
  public ownership of, 438–439
  rent on, 427–440 (*see* Rent: on land)
  total output maximum, 430
  value of, 427
Legal tender, 65–66
Leisure, under socialism, 503–504
Lenders:
  and loanable funds market, 445–447
  and rise of national income, 449
  households as, 473–474
  motives of, 442–444
  schedules of, 448
Liquidity:
  defined, 154
  function, 160–163
  interest and, 154–165
  preferences:
    changed, 173
    increased, 179
    of borrowers and lenders, 442, 444
  theory of interest rates, 117–118
Loanable funds, 441
  and aggregate investment, 447–449
  demand and supply of, 444–450
    equations of individual, 444–445
  market, 445–447
  interest rate, 479
Loans, bank, 53–54
Losses:
  probable, 463–464
  short-run, minimizing, 285–286
Luck, run of, and profits, 458
Luxuries, 262–264

M

Malallocation of resources with monopoly, 361–362
Management, variables to be determined by, 337–338
Managerial policy, governmental participation in, 511–512
Managers, plant, under socialism, 502–503
Manufacturers, in police state, 516
Marginal-efficiency-of-capital concept, 141–145

Market price, 42–43
Markets:
  and general welfare, 477–478
  closeness to, and rent, 433–434
  competitive, price determination in, 225–228
  defined, 225
  future and past, speculative linking of, 242–244
  spatial interdependence of, 239–242
  temporal interdependence of, 242–244
Maximizing profits, 336–337
Money:
  as means of payment, 66, 82
  balances:
    active, 160
    passive, 160
  cash balances approach, 77
  changes in stock of, 67–76
  circuit of payments approach (*see* Circuit of payments)
  circulation of, 91
  commodity theory (*see* Commodity theory of money)
  currency, 69, 71
  declining marginal importance of, 259–260
  defined, 66, 82
  demand for:
    and altered human attitudes, 171–172
    and income equilibrium, *graph*, 169
    effective, 200–202
    influence of, 169–171
    interest expectations and, 158–159
  functions of, 67
  hoarding of (*see* Hoarding)
  legal tender, 65–66
  marginal utility of, 257
  money box surfaces, 174–175
  national standard, gold content of, 80
  nature of, 65–67
  near money, 67
  new, government expenditures of, 99, 102
  paper, 80, 82
  price of, interest and, 157–158
  quantity of, meaning of, 82
  quantity theory (*see* Quantity theory of money)
  stock of:
    and effective demand, 201–202
    and income level, 161–162
    and interest rates, 157–158
    effect on income levels of, 171
    total, monetary outlays exceed, 84
  supply of:
    Federal Reserve influence on, 72–75
    increased, 179
  viewpoints re, 76–77
Monopolist:
  defined, 295
  demand as seen by, 296–299
  pure, price policies of, 296–303

Monopolistic competition, 217, 218, 219, 322–339
  composite nature of, 334–338
  interdependence among firms, 322–329
  price theory, 338
Monopoly, 204–205, 216, 368, 482
  and closed shop, 404
  and monopsony, 295–308
    concept of, 295–296
    long-run considerations, 306–307
  and private profit, 358–365
  and unfair competition, 367
  antimonopoly policy of government, 366–369
  bilateral, 217, 218
  defined, 204, 218
  extreme distortion, under capitalism, 511–513
  income distribution, 381–382
  malallocation of resources with, 361–362
  profits, maximizing, 300–301
    in market period, 302–303
  pure, price theory, 338
  with monopsony, 306
Monopsonist:
  calculations of marginal purchase cost, 304
  pricing by, 303–306
Monopsony, 217
  defined, 216, 218
  examples of, 365
  income distribution, 381–382
  monopoly and, 295–308
    concept of, 295–296
    long-run considerations, 306–307
  monopoly with, 306
  rareness of, 296

N

National economy:
  annual income in, 28
  goal of, 3
National factor income, 46, 47, 52
National income:
  accounting, 28–45
    basic ideas, 28–31
    estimates by Department of Commerce, 38–40
    factor cost approach, 42, 43
    government contribution, 40–42
    gross and net income, 31–33
    market price approach, 42–43
    personal income, 36–38
  and aggregate employment, 479–481
  borrowers and lenders and, 449
  components of, *table*, 39
  contribution and value, of firm, *table*, 23
  dual aspects of, 43–44
  estimates, by Department of Commerce, 38–40
  excluding net government interest from, 41–42

National income (*Cont.*):
  flows and stocks, 46–50
  general welfare and, 46–61
  investment and, 114–115
  methods of estimating, 43–44
  national defense and, 40
  nature of, 28–30, 33–36
  net national product differentiated from, 36
  saving and investment, 56, 57
National Loan Corporation, 499–502
National Planning Board, 486, 490, 493, 494, 498, 499
National policy, economic aims of, 471–484
National product:
  altered composition of, 58
  at market price, 33
  gross, 46
  gross and net, 31–33
Natural resources, preordained, 11
Near money, 67
Needs, 262–264
Negroes, and employment, 401–402
Net value, added, 22
New Deal, and devaluation of dollar, 81
Numeraire, 251–252

O

Oligopoly:
  defined, 204, 217, 218
  economic problem, 368
  increase of, 320
  price constancy of, 332–333
  price with, 323–327
Opportunity costs, 9–10, 360
Outlays, maximizing:
  for given total satisfaction, 552–553
  pleasure from fixed, 550–551
Outputs, 269–272, 527
  and price discrimination, 345
  defined, 269
  firm costs and, 274
  formulae for maximizing profits, 336–337
  long-run, 331–334
  of rivals, substitutability of, 335
  per acre or per worker, 431
  price ceiling to stimulate, 363
  private, unsold, 47
  specific tax to contract, 363
Overtime, economics of, 399–400

P

Packaging of goods, 320
Paper money, 80, 82
Payments:
  circuit of, 77, 91–106
    graph, 96
  expanding flow of, 96–97
    through active dishoarding, 97–98
    through bank credits, 98–99
    through government deficits, 99–104

Payments (*Cont.*):
  leakages in flow of, 92
  reasons for increase of, 104–105
Payrolls, wages, earnings and, 395–400
Personal income:
  and national income accounting, 36–38
  not disposable income, 38
Planning:
  curve, 276–278
    long-run, 277, 278
  of socialism, 485–488
Plant curves, 276
Pleasure, maximizing, from fixed outlay, 550–551
Point rationing, 489, 490
Police state, and regulation, 516
Political alternatives, 481–482
Politics and economics, 471–484
Polypoly, 217, 218
  price with, 323–327
Population, changes in, 60
Prejudice, and employment, 401–402
Prices:
  and quality, fixed, 311–312
  ceilings, 241–242, 472, 477
    effects of, 228–229
    to stimulate output, 363
  changes in:
    consumer's adjustment to, 553–556
    measuring welfare effect of, 558–562
    significance of, 88–89
    welfare and, 58
  constancy, oligopolistic, 332–333
  cross-elasticity and product interdependence, 249–250
  demand, income and, 260–262
  determination of, in competitive market, 225–228
  discrimination, 340–353
    based on income, 342
    basing point, 348–350
    between already separated markets, 342–345
    between separable markets, 345–348
    commodity sold at different prices, 342
    defined, 340
    economic desirability of, 350–353
    examples of, 340–342
    freight absorption, 348–350
    geographic, 341–342, 343, 348
    perfect, 340
    purpose of, 340
  floors, 477
  government regulation of, 241–242
    (*see also* Prices: ceilings)
  influence of supply on, 202–203
  interdependence of, 239–250
    export and import markets, 239–242
    spatial, 239–242
    substitutes and complements, 244–248
    temporal, 242–244
  interest as, 441

Prices (*Cont.*):
  isolation, when interdependent, 241
  leadership, 329
  level:
    and quantity of money, 82
    current thought on, 85–89
    measurement of, 86–87
    motives and, 85–86
    payments, gross and net, 87–88
    price-relation changes, 86
    theories, 79–90
  limits, 516
  policy:
    firm numbers and, 334
    of pure monopolist, 296–303
  product, and promotion, 309–310
  spiraling, 205–206
  supply, marginal costs and, 268
  systems, delivered contrasted with f.o.b., 348
  theory:
    dynamic, 222
    monopolistic competition, 338
    pure competition, 338
    pure monopoly, 338
    significance of, 211–212
    static, 222
    with oligopoly, 323–327
    with polypoly, 323–327
Pricing:
  by monopsonist, 303–306
  deliberate common, 332
  independent, 332
  market period, 302–303
  short-run, 300–302
Private enterprise:
  and government spending, 187–189
  and public works program, 134–135
Private profit:
  government antimonopoly policy, 366–369
  interpersonal utility comparisons, 357–358
  monopoly problem, 358–365
  real and money costs and revenues, 355–357
Probability, and investment, 463–465
Producer demand, iso-quant curves and, 563–564
Product:
  as variable, 310
  differentiation, 214, 320
  fabricated, 214
  marginal revenue, 377
  natural, 213–214, 215
  price, promotion and, 309–310
  specification, 214–215
  types of, 213–215
  unchanged, price effect of advertising, 315–316
Production, 30–31
  and distribution, communist formula for, 373
  consumer-goods, 30
  defined, 6

Production (*Cont.*):
  factors of, 6–9
    capital, concepts of, 7–8
    enterprise, 8–9
    labor, 6–7
    land, 7
  function, 269–272
  home, 47
  long-run national income, 50
  optimum allocation of, 476
  round-about methods of, 450
  self-interest and, 516–517
  subsidies for, 189–190
Productivity:
  changes in, 60
  investment in, 146–147
  marginal:
    determining, of factor from iso-
      quants, 564–565
    new inventions and, 385–386
  of capital, 443
Professional employment, 402–403
Profits:
  and price discrimination, 345
  as self-paid insurance premium, 462
  determining, 456–457
  entry and, 335
  increasing, with rising labor costs,
    399
  long-run, 330–331
  maximizing, output formulae for, 336–
    337
  of entrepreneurship, 454–468
  of single firm, 457–458
  private (*see* Private profit)
  private net, 354, 357
  reinvestment of, by firms, 51
  run of luck and, 458
  squeeze on, 329–331
  undistributed, 51
  usefulness of, 466–467
  what they are, 455
  what they are not, 454–455
Promotion:
  as variable, 310
  evaluating, economists' approach to,
    318–319
  price, product and, 309–310
  sales and price effects of, 315–317
Public works program, 133, 134, 186–189
  under socialism, 504
Pump-priming schemes, 150

Q

Quality:
  fixed, 311–314
  improvement in, 59
Quantity, unchanged, advertising with,
  313–314
Quantity theory of money, 76–77, 82–85
  crude version of, 82–85
  equation of exchange, 83–84
  value-of-trade version of, 82–85
Quasi-rent, 284, 286, 437

R

Rationing, 242
  commodity, bilateral trading and,
    568–569
  point, 489, 490
  under socialist regime, 488–489
Real income, defined, 5
Reallocation by government, 363–365
Reinvestment of profits, 51
Relief, unemployment:
  direct, 190–191
  under socialism, 505
Rent:
  ceilings, 222–223
  controls, peacetime, 518
  economic, defined, 427
  explicit, 438
  implicit, 438
  land, 427–440
    as unearned income, 427, 438
    basis of, 427
    comparisons of efficiency, 431
    concept of, 436–437
    defined, 437
    differential productivity theory of,
      432
    measuring, 433
    nature of, 427–431
    should it be paid? 437–439
    specific, 432–433
    stages of, 430–431
    urban site, 433–436
    varying factor proportions, 428–429
  quasi-rent, 284, 286, 437
Reserves, legal, of Federal Reserve
    System, 70–71
Resources:
  allocation of, under pure competition,
    359–361
  ideal arrangement of, 476
  malallocation of, with monopoly, 361–
    362
  natural, 11
Restraint of trade, 368
Returns:
  average, diminishing, 271
  diminishing, in short run, 204
  marginal:
    and average, 271
    diminishing, 271
  to scale, 272
Revenues:
  marginal derivation of, 297–299
  real and money costs and, 355–357
  total cost and functions of, 523–526
Rich, soaking the, 184–186
Risks, financial (*see* Financial risks)
Rivalry, potential, 459 (*see also* Com-
    petition)

S

Sabotage, 407
Saving:

Saving (*Cont.*):
  differentiated from hoarding, 96
  for emergencies, 155–156
  investment and, 540–541, 544
  plans, and investment plans, when they differ, 527–544
  propensities:
    changed, 172–173
    increased, 178–179
Savings:
  aggregate, 135
  and investment box surfaces, 175–176
  and investments, 545–547
  bogey of, 91–93
  defined, 111–112
  effect of interest and income on, *graph*, 167
  emergency, 185
  ex ante, 110
  ex post, 110
  from disposable income, 92
  intended:
    and investment schedules, *table*, 131
    reduction in, 136
  thrift and, 167
Scarcity:
  economy of, 10
  inevitability of, 10–13
Seasonal variations, 147, 148, 243
Self-interest, and production, 516–517
Sellers, surplus of, 229–231
Seniority, and employment, 404
Service, economic, defined, 5
Services, circulation of, 91
Social insurance, financing of, 19
Socialism, 373–374, 471, 481, 482
  firms under, 475–476
  households under, 16
  land under, 438–439
  problems of, 485–506
    absence of criticism, 487
    crude planning, 485–488
    decentralized managerial decisions, 502–503
    incentive incomes, 490–492
    individual consumer choice, 488–490
    interacting consumer and worker choice, 493–499
    leisure and unemployment, 503–505
    limited worker choice, 492–493
    rate of investment, 499–502
    rationing under, 488–489
Social security, 482
  in national income accounting, 37
Soviet Russia (*see* Union of Soviet Socialist Republics)
Special-interest groups, 477–478
  perverted government regulation for, 517–520
Speculation:
  and temporal interdependence of markets, 242–244
  in urban land, 435
  motive for saving, 156
Spending:

Spending (*Cont.*):
  consumer, 47
  government, 133–135, 186–189
  marginal periods, 102–103
  multipliers, vs. investment multipliers, 130–131
  nature of, 4–5
Squeezing of profits, 329–331
Static theory, 222–223
Subsidies, 41, 46, 189, 477
  sliding scale, 364
Substitutes and complements, interdependence of, 244–248
Substitution, marginal rate of indifference curves, 551–552
Suppliers' surplus, 230, 231
Supply:
  and demand:
    forces of, affecting price, 292
    interaction of, 291–293
    market schedules, 226
    of loanable funds, 444–450
    price elasticity of, 233–236
    wages based on, 403
  cost curves, 272–276
  forces of, 266–282
  influence on prices, 202–203
  joint, 246–247
  planning curve, 276–278
  production function, 269–272
  rival, 244–246
  schedules:
    collective, 266
    individual, 266–269
  time and, 278–280
Surpluses:
  buyer's, indifference curves, 556–558
  buyers' and sellers', 229–231
  government, 92
  suppliers' 230, 231
Symbols used in text, 574–575

T

Tangency equilibria, 331
Tariffs on imports, 518
Taxes, 100, 516
  business:
    altered, and welfare, 59
    indirect, 33–34, 46
  commodity, effects of, 231–233
  estate, 514–515
  excess profits, 100
  excise (*see* Excise taxes)
  gifts, 515
  income (*see* Income: taxes)
  inheritance, 478, 514
  leakages, induced, 100–102
  on varying capital, 515
  on venture capital, 515
  reducing, 191–193
  system of, and government regulation, 518
Teamsters' Union, 412
Tennessee Valley Authority, 187

Thrift, and savings, 167
Time:
 and supply, 278–280
 deposits, 67
Trade, restraint of, 368
Trades, overinvested, 512–513
Trading, bilateral, and commodity
  rationing, 568–569
Transactions, defined, 77
Transfer payments, 19
 business, 33, 35–36, 46
 government:
  to households, 41
  to individuals, 37–38
Treasury bills, 67

U

Underconsumption, unemployment and,
  91–106
Undistributed profits, 51
Unemployment:
 and socialism, 503–505
 and underconsumption, 91–106
 and wage rates, 413–414
 hoarding and, 91
 long-run and short-run, 407, 409
 mass, 109, 482
  and investments of firms, 147
  government policy and, 182–183
  under capitalism, 507–511
 technological, extent of, 407–410
Union of Soviet Socialist Republics:
 and sovereignty of household, 16, 475
 round-about productive methods of,
  450
 socialist economy of, 485
Unions:
 and labor supply, 407
 bargaining power of, 216, 421–423
 closed or open, 414–415
 industry-wide bargaining by, 512
 leaders of, and wage rates, 412–426
 wage arguments, 416–421
  ability to pay, 417–418
  comparable wages for comparable
   jobs, 420–421
  employee purchasing power, 416–417
  productivity of labor, 418–420
United Mine Workers, 412
United States, economy of, 374
United States Treasury and Federal Reserve System, 68, 75–76
Utilities:
 individual utility, and quantity consumed, 254, 255
 interpersonal comparisons, 357–358
Utility:
 defined, 4

Utility (*Cont.*):
 marginal:
  diminishing, 253–254
  of money, 257
 total, formula for maximizing, 256–
  257

V

Variables, determined by management,
  337–338
Varying proportions, principle of, 428–
  429
Venture capital, taxes on, 515

W

Wages, 395–400
 based on supply and demand, 403
 comparable, for comparable jobs, 420–
  421
 differences in, 400–407
  compensating, 400–401
  derived demand, 403
  non-competing groups in labor force,
   401–403
  union restrictions on labor supply,
   404
  wage and hour laws, 404–407
 earnings, and payrolls, 395–400
 employee's ability to pay, 417–418
 minimum, and labor monopsony, 406–
  407
 minimum wage laws, 404–407
 negotiations, bargaining power in,
  421–423
 or employment, 413–416
 output and, under socialism, 491–492
 rates, union leaders and, 412–426
 union arguments re., 416–421 (*see also*
  Unions: wage arguments)
Welfare, general:
 and dynamic change, 57–60
 and national income, 46–61
 and private profit, 354–370
Welfare state, 19, 478
Women, in non-competitive jobs, 402
Workers:
 choice of, interacting with consumer
  choice, 493–499
 in police state, 516
 limited choice of, under socialism,
  492–493
 soverign position of, in U. S., 475
 urban, and public works, 188
Working capital, 139
 investment, 140–141
World War II, bank financing of, *table*,
  25